Rhythms of
Academic Life

FOUNDATIONS FOR ORGANIZATIONAL SCIENCE
A Sage Publications Series

Series Editor

David Whetten, *Brigham Young University*

Editors

Peter J. Frost, *University of British Columbia*
Anne S. Huff, *University of Colorado*
Benjamin Schneider, *University of Maryland*
M. Susan Taylor, *University of Maryland*
Andrew Van de Ven, *University of Minnesota*

The FOUNDATIONS FOR ORGANIZATIONAL SCIENCE series supports the development of students, faculty, and prospective organizational science professionals through the publication of texts authored by leading organizational scientists. Each volume provides a highly personal, hands-on introduction to a core topic or theory and challenges the reader to explore promising avenues for future theory development and empirical application.

Books in This Series

PUBLISHING IN THE ORGANIZATIONAL SCIENCES, 2nd Edition
Edited by L. L. Cummings and Peter J. Frost

SENSEMAKING IN ORGANIZATIONS
Karl E. Weick

INSTITUTIONS AND ORGANIZATIONS
W. Richard Scott

RHYTHMS OF ACADEMIC LIFE
Peter J. Frost and M. Susan Taylor

RESEARCHERS HOOKED ON TEACHING:
Noted Scholars Discuss the Synergies of Teaching and Research
Rae André and Peter J. Frost

THE PSYCHOLOGY OF DECISION MAKING:
People in Organizations
Lee Roy Beach

Peter J. Frost
M. Susan Taylor

Editors

Rhythms of Academic Life

Personal Accounts of Careers in Academia

Foundations for
Organizational
Science
A Sage Publications Series

SAGE Publications
International Educational and Professional Publisher
Thousand Oaks London New Delhi

For information address:

SAGE Publications, Inc.
2455 Teller Road
Thousand Oaks, California 91320
E-mail: order@sagepub.com

SAGE Publications Ltd.
6 Bonhill Street
London EC2A 4PU
United Kingdom

SAGE Publications India Pvt. Ltd.
M-32 Market
Greater Kailash I
New Delhi 110 048 India

Printed in the United States of America

Library of Congress Cataloging-in-Publication Data

Main entry under title:

Rhythms of academic life: Personal accounts of careers in academia /
    editors, Peter J. Frost, M. Susan Taylor.
        p.   cm.—(Foundations for organizational science)
    Includes bibliographical references (p.).
    ISBN 0-8039-7262-8 (cloth : acid-free paper).—ISBN
0-8039-7263-6 (pbk. : acid-free paper)
    1. College teachers—United States.   2. College teaching—United
States.   I. Frost, Peter J.   II. Taylor, M. Susan.   III. Series.
LB1778.2.R59   1996
378.1′2′0973—dc20   96-10019

This book is printed on acid-free paper.

99   00   01   10   9   8   7   6   5   4   3

Sage Production Editor: Astrid Virding
Sage Typesetter: Andrea D. Swanson

To Nola McMorran Frost, who has been my partner, my confidante,
my friend, through all the rhythms of my academic life
Peter J. Frost

To my parents, whose lives have touched mine far more
than they know; and to Dan and Cassie, who "keep me from falling"
M. Susan Taylor

© Sandstone photograph by Thomas R. Knight.

Contents

———————

Introduction to the Series   xi
  DAVID A. WHETTEN

Acknowledgments   xiii

Introduction   xiv

Part I. Career Rhythms: Five Exemplars   1

 1. Lessons Learned Along the Way: Twelve Suggestions for Optimizing
    Career Success   3
      ARTHUR G. BEDEIAN
 2. On Becoming a Scholar: One Woman's Journey   11
      JOAN V. GALLOS
 3. Rhythms of an Academic's Life: Crossing Cultural Borders   19
      MIRIAM EREZ
 4. Transitions   31
      VANCE F. MITCHELL
 5. Creating a Career: Observations From Outside the Mainstream   37
      STEWART R. CLEGG, in conversation with JOHN M. JERMIER

Part II. Early Rhythms   55

 Becoming a Teacher   57
 6. Becoming a Teacher at a Research University   61
      CHRISTINA E. SHALLEY
 7. On Learning Why I Became a Teacher   73
      JOHN A. MILLER

8. Research/Teaching Boundaries   83
     WALTER R. NORD

9. Teaching as an Act of Scholarship   91
     STELLA M. NKOMO

   Doing Research and Getting Published   **95**

10. Using Programmatic Research to Build a Grounded Theory   99
     EDWIN A. LOCKE

11. Developing Programmatic Research   107
     MATS ALVESSON

12. The Publishing Process: The Struggle for Meaning   119
     SUSAN J. ASHFORD

13. Getting Published   129
     KEVIN R. MURPHY

14. Revising and Resubmitting: Author Emotions, Editor Roles, and the
Value of Dialogue   135
     J. KEITH MURNIGHAN

   Working With Doctoral Students   **143**

15. The Development of Doctoral Students: Substantive and
Emotional Perspectives   147
     LARRY L. CUMMINGS

16. Working With Doctoral Students: Reflections on Doctoral Work Past
and Present   153
     SUSAN J. ASHFORD

17. Mentoring Relationships: A Comparison of Experiences in Business
and Academia   159
     LINN VAN DYNE

18. Transitions and Turning Points in Faculty-Doctoral Student Relationships   165
     RODERICK M. KRAMER and JOANNE MARTIN

   Getting Tenure   **181**

19. Getting Tenure   185
     MARILYN E. GIST

20. Rounding Corners: An African American Female Scholar's
Pretenure Experiences   193
     TONI C. KING

   Pause Point 1: Integration of Work and Nonwork Lives   **201**

21. Thoughts on Integrating Work and Personal Life
(and the Limits of Advice)   203
     JAMES P. WALSH

22. Holding It All Together   207
     MARCY CRARY

Part III. Middle Rhythms: Traditional Paths

   Working Collaboratively   **219**

23. Working Together   225
     C. R. HININGS and ROYSTON GREENWOOD

24. Growing a Personal, Professional Collaboration   239
   JANE E. DUTTON, JEAN M. BARTUNEK, and CONNIE J. G. GERSICK
25. Three Voices Reflecting on Scholarly Career Journeys With
   International Collaboration   249
   JAMES G. (JERRY) HUNT, ARJA ROPO, and PÄIVI ERIKSSON

   Becoming a Reviewer   259
26. Becoming a Reviewer: Lessons Somewhat Painfully Learned   263
   ELAINE ROMANELLI
27. The Act of Reviewing and Being a Reviewer   269
   HUSEYIN LEBLEBICI
28. Balls, Strikes, and Collisions on the Base Path: Ruminations of
   a Veteran Reviewer   275
   ALAN D. MEYER

   Becoming a Journal Editor   283
29. Becoming a Journal Editor   287
   JANICE M. BEYER
30. Work as a Parade of Decision Letters: Pleasures and Burdens of
   Being an Associate Editor at the *Administrative Science Quarterly*   299
   ROBERT I. SUTTON

   Becoming a Department Chair and an Administrator   309
31. Alice in Academia: The Department Chairman Role From
   Both Sides of the Mirror   313
   NANCY K. NAPIER
32. Herding Cats Part Deux: The Hygiene Factor   321
   CYNTHIA V. FUKAMI
33. Becoming an Administrator: The Education of an Educator   325
   ALLAN R. COHEN

   Becoming a Full Professor   333
34. On Becoming a Professor   335
   RAY V. MONTAGNO
35. Becoming a Full Professor   341
   SARA L. RYNES

   Pause Point 2: The Overenriched Work Life   349
36. Dealing With the Overenriched Work Life   351
   SUSAN E. JACKSON

Part IV. Middle Rhythms: Nontraditional Paths

   Working as a Consultant   357
37. Midlife as a Consultant   361
   PHILIP H. MIRVIS
38. Working as a Consultant: Academic Imprimatur or Taboo?   371
   MARY ANN VON GLINOW

   Developing Innovative Teaching Materials   377
39. Rhythms of an Academic Life   381
   ROBERT D. MARX

40. Reflections on Championing an Innovation in Academe: The Case of
    Management Skill Education   391
    DAVID A. WHETTEN

    Working Inside the University   399
41. Breaking Out, Inside the University   401
    JUDY D. OLIAN

    Working With Policy Makers   409
42. Working With Policy Makers   411
    PAUL R. SACKETT

    Pause Point 3: Another Look at Integrating Work and Nonwork Lives   417
43. Confronting the Tensions in an Academic Career   421
    ROBERT E. QUINN, REGINA M. O'NEILL, and GELAYE DEBEBE
44. Professional and Personal Life   429
    ANNE SIGISMUND HUFF

Part V. Rhythms of Renewal

    Taking a Sabbatical   435
45. What's Next After 10 Years as Dean? Reflections of a Reemerging Professor 437
    ANDRÉ L. DELBECQ
46. A Sabbatical Journey: Toward Personal and Professional Renewal   443
    MERYL REIS LOUIS

Part VI. Rhythms of the Field

    A Look at the Future   453
47. Business Schools in Transition: A Brief History of Business Education   457
    RAYMOND E. MILES
48. The External and Institutional Context of Business Higher Education   459
    WILLIAM H. MOBLEY
49. The Changing Role of the Business School's Environment:
    The Threat-Rigidity Response Is Real   465
    ROBERT B. DUNCAN
50. Business Schools in Transition: An Associate Dean's Perspective   469
    MARCIA P. MICELI
51. Stakeholders and You   475
    JANET P. NEAR
52. Embracing Change: We Get By With a Lot of Help From Our Friends   481
    JAMES P. WALSH

    Commentary   485
    PETER J. FROST and M. SUSAN TAYLOR

    Conclusion   497

    About the Editors   501

    About the Contributors   503

Introduction to the Series

The title of this series, **Foundations for Organizational Science** (FOS), denotes a distinctive focus. FOS books are educational aids for mastering the core theories, essential tools, and emerging perspectives that constitute the field of organizational science (broadly defined to include organizational behavior, organizational theory, human resource management, and business strategy). The primary objective of this series is to support ongoing professional development among established scholars.

The series was born out of many long conversations among several colleagues, including Peter Frost, Anne Huff, Rick Mowday, Ben Schneider, Susan Taylor, and Andy Van de Ven, over a number of years. From those discussions, we concluded that there has been a major gap in our professional literature, as characterized by the following comment: "If I, or one of my students, want to learn about population ecology, diversification strategies, group dynamics, or personnel selection, we are pretty much limited to academic journal articles or books that are written either for content experts or practitioners. Wouldn't it be wonderful to have access to the teaching notes from a course taught by a master teacher of this topic?"

The plans for compiling a set of learning materials focusing on professional development emerged from our extended discussions of common experiences and observations, including the following:

1. While serving as editors of journals, program organizers for professional association meetings, and mentors for new faculty members, we have observed wide variance in theoretical knowledge and tool proficiency in our field. To the extent that this outcome reflects available learning opportunities, we hope that this series will help "level the playing field."

2. We have all "taught" in doctoral and junior faculty consortia prior to our professional meetings and have been struck by how often the participants comment, "I wish that the rest of the meetings [paper sessions and symposia] were as informative." Such observations got us thinking—Are our doctoral courses more like paper sessions or doctoral consortia? What type of course would constitute a learning experience analogous to attending a doctoral consortium? What materials would we need to teach such a course? We hope that the books in this series have the "touch and feel" of a doctoral consortium workshop.

3. We all have had some exposure to the emerging "virtual university" in which faculty and students in major doctoral programs share their distinctive competencies, either through peri-

odic jointly sponsored seminars or through distance learning technology, and we would like to see these opportunities diffused more broadly. We hope that reading our authors' accounts will be the next best thing to observing them in action.

4. We see some of the master scholars in our field reaching the later stages of their careers, and we would like to "bottle" their experience and insight for future generations. Therefore, this series is an attempt to disseminate "best practices" across space and time.

To address these objectives, we ask authors in this series to pass along their "craft knowledge" to students and faculty beyond the boundaries of their local institutions by writing from the perspective of seasoned teachers and mentors. Specifically, we encourage them to invite readers into their classrooms (to gain an understanding of the past, present, and future of scholarship in particular areas from the perspective of their firsthand experience), as well as into their offices and hallway conversations (to gain insights into the subtleties and nuances of exemplary professional practice).

By explicitly focusing on an introductory doctoral seminar setting, we encourage our authors to address the interests and needs of nonexpert students and colleagues who are looking for answers to questions such as the following: Why is this topic important? How did it originate and how has it evolved? How is it different from related topics? What do we actually know about this topic? How does one effectively communicate this information to students and practitioners? What are the methodological pitfalls and conceptual dead ends that should be avoided? What are the most/least promising opportunities for theory development and empirical study in this area? What questions/situations/phenomena are not well suited for this theory or tool? What is the most interesting work in progress? What are the most critical gaps in our current understanding that need to be addressed during the next 5 years?

We are pleased to share our dream with you, and we encourage your suggestions for how these books can better satisfy your learning needs—as a newcomer to the field preparing for prelims or developing a research proposal, or as an established scholar seeking to broaden your knowledge and proficiency.

David A. Whetten
Series Editor

Acknowledgments

The original impetus for this book was the creation of the **Foundations for Organizational Science** series by David Whetten and his sense that there was a need for a handbook in the series that dealt with faculty development. We jumped at the chance to do something with this concept, and this book is the result. We owe Dave a great debt of thanks for creating the opportunity for this to happen and for his continued encouragement through the several years that it has taken to bring it to fruition. We thank also other members of the FOS Board, Anne Huff, Rick Mowday and Andy Van de Ven, for their suggestions and critiques in the early days of the project, and we are very appreciative of the support we have received from Harry Briggs and Marquita Flemming at Sage. Several individuals have provided administrative and secretarial assistance for the project, and we have benefited enormously from their competence: Thank you to Stacie Chappell, Vivien Clark, and Cynthia Ree. The final product was influenced by the many constructive comments made by faculty and doctoral students at two presentations of the commentary of the book, one at the University of British Columbia and the other at the University of Massachusetts at Amherst. We are most grateful for those contributions. Finally, we thank our authors, who have shared their stories and reports and who provide the heart and soul of the book. We have more to say about their contributions in our introduction. We have shared equally in the shaping and editing of this volume, and take full responsibility for any errors and omissions. Creating this book has been a most interesting and rewarding experience for us. It has affirmed our enthusiasm for the academic life.

Peter J. Frost
M. Susan Taylor

Introduction

> Storytelling is fundamental to the human search for meaning, whether we tell stories of the creation of the earth or of our own early choices. . . . The past empowers the present and the groping footsteps leading to this present mark the pathways to the future.
>
> *Mary Catherine Bateson,* Composing a Life, *1990*

Perhaps the greatest impetus for our undertaking this volume was our surprise and disappointment when we realized how little information, conceptual or anecdotal, existed about the paths that academics choose to follow across the course of their careers. At the time of its beginning, we were both either experiencing or approaching forks in our own careers. Peter had just become an associate dean at a time when his faculty was entering a period of significant and rapid change; he frequently thought about what he had done in accepting his new position and wondered how he might better prepare himself to cope with the challenges that loomed on the horizon. Susan, fast approaching her promotion review for full professor, was surprised at strong feelings of having "been there, done that," in practice, if not in title. In thinking about the upcoming review, she seemed to hear the lyrics of the 1970s pop tune "Is That All There Is?" playing in her head. Thus both of us had our own set of career questions and were strongly motivated to discover some insights about various roles and activities that exist within the academic enterprise.

In the past, when concerns or questions about career issues arose, we had frequently relied on the experiences and insights of colleagues we knew and trusted. We generally chose as our advisers academics who not only had already faced similar transition points but were open and sharing enough to provide fairly objective assessments of the pros and cons of their choices. Further, we each recalled having assumed the adviser role when other colleagues called with their own sets of career questions. However, recognizing that the academic career path, never what one could describe as "a straight shot down Interstate Highway X," becomes even more convoluted after midcareer, we could easily envision our questions about career possibilities far outdistancing the experience base of our trusted advisers. Further, we suspected we were not alone in this respect. In short, we felt that much might be gained from the creation of a sourcebook describing the experiences of scholars in different roles and at different transition points and providing sets of guidelines that they felt might inform the choices of others; thus the vision for this book was born. In hindsight, we are quite pleased with how the book compares with its initial vision.

That being said, however, it is important to address early in this introduction a concern about the methodology used by the contributors who provide their accounts of their personal experiences. This issue was brought to our attention by James Walsh in the essay that appears here as Chapter 21. In that narrative, he urges us to view others' prescriptions about how to live our lives with caution, for, as he puts it, "A prescribed life is not a lived life" (p. 204). We think this is a useful caution. Each person needs to make his or her own decisions about life choices. Furthermore, those who have grown up in homes where the academic life has been lived may have little need for a book like this. Conversely, many of us had only brief, rather superficial exposure to the academic career before entering it, and found that it remained something of a black box even afterward. As Joan Gallos observes in Chapter 2: "I had no idea how that [the academic life] translated into day-to-day behavior. I was the first member of my family to attend college, let alone the first with any thoughts of teaching in one" (p. 12).

One the other hand, this is not just a prescriptive book; it is a very descriptive, quasi-experiential one. Even experienced and knowledgeable professionals sometimes find themselves in unfamiliar territory, having to tackle new tasks for which there is little lore on what to expect from the assignment. Anne Huff has likened the seeking out of assistance from others as equivalent to "making cement" for the first time. At a 1995 Academy of Management doctoral consortium, she observed:

When my husband and I wanted to make an addition to our house some time ago, we realized that one of the first tasks we faced was to prepare the foundations, and this was going to entail having to make cement. Since we had not done this before, we read as many books as we could about the process and began to understand what needed to be done. We were stuck, however, with knowing how to deal with the statement: "You will know when it is ready to pour when it has the right consistency, just like porridge"! No amount of reading could convey this desired quality. We needed to call on a friend who had done

this before. Once he had shown us the "right consistency" in a batch of cement, we were able to grasp the instruction. It was now up to us to do the job, to mix the cement and to pour the foundations according to our own judgment.

We intend the advice in this book to have the quality that Anne describes. We agree with James Walsh that each of us must live his or her own life, without becoming a carbon copy of someone else's admonitions about how to do this. At the same time, we agree with Anne Huff that reading about how tasks can be done and having others with expertise "show" us something about the more ephemeral qualities of the process ("the right consistency") may help to demystify what we need to do, thus inspiring and empowering us to move forward to put our own imprint on the task.

The title *Rhythms of Academic Life* originated from the input of our Foundations of Organizational Science coeditors—Anne Huff, Rich Mowday, David Whetten, and Andy Van de Ven—at our first staff meeting in 1992. They observed that the academic career is one characterized by recurrence more than by a progressive flow of seasons from spring to winter. Thus the seeds of this volume were sown.

In planning the book, we spent approximately 6 months identifying a group of contributors who could and would speak personally and informally about their experiences with particular paths that academics might take during the course of their careers. We strove for diversity in contributors along many dimensions other than their career choices—field of study, gender, career seniority, nationality, size and mission of employer, and so forth—because of the diversity within the academic population. Our invitations to authors urged them to tell the stories of their journeys along particular paths: how they came about, the people they consulted for guidance and support (before leaving as well as on the way), and the nature of the trips themselves. We asked them also to provide any advice they might have for those contemplating similar journeys.

The contributors' responses to our invitation were generally quite gratifying. Most expressed considerably more concern about *when* we needed their stories than about *why* we would ask them too undertake such a task. Further, their enthusiasm seemed to heighten as the first drafts began to reach us, with several reporting that initial doubts about the value of the project of their contribution vanished in the process of recalling and, sometimes, reanalyzing the personal meanings of their journeys. The results of their efforts proved to be quite extraordinary in the reading, and perhaps even in the telling.

As a collection, these essays provide rich, personal, sometimes poignant and often quite humorous accounts of common and unique journeys that may be taken during the course of an academic career, and of the "pause points" needed to reflect on the meaningfulness of life along the way. Often, while acknowledging favorable biases about their own experiences, con-tributors readily conclude that such journeys are not the best choices for everyone, and they explain why. Their willingness to share their experiences with others who know them only as colleagues, rather than confidants or even acquaintances, has greatly enhanced our understanding of career options; and yes, they have already informed, albeit *not predetermined,* some of our own career choices. We hope that reading this book will provide you with some insights, some affirmations, even some redefinitions of the way you choose to live your academic life. Should you wish to share your thoughts and reactions with us or any of the authors, that would be most welcome. Now we invite you to read on.

I

Career Rhythms

Five Exemplars

Developing a successful career is much like riding a train. Both require having one's ticket punched along the way.

Arthur G. Bedeian (p. 4)

A successful academic core is rooted in a clear sense of contribution (What do you want to do?), an honest assessment of talent (What do you do well?), a choice of method (How will you make your contribution?), and knowledge of what is joyful for you (What do you like to do best?).

Joan V. Gallos (p. 17)

Family life plays a major role in my conceptualization of what it means to be human. For this reason, I can reflect on the rhythm of my career life only by viewing it jointly with the rhythm of my family life.

Miriam Erez (p. 21)

Throughout my adult life I've been blessed with a wonderful wife, loving sons, challenging work, splendid colleagues, and a lot of luck.

Vance F. Mitchell (p. 36)

Some careers are a string of discontinuous projects, perhaps. Mine hasn't been like that—I see it as one big project that started with some builders on a building site, some analytic builders in some varied conceptual sites, and I've just negotiated the breaks that appeared along the way.

Stewart R. Clegg (p. 53)

In subsequent sections of this book we present reports of academics who have experienced one or another of the many rhythms in an academic's life. As might be anticipated, such experiences tend to take place in the context of other rhythms that have impacts on the lives of academics and those around them. In those later chapters, however, there tends to be an emphasis on particular sets of activities that are most engaging or pressing at the time or for which the individuals have primary responsibility. Some of the reports deal also with transitions—such as getting tenure, becoming a full professor, or taking a sabbatical—that provide individuals with significant opportunities for self-reflection.

In this part of the book, we present five extended reports by authors who describe their journeys through a number of academic activities and transition points in their careers. They draw inferences and offer suggestions based on having been in the field for many years and having engaged in many academic roles and stages in their careers. Although their stories are in many respects unique, as are all the stories in this volume, there are commonalities among their messages. Their reports foreshadow, in some cases even mirror, observations and experiences that others share in this section and in the more specialized sections of the book. Of course, there are important ways in which the suggestions from these five authors are different from one another and from those found elsewhere in the book. These differences are as illuminating as are the points of similarity. They help us see the nuances, the complexities, and the range of possible choices and paths we might take as academics.

The five authors whose chapters appear in Part I share an obvious enthusiasm for their work and for their field, as well as a deep commitment to the academic enterprise. All have been acknowledged for their work and

honored, in different ways, by their peers. Arthur Bedeian's 12 suggestions for optimizing career success are based on 25 years of experience in the United States as a researcher, teacher, and textbook writer and his view as a former president of the Academy of Management. Joan Gallos tells her story from the perspective of being the first member of an immigrant family to attend a university, to become a professor. She writes also as someone who embarked on a relatively nontraditional academic path, at least in a North American context. Miriam Erez provides yet another, different career context. She was born and raised in Israel, and she describes her experiences as an academic partly in terms of cultural values from within traditions in Israel that she sees as significantly different from those that women scientists encounter in North America. Vance Mitchell, although officially in his retirement years, is working on a third professional career, this one as a professor at Embry-Riddle Aeronautical University. His career experiences span a term of active duty in World War II and several years in the U.S. military as well as an academic career as a researcher, teacher, and organization builder. Stewart Clegg's story reflects his 25 years as a scholar in the United Kingdom and currently in Australia. Among other observations he brings to the discussion are reflections on his encounters and exchanges with other scholars in Europe, Australia, North America, and Brazil; on his great interest in history, philosophy, and sociology; and on the contributions of these influences to the books he has written on power and organization.

The stories of these five authors, which represent the culmination of many years in academia and in a variety of professional, cultural, and historical contexts, make interesting reading in and of themselves. They also serve as points of reference from which to view the contributions in the sections that follow.

1 Lessons Learned Along the Way

TWELVE SUGGESTIONS FOR OPTIMIZING CAREER SUCCESS

Arthur G. Bedeian

In prefacing my remarks, let me first note that they are based more on experience than on science. One may thus question their generalizability. My $n = 1$. At the same time, the scientific databases dealing with academic career success are quite limited.

My remarks result from my participation in more than a dozen doctoral consortia devoted to the "whys" and "wherefores" of career success, extended conversations over the past two and a half decades with respected peers in my academic cohort, and hours of personal reflection tinted with a liberal dose of agony.

Warning: My remarks are admittedly very prescriptive, with many "dos" and "don'ts." Additionally, they may seem, but are not meant to be, harsh or snide; I mean them only to be candid. To this end, they are organized into what might be termed suggestions for optimizing career success. Although my remarks may seem to be aimed only at individuals who wish to pursue high-profile academic research careers, in reality the proffered suggestions are directed to all those who seek personal and career success.

Suggestion 1: Hit the Ground Running

A large measure of career success is the ability to differentiate oneself. In this respect, every cohort has its standout Hi Ps—high-potential members—who announce their presence with an early and rapid succession of first-tier publications. The importance of timely publications and the notion of a greater multiplier effect for

AUTHOR'S NOTE: The helpful vetting of Achilles A. Armenakis, W. Jack Duncan, Hubert S. Feild, and David D. Van Fleet on an earlier draft of the manuscript for this essay is gratefully acknowledged.

publications authored earlier rather than later in one's academic career is supported by both experience and empirical research. Tuckman (1976) reports that those who publish are rewarded not only with higher salaries, but with larger incremental returns from early as compared with subsequent publications. As to be expected, his data also show an increasing probability of promotion with increased publication output.

With regard to differentiating oneself in the academic marketplace and announcing one's presence, various rules of thumb are commonly offered to doctoral candidates. Two publications, two to three paper presentations, and attendance at a doctoral consortium constitute a common benchmark. Fortunate are those doctoral candidates whose socialization has prepared them to make informed choices among competing activities and to pursue their craft effectively. My favorite query for consortia attendees is whether they feel guilty watching TV. If so, chances are they've been properly socialized, with a strong work ethic. I can easily identify several of my own peers who, after 25 years, still feel guilty watching television! So much for the traumas of graduate school.

It has been frequently observed that developing a successful career is much like riding a train. Both require having one's ticket punched along the way. Getting a quick start, or hitting the ground running, can do much to ensure that the journey from assistant, to associate, to full professor proceeds in a timely fashion, as one's ticket is properly punched at all the appropriate stations. This is not to say that all successful careers necessarily follow the same timetable. It took the immortal Abe Maslow 23 years to make full professor (Hoffman, 1988). Some trains are obviously slower than others, but nevertheless do reach their intended destinations.

Suggestion 2: Locate the Best Predictor of Future Performance

Several points are intertwined in the concept of predictors of future performance. First, the prestige of an individual's doctoral institution is a major determinant in his or her being selected for a position in a distinguished academic department. This has been shown to be true across disciplines, including in the field of

management (Bedeian & Feild, 1980). At the same time, whereas pedigrees may be helpful for obtaining desirable positions—especially early in academics' careers—at good universities they are of little value for keeping such positions. Few people are successful in sustaining entire careers on the basis of where they earned their degrees. (As an aside, I've long contended that if the first thing an individual mentions upon initially meeting fellow academics is where he or she received a degree, it's likely that person has little else to talk about.)

Thus, whereas choice of graduate school sets an indelible mark on a scholar's career, the cachet of a prestigious degree will ultimately wear thin unless bolstered by some degree of performance. Concomitantly, the handicap of initial identification with a less prestigious department can be surmounted through the establishment of a strong publication record and a professional reputation to match. Although graduates of prestigious departments do have a beginning advantage through their greater access to other distinguished departments, personality and ability are also key causal antecedents of career success (Rodgers & Maranto, 1989). Admittedly, as the graduate of an institution with no discernible cachet, my interpretation of these "facts" reflects a belief in advancement by merit rather than in particularistic criteria such as doctoral origin. Simply put, I've always believed in "hiring people, not schools." For my money, I've thus always favored job candidates with a high need for achievement over graduates of prestigious departments with little else to recommend them. Available evidence supports this practice (Taylor, Locke, Lee, & Gist, 1984).

As a second point concerning predictors of future performance, tenure and promotion committees are well known for discounting publications that are dissertation based. The extent to which such publications represent candidates' efforts or those of entire dissertation committees is seldom clear. Whereas collaboration is to be encouraged, some display of "independent scholarly ability" is almost de rigueur for tenure and promotion consideration. This is why sole-authored publications are seen as important in the evaluation of academic performance (Reichers, 1985).

As a third point, tenure and promotion committees are also known for stressing the importance of a "sustained level of academic performance." This, of course, places a premium on hitting the ground running and penalizes "late blooming." Consider a tenure/promotion candidate whose publications over the past 6 years have all been accepted within the past 6 to 12 months. Is the first 5 years or the last 12 months most representative of the candidate's scholarly ability? Believing that the best predictor of future performance is past performance, and realizing that some people respond only when their feet are to the fire, a risk-averse tenure and promotion committee is likely to return a negative vote.

In my personal experience, I have found that if new assistant professors don't publish within the first 3-4 years on the job, the odds are they never will. This may well explain why, other things equal, a new PhD's market value is generally greater than that of a seasoned PhD who has yet to publish. The former, at least, offers potential. The latter can only offer excuses.

Before leaving this issue, I want to acknowledge that some scholars labor their entire careers, making sustained and substantive academic contributions, and never attain great notoriety. This highlights the fact that in some cases careers are built on peak performances. Without listing specific names, I believe it should be quite easy for most readers to identify several management "stars" whose fame is bound to single theories or models. As a graduate student in the late 1960s, I remember thinking how fantastic it would be if I could just develop a theory or model that would bear my name. Maslow's need theory being popular at the time, I could just see it—Bedeian's hierarchy of needs. I'd be famous for life!

In her book *Men and Women of the Corporation*, Kanter (1977) argues that the job makes the person, not vice versa. Career success, she suggests, is at least partially determined by the nature of the social circumstances people find themselves in, rather than what they inherently bring to a job. Thus if an individual is a successful scholar, this may say as much about the surrounding environment as it says about his or her capacity to do research.

There is no doubt that whatever career success I may have enjoyed was largely determined by my being able to spend the first years of my career at Auburn University. The environment within the Management Department there was one of nourishment, excitement, and collegiality. Above all, no one was afraid of excellence and achievement in others. Why the critical mass that existed at Auburn in the mid-1970s formed is a question that still puzzles those of us who enjoyed the thrill of being part of what for many is a never-in-a-lifetime experience. Why it dissipated is unfortunately too easily explained as the result of poor university management. Without commenting further on this issue, let me simply note that, in my own experience, the old maxim that "good universities don't support bad departments, and bad universities don't support good ones" is generally true (Orr, 1993).

Nevertheless, whatever the circumstances, the bottom line is simply stated: Work with good people. I have collaborated with more than 65 colleagues—several of whom I've never met face-to-face. Playing to each other's strengths, we've complemented one another quite nicely. Commenting on this same point, and its relevance for junior and senior scholars alike, Nobel laureate Herbert Simon (1991) advises:

Suggestion 3:
Location, Location, Location

Realtors tell us that the three most important factors in selecting a site for home or business are location, location, and location. If I were asked to name the most important factor in a successful career, my answer would unhesitatingly be locating with colleagues one can work with—that is, having a critical mass of colleagues involved in researching, writing, and publishing.

To make interesting scientific discoveries, you should acquire as many good friends as possible, who are as energetic, intelligent, and knowledgeable as they can be. Form partnerships with them whenever you can. Then sit back and relax. You will find that all the programs you need are stored in your friends, and will execute productively and creatively as long as you don't interfere too much. (p. 387)

Suggestion 4:
Publish, Publish, Publish

One of the first lessons one typically learns upon entering graduate school is that publication is the primary basis of academic recognition. In economic analogy, publications are the major currency of the realm. Whereas there may be diversity in academic reward structures at the institutional level (e.g., teaching, research, service), the reward structure at the national and international levels is monolithic rather than plural. Thus, whereas scholars may draw their paychecks locally, academic recognition and the rewards that follow (e.g., editorial appointments, professional board memberships, fellow designations) are conferred elsewhere as a consequence of judgments made by the larger academic community (see Fox, 1985). Publications mean visibility, esteem, and career mobility.

In that the academic community is nationally rather than locally based, aspiring academics soon learn the necessity of adopting a "cosmopolitan" rather than "local" orientation (Gouldner, 1957). Cosmopolitans seek national recognition within a discipline as a whole, and feel separate from their immediate environments. They may work within institutions or departments, but they never belong to those entities. In contrast to locals, whose loyalties reside in their employing institutions, cosmopolitans may thus threaten locally vested interests.

The academic visibility, esteem, and career mobility enjoyed by successful cosmopolitans do, however, provide a measure of local independence. The rewards (e.g., editorial appointments, professional board memberships, fellow designations) that follow national recognition translate locally into what Hollander (1964) has termed "idiosyncrasy credits," operationally defined as the degree to which an individual may deviate from commonly expected behavior. Hence, as long as they are able to maintain a credit balance, cosmopolitans are able to engage in idiosyncratic behavior without fear of locally imposed sanctions. Stated differently, by expending discipline award credits, cosmopolitans are generally able to "get away with" actions unthinkable on the part of their locally oriented colleagues.

The benefits of a nationally based academic reputation should thus be obvious. This is not to say that local considerations can be ignored. When all is said and done, however, the aspiring scholar would do well to remember that "one's performance is the best tenure one can ever have" (Duncan, 1991).

In reflecting on this advice, one should not come away believing that performance is solely determined by research productivity or that excellence in teaching and research are at odds. The contention that teaching and research involve an either/or bifurcation implicitly establishes what I believe to be a false dichotomy. Complete academic success demands that those who wish to "play in the big leagues" be able to both "walk and talk," "hit and run," "teach and research." For any school even purporting to be a major university, only those scholars who excel in *both* teaching and research should be tenured and promoted. Establishment of a dual structure whereby faculty members are rewarded for excellence in *either* teaching or research will invariably result in three levels (or classes) of faculty—those who are notable teachers, those who are notable researchers, and, at the highest level, those major leaguers who are both. The internecine conflict that is likely to result as a consequence of such a pecking order is, no doubt, more than familiar to most faculty.

Suggestion 5: Be Proactive

In academia, as in any walk of life, an individual can be overwhelmed by meaningless activity. This underscores the necessity of making effective choices among alternative activities, given their potential payoffs. The aspiring scholar bent on a successful career must quickly appreciate that no individual has enough time to dispense effort endlessly to all comers without regard to the ultimate consequences. Given my previous emphasis on earning academic currency, my comments at this point are directed primarily at the individual's proactive management of workload so that he or she can transcend the immediate environment and establish a cosmopolitan role identity.

With sound teaching as a given, overinvolvement in administrative work or "service" can be an attractive distraction. Service activities such as committee assignments are often highly visible, easy, appreciated (in the short term), and, thus, nonthreatening (Taylor & Martin,

1987). At the same time, as Taylor and Martin (1987) note: "No one ever got promoted because of committee work" (p. 28). In such cases, all too often, the reward for doing a good job is another job.

The key to managing the service load proactively is the early development of an understanding of local norms. One should avoid overinvolvement in service activities, but should also take care to do one's fair share—otherwise, one will likely be resented. In this regard, there is typically a price to be paid for saying no. However, there is also always a price in terms of one's time for saying yes. In my own career, I've actually practiced saying no in anticipation of being "honored" with assignment to this or that committee. With experience, I've discovered that if I can't say no, I should at least avoid saying yes. Buying time with a noncommittal response has often afforded me the opportunity to seek higher-level intervention on my behalf.

Suggestion 6:
Do Different Things

It has long been my belief that academics should do different things at different points in their careers. This contention rests on several bases. The first involves the obvious need for beginning faculty to provide early evidence of their teaching competence and scholarly abilities, both being prerequisites of promotion and tenure. As a consequence, untenured assistant professors (and most associate professors) are generally advised to direct their efforts toward refining their classroom skills as well as establishing and executing deliberate research and publication programs.

As I have noted, faculty at the beginning of their careers are judged primarily by the quality of their research, and by journal publications in particular. Authoring textbooks may offer the promise of monetary gain, but it is an ineffective means for earning either promotion or tenure. Indeed, at many institutions, textbooks are not even examined as a part of judging publication performance, but are instead considered a form of teaching or service activity. Thus it is standard advice that one should consider authoring a textbook only *after* one has

received tenure and, depending on local norms, after one has been promoted to full professor.

A second basis for my belief that faculty should be doing different things at different points in their careers is the realization that, over time, they are capable of making different contributions to the academic enterprise. The "gray-hair" credibility of a seasoned senior professor is a distinct advantage in continuing education, outside consulting, and executive MBA programs. Senior faculty are also likely to be in a better position to divert time from their research to pursue research grants, accept administrative appointments, and become involved in such activities as faculty governance.

A final basis for my belief that individuals should do different things at different points in their careers is normative in nature. Simply put, I believe that each member of our profession should return something to the field, and those blessed with high standing have a special obligation to do so. Jack Duncan has labeled this obligation "Luke's Iron Law of Responsibility," after the Gospel of St. Luke, 12:48: *To whom much is given, shall much be required* (cited in Hunt & Blair, 1987, p. 207). Thus senior faculty involvement in mentoring junior faculty, accepting memberships on government panels, and so on are all means of giving something back.

Suggestion 7:
Achieve Academic Credibility

At some point in their careers, most faculty members at least entertain the possibility of accepting full-time administrative appointments. No doubt, higher education desperately needs better-qualified administrators. It all too often seems, however, that those who pursue administrative careers do so for all the wrong reasons—reasons having more to do with power and status than with fostering scholarship and classroom learning.

My one "tip" in this regard is more truthfully an opinion. That is, those who do go into administration should carry with them a measure of academic credibility. This is especially important because it avoids situations in which deans or department chairs demand that faculty members do things (e.g., conduct research, publish, secure grants) that the administrators have not done and perhaps could not do themselves. Unfortunately, this is an additional reason some faculty go into administration—they can't do, but they don't mind telling other people to do.

Suggestion 8:
Take Quantum Leaps

Whereas my preceding suggestion constitutes an opinion masquerading as a tip, here I offer an observation: At least two moves are typically required to maximize a career. The first involves that all-important initial academic appointment; the second is the seemingly mandatory quantum leap to secure a named professorship or endowed chair. Why the second more often than not requires a move from one institution to another is a conundrum. A partial answer might involve a second observation: An individual's academic accomplishments are almost invariably honored more by others than by those at his or her own institution. This, combined with the fact that one generally has less bargaining leverage at home than away, leads to a peculiar form of academic musical chairs. In one case, I actually witnessed an institution seeking to fill a chaired position forsake a deserving local candidate in order to hire an "outsider" who was half as qualified. The kicker is that the outsider was not only half as qualified, but required being paid twice as much. Meanwhile, those in charge seemed to delight in believing they were coming out ahead—another testimonial to the need for better-qualified administrators.

Suggestion 9:
Balance Work and Family

There is perhaps not much new that can be added to what has already been proffered in the popular press concerning the trials of balancing work and family. In my salad days, I could routinely spend 14-16 hours a day locked in my study revising a textbook. The burnout that ultimately resulted, and the death of a well-known contemporary, actually found dead at his desk, occasioned a simple question: Did I want to spend the rest of my life writing textbooks? My answer was no.

Looking back, I now see how I cheated not only my family but myself of irretrievable time together. Would I have achieved in my career as I have without such sacrifice? Who knows? Was it worth it? I honestly can't say. Materially, my family and I do have more than we would have had otherwise. And, admittedly, the additional income provided a sense of independence from the vagaries of state funding for salary increases. At the same time, let me caution those unreformed workaholics who may read this that rather than achieving fame and glory, they may simply die young and make their spouses' next partners rich.

Suggestion 10:
Continue Your Education

It seems strange to me that so many in our field fail to practice what they preach. We give entire lectures on career planning that stress the importance of investing in one's future by continuing one's education. We admonish our students that receiving a degree should be viewed as the beginning and not the end of a person's education. With no empirical proof, I would guesstimate that most faculty members acquire 80% of the knowledge they need in their careers *after* they've completed their formal education.

Perhaps the smartest decision I have made in my entire career involved "going back to school." I enrolled in my first multivariate statistics course while I was a faculty member at Auburn. I spent a sabbatical taking a course in research design. To this day, I take methodological notes on every issue of every journal to which I subscribe. Working with PhD students and younger colleagues has also been an invaluable means of updating and expanding my knowledge base. *Be forewarned:* When one submits to the temptation to jump from a research report's abstract to its conclusion, bypassing the methods section, it is time to go back to school.

Suggestion 11:
Become Involved in the Associations

The career benefits of professional association involvement extend well beyond those provided by formal paper sessions. Interacting with others in one's discipline is not only a means of establishing a professional identity, but a way to find points of reference for one's career. Networking, the informal job market, and an opportunity to develop name recognition are likewise benefits commonly attributed to association membership. In reflecting on the benchmarks of my own career, I am particularly proud of being the youngest person ever elected an Academy of Management fellow. At the time (1979), I was 32 years old. My DBA had been awarded only 6 years prior. I remain similarly proud of serving (in 1988) as the Academy's youngest-ever president. Both honors have afforded me a measure of academic credibility (not to mention a cache of idiosyncrasy credits) that would have been otherwise unattainable.

Less commonly acknowledged benefits are perhaps more subtle. In my own case, the opportunity to meet several times a year with my "reference group" of special colleagues has been more valuable than any therapy group. By coming together to ventilate our feelings and vocalize our frustrations, we provide one another with both social support and encouragement. The resulting friendships have meant more to me than all my academic achievements combined.

Suggestion 12: Have Fun!

Putting aside my earlier comment on the need for a strong work ethic, having fun (at work and play) requires that one not take one's career too seriously. There will always be conflicts and trade-offs. No matter how sharp one is, there is always someone sharper. And the more career success one enjoys, the harder it is to reach the next level of achievement. In the end, when that last lecture is given and that last manuscript is in the mail, one must define career success for oneself and find one's own personal happiness. Good luck! Enjoy!

References

Bedeian, A. G., & Feild, H. S. (1980). Academic stratification in graduate management programs: Department prestige and faculty hiring patterns. *Journal of Management, 6,* 99-115.

Duncan, W. J. (1991, March). *Beyond Baton Rouge: Dilemmas, choices, and (eventually satisfaction) after 20 years.* Address delivered at Louisiana State University, Baton Rouge.

Fox, M. F. (1985). Publication, performance, and reward in science and scholarship. In J. C. Smart (Ed.), *Higher education: Handbook of theory and research* (Vol. 1, pp. 255-282). Edison, NJ: Agathon.

Gouldner, A. (1957). Cosmopolitans and locals: Toward an analysis of latent social roles, I. *Administrative Science Quarterly, 2,* 281-306.

Hoffman, E. (1988). *The right to be human: A biography of Abraham Maslow.* Los Angeles: Jeremy P. Tarcher.

Hollander, E. P. (1964). *Leaders, groups, and influence.* New York: Oxford University Press.

Hunt, J. G., & Blair, J. D. (1987). Content, process, and the Matthew effect among management academics. *Journal of Management, 13,* 191-210.

Kanter, R. M. (1977). *Men and women of the corporation.* New York: Basic Books.

Orr, D. (1993). Reflections on the hiring of faculty. *American Economic Review, 83,* 39-43.

Reichers, A. (1985). Thirty-one reasons to disparage research productivity: A humorous (?) look at performance appraisal by the numbers. *Industrial-Organizational Psychologists, 22*(2), 30-31.

Rodgers, R. C., & Maranto, C. L. (1989). Causal models of publishing productivity in psychology. *Journal of Applied Psychology, 74,* 636-649.

Simon, H. A. (1991). *Models of my life.* New York: Basic Books.

Taylor, M. S., Locke, E. A., Lee, C., & Gist, M. E. (1984). Type A behavior and faculty research productivity: What are the mechanisms? *Organizational Behavior and Human Performance, 34,* 402-418.

Taylor, S. E., & Martin, J. (1987). The present-minded professor: Controlling one's career. In M. P. Zanna & J. M. Darley (Eds.), *The complete academic: A practical guide for the beginning social scientist* (pp. 23-60). New York: Random House.

Tuckman, H. P. (1976). *Publication, teaching, and the academic reward structure.* Lexington, MA: Lexington.

2 On Becoming a Scholar

ONE WOMAN'S JOURNEY

Joan V. Gallos

If your graduate school experiences were like mine, they conveyed the requirements for success in academia: Publish often and appropriately, teach acceptably, make some service contribution to your institution and discipline, and strive for professional recognition through scholarly contributions. General guidelines abounded for the appropriate number of articles to publish, the kinds of journals to target, and "tenure-friendly" time frames for cementing a scholarly reputation. I logged in the appropriate number of hours with fellow graduate students before graduation, testing future projects, sharing ideas and plans, making sure I knew the appropriate ropes to skip. From the postdissertation trenches, everything seemed straightforward. So, doctorate in hand, I set out in 1985 to begin my academic career. It was not long before panic set in. *So now that I'm here, how do I do it?*

The teaching part was relatively easy. Courses were assigned and classes needed to be taught. The structure and requirements were externally provided. The same was true of institu-

tional service: Committee assignments made it easy to keep busy. But what about research and scholarship?

I began, as advised, spinning off articles from my dissertation. I sent out three pieces within 4 months of receiving my degree. I was feeling good and right on track, especially in light of the fact that I also carried a full teaching load, was still nursing my infant son, and shared care for my mother, who now lived with us and was dying of cancer. I worked on additional articles while I waited for word on my initial submissions. Three letters came. I quickly interpreted them as three flat rejections—letters that I now realize, years later and a journal editor myself, were encouraging, complimentary, and much more suggestions for refocusing and revising than recommendations to throw in the towel. But, inexperienced and too quickly discouraged, I stopped writing articles. I put the three letters, my three initial journal submissions, and notes for additional pieces in the bottom drawer of my desk.

I turned to planning a book project. My dissertation was on dual-career marriage, a hot topic in the mid-1980s. I worked hard for a year, learning to write a solid book proposal and engaging query letters. With cold calls and unsolicited submissions to the major trade houses, I received serious consideration from several publishers, but a contract never quite materialized.

Knowing what I know now about the publishing industry, I should have been encouraged. As an unpublished author, I got a foot in doors that are usually tightly sealed. As a young academic, however, I was devastated. Rather than persist and seek alternative publishing outlets, I took each rejection as evidence that it was time to move on to something else. I had no external pressures to publish: I now taught in a graduate management program, at Radcliffe, that rewarded only teaching. My internal needs, however, were as strong as ever.

I floundered. I filled folders with promising ideas and unpublished manuscripts. After I had done much soul-searching, it slowly became clear. I had had my doctorate in hand for 3 years, and yet I did not know how to be a working scholar. I knew research methods and techniques. I had plenty of ideas. I wrote well. I did not know, however, how to translate all that into a productive scholarly life. I can look back now and name three critical steps in my own professional evolution: learning to appreciate what I now call the "human side" of scholarship, developing a research identity, and claiming my own scholarly voice.

Appreciating the Human Side of Scholarship

I entered graduate school with no plans to become a professor. I initially went to Harvard for a master's in educational administration. There were things I wanted to learn before returning to a university administrative career. A chance meeting during my first week on campus with Chris Argyris, the distinguished organizational theorist, and my delight in discovering that the field of organizational behavior existed turned my administrative career intentions on end. I applied and was accepted to the doctoral program at Harvard. I realized that I could teach. I was now on the path to becoming a professor.

I had little knowledge of academic life. Graduate courses and doctoral seminars did little to fill the gap. I knew that professors taught classes and published research. I had no idea how that translated into day-to-day behavior. I was the first member of my family to attend college, let alone the first with any thoughts of teaching in one. I envied two fellow students who had professor parents, whose home experiences seemed to give them the inside scoop on academic life—an implicit understanding of the expectations and academic rituals, the ability to see professors as fallible and approachable human beings, and the confidence to share their own ideas and critiques with those who write the great books.

My family's legacy was different. To an ethnic family like mine, which deeply valued education and accomplishment, professors were distant icons. They were larger-than-life people who performed sacred work—they were folks to respect, listen to, and admire. My parents, a high school-educated electrician and a homemaker who ended her formal schooling after the eighth grade so that she could go to work to support her immigrant parents, were supportive of a daughter who aspired to such a noble occupation. "Who would have thought a girl from Lyman Avenue could get that far?" my parents would repeatedly marvel. "Not just a schoolteacher. A college teacher."

That family legacy of awe and respect, and the implicit reminder that people like me don't usually "get that far," blinded me as a budding academic to what I now call the human side of scholarship—the fact that productive scholars are everyday people, not deities, who succeed in the face of life's daily challenges. They are men and women who work hard and long, establishing goals and responding to serendipitous opportunities. I knew I struggled, working long hours and alone to hide my fears, rewriting and reediting pieces that I was sure would never be good enough, but I assumed it must be different for the great names who wrote the great works.

I could not see the writing struggles, the confidence swings, the inevitable rejections, the critical reviews, the frustrations and blocks, the infrequent great breakthroughs, the risks and failures as things that all academics experience. I ignored the persistence and overlooked the guesses, speculations, and risk taking that are part and parcel of scholarly discovery for all. I saw only the finished products—the acclaimed models, published theories, and public achievements—of the great masters. I mistook their finely polished products for the scholarly process itself and perceived an ease and a mysterious genius in all this. I privately questioned whether the "girl from Lyman Avenue" had the right stuff for academic life. The hidden fears and self-doubts led to self-censorship. My folder of ideas and unshared manuscripts swelled.

A critical turning point in my own development as a scholar came when I learned to look behind the facade of scholarly mystery and ease. Unwilling to give up on myself as a contributing member of the academy, I reflected on a set of experiences I had early in graduate school and finally saw what I needed to see. The great commonsense philosopher Yogi Berra was right in my case: Sometimes you just have to look a long time to see what's really there.

Tired of living in an old graduate dorm but without the resources to navigate the Cambridge apartment market successfully, an enterprising friend and I had lived for years as resident dog walkers and house sitters for a professor and his wife. The professor was eminent even by Harvard standards—a man whose books, government service, and celebrity status have made his name a household word. Those were wonderful years for many reasons; I return often to the memories with fondness, deep gratitude, and affection for the family.

From a career perspective, however, those memories became an invaluable resource for clarifying the real secrets of scholarly success. There I was, struggling to figure out academic life, when I realized I had had a unique opportunity to take a behind-the-scenes look at how a seasoned veteran does it. What had I seen in those years? What could I learn from that experience that could facilitate my own research and writing?

When I looked carefully, I saw persistence, discipline, commitment, and hard work as the key elements for success. I remember, for example, the house rules about quiet in the morning while the professor wrote. He wrote every morning, rising early to work before the phone could start ringing and each day's endless stream of fascinating visitors began. He was a social man, but he did not want conversation in the morn-

ing. He took a breakfast tray and ate alone in his room. Then he worked. He was disciplined about setting aside time for his writing. It was an important personal priority, and he managed his schedule accordingly.

External structures to support the writing process are important, but from reflecting on the work life of this scholar, I saw more. He had a firm internal commitment to writing, and he honored that commitment even in the face of attractive distractions. Exhaustion from foreign travel or meetings with world leaders would be enough to keep the average author from a manuscript, but not him. At times, writing can be fun; more often, it is tedious, hard work. I'm sure it is more satisfying to offer advice that can shape the course of history than to struggle for the right words to convey an argument. As this professor's life illustrated well, however, the commitment to keep writing has to be deep and internal. External requirements are not enough for any academic in the face of all there is to do.

Even with discipline, focus, and commitment, all writing takes time. I remember seeing this great man sit long hours in front of an old typewriter in his study, then leave for his office to work some more. I saw him pacing the yard deep in thought, sorting out some new idea or maybe just looking for the right turn of phrase. I heard him many times climbing the stairs well before dawn to a large and airy third-floor room where he sometimes liked to write: unable to sleep, maybe excited by a new project or troubled by an old one, he would try a change of venue to free the creative juices. I remember the spirited debates and intense exchanges with valued others over meals to fine-tune old ideas or stimulate new ones. I knew about the hours of inevitable editing and rewriting that made his prose sing. There was no mystery and ease in this man's vast productivity. He established and maintained structures that worked for him. He persisted in the face of critical reviews, as well as temptations to rest on praise and past laurels. He wrote regularly. He worked long and hard.

When I allowed myself to demystify academic life and create a workable model for how to manage the scholarly part of my own life better, my writing and publishing soared. When I am home, for example, I set aside time to write 5 days a week; it may be hours, it may be only a few minutes, but the regularity helps. The more I write, the easier the words come. The more familiar I am with a project, the better I can take advantage of unanticipated free moments. I no longer wait for those long blocks of free time that never seem to materialize. If I'm tired or don't feel particularly creative, I'll use the writing time to draft ideas or edit some work in progress. I am more patient with myself about how long it takes to complete a project. I rejoice at those brief moments of divine inspiration in writing, but am equally happy to celebrate the slow, ordinary gains.

I find time and boundary management to be important and ongoing struggles affecting my writing. The freedom and ambiguity of academic life make it easy to find lots of relevant things to do. It is easy to feel overloaded, to feel there really isn't enough time to do research. I know for me, however, it is more a question of being honest with myself about the choices I make and of organizing myself to honor my espoused priority to publish.

I know, for example, the time of day when I am most productive, and I work to keep that time free for writing. I try to avoid feeling guilty for doing that. I will not, for example, answer phones during writing time, nor will I return phone calls for days if I'm on a creative roll and want to devote my attention to that. Those who know me accept that as given. I now accept that myself. I manage guilt less well when I think about time away from my children and husband. That has become easier, however, as I have let go of old, tenacious, gender-based myths about the things every good mother and wife should do. More often now I say no to fascinating projects and assignments that I am always sure in the moment are once-in-a-lifetime opportunities—the kinds of projects that, in the past, let me feel productive without publishing.

Developing a Research Identity

Even with structures to facilitate writing, you still need something to write about. Graduate training (and faculty development efforts) too often omits opportunities for budding academics to develop their own research identities. Finding your research identity is more than planning and carrying out a research project or learning how to publish in the right journal. It means claiming both a methodology and, implicitly, a definition of truth that is right for you.

I feel fortunate that my graduate training involved work with a number of respected academics who held vastly different beliefs about research and scholarship. In one year, for example, I took courses from a proponent of anthropological research and had opportunities to explore the intricacies of ethnomethodology, from a traditional researcher who ran rats through mazes to learn about human nature, and from a critic of traditional research who promoted single-case analysis and action research as the way to ground theory and practice, as well as from a host of others with beliefs and scholarly agendas that fell somewhere along a research continuum from highly traditional to radically innovative.

As a graduate student, I remember feeling fragmented and confused by such pluralistic teachings; I struggled to reconcile the contradictions in what I heard, and felt as if I continuously confused research apples with oranges. It turned out to be productive confusion. As I sorted through the options, I became energized by my implicitly acquired appreciation of epistemology. I was excited by the realization that I had real choices about how to define scholarship and my contribution to truth. I saw a variety of legitimate options. The choice was mine.

This was a freeing realization. All I needed to do, I told myself as a young assistant professor, was choose an arena and plunge in. I knew I was not passionate about empirical research. I enjoyed building theory by reflecting on my own and others' clinical experiences. There was my niche.

Identifying an arena, however, was easier than unambivalently throwing in my hat. I knew how I wanted to make my contribution, but I was wary. I recognized the potential costs of choosing a somewhat nontraditional path. I knew that traditional researchers, whose positivist paradigms still dominate academia, would sit on journal editorial boards and possibly my tenure and promotion committees. I feared their questions about the rigor and reliability of my work, and anticipating their questions triggered my own. It took time for me to muster the courage to confirm my choice of a research paradigm. It took experience for me to respond to critics with questions about their methods, rather than doubts about my own.

Winning the Fritz Roethlisberger Memorial Award in 1990 was an important boost. The award, presented by the Organizational Behavior Teaching Society, named "Developmental Diversity and the OB Classroom: Implications for Teaching and Learning" (Gallos, 1989a) the best paper on organizations and management education published in the *Organizational Behavior Teaching Review* in 1988-1989. This endorsement from a group of respected colleagues was a welcome confirmation that I was heading in the right direction. No longer burdened by requirements and standards set by other research models, I embraced my own with gusto. Five years after finishing my doctorate, I finally felt ready to run.

Claiming My Scholarly Voice

The decision to run my own scholarly race was even deeper, in retrospect, than settling on a method and means for doing my work. It involved resolving internal teleological and ontological struggles in order to claim my own scholarly voice. Why do I write? Why should I write? What is my purpose in all this? At Radcliffe, I had no external pressures to publish. What did I hope to accomplish by sharing my words on paper? What kind of contribution could I make to our understanding of the world?

Without realizing it at the time, I implicitly answered those questions with my decision, 2 years out of graduate school, to teach at Radcliffe. I left a more traditional, publish-or-perish university environment after a well-meaning senior colleague took me aside and warned that I'd have a limited future there if I continued to focus on gender and those kinds of "tangential" issues. I vividly remember that conversation and our long walk through campus on a lovely spring day. It was a critical turning point in helping me understand that my purpose in writing was not to please other academics who had power over my future. That was neither the work I wanted to do nor the position I wanted to be in.

It may have been arrogance or counterdependence, but I now see my decision to choose the teaching-centered environment of Radcliffe over other tenure-track possibilities as my teleological awakening—a defining moment when I clarified my purpose as a scholar. I had something to say, and I wanted an environment that would offer support and freedom for me to do

that. It seemed a risky choice at the time. I worried. If I step off the traditional tenure path, can I ever get back on? But more important, was I disciplined enough to be an independent scholar? Those fears gradually dissipated as I began to build my own body of work. The Radcliffe choice, on the other hand, offered priceless opportunities for me to learn about myself and to develop my own scholarly voice.

Having a clear scholarly voice involves the willingness and ability to speak out, but it is more than just taking a stand. It entails a personal commitment to your own research agenda and a push to explore multiple facets of that agenda before moving on to something else. It requires identifying a passion for some set of issues and setting out to explore that deep interest, even in the face of opposition and critique. It means believing you have a worthwhile contribution to make. It involves finding a style of writing and expression that is uniquely and comfortably yours.

I found my scholarly voice during my Radcliffe years. I reaffirmed my deep commitment to gender and learning issues, providing myself with a valued, long-term research thread. My teaching in the Discovery program for underemployed women served as a catalyst for my work on gender in the adult classroom. It also provided a magical experience and transformation for me as a writer.

Writing about the Discovery Women was not a task or job. It was an engaging mission of love. As these women worked hard each week to claim their voices as students and professionals, I guided and charted their efforts. I shared their struggles and worked at the same time to claim my voice as a scholar. I wanted to tell their story well, for them and for me (Gallos, 1992, 1993, 1995b).

I learned from working with the Discovery women that I write best when I write from the heart. I like to harness passion and wed it with intellect. I write to make a difference on issues that I consider important. I will no longer write about something unless I care deeply about it. I do not strive to be an objective observer. I am a very subjective interpreter of the world around me. I do not write to report; I write to teach—to stimulate, to provoke, to unsettle, to share how I make sense of things so that others are encouraged to do the same. I write for impact, placing articles where my intended audience will find them (e.g., Gallos, 1995a, 1995c) rather than only in those first-tier, refereed journals that my present institution's promotion committee suggests. I write and publish more when I do it my way. I am willing to take the career risk that more is better for all concerned.

Consciously identifying and embracing this has liberated my voice. It drives my writing style and content. I no longer, for example, feel the need to justify my claims and beliefs with multiple references. I now use references to identify alternative resources or borrowed ideas, but no longer for permission to take a stand safely in the company of distinguished others. I remember years ago, however, writing a chapter on women's development (Gallos, 1989b) and agonizing over how many references I needed in order to assert that men and women are different. I spent weeks thinking about the issue, rewriting and adjusting my claim. It was a watershed experience; I realized I was less concerned that readers would disagree with me than I was fearful that invisible critics would say I had no right to say that. That distinction facilitated my writing further; I, more than anyone else, had a right to describe my beliefs and perspectives. My scholarly voice was finally in place.

Well-meaning colleagues periodically ask me to reflect on the downside of writing from the heart, but thus far I have experienced more benefits than costs. I deeply enjoy my work and am happy doing what I do. All this has increased my productivity and, paradoxically, has made me professionally attractive in some very traditional academic circles. My directness and willingness to take a stand have given me a distinctive edge and reputation. I write persuasively enough that people take my work seriously, even if they disagree. I feel satisfied, rewarded, and at peace.

Reflections on the Journey: Advice to Young Scholars

Becoming a productive scholar is a developmental journey. It involves understanding the research terrain, comparing alternative routes, choosing a personal path, recognizing critical crossroads, navigating roadblocks, sustaining personal commitment, and celebrating the joys of the expedition. I acknowledge that this essay tells only part of my story. Other factors have

influenced my journey as well—motherhood, geographic commitments, marriage, economic factors, a supportive and academic spouse, family responsibilities, gender, opportunities, luck, and fate. I have chosen, mindful of page limits, to focus on three central themes—appreciating the human side of scholarship, developing a research identity, and claiming a scholarly voice. These substantive, core issues are critical for all who navigate the road to scholarly productivity. I do not mean to imply, however, that the personal context for the journey is unimportant.

As I reflect on my life as a scholar, what have I learned? What advice do I offer to those beginning their journey? Plan well. Follow your heart. Enjoy the travel. Replenish your spirit along the way.

A Good Map Is Valuable: Plan for the Journey

A good map makes travel easier. It helps you see the big picture, understand the terrain, compare roads and options, plan a workable itinerary, identify landmarks you want to visit, and mark alternative routes if necessary. The same is true of the scholarly journey. You can't wander aimlessly from project to project, hoping some combination of publishing luck and divine intervention will get you to your destination. You need some sense of the big picture: where you're going and how you'll get there.

Understanding research options and consciously choosing a methodology are important steps in this process. Map out the possibilities. Identify the route that is right for you. If you feel limited in your methodological options, you may want to broaden your horizons by sitting in on different methods courses at your campus, reading, and interviewing colleagues who do different kinds of work. Don't assume that there is only one way to do research, especially if the one you use isn't working for you. Experiment. Broaden your research horizons. Find a method that inspires you.

Understanding the institutional terrain is also critical. What does it really take to get tenure and promotion at your institution? What does that mean for your scholarly journey? Not all colleges and universities are alike. Learn about the norms, requirements, and expectations at yours. Use the information to sketch out an itinerary that will get you to your professorial destination. Take stock along the way, and adjust your route accordingly. Share your plans and progress regularly with deans and department chairs. Get letters of support from them that note your accomplishments en route.

Alternatively, you may find that the more you learn about the fit between you and your institution, the clearer it is that you need to be someplace else, where you feel fewer constraints and better supported. If so, test out whether the constraints you see are really there. Most academic institutions are willing to tolerate at least a few highly productive iconoclasts and free spirits. If not, don't be afraid to change venues.

Follow Your Heart

Maps are useful but always incomplete. Freeways change. Exits close. Routes shift because of accidents or detours. We hit dead ends. We find ourselves off the main road. Sketching out a travel plan is important, but experienced travelers are always flexible and prepared for the unexpected. Academic life requires the same.

It may seem contradictory for me to advocate both solid plans and flexible openness, but both are requirements for academic success. Academia requires creativity. It is hard to anticipate and plan for everything in jobs that are steeped in learning and ambiguity. Unanticipated roadblocks, wondrous discoveries, coincidences, major disappointments, chance, and learning can all change professorial lives and directions. Collaboration with a colleague, the impact of a powerful book, and contextual factors such as parenthood or a new dean can turn the best-laid plans on end. Staying open to catch the wind is a good way to turn surprises into productive outcomes.

At the same time, a successful academic needs an anchor. Those without plans for their journey flounder, filling folders with possible ideas they never develop, bouncing from project to project, searching endlessly for their niche. Tenure committees have looked at files filled with good published work and still decided no, because they found no coherence, no sense of direction or identity in the portfolio. The essential task for any successful scholar is to find an anchor: solid core, flexible application.

How do you find your anchor? For me, it has been a process of discovering my own path, learning about myself and my choices, and choosing to follow my heart—listening to my internal voice and identifying the projects and products in which I can openly and unambivalently invest. A successful academic core is rooted in a clear sense of contribution (What do you want to do?), an honest assessment of talent (What do you do well?), a choice of method (How will you make your contribution?), and knowledge of what is joyful for you (What do you like to do best?). Answer those questions honestly for yourself. Find your niche. Identify your contribution. Claim your voice. Follow your passion. Know yourself as a scholar. You'll be able to navigate with the sun.

Celebrate the Joys of Traveling

We embark on a journey to reach some destination. It is foolish, however, to focus only on the end point and miss the scenery along the way. Roads twist in surprising ways, unanticipated sights capture our fantasies, new vistas offer opportunities and unforeseen pleasures. We change plans, taking an occasional back road to places discovered en route. Being open to the unexpected makes travel rich and enjoyable.

University environments keep academics so focused on the external rewards of the scholarly journey—tenure and promotion—that budding professors can forget the intrinsic joys of the process. Enjoyment drives the creative juices. Learning and discovery are fun. They are what attract many of us to academic life. I have seen, however, too many colleagues frozen by a focus on publishing so as not to perish rather than energized by the process of discovery. They shortchange themselves, missing the pleasures of creativity and overlooking progress. The critical question for productive scholars is how to bring fun and playfulness into research and writing. It is harder to feel anxious and pressured when you're having a good time.

For me, that means thinking about what I choose to do, as well as when, how, and with whom I work. I know I need to limit better the number of projects I take on and to schedule my work with sufficient slack to allow me to meet deadlines. I am getting better at that, but the piles of "promised yesterday" folders on my desk tell me I've still got a long way to go. In the meantime, my perspective on the work becomes critical. If I frame my overload as overwhelming drudgery, it becomes just that. On the other hand, if I immerse myself deeply and completely in my present activity, reminding myself why I chose to accept this new challenge, I can dwell on the excitement of the learning moment rather than be dragged down by the reality of all else that waits for me. Working with good colleagues can keep you honest in all this and can be joyfully refreshing. Plan projects and work meetings to include time explicitly scheduled for fun, rejuvenation, and learning.

The "publish or perish" dictum also encourages academics to drive themselves so relentlessly that they miss creative twists and turns on their research routes. I know I have been too quick in the past to assume that an article or two is all I can do on a subject, instead of asking how research findings could be reframed and new implications developed for different audiences.

Replenish Your Spirit

The scholarly journey is long and difficult. The road seems forever uphill. Sustaining commitment requires that you periodically replenish your scholarly spirit. What nourishes you? What rejuvenates? The answers are different for different people. Find out what fits for you.

For some, work within the academy sustains and reinforces their commitment. Professional associations, presentations at conferences, positions as journal reviewers, conversations with colleagues on the Internet keep folks psychologically "close to home" and focused on their chosen destinations. For others, forays outside the academy—time in the community, in the corporate world, or just evenings at home with the family—put the meaning and pressures of the scholarly journey in perspective. University-financed sabbaticals are wonderful but too rare. Find ways to finance minisabbaticals for yourself.

Most of us need good traveling companions. Growth-filled collaborations are remarkable sources of support and learning. A good mentor can offer advice and serve as a welcome way station when the journey gets rough. Support groups and significant others provide camaraderie and acceptance as well as reality checks. Communities of faith with whom we can explore the meaning and purpose of life offer balance and perspective.

I am writing this essay a few months before I enter the valley of promotion and tenure review, and I've been reasonably diligent in building my file. I would like to try life with the new title and status, but I expect that even with them, I would do very little differently. Instead of holding some part of myself in abeyance until the big academic reward arrives, I am diving enthusiastically into my work. For me, the journey itself is my destination. My joy is in teaching and learning. My real commitment is to continue my journey—follow my heart, write about things I love, persist through times of anguish and self-doubt, and rejoice when I produce something that I think is pretty good.

No doubt your journey will be different from mine. We each need to find a path that is right for us. I share the struggles and joys of my academic travels as a bon voyage gift to you. May they speak in some way to your experiences, offer you support and guidance on your journey, and enable you to find a path that is productive and rewarding.

References

Gallos, J. V. (1989a). Developmental diversity and the OB classroom: Implications for teaching and learning. *Organizational Behavior Teaching Review, 13*(4).

Gallos, J. V. (1989b). Exploring women's development: Implications for career theory, practice, and research. In M. Arthur, D. Hall, & B. Lawrence (Eds.), *Handbook of career theory: Perspectives and prospects for understanding and managing work experiences.* Cambridge: Cambridge University Press.

Gallos, J. V. (1992). Educating women and men in the twenty-first century: Gender diversity, leadership opportunities. *Journal of Continuing Higher Education, 40*(1).

Gallos, J. V. (1993). Women's experiences and ways of knowing: Implications for teaching and learning in the organizational behavior classroom. *Journal of Management Education, 17*(1).

Gallos, J. V. (1995a). Editor's corner: Toward a new definition of faculty service. *Journal of Management Education, 19*(4).

Gallos, J. V. (1995b). Gender and silence: The implications of women's ways of knowing for effective college teaching. *College Teaching, 43*(3).

Gallos, J. V. (1995c, Winter). On management education for women: Faulty assumptions, new possibilities. *Selections: The Journal of the Graduate Management Admissions Council.*

3 Rhythms of an Academic's Life

CROSSING CULTURAL BORDERS

Miriam Erez

Over the spans of their careers, many of my close colleagues in the United States and Europe moved from one university to another within their own countries. Unlike my colleagues, I have had one university, the Technion, as my base, from which I departed many times on sabbaticals that took me across cultural borders in search of theories and research methods. After being away for a while, however, I always returned to my home port. As I accumulated knowledge and experience, I discovered that my frequent crossing of cultural borders serves as a major factor in my understanding of human behavior. In this chapter I focus on three major themes that have led me to recognize the important role played by culture: the impact of my culture on my self-image and, therefore, on my decisions and actions in composing my life of the two major rhythms of family and career; the influence of the crossing of cultural borders on the development of my career over time through sabbaticals; and the effects of crossing cultural borders on the development of my

interest in cross-cultural research. These three themes are jointly related; I separate them here only to give the reader a sense of what each involves. Toward the end of the chapter, I present a conceptual model that integrates the three themes.

Blending Work and Family: The Roles of Personal and Cultural Factors

Family and career life are interrelated, like figure and background. Figures have meaning only when contrasted with the backgrounds that surround them. Similarly, the meaning of information is shaped by the context in which it appears, and individuals end up making different decisions based on the same source of information when the context changes (Tversky & Kahneman, 1981). Nonwork domains, such as leisure time and family life, are often contrasted with work. Leisure time takes on positive meaning when it is perceived as a break from intensive work; however, it may have only marginal value for the unemployed person. In the same vein, career life may have different meaning for someone who has a fulfilling family life from that it has for someone who has no family life. Indeed, managers who allocate all their resources to the development of their careers at the expense of their family lives often end up unsatisfied and alienated (Korman, 1981).

Family life and career life interchangeably serve as figure and ground, and they compete for a pool of limited resources. A person's policy of resource allocation to family and career roles reflects the centrality of these two domains to his or her life and affects the extent to which he or she becomes engaged in each of the two roles. Allocation policies vary across individuals and cultures. For example, in some cultures, social gender roles are clearly distinct: Women are expected to be modest, tender, and concerned with family life, whereas men are expected to be more assertive, tough, and focused on materialistic success. In other cultures, social gender roles overlap, and both men and women are encouraged to allocate their resources to both career and family life.

Culture plays a major role in the development of a shared understanding of what it is to be human (Cahoone, 1988; Cushman, 1990). Culture shapes the criteria we use for self-evaluation and influences the development of positive or negative self-image. Across cultures, people strive to develop and maintain positive representations of themselves. Family and career roles are central to a person's self-concept, but their relative importance varies across cultures. The relative importance of these two life domains to a person's notion of self-worth and well-being influences his or her policy of resource allocation. In cultures that emphasize family and career roles equally, individuals use a policy of equal allocation to both life domains. In cultures where one role has priority over the other, people tend to allocate their resources in favor of the role they deem more important, in order to promote their own feelings of self-worth. In addition, there are individual differences among members of any given culture; individual characteristics and backgrounds strongly influence self-concept, over and above what culture contributes. Self-worth is a reflection of both the individual's

perception of his or her value and that person's value in the eyes of others (Brockner, 1988).

Our values determine the relative importance of the spheres of family and career as well as the amount of resources we allocate to each of these domains. Therefore, the extent to which each of these domains is allowed to grow is determined by our resource allocation policy. This policy conducts the rhythms of our career and family lives as they are composed by our perception of what it is to be human. The policy may shift emphasis from one rhythm to another in order to realize the full potential of each domain over time, and to keep them in harmony.

I was born and raised in Israel, and my resource allocation policy was shaped by Israeli culture and Jewish tradition, both of which value family life highly. According to Jewish tradition, men and women complement each other, but these complementary roles can be realized only in marriage (Richter, 1992). The family retains its central position in modern Israel, where it is seen as the basic cell of the society. The family role is so strongly embedded in Israeli culture that it is almost perceived as a natural development of a person from childhood to adulthood, as if one cannot be a mature person unless one is married and having children. By their early 40s, only about 2% of Israeli women have never been married, and a similar proportion of women at this age do not have children. The rate of divorce in Israel, in comparison with other Western societies, is relatively low (Richter, 1992).

In Israel, it is taken for granted that women care for children. The underlying assumption is that women will combine family and work, in that order of importance (Izraeli, 1986). Empirical data collected from women in academia show that the vast majority have families and children. A set of data collected recently at the Technion-Israel Institute of Technology shows that women constitute 9% (N = 48) of all faculty members, and among these women, 82% have children. Half of the women with no children were junior faculty members who had worked at the Technion for less than a year; they will likely have children in the future (Mannheim, 1990). Similar data were gathered at the Weitzmann Institute of Science in Israel (Toren, 1987), where women scientists with children were shown to be outperforming those with no children. Mothers of two children had the highest records of publication. In this sample, 62% of the female scientists argued that having families did not adversely affect their careers, 19% mentioned family and children as the reason for their relatively slower advancement in their academic careers, and only 5% said that having families affected their careers to a great extent. Thus the vast majority of Israeli women professors perceive both family and career roles to be part of their self-concept, and they successfully integrate these two life domains. This emphasis on both family and career roles has accompanied me from childhood to adulthood, and I share it with the vast majority of women scientists in the academic community in Israel.

In contrast to Israeli culture, American culture is more individualistic, less egalitarian, and more masculine (Hofstede, 1991). It is therefore less supportive of women who pursue both family and career roles. A recent comparative study of women scientists and engineers demonstrates that Israeli women consider success in private life and family relations to be significantly more important than do their American counterparts, and they experience less conflict between work and private life (Etzion & Bailyn, 1994). Perhaps for this reason, significantly more of the Israeli women were married and had children, compared with the American sample. Of the women in the American sample, 52% were married and 11% were divorced, compared with 76% married and 7% divorced among the Israeli sample. A total of 77% of the Israeli women had children, compared with 31% of the Americans (Etzion & Bailyn, 1994).

Perceptions of conflict between family and career roles seem to be the norm in the United States, and these perceptions serve as the underlying model of the vast majority of research on the relationship between family and career (Duxbury & Higgins, 1991). A number of different models serve to explain the relationship between family and career (Zedeck & Mosier, 1990). The conflict model seems to be the most prevalent, and most research demonstrates that family life is negatively affected by problems in the work environment (Zedeck, 1992).

Family life plays a major role in my conceptualization of what it means to be human. For this reason I can reflect on the rhythm of my career life only by viewing it jointly with the rhythm of my family life. The model that best describes the rhythms of my career and my family life is an integrative model in which family and career roles are equally important to my notion of well-being and self-worth. This model has led me to develop a policy of resource allocation that optimizes the development of both career and family roles over my whole life. This does not necessarily mean that I allocate my resources equally to both domains at the same time. Rather, I seek to optimize both areas over the long run. In certain periods more resources are allocated to one domain than to the other, taking into consideration special needs at any given time. Optimization requires determining when it is most effective to engage in family role or career role within a given time frame. My career and family lives have already progressed through four distinct phases: socialization and development of cultural values, early career, midcareer, and late midcareer.

Socialization and Development of Cultural Values

In my early childhood, the values and expectations of significant others shaped to a great extent my self-identity in terms of being both a family and a career person. My parents, members of my extended family, teachers, and friends expected me to be a first-rate student in school. Not only did they expect me to excel, they believed in my ability to do so. The combination of high expectations and strong belief in my ability fostered my perceptions of high self-efficacy. These perceptions were crucial for my success in school, and later in my academic career.

But academic achievement was not enough in my immediate social milieu. From age 8 to 16, I grew up in a suburban town dominated by four core values: collectivism, which advocated the subordination of personal goals to group goals; egalitarianism, which emphasized equality among human beings, regardless of sex and ethnic origin; humanism, which emphasized prosocial behaviors and good citizenship; and personal responsibility, which was conveyed by the phrase "Take yourself in your own hands." As a child I was involved in all kinds of extracurricular activities and social projects that reflected good citizenship. Sex role stereotyping was not prevalent because of the emphasis on egalitarianism; children were taught to be *persons* rather than *men* or *women*. Both boys and girls were expected to be good citizens and to be personally responsible for their actions. This emphasis on being a person and on personal responsibility has shaped my dual family and career roles. The lack of ethnic and sex role stereotypes certainly helped me to cross cultural borders and to relate to other people first and foremost as human beings, regardless of their ethnic identity, sex, or societal status.

Early Career

My family and career lives started to develop at about the same time. I got married after I earned my bachelor's degree, had my first child while I was a master's student, and had my second child as soon as I earned my PhD. Both my career life and my family life continued to grow and develop mutually. It did not occur to me that I had other alternatives, such as developing only one role or avoiding both roles all together. It was clear to me that my self-identity is derived from being both a family person and a career person. There was no selection process in which I considered the utility of various alternatives and made a choice. Rather, I have an image of what it is to be human, and that image has guided my goals, strategies, and behavior. Family and career roles are equally represented in my self-identity, and they jointly satisfy my needs for esteem and worth according to my personal and cultural values.

Beginnings are the most difficult part, in particular when both family and career lives begin at the same time. My belief is that children must come first when they are very young, because they are totally dependent on their parents. As they grow up they become more independent and require less attention on a daily basis; very often they serve as a great resource for their parents. The early stage of family development often parallels the crucial stage of early academic career development before tenure. In this early stage, I allocated more resources to my family because I believed that was necessary for the future development of my children and my marriage. On the career side, my goal was to survive the tenure process. Two important things in the career sphere helped

me survive the beginning. First, I was well prepared for an academic life by my graduate studies. In particular, there was an emphasis on independent thoughts and ideas, on being both critical and creative, and on self-management and independence. Second, my mentors served as invaluable resources. I was fortunate to have two distinguished mentors when I came to the United States for my postdoctoral year of research and study: Ben Schneider and Ed Locke, from the University of Maryland. Ben eased my arrival to the United States by sharing two important truths with me: that whatever I do should be fun and that the results of a study alone do not make an impact—rather, the impact is made by what one does with results, and how one interprets them and integrates them with existing bodies of knowledge. I embraced both of Ben's guidelines. I chose to study research topics that intrigued and challenged me. This helped me to become highly involved in my work, and to develop a programmatic stream of research that has challenged the existing theories of work motivation and tested their boundary conditions.

One theory that intrigued me was the goal-setting theory of motivation. I wondered what underlying mechanisms facilitate the link between goals and performance. My first hypothesis was that feedback plays a major role in linking goals to performance. I conducted my first study on this topic and found that people need feedback about their performance in order for goals to affect performance (Erez, 1977). I was fortunate to meet Ed Locke during my postdoctoral year at the University of Maryland. Ed encouraged me to publish my first study and was very helpful in assisting me through the publication process. Thus began a stream of research that explored the mechanisms and boundary conditions of the goal-performance relationship and the identification of methods that motivate employees to become committed to their tasks.

Receiving tenure served as a milestone; it represented the end of the beginning. I must confess that I barely made it. The dean of our faculty at that time told me that the curve of my rate of publications differed from his own and those of other male professors. They published more right after they received their PhDs and then slowed down, whereas in my case, I did not publish much right after I received my doctorate, but I started to publish more a few years later. He suspected that I wanted only to get tenure, and expressed concern that I might not continue to publish after I received it. He could not understand that my having given birth to my son right after I received my PhD could have been the reason my publishing had been postponed. One conclusion that may be drawn from my experience is that women may differ from men in their publication curves, and this difference should be respected.

The Influence of Cross-Cultural Sabbaticals on My Career Development

I have had the opportunity to take several sabbaticals at various universities in the United States and Japan. These sabbaticals have played a crucial role in my career development by providing me with opportunities to challenge my ideas and discuss them with some of the best researchers in our field. Furthermore, they exposed me to new research paradigms and knowledge that I did not have previously. My first sabbatical, which I spent at the Psychology Department of the University of Illinois, helped me progress beyond the exploration of boundary conditions to theory development, which focused on goal commitment.

At Illinois, I became acquainted with Fred Kanfer, a professor in clinical psychology who studied the effects of self-management and self-set goals on commitment to therapeutic goals and the effectiveness of therapy. We spent hours together in conversation, which led to a jointly authored review paper on the role of goal acceptance in goal setting and task performance (Erez & Kanfer, 1983).

Building upon the knowledge I gained from interacting with Fred Kanfer, I thought that employee involvement through participation in goal setting should increase goal acceptance and consequent performance. Kurt Lewin's work using participation to overcome resistance to change struck me as a potential theoretical basis for my research. I discussed these ideas with Chuck Hulin, my host at the University of Illinois. Chuck doubted whether participation in goal setting would lead to higher levels of commitment and performance than no participation, because commitment is anchored in the personal contract between employee and organization, regardless of participation.

The concept of a personal contract is not part of the Israeli culture, where employee-organization relationships for the vast majority of employees are defined by collective bargaining and collective contracts. Therefore, in Israel, employee commitment and goal acceptance cannot be taken for granted. My early discussions with Chuck Hulin led to the development of my interest in cross-cultural research 10 years later. At the time, we decided to do a study that tested the effects of participation on goal acceptance and performance. Chuck suggested that a PhD student, Chris Earley, should work on the project. Since then, Chris and I have continued to share research interests and have collaborated for the past 15 years. The research we conducted during that year in Illinois led us to conclude that participation in goal setting significantly contributes to goal commitment and consequent performance.

Our research on the effects of participation in goal setting contradicted the results of the line of research being conducted by Gary Latham and his colleagues, which failed to show a significant effect for participation. Ed Locke, who was a close friend of both Gary and myself, challenged us to conduct a study together to resolve the inconsistencies. The joint research I undertook with Latham and Locke was facilitated by my second sabbatical at the University of Maryland in 1985-1986. Our collaboration led to the development of a unique process of doing research in which the antagonists jointly design crucial experiments to determine the causes of their differential findings (Latham, Erez, & Locke, 1988). Reflections on this process are summarized in a book edited by Frost and Stablein (1992) titled *Doing Exemplary Research*.

During my second sabbatical, I also had the opportunity to meet Tamao Matsui, from Rikkio University in Tokyo, Japan, who conducted interesting research on goal setting in Asia. Dr. Matsui invited me for a visit, which provided me an opportunity to learn more about participative management in Japan. My visit was supported by two fellowships from the Japan Foundation and by the Israel Association for the Promotion of International Scientific Relations. Thanks to Dr. Matsui, I was able to interview top-level executives as well as shop-floor employees to learn about the Japanese culture and how it relates to Japanese management philosophy and practices. This visit stimulated my research interest in cross-cultural differences in motivational behavior, and it provided the foundation for the development of both theory and research in this area.

Midcareer Experiences

By the time I was promoted to senior lecturer, which in Israel is the level between assistant professor and associate professor, my family life was progressing smoothly. My children became more independent and developed their own life routines, personal interests, and various activities after school hours. At that point I did not deliberately decide to embark upon a programmatic stream of research on goal setting, but in retrospect that was what happened.

I am fortunate to have a husband with whom I share similar values and images of the family-career role relationship. He serves as an important resource, helping me to pursue both roles, and he supports all of my endeavors. The sabbaticals that played a crucial role in my career development required us to spend a great deal of time apart, as my husband needed to stay in Israel to run his construction company. I recall our friends saying that he deserved a great deal of respect for letting me go. They considered our arrangement to be a real sacrifice for him in particular. The challenges I had to face—going to a new place, always with our two children, and having to cope with both the career goals I wanted to accomplish on my sabbatical and the family responsibilities I bore alone—were somehow less significant in their eyes than his agreement to let me go by myself. I have come to see their reactions as a reflection of the fact that in Israeli culture, in general, the family-oriented role of women takes priority over the career role, and the expectation is that women do not sacrifice their families for their careers. However, from observation of my female colleagues in the Israeli academic community, I have the impression that their husbands share with my husband a very similar set of values pertaining to the family-career role relationship, and they support the career development of their wives even when sacrifice is needed in the short run.

The Development of Cross-Cultural Research Interests

My frequent sabbaticals spotlighted differences among the cultures I visited. I noticed differences in employee behavior and in prevailing managerial and motivational methods used by managers in various cultures. For example, lifetime employment stands out as a major factor in Japan. It influences human resource management practices, willingness to invest in training, and the long-term commitment of employees. In contrast, I noticed a high rate of voluntary and involuntary turnover in the United States. I also noticed that managers around the world use different methods to motivate their employees. In the United States, emphasis is placed on merit-based differential reward systems, whereas in Israel and Northern Europe, reward systems are more egalitarian.

My first research project in this area was to test for the effects of participation in goal setting on goal commitment and performance in the United States and Israel. Chris Earley and I conducted a line of research that showed that culture moderates the effects of participation and teamwork on performance (Erez & Earley, 1993). Participation is more effective in cultures that are egalitarian and highly collectivist than in other cultures. However, there was a missing link between the macro level of cultural factors and the micro level of individual behavior. An insight as to what this link might be was evoked during my third sabbatical, at the Department of Psychology, University of California, Berkeley, in 1990, where I worked with Sheldon Zedeck and his students.

The climate at the Berkeley Psychology Department was infused with cognitive theories, including cognitive theories of the self. This coincided with theoretical developments of self-regulatory models in industrial and organizational psychology, including the seminal work of Albert Bandura (1986), and self-regulatory models of motivation and leadership developed by Kanfer and Ackerman (1989), Lord and Maher (1991), and others. In the field of cross-cultural psychology, Harry Triandis (1989) and Markus and Kitayama (1991) published papers on the causal link between cultural characteristics and the two facets of the self: the independent and the interdependent. The former facilitates

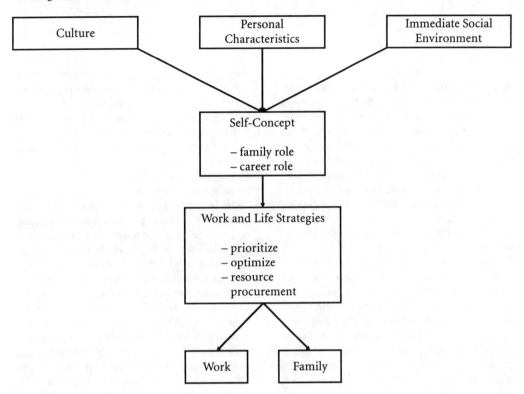

Figure 3.1. A Model of the Family-Career Role Relationship

behavior that is directed by the individual's internal repertoire of thoughts, feelings, and actions. The interdependent self is that part of the individual that sees him or her as part of an encompassing social relationship and recognizes that his or her behavior is shaped by the thoughts, feelings, and actions of others in the relationship. This research literature provided insights for the development of our model of cultural self-representation. In this model, Chris Earley and I propose that the potential effectiveness of various managerial and motivational techniques is determined by cultural values that shape human needs. In other words, motivational techniques derive their value from their contributions to individuals' perceptions of self-worth and well-being, which are largely shaped by culture.

My fruitful collaboration with Chris Earley on cross-cultural research and theory development resulted in two books: The first, *Culture, Self-Identity, and Work,* was published in the summer of 1993; the second is a trade book titled *The Transplanted Executive: Challenges for*

International Management Success, which is currently in press. In addition, I am currently working on two projects that review the micro and macro levels of research on cross-cultural organization behavior. On the micro level, Chris Earley and I are editing a volume for the Frontiers of Industrial and Organizational Psychology series on international industrial and organizational psychology. At the macro level, Sam Bacharach, Peter Bamberger, and I are editing a special issue of *Research in the Sociology of Organizations* dealing with cross-cultural analysis.

In an attempt to generalize from my personal experience to a model of family-career role relationships, I borrow from the model of cultural self-representation to provide a conceptual framework. The model is presented in Figure 3.1. The self-concept depicts the multiple roles played by individuals. These roles vary in relative salience and importance. The self-concept is formed through direct experiences and evaluations adopted from significant others (Bandura, 1986) and is shaped by the shared understanding within a particular culture of what it is to be human (Cahoone, 1988; Cushman, 1990). This belief shapes to a great extent the family-career role relationship.

The impact of culture on the family-career role relationship is the focus of a special report in a recent issue of *Science* titled "Comparisons Across Cultures: Women in Science '94." According to the author of the section's overview article, societies may be classified as family-friendly or non-family-friendly (Barinaga, 1994). Latin countries such as Spain, Portugal, Argentina, and Mexico, and Mediterranean cultures such as Italy, Turkey, and Israel, are family-friendly. In contrast, the United States, Great Britain, and Germany are non-family-friendly societies.

There are several reasons for the differences between the two types of cultures. First, the cultural values in Latin and Mediterranean cultures emphasize the importance of the family for both females and males. Therefore, it is legitimate for mothers of young children to be absent from work when their children are ill or on special occasions, such as the celebration of birthdays and school programs in which parents are expected to participate. Astronomer Sara Beck contrasts the United States, where she was educated and held her first faculty job, to Israel, where she is a tenured professor at Tel Aviv University: "When I was working in the U.S.A., if I missed a half-day of work because my kid had a temperature of 104, I was lectured on how this let down the department. In Israel if you don't take off from work for your kid's birthday party the department chairman will lecture you on how important these things are to kids and how he never missed one while his kids were little" (quoted in Barinaga, 1994, p. 1472).

Further, it is relatively easy to find decent child care in most Latin and Mediterranean countries; in Italy, for example, many universities have free on-site child-care centers. It is very difficult to secure good day care for children in the United States. Additionally, the extended family provides a great amount of support in all the Latin and Mediterranean countries. A female physicist in Turkey who was interviewed for one of the *Science* articles said that she could take a sabbatical in Italy because her mother-in-law came with her to take care of her son. I had a similar experience when I came to the United States for my postdoctoral year and for my first sabbatical.

In addition, Latin and Mediterranean cultures tolerate a relatively slow pace of career progress for women scientists with young children. The Italian system, for example, allows a young physicist to stay in lower-level positions for as long as 10 years while starting a family, and then to move up later without the stiff penalty an American physicist would pay for delaying career progress. In Sweden, women can take a full year off when they give birth. Because of these various support systems and cultural expectations, women in family-friendly cultures have become more prevalent and firmly established in the scientific community. Young women thus have role models to emulate, which serves as another important factor in facilitating scientific careers for women. Prominent women scientists who lived in Italy at the beginning of the century serve as role models for many women scientists in Italy: "There was a tradition of women in physics, so I knew that it was something I could try for," notes Ida Peruzzi (quoted in Flam, 1994, p. 1480). Indeed, the statistical figures show that in Portugal, 36% of scientific researchers are female. In Mexico and Argentina, 20-50% of scientific researchers are women, compared with less than 10% in the United States, Great Britain, and Germany. In Italy, women physicists constitute 23% of the national sample, compared with only 3% in the United States.

An interesting factor that influences the likelihood of a woman's becoming a scientist in less supportive countries is enrollment in a single-sex school. Survey findings in Great Britain and in the United States suggest that the microculture of the school system influences the extent to which women develop self-confidence in their academic ability and thus their subsequent career decisions.

It is therefore reasonable to argue that the extent to which women are able to integrate both family and career roles in their self-concepts is affected by their cultural values and the opportunities offered them. Cultural values affect resource allocation policies, which determine the specific strategies individuals will adopt to meet the demands of their dual roles. Individuals who have a clear representation of the dual family-career role relationship will develop strategies that help them to fulfill both roles equally over time. When the family-career role relationship is not clearly integrated in an individual's self-concept, he or she may not be able to develop a clear policy of resource allocation, and thus may face a conflict between the two roles when both roles are highly demanding.

The different patterns of family-career role representations are modified by individual difference characteristics and sociocultural factors. The Israeli culture, for example, is characterized by higher levels of collectivism, egalitarianism, and femininity than are found in the American culture. The family is of utmost importance in Israeli culture, for both men and women; the culture provides a supportive environment in which women can develop their careers, and women share responsibility with their spouses for preserving family life.

In contrast, American culture is known to be more individualistic, more masculine, and less egalitarian. Therefore, Americans are more likely to segregate work and family roles (Lobel, 1991). When the situation calls for equal representation of family and career roles, Americans are more likely to experience high levels of role conflict than are members of the Israeli culture.

To summarize, self-representation of the family-career role relationship is shaped by cultural values and translated into role behavior. In individualistic cultures the two roles are segregated, and the value system does not support an integrative model that gives equal weight to both roles in the self-concept. Therefore, the highest level of conflict is experienced when both roles make equal demands for time. On the other hand, the Israeli culture supports an integrative model of self-representation of the career and family roles, and therefore women are more prepared to cope with exceeding demands. Compared with career women in the United States, they tend to get more support from their immediate and extended families, as well as from their social environment.

Late Midcareer Reflections

In retrospect, the end of my 1990 sabbatical at Berkeley was a milestone for me; that was the time when I was entering the midpoint of my career. This is best characterized by recognition I received from my colleagues, as expressed in the following: (a) nomination as a fellow of the Society of Industrial and Organizational Psychology and the American Psychological Asso-

ciation; (b) selection as a member of the editorial boards of the *Journal of Applied Psychology, Organizational Behavior and Human Decision Processes, Applied Psychology: An International Review,* and *Human Performance;* (c) receiving the Academy of Management's award for outstanding publication in organizational behavior for the study I conducted with Gary Latham and Ed Locke; and (d) becoming involved in the International Association of Applied Psychology (IAAP) as a nominated member of the executive committee and elected as the president-elect of the Division of Organizational Psychology.

The midcareer stage is also often characterized by the taking of administrative roles at one's university. Upon my return from the sabbatical at Berkeley, I became the head of the Area of Behavioral Sciences and Management at the Technion. One year later, I was asked to be the associate dean of our Faculty of Industrial Engineering and Management. I became heavily immersed in the role of associate dean, which consumed a large portion of my resources. In this position, I learned a great deal about the academic system and had the opportunity to develop new skills of persuasion, influence, and decision making. I focused on improving both the quality of teaching and faculty-student relationships.

In addition to my heavy administrative load, I was interested in the empirical testing of the model of cultural self-representation. I was fortunate to have very good master's and PhD students who were interested in my research. Swept away by my enthusiasm to do research, I ended up working with about 15 students. I like the metaphor that Mary Catherine Bateson uses in her book *Composing a Life* (1990) for a similar problem of work overload; she says that "we all talk about time as if it were a flower bed continually invaded by wild-flowers that we are reluctant to pull out" (p. 178). From this experience, I learned a lesson for the future: I should monitor and more carefully control the number of students I work with, as well as the number of obligations I undertake.

At that point in my career, my children reached adulthood, so I allocated fewer resources to my family. My older daughter got married, and my son finished high school and started his service in the Israeli Defense Forces. Working under the pressure of multiple, highly demanding academic roles, I discovered that my family serves as a valuable resource, supporting me and sharing the load. In my midcareer life, my resource allocation policy clearly shifted from the family to the career role. My time resources were divided among five major subroles: academic administration, mentoring and advising my graduate students, integrating research and theory in two published books, serving the professional community by being on the editorial boards of four journals, and getting involved in the IAAP.

At the end of 3 intensive years as associate dean, I felt the need to take another sabbatical to shift my resources back to research and writing. I recognized that I was not ready to give up my research for academic administration, and taking another sabbatical seemed to be a good way to facilitate the shift toward research and writing. In autumn of 1994, I began a sabbatical year as the Kermit O. Hanson Endowed Visiting Professor at the University of Washington's School of Business Administration in Seattle. The future looks promising for the development of new research with my colleagues here. I have already started brainstorming new ideas for future research with Terry Mitchell, Tom Lee, Vandra Huber, Sally Fuller, and Marilyn Gist.

While on sabbatical in the United States, I maintain contact with my family by commuting back and forth to Israel during long holidays, using e-mail, and making phone calls. I have reached another milestone in my family life; I have become a grandmother, and perhaps the first grandmother to communicate on a daily basis via e-mail on baby's affairs.

References

Bandura, A. (1986). *Social foundations of thoughts and actions: A social cognitive theory.* Englewood Cliffs, NJ: Prentice Hall.

Barinaga, M. (1994). Overview: Surprises across the cultural divide. In J. Benditt (Ed.), Comparisons across cultures: Women in science '94 [Special report]. *Science, 263,* 1468-1469, 1472.

Bateson, M. C. (1990). *Composing a life.* New York: Penguin.

Brockner, J. (1988). *Self-esteem at work.* Lexington, MA: Lexington.

Cahoone, L. E. (1988). *The dilemma of modernity: Philosophy, culture, and anti-culture.* Albany: State University of New York Press.

Cushman, P. (1990). Why the self is empty: Toward a historically situated psychology. *American Psychologist, 45,* 599-611.

Duxbury, L. E., & Higgins, C. A. (1991). Gender differences in work-family conflict. *Journal of Applied Psychology, 76,* 60-73.

Earley, P. C., & Erez, M. (in press). *The transplanted executive: Challenges for international management success.* New York: Oxford University Press.

Erez, M. (1977). Feedback: A necessary condition for the goal setting-performance relationship. *Journal of Applied Psychology, 62,* 624-627.

Erez, M., & Earley, P. C. (1993). *Culture, self-identity, and work.* New York: Oxford University Press.

Erez, M., & Kanfer, F. H. (1983). The role of goal acceptance in goal setting and task performance. *Academy of Management Review, 8,* 454-463.

Etzion, D., & Bailyn, L. (1994). Patterns of adjustment to the career/family conflict of technically trained women in the United States and Israel. *Journal of Applied Social Psychology, 24,* 1530-1549.

Flam, F. (1994). Italy: Warm climate for women on the Mediterranean. In J. Benditt (Ed.), Comparisons across cultures: Women in science '94 [Special report]. *Science, 263,* 1480-1481.

Frost, P. J., & Stablein, R. (Eds.). (1992). *Doing exemplary research.* Newbury Park, CA: Sage.

Hofstede, G. (1991). *Cultures and organizations: Software of the mind.* New York: McGraw-Hill.

Izraeli, D. N. (1986). The perception of women's status in Israel as a social problem. *Sex Roles, 14,* 663-678.

Kanfer, R., & Ackerman, P. L. (1989). Motivation and cognitive abilities: An integrative attitude, treatment interaction approach to skill acquisition. *Journal of Applied Psychology, 74,* 657-690.

Korman, A. K. (1981). Career success and personal failure: Alienation in professionals and managers. *Academy of Management Journal, 24,* 342-360.

Latham, G. P., Erez, M., & Locke, E. A. (1988). Resolving scientific disputes by the joint design of crucial experiments by the antagonists: Application to the Erez-Latham dispute regarding participation in goal setting [Monograph]. *Journal of Applied Psychology, 73,* 753-772.

Lobel, S. A. (1991). Allocation of investment in work and family roles: Alternative theories and implications for research. *Academy of Management Review, 16,* 507-521.

Lord, R. G., & Maher, K. J. (1991). Cognitive theory in industrial and organizational psychology. In M. D. Dunnette & L. M. Hough (Ed.), *Handbook of industrial and organizational psychology* (2nd ed., Vol. 2, pp. 1-62). Chicago: Rand McNally.

Mannheim, B. (1990). *A statistical report on the distribution of women in different ranks of professorship at the Technion-Israel Institute of Technology* (Research report). Unpublished manuscript.

Markus, H. R., & Kitayama, S. (1991). Culture and the self: Implications for cognition, emotion, and motivation. *Psychological Review, 98,* 224-253.

Richter, J. (1992). Balancing work and family in Israel. In S. Zedeck (Ed.), *Work, families, and organizations* (pp. 362-394). San Francisco: Jossey-Bass.

Toren, N. (1987). The status of women in academia. *Israel Social Science Research, 5*, 138-146.

Triandis, H. C. (1989). The self and social behavior in differing cultural contexts. *Psychological Review, 96*, 506-520.

Tversky, A., & Kahneman, D. (1981). The framing of decisions and the psychology of choice. *Science, 211*, 453-458.

Zedeck, S. (1992). Introduction: Exploring the domain of work and family concerns. In S. Zedeck (Ed.), *Work, families, and organizations* (pp. 1-32). San Francisco: Jossey-Bass.

Zedeck, S., & Mosier, K. L. (1990). Work in the family and employing organization. *American Psychologist, 45*, 240-251.

4 Transitions

Vance F. Mitchell

I have been through a number of transitions during my adult life. In the fall of 1941, I was a student at the College of Wooster in Ohio. A number of us had joined an organization called the Oxford League, in which we pledged to go to jail rather than fight in "Roosevelt's war," which we were convinced was coming. Pearl Harbor changed all that, and by August 1942 most of us had joined one of the armed services. Having no desire to be drafted into the infantry, I opted for aviation cadet training as a navigator in the then Army Air Corps. After completing navigation training, I was assigned to the newly formed 398th B-17 Bombardment Group. Then followed 3 months' training at the Rattlesnake Bomber Base in the west Texas desert. We were then assigned to another 3 months in Rapid City, South Dakota, where we continued our training, flying in unheated B-17s in outside temperatures well below zero. Our group was then assigned to the Eighth Air Force in England.

Fortunately, during the training phase my pilot insisted that we work together to hone my navigation skills and develop his confidence in my navigational instructions. This work paid off, as shortly after arriving in England he and I were designated a lead team. As a lead team, we would lead a formation of bombers on raids over Europe. For a youngster just turned 21, this presented the greatest challenge yet. The flak-free corridors through which we flew were so narrow that my navigation had to be near perfect. If I let the formation get as much as a quarter mile off course, some of the aircraft on the edges of the formation were certain to be right in the path of German antiaircraft guns. Of course, our lead aircraft was a favorite target of the German fighters. We must have been charmed; both of us came through our tour without a scratch.

I returned to the United States in December 1944 and met my bride-to-be, Fran, just 3 days before Christmas, for the start of a whirlwind courtship. Then it was off to a series of replacement depots, ending up finally at Memphis, Tennessee. This was a boring period when I had literally nothing to do. I kept asking for a job, any job, and one fine day the person in charge of the officer personnel section at base headquarters granted my request. He had just received transfer orders and offered me his job.

Talk about a transition! From idle navigator to officer in charge of a section with an average strength on base of about 1,500 combat returnee officers who were joining from all over the world and soon thereafter leaving for some new destination. But I learned a great deal and was blessed with an excellent staff who managed to keep me out of trouble.

When the war ended in August 1945 I was anxious to join the flood of those leaving the service. Before the war I had aspired to become a professor of English, but the prospect of years of study did not then look very attractive. At my dear wife's suggestion, we decided to stick with the Army Air Force for a while. Shortly thereafter, I was offered and accepted a regular commission. From then until my retirement in December 1963, each new assignment was a transition, frequently to a new type of work. I served, for instance, in various facets of military and civilian personnel administration, in command of a squadron, and as executive officer of a maintenance and supply group. I did a tour in the Air Staff, handling the enlisted portion of the macro manpower program and the enlisted requirements for new weapon systems under development, and I also spent a number of years as an organizational analyst. In this last capacity, our teams were responsible for evaluating subordinate commanders' requests for additional personnel and for reviewing the formal organizational structure of the units concerned. It was an unparalleled learning experience, as we studied in depth a wide variety of operational and support organizations. (This knowledge was to prove extremely valuable when I later started teaching about organizations.) After the first few years, I found that there were always friends from previous assignments to ease the shock and help with the learning that came with each transition. Meanwhile, I was working at night to complete my bachelor's degree in the University of Maryland's off-campus program. In all, 17 years elapsed between the time I started college and the time I graduated in 1957.

At the conclusion of my tour in the Pentagon in 1957, the Air Force sent me to George Washington University to earn an MBA. This too was a challenging transition, because we were allotted one calendar year to complete 56 semester hours. I've always believed that the Air Force goofed in my assignment from George Wash-

ington. Instead of sending me to an operational command, where my newly acquired knowledge could be put to good use, I was assigned to head the Air Force ROTC at the University of California at Berkeley. Those were enjoyable years. For the upper-division courses we threw out the Air Force texts and adopted in their stead standard college texts. As a consequence of this, one of those "fortuitous encounters" occurred. I met Lyman Porter, then an assistant professor in the Psychology Department, who was destined to become my good friend and later my mentor. This assignment, together with the lack of opportunity then available for further advancement in the Air Force, convinced me that I should take early retirement and, after all those years, pursue a doctorate. I still had 18 months to serve before I could do so and still hold on to my grade as a lieutenant colonel. In another fortuitous encounter, an old friend then at Fifth Air Force headquarters in Tokyo requested that I be assigned there. My wife, Fran, was teaching business in the Contra Costa County schools to augment the Air Force's meager pay, and we decided that I would do the tour in Japan without her and our two teenage sons. Those were lonely months, but they were softened by the presence of old friends and the experience of becoming acquainted with Japan and its history, culture, and art. The job was not very demanding, so I filled the time by teaching for the University of Maryland and gathering data that later provided the basis for two articles in the *Journal of Applied Psychology*.

Perhaps the most difficult transition of all came in December 1963, when I retired from the Air Force and started my doctoral work at Berkeley. The Air Force, although large, becomes quite small after a few years as one advances in grade and gets to know most of the people in one's field. Suddenly, after years as a senior officer with plenty of support staff, there I was—1 of 18,000 graduate students, most of whom were still in their 20s, and in a campus community as turbulent as that at Berkeley. To complicate matters, my first course work was in mathematical economics—and it had been 10 years since I had studied college algebra!

Shortly after I started, one of the senior accounting professors called me in to advise me to withdraw from the program. He said that I was really too old for doctoral work. He stated that even if I completed the program, no school would wish to hire me and I should save myself and the faculty time and trouble by withdrawing and seeking some other line of work. Not long after that, the dean offered me a half-time job as an administrative assistant, where my principal duties would be managing the school's Alumni Association. He particularly wanted a reasonably mature person in this role, because it involved dealing with the senior business executives who constituted the association's board of trustees. As the position carried with it a private office and a secretary, the reader can imagine the alacrity with which I accepted. My relations with the board members were pleasant and led to several lasting friendships. Also, my relationships with faculty members were quite different from those of most of my fellow students, because as a member of staff, I had access to the faculty coffee room. During those 3 years, Raymond Miles, then a newly minted assistant professor, became a valued friend and mentor.

The Allied Social Sciences met in San Francisco the year I entered the job market. Contrary to the earlier prediction of the accounting professor, a number of universities expressed interest in hiring me. Organizational behavior people were much in demand. Philip White, then dean of the Faculty of Commerce and Business Administration at the University of British Columbia, made the most attractive offer—associate professor. He was then engaged in building a strong faculty and wanted me to help in building the Division of Organizational Behavior and Industrial Relations. At Lyman Porter's urging, I had regularly attended meetings of the Academy of Management and the Western Academy as well. Again at his urging, I had made it a point at these meetings to become acquainted with the leading scholars in the field. The Academy was quite small in those days, so making these acquaintances was no problem. These associations proved valuable as my close friend Larry Moore and I drank the heady wine of building a strong group of colleagues over the next few years.

Dean Philip White called on those of us who formed his executive committee to assist him in hammering out new policies and procedures to rationalize the faculty's governance. These efforts and several years of aggressive faculty recruiting made it possible to transform the faculty from a body where traditional teaching was

the principal mission to one where both teaching and first-class scholarship were important.

For 7 years, my duties as division chairperson brought with them the responsibility of mentoring our newly hired junior colleagues as they learned their craft, launched their research programs, matured, and passed through the gate for promotion and tenure. The key to this process was the successful development of strong collegial relationships, both professionally and socially. These relationships encouraged all of us to discuss any problems that arose and enabled me to offer guidance as I thought appropriate—guidance that was often, but not always, followed. Indeed, our group's relationships were noted by colleagues at other universities and prompted the question by several, "How is it that you are all friends?" Apart from frequent social gatherings in each other's homes, the annual fishing trips to the outback of British Columbia that Merle Ace organized greatly helped in team building. These kinds of things were possible then, but I doubt they would be practical today, owing to the increased pressure more recently hired faculty feel concerning research and publication as well as the increased size of the group. In any event, in the mid-1970s, as the faculty's leadership changed and became more centralized, I gladly passed on the administrative role to other hands so as to concentrate more on teaching and research.

My research went well in spite of the pressure of administrative duties, and so did my teaching. Peter Frost, Walter Nord, who was visiting one year, and I began to develop the collaborative style of teaching that has proven so effective. In a recent interview in the *Journal of Management Studies*, Peter credits me with mentoring him. I suppose that was true during his first few years at UBC, but he quickly became a role model to me.

Also, I helped to organize the Administrative Sciences Association of Canada, a counterpart to the Regional Academies of Management, was honored to be its first president in 1972-1973, and obtained the Association's membership in the Social Science Research Council of Canada. Then, in 1977, I was again honored by election as president of the Western Academy of Management and in 1980 by election as a representative-at-large on the Board of the National Academy of Management.

The undergraduates and MBA students at UBC were a challenging and, for the most part, fun group of people with whom to work. In those days the faculty did not have the excellent Career Center that now exists, and I did a good bit of career counseling and helped with résumés, particularly with the students in their final year. As the years passed, it was rewarding to see our graduates succeed in both business and government and, in no few instances, rise to senior executive positions. Work in executive programs on campus, with a variety of government agencies, and at institutions such as the Banff School of Advanced Management provided close contact with practitioners from a cross section of business and government. These contacts led to opportunities for consulting that helped immeasurably to broaden my knowledge of the real world of civilian organizations and, I hope, to help the organizations for which I consulted become better and more effective places in which to work. It is interesting in light of my present affiliation with Embry-Riddle Aeronautical University that my most extended consulting relationship was with Canadian Pacific Air, now Canadian Air.

Without doubt, however, as our doctoral program in organizational behavior became recognized, the greatest reward came from guiding 15 students through their training and dissertations, either as chair or as a member of their dissertation committee. By the time I retired from UBC, I had chaired more dissertations than any other member of our faculty. Several of these students were interdisciplinary, with backgrounds in health care professions. I'm convinced that, in addition to encouraging rigor and creativity, an important part of a doctoral student's success lies in the supportive relationship he or she develops with faculty mentors. Of equal importance is insistence on a detailed, well-thought-out dissertation proposal. The results of these efforts have been repaid many times over. With only one exception, these individuals have been very successful in their academic careers. Several have achieved worldwide recognition in their chosen fields of activity. It is a source of pride that virtually all are good friends. We hear from many of them each Christmas.

In late 1983 I recognized that current law in Canada would force my retirement in 1988. Fran and I began to explore the question of where to retire. Would we remain in Vancouver, where we had established a wide circle of friends

and acquaintances? If not, where would we make our new home? After many discussions, she asked that we return to the United States. Because she had cheerfully accompanied me through my various Air Force assignments, graduate school, and what would be 21 years as an expatriate, I willingly agreed. The question of where was not too difficult. Fran is almost phobic about ice and snow, and I can't take hot, humid climates. Besides, after one has lived in the Pacific Northwest, the rest of the country does not hold much attraction. After much soul-searching, we decided that our retirement home would be on Whidbey Island in Oak Harbor, Washington. For years we had kept a boat in the municipal marina there, and had made a small number of friends in the community. There is a large naval air station on the island, so we would be able to shop at the base exchange and commissary and obtain outpatient health care at the base hospital. Some years earlier, we had purchased as an investment a lot on the island with a beautiful view of both mountains and water. So, early in 1984, we contacted a builder and began the process of designing and building our new home. In October 1984 we moved into our new home and placed our Vancouver home on the market. In April 1985 the house sold while I was visiting at the Chinese University of Hong Kong, and Fran rented a small apartment just off the UBC campus. From then on, we spent the weekends in our new home, traveling to Vancouver only to meet my teaching assignments, continue work with my last doctoral student, and enjoy associations with colleagues and other friends.

As is apparent, the period from 1985 to June 1988 was one of gradual disengagement from the faculty at UBC. I believe my colleagues understood that this process was taking place, although I discussed the matter with only a few. I continued to be active in executive programs but gradually withdrew from participation in faculty committees. The leadership of our division was in excellent hands, and I was content to play only a passive role. Dean Peter Lusztig generously granted me complete relief from teaching during the spring term of 1988, further easing the transition to retirement. Fran and I were then spending nearly all our time in Oak Harbor, although we continued to maintain the apartment in Vancouver.

Actual retirement was a time of both joy and sorrow: joy because of the wonderful surprise party given us by my colleagues and friends—one could not ask for a more wonderful expression of friendship and good wishes for the future—and sorrow in the realization that the most rewarding chapter in my life was now ended and that of necessity we would be seeing less of friends of many years. There was sadness also that I no longer would be an active part of the university. Several weeks later, Dean Lusztig added his thanks at a formal luncheon in the faculty club and generously announced the establishment of a special annual prize in my name for an undergraduate student of organizational behavior. My ties to UBC were not completely severed, however, as I continued to participate in executive programs for several years, further easing the transition.

Conventional advice for retirees urges caution in selecting where one will live lest one find oneself in strange surroundings among strangers. We had avoided this problem by our decision to live in a community we knew well and where we were known. We settled into the community easily and continued our hobbies of boating and fishing and participation in the activities of the local yacht club. Retirees are also urged to plan how they will fill their days. I must confess to having given little thought to this question beyond a desire to work with functional illiterates and perhaps teach the odd course at the local community college. I did know that the last thing I wished was to annoy my dear wife by sitting around the house all the time. The solution appeared even before my formal retirement. One afternoon, as I worked on my boat at the marina, I was approached by Dick Hopper, whose boat was moored nearby. At that time Dick was the northwest regional director of Embry-Riddle Aeronautical University's College of Career Education.

For those readers who are not familiar with Embry-Riddle, the university is recognized throughout the aviation and aerospace industry as the world's leader in aviation education. Besides the university's residential campuses in Daytona Beach, Florida, and Prescott, Arizona, the College of Career Education offers associate's, bachelor's, and master's degrees in a variety of aviation and aerospace management and operations fields at more than a hundred residential centers throughout the United States and Western Europe. Although most of these centers are on military bases, several are located at aerospace plants and civilian government agencies such as the FAA. Dick's need was to fill a newly established position for a regional faculty adviser to monitor the academic programs at the centers in his region. I just happened to fit the criteria for the job, which consisted of previous aviation experience, an earned doctorate, and experience in a traditional university. Was this another of those fortuitous encounters?

After interviews at the parent campus in Daytona Beach, Florida, I accepted the position with the rank of professor. Because our region includes bases in Montana, Idaho, Washington, Alaska, and Hawaii, I agreed to teach only two 9-week terms each year here at the nearby Naval Air Station Whidbey Island rather than travel to teach in other centers in the region. Until 1995, there was no graduate program here at Whidbey. Meanwhile, I've been teaching upper-division undergraduate courses, but on a much broader scale than while at UBC. When I accepted the position, I had no idea of the extent to which it would grow. As our Faculty Senate matured, I soon found myself appointed or invited to participate in a number of faculty governance activities that I thoroughly enjoy. As chair of our MBA program, I sit on the University Graduate Council; I am also a member or chair of three other Senate committees. (One of these is the Faculty Handbook Committee, and in that capacity I sit on the Joint Senates' Coordinating Committee, which exists to coordinate the activities of the three Faculty Senates—ours and those at Daytona Beach and Prescott.) To help ensure that our students at different locations receive comparable education, we designate various professors as "course monitors." These individuals select one to three texts and develop a master course outline to guide other faculty in preparation of their syllabi. I am currently monitor for three graduate courses.

As one might guess, the position calls for a considerable amount of travel, so my frequent flyer accounts are not lacking. In addition to visits to our centers, meetings of one sort or another take me to Daytona Beach nearly every month. My colleagues are a delightful group of people with varied and interesting backgrounds. Although the job is nominally full-time, my office is in my home and I handle much of the work through electronic mail, so there is adequate time left for other activities. All things considered, I couldn't ask for a more ideal third career.

How long will I remain with Embry-Riddle? The answer is simple—as long as I am able. Too often one sees people who have retired completely wither and die within a few years. I am convinced that one of the secrets of longevity is to remain active and mentally stimulated.

So, there is the story of my transitions. Throughout my adult life I've been blessed with a wonderful wife, loving sons, challenging work, splendid colleagues, and a lot of luck. To all of you who may read this brief story, I wish the same.

5 Creating a Career

OBSERVATIONS FROM OUTSIDE THE MAINSTREAM

Stewart R. Clegg
in conversation with **John M. Jermier**

John: Let me start by asking you to situate your early years of study in a social, political, and intellectual context.

Stewart: In 1971 I started a PhD at Bradford University under David Hickson's supervision. I chose Bradford for several reasons. One reason was that I had become interested in power and uncertainty as related concepts, and these were David's interests. Second, I was born in Bradford. It was a good place for being close to family networks.

I returned to the North again in the summer of 1971. During the summer, before starting the doctorate, I had worked on a building site as a joiner's laborer, something that was to have some impact on later work, although I didn't know it at the time. I decided that I would do a PhD on "power and organizations." As an initial exercise to get me into the research, I did a replication of the Hickson et al. "strategic contingencies interorganizational power" study on a brewery near to where I was living. At this point, I was taking a qualitative and phenomenological approach based on reading Wittgenstein, Schutz, Winch, Glaser and Strauss, and others, and based on research

I did in hospitals as part of my BSc honors degree in behavioral science at Aston University. From this perspective, the "strategic contingencies" approach seemed overly constraining, and ungrounded—it didn't relate to the members' experiences much at all.

The first year or so of the doctorate I read through the power literature and the debates in political science and sociology, also trying to follow up more of my philosophical and theoretical interests. This meant reading Bachrach and Baratz's critiques of Dahl. I tried to sort out what was happening, what was going on in the debate, and how it related to organizations, sociological theory, and what the organizational research implications were. Simultaneously, I was continuing my reading in more phenomenologically oriented material and was also reading much Wittgenstein, to whom I'd been introduced in undergraduate philosophy classes, by Mike Hall.

I became convinced, because of reading Bachrach and Baratz, that to understand power it wasn't enough just to look at behavioral outcomes in the way in which Dahl stipulated. Bachrach and Baratz sug-

AUTHORS' NOTE: A different segment of this conversation was published previously as John M. Jermier and Stewart R. Clegg, "Critical Issues in Organization Science: A Dialogue," *Organization Science*, vol. 5, 1994, 1-13.

gested that one should look to the motives
and the intentions of the actors, the way in
which they were constructed, to be able to
see the hidden face of power. About this
time I heard a paper presented by a British
sociologist of deviance, Laurie Taylor, that
used C. Wright Mills's "social ascription of
motive analysis" applied to data collected
from sex offenders in a long-term prison,
looking at their differently situated motivational accounts. This opened up some
new ways of thinking for me.

I became intrigued by the idea of socially structured motive accounts as a way
of getting some purchase on the Bachrach
and Baratz contributions to the community power debate. If people didn't raise
some issues that one might have thought,
for various theoretical reasons, would have
been issues, then one needed to understand their motives. The notion of motives
that I was using was sociological rather
than psychological: how typical motive
structures of available accounts became
constructed. Today we might say it was
quite close to Foucault, although at the
time it wasn't as he hadn't done the work.
Anyway, I'd never heard of him then.

In late 1971, Allen Blum and Peter
McHugh published a new piece on "motive" in the *American Sociological Review*.
This theoretical revision of Mills's work on
motives intrigued me. Their account of
motives was characterized by an extreme
reflexivity. Besides, it had recourse to
Wittgenstein. It touched many chords, and
I began to follow up the references. Some
were to Jack D. Douglas's *Understanding
Everyday Life,* some of which I had already
read. This book contained separate chapters by Blum on "theorizing" and McHugh
on "positivism." From McHugh I began to
get a more systematic version of the things
already coalescing from my reading. It was
very exciting work, intellectually. It seemed
theoretically radical in a way that was unlike any other work that I'd read to that
date, except Wittgenstein. It was ethnomethodology with a difference.

Ethnomethodology arrived in Britain almost like a social movement, in terms of its
projection and its reception. It became well
established in two particular sociology de-

partments. One was the Manchester department, which tended to be more focused on the mechanics of conversation
analysis. The other was Goldsmith's College at London. This brings up another of
the important connections.

One significant person in Goldsmith's
College at London was David Silverman.
In 1970-1971, when I was finishing my
studies at Aston, I discovered Silverman's
The Theory of Organizations. It was a phenomenologically influenced critique of systems and positivist models. I thought it
was the best thing that I had read up to that
time in the organizational literature. It did
one thing that nothing else did: It bridged
the debates in sociological theory with debates in the analysis of organizations.

In 1972, under the editorship of Paul
Filmer, a group of sociologists at Goldsmith's, including David Silverman, published one of the first British phenomenologically influenced texts, called *New
Directions in Sociological Theory*. I contacted Paul, whom I'd seen give a paper
when I was an undergraduate at Aston,
and, presuming on that slight acquaintance,
I arranged to go down and meet and talk
with people at Goldsmith's. I did this because I wanted some advice on how to
follow up the links between phenomenology and power. Thus it was with great
anticipation that I set off on the south-
bound train for Kings Cross station in London, and from there to New Cross tube
station and Goldsmith's.

During the early 1970s Goldsmith's had
several visiting American academics. First,
I think, was Aaron Cicourel. Peter McHugh,
whom I was fortunate to meet while he was
in London, followed. Allen Blum had been
visiting Oxford, where he was on study
leave. These figures had a considerable impact on the group at Goldsmith's, reflected
in a very lively seminar. The year, I think,
was 1973. I came to participate in these
informal seminars because of that visit.

The seminars proved puzzling: I found
them somewhat bizarre and increasingly
difficult the longer I participated in them.
Some members of the group were very
much under the influence of Blum's theorizing, and Blum's theorizing was becom-

ing ever more complex, at least in terms of my ability to grasp it. What had started out as an opportunity to learn more about the analysis of rules in ethnomethodology, that I could then relate to power in organization theory, was turning into a weird scene. I taped the seminars and as I drove back north on the motorway would listen to the tapes repeatedly, trying to make sense of the seminar that I had been in.

The journeys to London were not the only ones that I was making. Also, I traveled to the field on a regular basis. Recall that I had once worked as a joiner's laborer on a building site. My supervisor, exasperated at my theoreticism and its expression through concepts and texts that were foreign to his way of thinking, insisted that I "get some data." After some false starts, in desperation I turned to the only organization I had relatively recent experience of and contact with—to a construction site in a nearby northern town, where I was also collecting data by tape-recording construction site managers, subcontractors, and employees talking about building a bus station and multistory car park.

I felt a stranger to both worlds, almost equally estranged from each. I decided I would never make sense of either. At the same time there was my increasingly anxious, albeit remote, supervisor to negotiate with. The three life worlds could not have been more different. There was constant tension that I sought to intermediate. At the same time, because of David Hickson's insistence on empirical work, I was trying to intermediate the pressure to collect data as well, such that from about 18 months into the doctorate I started fieldwork.

My approach to the texts that I collected was interpretive, concerned with deconstructing stories that I heard on-site. I always had in mind Georg Simmel's version of the Hobbesian question: "How is society possible?" I interpreted it as "How is this talk possible? How is it possible that these actors could have produced that kind of talk?" So my interest was more in the everyday organization of the talk than in formal conversational mechanisms of its production.

My interest in the second face of power, as Bachrach and Baratz called it, had co-

alesced around the concept of rules. It seemed that the way in which rules were constitutive of particular social settings and structures was the undercurrent, what I was to call, after Wittgenstein, the "deep structure." The deep structure/surface structure distinction from Wittgenstein was tied into a reading of Weber on *Macht* and *Herrschaft*. I interpreted *Macht* as "power." *Herrschaft* I interpreted in two ways, depending on the context in which Weber used it: as rule and as domination.

Power was often represented in the literature as the manifest doing of things. Given this, I thought that it was necessary to get beneath the surface to the "hidden face" of power, as Bachrach and Baratz called it, to look at the rules that underlay these manifest doings. I argued also that, in turn, they were embedded in a third level of analysis, the title of which also came from Wittgenstein, the notion of "form of life."

I was fortunate in collecting data from meetings on the building site. The site meetings were about issues. The whole discussion was about what an issue is, how it's an issue, what the responsibility is for it as an issue. This fit very well into the power framework I was developing. I would like to say it was because of great foresight and research design and planning, but it was not. Like many other things in my professional life, it was a random choice with chaotic implications.

The randomness of the choice can easily be gauged. I ended up on a construction site because I had worked on one. I had worked on one to earn some money to make a deposit to buy a house. That the job I took to do this was a joiners' laborer on that particular construction site was only because of my wife's father, a policeman in that northern town who policed the site and so had some influence with the project manager. The chaotic implications were that it placed me in an empirical situation where I had to try to research naturalistically a concept that had been dealt with extremely nonnaturalistically, "objectively," in the literatures that were available. Empirical realities proved chaotic for preexisting theoretical conventions that saw power wholly in objectivist, in action, terms.

I had a great deal of data. They took a long time to transcribe. In treating them, I sought to regard the people on the construction site as theorists in the same way that I would have treated the theorists I was reading in books. I developed this idea from the Goldsmith's seminars. What I sought was to try to theorize reflexively how the form of life of the stories and data that I collected on-site was possible. So I began to do with the builders what my Goldsmith's colleagues seemed to be doing with their philosophers.

I saw power as nested within the conception of rule, where rule centered on the indexical interpretations made of contractual documents on the construction site. By "indexical" I meant, following Garfinkel, how different interpretations indexed, or made use of, a different context of understanding—in both a temporal, occupational knowledge and organizational position sense. In turn, I thought, these reflected the way in which capitalism, as a form of life, infused these settings. Indexicality helped secure profit. Different readings of the contractual documents, always open to interpretation, sought to secure the legitimacy of different actions, and the costs attached to them, that flowed from different interpretations. Indexicality was ineradicable. The complexity and quantity of documentary material meant that it could never provide its own meaning. Formulated as a rule it would be: Always seek to exploit the indexicality of the contract.

In brief, it seemed that on the construction site, the institution of contract had a central and particular role to play. The contract specified who could do what, where, when, how, with whom. It specified almost every variable except, and this was the Wittgensteinian twist, its own interpretation. There were no rules for the interpretation of the rules contained within it. This insight related to the ethnomethodological concept of indexicality, as I have said. I treated indexicality in terms of empirically different forms of interested readings and interpretations of the contractual and other documents. The interested read-

ing from the project manager, from the consultant engineers, from the clerk of works, and so on: These were my texts. What I ended with was an analysis of power not as condensed into one person, one body, or one institution, but as power in process. Power worked through various "language games," to use Wittgenstein's term.

I finished the research and submitted the thesis in 1974. David Silverman was my external examiner. A year after I completed the degree, Routledge and Kegan Paul published a slightly revised version of my dissertation. I knew that publishability was a criterion for the award of the doctorate, so I had negotiated a contract to publish the book before I submitted the dissertation. I even had a literary agent (a couple of people had suggested this)! Armed with my doctorate and a forthcoming book, I went on the labor market and got a job as a lecturer in industrial sociology at Trent Polytechnic, in Nottingham. This was in 1974, in September. Shortly after, in about November I think, Steven Lukes's book *Power: A Radical View* was published. Was I depressed! This was an elegant and economical book, published by someone famous and prestigious, which, without any of the struggle and difficulty that attended my own investigation into power, seemed to say everything that I had, but said it so much better. Would anyone even want to read my book now, I thought? It seemed like the intellectual struggle to make sense of things as a trinity of power, rule, and domination had been undercut, effortlessly, by Lukes's trinity of a one-, two-, and three-dimensional view. If only I had been able to read this while still doing my thesis—how much easier it would have been. Later, I was glad I hadn't; at least I'd made my sense, not applied someone else's. But it took a while to see things that way.

Lecturing was another shock. I'd been 3 years working on what, I realized rapidly, was a set of issues with little relevance to the demands of the classroom. Wittgenstein, Weber, Simmel, the community power debate, ethnomethodology, and empirical data collected on construction sites did not have much relevance for teaching 16 hours a week across five courses to students doing accounting and business degrees, who, in general, had little interest in these things. Nor was there any reason they should have. Unfortunately, it was all I knew at the time. It was a fast learning curve for me. It had to be.

The fast learning curve had two sides to it. First, I had to learn to teach a lot more than I knew. Second, I appreciated that if I was going to continue to write and re-search as I wanted to do, I'd be better off getting some other kind of position, one where my time was less besieged. Another factor exacerbated the sense of besiege-ment. For a while, I was traveling $3\frac{1}{2}$ hours each way to work and home, every day. We couldn't sell the cottage and couldn't af-ford to rent elsewhere initially. After a few weeks we did, and traveled home on week-ends. One weekend I saw David Hickson, and he learned of my plight. He was fre-quently on the continent of Europe push-ing for greater collaboration among or-ganization theorists in what was to become the EU. The European Group for Organi-sation Studies (EGOS) had just started as the vehicle for this. Lucien Karpik, David Hickson, and Walter Goldberg, among oth-ers, were the prime movers. They decided that it would be a fine thing to fund an EGOS research fellowship. Walter Gold-berg, who then was director of the Inter-national Institute of Management In Ber-lin, made one of their fellowships available for EGOS. I was successful in gaining this fellowship, because of David Hickson's be-hind-the-scenes influence, I guess. For the next 18 months or so, I was the EGOS fellow, leaving Trent Polytechnic after only 6 months in early 1975. The EGOS fellow-ship brief was very simple and very broad. It was to work on European perspectives on power in organization theory. In a way, it wasn't a great brief to accept, having just finished a PhD in the area, but probably I couldn't have done anything else anyway. Power was my topic. I had just come out of doing a dissertation on power and now I had to try to find more things that were fresh and novel to say, at book length, be-cause I wanted to write a substantial report and I wanted to publish it as well. And I had to try to steer around, or engage with, Lukes's

book, which I admired greatly, even as it boxed me in. I felt little room to maneuver.

There were various ideas floating around as to what I might do. I sought to construct what a European perspective on power in organizations might look like. In the early 1970s in British sociology, various forms of Marxism were influential. During my work on my doctorate I had not kept up with these currents. I knew about Marx, had read him as a social theorist as an undergraduate not read widely. An unob-trusive measure of what I was reading still sits on my bookcase. It is a dog-eared copy of *Social Research*. *Social Research* was there because it had an article by Habermas called "Why More Philosophy?" as I was reading some Frankfurt school at the time. That was about the extent of my reading in con-temporary debates. What I had not read was structuralist Marxism.

Althusserian and Poulantzian Marxism was very fashionable. This approach sought to analyze the "objective" properties of capi-talism as a "mode of production." I under-stood the debates hardly at all when I first encountered them. If I had, I might not have persisted. But I was stubborn and persistent. I didn't like to be beaten by a theory—I wanted, always, to try to master theories, to understand them. In part, I think, this was because of a degree of the-ory anxiety on my part. Not having had a "proper" sociological training at one of the accepted centers of excellence, I think that I overcompensated through the time and energy that I gave to grasping debates that others, better advised, might have coun-seled less enthusiasm for. So I set out to teach myself Marxist theory!

I thought that I could use this material to construct what a European perspective on power in organizations might look like for the EGOS report. I began to read exten-sively, concentrating on the "structuralist Marxist" literature. In part I was predis-posed to do so because during the work that I did for the dissertation, one paper that was very influential in shaping my thinking, in an indirect way, was by Maurice Godelier, a French anthropologist. The pa-per compared Lévi-Strauss and Marx, pro-viding a structuralist analysis of Marx's

Capital. In fact, I think he may have used the deep structure/surface structure distinction that I already knew from Wittgenstein. This affinity would have excited me. At this distance, I can't recall.

I also had another job to find. My fellowship was due to run out at the end of 1976. It was a bad time to be coming onto the academic labor market in the U.K. In fact, many years later, when we met in the United States, Anthony Giddens reminded me that I had suggested that I might pack the academic life up and become a farmer! I must say, this sounds an absurd suggestion, but I think that I was thinking in those terms. I guess I was feeling pretty estranged. I couldn't get a job. The U.K. was having one of its periodic economic crises during that summer of 1976. The International Monetary Fund placed the economy under its stewardship, because of a £3 billion sterling loan. The government had to accept IMF discipline, part of which was to cut public expenditure. It usually is. One area of public expenditure that was cut was university appointments. Many were frozen. In particular, sociology suffered. There were few jobs, and I didn't get any of them. I tried both sociology and management departments and seemed to fall between two stools—too sociological for one, not sociological enough for the other.

During the spring of 1976, someone told me of an opening in Australia. It was a job advertised at the Australian National University (ANU). It was a research post, designed to study power in Australia. The deadline was about 5 days away. In those days, before word processing, and with no secretarial support from anywhere, I typed all my own material—a habit that persists to the present day. I did it, clumsily, on a small portable typewriter. I didn't have time or energy to write a fresh application, so I just photocopied an earlier application that I had on file and pasted a new address on the top of it and photocopied it again. It looked a bit scrappy, but I sent it off.

Well, I made a big mistake. The application that I'd sent was one that I'd formatted for a job in a department of sociology in a small European country, a position where I thought they wanted someone extremely theoretical. The person in Canberra who read it was a professor well known in Australian sociological circles, then and now, for his commitment to quantitative approaches and methods. The kind of profile that I offered would not have been attractive to him. Still, he passed my particulars on to a colleague in the ANU's Research School of Social Sciences, who had just been appointed as a foundation professor of humanities at Griffith University, a new university in Brisbane. Griffith subsequently invited me to join them as a lecturer after the foundation professor joined them. He knew Blum's work, and that of the philosopher Stanley Rosen, whom I had cited in a *Theory and Society* article developed from the thesis. As a political philosopher, he had been a student of Rosen's. What luck!

By the end of 1976, Lynne (my wife) and I started a new life in a very different context, both personally and professionally. Previously I had worked in technological universities in schools of management. Now I had joined an interdisciplinary school of humanities. Griffith was very important for me. Colleagues worked in areas as diverse as history, comparative literature, semiotics, anthropology, political theory, media studies, women's studies, Australian studies, Marxism, and many other areas. It was a very exciting place to be, very challenging. It had great energy and there was a terrific fusion of ideas. It was also a world away from Britain and Europe, the entirety of my experience to that date. By contrast, it was a place of easy informality, hot days, cold beers, and superb beaches. It was Queensland. It was also the most redneck and reactionary state in Australia, under the elective dictatorship of a Huey Long figure, Premier John Bjelke-Peterson. These contextual factors had a marked intellectual influence. Power was pretty transparent in Queensland, for instance. The "theory of the state" debate, developed in a Western European context, was not necessary to group the political realities of a state in which a gerrymander, authoritarian populism, and corruption combined to run the state in the interests of a "development" minority of property developers, primary producers, and extractive, logging- and minerals-based multinationals.

The main course that I taught initially at Griffith was "Power in Organizations." The foundation professor, Hiram Caton, set this up for me. I hadn't finished writing the report for EGOS, so I combined teaching the course with writing the report. I think there is a strong Griffith influence on the book that I produced, *The Theory of Power and Organization,* largely through the importance of the concept of "hegemony." I had discovered Gramsci shortly before coming to Australia, initially through Lukes, and when I did I could have kicked myself, because it seemed that the Gramscian idea of hegemony said what, painfully, obliquely, and opaquely, I had been working my way toward through Wittgensteinian analogies and metaphors. I've often wondered about the role of Pierro Sraffa, the famous economist, who was a friend and confidant of Gramsci in Italy (and the executor of his will) and of Wittgenstein in Cambridge: It was to a particular Sicilian gesture that Sraffa made that Wittgenstein attributed his retreat from the correspondence views of language that he developed in the *Tractatus* and replaced with the *Philosophical Investigations,* and their view of "language games."

At Griffith there happened to be an Italian studies program in the school and there were people I could talk to about Gramsci, particularly David Saunders. It was very stimulating and interesting and helped me clarify ideas considerably. When I finished writing the course that became both the EGOS report and *The Theory of Power and Organization,* it focused on debates and issues around the idea of hegemony.

John: It was not this, but *Critical Issues in Organizations*—that was the book I think many us in the United States first saw. From it we learned about the work that you had done on power, and saw it as first development of a critical perspective on organizations. How did this project develop?

Stewart: The title was a pun. I don't know whether many people picked it up. It was the joint Althusserian idea of "symptomatic absences" that what is not present in a text may be its most significant feature in light of later developments, "nonissues" that were absent from the expression of politics, but nonpolitical in their absence, which led me to develop that title. By "critical issues" I did not mean that the issues selected for topics in the book were critical, because of their presence, but because of their absence: issues like feminism, the state, and power.

During my last summer as a doctoral student at Bradford I met and became friends with David Dunkerley, who had been appointed recently to the Sociology Department at Leeds University. David Dunkerley and I took the idea for *Critical Issues in Organizations* to Routledge in London. Routledge agreed to publish it, but said that a reader was not what they really wanted from us. What Routledge wanted was a book on organizations that performed similarly in its field to *The New Criminology,* the best-selling Routledge book at that time. It would be one that started historically from the very beginning and brought the reader right up to the present and did so with a strong critical edge to it.

We agreed with Routledge that we would do what we came to call the "Big Book" on organizations and they would do *Critical Issues.* Because I'd moved to Australia and David had moved to Plymouth, there was a delay before we got started on the book. Also, I was working on *The Theory of Power and Organization.* Once I'd finished that book, it made writing *Organization, Class and Control,* the final title of the Big Book, much easier. Theoretically, the earlier book prefigured the structure of the later one.

We completed work on *Organization, Class and Control* when David was a visiting scholar at Griffith University, toward the end of 1978. During that period we worked ferociously on the book; before that I had spent a month or two in David's house in Plymouth at the end of 1977. Our production there was somewhat Dickensian. We worked mostly in his attic, a high little garret with a view of the sea if you craned your neck. I'd be scribbling away, everything in longhand of course, lots of 2B pencils, pencil sharpeners, and erasers at the side. I'd be writing in one room,

David would be writing in another room. It was a textual production line. We kept this production line going later on the verandah of our house in Brisbane.

We worked out a structure and a rough idea of what the orientation of the book would be as we wrote it. During the process of writing the volume, we began to coalesce our ideas around the notion of control. *The Theory of Power and Organization* came to be concerned with the labor process debate, and this became the main edge for *Organization, Class and Control,* around the idea that organization could be regarded as control of the labor process.

I learned a great deal about organization theories because of writing *Organization, Class and Control.* It meant reading lots of new things as well as rereading some familiar things and seeing them differently.

John: What made you start to shift your focus from the concept of power to that of control? I see those concepts as related but not identical. I wonder what led to that transition? Were there any specific works or was it just the development in your thinking as a product of a long period of study? Perhaps they're not even that clearly differentiated in your view? You did mention Braverman, implicitly, or at least labor process theory.

Stewart: Initially, it was not the labor process literature. I came to that late and not through Braverman but through material produced by the Conference of Socialist Economists. The interest that I developed in Gramsci, Poulantzas, and Althusser led me to the Marxian idea of ideology. Much of the debate in the School of Humanities was about the way that ideology functioned in drama, in texts, of various kinds. The major theorists of ideology then were Althusserian or Gramscian. The Althusserian emphasis on ideology was on a concept of control by other means. Where one didn't have control by repression one had control by the ideological state apparatuses. That was probably the point of transition. As that agenda became more apparent in the work, I guess there was a shift from a more agency-centered view of power to a more structuralist-oriented conception of control. In part I saw that as a way of redress-

ing the balance of the early work. What I should have done and didn't seek to do until much later was to achieve some form of synthesis between agency and structure rather than to move from one side of the polarity to another.

If there had been other organization theorists to talk to, or graduate students, I probably would have approached "control" through a more obvious route. But there weren't such people. Nor was there fax or e-mail, and I knew few people in the "organizations" field very well. Those I did know, on the whole, were not on the same intellectual wavelengths. I corresponded, intermittently, with one or two British scholars, and frequently with David Silverman, but none of them worked in areas that connected with the debates I encountered at Griffith.

I like to talk to people, and there just wasn't anyone to talk to about organization theory at Griffith, so I gravitated toward those areas and those people where discourse was possible. The people I talked to were not sociologists, not management theorists, not organization theorists. None were there initially, but they did constitute the intellectual community in which I was living. Also, the broader sociology scene in Australia during the 1970s focused on questions of culture and control, of dominant ideology and social reproduction, particularly in Bob Connell's influential work on Australian identity and history. In addition, there was the impact of the labor process debate that I was reading in some British literature and then in Braverman and responses to his work. All these fed into *Organization, Class and Control* from my side.

John: *Organization, Class and Control* was very well received and influential.

Stewart: Yes, I guess that it was, although, like just about all of my books, with the exception of the first two, it was never reviewed in the *ASQ,* not that I ever noticed, anyway. That was a bit frustrating. At the time there was only the *ASQ* in the field, and my books didn't seem to get reviewed in it. I began to feel paranoid about this, taking it as a judgment of the relevant lack of interest in my work by North Americans. I don't know how influential the absence of a review is, but I must say that I have found the typical *ASQ* silence that has greeted the publication of all my books, since the first two, surprising. They have been well reviewed in many places elsewhere, but if all you knew about what was in the marketplace came from reviews in the leading U.S. organizations journal, then my product, as it was defined by books, didn't exist. We're talking about 9 books over 15 years that have gone unremarked in a lead journal. For anyone familiar with power theory, when you see a recurrent pattern of "nonissues," you're inclined to ask, What's going on?

John: What audience were you writing for?

Stewart: Well, initially, I never thought about an audience much at all. When I did my doctoral dissertation, which became *Power, Rule and Domination,* my audience was very specific: It was David Silverman, who I hoped would be an external examiner; Alan Dawe, who was at Leeds University and used to read some of the things that I drafted; David Hickson, Bradford, who would examine me; and anybody else I could persuade to read it. I knew very little about what a U.S. audience might be. I thought more about disciplines: about sociology, and schools of thought within it. I was wrapped up in trying to see the thesis through in the terms that I had embarked on. When I sought to get it published, then it seemed I'd hit the audience appropriately, in the judgment of the literary agent and the publisher, Routledge, that the agent approached.

John: When did you first start to address a U.S. audience?

Stewart: It was in 1980 that I went to America for the first time, to attend an American Sociological Association meeting in New York City. That was a great experience. I just walked for miles and miles, past and through all the landmarks: the New School for Social Research, where the Frankfurt school émigrés went to; 42nd Street, where Charlie Parker used to play, where all the jazz clubs were that many of the records I had bought over the years had been recorded; past the big brownstone where I knew John Lennon lived; through the city

I'd seen in so many movies, from Warner Bros. classics to contemporary Woody Allen films, like *Annie Hall* and *Manhattan.* (*Manhattan* had not been out long—I'd seen it in Denmark the previous year during some time I spent at the Technological University.)

In New York I met heaps of sociologists—more than I'd ever seen before. Some were famous people, and it was good to see what they looked like; some were graduate students or assistant professors, and it was among these people, in particular, that I found there was an audience for some of the things that I'd done. Some, like Charles Perrow, Peter Blau, and Howard Aldrich, I had met already in Europe. But I also met lots of new people. I'm still in touch with some of the people I met then. After this I didn't feel quite so isolated—I knew that there was an audience even if it was on another continent. About the same time, I published a piece on organization and control in the *ASQ* as well. This was interesting—the piece published wasn't the piece I'd written but the piece that someone at *ASQ* rewrote. It may have been a better paper—it was certainly a different paper.

I learned something new from that visit to the States as well. You're not supposed to write books. You write articles. I didn't know this; from my background in the U.K. and currently in a school of humanities, it was fine to write books. But I learned that in North America books don't count. I think it was both Charles Perrow and Howard Aldrich who told me this. Again, it was a bit depressing. Not only were my books not being reviewed, they didn't count much, whether they were favorably reviewed or not. I had thoughts of locating in the United States, because of the professional opportunities, but it never came to anything: I didn't know the U.S. graduate school culture and norms of "the presentation," nor was what I had achieved seemingly recognized in the United States.

I returned to Griffith restless from a period overseas. I'd enjoyed living in Europe. Queensland at that time was a politically depressing place to be because of the corrupt political culture of cynical authoritarianism and development at any price (there used to be a joke that the prevailing political philosophy was "If it moves, shoot it; if it stands still, chop it down"). I wasn't sure where I wanted to be. I wasn't sure what I wanted to do. I could see that my career could be at a crossroads. Either I translated myself into a proper sociologist, in a sociology department, I thought, or I rejoined the ranks of management as an organization theorist. My present position, as a reader in a school of humanities, seemed anomalous and made the latter option almost impossible, given the then prevalent conservatism of Australian business schools and the marginality of organization studies within them. I felt as if I couldn't go on forever working in the organizations field in virtual physical isolation, with no one to talk to on a day-to-day basis, surviving on the once-a-year overseas conference. The only route out seemed to be to become more involved in the interdisciplinary life of the School of Humanities and to try to build a network with the Sociology Department at nearby Queensland University.

I did both of these things. Together with Paul Boreham, from Queensland University, who was a sociologist, not in the Sociology Department but in "external studies," and Geoff Dow, from the School of Humanities, who, although primarily a political economist, was a genuinely interdisciplinary person. I decided to try to organize an event at Griffith that might put the place on the social science map. This was the OES (Organization, Economy and Society) Conference that we held in 1981. We got a small seed grant from the School of Humanities and started to organize what turned into a conference with about 350 participants. We invited all those people whose work we all knew and who we could all agree on really liking. Some of them came, including Claus Offe and Harvie Ramsay, the latter whom I knew from my English days, the former whom I'd never met, but admired greatly. Out of this conference came several things—one was negative, the others positive. The negative was that there was some resentment that the conference had been organized by three men. We got the reputation for having or-

ganized a "boys'" conference among the increasingly important constituency of feminist theorists. We all came to regret this perception—there was probably some truth in it because we had, of course, concentrated on the "public sphere" at a time when feminism was reclaiming the personal as political. I wish that we had been more sensitive to the possible perception of exclusion on our part—in our defense I can only say that we did not try to do this, but it did not stop us being labeled.

The positives were that we created two things from the conference. One was a book, *Class, Politics and the Economy*, which came out in 1983. I don't think a lot of people know this book.

John: I've seen it.

Stewart: Oh well, at least someone has. This book marked the beginning of a collaboration with Geoff and Paul that was to last for about 5 years. The only previous writing collaboration that I'd had, with David Dunkerley, had been a "marriage of convenience" arranged by the publisher for the purposes of *Organization, Class and Control*. We had some fun, and some tensions, writing that book, and after it was over we never really got together again. After all, we lived on opposite sides of the world. Paul and Geoff were different. For a few years we lived close to each other in adjacent suburbs of the same city. We wrote together because we wanted to.

While Paul was on study leave in the U.K., a colleague at Leicester University, where he was based, living in a shiveringly cold flat, by his account, approached him. A publisher wanted the colleague to write a book on "the politics of social class." The colleague was too busy—he probably knew that you don't publish books—and so asked Paul if he was interested in doing it. Paul brought the idea back with him and the three of us decided to write the book together. Eventually, about 4 years later, it was published under a different title, with a different publisher, Routledge again, as *Class, Politics and the Economy*.

About the time the OES Conference occurred I was approached by the outgoing editor of the *Australian and New Zealand Journal of Sociology* to see if I would take over the editing of the journal. That would have meant its coming to Griffith. I knew that many of my colleagues, none of whom were sociologists, with about two exceptions (and they were junior people), wouldn't want a part of this: the argument would be that we shouldn't be sponsoring disciplinary activities from an interdisciplinary school. There were other, more locally political reasons, as well. Also, I felt nervous about doing this; after all, in the same city was one of Australia's best-known sociology departments, at the University of Queensland. I suggested that the editors approach the professor of sociology there, John Western, to see if there was interest in joint editorship of the journal by the two of us. There was, and John and I became coeditors and Paul the book review editor. We did this from about 1982 to 1986. We had great fun.

Eventually, as a result of work that Paul and I were doing with Geoff on "class debates," work that for me followed on from the direction of *Organization, Class and Control,* by developing organizationally influenced ways of conceptualizing class and political issues, taking organizations to class following on from bringing class to organizations, John, Paul, and I found ourselves in correspondence with Erik Olin Wright in Madison, Wisconsin. He had "operationalized" structural class measures, and we were keen to do some empirical work after all the work we had done on conceptualizing class. John was an experienced and skeptical survey researcher, and slowly we built a team and secured research funding to conduct the "class project." This grew into a massive project, with about 10 people working on it at any one time. Another friend, Mike Emmison (through whose influence I became aware of Laclau and Mouffe's work on power), got involved, and we recruited graduate students to the project. Many papers were produced, some of which found their way into prestigious journals, and eventually the team produced a book from the project titled *The Class Structure of Australia.* Also, related to it, but separate, I produced *Organization Theory and Class Analysis* in 1989, out of interest in the project and the two earlier books on "class."

One interesting spin-off from the project was that I think all of the people who were involved in it ended up with a very skeptical attitude toward the explanatory power of class, in any of its various conceptualizations, as a variable. It didn't make much difference to the interpretation of the data which class or stratification model one used. Nor did it explain much of the variance that conceptual claims had suggested that it might. Still, good links were forged with Erik, and some of the graduate students spent very valuable and productive time there. There was another Australian connection, in that the émigré Hungarian sociologist Ivan Szelyni, who had worked at Flinders University in Adelaide, was also there.

About 1984, the chance came to redefine myself and resolve the ambiguities that had troubled me to that date. Actually, there were two chances. One was to apply for a professorship in the new School of Social and Industrial Administration that had been created at Griffith. However, even though I had a role in setting the school up, for various reasons I was not confident that if I applied for the position that was available, I would get it. There was a strong "public administration/public policy" culture emerging in the school, but not one of organization theory. Anyway, nobody really defined me as one of those; organization theory was a minor discipline in Australia, and generally in Australia I was thought of, if at all, as a sociologist. Overseas, in the United States or the U.K., it was probably more likely that I'd be thought of as an organization theorist, I think. Actually, at this time, formally, I was neither—I was a reader in a school of humanities.

Although I applied for the job at Griffith in the new school, I withdrew because, at the same time, in 1984, I was offered the chair of sociology at the University of New England (UNE). Incidentally, Bob Hinings was a confidant. Bob was visiting the new School of Social and Industrial Administration at the time and we talked things over, as we were wont to. Sociology came up trumps. So I thought that the duality was about to be resolved finally.

John: Earlier, you mentioned two things, that the OES Conference led to two positive things. What was the second?

Stewart: Oh, I haven't mentioned that. The other was something called APROS. Originally, this acronym stood for Australian Pacific Researchers in Organization Studies. Later we came to change it Asia Pacific Researchers in Organization Studies. A lot of people, including Jane Marceau, who like me knew EGOS in Europe, had enjoyed the Brisbane conference in 1981. We wanted to keep the momentum going. A number of people networked, and the following year, at a wonderfully faded hotel at Medlow Baths in the Blue Mountains, outside Sydney, about 30 or so people came together to form APROS on a rough parallel of the EGOS model. Being Australians, we didn't go in for any of the elitist stuff that EGOS delighted in—there were no "SuperEGOS" as a self-appointed cadre of "senior people" in the field. It was much more democratic and loosely coupled than EGOS—for one thing we had no resources to speak of, and we couldn't play off national rivalries to hold ever more elaborate conferences in a continuing game of intellectual and resource one-upmanship. In 1985, we held our first meeting offshore in Hong Kong, when we began to approach the organizational efficiencies of an EGOS Conference, through the resources that Gordon Redding could contribute from Hong Kong University Management School, where he was head of department. From this conference came the interest in East Asia that has manifested itself in several subsequent works, including the book that came out of the conference that Gordon Redding, Dexter Dunphy, and I edited and published through the Center for Asian Studies at Hong Kong University. This one was called *Enterprise and Management in East Asia.* I had seen Dexter give a paper on Japanese management in Sydney and wanted to get him and Gordon in touch with each other. The conference was an opportunity.

John: How did you get to meet Gordon? This must have been an important meeting, as it contributed, by your own account, to the inclusion of East Asian material in your work, in *Modern Organizations* and *Capi-*

talism in Contrasting Cultures, at a time when not many people knew much about this part of the world.

Stewart: Yes, that's right. In 1983, on the way back from Stanford, where I'd been on study leave (another story in its own right— briefly, don't negotiate access in elite U.S. institutions through junior people, was what I learned from that experience; when I got there I found that Stanford was a little surprised to see me, but eventually it worked out fine), I wanted to stop off in Asia on return from the United States via the U.K. David Hickson knew Gordon Redding by name, because Gordon had a paper in *Organization Studies* (which had started up in the early 1980s), and David suggested that I contact him. I wrote to Gordon, he invited me to stop off, and we had a great time. We've become great mates. I had expected to see an exploited proletariat and I found instead a dynamic, different, and economically successful capitalism with a culture that confounded the familiar Weberian hypotheses about the rationalization of the world. Quite an eye-opener. Since then I've been back to and through Hong Kong many times. APROS has held two conferences there.

In fact, the success of APROS, particularly from 1986 onward, when we changed to an Asia Pacific focus, helped to keep the dualism alive. Just as I'd moved into sociology I found an audience and renewed data in the organization theory field. It was in the latter half of the 1980s that I returned to organization theory again after being out of it, effectively, from about 1980, after the publication of *Organization, Class and Control.* During the early 1980s I didn't publish in the organizations field. I had thoughts of moving out of it altogether.

At UNE I had to give an inaugural lecture as a professor sometime in 1986. I wasn't sure what I could talk about that would interest a wide cross section of the community, so, given the interests that I'd had with Geoff and Paul, I decided to write about socialism from an organizational point of view, revisiting some classic debates. I chose this because I was already working on such themes in a paper with Winton Higgins that, eventually, was published as

"Against the Current" in *Organization Studies*. This arose from a paper that Winton gave to the department. From that period on I became reinterested in organization issues, in part because I thought that there was more of an audience than there had been previously, in part because Lex Donaldson's "defense" of orthodox organization theory presented me with several opportunities to readdress some old issues.

At UNE I took over the teaching of a course in "power." From the teaching notes that I produced for this course, some new ideas began to take shape. At Griffith I didn't teach Foucault because lots of other people did it already. At UNE no one did. He had to be in a curriculum on power. My thinking, which had been changing anyway, got to be redefined through the encounter with Foucault. I wrote a hurried paper to give to a small conference of American and European organization theorists in the Netherlands. There I realized, when I heard Richard Scott on "institutional" theory, that maybe my work was moving in a related way. I don't think anyone else did. The paper met with the puzzled and irritated response that I had become used to, although later, when I submitted it as "Radical Revisions" to *Organization Studies,* it was accepted. After realizing that there was still something to say about power—it had been nearly 10 years since I had written on it—I decided to write another book on power. This was a break from pattern—previously I'd always written the books first and then tried to write papers from them; this reversed the causality.

So I resolved to write a book around the notes that I had prepared for the power course. And that became *Frameworks of Power.* It turned out very differently from how I'd initially conceptualized it as a really short book like Lukes's.

John: Let's pause here. So you were a sociology professor, you'd resolved the duality, you wrote what was to become a critically acclaimed book with *Frameworks* . . .

Stewart: *ASQ* didn't review it . . .

John: So, *ASQ* didn't review it, but it was very well received. The question is, why did you choose to leave Australia and go to St. Andrews to take a management chair?

Stewart: It's a question I've asked myself many times. Let me try to construct an answer. St. Andrews wrote to me when I was visiting professor at Hong Kong, asking if I would be interested in applying for the job. John Child had proposed me to them—he knew I was restless. I thought long and hard about it. I was bored in Armidale. I didn't think that the chances of moving to another chair of sociology in Australia were good, and I didn't think there was any chance of moving from a sociology position to a management position within Australia. To the extent that I was known at all in Australia it was, largely, as a sociologist. The standard business school attitude to sociology was that it wasn't relevant. So I felt stuck.

I'd written *Frameworks* and was starting to write *Modern Organizations* straight after it—I wrote them back-to-back in about a year. Also, after doing the two books, I really didn't know what I was going to do next. I've often felt like this after completing books. In fact, it's characterized the postbirth experience of nearly all of them. There's been that sense that what you know has just been laid out for the world—what on earth will you do for an encore, what next? Actually, it's never been a problem, but there is that feeling of emptiness after you've finished a big project, seen it through. You know you don't have another book in you immediately—well, *Modern Organizations* was the exception there, and, come to think of it, *Organization, Class and Control,* that followed hard on the heels of the previous one. I guess if you routinely write 6,000- to 8,000-word papers, that is not a problem. Also, no one reviews them in public. No wonder North Americans don't write books so much. They're too smart! Why write a 100,000 word book for one hit, when you could write heaps of articles instead? Why, indeed? I guess that it's just that for some ideas you require a big canvas—I think that part of me is a "big-picture man"—someone who likes to write large on a big topic. Of course, I do the smaller-scale and more specialist stuff as well, the miniatures, but I do like the freedom to roam over a large and historical canvas. I think that roaming probably characterizes most of the books that I have written, roaming historically, philosophically, across disciplines. Nomadic theorizing with a power compass. So there was a sense of what next. In the past new places had led to new avenues of work. Why not again?

There were other factors as well. Armidale is a pretty, but remote, country town—not a lot to do if you like city things. I was bored with living there. I enjoyed the cycling, but that was about it. Universities in Australia were changing rapidly as a result of government policies. At UNE, in particular, there was a feeling of siege, of panic, about the future, as we were being forced to merge with other entities by application of government policy. I feared being stuck there for the rest of my life—missing all the movies I wanted to see (there was no cinema), bands I wanted to hear, and so on. I was quite isolated in the department. My interests had swung back to organization theory, but there was no community of scholars around me. There was APROS, but it was intermittent.

St. Andrews appealed to my vanity. At a distance it had an Ivy League quality. I thought that going back to the U.K. as a professor was a kind of recognition. We thought that it would be fun to live in Europe again. They offered me what seemed a lot of money compared with Australian salaries, which had been in a period of relative decline, as had the Australian dollar. Almost the last thing was going back to the U.K. Over the years I had become fiercely Australian nationalist. I didn't define myself as "English" anymore. I had spent very little of my career there. My children were born in Australia. We had Australian citizenship. I had never lived in Scotland, and in fact, had only ever visited it twice. In fact, when we returned, I remained staunchly Australian, which must have confused people who tracked identity by birthplace and accent.

So, ready for a change, any change, from Armidale, we packed our bags and went. What a mistake! First, there was the climate. Armidale, with its Tableland climate, was cold in winter, it snowed sometimes, but nothing had prepared us for the dis-

mal, damp conditions of Scotland compared with Australia. Then there was the homesickness: We all missed Australia enormously. Though my wife had family in England, mine lived in Australia. I missed the politics, the culture, the lifestyle of Australia. I resented the unthinking arrogance of some of the old fogies who inhabited St. Andrews, the university. Most of all, I resented the ways in which what had been represented to me as opportunities for the department were, *in situ,* a mirage, which never materialized. It ended up being a very difficult period in my career and life, one where the sense of estrangement that I had always felt to some extent was massively heightened.

John: You became editor of *Organization Studies* in this period as well, didn't you?

Stewart: Yes, that's right, for a year or so, as it turned out. Not long after I took over the editorship the situation at St. Andrews went from worse to appalling, as resources disappeared, staff left what appeared to be a sinking ship, and the politics got pretty nasty. Editing *Organization Studies* was a job that got pushed, increasingly, to the margins of an increasingly disagreeable professional life. There was another thing. I agreed to be *OS* editor shortly after returning to Scotland, about a month after, in fact. However, about 9 months after being at St. Andrews I had resolved but not entirely admitted that I wanted to return home to Australia. We all did. Eventually, I told David Hickson about this, funnily, once again, after I'd discussed scenarios with Bob Hinings and Mary, his wife, over dinner in the staff club at Alberta, during some time that I spent with Albert Mills and Richard Marsden as a visiting professor in Athabaska. Bob said I shouldn't feel guilty about quitting the editorship, about wanting to go back to Australia. When I returned I rang David up and told him I was thinking of leaving, and why. He was concerned about the journal editorship—it had to be published from Europe by a European, and it was impossible that it be published from Australia. That was his focus. It wasn't mine. That wasn't why I rang him.

I had an agreement with St. Andrews that I could spend what was called summer in Australia, as a visiting professor at Bond University. This was a great opportunity to look for a job in Australia and stay with my parents. It was from there that I flew, in the Queensland winter of 1992 (better than any British summer), to the EGOS meeting in Vienna. Through the fog of a 36-hour flight jet lag, the end of my editorship was negotiated. Strangely, although a bit depressed to be giving the job up so soon, I was relieved as well. It meant the end of obligations, of doing things because, in a professional sense, I thought that I ought to do them, like work in cold old places (even if they did pay heaps of money, most of it went to trying to keep warm), edit journals because I was asked to rather than because it was what I really wanted to do, defer to people who thought I owed deference to them. So I redefined professional obligation. I made some cuts to my networks. I ceased deferring. And I returned to Australia.

It was in 1992 that I was appointed to the present job, but once again the British economy played a determinate role in shaping opportunities. In August/September 1992, the pound sterling fell out of the European Monetary System and lost 25% of its value overnight; interest rates shot up, and a stagnant property market collapsed with the loss of economic confidence. It took a year to sell the house, and so we had to delay our return considerably.

It was out of this period after the Vienna EGOS meeting that I decided to produce the *Handbook of Organization Studies*. In part, it was born from a desire to do something professionally that would make a difference. Editing journals doesn't—all you can do, really, is respond to what comes in from reviewers and from contributors. Of course, you can shape it to some extent, but the chances of doing that with a journal such as *Organization Studies* was at that time were very remote.

Actually, the last 18 months or so that I was at St. Andrews, apart from the weather and some other little local irritants, were quite pleasant. I was able to write a great deal and the period proved very productive. I wound down the editorship of *Organization Studies* and handed it on to John

Child. I started to tie up lots of loose ends—projects on Weber, on European organization theory, on missing links in institutional theory, and some other things. Since returning to Australia, the roll has continued. I've consulted to government for a major review of "Australian leadership and management needs for the twenty-first century." The *Handbook* is nearing completion, and I've had the most productive writing and editing relationship of my career working on it with Cynthia Hardy. A number of other projects are coming to fruition. At last, I'm happy in a city, Sydney, that I think is without parallel as a place to live, and, although I don't work in an institution that could be construed as a glittering prize, it has great potential. Things seem to have worked out okay in the end.

John: What was the process of getting the *Handbook* off the ground?

Stewart: In 1990, at the request of Suzana Rodrigues and Roberto Venosa, colleagues I knew from a past point of connection at Bradford, and from International Sociological Association and European Group for Organization Studies meetings, I went to Brazil for the first time. Brazil proved pivotal: Here was warmth, conviviality, surf, sun, fun—all of the things that, predictably, reminded me of Australia. It was the first time since leaving Australia that I realized that I felt warm and relaxed.

Quite soon after returning from Brazil, a matter of a week or so, I went to Florida, to the University of South Florida, Tampa. You had arranged this visit. Earlier that year you had visited St. Andrews when in the U.K. Working with you at Tampa was Walter Nord, whom I had met fleetingly in the past, but didn't know well. The trip went well, and a good relationship was forged with Walt.

Back to Scotland and winter had set in. I negotiated with St. Andrews that Suzana Rodrigues and Roberto Venosa be visitors to the department that I headed at that time.

October 1991 rolled around. Suzana and Roberto arrived in St. Andrews. Suzana and Roberto suggested a project: They wanted to edit a "handbook of organizations" in Portuguese with the help of

Clóvis Macahado in Brazil, and they asked me to join in this endeavor with them. Rapidly we began to map out some preliminary ideas. Then I had a suggestion. Why not do such a book in English as well? Maybe Stephen Barr and Sue Jones at Sage might be interested in this idea?

I phoned Sue Jones and, to my surprise, found that she had been in the process of coming to me with a similar suggestion. A meeting was arranged with Sue and with some other senior editors at Sage, including Stephen Barr. A stumbling block was immediately placed in the way of the project by Sage. The type of project that they were envisaging had to have the editorial involvement of some senior people from North America because of the realities of marketing in English; also, it had to have a team of senior academics for whom English was their first language, in order to manage the complexity that editing such a project would entail. They were adamant that the project could not be managed by one person on his or her own and that the coeditors would need to be from North America for reasons of marketing. Reluctantly, I was enrolled to their way of thinking, and the search began for some North American colleagues with whom to work on the editorial task.

I think that Sue and I drew up a short list of various people we could both work with over what was projected as a 3-year period, who we knew had academic standing and covered a range of potential contributor knowledge bases. Most of all, they had to be fun to work with. It didn't take long to come up with Walt and Cynthia. We both knew them. We liked them both. Also we thought that we would all get on well with each other. It proved a good choice.

The three of us got together at the Academy of Management meetings in Las Vegas in 1992 with Sue Jones and Stephen Barr, and the structure of the *Handbook* was mapped out from the sketch that Sue and I had already worked up. There was some urgency to stitching it up on this occasion: I had accepted an offer to become the foundation chair of management at the University of Western Sydney, Macarthur, and knew that I would definitely be returning

to Australia, although not exactly when I would be able to start. It could be difficult for the three of us to meet easily again. In fact, we didn't, not until the project was almost completed. Hence the project was managed largely through faxes and e-mail, and it was through these media that a great deal of the collaborative work of writing was accomplished.

Letters were sent, phones buzzed, faxes transmitted and received. The book began to take shape. There were disappointments, of course, but these paled into insignificance when I received the awful news that Walt had been taken seriously ill and the prognosis was that he should not work for some time, until he recovered. (We were all relieved when Walt subsequently made a full recovery.) Now we were all really glad that we had triadic strength; with Walt out of action, Cynthia facilitated coordination from Montreal while I moved back to Australia in 1993.

Deadlines drew near and some contributors were exemplary. They sent us great copy the first time, on time. Others were somewhat more "recalcitrant," shall we say? Anyway, deadlines passed, exhortations were made, occasional dark thoughts found utterance in the ether as the project moved into full e-mail mode for communication among the three editors, contributors, and Sage. On the schedule that events imposed on us (such projects are never any faster than the slowest contributor), Cynthia was going to be in Sydney during the months of April and May 1995, in the period prior to the final compilation of all the chapters.

During the period that Cynthia was in Sydney, we wrote the introductory and concluding chapters, sending drafts to Walt and to Sue by courier and e-mail, keeping in close contact with them. We felt that we were in the downhill stretch of what had turned into a far more consuming project than imagined at the outset. I believed strongly in the project and knew that it was impossible to accomplish other than as an edited venture. I knew that it would be demanding, but the demands of the experience exceeded my expectations (but not, I think, Sue's). I think it was Sue's canny knowledge in insisting that there be three editors that saw the project through the stickier moments.

Cynthia started the writing and then I worked with the materials that she had produced. We argued forcibly but amicably. She thought she was usually right. She proved herself more stubborn than me. Many times she pushed me to make more transparent ideas that were quite clear to me, and so I assumed that they would be to others as well. In our work relationship she sought to exercise control and invariably I resisted, usually by colonizing the physical space of my Macintosh keyboard when we were redrafting.

John: Has all the effort been worth it?

Stewart: I think so. Well, no, I'm sure, really. Seriously, its been a privilege to be involved in the production of what we are sure will be a significant statement for our profession. That opportunity alone should make all the effort worthwhile.

John: Yes, but what about the rest of it, all the moves, tensions, dualities? Have they been worth it?

Stewart: It's hard to say. I don't have any other benchmark. I know that each move has brought new learning and opportunities, so if I hadn't made some of the moves I'd have done different things, that's for sure. For instance, at Griffith I learned a lot about Foucault but I didn't start to apply it until I'd moved to UNE. As a result of the OES Conference we founded APROS, and without APROS and Gordon Redding's involvement, I wouldn't have accessed material on East Asia. As a result of teaching the power course at UNE I wrote *Frameworks,* and without *Frameworks* I would never have struck up such a productive relationship with Sage, done *Modern Organizations* at their request, so that we'd each get the confidence to do the *Handbook.* And so on.

There have been a lot of moments of doubt and uncertainty, but I think that's normal. It is an odd kind of life—you are a kind of performance artist, both in the universities that hire you and in the broader professional life. Constantly you are presenting yourself even as you present quite abstract ideas. And that means, or at least I think it means, a constant pressure not only to display some elements of consistency, as one presents a self to the world, but also to innovate, to be doing something that takes further something that you did previously. Some careers are a string of discontinuous projects, perhaps. Mine hasn't been like that—I see it as one big project that started with some builders on a building site, some analytic builders in some varied conceptual sites, and I've just negotiated the breaks that appeared along the way. There was never any grand plan to do anything in particular. One thing tended to lead to another. There was a consistency to the analytic directions, always navigating around "power," but the course was often charted as a result of some unforeseen opportunity or reef, some aspect of professional life that one couldn't anticipate developing the way that it did: the success of APROS from the OES Conference; the short duration of the *Organization Studies* editorship, due to recoil from St. Andrews and Australia's pull on me; and the idea of the *Handbook* as something to fill the gap before returning and to tide me over. Finding that the work that I'd done on "postmodern organizations" tied into government concerns about the future of management, for instance, this was a real surprise, real serendipity. People ask you to do things; Australian males value "mateship" highly, so if my mates ask me to do something for them I usually say yes. A lot of things have got written that way. Much of it has been like that. I tend to think of it, as I said earlier, as a degree of randomness upon which one seeks to impose a pattern. That's my view of the meaning of life, that there is none, other than that we configure, or others configure for us, using whatever resources are available. Devices like this interview then become part of the pattern making.

II

Early Rhythms

The initial rhythms in an academic's life are likely to revolve around two fundamental crafts: teaching courses to students and starting to carve out a career as a researcher. In some schools, the primary (even the only) task is to teach, whereas in others it is to do research. Finding one's way as a teacher, getting one's research project or program under way, getting one's work published (this can apply to teaching as well as to research), and beginning to work with doctoral students are all part of the early years of activity for scholars in most academic settings. For most scholars, getting tenure based on research and/or teaching performance is the major career objective of this period. Doing all this and still striving/hoping to have a personal or private life constitutes a full and challenging, even daunting, undertaking.

Becoming a Teacher

My view is that it is entirely possible to be both a good researcher and a good teacher, but one has to be fairly deliberate about managing the process and realistic about the rewards.

Christina E. Shalley (p. 62)

I now spend a lot of time talking with business school colleagues about curricula, audiences, and techniques in management education. In these conversations, I am consistently struck by the realization that most of us, most of the time, frame our decisions about teaching as if they were primarily about subject matter, secondarily about technique, and hardly at all about students. I lament the degree to which we take these priorities for granted.

John A. Miller (p. 75)

Teaching can be viewed as an ongoing process that both promotes teachers' continuous learning and helps to prepare and stimulate others for continuous learning.

Walter R. Nord (p. 83)

I had decided to become a professor because I wanted to teach others. My own life had been profoundly changed by education.

Stella M. Nkomo (p. 91)

The two tasks of teaching and conducting and publishing research generate quite different rhythms, particularly in the initial phases of an academic's life. Teaching has an immediacy that flows from the need to perform in front of others and from the rapidity of feedback from students to the teacher about how well the job is being done. Research has a much slower cadence. It requires a longer start-up than does teaching. Teaching can be both agonizing and seductive. One might have to wait until after the end of a school term or semester to get a complete picture of one's impact as a teacher, but the visceral effects of one's efforts are available even before the end of a single class session. Further, teaching tends, for the most part, to create a reputation that is local and internal to the organization, to the school in which the scholar is employed. This can affect the way one's colleagues frame one's contributions, as being to teaching rather than to research. It may draw additional teaching assignments and expectations. If employed by a school that prizes good teaching, a scholar may find high-rated performance in this craft to be beneficial to his or her career. On the other hand, if the setting is one in which research is the primary task, or is valued above teaching, then outstanding teaching may reflect negatively on the junior scholar and make it difficult for him or her to survive in that institution. Being a good teacher in a research-oriented school requires careful attention to managing the boundaries between the two activities.

In Chapter 6, Christina Shalley tackles many of the issues and experiences faced by individuals who join business schools that place primary emphasis on research: "In fact, a common message that is communicated is that one needs only to be competent at teaching, that research should be the number-one priority" (p. 62). She found becoming a teacher stressful, and acknowledges the benefits of the training in teaching she received while in her doctoral program. Along the way, through her early years as an academic, she has had some surprises; "How oddly things have turned out," she comments. Some of this has to do with her discoveries about herself as a teacher. Some of it has been contextual; teaching was becoming more salient in business schools, including her own. She experienced the danger we note above, that doing a good job of teaching

can lead to being typecast as a "natural" and as being expected to pick up additional courses. This pressure set up a tension in her between meeting this demand while fulfilling the requirement also to publish research in top journals. It forced her to become explicit and quite political in her strategy for managing her career as a teacher and a researcher, and her solutions are instructive. Her discussion of these challenges points up many of the dilemmas that are facing junior scholars who want and need to do well as teachers while keeping their eyes on the primary task of being effective researchers.

Balancing teaching and research, ruminating on the boundaries and bridges between the crafts, is the central issue in the discussions offered here by both Walter Nord and Stella Nkomo. Whereas Christina Shalley's progress through doctoral training and early career experiences appears to have been rather structured and bounded, requiring considerable effort to break the mold, Walter Nord's early days as a scholar were extraordinarily open-ended and experimental. We suspect that his career path, with its heady mixture of freedom to explore and invent, coupled with access to a wide range of interesting and accomplished scholars and students, has been more typical of the emergence of the fields that constitute what we now call organization studies (or some similar name). One wonders what we may have given up or lost as our fields and our disciplines have become more systematic and focused in their training and more standardized in their evaluation of performance.

From Nord's reflections on his career we gain a very useful insight about the possible meeting ground of research and teaching. He sees both as having to do with continuous learning. He discusses how work as a teacher and his activities as a researcher have advanced the continuity of his own learning. He notes:

One thing I did—which is a bit embarrassing to own up to publicly—that was important for me in blurring teaching/research boundaries was to make what I wanted to learn something that I taught. To illustrate, particularly in advanced courses, when there was something I thought I should know better than I did, I made it part of a course and learned it along with the students. (p. 86)

Whereas Nord came to embrace teaching through his excitement about research, Stella Nkomo, as a first-generation college student, discovered the research craft through her passion for teaching: "I had decided to become a professor because I wanted to teach others. . . . For me, teaching was about changing lives and, eventually, society" (pp. 91-92). She also comments, "I do research on race and gender because I want to see an end to racism, sexism, and other forms of domination in organizations" (p. 92). Her career choices and her willingness to extend herself through education were shaped by significant mentors at crucial points in her life. Nkomo points to the concept of scholarship as articulated by Ernest Boyer as a bridge between research and teaching. She discusses some of challenges we face if we are to have teaching taken seriously as a form of scholarship.

There seem to be moments for many of us that are truly transformative. Something happens *to* us during or at a certain point in our careers that touches something *in* us, and the result is a change in the direction of our work, whether it be in research or in teaching. We might shift our thinking and our research in ways that put us in a different frame or paradigm. We might change dramatically what we teach, or how we teach, or what we think is the purpose of education. John Miller's story is about a shift in perspective about teaching that reflects all of these elements. He was jarred by a comment of a student into seeing differently his whole rationale for teaching:

Late on a Tuesday afternoon in October 1977, I finally began to understand why I had become a teacher. Over the course of about 90 minutes that afternoon, more than a dozen years after I stepped onto this career path, it dawned on me that some things about teaching that I had taken for granted—assumptions about what and how I was teaching and, especially, *to whom* and *why*—had been (at best) incomplete. In that moment, a student taught me that somebody really did *need* me to do what I was doing. (p. 73)

Miller spent a number of years putting that shift into practice through the development of an entirely different management course that was every bit as programmatic as one might find in a significant stream of research work. He makes clear the enormous investment of time and ingenuity and effort that is needed to bring an interdisciplinary experience to the learning experience of students.

It is unlikely that good teaching can endure without serious attention to newly created knowledge, whether it is done by the teacher or by others. The connection between the two activities must be made and encouraged. In a professional school that has a mandate both to create and to disseminate knowledge, it is important that time and rewards be provided to foster and sustain an enthusiasm for teaching among junior scholars. The alternative is to diminish the performance repertoire of such an institution. It will drive away the best students. At the end of the day, taking teaching seriously can be enriching for both academics and those who learn with and from them.

6 Becoming a Teacher at a Research University

Christina E. Shalley

I was approached by one of the editors of this book to write this chapter after I had given a talk in a symposium Peter Frost had directed at the Academy of Management annual meetings on teaching doctoral students to teach. I thought the idea of the book was great and the topic of the chapter important, and I was happy to be asked to participate in this project. When I agreed to write this chapter, I knew that it would be challenging for me, but it was even more difficult than I had expected. First, I knew that writing about the content required would necessitate my using a very different approach from what I use in other writing. Basically, the chapter demanded that I talk personally about myself, my perceptions and opinions, instead of about theory and data. What I did not anticipate was that it would also be difficult to shift gears in terms of writing style. Like most academics, I am very used to writing in a particular scientific way, with third person being the dominant voice. It was difficult to write more informally, and my bet is that a nonacademic reading this chapter will still believe that my style is too formal for telling a personal story. In any case, what follows is my perspective on the role of teaching at a research university and how to manage the process of balancing teaching and research. In writing this chapter I have learned more concerning my own views about both teaching and research, and my opinions in some ways have evolved in the process.

I think the process of developing into a good teacher at a research university is different than at a primarily teaching-oriented university, for a number of reasons. First, those who have been trained to be researchers and to strive for employment at research-oriented universities probably have not been trained fully, or possibly at all, in how to be good teachers. Generally, good doctoral programs focus on training students to do quality research. The job of doctoral students is to learn the analytic and research-oriented skills that will enable them to become productive scholars. The overarching goal of most doctoral programs is not to turn out good teachers; in fact, some academics would argue that their students don't need to be trained in how to teach, because if they know the material well they should have no problem communicating it to others. There is a wide variance in how much and at what level of exposure graduating doctoral students have learned how to teach, from having had the opportunity to teach a few courses to having had no classroom experience at all. In fact, a common message that is communicated is that one needs only to be competent at teaching, that research should be the number-one priority. I agree with this focus on research and think it should continue, but I believe that teaching can be better integrated into doctoral curricula so that new faculty members are prepared to do both successfully, particularly in business schools, where it is increasingly important to be a good teacher. Therefore, just as there has always been the emphasis on junior faculty to develop into independent, productive researchers, more programs could focus on helping students to develop techniques for quality teaching.

A second issue is that the reward and evaluation systems at traditionally research-oriented schools are not set up to stress or fully address quality teaching. At teaching schools, this is the main focus of evaluations. That is, research universities by their very nature implicitly or even explicitly make it clear that faculty are to concentrate on research. This is the evaluation criterion, and rewards are based on successful research. Thus at research universities it is typically unclear how teaching fits into the promotion and reward equation. If one accepts the premise that at research universities one must be a competent teacher, the issue is whether one should go beyond competence and strive to be very good or excellent at teaching.

Given the emphasis on research, why should one try to be better than a merely competent teacher? Is this something that junior faculty members should be expending their efforts on? I'm sure there are differences in opinions regarding these questions, and I don't know if there are any right answers. I do know that I personally feel that it is important for me to do well at teaching, for two basic reasons. The first is an intrinsic reason, and that is what initially motivated me: If you are going to do something, then do it well. Second, there is a more practical reason that I've just started becoming aware of during the past couple of years, as the

emphasis in business schools has started to change toward quality teaching. Specifically, it seems to be becoming increasingly important to have faculty who can teach well and at all levels, including executive programs. Although I haven't seen corresponding changes in the compensation structure to support this, I am starting to see and hear about it being reflected in how selection and renewal decisions are being made for faculty.

My view is that it is entirely possible to be both a good researcher and a good teacher, but one has to be fairly deliberate about managing the process and realistic about the rewards. Of course there are individual differences and various constraints, but I believe both can be done successfully, and are done well by many individuals. The demands on scholars' time have been increased by the addition of greater emphasis on teaching to the continuing primary emphasis on research. Just as we work at developing the skills, norms, and values that enable our doctoral students to become productive researchers, we can instill values concerning teaching so that our students are successful in both areas as junior faculty. Basically, I view teaching as an essential, though not necessarily rewarded, component of my job. Therefore, I try to do well at it. I really couldn't see spending so much time in the classroom over the years and not doing a good job. I don't know if it is achievement motivation, ego involvement, or both that's the explanatory factor driving me, but it is logical to think that most of us may not have chosen academia as a profession if not for having had some good teachers. So why not continue the tradition?

As for my story, I see my developing into a good teacher as a definite passage. Quite simply, I did not choose this as a profession based on my desire to teach. In fact, the idea of teaching was almost a deterrent to my choosing to go into academia. Plain and simple, I chose this career in order to be free to pursue research in which I was interested and to work in a stimulating intellectual environment. Today, I would be uncomfortable stating this so plainly to my undergraduate or master's students. When I started teaching I was concerned with being competent, but as I progressed and did better (and realized I could do better), teaching became more important to me. In fact, I can honestly say that I really enjoy teaching and have enjoyed getting to know many of my students—although I still do complain about the amount of time teaching takes away from my research.

In the following pages I present my perspective on the process of becoming a good teacher at a research university. I tell you about my background, discuss some of my experiences, highlight some key issues to consider, and, finally, offer some recommendations to others that may enhance their own experiences and help them avoid some of the apparent and not so apparent pitfalls. Although much of what I say here concerns my own experience balancing research and teaching demands as a doctoral student at the University of Illinois and as assistant professor at the University of Arizona and some of the experiences of colleagues at the same and different academic institutions, I think that the majority of the issues discussed and experiences mentioned can be generalized to most research universities. Given that I am speaking in general, I realize that there are some exceptions to what I am saying. For example, there are a few top research universities where MBA and executive teaching always have been heavily emphasized. However, at many research universities, particularly public land grant universities, this has not always been the case. Also, I discuss below some fundamental changes in business schools regarding teaching that have occurred (and are still in the process of occurring) since I started in the late 1980s.

From Whence I Came

In sitting down to write this chapter, reflecting on how I became a good teacher while attaining the research productivity desired at a research university, I had to think about how oddly things have turned out—from where I started to where I am now. As an undergraduate social psychology major at SUNY Albany, I was committed to getting a PhD in applied psychology or a related field in order to do empirical research. As I neared graduation from college, I realized that graduating PhDs in social psychology were not getting jobs. Being ever so practical, I started to look for related areas. During that time, one of the last undergraduate classes I took was an organizational behavior course taught by Tom Taber; I loved it, and

right then I knew this was the area for me. After graduation I worked for a while, and then went to the University of Illinois for a master's degree in labor and industrial relations, with the intention to continue on for a PhD. I chose this program because it had an organizational behavior concentration and a variety of courses in labor relations and labor history, which had always been an interest. Once in the labor program, I started on my master's thesis under the direction of Greg Oldham. As we began to discuss my prospects for a PhD, the issue of teaching first arose as a potential stumbling block. Greg was very supportive of my pursuing a PhD (which I did do at Illinois, in the business school), but he wanted to know what I planned to do with it. I informed him I wanted to do research. I remember Greg talking to me about the job of a professor, in which of course I would be expected to teach. It might seem naive now, but I really hadn't thought seriously about teaching. As an undergraduate in social psychology I had the opportunity to work on several research projects (everything from keypunching data to conducting my own small survey study). Developing and conducting research was what ignited my interest. The idea of teaching being an integral part of my job was fairly unappealing to me at that point, particularly as I tended then to shy away from public speaking. I know for many doctoral students and faculty it might seem odd that I would not have really thought about teaching when choosing to get a PhD, but I was focused on the research part. Greg and I discussed other options available for someone with a PhD in organizational behavior who wanted primarily to do research (e.g., research groups, consulting organizations, positions in companies), and our discussion led me to believe that given my interests, academia was the place for me, as long as I could deal with teaching. I thought about all this for a few days and later told Greg that I was firmly committed to being a research professor, even if that included teaching. So, that's where I started. Funny, reflecting on that now; I never would have expected to enjoy teaching, never mind to be good at it—but I do and I am. I am proud of how far I have come and I think that how I started probably helped me to retain the "research is top priority" focus that I needed to make it at a research university.

Initially I found teaching to be a very stressful experience and difficult to do. We all have views of ourselves that may not always be in sync with how others view us, but I did not think I would be good at teaching. In some ways, looking back, it might have been fortunate that I had no choice but to teach from the first semester in the doctoral program, or I might have avoided the experience for as long as possible. The way funding was then set up at Illinois, doctoral students taught 10 hours per week and were research assistants for 10 hours. During my first semester in organizational behavior, I was assigned to teach an introductory management skills course under Dave Whetten's direction. This course was a precursor to the organizational behavior course and, as such, the material was dealt with in an introductory manner, with a strong emphasis on the use of experiential exercises for skill building. Because of this, the instructor's job was more facilitation than lecturing. As someone who had never taught and was not used to public speaking, I found this difficult. Dave had the new group of teaching assistants participate in a fairly comprehensive training session about teaching techniques and course material for about a week, and we were given a textbook, syllabus, and sample exercises. Even so, I found it daunting to go into that first class and facilitate discussion. I can say that I did all right, no complaints to the dean, but I was by no means wonderful. The next semester I repeated the process and improved slightly, but still did not enjoy it. I would probably go so far as to say that I worked at getting through my teaching days. I definitely did not look forward to teaching and did not really enjoy the students at that point.

Fortunately, things changed in my second year of the program. There was an opportunity for one of the doctoral students to teach a human resources course. That person would be given full responsibility for the course—and it was lecture/discussion! I lobbied to be assigned this course for a variety of reasons. I had a master's in the area, so I was well qualified to teach the material, I felt that I would be better at a class that was structured primarily around lectures rather than facilitation, and I thought I would enjoy teaching this material. I was given the course and set to work developing it. Initially, I had to invest a significant amount of time in structuring the course, because I'd never taken a basic human resources course, even though I had taken courses in a number of the

topic areas covered. Without a syllabus, with no book selected, and without the kind of training and structure Dave had provided, it meant quite a time sink. This was probably not what I should have been doing as a second-year PhD student, but it was worth it. I was much more comfortable with this type of material, and the lecture format, and I did better. As I kept improving and my ratings went up, I started to enjoy teaching and really came to enjoy my students.

What's interesting now is that my teaching has come full circle. My teaching style now is very facilitative, even in large lecture courses, but still very factually oriented. So ultimately my initial experience was good for my development—and I still use many of the techniques that I learned in Dave's training course. However, I am glad that I opted to put time into developing my own course that second year—or I might not have felt as good as I eventually did about teaching. I think that this has been a recurring theme for me—that sometimes it is worth putting in the time because of the rewards that I ultimately get. One of my last semesters teaching at Illinois, I was named to the TA Teaching Distinction List; this recognition of my efforts was a nice addition.

Managing the Process as a Junior Faculty Member

When I started at the University of Arizona, I felt confident that I could be a competent teacher, but wanted to continue my upward trajectory of doing well teaching. Let me stop and say that by no means was I then, or am I now, aspiring to be the best. What I wanted was to do very well at teaching. Basically, I refuse to commit the effort needed to be rated excellent. Of course, when I receive an excellent rating I am very happy, but I don't feel I can commit the time and resources to do that well consistently. I think I had very realistic training in how I was to make it in academia—publish, plain and simple, and be competent at teaching so they don't have to get rid of you. My training at Illinois prepared me for Arizona, where, as in any other research-oriented school, to do well I had to publish in quality outlets. Teaching was documented, but teaching alone wasn't going to lead to promotions. Looking back, given the demands on my time and the evaluation process that was in place, the strategy I chose may not have been the best, but there were subsequent changes that occurred at Arizona that resulted in teaching quality being more carefully scrutinized, so that I actually benefited in the long run by the decision to focus on producing quality research while still striving to do very well at teaching.

What I found unexpectedly at Arizona was that even though we weren't rewarded for teaching, our ratings were made public. I think this was a way to try to motivate faculty to be at least average teachers, if not better. At the end of each semester, faculty members received a list of the summary teaching scores of all members of the department. At Arizona there were quite a few good teachers, and many also were very productive scholars. One in particular, Greg Northcraft, provided a good model for me. Greg has always been an excellent teacher, besides being highly productive. It appeared to me that Greg personally valued both and could do both well, which I found motivating to see in a senior colleague. At Arizona it really became a circular process for me; as I did better at teaching I liked it more, and the more I enjoyed my students and teaching the material, the more my ratings increased. I found that teaching can be very seductive when you do it well, in that you can make an immediate contribution that can be seen when students get excited about topics in class, want to pursue graduate studies in the area, and so forth. It really does feel great. I think in this way it is very similar to research—once one gets that first publication or first solo publication, one feels legitimated, one thinks, "I can do this." It is the same with having a really good class session, receiving good ratings, and winning teaching awards. I think once one becomes legitimate in the process, one knows what one is capable of doing, and so it becomes more important to do well. The more I started to get named to the top teaching list in the College of Business at Arizona, the more it became an expectation or goal of mine. By the time I left Arizona, I consistently was named to the list each semester and had received numerous other teaching awards and distinctions. As in our research, if we are to continue to develop, the benchmark must keep rising.

At Arizona I continued teaching courses in human resource management. During my first year, I was given three different course prepa-rations (one of which was similar to the human resource course taught at Illinois) and was asked to prepare another new course my second year. By my third year I had prepared five courses (three undergraduate and two graduate). Although these were all under the broad framework of human resource management, there was quite a bit of time involved in developing each class. Additionally, because I commonly had students take all three of the undergraduate classes, the course materials could not overlap too much. Even though this took quite a bit of work, I believe my efforts paid off down the road. I began to think more strategically about my teaching during the middle of my second year there. I decided that I could not keep preparing different courses, and that I really needed to teach ones that were regularly offered so that I would start to benefit from my investments. Given this, I volunteered to teach the last course I prepped there, which was my fifth preparation, with the aim of ultimately cutting down on my workload. There were a few reasons this made sense. First, I knew that no one else in the department was really interested in teaching this course on human resource policy. It was required of all graduating majors and, as a result, had to be offered every semester. As such, I should be virtually guaranteed the same course every semester, which in effect would lock my teaching in and prevent me from having to prepare other service courses. In general, my teaching has been focused on critical courses that are needed, and so are somewhat valued by the department, but that most people don't or can't teach. That way I know that once I have invested the time, it is basically my course (or at minimum I will be able to teach it relatively often). For this reason, while I was at Arizona I opted never to teach an organizational behavior course, because there was too much demand among the faculty for those courses.

Looking back, what I find interesting is that in the first two or three years of my academic career I worked very hard at making sure that I didn't put too much time into teaching at the expense of research. Also, I was very concerned that my colleagues never have the perception that the reason the students liked me and I got good ratings was because I put too much time into teaching. Therefore, I consciously tried to minimize the visibility of my teaching efforts while trying to make my research activities salient. This strategy changed somewhat after a few years. After my fourth-year review, when I had basically passed a major evaluation hurdle, I decided that I needed to have people recognize that besides being a productive researcher, I was doing quite a bit of service for the department with my teaching. My teaching consisted almost exclusively of core required courses, and I was doing a good job of it. I think that some of my colleagues had started to take what I was doing for granted, and in some ways teaching was seen as being easier for me than for others, although this was not true. Therefore, I started to work at reminding my colleagues that it did take real work for me both in and out of the classroom, as I had taught many students and was also the primary adviser to all our undergraduate majors. I felt that I had paid my dues and that good teaching was not without its costs for me, and that this should be recognized. It was an interesting switch, and one with which I was not totally comfortable at first. I went from downplaying the amount of time spent investing in teaching to saying, "Look, this takes real work for me, it benefits the department and college, and I would like this contribution realized." I think my colleagues were responsive to these messages. We often don't realize the contributions others are making until they are made salient. It was odd to have to say, "Yes, I am a researcher, but I also want you to recognize my teaching and how that contributes to our mission."

Subsequent changes at Arizona resulted in research still being strongly weighted while quality teaching became more of an expectation. As at most other public universities around this time, in the early to mid-1990s, because of concerns and criticism from the legislature and public about how little of professors' time is spent in the classroom, there was more of a demand to justify our time and document the quality of teaching. Even though there are differences across institutions, increasingly, research universities have begun talking about and further emphasizing teaching quality across all levels—undergraduate, graduate, and executive education. Therefore, ultimately, in reviews my teaching started to be recognized and rewarded at Arizona.

What I Have Learned (or Am Still Learning)

I feel I have been fortunate in this process because the paths I have chosen have worked out well for me and I am satisfied with my performance and career progression. Timing is very important, and in some ways I was lucky to have started my career at the time I did, because my values with regard to emphasizing research while still valuing quality teaching are being reflected in changes going on at research universities. The environment in business schools at research universities is in the process of change, in that there is more need for faculty to develop into good MBA and executive education teachers. Although teaching is becoming more important and may be given greater (or at least some) weight in the evaluation/reward equation, I doubt it will ever completely overshadow research. Therefore, quality teaching may become a more important minimum requirement of our jobs. Because teaching can take an enormous amount of time and there are fewer tangible rewards attached to quality teaching, we need to focus on some of the intangible benefits, such as helping with research, keeping fresh and up-to-date, and potentially helping to gain access to future field sites for research from MBA or executive education contacts.

So what are the main issues that junior faculty have to consider in learning to balance teaching and research and in determining whether they are going to strive to be very good teachers at research universities? When one is a faculty member at a research university, it is accepted that one needs to immerse oneself in research and publish the results of this research in high-quality journals. In the past, typically when performance has been reviewed at a research university, research has been by far the dominant focus; teaching may have received some consideration (but often none at all) and evaluation of service has been more perfunctory. Therefore, it makes sense that the bulk of a junior faculty member's time would be focused on developing and executing the skills and behaviors needed to be a productive researcher. So if one wants also to develop as a good teacher, or if there are external pressures to do this, what are the important issues that need to be dealt with?

Long-Term Versus Short-Term Rewards

From a junior faculty perspective, it is rationally known that tenure is based on one's research record, and that this probably will never significantly change at research universities. The tenure clock is interesting in that, in some ways, it seems to be fairly long when you think about going through your day-to-day activities for 5 or 6 years, yet in reality it is very short, because in order to have enough work in process at various stages and to have it complete the publication process by the time you are reviewed for tenure, you need to conduct a great deal of research in the first few years of your career. Thus junior faculty have always had to keep from being sidetracked, particularly in their first few years. Now add to that the fact that teaching quality is being stressed, with possibly some short-term rewards attached. Here there is much more of a danger in emphasizing the wrong components of the job. For example, when I arrived at Arizona I found that teaching was stressed by my department and college much more than I had anticipated, particularly given the publication expectations. Because teaching ratings were public among the faculty in my department, teaching results were both visible and salient. However, at promotion and tenure time, research was really the only factor that mattered.

Over the past few years this has changed somewhat. At Arizona there has been more of an effort to evaluate teaching rigorously and to reward teaching success, primarily thorough different department and college teaching awards. Faculty are given more feedback and there are better qualitative data to be used at promotion and tenure review. How much these data are weighted in the review is unclear. What is clear is that more material than previously is being collected and evaluated, and feedback is being given concerning teaching quality, improvement, and so forth. Another good example of the increasing emphasis on documenting teaching is that structured interviews with student focus groups are used in evaluating junior faculty members' teaching performance. In our department, senior faculty lead the focus groups

and have to provide feedback to the junior faculty. Thus they become even more aware of how junior faculty are performing in the classroom. This helps because some of the senior faculty have not taught undergraduates and/or MBAs recently and may not realize what the demands are, how much work it takes to do a good job, and who does well.

As these changes were being made at Arizona, some junior faculty found themselves caught between earlier standards, in which teaching wasn't at all important, and newer standards, in which they were expected to be at least good teachers. So, basically, they had only a short time frame in which to improve their ratings. Given all this, it would have been easy for them to get sidetracked into improving teaching in the short run and losing sight of their research progress. If junior faculty picked up on the short-term emphasis on teaching and stressed it too much, ignoring their research, it would not have boded well for their future on the faculty. Although across universities teaching quality may be more important now, the overall reward systems at most universities have not changed significantly to address this. Some universities are grappling now with these issues, but I don't think there have been many fundamental changes yet. Essentially, a faculty member has to deal with how to balance these priorities, with potentially no payoff, or perhaps only an unknown payoff, down the road.

Number and Types of Preparations

Every junior faculty member knows to keep the number and types of course preparations down when beginning a career. However, the reality is that many departments ask their junior people to teach a variety of new courses. From the department's perspective it makes sense, because the new person generally has to prepare a course anyway, so why not give him or her a new course or courses that no one else wants to teach? Unfortunately, this can be very demanding for new faculty members, particularly if they are asked to teach a diverse portfolio of courses. Depending on the composition and philosophy of the department, a junior faculty member may end up doing some of the "harder teaching," what others can't or won't do. If senior faculty have not wanted to do or have never done what they are asking their juniors to do, they may not realize how labor-intensive certain preparations are, how difficult it may be to get good teaching ratings in those courses, and so on. Therefore, they may not be totally aware of some of the pressures junior faculty are under. I think junior faculty need to find a way to bring such issues to their departments' attention without appearing to be complaining. They need to make their colleagues aware of how labor-intensive some preparations are and how every course one is asked to teach may require new preparation, which may not be an appropriate load for a junior faculty member's first few years.

How Good Should You Strive to Be?

When we speak about good teaching, how good is good enough? Let's assume that the individual, the institution, or both value teaching. If the goal is to be an effective teacher, what does that mean? There are decreasing returns to scale for putting time into one's teaching. It takes a certain amount of work to be good, and the time spent raising the level of teaching from competent to very good is not much more significant (see Figure 6.1). However, the time spent to become excellent may require quite a bit more work. Where does one want to be? A junior faculty member must consider seriously how much is enough in terms of quality, and whether being excellent at teaching is worth the investment of time and psychic energy required. Time is not the only issue when we talk of being an excellent teacher; there are also individual differences in ability that might make it more feasible for some to be consistently excellent teachers. Therefore, each faculty member needs to decide where his or her values and strengths are as well as how much time and resources he or she needs to commit, and can afford to commit, to developing into a very good teacher.

Managing Perceptions

Let's assume that junior faculty members have their priorities straight and are capable of balancing teaching and research effectively. They still need to worry about managing the perceptions of their colleagues. They do not want to look as if they are spending too much time on their teaching to the detriment of their research. Even if their university values quality teaching, as junior faculty members, the last impression they want to give is that they are devoting significant amounts of time to teaching and student-related issues at the expense of their research productivity. On the other hand, they don't want to look as if teaching is effortless for them. If a junior faculty member does manage to do a good job in the classroom and does not look as though he or she needs to spend a significant amount of time to do so, he or she may be labeled a "natural." This is not necessarily a desirable attribution. The danger in this assessment is that the faculty member is not receiving the credit he or she deserves for the amount of work expended. Furthermore, such a faculty member may get more work piled on him or her than someone who hasn't tried as hard or done as well, or who has struggled in the classroom. Because quality teaching takes time, one should want it recognized that one has worked hard to learn to manage time effectively in balancing teaching and research. I say all of this with the assumption that one's research is progressing. If one is at a research university and is in the position of spending time and doing very well at teaching but has not been publishing, probably the last thing one wants to do is lobby to have one's efforts at teaching recognized.

Executive Education

Finally, executive education is potentially a very ambiguous issue for a junior faculty member. It varies across business schools, but at some universities only a few of the faculty (some of whom are not considered research faculty) are involved in executive education programs. In fact, in many departments some senior faculty are not interested in participating in executive education and also may not value it. Yet increasingly, when business schools hire, they want new candidates to have some potential for or interest in participating in executive education programs. Many research universities never before expected their research faculty to teach executives. As more business schools develop executive MBA programs and other executive education programs, it is increasingly neces-

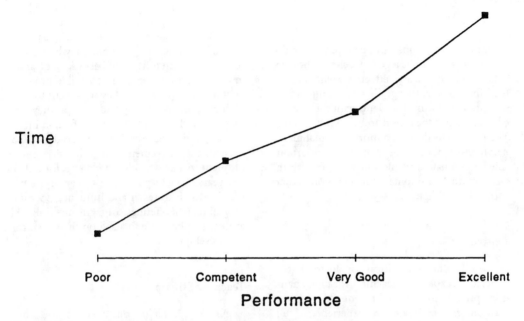

Figure 6.1. Amount of Time Spent Preparing Relative to Teaching Quality

sary for them to hire faculty who are willing and able to teach executives. Of course, there are exceptions—schools that have always had a strong research focus while having high-profile MBA or executive programs—but this is occurring across the majority of research-oriented programs now. An important issue, then, is whether a junior faculty member should be involved in executive education before receiving tenure. It can be helpful for junior faculty to talk with senior faculty members at their institutions and with other colleagues about these issues.

There are many questions that need to be considered in addressing the issue of whether or not to participate in executive education and how much participation is necessary or desirable. For instance, will such participation be seen as a worthwhile contribution that will be considered in a promotion decision? It may be that the dean's office will value an individual's contribution to these external programs, but will the senior faculty? And even if the dean's office does value it, will the dean exert influence concerning this area to make sure it is positively factored into the promotion and tenure decision? If a junior faculty member doesn't think it is worthwhile at this point for his or her

career development, but the dean wants the individual to do it, should that person say no, and what are the potential repercussions of declining this opportunity? Does participation in executive education look bad? In other words, will it hurt promotion and tenure cases by reflecting that a person's priorities are not in the right place? On the other hand, does one need to be able to demonstrate competence in executive education? And if so, how much is necessary and when does it potentially become too much? For instance, if an individual participates in executive education and does well, he or she will probably be asked to become more involved in the program. How much executive education teaching is considered appropriate for junior persons, if any, to demonstrate that they can be effective with executives? And when is participation viewed as too much, leading to the perception that the individual will be seduced by the money to do executive education and consulting exclusively after tenure. The start-up costs for executive education can be quite large. Therefore, a junior faculty member really needs to evaluate whether there is a payoff aside from the immediate monetary compensation, and whether the costs are worthwhile relative to the benefits.

Epilogue for Future Researchers/Teachers

Unfortunately, most graduate programs do not address how to be a good teacher or how to balance quality research effectively with quality teaching. I believe that graduate training can be used to help doctoral students gain the knowledge and skills they need to be good teachers. The rest can be done in a more informal manner; mentors, for instance, can fill an important role for graduate students and junior faculty. In any case, there are some important points that should be highlighted.

Experience

First, I think it is critical for doctoral students to get experience teaching, ideally by handling preparation and full responsibility for at least one course. Having the experience of full preparation of a course is invaluable, and having the opportunity to repeat the course and make improvements is also worthwhile. There are enough things for a junior faculty member to learn without being at the disadvantage of never having taught a course. On the other hand, I don't think a graduate student needs experience in preparing a large number of courses, because it is always unclear what one will be teaching as a faculty member. I have seen some doctoral students try to collect courses so that they can list them on their vitas, in the belief that this will help them when searching for a job. I think this is a waste of time, especially when the courses are in specialties that may not be duplicated at other universities. I believe that the highest payoff comes from choosing a good mainstream course (e.g., human resources, organizational behavior, organizational theory or strategy) or a marketable elective course (e.g., bargaining and negotiation, groups, or power and politics) that most schools offer in some form. This will help the student both in building the skills and confidence needed to prepare courses that he or she potentially will teach again and in competing in the marketplace for that first job. Doctoral students should be encouraged to try numerous teaching methods, because teaching performance in graduate school tends to be less visible than it will be on their initial jobs.

I would discourage new faculty members from continually developing new courses, particularly doctoral-level courses, which, depending on the size of the program, may be offered sometimes on an infrequent basis. A lot of times new graduates are excited to be able to teach doctoral-level courses—they may want to give their students what they had or what they feel they should have had, and this is fine, in moderation; it is a great service to the students and department. But remember, a university's commitment to a new faculty member is for only a few years. A faculty member has an entire career in which to teach and influence doctoral program course offerings, so new members should at this time be more focused on their own career development.

Teaching Stream

Once one has a job, one needs to work consciously at developing a teaching stream, exactly as one does with research streams. One needs to think about establishing a teaching niche that will pay off in multiple ways. For example, one might develop a portfolio of courses that build on and complement each other. Also, one needs to be as efficient as possible in developing teaching materials and techniques that could be used at all levels—cases, experiential exercises, and discussion of timely issues that could be used with executives, MBAs, and undergraduates. Different techniques work with different audiences, but a lot of the same material can be used well at all levels. I know that many doctoral students looking for jobs are stretching the areas they can teach—from micro to macro, and so on. Given the market, that's understandable, and it is good to be flexible. Once in a job, however, one needs to be more deliberate in choosing courses. Unless one's interests are diverse, one's teaching shouldn't be. Ideally, it is nice to teach in the same areas as one does research, but often that is not possible, and one is asked to stretch. Still, choosing where one stretches is critical. One should choose to invest time in courses that cover areas that can enhance one's research stream or provide new directions for research. Also, it is preferable to focus on courses that will always be offered, to stay away from one-time preparations. It is desirable to choose courses that are offered on both graduate and undergraduate levels (so that, with some appropriate changes, one is well on the way toward another preparation). Along the same lines, it is wonderful if one can teach courses that are also of interest to the executive program. Always keep in mind that one should spend one's time efficiently. Don't let teaching suck up more time than it needs. I have talked about how things are changing at universities with regard to teaching, but in part because of these changes, the demands on faculty time have increased. Therefore, one cannot put much more time into teaching; rather, one needs to be more deliberate in planning how to balance teaching and research.

Maintaining Research as the Top Priority

Finally, it almost goes without saying that a junior faculty member at a research university should always maintain research as the top priority. I don't think the rewards for teaching are clearly figured in the promotion equation, but as there is increasing pressure to do a good job in the classroom and there may be some short-term rewards, junior faculty need to focus on how to manage the process while not losing sight of the fact that high-quality publications will probably always be the dominant criteria for promotion at research universities. They also need to think very carefully about whether they should be involved in executive education—before making this decision, they should find out as much as they can about what the culture and values are at their institutions.

In closing, I have tried in this chapter to share my experiences and what few insights I have with the hope that this can encourage others to balance high-quality research and teaching in order to be successful at research universities. As for me, I am still actively trying to manage this process. I had a great start at the University of Arizona, and have recently moved to the Georgia Institute of Technology. It is interesting how the impetus for the move came about, given that I really hadn't been looking to leave Arizona. The year before I would have gone up for promotion and tenure review, I was approached by a friend and colleague, Don Fedor, about whether I would be interested in applying for a job at Georgia Tech. During my time at Arizona I was totally focused on developing my stream of research and on becoming a quality teacher, with the ultimate goal of making tenure. I had been so focused on the goal of tenure that I really hadn't thought seriously about what lay beyond tenure. Don's request that I apply for the position at Georgia Tech prompted me to start considering more fully what type of environment would be desirable for this next stage of my career and personal life. This is not to say that I am not an introspective person—actually I am very much so. However, I had so much on my plate during those years, balancing career and family while still trying to have some leisure pursuits (though not nearly enough), that I was just too busy and focused on attaining my goals. It was interesting that once I was so close to goal attainment, I came to realize that I had a number of important needs that could be met better at Georgia Tech. For example, Georgia Tech had a core group of organizational behavior/human resource researchers with a number of research interests that would lend themselves to collaboration. At Arizona I had worked with a few of my colleagues, but there were not as many natural connections. More important, when I began to reflect on what direction my research was going, I felt that there were more growth possibilities for my work at Georgia Tech, particularly regarding the possibility of more field sites in Atlanta and collaboration on survey research. Finally, the School of Management at Georgia Tech was just starting to develop a number of executive education programs that could potentially provide me with more opportunities.

So far, all of my expectations have proven to be true. Already after spending a year at Tech I have seen my research areas broaden in positive ways, and I am collaborating with a number of colleagues and doctoral students. Also, I like the philosophy of the group, with a strong emphasis on group cohesiveness and an overall collegial atmosphere in the school. Another issue was location. Relocating to a major city provided much better employment possibilities for my spouse, who has always been very flexible about moving where it would be best for my career. Finally, there is always the economic reality that we must not forget: With any voluntary move, salary improves. Thus here I am, an advanced assistant going up for tenure. Once again, I am dealing with trying to balance quality research with new course preparations and other work demands. At this stage of my career, I am beginning to get involved in executive educa-tion programs and am achieving high quality in this arena as well. As always, I am endlessly wishing that there was more time in a day.

7 On Learning Why I Became a Teacher

John A. Miller

Late on a Tuesday afternoon in October 1977, I finally began to understand why I had become a teacher. Over the course of about 90 minutes that afternoon, more than a dozen years after I stepped onto this career path, it dawned on me that some things about teaching that I had taken for granted—assumptions about what and how I was teaching and, especially, *to whom* and *why*—had been (at best) incomplete. In that moment, a student taught me that somebody really did *need* me to do what I was doing. Her comments seemed to me to justify my journey up to that point, and they triggered a process, still ongoing, that has served to energize and direct the rest of this adventure.

At one level, this story is simply about how I identified and adjusted to a new audience—in familiar jargon, about how I started to listen to and meet the expectations of new "customers" in a new "market niche." I want to argue, however, that at a more fundamental level, it is about the excitement that comes from looking beyond the sorts of tactical, "micro" decisions around learning objectives, student preparation, course administration, and so on that teachers make continuously, to focus on strategic,

"big picture" configurations of *who* and *what* and *how*. For me, the passion of this enterprise is tied to a sense of purpose—a *why*—that entails simultaneous attention to audience, subject matter, and technique.

Like all teachers, I seem to rewrite my job description continuously, as audiences, subject matters, and techniques themselves appear to change continuously. Because such changes are so frequent and so customary in the lives of teachers, it may be too easy to overlook the opportunities they provide for fundamental rethinking. Our basic strategies therefore seem to evolve from efforts to muddle through—and are discerned in the results of that muddling—with minimal discontinuity.

By 1977, I had had considerable experience with certain sets of topics, techniques, and audiences, and had devoted some thought to relations among them in specific situations, but I had little appreciation of the richness and variety of patterns possible among the three sets of them together. Like most of the teachers I know, I learned how to make micro decisions about shaping techniques and content to specific audiences. Competent teachers are expected to be micro flexible about (for example) techniques that work less well in seminar discussions than in large lectures, and not at all in individual counseling or advising sessions, or about how to adjust learning objectives to students' backgrounds—and to implement necessary calibration and feedback methods. We all struggle with decisions about the relevance of this or that concept and research result to this or that specific audience. None of that experience had provided me with compelling answers about why any particular pattern mattered to anybody. I simply hadn't thought much about big pictures.

This "before-and-after" story—uncritical application of received wisdom and acceptance of institutional constraints, increased frustration, an "upending intervention," reframing, redesign and experimentation, and refreezing (all with a lot of help from my friends)—has an undoubtedly oversimple plotline, marked by a symbolically dramatic discontinuity. In this chapter, I try to fill in enough details and provide enough interpretation (or retrospective rationalization) to convey a more complex reality and still preserve the excitement I felt, and still feel, in this adventure.

In retrospect, I view that October afternoon as a critical turning point for how I define my professional identity and my purpose as a teacher. I will first describe that turning point and comment briefly on how I view its central implications. I will then sketch some personal and contextual factors that I now think helped me recognize the value and make sense of that incident. Following that, I will try to describe a few of the lessons and results drawn from my experience since then. In particular, I want to outline key features of the general education course in management—the direct descendant of that autumn afternoon—that students and colleagues have worked with me since then to develop. In the process, I will suggest a critique, given these experiences, of "received wisdom" about priorities in management education. Finally, I want to emphasize that "general education in management" implies expanding the boundaries around our territory—and thus the limits on the challenge and excitement of our adventure—without apparent limit.

In October 1977, about halfway through my introductory upper-division elective management course at Yale, three or four students and I were standing around the podium in the well of a large lecture hall. I had just finished a lecture, to about 120 students, on the blessings and banes of matrix organization designs and, in particular, about what it takes to deal with being squeezed between conflicting bosses. I had highlighted the point—it always gets a knowing laugh—that, despite the administrative classics, there's nothing "unnatural" about dual- or multiple-authority structures: "After all, we all learn how to whipsaw our mothers against our fathers by the time we're 5 years old . . . and we've spent every semester since then practicing those skills on our teachers."

Apparently, the combination of group process problems in the class and the family reference provided a personal hook—a "teachable moment"—for at least these few students, and for me. We had talked a bit about sources and varieties of authority and the usefulness of political skill in organizations, in classrooms, and in families, when June W. started telling us about her family's company.

"I grew up in this company," June said. Her grandparents (as I recall the story) had turned the business over to her father some years before, but they still came to work every day. Some other relatives worked there also. "And I guess I'm supposed to go to work there, too, and eventually take over, although up to now I wasn't sure I wanted to." She couldn't remember a family get-together where the subject wasn't some management crisis, or a dinner when everybody wasn't complaining about some awful mess at work. "I've been around managers for 20 years now, but this [course] is the first time I've had the slightest idea what managers really do . . . or how much fun they could have doing it."

I thought hard about June's comments that afternoon—and for many hours since then. What she said pushed me to reconsider my assumptions about audience, and, ultimately, to see that the stakes of my game had changed radically. From that afternoon, I resolved that whatever other function my role as a teacher might serve, its central focus had to be on the pressing need for otherwise well-educated people to understand—and to be able and willing to deal effectively with—the key institutions of their societies. From that turning point, my teaching has taken on the attributes of a General Education Mission.

I am still shocked, but no longer surprised, to hear excellent students from the humanities, social sciences, and sciences, as well as from professional schools of education, journalism, and engineering—that is, students from among that great majority of undergraduates who will eventually run our hospitals, governments, schools, media, churches, and families, as well as most of our businesses—declare that they wouldn't be caught dead in a business school course, even if they were permitted to take one.

"Reality shock" reports from business school graduates are even more dismaying. I have continued to run an informal survey of college graduates from (other) fine institutions of higher learning, with the finding that virtually none had had clear notions, before entering the working world, about what it takes to undertake collaborative efforts to solve complex economic, social, and political problems. Ignorance about the structure and functioning of collaborative enterprises frequently seems to approach the dimensions of a national disaster—see, for example, any newspaper's front, editorial, and letters-to-the-editor pages.

In the years since 1977, I have worked continuously to extend the boundaries around what I ought to be teaching and to whom and how, and, in the process, have learned that management education can assume a role as an essential component of everybody's general education. Moreover, I have become convinced that it must assume such a role; the stakes are even higher now than they were in 1977.

I now spend a lot of time talking with business school colleagues about curricula, audiences, and techniques in management education. In these conversations, I am consistently struck by the realization that most of us, most of the time, frame our decisions about teaching as if they were primarily about subject matter, secondarily about technique, and hardly at all about students. I lament the degree to which we take these priorities for granted.

There were no management or business courses in my undergraduate school (Stanford), or in my graduate year in Germany, and I went through my MBA program (at INSEAD) with classmates for whom the standard U.S. model of "professional" education in management was an unheard-of novelty—and of questionable legitimacy compared with the importance of prior general educational experiences, including broad familiarity with the liberal arts, social and language skills, cosmopolitan street smarts, and old school ties.

It has taken me a long time to acknowledge, with great regret, some glaring holes in my own education about the realities of collaborative enterprise in general and corporate business organizations in particular, and, with great ambivalence, the likelihood that my interpretations and prescriptions, like the classic academic joke, reflect my own obvious shortcomings. On the positive side, I treasure a wonderfully diverse collection of models from English and Latin and German, music, calculus, biochemistry, and physics, as well as economics, psychology, and political science—much earlier models, and rather different from those I encountered in management and business—for what good teaching ought to be. I have very clear and very happy memories of my formative general education years.

Second, I was lucky in timing my main business school socialization stage to coincide with the Age of Aquarius. I was especially lucky to have mentors and colleagues who were competent, critical, and supportive guides for people like me who were exploring the technologies of that age. I was above all lucky to be a skeptical explorer of those technologies, after having spent half a dozen years working with practicing managers in nonacademic settings both in the United States and abroad.

In the Management Research Center at Rochester, Bernie Bass, Gerry Barrett, Ed Ryterband, Jim Vaughan, Ed Deci, Richard Franke, Judy Krusell, Ralph Alexander, Seenu Srinivasan, and many others joined to create a Camelot in which the domains of traditional, subject-matter scholarship and assertively nontraditional (in the late 1960s and early 1970s), process-oriented experiential learning were put in constant tension, to their mutual benefit. Rochester's MRC forged links for us to NTL workshops in Aspen and Bethel and elsewhere; my memories of work with Edi and Charlie Seashore, Marilyn Harris, and Lee Bolman remain particularly sharp more than 20 years later.

And finally, I have been extraordinarily lucky to have been employed by institutions and clients, both inside and outside academe, that invited me and pushed me—or at least left me alone—to design and implement active learning strategies, to ignore traditional boundaries among disciplines and functional areas, and to take the kinds of risks involved in experiential methods. INSEAD, AMA's Management Learning Center, Rochester's Management Research Center, and Yale's School of Organization and Management were all self-proclaimed "pioneering" entrepreneurial ventures that formally incorporated interdisciplinary, group-based, active, and participative pedagogical methods when I first joined them.

In the early 1960s at INSEAD, I worked on group discussion modules to accompany a prototype IBM-Europe computerized business game. In the mid-1960s I ran a management training program for Ethiopian Airlines in Africa and the Middle East that was designed to involve people from multiple ethnic and cultural backgrounds in group-oriented study. In the late 1960s, I was part of AMA's Learning Center group, charged with designing and evaluating an innovative top management team long-range planning process, and in the early 1970s at Rochester, I wrote and tested group- and self-administered career planning exercises explicitly designed to shift power over critical career decisions from organizational systems to individual managers.

In short, my own educational route was amply punctuated with fortunate detours through a wide variety of audiences, techniques, and subject matters (for which I am deeply grateful)—as well as a few rest stops and potholes. These occasionally amusing diversions and painful delays have, I now think, made me more than ordinarily alert to the wide variety of ways technique interacts with audience and subject matter to produce education. More important, they have helped me feel free to experiment with uncommon combinations. Above all, they have taught me to value the potency of active and experiential learning methods as components in strategies for linking content, audience, and technique. I have also learned something about the costs and risks inherent in those methods, and thus about the need for prudence in selecting particular combinations.

By the mid-1970s, assumptions about audience had become the critical issue for me. At that point, my presuppositions about audience, again like those of most of my academic colleagues, had essentially been shaped by business school curricula charted in the 1959 Ford and Carnegie Foundation reports on the (then allegedly lamentable) state of management and business education. The Gordon & Howell and Pierson prescriptions for academic rigor and scholarly respectability implied *inter alia* heavy investments in graduate-level professional programs and relative disinvestment in, if not outright disdain for, undergraduate management education. Despite the fact that none of the authors of these critical reports was at the time a business school faculty member, and despite their appeals to replace "training" with "education," it is clear to me, in retrospect, that their prescriptions remained entirely for and about professional audiences in separate schools of business and management.

Even in prescriptions for undergraduates, management education was not to be confused with general education. The American Association of Collegiate Schools of Business (AACSB) "Common Body of Knowledge" guidelines for introductory organization and management courses, for example, defined them as core courses for specialized, professional, or "pre-professional" students, not to be offered before junior year, major standing. CBK curricular guidelines have consistently held that students should complete liberal and general education distribution courses prior to declaring their majors and taking management courses. Along with purported benefits comes a perverse message, learned well by students in professional programs, that liberal education consists mainly of some childish things to put away before getting to the really serious stuff.

What was supposed to happen in standard business school classrooms was, in this model, fashioned primarily to meet the needs of MBA students with significant full-time work experience. These subject-matter and pedagogical design parameters reflected the realities of leading professional school faculties, with their own carefully selected, relatively mature, and street-smart student audiences, and were then largely confirmed through corporate experiences with their alumni, their executive program students, and consulting clients—and, until quite recently, the business press.

The MBA model has dominated management education at both graduate and undergraduate levels for more than 30 years, institutionalized in business school accreditation guidelines—and even more firmly in textbook markets—that have, despite extensive and prolonged criticism, only recently been relaxed. At the time and until quite recently, however, the focus of critical attention seemed to remain primarily on issues of subject matter (e.g., model course syllabi) and technique (e.g., sharing experiences with group-oriented learning methods and team building), and not audience.

By 1977, I knew that the MBA model didn't fit my undergraduate student audiences. By then, I understood that it was one thing to follow the AACSB guidelines with students who had significant, often full-time, experience in complex organizations, but quite another to work with novices. People who had seen the inside workings of corporations, government agencies, or other work organizations were readily convinced both of the complexity of the pieces and the need to tie them all together. Without such experience, however, the components of a management curriculum appeared to represent little more than a disjointed sequence of abstract exercises.

For example, in introductory management courses for graduate students or practicing managers, I never needed to spend a lot of time arguing for, or demonstrating, the "relevance" of theory and research. For undergraduates, however, the distance between experience and cases, or between real concerns and structured class exercises, often seemed so great that cases became, at best, interesting stories (and occasions for demonstrating analytic, writing, and presentation skills identical to those used in literature and composition classes), and structured exercises became games to be figured out and played on their own merits, with few transferable lessons.

By 1977—toward the end of what many management teachers now call the Foundation Reign of Terror—leading business schools had deemphasized if not abandoned undergraduate programs. The conventional wisdom among business school faculty members, even including teachers who were by then using active, participative, and experiential techniques, was that undergraduate teaching was a low-priority venture—important in numbers, perhaps, but not for first-rank schools—and certainly not "where the action was." Some even argued (probably with justification, given available techniques and materials) that any attempt to teach management to inexperienced undergraduates was a futile exercise and certainly an unproductive use of scarce faculty talent. That teaching itself was a low-priority venture, without much explicit attention in graduate curricula, and evidently all but irrelevant for tenure, served only to underline the point.

Yale had just inaugurated its graduate, professional School of Organization and Management faculty, which was in the process of "absorbing" Yale College (i.e., undergraduate) and Graduate School (i.e., PhD programs) administrative sciences faculties. Despite some official words to the contrary, the establishment of SOM clearly relegated undergraduate management education to secondary status at Yale.

I had been hired, in 1973, to join the new SOM faculty, and had been assigned some undergraduate administrative sciences course duties, in part to "mark time" until the professional master's program was launched. I had never taught undergraduate classes before.

Ad. Sci. 228 was the introductory survey course in organization and management, designed to meet core course requirements for the administrative sciences major, but also to serve as an open elective, without prerequisites, for Yale College undergraduates. I had taught it several times between 1973 and the fall of 1977.

Virtually all of the 25 or so students in the earliest versions of the course—a relatively perfunctory lecture/discussion model, organized around a standard introductory management text with a companion supplementary readings package ("written for first-year MBA and upper-division undergraduate students")—were junior administrative sciences majors. It all went very smoothly. There wasn't much participation, but I was animated and the occasional laughter kept most students alert. Teaching evaluations (and, apparently, "word of mouth") were quite flattering.

Elective enrollments grew substantially between 1975 and 1977. "Discussions" increasingly turned into contentious debates among vocal partisans. I saw and heard escalating signs of frustration about airtime from nonparticipants, including requests that I "exercise more control"—in particular, that I should lecture more and limit discussion to Q&A formats. By the fall of 1976, we could justify multiple discussion sections to supplement the large lecture, which helped somewhat with the airtime problem but not with the discord.

I had ongoing consulting advice and considerable TLC from Yale colleagues—at the time, Yale's administrative sciences organizational behavior group was arguably the locus of expertise in teaching about group, intergroup, and large-system process consultation—including Dick Hackman, Clay Alderfer, Maddy Heilman, and Doug Yates. With substantial encouragement, I decided, in the spring term of 1977, to call a time-out from the syllabus, quickly switched some reading schedules around, moving chapters on group process and OD (particularly, survey feedback techniques) forward, and turned the class's attention from Bethlehem Steel, Western Electric, and air force bomber crews to the organizational and managerial issues that were right in the middle of us.

We figured out a few key things immediately. The majority of "us" were no longer administrative sciences majors; rather, the group was widely representative of the humanities, social sciences, and sciences programs in Yale College. For this new, liberal arts majority, "contentious debate"—particularly about the efficiencies of impersonal, bureaucratic machines and the political power of industrial and government organizations—was the norm. Administrative sciences majors, often clearly playing defense, participated very actively. Indeed, most of the students (and the instructor) thought the arguments were exciting and valuable—sometimes even more fun than lectures; virtually everybody wanted to say more, not less. We would need to design a new structure to make the class work the way we wanted. We did, and muddled through with some excellent results.

I built some of the main lessons of the previous semester into the syllabus for fall 1977 (my "critical turning point" semester). We would employ "cross-major" groups for certain assignments, including debate preparation. Groups could divide and assign work to members, and also could negotiate with other groups to specialize. Members of discussion sections, with support from section associates, could call for "parliamentary sessions" in the combined lecture session to propose and debate agendas, evaluation criteria, and deadline changes.

I know that this story is only one of many similar "unfreezing/changing" experiences of an era in which there was an explosion of experiential exercises and simulations that were subsequently "refrozen" in various active, skill-oriented, and experiential pedagogies. In the years since 1977, I have continuously reinvested learnings from the experiments started in that era in attempts to develop a comprehensive organization and management course for general education students. In recent years, colleagues from other institutions have begun to offer versions of that course, and to share experiences. The central objective of our courses, now collectively known as the "organization-as-classroom" model, is to take experiential learning principles to their logical conclusions, to provide a coherent, relevant, comprehensive, and integrated introduction to management theory and practice in a single-semester course—for *everybody*.

Management 101 is the course label I chose at Bucknell to represent much more than a catalog number. It is designed to be a comprehensively integrating management experience for undergraduate general education students, whether or not they will take other formal management courses before being assigned important managerial duties in companies and communities. For those students who do follow a business curriculum, either in an undergraduate program or later, in an MBA program, MG 101 strives to provide a meaningful conceptual framework—a "practical theory" of how the essential pieces all fit together—and a compelling argument for paying attention to the important details that follow.

Since 1977, more than 4,000 students have worked in several hundred project companies, each consisting of about 20 to about 40 students, in courses now offered at a dozen or more colleges and universities. Over the years, those students have worked with teaching assistants and instructors, in what we have since learned to call a Kaizen continuous improvement process, to develop a basic course structure—course policies, performance expectations, and procedures—around which students can, and unfailingly do, invent endless variations and surprises.

Although no two companies are ever identical, central features of the course have now evolved to a pretty stable pattern. In the current version of the course that I teach, MG 101 company activities take place in three phases. In the first, participants decide on the collective missions and strategies of their companies, and they build a sense of themselves as teams. In the second, they design organization structures and operating plans to achieve their missions. In the third, they carry out their plans and report on activities and results. MG 101 companies are real management experiences, with real customers and clients, not traditional "simulations" or "structured exercises." Project budgets of several thousand dollars each are common, and service project activities have earned national and international recognition.

The centerpiece of MG 101 is a set of three organizational and managerial projects. In their campus or community service projects, MG 101 companies have provided a wide variety of services and have been important contributors to local, national, and international charities. In their business projects, companies must produce sufficient revenues to fund their service projects by conducting profitable business projects; over the years, MG 101 companies have manufactured products, invested in inventories to be sold at profit, and provided revenue-generating services. The third project, a "final test" for leadership and integration, is the company's public report project. These projects challenge students to create and run collaborative enterprises—to apply theory and research in coping with actual management problems, to identify and develop managerial skills, and to think critically about management as a career, as a set of methods, and as a body of knowledge devoted to the accomplishment of valued social and individual goals.

The academic goals of MG 101 are derived directly from the developmental needs of MG 101 projects. The most effective and efficient way for general education students to learn this material is, in my experience, to tie reading and lecture/discussion assignments directly to company project activities, emphasizing the students' "need to know," "just in time." Concepts and models must be introduced when students need them to solve actual problems; theory and research results have to provide meaningful interpretations of real events (as experienced by those who will use them); and assertions of relevance, including the relevance of definitional and methodological quibbles of the sort that generate PhD theses and journal articles, must be demonstrated in practice. The priority throughout is on linking concepts to experience.

The evidence is compelling: Under this model, students are highly motivated and sufficiently skilled to enjoy the challenge of creating, experiencing, and making good sense out of a managerial organization. By the end, students can demonstrate some mastery of fundamental management skills and command of a theoretical language of management sufficiently rich to support further learning about organization and management. And they (and we) have fun.

I have worked with at least four MG 101 companies virtually every year since 1977. My greatest source of excitement—in retrospect, the most important energizing force in my teaching career—is that moment when all of us, students and instructor alike, encounter a novel situation and work through it together, linking the best of our collective skills to scholarly resources. Fortunately, such moments occur regularly. Even more fortunately, we have developed ways to capture and document such moments; successful innovations diffuse rapidly—as does the catalog of red flags. The course's archives of "critical incidents" represent, with all their pains and frustrations, endlessly satisfying variations on June's message: "This is the first time I've had the slightest idea what managers really do . . . or how much fun they can have doing it."

For me, the most important lessons learned on this adventure have been about the tight interdependencies that exist among questions of subject matter, technique, and audience. In retrospect, the lessons of MG 101 started to be fun for me too only once I started to make choices that explicitly took all three issues into consideration. I have learned, above all, that when teaching is not fun, it is probably because I am too stuck on one, and have stopped paying close enough attention to another, of those three elements.

I have tried in the preceding pages to sketch my awakening to issues of audience. I would now like to mention briefly some of the things I have learned about subject matter and technique, given my primary commitment to undergraduate general education audiences. In particular, I want to focus on efficiency, because that issue inevitably raises the most intense and serious questions among my colleagues. Efficiency has clearly been out of fashion in academe, especially among enthusiasts of active and experiential teaching techniques, even in professional schools.

Many of us who became teachers in the 1960s and 1970s viewed efficiency as the antithesis of humanity. The demonstrable power of apparently unstructured, go-with-the-flow pedagogies for dealing with the special case in which subject matter was audience undoubtedly convinced many of us of their general utility. We learned to be skeptical and cynical about efficiency in general, and particularly in the classroom. As long as we quit talking soon enough to keep students from being late to their next classes, didn't egregiously violate contracts implied in the "tentative syllabus" handed out on the first day of class, and administered testing, feedback, and evaluation procedures pretty much according to norms, that was good enough, and nobody expected that we would actually ever talk about the last two chapters of the textbook. In any event, nobody checked.

Exceptions only seemed to make efficiency issues even less relevant and more onerous to individual teachers. Where large numbers of students followed structured sequences of courses, it obviously paid to rely on mechanisms for efficiency that limit instructor variation—namely, accreditation and textbook standards. When, in addition, student audiences were homogeneous and subject matter complex, it paid to develop mechanisms that imposed special burdens on instructor time or skill—namely, group project, structured exercise, and case methods. Thus, in circumstances in which efficiency was a clear priority, design and implementation decisions about technique tended to be further removed from the "here and now" of teachers in their classrooms.

Efficiency simply wasn't very important to me before MG 101, but the pressing need to be comprehensive in that course has taught me to pay very close attention to pedagogical efficiency. Unlike most classes, MG 101 is not a loosely coupled, temporary system, designed to disintegrate long before running out of energy. When there are tight interdependencies among class members—or among courses in a sequenced curriculum, or when students in one semester depend on archives from past semesters, as in MG 101—energy failures can't simply be chalked up to individuals without threatening the collective. If we don't "cover" Thursday's assignment schedule, we don't have the option to finish it next Tuesday, or skip it altogether.

MG 101 is hard work for teachers and students alike. Over the years, we have been obliged to develop a framework for deciding about subject-matter priorities and procedures for efficient assignment schedules and classroom management to bring those burdens in line with those of other standard one-semester courses.

Efficiency with respect to subject matter presents ongoing decision problems. Our definition of the essential topics in an introductory management course has shifted and expanded rapidly. At the outset, "essential topics" were largely defined in familiar management process textbook terms—planning, organizing, directing, controlling—but as project activities drove us to add topics, it quickly became clear that that framework simply wasn't sturdy enough to guide choices about what to include and what to exclude.

The pressing need to emphasize interpersonal, group, and intergroup process issues that crossed all course phases was immediately obvious. Indeed, these traditional organizational behavior topics remain central hallmarks of the course. In our experience, for example, everything else depends on close and systematic attention to issues of team building, organizational development, and organizational politics from the outset and throughout the course. Many MG 101 alums who have jumped into the world of work organizations upon graduation report that their most important MG 101 experiences were those that helped cushion "reality shock" about teamwork, communications, motivation, organizational politics, and leadership.

We have discovered that treatment of these topics in introductory texts is inappropriately organized and sequenced for our needs and, frequently, misleadingly and superficially labeled, so we have had to develop supplementary indexes, glossaries, and, finally, a synthesizing conceptual framework that keeps us focused on these process issues. Without doubt, these efforts to develop a "practical theory" have turned out to be among the most intellectually challenging and satisfying scholarly activities I can imagine.

In recent years, as projects have evolved into quite complex and sophisticated sets of activities, MG 101 has incorporated specific techniques from course materials typically found in intermediate-level functional area courses (e.g., survey and focus group techniques in marketing research, cash-flow and managerial accounting techniques, matrix organization design, Gantt and critical path charting, quality of work life and performance appraisal systems) as well as in such "advanced" courses as organizational politics and organizational culture.

Although the outcome of continuous adjustments in course processes—a tightly structured, "well-oiled machine"—has often seemed inconsistent with our commitment to active, experiential learning, we have (re)learned, with repeated surprises, that firm deadlines, clear performance expectations, and unambiguous process structures facilitate the sense of freedom and experimentation that we all need for this course. Efficient "bureaucracy," high-quality, innovative outputs, and a strong sense of community are not inconsistent with each other—or indeed with the individual growth objectives of a general education course.

It has become increasingly clear to me that a commitment to general education in management is not the same as a commitment to any particular configuration of audiences, techniques, or contents. On one hand, knowledge about the meaning of work and the challenges of collaboration, about the activities and skills of managers, and about how society's key institutions are structured and governed is an essential component of everybody's general education. On the other, those who will bear managerial responsibility and exercise formal authority in professional roles will do so efficiently, effectively, and cooperatively to the extent that they have been broadly educated about their roles in society. We simply must ask all students to think expansively and critically about what it means to work with others, to experience and assess some of what it takes (beyond "common sense") to organize and manage, and to grapple with the question of what is worth managing.

I have learned, for example, about marked differences between audiences of sophomore nonmajors and senior management majors, primarily in issues surrounding developmental stages, learning styles, social agendas, and classroom norms, that shape my decisions about technique and about content. I know there are critical distinctions between audiences of novices and audiences in which many have significant full-time organizational experience that determine whether and how I use cases and simulations, experiential exercises, and group or individual assignments. And, of course, differences between small and large audiences, or students and executives, or manufacturers and hospital administrators, or Japanese and French—all obviously affect decisions about how I teach and about the scope of my subject matter; indeed, about the very definition of *management.*

There are likewise differences among lectures, project assignments, writing exercises, case discussion techniques, group exercises, and so on that enable me to capitalize on some audience characteristics and suppress others, and to highlight certain organizational and managerial issues in favor of others. And, of course, there are differences in subject matters, text assignments, course objectives, and class agendas that generate audiences of certain qualities and quantities and render some techniques more efficient than others.

But for me, none of these differences defines the boundaries around general education in management. Sophomore psychology and music majors can (and should) be just as engaged in general education in management when they struggle with income and cash-flow statements, performance appraisals, and sales schedules as are senior accounting majors debating corporate social responsibility, or corporate executives discussing *King Lear.* For me, management education, at all levels, must be "liberal education"—liberating, in the classical sense: How free can people be who do not know how, or when, or why, or with whom, to set and achieve worthy objectives?

Here then is the crux of the matter—the excitement and the challenge—for me: In the years since 1977, I have not been able to identify the limits of this territory, and I have come to suspect that there are none. Wherever I start—with subject matter, with audience, or with technique—I find new regions to explore across the confines of my all-too-obviously limited command of subject matters, access to audiences, and technical competence. None of these three components of the teaching process remains a "given" for me. Because variation in any one of these elements alters the success of the blend, I have to take responsibility for deciding simultaneously *what* to teach, to *whom,* and *how.*

I freely acknowledge that advocating general education objectives for management teaching comes across to colleagues as inordinately abstract, idealistic, and even crusading. Even for teachers in the humanities and social sciences, for whom broad questions of value, context, validity, criticism, and interconnectedness are supposedly second nature, operational definitions of general education are ill defined and controversial, moving into and out of fashion in academe; they can't be pursued effectively without broad understanding and support.

I have benefited greatly from the help of colleagues who appear increasingly to share such aims, both through team teaching—in a rare, stable, and enormously productive collegial relationship with Gordon Meyer, through curricular integration with colleagues in related courses, and through the encouragement and critical observations of colleagues in other schools and in the OB Teaching Society. I have also come to depend on support from administrators, technicians, and teaching assistants, and, above all, creative and energetic students. In my experience, teaching is decidedly not a loner's job.

Clearly, therefore, I intend this chapter to serve as an invitation to colleagues to join me, to continue to push beyond current assumptions about the boundaries of our audiences, our technical skills, and even our disciplines, and to extend a conversation about broader, more ambitious purposes for management education.

Research/Teaching Boundaries

Walter R. Nord

process/product def.

In this chapter I will explore the "boundaries" between teaching and research by addressing who I am as a teacher, as a researcher, and as a person. I will explain how teaching and research have or have not meshed for me, describe my view of the roles that the institutions in our field play in these boundaries, and examine how I have experienced the teaching and research relationship. I will touch on all of these, but for the most part I will do so through an autobiographical narrative rather than going point by point.

However, before I begin the narrative, it is necessary that I pay brief attention to the concepts of boundaries, teaching, and research. Clearly, any consideration of the boundaries between two sets of things, such as teaching and research, depends upon definitions of the two things themselves, and there are many ways to define both research and teaching. Some time ago, I ran across a definition of research proposed by a physical scientist whose name I do not remember. The scientist defined research as the process of continuously learning about something. As this view suggests that research is an ongoing process, I will call it the *process* definition.

In contrast to this view is the more pragmatic one that impinges on academic careers, which defines research in terms of the work an individual has published. This approach implicitly defines research as a product. I will call this the *product* definition. Although the product definition of research is not necessarily incompatible with continuous learning, in use its emphasis on getting the products of our individual continuous learning into print often leads to an emphasis on the appearance of completed parts and makes continuous learning appear somewhat incidental.

Similarly, teaching can be viewed in both process and product terms. Teaching can be viewed as an ongoing process that both promotes teachers' continuous learning and helps to prepare and stimulate others for continuous learning. Of course, many of us experience teaching more in terms of a *product*—as an activity that puts us in classrooms (sometimes in auditoriums and/or in front of TV cameras) where several hundred students can see and hear us. These people may be interested in continuous learning about some things, a few of which (and often only very few) may even have some relationship to the subject matter specified in the descriptions of the classes we are assigned to teach and/or we believe are part of continuous learning. At the end of a term, the product is reflected in credit hours toward the students' degrees and student credit hours on our departments' balance sheets.

When I analyze the teaching/research boundaries using these definitions, in my experience there have been as many significant boundaries between the two definitions of research (i.e., the process and product definitions) as there have been between the process definition of research and the process definition of teaching, which both emphasize continuous learning. In contrast, the product definitions suggest high levels of conflict between the two, given that time taken to orchestrate the classroom (or auditorium) is time that is not available for the production of publications.

The extent of the boundaries depends upon which sets of definitions are most descriptive of the individual's experiences. Thus the boundaries are not necessarily general ones; rather, they are apt to be highly idiosyncratic. Their strength is a function of who an individual is as a person and the environment in which he or she exists. Consequently, I will examine who I am personally *and* assess how the particular contexts I have lived in have affected the boundaries I have experienced and not experienced.

First, on a personal level, I am Myers-Brigg INTP. As Keirsey and Bates (1984) note, INTPs typically prize intelligence in themselves and in others, but are apt to become intellectual dilettantes as a result of their need to amass ideas, principles, and understanding of behavior. INTPs can become obsessed with analysis. Once caught up in a thought process, an INTP may find that that thought process seems to have a will of its own, and will persevere until he or she comprehends the issue in all its complexity.

For INTPs, the world exists primarily to be understood. Reality is trivial, a mere arena for proving ideas. It is essential that the universe is understood and that whatever is stated about the universe is stated correctly, with coherence and without redundancy. This is the INTP's final purpose. It matters not whether others understand or accept her or his truths.

The INTP is the logician, the mathematician, the philosopher, the scientist: Any pursuit requiring architecture of ideas intrigues this type.

INTPs should not, however, be asked to work out the implementation or application of their models to the real world. The INTP is the architect of a system; he or she leaves it to others to be the builders. Clearly, one with these inclinations would be quite comfortable with the activities involved in the process views of both teaching and research and the continuous learning they both entail. The major contexts in which I have spent my academic life have accentuated this bent.

I attended Williams College—a small liberal arts college in a small New England town. At the time I was there, 1957-1961, the climate emphasized the broad development of a person's intellect. In a sense, boundaries were always blurred in this context. To illustrate, there was a requirement affectionately known as "compulsory chapel," which meant that seven times a semester one had to demonstrate having attended a church service. Operationally, such a demonstration entailed seven times/semester turning in a written document certifying that one had attended a religious service. Such documentation could be made either by actually attending a service in Williamstown and signing an appropriate card or by having a friend sign a card for one at a local church service. More cosmopolitans found it better to meet the requirement by persuading an out-of-town minister to sign a note indicating that in fact they had attended services at home or elsewhere. As you might expect, compulsory chapel was not popular. What is interesting about this requirement at Williams as it relates to boundaries is the rationale that the administration used to defend the chapel requirement. The rationale denied boundaries for human development. It entailed blurring secular and religious boundaries. It was not asserted that one ought to go to church or have faith, but rather that a complete education includes experience with religion.

One of the greatest things about Williams was the quality of my classmates and the interrelationships they helped me to see. I learned more about thinking from my sophomore roommate, Tad Day, than from almost any other source. Tad's mind was so open and insightful that he would routinely leap from an idea in physics to an understanding of something in political science or economics. Tad had an enormous impact on me in demonstrating that learning entails thinking about the relationships among things, not just amassing information. Also, almost every examination at Williams emphasized the comparing and contrasting of different things and ideas. Thus, to prepare, students came to blur boundaries constantly.

The graduate schools I attended also discouraged boundaries. When I attended the School of Industrial and Labor Relations at Cornell in the early 1960s, it was a remarkably interdisciplinary setting, with much interaction among the members of the small, talented faculty. Also, most faculty urged students to think across areas and voiced an appropriate amount of cynicism about "accepted truths" (Larry Williams stands out in this regard).

My PhD work at Washington University was in social psychology. At that time the social psychology faculty was quite small. There were very few seminars in this subfield, and the faculty didn't know exactly what to do with me. Fortunately, it was a long time before the administration set out to abolish the Sociology Department, which at this time was excellent. I was encouraged to go outside of the Psychology Department; as a result, I took a lot of work in the Sociology Department, which at that time was led by people such as Alvin Gouldner, who was beginning his critique of modern sociological theory by studying Plato, and Robert Hamblin, who was a rarity in sociology—he was a Skinnerian. Also, I was funded by a program in community mental health led by Jack Glidewell and composed of students from many departments: psychology, sociology, anthropology, economics, and political science.

I mention all this to suggest that both my personal inclinations and my early intellectual experiences put me in situations where boundaries were constantly challenged—at least they were not revered. I think the smallness of the institutions and the high-quality individuals I met there played important roles. The model of scholarship that I have and value that emerged from these contexts is very consistent with the process definition of continuous learning (unconstrained disciplinary boundaries).

My early experiences as a professor were very similar in these respects. I was hired as psychologist by what was then a small business school—one that had been very slow to get with the trend of the time of hiring social scientists. I was the school's first social scientist, and it was my first contact with a business school (I had never taken a course in a business school). Because there were few people like me in the business school, and no one, including me, knew exactly what an organizational psychologist should do, I had a great deal of latitude. As a result, I was in a situation where I had room to experiment and introduce things that I was interested in. My first major teaching assignment was the introductory organizational behavior class. I was fortunate that Sterling Schoen was the senior instructor in the course. When we first met to talk about what we would do, Sterling said to me, "Well, we hired you to introduce psychology into our curriculum. What do you think belongs in the basic course?" I introduced a lot of ideas from psychology, including having the first-year MBA students read *Walden Two*. Sterling was very enthusiastic and supportive of these moves. Thanks to Sterling, I was not really forced to choose between what I thought was important about psychology and organizations and what I was teaching. I was allowed to be a "self-organizing system." As I learned more about what was being taught in business schools about motivation, I saw many commonalities with the Skinnerian ideas I'd gotten in sociology from Hamblin—my first operant conditioning paper compared and contrasted these sets of ideas (Nord, 1969). Thus it was stimulated by what I was teaching.

Several other things about my early career are important. First, I began my career at almost the same time I married my wife, Ann. Ann's excellent inquisitive and irreverent mind, with its agnostic bent, has helped me see how most boundaries in human thought are porous and mindless. I have been fortunate that this orientation is highly contagious, and I have learned much from her. I was also fortunate that Karl Hill was my dean early in my career. Whenever Karl met someone else on campus who he thought might share my interests, he usually found a way to get me in touch with that person. Often some committee assignment was the vehicle; many of these had to do with teaching programs—only a few of these committees were research related.

As a result, very early on I had working relationships with people from many disciplines and professional schools. I became part of a local network in which I knew people from education, history, and other disciplines who otherwise I would not have met. A positive by-product was that I learned a lot about other disciplines. Doctoral students, of course, served similar functions. Most of the departments in social science at Washington University were too small to have self-contained PhD programs—interdisciplinary exposure was an almost inevitable result. Moreover, because I had stayed on at the university where I had gotten my doctoral degree, I had many previously established contacts in psychology and sociology.

So far, much of this may seem somewhat distant from the issue of research and teaching boundaries. However, in retrospect there is a relevant, underlying pattern operating to submerge boundaries. The pattern is driven by the fact that because I did not fit into the established routines and was surrounded by developmentally oriented people, I was always allowed and encouraged to introduce and/or keep open to a variety of perspectives, which is what I do in my research. I had the opportunity to be a self-designing system by constructing much of my teaching in ways that were consistent with my other intellectual interests. However, the students (especially the part-time ones) pushed me to make linkages to practice. Initially, this made me defensive, but as I became more confident, it became a stimulus for learning. For example, when I was promoting job enrichment to part-time MBA students and they said it would not be accepted in their organizations, initially I discounted their objections as showing a lack of imagination. However, they began to convince me, and this stimulated a productive tension. The tension between what made such great psychological sense and what might be possible became part of the stimulus for my seeing the relevance of Marx (Nord, 1974).

The opportunity I had to self-design was promoted by the fact that I was frequently teaching courses that had never been taught locally before. Thus there was no particular set agenda, and I was free to bring in things that I wanted to learn about. One thing I did—which is a bit embarrassing to own up to publicly—that was important for me in blurring teaching/research boundaries was to make what I wanted to learn something that I taught. To illustrate, particularly in advanced courses, when there was something I thought I should know better than I did, I made it part of a course and learned it along with the students. My most memorable experi-

ence with this was some time ago, when I used Buckley's (1968) monumental volume on general systems theory as a textbook in a doctoral seminar before I had absorbed the material thoroughly myself. I admitted to the students at the outset what I was doing and asked them to trust my intuition that the material was very important and we would learn it together. I learned a great deal from the seminar, and I think if you were to go back and talk to the students who were in it, they would say they did too. I have done similar things, although not quite as risky, since then. In many ways, I think some of my best teaching has been done at these times; certainly such experiences have helped me to continue to learn.

Teaching has advanced my continuing learning in other ways. One of the things that bothered me early in my career as a teacher was the lack of availability of teaching materials for business school students that conveyed what was known about human behavior—in ways that would provide them with a basic foundation of our understanding while at the same time convey an appropriate tone for how temporary and contingent this understanding might be. As part of an effort to solve the teaching materials problem, I expanded the reading list that Sterling Schoen and I had developed for our course. These materials attempted to do the two things I've indicated above—provide the students with an understanding of the conventional wisdom while simultaneously challenging the conventional wisdom in an appropriate manner. Out of this effort came the collection of readings I put together called *Concepts and Controversy in Organizational Behavior* (Nord, 1972, 1976). Although it is open for debate whether or not an edited book of readings constitutes a research product, in my context it did; more important, that book played a very important role in my continuing learning. For one thing, to write the introductory essays as well as the papers that filled in the existing gaps, I was forced to go restudy the foundation areas and package the material in ways that related to what students appeared to need. Equally important was the external world that book opened up to me. Among its early adopters were members of the faculty at the University of British Columbia. That faculty included not only Peter Frost, who is an editor of this book, but also such other fine scholars as Craig Pinder, Merle

Ace, Skip Walter, Ron Taylor, Larry Moore, and Vance Mitchell. Their enthusiasm for the book led them to introduce themselves to me and to invite me to visit on their faculty in the mid-1970s. The year that I spent at UBC was undoubtedly one of the best I have ever had in terms of opening me up to continuous learning. In addition to being surrounded by intelligent and wonderful colleagues, we were teaching an introductory organizational behavior class. For the first and, I hope, last time in my teaching career, I was in a position of having to use a conventional textbook—as the first edition of *Concepts and Controversy* had aged and become dated, they were no longer using it. However, they were an extremely innovative group of people, and to supplement the textbook, they used a novel called *Wheels*. The reaction to that book led Peter, Vance, and me to recognize how much could be learned from nonacademic literature, including fiction, the *Wall Street Journal* and *New York Times*, and so forth. This led us to put together the first edition of *Organizational Reality* (the fourth edition of which was published in 1992). That process had a major positive influence on how I and, I'm pretty sure, Vance and Peter think about organizations. We found that we could capture our own experiences in organizations well by dealing with the concrete experiences other people reported having with organizations. We found that we could improve our teaching by attending to these materials more fully than we had before. This opened up a whole host of sources of information that I would not have been interested in or given much credence to before. Boundaries between academic and nonacademic bodies of knowledge became far less salient for me as a result.

Another instance in which teaching influenced how and what I learn about organizations came later in my career at Washington University, when I became concerned with the inadequacy with which I felt I was teaching cases. I wanted to do this better, and a colleague, Nick Baloff, suggested that I try to sit in a few days with some of the faculty at Harvard to observe their use of the case method. My dean at the time, Bob Virgil, was extremely supportive. He took the initiative, and through the appropriate administrative channels got to Paul Lawrence and Mike Beer, who were kind enough to host a visit for me of several days' duration. I was extremely impressed by what I observed

and came back much more confident in my knowledge of what could be done with cases and how to try to accomplish what I had in mind. One of the things that I found very interesting about this is that my anxieties about using cases had stemmed from my lack of confidence in knowing the "answers"—that is, what *should* be done in many of the cases. In the past, that lack of knowledge had scared me. But knowing the answers didn't seem to be a concern for the Harvard people. They were not striving for *the* answer to any given case. When I shed that concern, it became possible for the lack of an answer to create a productive tension. Perhaps the best illustration I can give is the aerospace lab case. As most readers probably know, this case deals with how a company can do needed basic research and have it lead to some type of profitable product development. After using that case, to this day, as a result of that tension, anything that I see related to this issue in *Fortune*, the *Wall Street Journal*, or anywhere, I read very actively with a very specific context in mind. I have learned much as a result, although I still don't know *the* answer.

To conclude, in my experience teaching and research, viewed as processes, have been mutually reinforcing. There have even been instances where teaching has facilitated research, even defined in product terms. This happens most when I have had the opportunity to work with talented and enthusiastic doctoral students, especially ones from other disciplines. In fact, a good portion of my first writings on Marx and organization theory stemmed from a conversation with a doctoral student, Ken Runyon, who was taking a course in the Sociology Department in which he read a book by Robert Tucker titled *The Marxian Revolutionary Idea* (1969). Ken had taken the introductory organizational behavior MBA. One day he mentioned that he was reading Tucker's book and said, "There are a lot of similarities between what you taught in organization behavior and some of the things that Marx wrote about. You really ought to read this book." I did, and I saw the parallels too, but I also became much more aware of the macro side of things that organization behavior did not deal with at the time.

Not only has teaching helped my research, but the reverse has occurred also. When I was doing the first edition of *Concepts and Controversy*, I was fortunate to have Jane Warren serve as an editorial consultant. Jane taught me much about how to convey ideas in writing. What I learned from her has helped me to help students and colleagues with their work.

Other examples of how teaching has led me more directly to traditional research work come out of seminars and independent studies. The paper I published with Ralph Stablein grew directly out of a paper he wrote in a seminar I taught when I was visiting at Northwestern (Stablein & Nord, 1985). Independent studies also have been helpful, although they take time and often lead to no concrete output. In at least one case, an MBA student by the name of Bob Costigan wanted to do an independent study. He indicated that he was interested in studying a plant in town that had just gone to the 4-day workweek. We built a research project around that, and it turned out to be a paper that at the time was quite well received (Nord & Costigan, 1973). Also, undergraduate honors theses have served as places to do some pilot work.

Clearly, the tone of what I've said so far is that, at least in my experience, teaching and research as I have defined them have been mutually supportive. Much of the mutuality has come when there have been strong students who have pushed me and when I could be open and avoid being defensive when their pushing was rooted in skepticism and dissatisfaction with what I was teaching. Also, the mutuality of research and teaching has been fostered by my own skepticism and dissatisfaction in settings where I was encouraged to experiment. (Much of this experimentation occurred prior to standardized course evaluation forms, which, when I was young and not tenured, I think might have discouraged my innovative proclivities.) However, these experiences must be interpreted quite carefully. Like all experiences, they occurred in particular contexts. For the most part, the contexts that I have been fortunate enough to be in were ones where people valued quality and were not committed to any particular narrow definition of what types of things one could make quality judgments about. (Unfortunately, such latitude may not exist in many contexts today, when the product definitions of research and teaching are dominant.) In more rigid systems, it would have been more difficult to obtain mutual benefits from seemingly diverse activities. Also, the approach I have followed has serious deficits. The pattern reflects a bouncing

around that is inconsistent with programmatic research.

In addition, there are boundaries that I have put up for myself. The most salient one relates to my research, particularly with the work on Marx. Except in doctoral seminars, I have always made an effort to keep this work out of the classroom, in order to avoid appearing to impose my particular set of political values in circumstances where they might not be seen as academically relevant. I am not sure that has necessarily been a good thing to do, but it has been a boundary between teaching and research, albeit a boundary that I introduced myself.

Conclusions

The foregoing observations represent one individual's potentially self-serving recall of experiences that took place some time ago, in settings that were probably atypical even in the time they occurred. Drawing conclusions from them can at best be very risky. However, given that boundaries are experiential and most experiences occur in contexts that are in many ways idiosyncratic, it seems useful to highlight any patterns that appear so that others may compare their experiences. Such comparisons might provide general guidelines for helping to create contexts for ourselves and others within optimal boundaries.

As I reflect back on my experiences, it seems that the most significant boundaries between teaching and research that might have occurred would have been products of the social systems and the people who had significant influence in them. Quite likely, these would have emerged when individuals in the system had strong convictions about the nature of reality and/or about how something ought to be. The processes that such convictions appear likely to have spawned would be ones serving to direct my energies into certain predefined modes. In the absence of such convictions, the processes I experienced avoided boundaries by encouraging me to self-direct and, consequently, to self-organize.

Several factors—some personal and some contextual—seemed to me most important in encouraging such self-direction. First, I was often surrounded by supportive individuals who valued quality and continuous learning. Second, the social settings of which I was a part were low in established routines. Third, I have long had a somewhat anarchistic, iconoclastic bent.

Which is more important, the context or the personality? I do not know, but as I look around at the systems in which my junior colleagues and doctoral students exist, I suspect that, had I been in their shoes, I would have experienced much more in the way of boundaries than I did. In fact, some of my own efforts to help them succeed in today's world may help introduce boundaries. Somewhat paradoxically, and unfortunately, in trying to help them create products and/or present themselves in ways that will be well received by significant gatekeepers, I may socially construct boundaries for others that did not exist for me in my own personal experiences. I believe I am most apt to do this when I have fairly strong convictions about what is and/or should be.

References

Buckley, W. (Ed.). (1968). *Modern systems research for the behavioral scientist.* Chicago: Aldine.

Frost, P. J., Mitchell, V. F., & Nord, W. R. (1992). *Organizational reality: Reports from the firing line* (4th ed.). New York: HarperCollins.

Keirsey, D., & Bates, M. (1984). *Please understand me: Character and temperament types* (4th ed.). Del Mar, CA: Prometheus Nemesis.

Nord, W. R. (1969). Beyond the teaching machine: The neglected area of operant conditioning in the theory and practice of management. *Organizational Behavior and Human Performance, 4,* 375-401.

Nord, W. R. (Ed.). (1972). *Concepts and controversy in organizational behavior.* Santa Monica, CA: Goodyear.

Nord, W. R. (1974). The failure of current applied behavioral science: A Marxian perspective. *Journal of Applied Behavioral Science, 10*(4).

Nord, W. R. (Ed.). (1976). *Concepts and controversy in organizational behavior* (2nd ed.). Santa Monica, CA: Goodyear.

Nord, W. R., & Costigan, R. (1973). Worker adjustment to the four-day week: A longitudinal study. *Journal of Applied Psychology, 58,* 6-66.

Stablein, R., & Nord, W. R. (1985). Practical and emancipatory interests in organizational symbolism: A review and evaluation. *Journal of Management, 2*(2), 13-28.

Tucker, R. C. (1969). *The Marxian revolutionary idea.* New York: W. W. Norton.

9

Teaching as an Act of Scholarship

Stella M. Nkomo

As I read Walter Nord's essay in this volume about who he is as a teacher and scholar, I was struck by the smooth and seemingly integrative and complementary relationship between his teaching and research. They do not take away from each other, but are acts centered in a philosophy of continuous learning. The boundaries are not distinct, but permeable, with frequent exchanges between the two elements of being a management scholar. I was also struck by the profound impact other scholars have had upon not only Walter's intellectual development but his beliefs about education. We could conclude from his self-reflection that only those whose research interests coincide with class content are able to integrate research and teaching effectively. So we could easily attribute Walter's ability to bridge research and teaching to this and conclude that this may not be the case for most of us. Walter himself acknowledges that for others, teaching and research may not blend as easily. Some of us may feel teaching and research are irreparably unbalanced. Often our research may not be in areas directly correlating with our teaching, especially our undergraduate teaching. But if we

examine Walter's essay thoughtfully, we can see that he has found a common denominator for teaching and research: continuous learning. He does not separate the two. He envisions his work as that of a scholar, whether in the classroom or in preparing a paper, engaging in continuous learning.

After reading his essay, I could not help but reflect upon my own academic career. When I decided to pursue a PhD, I had no inkling that in my career I would confront the teaching-versus-research dilemma. I had decided to become a professor because I wanted to teach others. My own life had been profoundly changed by education. I wanted to attend college upon graduation from high school but was told by a misguided guidance counselor that I was too poor (and, although he did not say it, the implication was that I was "too black") to go to college, and that I needed to go to work. So I went to work. Eventually, however, I started working on my undergraduate degree at night at a community college. It was my faculty adviser, a lecturer in sociology, who told me about possibilities I thought were beyond my reach. She herself was pursuing her own doctoral degree at the time and encouraged me to continue my education. Faculty roles were clear at that community college—faculty spent a lot of time teaching and advising students.

When I completed my undergraduate degree, I found myself going on for an MBA and finally my PhD. For me, teaching was about changing lives and, eventually, society. What more impact could one have? As I look back now upon my naïveté, I see that it was only when I entered the PhD program at the University of Massachusetts that I finally discovered the significance of research. My classes were about learning to do top-quality research, not about teaching. Yet I found the research fascinating. I thought, If this is what I must do in order to teach, then this isn't bad at all! It never occurred to me that I would have to choose one over the other.

Luckily for me, the late George Odiorne agreed to be my major adviser. If there was ever an exemplar for balancing teaching and research, it was George Odiorne. He was a charismatic and inspirational teacher as well as a prolific researcher and writer. He influenced not only me but many other students. He pushed all of us to new heights, but above all, he thrived being a professor.

My favorite and best-remembered class with George was a seminar on human resource management that I took with five other doctoral students. The course had one requirement for passing—a published article. We met once a week over lunch, and about midway through the meal, George would turn to one of us and ask, "What are you thinking about?" Or he would share with us some new insight he had gotten from teaching management, consulting, or just reading. The first article I wrote in my career was sparked at one these luncheon gatherings. I remember scratching out the first paragraphs on a paper napkin.

It has been a long time since that seminar. When I graduated with my PhD, I chose to be at a university that valued good teaching, and I also wanted a chance to teach students who were like me—first-generation college students. I learned a lot from George about being a scholar. Teaching and research are both intimately part of being a scholar. I admit I have never tried to "balance teaching and research" as if they are things that can be weighed on scales. In a way, my only standard has been emulating George

Odiorne. I am a teacher and researcher. There is no *versus* between these identities for me. For me, both are about change. I do research on race and gender because I want to see an end to racism, sexism, and other forms of domination in organizations.

Yet I do know that it can be hard to achieve a balance between research and teaching when many of the conventions and rewards around us reify the status and importance of research compared with teaching. This has been particularly problematic for management scholars because we have spent the past 30 years trying to overcome an image of our discipline as vocational rather than academic (Laidlaw, 1992, p. 2).[1] We may sometimes feel we are living a schizophrenic existence, constantly torn between two identities, as teachers and as researchers.

Perhaps some of those reading this essay and Walter's essay may dismiss our experiences as unique. It occurs to me that we all need some common denominator to help us out of the overwrought teaching-versus-research debate. A common denominator may allow us to see value in both teaching and research, without one detracting from the other. I believe for Walter this is the idea of continuous learning.

Scholars of education have suggested that one way out of dichotomous thinking about research and teaching is to redefine the concept of scholarship in higher education. Ernest Boyer (1990) offers a new paradigm for understanding our work as scholars:

> What we urgently need today is a more inclusive view of what it means to be a scholar—a recognition that knowledge is acquired through research, through synthesis, through practice, and through teaching. We acknowledge that these four categories—the scholarship of discovery, of integration, of application, and of teaching—divide intellectual functions that are tied inseparably to each other. (pp. 24-25)

Boyer suggests that we think of research and teaching as different aspects of scholarship. Teaching, like research, should be seen as an act of scholarship. Thus scholarship becomes the common denominator for what we do as professors.

What does it mean in practice to think of teaching as an act of scholarship? If teaching is seen as a scholarly activity, we can put more time into learning about its theoretical content (pedagogy), evaluating it, sharing our knowledge about good teaching with our colleagues, and, most important, changing the lives of students. These practices may not be isomorphic with how we approach research. But notice that we spend a great deal of time learning research methodology, not only in our doctoral education but throughout our careers. We have conventions for evaluating research (albeit not perfect conventions). We also expect good research scholarship to have an impact on the discipline and ultimately on practice. But most of all, we share our research knowledge with fellow scholars by publishing our findings or presenting papers. Our research is held up to public scrutiny. It is this last convention, according to Lee Shulman (1993), that most greatly hinders the congruence between teaching and research:

> I now believe that the reason teaching is not more valued in the academy is because the way we treat teaching removes it from the community of scholars. Universities do not diminish the importance of teaching because they devalue the act itself; investigation is not seen as having more intrinsic value then teaching. Rather, we celebrate those aspects of our lives and work that can become, . . . *community property..* And if we wish to see greater recognition and reward attached to teaching, we must move teaching from its current private status to community property. (p. 6; emphasis added)

Whether or not everyone agrees fully with Shulman's argument, many universities are beginning to reexamine the ways they evaluate and reward teaching. Some schools are requiring job applicants to present teaching colloquiums (where they talk about their philosophies of teaching and how they approach their subject matter) in addition to research colloquiums. Other universities are sponsoring projects to develop prototypes for peer review of teaching.

I believe, however, that the major change that must take place is in how we think about what we do as professors. I agree with Walter that we must attend to both the process of our teaching and the products of our teaching. Sharing knowledge with students presupposes that I am at the forefront of my discipline,

aware of its major philosophical and theoretical debates. I do not avoid paradigm shifts, but embrace them through my own continuous learning. Like Walter, I do not avoid new ideas or unfamiliar theories, but instead find ways of acquiring and understanding new knowledge. This is the only way I can hope to transform and extend knowledge. Thinking of my teaching as scholarship also means I have a philosophy of pedagogy. What beliefs do I hold about how students learn and the best ways to convey management knowledge? I also engage in developmental activities that will help me to improve my teaching. Foremost, I make my thinking about teaching and the products of my teaching "community property." I am willing to have my colleagues review my teaching and to make judgments about my scholarship as a teacher.

If we are going to challenge the boundaries between teaching and research, we must change not only our conceptualization of scholarship but the traditions and conventions that have kept us locked in a paralyzing debate. As faculty, we may want to believe that we have long abandoned the view that the essence of scholarship is research. Often for justifiable reasons we point the finger of guilt at the administrators of our institutions. There is still a wide gap between administrators' voiced commitment to teaching and the use of reward structures that valorize research performance over teaching performance. But we must ask about our own role in perpetuating the privileged status of research in the academy. For the most part, we are the ones who make promotion and tenure decisions, we are heavily involved in the recruitment of new faculty, and we are primarily responsible for the preparation of doctoral students. It is here that we can begin to extend our definition of scholarship by the value we attach to teaching in each of these activities.

Note

1. Laidlaw (1992) points out that in late 1950s and 1960s, major reports on the field of management education were sponsored by the Ford and Carnegie Foundations. Among the findings of those reports were that business schools were too vocational, lacked academic rigor, and taught subjects that were not founded in basic research.

References

Boyer, E. L. (1990). *Scholarship reconsidered: Priorities of the professoriate.* Princeton, NJ: Carnegie Foundation for the Advancement of Teaching.

Laidlaw, W. K., Jr. (1992, July). *Defining scholarly work in management education.* Report prepared for American Assembly of Collegiate Schools of Business.

Shulman, L. S. (1993). *Displaying teaching to a community of peers.* Paper presented at the American Association for Higher Education National Conference on Faculty Roles and Rewards, San Antonio, TX.

Doing Research and Getting Published

To build a theory, you have to know what it is you are talking about . . . , provide evidence for it . . . , and integrate it with other relevant theories (e.g., to resolve contradictions . . .). The bulk of the work in theory building involves gathering evidence.

Edwin A. Locke (p. 100)

Frustration with the preoccupations of the mainstream functionalist and managerial literature, as well as concern about ecological matters and the danger of "corporate colonization" . . . turning us all into consumers and clients, inspire me to produce a steady flow of critical work.

Mats Alvesson (p. 112)

Some successful academics work from 8:00 a.m. to 6:00 p.m. every day in a regimented style that keeps them focused on the work at hand and away from the many distractions present in the workplace. Others work when their emotions move them, putting in perhaps more hours, but spending many of those hours reacting to the various interruptions of the day; these individuals definitely put in many hours at odd times (when the spirit moves them).

Susan J. Ashford (p. 121)

I publish mainly because I want to influence others and because I want to build and maintain a reputation in the community of scholars who do similar work, and I think most of my colleagues publish for the same reasons.

Kevin R. Murphy (pp. 129-130)

I also think we [editors] really do act as our authors' true friends, friends authors need when we decline to accept their papers. If we accepted papers that shouldn't be accepted, we would not be protecting authors from publishing works that, in the end, they don't really want to have in academia's archives.

J. Keith Murnighan (p. 142)

There are many reasons scholars do research, and many ways they engage in the process (see, e.g., Frost & Stablein, 1992). There also are many ways to get one's work into the public realm, where it can be read, evaluated, and learned from (see, e.g., Cummings & Frost, 1995). In this section of the book, our contributors provide reflections and insights about research and about the process of publishing completed work. Of all the things academics do, research has the most extended rhythms. It usually takes a long time to develop and test one's ideas, whether it is empirical or conceptual work. It can take even longer to get that work published. Electronic media can hasten the sharing of ideas with others, but the typical journal article or book or book chapter can be in process for months or even years.

It can take a lifetime for the fullness of an academic's research contributions to a field to be appreciated. Edwin Locke points out that it has taken 25 years of work on goal-setting theory to give it the depth and rigorous testing needed to make it valuable. Long intervals of sustained attention and persistence are required to produce good research. Susan Ashford observes that research is a manifestation of both the individual's creative urges and the need to survive and prosper in an academic career, particularly during the buildup to a tenure decision in a research-oriented institution. Authors Locke, Alvesson, Ashford, Murphy, and Murnighan are very different people, with different worldviews, research agendas, and outputs, yet they share an enthusiasm, even a passion in some cases, for the work they do, for their topics of study, for the need to publish their work so others can read it. They understand the importance of being open to feedback. Locke writes about the value of "theory builders" and the dysfunctionality of "theory defenders." As Ashford notes, "Defensiveness would seem to muck up [the research]

enterprise at both the early and later stages of one's career" (p. 125).

In our field, research contributions and careers seem to emerge rather than to develop as the result of some grand design or master plan. Locke puts it this way: "Goal-setting theory, I would have to say, was built piecemeal, without a grand plan. Every study, I believe, had a specific purpose, and this purpose built upon previous work" (p. 100). It is likely, however, that as researchers make progress in their work and become increasingly confident in their ideas and skills, they have the "luxury" to focus their efforts on long-range projects. (A positive tenure decision can reinforce this opportunity, particularly in institutions that have adopted the academic career model prevalent in North America.) Alvesson states:

> Up until this point in my career (around 1990), it makes little sense to talk about my work in terms of research programs, as my projects were usually conducted without any long-term plans or the intention of achieving consistency among individual projects. . . . At the beginning and middle of the 1990s, my rather wide range of research activities could be neatly summarized in terms of . . . five research programs. (p. 109)

Other shifts may occur that can encourage and even shape the focus of researchers' investigations at the time when they become known for their published work. One trend is toward a greater frequency of collaboration on research projects. Of course, as Ashford points out, collaborative work can occur at any stage in a research career. Nevertheless, it seems it is when one proceeds beyond the early stages of a career, which typically require production of individually authored work to demonstrate one's competence, that there is increased contact with other like-minded scholars. One's reputation as a competent scholar becomes more widespread in the academic community. There is also likely to be an abundance of ideas and potential lines of possible inquiry that spin out from one's earlier work, and it is impossible to engage these ideas unless one combines the talents of others with one's own.

In their chapters, Locke and Alvesson focus on a fairly grand sweep of rhythms associated with doing research. Each continues to conduct research and to publish findings that are influential in the field. The audiences for these two authors are likely very different. We offer their stories not as prescriptions, but as illustrations of interesting research paths taken and research done competently, and to underscore the plurality that exists in the field about what constitutes scientific knowledge, its undertaking, and its assessment.

On a more pragmatic level, whether one is doing programmatic research or not, there are some basic issues to address, such as how one manages one's research efforts and how one gets the products published. Some interesting insights are reported in these chapters. (The reader will find ideas on these two questions scattered across many of the other chapters in the book as well.) Ashford discusses the importance of keeping several projects going simultaneously, especially for individuals who are still establishing their careers. While acknowledging the legitimacy and potential value of pursuing a single-project strategy, she warns that it can become "the Waterloo of younger faculty members. If your single product is not accepted at the journals, you don't have much to fall back on" (p. 122). She provides tips on the use of time, including making appointments with oneself to protect and harness research time, and deals with the tensions between research and teaching roles:

It occurs to me that for half of our job we are really novelists (the research, writing,

and publishing parts) and for half we are talk-show hosts (the teaching and executive teaching parts). I try to identify to myself which part I am playing . . . and am careful about bringing the rules of one into the arena of the other. (p. 123)

Ashford also describes some of her preferred strategies and behaviors when she is in her novelist role: "A novelist doesn't need to go to an office (in fact, that might be the worst place for her to work); she doesn't need to work 9:00 to 5:00, and she doesn't need to dress up" (p. 123).

Getting published is clearly a crucial part of the research process. It brings one's work to a public forum, where it can be evaluated and where it can have potential influence. There is no surefire, best way to get one's work published. What it takes to have work accepted in a top-ranked journal differs somewhat from what may be required for other journals, and the publishing process for books is different again. Nevertheless, there are some useful lessons about journal publication that one can take from the comments of Murphy, Murnighan, and Ashford.

Kevin Murphy suggests that many of us publish because we want to influence others and to be "players" of note in our particular academic communities (note the quote from his chapter at the beginning of this introduction). He brings into focus several strategic questions that can influence an author's decision to publish: "Why should you publish? Where should you publish? What should you publish?" (p. 129). He astutely identifies the gaps between good research and good publication and provides suggestions for dealing with such shortcomings. He explicitly encourages persistence in efforts to get published: "Knowing that the publication process is fraught with uncertainty, I have learned to be persistent and active. The only way I know to publish a lot is to submit a lot, and to hang in there with papers that I think are really good" (p. 132).

Murnighan discusses the publishing process mainly through the lens of an editor. He acknowledges the strong emotions that authors feel when their manuscripts are rejected, and he stresses the value of an informed dialogue between editor and author that can significantly improve the quality of a paper and its chances of being accepted. He provides an example of such a dialogue and then notes:

> The extended interchange depicted above was incredibly important—for the paper, for the authors, and for me as an editor. . . . We [the editors of *Administrative Science Quarterly*] don't want any misunderstandings about what we are looking for; we want to share a vision for the paper with the authors. If we can agree on how a paper can be improved, then it's likely to become a much better paper, which is something we all are hoping for. (p. 140)

Ashford, as an author, discusses receiving feedback from journal editors and reviewers. Her strategies for approaching reviews of her work reflect her sensitivity to the importance of timing, place, attitude, and response. She notes, "I always read my reviews in a secluded place (not my office). . . . I tell myself that the feedback that I am about to receive is about my *work*, not about me" (p. 124). She goes on, "Shortly after I get the reviews, whether

the decision is a revise and resubmit or a reject, I break each review up into specific points. I then create a setup for responding" (p. 125).

Doing research is a complex process. It involves a great deal of passion *and* persistence. We need to develop and use our own voices as researchers to harness the creativity, experiences, and rhythms that inform and excite our intellects. Our work can be shared with others when we bring sufficient instrumentality to it to ensure that it is completed and that we get the products into the publication process. Our research capabilities are likely to endure and flourish when we pay attention to renewing our skills and our knowledge base, as Arthur Bedeian and other contributors to this book recommend. We will also continue to grow as scholars by being open to disconfirmation of our ideas, as Locke and Ashford suggest; by being attentive to our audiences of editors, reviewers, and authors, as Murphy points out; and, as Alvesson argues, by thinking critically about our subject matter and about our field. We need to manage our research wisely, and we need to encourage our institutions to support it.

References

Cummings, L. L., & Frost, P. J. (Eds.). (1995). *Publishing in the organizational sciences* (2nd ed.). Thousand Oaks, CA: Sage.

Frost, P. J., & Stablein, R. (Eds.). (1992). *Doing exemplary research*. Newbury Park, CA: Sage.

10 Using Programmatic Research to Build a Grounded Theory

Edwin A. Locke

We are constantly told in the social sciences that we should build theories, that there is nothing as practical as a good theory, and that data without theory have little or no utility. I would agree with this for the simple reason that no one could retain or integrate thousands of disconnected facts divorced from some wider set of principles or theoretical framework. The unanswered question for most aspiring theorists, however, is, *How* do you build a theory?

A common procedure is to invent a theory a priori based on one or more of the following: a small, preliminary data set from which grandiose deductions are made, guesswork, hunches, arbitrary hypotheses, intuition, qualitative observations, and deductions from other, marginally related, theories. Inventors of such theories may then spend the rest of their careers (a) defending their premature speculations to the death or (b) alternating between defending their speculations and scrambling to make post hoc revisions of the theory when additional evidence contradicts it (often accompanied by post hoc reinterpretations of the contradictory studies).

I do not think this is a very good way to build a theory; I never have thought so. It's too deductive and results in an excessive focus on "defending territory" rather than looking at the facts. I followed a different approach in constructing goal-setting theory. I did it with full realization of the limitations of the conventional approach, but without knowing what to call what I was doing. I later realized that I was using the "grounded theory" approach described by Glaser and Strauss (1967; see also Locke, 1991). The grounded theory approach is inductive: Theory emerges from the data rather than being deduced or guessed at in advance.

The grounded theory approach implies that it takes a long time to build a theory, because a great many data have to be collected first. Central to the process of theory building, I believe, are seven key tasks:

1. Definition of the core concept(s)

99

2. Validation of the main theoretical ideas and/or measurements

3. Replication by other investigators

4. Documentation of the generality of the results (e.g., across settings, tasks, and subjects)

5. Identification of boundary conditions for the theory (boundary conditions are, in fact, the same as moderator variables)

6. Identification of causal mechanisms

7. Conceptual integration with other theories, especially in cases where those theories might seem to conflict with or compete with one's own

One might ask, *Why* are these the key tasks? My answer is that to build a theory, you have to know what it is you are talking about (task 1), provide evidence for it (tasks 2-6), and integrate it with other relevant theories (e.g., to resolve contradictions; task 7). The bulk of the work in theory building involves gathering evidence.

I know of no readings in the theory-building literature (most of which have been written by people who have never built a theory or studied, in depth, the procedures of those who have) that identify the activities that constitute the essence of theory building, indicate how these activities are to be carried out, or specify the order in which the various tasks are to be done. I cannot answer the second and third points even today. Goal-setting theory, I would have to say, was built piecemeal, without a grand plan. Every study, I believe, had a specific purpose, and these purposes built upon previous work, but there was no grand design involved, no overall blueprint. This was simply because no one really knew how to go about building a theory.

On the other hand, I was implicitly aware of the need to address in some fashion the various theory-building tasks. These tasks were accomplished by Latham and me and by many others over a 25-year period.

Key Tasks

The Core Concept

Let me state right away that I no longer use the term *construct,* and I discourage doctoral students from using it.[1] The reason is that the

term *construct* is a Kantian idea. Kant has been called the "great destroyer" in the history of philosophy. This is true in two respects: epistemology and ethics (Peikoff, 1982). I will focus here on epistemology. Kant was the first philosopher to declare that the real (noumenal) world is unknowable and that we can be aware only of the phenomenal world, the world of appearances. The world of appearances, he argued, is a creation of the human mind, a set of constructs if you will, that do not give us any knowledge of things in themselves. Thus Kant totally severed reason from reality (his motive for destroying reason was to make room for Christian faith). Social scientists, unfortunately, have uncritically accepted the idea that their terms are arbitrary inventions of the human mind, or *hypothetical constructs,* to be "validated" by correlating measures of them with measures of other hypothetical constructs! It is not clear how this could ever work if all terms and/or measurements are arbitrary.

The proper term to use in place of *construct* is *concept,* which may be defined as "a mental integration of two or more units which are isolated according to specific characteristic(s) and united by a specific definition" (Rand, 1990, p. 10). A valid or objective concept is not an arbitrary invention but an integration material provided by the senses or derived from such material. In psychology, the units of relevance are conscious experiences and thus are validated by introspection.

I first got the idea of using goals as a motivational concept from one of the faculty at Cornell, T. A. Ryan, who was writing a book on intentions, and from the work of C. A. Mace, a British psychologist whose work on goal setting Art Ryan and Pat Smith had cited in their classic 1954 textbook *Principles of Industrial Psychology.*

The *concept* of goal, however, is *validated* by observing that we have ends that we desire to attain and that these guide our choices and actions. (Later we observe that not all goals are consciously directed—that is, not all are purposes; some goal-directed activity occurs automatically and is inferred from its life-preserving consequences. See Binswanger, 1990.) No further validation of the concept of goal (or of any other concept) is necessary beyond identifying the observed facts that gave rise to the concept and integrating those facts into a coherent definition.

How to *measure* the content of the goals of particular individuals in particular contexts is a different and separate matter. The simplest way is just to ask people what their goals are; for many purposes such questions yield valid and useful answers. A related question is how to ask the question. For example, Mento, Locke, and Klein (1992) found that the most useful way to measure an individual's personal goal on a task is to ask what *minimum* level of performance he or she is trying for.

Another question is how to obtain variation in goals. A simple way is to persuade people, for the purposes of an experiment, to pursue different kinds and levels of goals (i.e., goal assignment).

Observe that there is *no* attempt here to "triangulate the construct" of goal through multiple measures, although there is nothing wrong with trying different measures to see what works (Mento et al., 1992). But the concept must be defined first. Then ways are found to measure it that are consistent with the definition and appropriate to the proposed context. (For example, asking a person to report his or her personal goals might not yield accurate information if the individual has poor self-insight or if telling the truth will result in punishment.)

Core Evidence

To support a theory, you need at least some initial evidence. The key problem here is, What constitutes evidence? For example, Freud claimed to validate his ideas based on clinical experience, but much of what he claimed was evidence could have been interpreted in other ways, as many critics of Freud have pointed out. Experimental evidence is especially helpful, because well-designed experiments can rule out alternative explanations. Some phenomena in the sciences, of course, are beyond controlled experimentation (e.g., astronomy, history, most of economics), but, fortunately, goal setting can be studied in the laboratory.

For my dissertation I did several laboratory studies of goal setting and they all worked, so I decided to keep at it. I took my first job, in 1964, at the American Institutes for Research (AIR) in Washington, D.C., then under the direction of Ed Fleishman. Ed suggested that I might get funding from the Office of Naval Research (ONR), which I did. I hired Judy Bryan as my research assistant.

We conducted a series of additional goal-setting studies, and they too were successful. We compared "do best" goals with specific, difficult goals and hard goals with medium and easy goals. We used a variety of different tasks (brainstorming, addition, and others) and experimental designs, including one where we took naturally low-performing subjects and improved their performance through the setting of specific goals. After a couple of years, ONR cut us off, because, as I was told confidentially, our studies had come out so well that ONR did not have to justify its past support with further support, as in the case of other contracts! There is nothing like being punished for success.

However, I obtained another grant to study goal setting in relation to feedback. The idea for this work also came from C. A. Mace. He had suggested that goals and intentions might mediate the effects of other incentives on performance. We conducted a series of studies that showed (a) when goal setting was controlled, there was no effect of knowledge of score-type feedback on performance; (b) feedback often led to spontaneous goal setting and thence to performance effects; but (c) when goal setting was statistically controlled, the feedback effect was vitiated. In sum, the feedback effect on motivation was mediated by goal setting (for a summary of this work, see Locke & Latham, 1990, chap. 8).

Just before I left AIR, I completed a paper (later to become a "Citation Classic")[2] titled "Toward a Theory of Task Motivation and Incentives" (Locke, 1968). It summarized the results of about a dozen of our goal-setting studies plus other relevant studies in the literature. I remember specifically *not* wanting to call it a theory and being questioned by a number of people as to why. At this point I had not read any literature on theory building, but my caution was based in part on the philosophy of Objectivism (Rand, 1990), which argues that knowledge comes from reason applied to experience—which implies that theories should be tied to reality, that is, based on actual knowledge rather than speculation.

Replication

In medicine and biology replication across laboratories is considered to be very important, because research procedures in these fields are highly complex, and sometimes idiosyncratic elements of procedure can affect outcomes. The same principle holds for social science research, even though research procedures here may be less technically complex.

Replication of goal-setting results began, I assume, when people read about our results in the journals. When I was a doctoral student, everyone was trying to test Herzberg's theory, and expectancy theory was just starting to create a stir in industrial and organizational psychology (Vroom, 1964). I believe that the most obvious reason people keep doing research in a given area is that previous research has yielded positive results. When a long series of studies come out with negative or questionable results, people begin to lose interest. Goal-setting studies typically came out well, thus encouraging further work.

However, there is another factor involved in the spread of research on a given topic that, for want of a better term, I will call *theoretical growth*. If a theory remains focused around one narrow topic or subtopic, people get bored because they find nowhere new to go with it. I constantly tried to help keep goal-setting research going in new directions (see below). The result is that the more new directions you go in, the more additional directions other people think of (e.g., goals and self-efficacy, group goals, goals and leadership, goals and intrinsic motivation, goals and personality). In the end, there are literally hundreds of possible studies to do that nobody else has thought of doing.

A final factor that I think helped the growth of goal-setting research was my attitude toward young researchers. I always tried to be encouraging to such people (except in those few cases where they claimed to have invented goal theory themselves or were too arrogant to take good advice). This has involved such actions as commenting on past research, making suggestions on how to analyze and present results, and offering commentary on the design of future studies (including dissertations). Even when negative results were obtained, I tried to figure out the possible reasons and suggested ways that the hypotheses could be verified or the errors eliminated in future studies. Typically these researchers were grateful for the interest and open to suggestions, which led to additional goal-setting studies and additional discoveries.

Generalization

Generalization involves induction. Philosophers of science have not yet discovered all of the factors that would have to be considered to make valid generalizations from one set of results to other settings and situations. Obviously, the notion of similarity is relevant, but similarity in what? In every detail or just essentials (Locke, 1986)? And what is essential in an experimental situation? In psychology we are concerned with differences in subjects, settings, and tasks, among other things. If a phenomenon comes out with many types of subjects, in many different settings, and with many types of tasks, we usually have more confidence in the generalizability of the results than if it works only in more limited circumstances. Goal-setting studies have been conducted with more than 40,000 subjects in seven countries, in both laboratory and field settings, and with at least 88 different tasks (Locke & Latham, 1990, chap. 2).

I think that I worried most during the early years about settings. I especially wondered about the difference between laboratory and field settings. Enter Gary Latham. At the same time I was doing my early lab studies, he was doing research in lumber companies and was obtaining results similar to mine, although at first he did not know about my work. I was very gratified when, in field study after field study, he obtained significant goal-setting effects. He played a significant role in making my work believable. He also did the bulk of the early research on assigned versus participatively set goals. I had no particular personal interest in this topic, but both of us, imbued with the zeitgeist of the 1960s, assumed that participatively set goals would lead to higher commitment than would assigned goals. We were both surprised when this was not found. But this added to the generalizability of goal-setting results, because we later realized that there are many ways to get people committed, one of which is visionary leadership (Locke & Associates, 1991). I was less worried about generalizability across tasks because, in logic, there did not seem to be any reason goal setting would fail to work on any task or outcome. However, it did occur to me that simply having a goal or full commitment to a goal was no guarantee that one would reach it; one's desires do not *automatically* lead to successful action. There were two issues involved here, although it look me years to grasp them fully: The first was knowledge and ability, and the second was volition (see Binswanger, 1991; Locke & Latham, 1990, chap. 1).

Generalizability across subjects did not concern me very much either, because I considered conscious goal-directedness to be a fundamental attribute of all human action (Locke, 1969), regardless of culture. At a deeper level, goal-directedness is an attribute of the activities of all living organisms, including those that are not conscious (Binswanger, 1990). The goal-setting work in other countries got done simply because researchers in those countries became interested in the topic (e.g., Gary Latham in Canada, Bob Wood in Australia, Miriam Erez in Israel, Uwe Kleinbeck in Germany, C. A. Mace and, just recently, Ivan Robertson, in England).

Boundary Conditions

Boundary conditions for a theory are the conditions that specify when it will work and when it will not. Conceptually, they fulfill the same theoretical function and are really the same idea as moderator variables. Erez (1977) identified one important boundary condition I had overlooked, feedback. I had been so focused on goals as a *mediator* of feedback, I had neglected to pursue the idea of feedback as a *moderator* of goals. I had identified goal commitment as important in 1968, but little was done to measure it for many years—probably because commitment was so easy to get in laboratory settings due to the authority of the experimenter and the fact that it was a volunteer subject population. However, a number of more recent studies by Hollenbeck and others have shown that commitment is often significantly associated with performance for subjects with difficult goals, because these subjects are more tempted to set personal goals that are lower than their assigned goals (Locke & Latham, 1990, chap. 6).

A third moderator, which I had suspected for some time, was task difficulty or complexity (Wood, Mento, & Locke, 1987). I reasoned that on complex tasks there are many alternative methods of pursuing the goal—that is, many possible task strategies—many of which will not work. Thus establishing the proper link between goals and goal-relevant outcomes, which means identifying correct strategies, is problematic. The chances of error will be greater on complex tasks than on simple tasks, where the correct path to the goal is more obvious. Thus, as expected, Wood, Mento, and I found a smaller effect size for goals on complex tasks than on simple tasks. There are other moderators, such as ability and situational constraints, but these have been less extensively studied than those mentioned above.

One unique aspect of our 1990 book, which no reviewer ever pointed out, is the analysis of *every* negative goal-setting study that we knew about. The reason we included this analysis was the *law of contradiction*: A theory cannot be both true and not true at the same time and in the same respect. Thus a negative result must mean either (a) that the theory, as stated, is wrong and needs modification (e.g., the formulation of an additional boundary condition) or (b) that the theory was not tested properly. Thus we attempted to identify the probable cause(s) of every negative result. Some of these analyses had to be a bit speculative, owing to the post hoc nature of the interpretations. One of the more intriguing propositions we offered (which was never taken up by anyone) was that certain personal traits, such as persistence, might operate motivationally as "goal equivalents" in that they may motivate a person to perform highly in the absence of explicit goals (Locke & Latham, 1990, chap. 2).

Causal Mechanisms

It has always puzzled me how little attention is paid in the theory literature to the need to explain the mechanism(s) by which independent variables affect dependent variables. The issue is especially important in the social sciences, because these mechanisms or mediators always involve some internal ones (namely, beliefs, values, expectations, knowledge). Behaviorism, despite being irrational on the face of it (Locke, 1980), was able to create the illusion of explaining human action only because nobody bothered, until Dulany asked it in 1968, to ask the question, By what means do so-called reinforcers reinforce? I consider mediation studies to be among the most important types of studies done in the psychological sciences, although not many people seem to agree with me. The three core causal mechanisms for goals were, in a certain respect, self-evident, because they could be identified through introspection—effort, persistence, and the direction of action and attention. Empirical studies of these mechanisms turned out to be surprisingly difficult due to the need to make fine, internal, micromeasurements of subjective and partly automatic experiences or functions (e.g., effort), but, over the years, relevant experimental studies were forthcoming (see Gellatly & Meyer, 1992; Locke & Latham, 1990, chap. 4).

More complicated to understand is the effect of the fourth type of goal mediator, task strategies. Even on simple tasks, more than one strategy can be used to pursue the goal. As noted earlier, on complex tasks there are many more possibilities, and thus goal effects are less reliable (Wood et al., 1987). Furthermore, although many strategies may fail entirely, others may work, but with different degrees of speed and efficiency. The realm of task strategies implicitly connects the goal-setting realm to three other research realms: problem solving, decision making, and group dynamics. Actually, more than three could be listed (e.g., I could add cognitive psychology, leadership, training, and more). I am sure the reader can now see that if you think of *all* the implications of a given line of work, eventually everything connects to everything else.

Thus it is a genuine challenge to understand what types of goals lead to the best choice of strategies on what tasks and the processes that lead to the different strategy choices. These problems alone could occupy many researchers for a lifetime. The existence of groups adds another layer of complexity, because group members communicate and work with one another, which means that the ideas, abilities, and motivations of each person can affect those of other people. Such complexity, of course, also adds to the fun and challenge of goal research.

Conceptual Integrations

Just as individual findings cannot contradict a valid theory without the theory being modified or the findings invalidated, a valid theory cannot contradict another theory without at least one of the theories requiring modification

or clarification. The most glaring contradiction from the beginning seemed to be between goal theory and expectancy theory, in that one claimed to find a positive association between performance and goal difficulty (which was inversely related to probability of success) and the other claimed to find a positive association between performance and probability or expectancy of success. In this case, it turned out that both theories were correct and that the contradiction was only apparent. When the level or difficulty of the goal was controlled, probability of success was found to be positively associated with performance; the same was found for self-efficacy (Locke, Motowidlo, & Bobko, 1986).

Another apparent contradiction was between "human relations" theory in the form of the findings of Erez and her colleagues regarding the positive benefits of participation in goal setting and those of Latham and his colleagues, which showed a null effect of participation. In this case the apparent contradiction turned out to be caused by different experimental procedures used by the two camps. The solution to this riddle turned out to be fascinating and involved a unique scientific collaboration between the opposing researchers moderated by myself (Latham, Erez, & Locke, 1988).

On the other side of this coin, goal theory and social cognitive theory fit together from the beginning like hand and glove. Bandura's theory is very broad in scope and pertains to an impressive array of situations, from sex to cultural innovation to task performance (see, e.g., Bandura, 1986; Bandura & Cervone, 1986). In contrast, goal-setting theory is narrow in scope (pertaining to performance in work and, to an extent, sports tasks), but the theories intersect in the realm of task performance. Two concepts of social-cognitive theory are especially relevant to goal setting: role modeling and self-efficacy. Role modeling can affect both goal choice and goal commitment (Locke & Latham, 1990). Self-efficacy has a main effect on performance and affects choice of personal goals, goal commitment, and the quality of chosen task strategies (Locke & Latham, 1990, chaps. 3-4). Further, self-efficacy helps to mediate the effects of feedback on subsequent performance (Locke & Latham, 1990, chap. 8).

The reader will note that I have said nothing about integrating goal theory with control theory. I have made it clear elsewhere that I do not regard control theory as a valid theory (Locke

& Latham, 1990). It is not a grounded theory; it has no database at all. As a model, it is based on a misleading machine metaphor (Binswanger, 1991). Piled on top of this metaphor is a random conglomeration of propositions, all borrowed from other theories (Locke, 1991). In my opinion, control theory is everything a theory should not be.

Goal-setting theory was also integrated with satisfaction theory (Locke, 1976) by showing that goals serve as value standards for appraising the adequacy of one's task performance. Outcomes below one's minimal goal level are judged to be unsatisfactory. Outcomes that exceed the minimum goal level are appraised as increasingly satisfactory (Mento et al., 1992). By adding in causal attributions made for performance, goal theory also can be connected to attribution theory. The satisfaction research led to an interesting paradox, which reflects back on expectancy theory. Hard goals lead to higher performance than easy goals because more is required for one to be minimally satisfied with one's performance when goals are high. Thus anticipated satisfaction, which is the recommended measure of the concept of valence in expectancy theory, is negatively associated with performance, but only when goals differ across individuals. As in the case of expectancies, when goal level is controlled, anticipated satisfaction is positively associated with goal choice and performance (Klein, 1991). Instrumentality is also positively associated with performance.

There are other studies now ongoing that will connect goal-setting theories and other theories. For example, there are studies showing that goals and self-efficacy mediate or form a link in a causal chain leading to performance from money incentives, job responsibility, personality, and charismatic leadership.

Conclusion

I hope it is now evident why genuine theory building (as opposed to making up guesses, putting them in boxes, and connecting them with arrows) is a gradual, slow, and painstaking process. There are many tasks to be performed, and each one can take years—none is ever really finished because new knowledge is continually being discovered and thus new integrations must continually be made. I personally doubt that true theories can be built in any other way. For example, could a valid theory of cancer be built in any way other than incrementally—by conducting hundreds of thousands of studies and piecing them together into a coherent whole?

I believe that one requirement of successful theory building (even if it is a theory within a theory, e.g., a theory of goal commitment) is that one stay in the same research area for many years. The reason is that grounded theories are built on data, and it takes a long time to accumulate data. It is unfortunate that few researchers seem to have the interest or tenacity to stick to one area. Fewer still may have the stomach to tolerate the journal review process, which I believe is becoming increasingly onerous (and lower in quality). I hope that I have at least suggested the specific processes that are required for building a viable theory and perhaps have even inspired others to follow the same steps. It has been a fascinating process for me and I have enjoyed doing it, even though I was not exactly sure where it was all going until about 1988, when Gary Latham and I decided: Now there seem to be enough data actually to build theory; let's do it.

One might ask how one can ensure that a theory will be built at all without a grand plan. The answer is that one cannot. But there are steps one can take that will facilitate the process. Most important, I believe that a theory needs a *champion*.[3] The champion's main tasks are to articulate the basic idea or concept, to conduct preliminary and ongoing research, to inspire others (by example and personal contact), to do relevant research in order to replicate and extend the findings, and, finally, when there are sufficient data, to formulate the actual theory. If enough people with a variety of perspectives get interested, the key tasks of theory building eventually get done. Theoretical "holes" get identified and filled in. Integrations with other theories get made.

In the case of goal-setting theory there were cochampions: myself and Gary Latham. This worked out very nicely, because I was more at home in the laboratory and Gary was very skilled at field research, and each of us inspired others like us. Would things have worked out differently if either Gary or I had not been around? Of course. Does this mean that there is an element of chance in theory building? Not in the sense of *uncaused*; only in the sense of *not predetermined*. Research is partly a matter of personal interest and creative ability, but it is also a matter of volitionally directed thinking and the choice to act on that thinking (Binswanger, 1991). Because people have many options in what they study, one cannot know in advance the direction that a given field will take.

In closing, I would like to stress that I believe the *mental frame* of the theory champion is critical to the success of theory building. If a champion takes the role of *theory defender*, the tendency will be to attack the authors of disconfirming studies and theoretical critics rather than to learn from them. As a result, the theory may stultify. In contrast, if a champion takes the role of *theory builder*, new (relevant) discoveries and insights will be welcomed, and the theory will grow and develop. (Theory defending, of course, is appropriate when a theory has been clearly misrepresented.)

Notes

1. Constructs are sometimes called *social constructs*, and it is often asserted that people engage in the *social construction of reality*. I can think of no more epistemologically debilitating idea than that reality is socially constructed. It implies that instead of focusing on reality (evidence and facts) to discover knowledge and build theories, one should focus on the consciousness of other people. But if your own mind cannot perceive reality, how can the minds of other people do it? And if reality is really constructed, rather than perceived, by people's minds, then why not just make up anything you want, call a group together, get a consensus, and declare it real?

2. This means it was cited 400 or more times.

3. I would like to thank Peter Frost for guiding me to the idea of a theory champion.

References

Bandura, A. (1986). *Social foundations of thought and action: A social-cognitive theory.* Englewood Cliffs, NJ: Prentice Hall.

Bandura, A., & Cervone, D. (1986). Differential engagement of self-reactive influences in cognitive motivation. *Organizational Behavior and Human Decision Processes, 38,* 92-113.

Binswanger, H. (1990). *The biological basis of teleological concepts.* Los Angeles: Ayn Rand Institute Press.

Binswanger, H. (1991). Volition as cognitive self-regulation. *Organizational Behavior and Human Decision Processes, 50,* 154-178.

Dulany, D. E., Jr. (1968). Awareness, rules and propositional control: A confrontation with S-R behavior theory. In D.

Horton & T. Dixon (Eds.), *Verbal behavior and general behavior theory.* New York: Prentice Hall.

Erez, M. (1977). Feedback: A necessary condition for the goal setting-performance relationship. *Journal of Applied Psychology, 62,* 624-627.

Gellatly, I. R., & Meyer, J. P. (1992). The effects of goal difficulty on physiological arousal, cognition and task performance. *Journal of Applied Psychology, 77,* 694-704.

Glaser, B. G., & Strauss, A. L. (1967). *The discovery of grounded theory: Strategies for qualitative research.* Chicago: Aldine.

Klein, H. J. (1991). Further evidence on the relationship between goal setting and expectancy theories. *Organizational Behavior and Human Decision Processes, 49,* 230-257.

Latham, G. P., Erez, M., & Locke, E. A. (1988). Resolving scientific disputes by the joint design of crucial experiments by the antagonists: Application to the Erez-Latham dispute regarding participation in goal setting [Monograph]. *Journal of Applied Psychology, 73,* 753-772.

Locke, E. A. (1968). Toward a theory of task motivation and incentives. *Organizational Behavior and Human Performance, 3,* 157-189.

Locke, E. A. (1969). Purpose without consciousness: A contradiction. *Psychological Reports, 25,* 991-1009.

Locke, E. A. (1976). The nature and causes of job satisfaction. In M. D. Dunnette (Ed.), *Handbook of industrial and organizational psychology.* Chicago: Rand McNally.

Locke, E. A. (1980). Behaviorism and psychoanalysis: Two sides of the same coin. *Objectivist, 1*(1), 10-15.

Locke, E. A. (1986). *Generalizing from laboratory to field settings.* Lexington, MA: Lexington.

Locke, E. A. (1991). Goal theory vs. control theory: Contrasting approaches to understanding work motivation. *Motivation and Emotion, 15,* 9-28.

Locke, E. A., & Associates. (1981). *The essence of leadership.* New York: Lexington.

Locke, E. A., & Latham, G. B. (1990). *A theory of goal setting and task performance.* Englewood Cliffs, NJ: Prentice Hall.

Locke, E. A., Motowidlo, S. J., & Bobko, P. (1986). Using self-efficacy theory to resolve the conflict between goal setting theory and expectancy theory in organizational behavior and industrial-organizational psychology. *Journal of Social and Clinical Psychology, 4,* 323-338.

Mento, A. J., Locke, E. A., & Klein, H. J. (1992). Relationship of goal level to valence and instrumentality. *Journal of Applied Psychology, 77,* 395-405.

Peikoff, L. (1982). *The ominous parallels.* New York: Stein & Day.

Peikoff, L. (1992). *Objectivism: The philosophy of Ayn Rand.* New York: Dutton-New American Library.

Rand, A. (1990). *Introduction to objectivist epistemology* (2nd ed.). New York: New American Library.

Vroom, V. (1964). *Work and motivation.* New York: John Wiley.

Wood, R. E., Mento, A. J., & Locke, E. A. (1987). Task complexity as a moderator of goal effects: A meta-analysis. *Journal of Applied Psychology, 72,* 416-425.

11 Developing Programmatic Research

Mats Alvesson

Life After the Dissertation

I completed my dissertation, *Organization Theory and Technocratic Consciousness,* in 1983. As the title indicates, it did not pass without problems and resistance. My major source of inspiration (the critical theory of the Frankfurt school) represents an intellectual tradition well outside the mainstream of academia, especially with regard to disciplines such as business administration and applied psychology. It was during my time spent as a PhD student at the University of Lund in southern Sweden that I became associated with both, owing to my wish to reduce dependence and minimize constraints regarding intellectual space.

The idea of maximizing autonomy from social domination (perhaps an illusory project, at least according to current postmodernist fashion, although this does not prevent it from being an inspiring and constructive idea) is also the governing idea of the Frankfurt school—knowledge in social science is or rather should be a matter of facilitating emancipation from socially unnecessary constraints.

When I, as a student and PhD candidate, came across the writings of critical theory, I felt

(a) that my intuitive understanding of society and people in terms of rationality, autonomy, and consciousness was clarified and raised to a higher intellectual level; and (b) that large parts of education and research in management and organization studies draw upon and produce a technocratic consciousness—for example, a narrow focus on optimizing means while basic political and ethical issues are taken for granted and unreflectively reproduced. The ideological nature and functions of management and organization theory—as taught in most business schools and management departments, not only in the United States but also in Europe—are strong. I felt fooled by and a bit angry toward the education I had gone through, but used the energy productively in my dissertation project.

The dissertation passed—and almost my academic career as well. I had a great deal of difficulty in finding employment for some time. I received a minor research grant, taught in Finland for a term, in Canada for another, and then came back to Sweden and obtained a position as an assistant professor. This was in 1985. Around the same time, I began to take an interest in organizational culture, mainly because everybody else seemed to be talking about culture, which caused me to become curious. I approached the field with the deepest suspicion—an attitude cultivated by all the readings of Horkheimer, Adorno, Fromm, Marcuse, and Habermas and other critically minded researchers (e.g., Habermas, 1984; Horkheimer & Adorno, 1947/1979). My first writings expressed skepticism toward this field and tried to account for its enormous and rapid popularity in the beginning of the 1980s. Some reviewers expressed an even more profound skepticism against my accounts—one person actually became very upset and called one paper "rubbish." But I also received some positive feedback, and I eventually began to publish a series of conceptual papers on organizational culture.

I then wrote a book with P. O. Berg, a Swedish pioneer in the field of organizational culture. At first our idea was to write an overview paper for a reader. The reader never materialized, and our overview paper soon became rather long, and we then felt that the best solution was to produce a short book. It appeared in Swedish in 1988 and in an extended and revised version in English 4 years later (Alvesson & Berg, 1992). P.O. is my complete opposite in a number of ways. He had enthusiastically started to work with organizational symbolism around 1980, but had begun to feel slightly tired of organizational culture toward the end of the 1980s. I was more critical, but felt increasingly positive toward organizational culture research as the years passed. I was—and am—skeptical about a lot of it, but also acknowledged that there was some good work and potential in anthropological approaches to organizations. Our different sentiments and trajectories with respect to organizational culture and styles mixed, and we produced the book, an advanced state-of-the-art piece. In the book we discuss the development and popularity of organizational culture as a field of academic interest and provide a theoretical overview in terms of object levels, cultural phenomena, and conventions and perspectives in the research field. We also discuss practical applications—symbolic management—and cover current debates, including the omnipotence syndrome, romanticism, manipulation tendencies, and symbolic pollution in the use of the culture concept in theory and practice. A final chapter addresses postmodernism and its implications for organizational culture studies.

I began to feel that it was about time I conducted an empirical study of my own, having worked conceptually with organizational culture and having criticized large parts of the research for various things (lack of reflection, blending culture and ideology, assuming that organizations are unitary and unique, naive promanagement bias, overconsumption of cultural concepts, and so on; see Alvesson, 1993b). Social pressures facilitated the decision: Empirical work is almost obligatory in Swedish business administration and organization theory. I had, prior to that time, conducted only moderate empirical work within a narrow sector (psychiatric hospitals). Reluctantly, I decided to do a case study within the field of organization studies in Sweden. Empirical work usually means case study based on qualitative method. Glaser and Strauss's (1967) notion of grounded theory is referred to, and this provides a certain level of legitimation. Typically there is little sympathy for hard-boiled quantitative studies: "Boring," "abstract," "no real understanding," "always explains 20% of the variance," "narrow," and "ritualistic" are some examples of the pejorative remarks that I have heard. A qualitative case study is therefore not very original in a Swedish context. Despite my inclination to depart from the mainstream—an inclination that seems to decline with age, at least in my case—I followed the qualitative case study route.

Initially, I was not interested in spending much time with this study, as I was not very keen on empirical work. But at the same time, cultural research calls for closeness to the subject of study, and therefore I could not escape doing a considerable amount of empirical work. I was interested in deep access and closeness to the subject, which meant that I preferred to study an open-minded company. (Swedish companies are often open-minded, which means that it is not very difficult to get good access. Sometimes when we explain the differences between U.S. and Swedish organization studies, we point to the fact that we have better options for conducting deep-level studies.) A colleague who had seen something on television about a computer consultancy company suggested that it could probably offer rapid access. This proved to be the case, and I was able to do a case study of this company, which turned out to be a kind of "in search of excellence" company, at least as far as the market for its services continued to grow: rapid corporate growth, high profits, low personnel turnover, excellent client evaluations, reputation for innovativeness and creativity.

I conducted the empirical work in 1987 and 1988. I did interviews, had informal conversations, observed particular events, and analyzed artifacts (buildings, interiors). I participated, for example, in the company's week-long introductory course on Rhodes, Greece. The project was more interesting to do than I had expected. It was particularly interesting to interpret the data and write about the findings, especially as more ideas began to form. I decided to cover a wide spectrum of the dimensions of the company and, based on a combination of the case and more general analysis, to say something of broader relevance on themes such as socialization, organizational structure, leadership, service marketing, and strategy in adhocracies. The cultural perspective informed my work, but I also discussed and used many other management theories of a more conventional type. I finally published a 400-page volume titled *Management of Knowledge-Intensive Companies* in 1989 (in Swedish; revised version in English, Alvesson, 1995). The title appeared to be well chosen, as the book sold surprisingly well, even though it was written as a research monograph. I discovered that the cultural perspective—focusing on shared meanings and symbolism—was productive for understanding how organizational structures, leadership processes, team building, and even the business concept (mission statement) worked. A key concept of the study was social-integrative management. In this kind of company, management works by counteracting the fragmentation tendencies involved in this kind of activity: downplaying hierarchy and developing community, facilitating emotions and cohesiveness, making people identify with the workplace, synchronization of meanings and values on work style, social relations, client interaction, and so on.

This book appeared to give me legitimacy in the context of Swedish business administration (as the discipline is called in Sweden). Together with the publication of the English version of my dissertation, which received rather positive reviews, and a couple of other books and a number of journal articles, I became rather well established on the Swedish research scene in this field. I even received a full professorship in

1992, at a relatively young age. (In Sweden, as in the United Kingdom, a professorship means something special. You do not get promoted to it, but apply for an advertised job in open competition. In business administration, only one out of every six to eight faculty members is a professor.)

Developing Programmatic Research

Up until this point in my career (around 1990), it makes little sense to talk about my work in terms of research programs, as my projects were usually conducted without any long-term plans or the intention of achieving consistency among individual projects. By the end of the 1980s, the situation began to change. At the beginning and middle of the 1990s, my rather wide range of research activities could be neatly summarized in terms of the following five research programs:

- Critical theory and management studies (e.g. Alvesson, 1996; Alvesson & Willmott, 1992a, 1996)
- Organizational culture (e.g. Alvesson, 1993b; Alvesson & Berg, 1992)
- Metatheory, interpretation, and reflection in qualitative methodology (e.g. Alvesson, 1993d; Alvesson & Sköldberg, 1996)
- Knowledge-intensive companies (Alvesson, 1993a, 1993c, 1994b, 1995)
- Gender and organizations (Alvesson, 1994a; Billing & Alvesson, 1994)

By *research program* I mean a stream of research pursued without too great intervals between studies. Research programs are regularly activated or deactivated. Almost every year since the beginning of the late 1980s, I have carried out some work within all of the programs. I also have research grants for research within the different areas. Compared to many other ways to conceptualize research programs, mine are basically idea driven rather than data driven. Especially in the area of knowledge-intensive companies, empirical studies are significant, but also here the "data" are seen as ambiguous and open for various kinds of interpretation and reinterpretation, making the idea and inspiration elements of research more crucial than the "data dredging."

I have been and still am very reluctant to sacrifice freedom and flexibility for planned, long-term projects. I feel frustrated by the thought of being forced to work with a particular, clearly defined area for 3 years or so (I will return below to how I have tried to solve this problem). How is it that I have become engaged in these research programs? It is difficult to distinguish between intrinsic motives and external forces. The concept of motives is also very tricky. Even if they should "exist," we may not be able to say anything about them. As Mills (1940) points out, we are caught in the vocabulary of motives of our time. Nevertheless, a few remarks appear rather unproblematic.

Of course, the wish to do a good job (manage one's career, say something socially important) means that a certain persistence is needed. Time pressure also increases over time, in the sense that it is difficult to find time to read as much as was previously the case, when one was a PhD student, an assistant, or a young associate professor. (In Sweden we do not have the "publish or perish" syndrome, which means that people can be more oriented toward long-term payoffs than in the United States. Unfortunately, it also means that people can get away with work that would never pass a peer-reviewing process.) Being "established" for some time usually means that a very large part of one's time is occupied by supervising PhD students, doing reviews for journals and publishers, evaluating research grant applications, doing administrative work, and so on.

Over time, a certain "locking in" takes place as a consequence of the job situation. It becomes important to utilize one's aggregated competence and stick to the research possibilities that are in line with this. In addition, the following social mechanisms have contributed to my loose foci on the five research areas previously mentioned.

Given the slowness of the production and dispersion of work results (texts) in academic life, there is often a considerable time lag between what one does and what people know of one's work and interests. On a couple of occasions, I have received invitations to present (keynote) papers at conferences some years after I have actually worked on the topic that I am asked to address. As stated above, my disserta-

tion, completed in 1983, appeared after revisions and extensions in English in 1987 and led to an invitation to speak at a conference titled "The Frankfurt School: Its Relevance Today" in 1988. I had not worked on critical theory for some years, but the inclination to "social responsiveness" (Asplund, 1987) reactivated my commitment to this line of thought so that I wrote a paper with Hugh Willmott for the conference. The conference paper was too long for an article, so we decided to turn it into a book instead. (This is perhaps an emergent strategy in the Mintzbergian sense: Write a paper that becomes too long and turn it into a book. I have done this on three occasions.) We felt strongly that there was a need for a critical management text, useful to both scholars who are sympathetic to but not experts in the field and students. The idea was to look at the entire field of management studies—from organization theory to strategic management, information systems, accounting, and marketing—from a distinct critical perspective. This project began slowly in 1989. We felt a need for an overview of what was going on, so we decided to publish a reader and invited a dozen scholars from various management subdisciplines to a workshop in Shrewsbury, UK, where Hugh lives. The reader appeared in 1992 (Alvesson & Willmott, 1992a) and the textbook in 1995. Another invitation to speak at a conference titled "European Approaches to Organizational Communication: Critical Perspectives" for a society of communication scholars also reinforced my interest in critical work, as did a call for papers for a special issue of the *Academy of Management Review* on new theories, edited by Linda Smircich, Marta Calás, and Gareth Morgan (Alvesson & Willmott, 1992b). In much of our work we try to develop ideas from critical theory in order to make them more relevant for a management context—for example, perhaps to inspire more reflective organizational practices. We also take seriously the critique of postmodernists against the project of emancipation and the power-knowledge relationship (Foucault, 1980). We therefore developed the concept of "micro emancipation" as an element in critical management theory.

A similar effect of reinforcing an interest to continue or reactivate earlier work was accomplished by two sponsored invitations in 1992 to conferences on professional service organizations (Alberta, Canada) and the knowledge worker in organizations (Lancaster, U.K.). I managed to produce the book as well as some articles and, after having completed my study of the computer consultancy company, I had no specific ideas about continuing with this empirical area. (I was, as I will elaborate on below, engaged in a project concerning advertising agencies and did not think carefully about the links between this and the study of the computer consultancy company.) The invitations had an immediate effect in that I wrote two papers, and also affected my thinking in terms of this field. At least for many people in my position (i.e., not being an international star), such invitations are forceful signals. They trigger specific actions as responses (the production of papers), but also affect one's thinking about what is interesting and about one's own identity. Other people's perceptions influence the self-perception. The combination of the market evaluation (What are others interested in? How do I become appreciated and famous and—above all—cited?), the encouraging signals reinforcing one's self-esteem, and the confirmation/reinforcement of a particular identity, followed by participation in the conference ritual (an identity-constituting event in this profession), contributes to one's locking oneself onto a particular path (or, in my case, one of several different paths). Broadly speaking, people's (positive) reactions to earlier work and offers (conference invitations, contributions to readers, and so on) encourage further work along similar lines.

Another mechanism that made me concentrate my research efforts was the possibility of receiving research grants. Swedish universities have limited resources for research, but there are large national funds for research grants. (These can be used for expenses, for employing research assistants, or for paying oneself in order to lower or even eliminate one's teaching load for one or more years.) I was able to get money for broadly defined projects, in particular, studies of knowledge-intensive companies, organizational cultures, and gender and organizations. One reason to apply for these grants is simply that they are there; it is hard to resist. It is like mimetic rivalry: you want what other people value. Associated with a research grant is the ability to purchase equipment, to travel, to buy books. It is also prestigious to receive a grant, and this is

something that is expected of senior people for the benefit of their departments.

PhD students in particular benefit from faculty members' receiving grants, as this means they may be employed as research assistants with decent salaries. I have during the 1990s kept two or three assistants occupied and well financed. Such support of PhD students is considered to be an important task of senior faculty members in Sweden, especially full professors.

PhD students are sent out to do ethnographic fieldwork. They conduct (most of) the interviews, observations, and so on, and then we analyze the material together and write different parts of the research report (normally a book, e.g., Alvesson & Björkman, 1992; Alvesson & Köping, 1993). The research approach is usually open, the research questions are initially very loose and become clarified and sharpened gradually throughout the research process. As ethnography is a matter of combining closeness and distance, I have found this to be a good model of work. The research assistant stands for closeness, empathy, and empirical detail, and I represent distance, overview, and conceptual abstraction. It is difficult to perceive social reality not as natural, rational, and self-evident but as historical, arbitrary, and exotic—which is crucial in cultural studies (Alvesson, 1993b)—but this perception is facilitated if you have some distance on it. The division of labor is not very strict, as the research assistants also read, think, analyze, and write, and I also do some empirical work. The ethnographic work becomes more efficient compared with that of inexperienced PhD students who conduct the work by themselves with only an ordinary level of supervision, and this method also saves me a lot of time. It is of course important that the research assistant have all the traditional competencies called for in ethnographic work—that is, the ability to tolerate ambiguity, sensitivity to social contexts, an extroverted attitude—but perhaps even more important that he or she be a good writer. These skills are difficult to acquire. Methods courses, familiarity with the theoretical literature, and sharing of experiences with people who are or have been in similar situations may be of assistance. Reading social science literature that is well written and indicates an awareness of detail may also be inspiring and helpful (good examples in organization studies include the work of Kunda, 1992; and Rosen, 1985).

Another factor that accounts for the development of my kind of programmatic research is interpersonal in nature. I like to collaborate with people and have written with colleagues across a broad range of subjects, either because we have had similar theoretical perspectives or because we have found ways of synthesizing rather different orientations. Together with one colleague, Lars Lindkvist, an expert on transaction costs analysis, I wrote a piece on transaction costs and organizational culture in ambiguous, knowledge-intensive work settings, where complexity rules out a strong reliance on market and bureaucracy for surveillance (Alvesson & Lindkvist, 1993). I persuaded my wife, Yvonne Billing, to direct her general interest in gender studies toward work and organization, and it later felt natural—as well as time-efficient—for us to collaborate on a number of writings in that area (e.g. Billing & Alvesson, 1994). My interest in metatheoretical aspects of research and theory—cultivated by critical theory and the sociology of knowledge discussions of organizational culture theory—was reinforced by discussions with Kaj Sköldberg, an organization theorist who is well read in the philosophy of science, about a joint book project (Alvesson & Sköldberg, 1996). Thus a particular interest that would have been too demanding for me to follow up fully on my own, in combination with options for research collaborations, brought about programmatic research in the fields of gender, work and organization, and reflective methodology.

Another significant driving force is related to my interest in critical thinking on a broader social level and my view of knowledge as a potential source of emancipation. Frustration with the preoccupations of the mainstream functionalist and managerial literature, as well as concern about ecological matters and the danger of "corporate colonization" (Deetz, 1992) turning us all into consumers and clients, inspire me to produce a steady flow of critical work. In general, I think it is very important for researchers to reflect upon what knowledge they are developing and why. Such reflection should, in my opinion, go beyond a myopic preoccupation with techniques and hypotheses and subordination to what researchers believe is of interest only for managers. (I am certainly not against developing knowledge for managers. I often lecture for practitioners. However, I think

that management research and education should reflect several viewpoints and interests, including subordinate, gender, consumer, and ecological interests. Researchers should pursue a balance among different cognitive interests.) It appears reasonable to assume that status, being liked and accepted, doing something that reaches an audience, confirming their own social identity, and adapting to the zeitgeist all help to account for what researchers are doing.

Among academics, in general, individuals' interest in their careers seems to be more significant than their interest in contributing to socially important knowledge. Despite academics' frequently espoused values arguing the opposite, I believe that the inclination toward conformity is strong in academic settings. We all tend to be subject to the rules for achieving cultural and/or economic capital. In addition to career and financial motives, the hegemony of 3M (mindless mainstream managerialism) is at least a large part of management and organization studies. Cultural parochialism and the taken-for-granted idea that relevant knowledge is subordinated to the dominance of instrumental rationality (Alvesson, 1993b; Alvesson & Willmott, 1996) play significant roles here. But less conformist motives and driving forces also matter. In my case, this is expressed through suspicion against fashions and cultural parochialism within the field and a wish to combat forms of social domination. Here it is important to avoid self-indulgence. Even though such wishes are often blended with more or less successful efforts to reinforce one's own position within the research field and the strengthening of the wing to which one belongs (Bourdieu, 1979), I still think that elements of individual responsibility and integrity have their place in academic reflection and research practice. The wish to raise alternative, critical voices against the domination of managerialism and its tendency to reinforce the exploitation of nature as well as asymmetrical relations of power in organizations and society has guided much of my work. My frequent frustration with the state of affairs in mainstream management research and education has led me to a steady stream of critical work.

To summarize, the five programs that have characterized, with varying intensity, my research since the end of the 1980s have been influenced by several very different factors: (a) the wish to use developed competence, (b) difficulties in radically departing from the developed lines of work after 10 years in the field, (c) reactions from the environment encouraging me to continue to work in areas in which I had earlier published and thereby obtained a reputation, (d) financial motives associated with the possibility of obtaining research grants for projects in areas where I had shown my competence, (e) the expectation to help PhD students financially and with project experience, (f) the wish to work with colleagues in joint research projects, and (g) my opinion of the character of mainstream management and organization studies and repeated impulses to engage in critical reflection. These factors are to some extent contradictory; there is a complex interplay between conformist impulses and efforts to negate such tendencies. All these factors do not necessarily point in the direction of programmatic research, and in some cases the programs are composed of loosely coupled projects. Nevertheless, there are synergy effects and a sense of direction within each of these programs.

On Multiprogrammatic Research

An important dilemma, at least for me, is the choice between remaining flexible and engaging in a specific long-term project. As noted above, I prefer to have a high degree of discretion and to avoid locking myself into a particular route. The idea of tying my research into a particular planned long-term project is very frustrating, as such a commitment eliminates or reduces my option to be able to engage in new ideas and projects without too many constraints and obligations standing in the way. There are so many interesting research areas, and life is short. As I remarked previously, scholars in Sweden do not have the pressure they have in North America to achieve a high output of journal articles rapidly—something that appears to force many junior faculty members in the United States to work within narrow, safe fields with high and predictable payoffs in terms of publications, often closely related to the dissertation. The Swedish (and, on the whole, European) system provides individuals with somewhat better chances to develop their interests in new directions. By working with a few different programs, it is possible to combine variation

with concentration. Researchers can accomplish variation and flexibility by going back and forth between their different lines of interest. One solution to the dilemma is thus multiprogrammatic research.

I assume that the dilemma between being, on the one hand, exploitative in one's competence and achieving a steady output in terms of annual publication and, on the other hand, developing new areas of research is normally solved through gradual change, in which bridges are created between early fields of interest and new fields. I myself bridged research areas in the following ways. First, I developed a good understanding of critical theory as a PhD student. I used this perspective when I started to look at organizational culture. An advantage here was that whereas organizational culture studies normally look at the functional side of cultures— the good things that culture accomplish—critical theory draws attention to the constraining elements of ideas, values, and meanings: the freezing of existing social reality. Critical theory thus facilitates the development of a broader understanding in organizational culture studies. Gradually, I moved from a critical/radical humanist approach—or rather, expanded my repertoire—to include a more interpretive position and an interest in ethnography. I utilized this as the major framework in my empirical studies of knowledge-intensive companies as well as in studies of gender and organizations. The combination of cultural and gender approaches is, I think, productive. Seeing the genderedness of values, ideas, vocabulary, and social practices in organizations provides one way of interpreting cultural material. A cultural approach is a good way to get beneath surface patterns in gender relations at work. My studies of knowledge-intensive companies and gender also called for me to review other readings and literature, but my familiarity with culture research greatly facilitated the work. I employed all these streams of work—critical theory, organizational culture theory, ethnographic work, gender studies—in the metatheoretical research program. At the same time, reflections on a metatheoretical level have always been an integral part of theoretical and empirical work. For me, social science is not a matter of following procedures; it is about reflection (Alvesson & Sköldberg, 1996). A major obstacle to reflection is the following of procedures and preoccupation

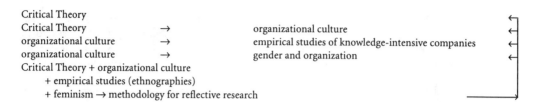

Figure 11.1. Linking Research Programs Over Time

with protocol and technique. My metatheoretical research reflects back on and inspires empirical studies and theoretical work. I have found that working with in-depth case studies greatly facilitates multiprogrammatic research, as case studies of organizations make it possible to take many aspects into account. Broad empirical work allows for connections in different directions.

The relationships among research programs can be represented as shown in Figure 11.1, which also illustrates their development over time. The reflective methodology (Alvesson & Sköldberg, 1996) is thus partly an outcome of all the ideas and insights developed during more than a decade of metatheoretical, theoretical, and empirical work. The basic argument is that good science does not follow from the use of a set of techniques associated with scientific method—whether quantitative or qualitative—but from the salience and quality of the reflexive elements in the research process and the completed text. Developments in the social sciences, philosophy, and linguistics have provided us with a wide range of reflective areas in social science: on gender and ethnicity, the power-knowledge connection, language, texts, rhetoric, the situated nature of "data" (often conversational in nature), the metaphorical nature of knowledge, and so on. The methodology is called *reflexive interpretation,* and consists of a flexible framework for coping with four cornerstones of postempiricist qualitative research: (a) the raw or preliminary interpretations involved in data construction, (b) the hermeneutics of in-depth (beyond surface) interpretation, (c) the political contextualizing of interpretation, and (d) the problematization of language use, authorship, and the establishment of authority. The experiences with reflection-significant areas, such as critical theory and gender studies, and empirical studies in which the interpretive character of research is salient bring about a play of

ideas that facilitates broader synthesis. In our case it involved a pragmatization of ideas from philosophy to make them relevant in empirical studies and an intellectualization or detechnification of ideas in qualitative method to provide more emphasis on the reflexive elements.

Research Programs and Synergy Effects

As indicated above, I prefer that my projects, as well as elements within a given program, be loosely coupled. In a series of case studies of knowledge-intensive companies (a computer consultancy company, advertising agencies, a newspaper, a law firm, and so on), for instance, each case study is carried out and reported as a separate project. The idea is not to test hypotheses, but to provide deep and multifaceted credible empirical descriptions and to develop new ideas. It is important in such projects to give research assistants considerable leeway. Of course, insights and experiences from earlier case studies influence the work, and new ideas also emerge as comparisons are conducted and as the researchers draw upon the accumulated empirical material (see, e.g., Alvesson, 1993c), but this is done in an ad hoc way. The more interesting synthesis cannot be predicted or achieved through rigorous research designs. What is interesting is normally what is unexpected. In a "rigorous" study, normally most things are thought out in advance, and the space for the unexpected is limited. As Astley (1985) points out, the most celebrated theories in administrative science have attained this position in spite of clear empirical support for them. Rigorous empirical research seems thus to be decoupled from what are considered to be interesting theoretical contributions.

By developing a number of research programs, one creates possibilities of synergy effects, not only between individual projects and writings within programs, but also between programs. It is important to develop research programs that are different but at the same time also share some basic affinities, such as being interpretive. The trick is to find an appropriate degree of difference/supplement. The differences may be on a similar level (e.g., different theories or empirical fields), but may also be on different levels. In my case, the five research programs with which I have been involved concern the three levels of empirical inquiry, theoretical perspective, and metatheory (reflection).

A particular project may lead to unexpected results that can be fully utilized by approaches other than the one originally guiding the project. This is the charm of qualitative research—ethnography provides rich empirical material that can be interpreted from various perspectives. Of course, a precondition—if one is not very creative—is a good grounding in various fields, so that one can develop and exploit interesting ideas and interpretations. Here a vital concept is an interpretive repertoire (Alvesson & Sköldberg, 1996) that points to the prestructured understanding and broadens the capacity to see aspects and conceptualize issues. If one is narrowly specialized and in love with a particular framework—such as behaviorism, psychoanalysis, or pluralism theory—one is able to see only a limited number of phenomena; conversely, if one is widely read and has sympathy toward various types of theories, then one's interpretive repertoire is broad and one can consider more interesting angles. A powerful interpretive repertoire makes it likely that one may produce rich research results from any empirical material, without being forced to use one's favorite theory on anything.

Among the drawbacks of the idea of a broad interpretive repertoire are that such a repertoire may take a long time to develop and it may also be difficult to use. There is also the risk that it may lead to shallowness. Another problem is that the journal format generally allows authors less text space than they sometimes need to present studies based on the use of broad interpretive repertoires. This type of repertoire may, however, be seen as something that may encourage the researcher to develop studies in many different directions. The repertoire may thus be actively used only in the first phases of the research process. When something within the repertoire, aided by the researcher's interpretive-creative powers, hits upon or is hit by an interesting empirical theme, this line of inquiry may then be fulfilled and the repertoire deactivated until the researcher embarks upon the next research project or the next phase of the current project.

In my case, an ethnography of an industrial company—basically carried out from an interpretive, cultural perspective—included an observation of an event that lent itself perfectly to intensive interpretation from various critical perspectives. I used culture theory, Foucault and Habermas, to illuminate the specific empirical situation, which exhibited interesting themes of leadership, power, communication, and organizational change (Alvesson, 1996; this book develops some general ideas about how to work with multiple interpretations). In this case I used a broad interpretive repertoire throughout the study. In a project on advertising agencies, I found the gender division of labor and gender relations so striking and interesting that they called for a special investigation (Alvesson, 1994a). In this case the interpretive repertoire—including gender theory—allowed me to take the gender relations in the organization seriously and to proceed with an inquiry into the topic. A very strong gender division of labor—with all those in professional positions being male and all but one of the persons in assisting positions being female—coexisted with unitary accounts of the workplace in feminine terms: According to interviewees, feelings and intuition dominated work; close social relationships, community, and antibureaucracy characterized the organization; and subordination characterized the agencies' relations with clients. Very briefly, my interpretation was that in a strongly feminized work context, where the authority of the advertising professionals was regularly challenged, there was considerable need for identity work and, relatedly, for a strengthening of the masculinity of the male professionals. A clear-cut gender division of labor may have been helpful in this regard. The employment of young, attractive women in subordinate positions, along with sexualized interaction patterns, confirmed the identities and maleness of the men.

116   EARLY RHYTHMS

Final Comment

My research story bears imprints of a slightly obsessive drive to write and to make something of my ideas. It is likely that social commitment adds something to the career and identity-securing motives that are salient for the modern person, especially, perhaps, ambitious academics. (I should perhaps add that I certainly believe that intellectual curiosity and the urge to be creative are also important driving forces for most academics. In addition, there are probably deep existential issues at stake, but these I have not tried to sort out here.)

My research covers relatively broad areas, and I have tried to find ways of combining various ideas and projects in order to get synergy effects. This often takes place in an adhocratic manner. Having concentrated on and completed a particular project, my next step is the development and pursuit of a new idea that takes elements from the completed project in a new direction, perhaps through synthesis with ideas from other projects. Theoretical ideas, for example, can be used for the reinterpretation of an ethnography or to inspire more basic, metatheoretical work. My way of doing programmatic research may, like so much else, be illuminated by the garbage can metaphor (March & Olsen, 1976). The outcome of a particular research text is a result of interactions among five varying streams of research interest (programs). These are in turn affected by a variety of individual and social forces that also interact with the streams and activate, reinforce, and deactivate the streams and various combinations of these at different points. Multiprogrammatic research is a combination of flexibility and direction. Drawing upon earlier experiences and utilizing competence points toward continuity and specialization, the flexible and adhocratic combination of ideas and results from a variety of interests means that variation and broader possibilities are kept open. Of course, the dilemma of combining direction and flexibility, focus and variation, can be dealt with in many ways. I hope that my account here of my approach and my experiences may also have some relevance for others.

References

Alvesson, M. (1987). *Organization theory and technocratic consciousness: Rationality, ideology and quality of work*. Berlin: de Gruyter.

Alvesson, M. (1993a). Cultural-ideological modes of management control. In S. Deetz (Ed.), *Communication yearbook 16*. Newbury Park, CA: Sage.

Alvesson, M. (1993b). *Cultural perspectives on organizations*. Cambridge: Cambridge University Press.

Alvesson, M. (1993c). Organization as rhetoric: Knowledge-intensive companies and the struggle with ambiguity. *Journal of Management Studies, 30*, 997-1015.

Alvesson, M. (1993d). The play of metaphors. In J. Hassard & M. Parker (Eds.), *Postmodernism and organizations*. London: Sage.

Alvesson, M. (1994a). *Gender, sexuality and identity at work: A case study of an advertising agency* (Working paper). Göteborg, Sweden: Göteborg University.

Alvesson, M. (1994b). Talking in organizations: Managing identity and impressions in an advertising agency. *Organization Studies, 15*, 535-563.

Alvesson, M. (1995). *Management of knowledge-intensive companies*. Berlin: de Gruyter.

Alvesson, M. (1996). *Communication, power and organization*. Berlin: de Gruyter.

Alvesson, M., & Berg, P. O. (1992). *Corporate culture and organizational symbolism*. Berlin: de Gruyter.

Alvesson, M., & Björkman, I. (1992). *Organisationsidentitet och organisationsbyggande: En studie av ett industriföretag*. Lund: Studentlitteratur.

Alvesson, M., & Köping, A.-S. (1993). *Med känslan som ledstjärna: En studie av reklamarbetare och reklambyråer*. Lund: Studentlitteratur.

Alvesson, M., & Lindkvist, L. (1993). Transaction costs, clans and corporate culture. *Journal of Management Studies, 30*, 427-452.

Alvesson, M., & Sköldberg, K. (1996). *Towards a reflexive methodology*. London: Sage.

Alvesson, M., & Willmott, H. (Eds.). (1992a). *Critical management studies*. London: Sage.

Alvesson, M., & Willmott, H. (1992b). On the idea of emancipation in management and organization studies. *Academy of Management Review, 17*, 432-464.

Alvesson, M., & Willmott, H. (1996). *Making sense of management: A critical analysis*. London: Sage.

Asplund, J. (1987). *Det sociala livets elementära former*. Göteborg, Sweden: Korpen.

Astley, G. (1985). Administrative science as socially constructed truth. *Administrative Science Quarterly, 30*, 497-513.

Billing, Y. D., & Alvesson, M. (1994). *Gender, managers and organizations*. Berlin: de Gruyter.

Bourdieu, P. (1979). *Outline of a theory of practice*. Cambridge: Cambridge University Press.

Deetz, S. (1992). *Democracy in an age of corporate colonization: Developments in communication and the politics of everyday life*. Albany: State University of New York Press.

Foucault, M. (1980). *Power/knowledge*. New York: Pantheon.

Glaser, B. G., & Strauss, A. L. (1967). *The discovery of grounded theory: Strategies for qualitative research*. Chicago: Aldine.

Habermas, J. (1984). *The theory of communicative action* (Vol. 1). Boston: Beacon.

Horkheimer, M., & Adorno, T. (1979). *The dialectics of enlightenment.* London: Verso. (Original work published 1947)

Kunda, G. (1992). *Engineering culture: Control and commitment in a high-tech corporation.* Philadelphia: Temple University Press.

March, J. G., & Olsen, J. P. (1976). *Ambiguity and choice in organizations.* Bergen, Norway: Universitetsforlaget.

Mills, C. W. (1940). Situated actions and vocabularies of motives. *American Sociological Review, 5,* 904-913.

Rosen, M. (1985). Breakfast at Spiro's: Dramaturgy and dominance. *Journal of Management, 11*(2), 31-48.

12 The Publishing Process

THE STRUGGLE FOR MEANING

Susan J. Ashford

For 10 years before I entered the field of organizational behavior, I played with clay. Happily pinching, pulling, centering, sculpting, and glazing, I learned and joyfully engaged in the creative demands of the ceramist's craft. When I was 15, my dad lost his job and had little hope of getting another. My five siblings and I were left with an uncertain financial future, questionable opportunities for college careers, and a feeling of fear in the pits of our stomachs that has never quite gone away. For me, publishing in the organizational sciences has always been a mixture of these two realities: the creative and the pragmatic, the expressive and the instrumental, the sacred and the profane.

In my profession, I write because I want to say something: to create a message that is clear, pleasing to my ear, and meaningful to me and, I hope, to others. I write because I have an urge to create. I also write because my livelihood depends on it. The publication process is highly charged because it involves making my inner self tangible and opening it up for assessment of the adequacy of its products. It is also charged because my survival depends upon those assessments. The publication process, for me, has been a struggle between these two realities. In that struggle, I have had extremely fortunate times (such as the acceptance of three articles in the 6 months just prior to tenure) and unfortunate times (such as the rejection of three articles in the 3 months just prior to my writing this essay). The former periods let my creative side take wing; during those times I feel like an especially imaginative, successful person. In contrast, in the latter periods I feel the perhaps irrational but just as real instrumental panic that I felt as a 15-year-old, wondering how I (the family) would survive.

I have seen these two realities manifest themselves in others, too, and in the field in general. In the best people I know in the field, the creative side burns brightly (and in watching and interacting with them, I am able to nurture this side of me). The symptoms of the creative side are readily recognizable: the inability to go home

119

until words are on paper and a particular idea is expressed (I have walked out of my workplace at midnight as excited and happy as I have been at any other time in my life), the satisfaction of an argument well crafted, the pure joy in the choice of words and their arrangement on a page, the intense desire to share ideas with others and the enthusiastic engagement of any feedback those ideas bring.

The instrumental side, however, also seems omnipresent. You can see it in the anxiety people express over computer output—not because it presents a complex picture that will be difficult to interpret, but because the results portend whether they will have a "good year" with fresh manuscripts to submit or will need to start over, with the time already devoted to this project "wasted." (One colleague likens getting the computer output to pulling the handle on a slot machine—there is a lot riding on the results, and both situations seem at times equally uncontrollable.) You can see it in the numerous conversations between colleagues in which an instrumental language predominates: Publications become "hits" and journal names are used as nouns in a different sense than usual (as in "He has three *AMJs* and two *ASQs*"). You can hear it in the preconference workshops offered at the academy meetings for doctoral students and junior faculty, where it is difficult to turn the talk *away* from the instrumental (e.g., "How many publications do I need to survive in this field?"). And finally, you can see it in the proliferation of articles on "how to" get published (making me wary of the incremental contribution of this one).

In writing this chapter, my biggest regret is that I will say more about the instrumental than the creative side. The creative side seems amorphous to me—idiosyncratic to individuals and not amenable to advice. Further, although I could share some of the strategies that have helped me feel more creative, even that has a disappointingly instrumental tone (how to "get better" at the creative side). The most important message that I can convey about the publication process is that authors should not forget the creative aspect of our enterprise as they engage in the often instrumental actions that this process requires. Most of us entered this field because of a desire to create (to say something or discover something—other words that express what I mean by "create"). I am the least

satisfied with my chosen career when this side is neglected and abused. When the instrumental dominates, nothing works. The more in touch I can be with the creative aspects of my undertaking, the more I can be open to feedback from reviewers and editors, face the publication process with hope and dignity, and feel great and deep satisfaction in the results.

So, with that caution in mind, I would like to address a couple of aspects of the publication process about which I feel I might have something to say. The point of the essays collected in this volume seems to be the "lessons" that may be extracted from the contributors' reflections on their experiences. As I think back, I come up with a few lessons, but I would also like to begin with two caveats. First, the publication process in some ways remains as ambiguous and frustrating today as it was when I started in this field (in 1983). As my recent experiences (noted above) attest, although there may be (and I believe there is) a learning curve involved in the publishing process, it is by no means a perfect one. Second, I comment on this process as one voice among many. There are certainly others who have published more, and more often, than I. Thus I approach this task with a great deal of modesty. What I bring to this essay is a lot of time spent in self-reflection (as I prepared to write) and an intense involvement with the other side. I have been on an editorial board since my first year in the field, and have served as a consulting editor for one of our journals for the past 3 years. In short, I have reviewed a lot of manuscripts. This has given me a sense of what works and what doesn't—some dos and don'ts.

Realistic Expectations

My first paper (the theory section from my dissertation) was conditionally accepted on the first review. This experience is probably not uncommon (I have had many people tell me that they had or know of someone who had a similar experience), but it gave me a warped view of the publication process and left me utterly unprepared for the much more difficult task of publishing the first empirical article from my dissertation. This latter effort involved several rounds at two different journals and was most discouraging to one starting out. The lesson? Being new to the field may give one fresh eyes, leading to fresh theoretical insights that, if they can be well crafted into a paper, may be seen as a contribution (i.e., may be accepted for publication). I think this is what happened in my case. However, my sense is that the freshness of one's eyes erodes quickly, and that this is not a bankable strategy for tenure or a lifelong contribution to the field. Second, perhaps the hardest paper you will ever write will be the one that you pare down from a 250-page tome rather than build up from a blank sheet of paper. Third, it is important to develop fairly realistic expectations early on regarding the publication process. It is very hard. This reality seems almost universally true (i.e., true for everyone). The process has almost never gone easily for me since that first time. The feedback is harsh, the work involved in revisions is intensive, and the battle is uphill. Having this expectation allows one to handle the process better, without feeling that one is singularly (and uniquely) unsuited for this profession. This expectation is critical for continued persistence—the essential behavioral strategy—but more on that later.

The Way We Work

I have often been struck by the differences in work styles across successful academics. One has only to sit on a career-oriented panel (say, for doctoral students or for junior faculty) once to get a sense of the real differences in how people work—and these are people describing styles that have seemingly led to success. Some successful academics work from 8:00 a.m. to 6:00 p.m. every day in a regimented style that keeps them focused on the work at hand and away from the many distractions present in the workplace. Others work when their emotions move them, putting in perhaps more hours, but spending many of those hours reacting to the various interruptions of the day; these individuals definitely put in many hours at odd times (when the spirit moves them). The bottom line seems to be the importance of self-discovery—finding the style that best suits you, knowing your weaknesses and building in safeguards against them. Given that, I can only report what works for me. It is clearly not a guide for anyone else. If a description of my

style gets you to think through the issues for yourself, then it has served its purpose. Although many of these issues will probably be touched upon in other chapters in this volume, also, I will mention a couple of work style issues that, in my mind, are directly related to the publishing process.

Multiple Projects

I get excited by a lot of different things. Hazel Markus's theory of possible selves must have been written with me in mind. I find many different literatures interesting, and I can see myself doing various different types of research. I used to worry a great deal about being "scattered" until someone told me about Lyman Porter's metaphor of the carnival plate spinner (now I only worry sometimes). At carnivals (it must be carnivals of old, for I have never seen this) there is a man who spins plates on top of various poles (this is actually a performance act that people pay money to watch, but enough editorializing). The plate spinner gives one plate a vigorous spin and moves on to the second. As he walks back and forth across the stage, he amazes the audience with the number of plates he is able to keep up and spinning. Porter argues that those who are most successful in the publication process (at least this is how his views have been recounted to me) follow the behavioral repertoire of the carnival plate spinner. They have several projects going, but projects that do not all need their attention simultaneously. Rather, they give one project a "spin" (send out a survey or analyze data and send them to a colleague) and then move on to the next (paying the first only partial attention to ensure that no sudden gusts of wind knock the first plate off its pole). My sense is that when we are new to the field and lower on the learning curve, the number of plates we can spin at once is fewer than the number we can handle later in our careers. In any case, the goal is to keep the plates all spinning (even if they are wobbling at times) without having any fall and crash. When things are going well for me, I have the sense of giving plates a spin as I move from project to project, with some requiring a vigorous spin and others needing just a gentle touch to keep them steady and on course. In my mind's eye, I also have a few plates (additional projects and ideas) on the shelf, ready to be put up on poles as I gain capabilities (get better at the research process) or take other plates off their poles (as projects are completed).

I like this metaphor because it fits my preferred work style. Others work more as single-product producers. I have had the good fortune to know a few of these, and they are people I admire very much. These people move at a slower pace as far as getting things into print, but (ideally, or this strategy is woefully ineffective) each piece has significant impact. This strategy clearly works well, but it can be the Waterloo of younger faculty members. If your single product is not accepted at the journals, you don't have much to fall back on. I have found the tendency to think in terms of multiple projects at different stages (requiring different degrees and levels of spinning) to be important to succeeding in the publishing process. And yet this is something new academics are rarely told. They enter the field with one project in hand (their dissertation) and often by the time they take that project through the publishing process, they are in the mind-set of, What next? They are already thinking in terms of what single project to take on next. This strategy can be successful, but it seems more risky than a multiple-plate strategy.

Coauthors

I both love and hate the solitary nature of our profession. I am enough of an introvert to love the quiet and to value time alone, but I am also a social being. I find that I learn most through interaction with others (even more than through the written word). Since graduate school, my main sources of learning have been my coauthors. My success in the publication process has been enhanced by my interactions with coauthors. They both make it possible for me to keep more plates spinning (it is a great feeling when, after a long day of teaching and meeting with students, I get a phone message saying that my coauthor has just completed a draft of the discussion section of our paper or just sent me the draft of our survey—cha-ching! Another plate spun!) and make the process a whole lot more fun. Clearly to have this work, one needs the right coauthors—and one also needs to hold up one's own end of the bargain.

The right coauthor can be anyone (and I wouldn't begin to presume to tell anyone how to pick coauthors). I have found my coauthors mostly on job interviews. After my job talks at their institutions, we have started talking and then have soon begun working together. I haven't always gotten the jobs, but I would take what I *have* gotten out of the process any day! One coauthor and I met at a junior faculty consortium—I asked her to lunch because she looked as if she had no one to eat with. We have published three papers together. My coauthors have typically been young people in the hunt for tenure (I think this is important) with strong research values. They often have strengths that are different from mine (and although this has been fortuitous, I think it is also important). For example, one of us might have a strength in data analysis, the other in building theoretical arguments; one might be better at crafting first drafts and the other in working revisions; one might have access to research sites or subjects and the other access to the money to pay for subjects or travel. My coauthors and I have divided the work and credit pretty evenly. One of us usually takes a first crack at the theory section while the other does the analysis and writes it up. In dividing up credit, we typically have followed a "logrolling approach" (a term that comes from my negotiation-oriented coauthor). We presume that we will write multiple papers together. One becomes first author on the first, with the understanding that the other will be first author on the second. We usually include an authors' note containing the disclaimer that "the authors contributed equally to the effort," and this is true. I can think of at least one occasion when we switched the ordering of authorship because of the demands of one coauthor's personal situation (i.e., one of us was coming up for tenure). I value my coauthors highly. They have served many functions for me. They were my "research cues" for the 8 years that I spent in a (relatively more) teaching-oriented environment. They have been my main source of learning over the past several years, and they are my personal friends. The publishing process is a lot more warm and fuzzy for me because of them. I wouldn't undertake this process in any other way (no matter how committees "count" things at tenure time). My sanity and growth depend on my coauthors. However, you need to do what works for you.

A coauthor strategy requires interacting with others (which is not attractive to everyone) and carries some career risks (after all, those committees do count at tenure time, and they often count dual-authored papers differently from single-authored ones). I was and am willing to take those risks (whereas I am less willing to take the risk of the single-project focus—different strokes . . .). Your goal should be to find your own preferences.

The Use of Time

The scarcest resource in our professional life is time. I am constantly monitoring my time, fretting over my time, saving my time, and spending my time. I consider the management of time to be critical to the publishing process, because research time is the most fungible. It is the time that no one is particularly clamoring for. Journals will wait forever for your papers, but students demand that you be prepared on Tuesday. It is probably not surprising, then, that your time gets pulled toward teaching. You oil all the squeaky wheels and only then notice that there is nothing left for the work that is not only the most important to long-run career survival, but also your most creative and satisfying. Saving time for research is critical, for it is a task that requires time, lots of it, and quality time to boot. I have done a couple of things to help save time for the research/publication process.

First, I recognize Kaye Schoonhoven's law (or at least the person who told me this attributed it to her). That is, young scholars keep waiting for big demands on their time so that they can be sure to turn them down to save themselves for research. What they don't understand is that the process is more like being eaten away by ants; big demands on time are not the problem. It is the person who needs just 30 minutes of your time (and how can you turn down a request for 30 minutes?) who is the biggest danger to you. Such requests, like ant bites, are small, but they come with such frequency (and increasing frequency as one gains tenure; increasing frequency if one is female or minority) that soon all your time is eaten away. You're left with a tattered day that has an hour free here and 15 minutes there. It is very difficult to conduct a research life with such time. Once I understood the ant problem, I had a much easier

time turning down "reasonable" requests for my time and, by so doing, have preserved more time to devote to the publishing process.

Second, I make appointments with myself. All of us are very professional. If we make appointments with colleagues or staff persons at our universities, we keep them. If someone else asks for that time, we have little trouble saying that we have prior commitments, but would be glad to meet another time. A few years back, I asked myself why I didn't offer myself that same courtesy. I began not just blocking time out for writing and attention to the publishing process, but making appointments with myself. I now have no trouble saying to someone who wants my time on a Tuesday that I have blocked out: "I can't meet then, I have an appointment; I would be glad to meet another time." With this strategy, I feel much more in control of my life, and I also feel good about respecting myself.

Third, I pay more attention to what I am doing and what it really demands. It occurs to me that for half of our job we are really novelists (the research, writing, and publishing parts) and for half we are talk-show hosts (the teaching and executive teaching parts). I try to identify to myself which part I am playing at any given time (during the times of the year that they can be separated) and am careful about bringing the rules of one into the arena of the other. For example, a novelist doesn't need to go to an office (in fact, that might be the worst place for her to work); she doesn't need to work 9:00 to 5:00, and she doesn't need to dress up. When I am in a heavy research mode, I let myself sleep in if that is what I need, I work all hours (and odd hours), I never get out of my sweats, I do things that spur my creativity (such as exercise), and I leave the house only once a day, to pick up my kids. When I go into talk-show mode, I feel better about it (and get into the spirit of it) if I go to the office, dress up for the part, and read professional books. This discussion pertains to the publishing process in the following way: I do my worst at writing (coming up with responses to reviewers and so on) when I try to shoehorn that activity into the work mold of a professional. I do my best thinking while lying down (sometimes), during exercise, in sweats, and late at night. I am happiest when I take advantage of my flexible career and live my life this way when I am focused on writing.

One thing that I am always searching for in my career are ways to extend the novelist portion of my work year. The institutions that I have been a part of, for example, have allowed me to "bunch" my teaching (e.g., all into one term), allowing for an extended period to be devoted to writing. Bigger institutions, also, have a larger set of demands. Sometimes these can be traded for novelist time. For example, the dean asks you to take on a large administrative role? Negotiate for reduced teaching time. The field honors you with an appointment as a journal editor? Negotiate hard for fewer teaching commitments. Within reason, I find that the more time I am able to call my own as a novelist, the better. However, if this free time extends too long, I find I have diminishing returns. Sometimes the deadline of the impending return to the classroom is a useful discipline for my writing. I often get a lot done in that last month. I find that 6 months without teaching commitments works well for me, whereas with 9 months, I am slow in the start-up phase (because I have "so much" time to use).

Dealing With Feedback

I consider dealing with feedback to be the most important part of the publishing process. Therefore, in this central section of the essay, I will share how I deal with feedback and the attitudes and behaviors I have come to see as important from my observations of myself, my colleagues, and the authors with whom I have interacted in the reviewing/editing process.

I always read my reviews in a secluded place (not my office). I know several others who do this as well. One of the worst aspects of being as involved as I am in the reviewing/editing process is that I sometimes mistakenly open mail containing feedback on my own papers thinking that it is a reviewer report or a letter in which the journal editor is sending me copies of feedback for an author of a recent submission. In these cases I have taken in the feedback on my own work almost "intravenously" (without any mental preparation). This feedback is always the toughest on my soul.

So what preparation do I do in this secluded place, with my reviews sitting unopened on my knees? I tell myself that the feedback I am about to receive is about my *work*, not about me, and

that my work is only a small part of myself. (It is nearly a mantra: "I am an effective teacher, I do good reviews, I am a good wife, I am a much-loved mother. . . ." I usually stop when I get to "I have my health.") It is a myth that people who write about the importance of feedback enjoy getting it themselves. I prepare myself for pain and I open the letter. In most cases receiving feedback has been painful, and perhaps there is a lesson here. The reviewing process has some inherently negative aspects. Reviewers staring at manuscripts, particularly new reviewers (I know this was true for me when I was starting out), feel that they haven't done their job unless they have found a study's flaws. They also worry that they will look bad in the eyes of editors if they think an article is just fine when two other reviewers return 16-page single-spaced analyses articulating its many shortcomings. These realities lead to what can sometimes be (and often is) a negative tone. Many of the acceptance letters for my articles have read something like: "This work isn't much good, but we've run out of steam so we are (against our better instincts) going to go ahead and publish it."

Recognizing that the process has some inherently negative aspects makes it easier to deal with. The most important suggestion implicit in the previous paragraph is that you should not take it personally. Remember that the article for which you just received feedback is but one piece of your work and that your work is but one piece of who you are. This attitude underlies what I think are the two most important attitudes for an author to have in the publishing process: openness to feedback and a willingness to persist.

Openness

I have been told by several of the authors with whom I have written that I am more open than they would naturally be to feedback from others on our work. I believe in the review process. Having spent countless hours laboring to give feedback to authors as part of the review/editing process, I believe that I should take the feedback offered me and try to learn from it. Thus I feel very open to suggestion and criticism (not that I always like it). I actually like the revise-and-resubmit part of the publication process. Suddenly, instead of having to deal with every possible criticism of your work that you can imagine (or might hear from the wide variety of colleagues you might have gotten a "preread" from), you have to deal only with a constrained set of critiques (though with the length of some reviews, the set doesn't always feel that constrained). With reviewers' reports in my hands, my uncertainty is reduced, my sense of self-efficacy goes up (usually), and I generally learn a lot. I find that as time goes on and we all get busier, it is very difficult to get colleagues to spend serious time with my work on an informal basis (and I am extremely grateful to those who have). Reviewers generally spend time with my manuscripts and have something valuable to say. Although the negativity does get me down, if I can wade through that, I learn a lot. I especially learn a lot if I am working with a coauthor and we have a series of meetings in which we discuss how we will respond to reviewers' criticisms. The push that reviewers give to our thinking and the creative process in which we engage in responding is generally very stimulating—and fun!

It is interesting to note two recent comments from colleagues of mine that are relevant to feedback openness. First, in evaluating our PhD students recently, one faculty member summarized the discussion of seven different students by saying that what seemed to differentiate the top and bottom performers was their openness to feedback. Top performers were open to faculty input, actively sought it, and incorporated it into their work. Less effective students were defensive regarding feedback and, occasionally, openly hostile. Second, another colleague observed that several senior members of our field have essentially dropped out of the publication process, viewing the feedback they get from it as coming from "unqualified, incompetent reviewers." Although it may be true that reviewer quality is deteriorating, the generality of this statement reflects a degree of defensiveness toward feedback. This defensiveness may inevitably creep into an individual's personal style as he or she gains experience in the field. However, to my mind, this is disappointing. Our field relies on the participation of a community of scholars to shape the body of work that is our literature. The way each of us participates in that community is by putting his or her ideas out there to be tested and by providing feedback

on each other's ideas. Defensiveness would seem to muck up this enterprise at both the early and later stages of one's career.

One practice has helped me remain open to reviewers and to keep my spirits up for responding. Shortly after I receive reviews, whether the decision is a revise and resubmit or a reject, I break each review up into specific points. I then create a setup for responding to each review (I typically dictate this and have a secretary type it up), a template in which I state the reviewer's points in order, each followed by "Response:" and room for my future response. Thus I create a lengthy document, most of it blank, awaiting my responses. No matter how gloomy I feel after receiving the reviews, I get this done. Then, after several days (sometimes weeks), I pick up the response templates and begin by answering those points that are easiest (sometimes all I can do at that time is fix typos and find missing references if my self-efficacy is still low). Once I am engaged in the task and the task is broken into small pieces, I generally can keep going and soon build a head of steam to deal with the more difficult issues. This procedure has two additional benefits as well: First, it allows me, in very busy times, to keep going, finding small things that I can tackle in the few minutes that I can squeeze out of a day for research. Second, it sets up my responses to reviewers in an ideal way for resubmitting the manuscript to a journal.

Having reviewed a lot, I have strong feelings regarding how response memos should be constructed. First, they should repeat (summarize) the reviewer's concerns (so that he or she doesn't have to go back to the initial report to check). Second, the author should be very clear regarding what he or she has done to address particular reviewers' comments and where those changes can be found in the new manuscript (i.e., the author should cite page and paragraph numbers). As a reviewer, I hate getting response memos that say something like, "Point 1. Done." This tells me nothing regarding what my point was, what was done, or where the change can be found. My philosophy as an author is to make things as easy as possible for the reviewer (thus, for example, I repeat my responses for each reviewer who asked a particular question, rather than refer reviewers to my responses to other reviewers). Not everything I do is necessary (and indeed there may be a rationale for not doing some of it), but everything I do does make the process less effortful for the reviewer. I figure that can't hurt (and I appreciate such efforts as a reviewer).

Persistence

This theme is intricately interwoven with the theme of openness. Part of my struggle with remaining open to feedback lies in how not to become overwhelmed by it. And yet I think winning this struggle is central to succeeding in the publication process. Persistence in the face of adversity is crucial. There are many out there who are smarter than me, but they couldn't handle the feedback and gave up. Many of us know colleagues from graduate school who fit this profile. They were (are) very smart, but they haven't published. The publishing process is a discouraging one, and success at it requires persistence in the face of that discouragement. The most important advice that I can give is to keep going, whether it is in redoing the study with better measures and more constructs or in revising the article and resubmitting it to the journal (or to another journal following a rejection), the important thing is to keep moving. Perhaps what you thought was going to be the definitive study you will need to consider a pretest. Perhaps you will have to redo the manuscript and hope for a more sympathetic reading from a different journal—whatever, just keep moving.

One ability that is important to the maintenance of persistence is the ability to interpret feedback appropriately (or to find someone who can). Given the negativity of the review process, it is critical that you figure out what the messages you are given mean. Early on in my career, two colleagues and I submitted a paper to *Administrative Science Quarterly* and received very detailed (read "long") reviews with lots of negative comments, along with an invitation to revise and resubmit the manuscript. We figured that with so many criticisms and concerns, how could the paper have a chance? We sent it elsewhere, to a lower-tier journal, and it was accepted there. Since then, we have learned that ours was actually a quite positive outcome from *ASQ!* To be invited to resubmit is a significant achievement, and the reviews that we received for this paper were no more negative than many

that we pursued vigorously (and with success) subsequently in our careers. In retrospect, it is clear (to us, anyway) that we didn't interpret the feedback correctly, in its proper context. One has to read the levels of negativity to make a judgment regarding the chances of success. The task of revising is usually daunting, but the size of the task shouldn't be the measure of whether it is doable or "worth it." I now believe that an invitation to revise and resubmit is extremely positive news (and I don't pay much attention anymore to the phrase that editors like to use, "high-risk revise and resubmit"—it is used so frequently that it is not a differentiator). Since that early *ASQ* paper, I have turned down only one opportunity to revise and resubmit, and I always have someone else read my reviews to give me an assessment of how bad it seems (somehow, others don't take the comments as personally).

Clearly, there are some rules for persistence. Never submit to a second journal without fixing (to the extent possible) the problems noted by reviewers at the first journal. Failure to do so will come back to haunt you with startling regularity. (We are indeed a small field, and most people I know have gotten an article to review twice. When an author hasn't taken advice the first time around—if only to rebut—it tends to anger a reviewer.)

There are also some persistence practices that I have not used personally, but that are probably worth mentioning, as I have seen others use them successfully. These involve interacting directly with journal editors (something I am much too shy to pursue). As a reviewer, I have seen articles published that were previously rejected. The authors in these instances have gone directly to the editor (usually in writing, but, I gather, often preceded by phone calls) to make a case for the unfairness of the reviews or their ability to deal effectively with the comments raised. These are rare events, but they do suggest that no word is necessarily final. Instead of taking feedback personally and crawling off to find a rock to hide under, one might (at least others have) examine one's reviews for their fairness and consider whether or not one can deal with the concerns raised in a convincing manner. Then one has to make the phone call to the editor (here is where I typically fall out of this imagining). Of note, however, is that whereas *as an author* I would feel that such a phone call would prejudice the editor and reviewers against me, *as a reviewer,* I have seen little evidence of this. The review process is a human process, and reviewers and editors seem open to hearing about it if an author feels that he or she wasn't treated fairly in it.

Conclusion

I just finished reading a novel by Kaye Gibbons. It was only fair, but the title has stuck with me and haunts my recent thoughts: *A Cure for Dreams.* Now, as professionals, we avoid many horrible cures for dreams that are daily realities for others in our world (such as poverty, urban violence, and famine). However, our dreams die just the same, and they often die in the publishing process. A researcher fueled by passion, whether that passion is for a solving a practical problem, resolving a theoretical puzzle, or figuring out the implications of a new methodological insight, is a beautiful thing. This type of passion seems to fuel a career and leads to success in the publishing process almost as a by-product. The cure for dreams that we encounter in our world lies, in part, in the instrumentalism that I described earlier. Doing re-

search that "they" seem to want, doing the types of studies that seem to be all that the journals are publishing (as opposed to what will best answer the question), and choosing a topic based on what is hot or accepted rather than because you are passionate about it are all examples of letting the instrumental dominate. Making such choices amounts to choosing death. These are small deaths, to be sure, and may go many years without detection, but it seems to me that they are death all the same. Clearly, the instrumental requires some thought and, particularly early in one's career, can seem of paramount importance. I have never been able to rid myself of the instrumental completely: Posttenure, the annual performance review and that section where you are asked to list your articles accepted now looms large in a way that I seldom thought of prior to tenure. But I catch myself. I sometimes see that the instrumental is dominating and the creative, inner-directed side is withering away and in dire need of feeding. In my mind it is a matter of balance—the question of "Why am I doing what I am doing?" is one worth continual reflection. I prefer dreams and hope not to encounter their cure in my professional lifetime. Thus, to me, the struggle seems one well worth engaging.

13 Getting Published

Kevin R. Murphy

The process of getting published is critically important, steeped in secrecy and mystery, and often poorly understood. Although success in an academic or research career is not the same thing as success in publishing, it is very difficult to get and keep a good job, influence the field, advance science, make a name for yourself, and so on without developing skills in this area. My goals in writing this chapter are to share some of the things I have learned as an author, reviewer, and editor and to give advice and suggestions to others, particularly those who are just starting their careers in research and/or academics.

I first consider three questions: Why should you publish? Where should you publish? What should you publish? I then discuss the distinction (which took me several years and many rejected manuscripts to learn) between good research and good publication. Next, I comment on the roles of uncertainty and luck in the publication process, and their implications for researchers. Finally, I suggest some strategies for thinking about and presenting your research that might aid you in the publication process.

Why Publish?

In the early stages of your career, the question of why you should publish probably will seem a rhetorical one. There is a substantial element of truth to the axiom "Publish or perish," and you are unlikely to give much thought to why you invest so much time and energy in publishing. That's a shame, because there is much to be learned by thinking through exactly why you publish.

Once you get beyond the fact that most early career researchers publish because they have to (e.g., for promotion and tenure), you will find many of your colleagues and mentors surprisingly inarticulate and/or unconvincing when they tell you why they publish. When colleagues tell me that they publish to disseminate knowledge, or to help others, or to advance science, I doubt that they are being fully frank (or that they have a great deal of insight into their own behavior). Perhaps I am too cynical, but I think that most publication has a much more personal motive—that is, the desire for influence and reputation. I publish mainly because I want to influence others and because I want to build and maintain a reputation in the community of scholars who do similar work, and I think most of my colleagues publish for the same reasons.[1] These motivations have substantial impacts on both where I publish and what I publish.

Where to Publish

If your motivation to publish is to influence others, it follows that you should always try to publish in outlets that your peers read and pay attention to. A paper published in an obscure journal might as well remain unpublished; it will reach your colleagues' attention only if it is frequently cited in the journals they read. Similarly, a paper in a nonrefereed journal will not cut much ice; the presumption is that a good paper would have appeared in a better journal, and that papers appearing in outlets that publish whatever is sent to them are probably not very good. This is sometimes unfair, but it is nevertheless true that papers in less selective journals get less attention.

You might notice that I have talked only about journals, not about books, chapters, and so on. In the past few years, I have spent more time writing books, chapters, and the like than articles, but that is because books are more fun, not because they are more functional. In writing a book, you can pursue a topic in depth, pursue tangents that seem interesting to you, speculate to your heart's content, and more, without the normal constraints of a journal article (e.g., an article needs to be to the point, brief, and precise, which can add up to boring). The downside of book and chapter writing is that your work is less likely to reach the audience you most want to influence. There are some books that reach wide audiences, especially those that appear in series that are most like journals (e.g., Research in Organizational Behavior, Research in Personnel and Human Resource Management), but for the most part, book and chapter writing should be done because it is interesting, fun, and sometimes profitable, not because it is an efficient way to influence the field.

Even if you don't succeed in publishing in the top journals in your field, it is usually worth your while to submit papers to them. My own experience is that the best journals also give the best reviews. The caveat is that they are also the most likely to be critical (and to reject your paper), and it is necessary to develop a thick skin if you are going to submit papers to these outlets. Nevertheless, reviews from good journals are usually quite useful. I can recall only one paper I submitted to a journal in this category that was not improved by the reviews I received, and in that case I attributed the truly awful review that led to the paper's rejection to the fact that the one reviewer who provided detailed (and devastatingly critical) feedback was dying of cancer when he reviewed my paper, and simply wasn't paying attention to what I actually said in the paper. In that case, I wrote to the editor, explained why I thought the reviewer had missed the point, fixed the fairly minor problems noted by the other reviewers, and resubmitted the paper, even though it had been rejected in no uncertain terms. Much to my surprise and relief, the paper was accepted. In any case, the main point still holds: Reviews, even those that question your competence, sanity, and parentage, usually contain suggestions, ideas, and questions that can help you improve your paper.

What to Publish

Most publications can be classified as data oriented, idea oriented, or integration oriented. The first category includes empirical studies of all sorts, as well as quantitative reviews of the research literature (e.g., validity generalization studies, meta-analyses). Idea-oriented publications include methodological pieces, review papers that do not rely exclusively on quantitative summaries of study results to make their points, essays, and critiques. Integration-oriented publications include textbooks, summative reviews (e.g., *Annual Review* chapters), and chapters designed to educate readers in other disciplines.

Most researchers concentrate on data-oriented publications, at least during the first 5-10 years of their careers. This is a sensible strategy for a number of reasons. Data-oriented studies are most likely to appear in journals, as opposed to other, less accessible sources. (There are exceptions. I have a data-oriented chapter in a book I will not name, and I doubt if there are 20 people living who have read it.) More important, data-oriented studies are easier to assess and predict than are idea- or integration-oriented works. The evaluation and review of data-oriented papers follow a pretty standard course (Is the question important? Do the data address the question? Does the answer to the question get us anywhere?), and experienced researchers can usually predict which papers will be published or rejected. There is much more subjectivity and unpredictability involved in the evaluation of idea-oriented and integration-oriented papers. I have submitted several papers of this kind and found the reviewers perfectly split between those who said my ideas or suggestions were clearly wrong and those who said my ideas were correct, but so obvious that everyone already knew whatever it was the papers said. It is a very risky strategy to hang your hat on nonempirical papers as a means of establishing your career in publication.

It is very tempting for new researchers to concentrate on books and chapters, because these represent almost certain publications (assuming you ever finish them). This strategy can work, but it has some hidden costs. In particular, if most or all of your work appears in what are essentially nonrefereed sources (most books and chapters go through some sort of review, but they are very rarely rejected, no matter how dreadful), people will start to wonder why. The inference is often that you are either unwilling to submit your work to review or that your work never survives the review process. In either case, books and chapters often involve a lot of work for relatively little credit, especially if this is the only outlet you pursue.

Publication Versus Research

It is important not to confuse good research with high-quality publication. Good studies are not always published in good journals (and sometimes are not published at all), and poor studies are not always rejected. As someone heavily invested in the publication process (as a frequent reviewer and an editor), I am probably biased in thinking that relatively few poor papers make it into good journals. In reality, it is probably a good idea for authors to be persistent, even with relatively weak studies. Virtually every piece of research you do will eventually find a home if you look hard enough.

My concern in this section is not with the poor studies that manage to make it into the journals, but rather with the good ones that never get published. There are at least three reasons good studies may fail to appear in print. First and foremost, many researchers can't write (a colleague once neatly summarized a terribly written paper by noting, "This isn't writing, it's typing"). Like any other skill, good writing requires lots of practice and lots of feedback, and too many researchers fail to develop even the most minimal skills in this area. No matter how good the study, a manuscript that is impossible to understand will never be published in a respectable journal.

Second, authors often fail to understand their audiences. Journals differ considerably in their emphasis and scope, and a particular paper might receive very different evaluations at two journals of comparable quality and selectivity. You need to think carefully about who reads any given journal, and what they expect to see in a paper. This is especially important when you are submitting a paper to a journal in which you don't ordinarily publish.

Third, many authors never learn how to read or interpret reviews. The journal review process is a good place to learn humility. No matter how good the initial submission, reviewers are likely to criticize some aspect of your work or its presentation, and many researchers take such criticism badly. In particular, when journal editors write to tell them their papers have been rejected, many authors decide to give up. It is important to understand that virtually *every* paper is rejected, at least the first time around. In my life, I have had two papers accepted for publication in the form that they were first submitted, and in one case this happened only because the editor needed to fill a particular issue. One key to successful publication is to learn how to read letters of rejection.

There are a few basic variations on the standard rejection letter. First, there is the letter that says the paper is rejected as it is, but that with specific revisions it will be acceptable for publication. For all practical purposes, this is an acceptance for publication, and it requires a pretty significant screwup on the author's part (such as not making the requested revisions) to fail. On the other end of the spectrum is the letter that identifies specific fatal flaws (e.g., the data do not address the research question, there is an unsalvageable confound in the design) that cannot realistically be addressed. For all practical purposes, the paper that stimulates this letter will never be published, except perhaps in a journal that publishes virtually everything it receives. In the middle is the letter sent to the author whose paper presents some problems, but is potentially salvageable. My advice is that whenever an editor encourages, calls for, or even mentions a revision, do it. Most journals will not invite a revision unless the editor thinks that it has a reasonable chance of success. Once or twice I've been burned by following this rule (i.e., have made all the requested revisions and still been rejected), but I still always revise and resubmit when the option is suggested.

Earlier, I suggested that you should be persistent, even with a relatively weak study. At some point, however, you do yourself more harm than good by publishing studies that are clearly flawed. It is difficult (but very important) to learn the difference between a weak study and a bad study, and to avoid publishing bad studies. A weak study is one that is unlikely to have any substantial influence in the field, either because the question is a bit narrow or because the methods do not provide a definitive answer to the question. I am currently working with some colleagues on a series of studies conducted in organizational settings. It has not been possible to obtain large samples in any of the organizations, and we will probably not be able to draw very strong conclusions, no matter how clever our data analysis. I expect that this set of studies will be published somewhere, and that it will make a modest contribution, but I also know that these are relatively weak studies. Bad studies, on the other hand, are ones that have no possibility of answering a worthwhile question, either because the original research question was not a very sensible one or because the methods are simply inappropriate for addressing the question.

Weak studies probably do little to either advance or harm your reputation. They will probably end up in fairly obscure journals, will be only rarely read and even more rarely cited, and very little would be different (for you or for the rest of the world) if they had never been done at all. Bad studies, on the other hand, make you look foolish or incompetent. Another line on your vita is small consolation for a reputation as a sloppy researcher. Some judicious gatekeeping is probably a good idea, and there will be instances in your career (at least there have been in mine) when the decision not to publish, or the failure to persuade any journal to publish, a particular paper will probably do more good than harm, both to the field and to your own career.

Publication and Luck

There is an old baseball saying: It's better to be lucky than to be good. Although it might stretch things a bit to apply that same thinking when submitting a journal article, it is nevertheless true that luck plays an important and usually unacknowledged part in the publication process. Early in my career, I had the good luck to choose an area of research (cognitive processes in performance evaluation) that was just getting hot, and it helped me immeasurably. In fact, I was doubly lucky, because my "choice" of a research area was not so much a well-considered decision as an act of desperation. My original area of research was in judgment and decision making, and I had the good luck (although it did not look like it at the time) to fail so miserably in this area that I needed to choose another quickly, and I drifted into the right one.

There is an element of luck in choosing the right topics, in getting sympathetic reviewers, and even in choosing the right journals. One implication is that the publication process is filled with uncertainty, and no matter how good or how experienced you are at it, you can never count on a paper being published. The lesson I take from all of this is that if you are not born lucky, you'd better be born persistent. No matter how good (or how bad) the underlying research, you can never be certain of the outcome when you submit a paper for publication, and you should learn to expect the unexpected. I've lost count of the number of times I thought that a particular paper I submitted was good and one or more journals did not. Knowing that the publication process is fraught with uncertainty, I have learned to be persistent and active. The only way I know to publish a lot is to submit a lot, and to hang in there with papers that I think are really good.

Some Maxims to
Write and Publish By

You can succeed in publishing by being very smart (so that the extraordinary quality of your work makes up for the poor quality of the writing, the poor choice of outlets, and so on) or very energetic (if you submit enough things, something is bound to be published), but neither of these avenues seems all that appealing or practical to me. My advice is to learn as much as possible about the strategy of the publication process, and to apply this knowledge to your own work. My understanding of the strategy of publication can be boiled down to nine maxims:

1. *Nobody cares.* This is the advice a boy receives from a gangster in the movie *A Bronx Tale*. It is not a bad thing to keep in mind when criticizing your own research. In writing articles, chapters, and so on, it is critical to remember that problems, questions, and the like that strike you as fascinating are likely to bore other readers. Always assume that nobody cares about your research problem, and that your first task in writing a paper is to make them care. That is, never assume that your problem is so interesting and important that you don't have to convince your readers of that fact.

2. *No one ever went broke underestimating the American public.* The same is true of your readership. If you assume that your readers will be willing and able to wade through unclear prose and complicated presentations to glean the insights implied in your work, you are in for a rude shock. You have to present your research in such a way that readers can understand with a minimum of effort what you did, why it is important, what you found, and what it means. You cannot be too helpful to the reader.

3. *Add simplicity and lightness.* This was the design motto of the team that created the legendary F-5 fighter, and it is a good motto for both research and writing. If your research question can be settled with a single *t* test, piling on structural equation models, meta-analyses, corrections for deviations from normality, and so on does not make it a stronger paper. Always look for the simplest and most direct way of getting at the question.

4. *Ask Aunt Clara.* If you want to find out whether your writing is clear, don't ask a colleague who is equally steeped in the jargon of the day—ask your Aunt Clara. That is, your papers should be written in such a way that any reasonably intelligent person would be both willing and able to understand what you say.

5. *Who needs paper?* For me, the acid test of a paper is the feeling that I could stand up in front of an audience and read it to them without feeling stupid, and without confusing them. Read your papers aloud. Better yet, compose them as talks before you write them.

6. *The importance of the information on a written page is inversely proportional to the page number.* This is a hypothesis of mine that many other researchers and writers will hotly contest. My preference is to front-load a paper. The farther you are from the first sentence of a paper, the less important the material is likely to be. The key to a good paper is the problem, followed by the method. The results are likely to be mildly interesting (in a good piece of research, you already know pretty much what you are going to find), and the discussion hardly interesting at all (in a good paper, you already know what it means). A colleague claims that I once said that a discussion section longer than four pages means that the author is trying to hide something. I don't know if I really said this, but if I didn't, I wish I had.

6a. *The quality of a paper does not depend on its results.* If the question is truly compelling and the methods are appropriate and powerful, any result should be interesting and informative.

6b. *Surprises are bad for the heart and the vita.* In thinking about my own research, one way I clearly distinguish the good stuff from the bad is that in the bad studies, I had no clear idea how the data would come out (or I had a clear idea, but was completely wrong). If you know the domain well enough to predict in some detail your results, you are more likely to ask good questions and less likely to run studies that fail.

7. *The quality of your work counts, but you also need quantity.* One really good paper is better than three or four or five mediocre or poor ones. You could conceivably make your name, win tenure and promotion, and more, on the basis of one excellent paper, but don't hold your breath. Really good papers are quite rare,

and we all tend to overestimate the quality of our own work. It is best to assume that *none* of your papers is so good that people will ignore the volume of your work and pay attention only to its sterling quality. Self-enhancement biases are so ingrained in our culture that even if you did happen to write a gem, you will probably find it difficult to distinguish its quality from that of several other of your works. As I noted earlier, a bad paper may be worse than no paper at all, but assuming that you can identify reasonably interesting research questions and apply reasonably sensible methods to the problem, my advice is to crank papers out at a pretty regular pace.

8. *The quality of the journal probably counts more than the quality of the paper.* I say this for a number of reasons. First, people pay attention to high-quality journals. When your paper is published in one, the halo effect alone will lead people to pay some attention to it. Second, as I have noted before, good journals usually give the best, or at least the most useful, reviews. They may not like your paper as much as the less demanding journals, but they are much more likely to help you improve both that particular paper and your research in general. Third, people read high-quality journals. Take a look at your own bookshelf and the shelves of a few colleagues, professors, and others, and you will see the same four or five journals on every shelf. You can always find some journal that will publish your work, but unless some of that work gets into the journals that someone reads, you might as well not bother publishing.

9. *It's only business.* The film *The Godfather* includes a line like this—one mobster is reminding another not to take his impending death personally. You should keep this saying in mind whenever you read reviews of your papers. Don't take negative reviews personally, don't assume that the reviewers are motivated by personal animus, and don't get offended or discouraged. Anyone who hasn't been called a

fool by reviewers hasn't submitted enough papers to the journals. It comes with the territory.

Replies, Rejoinders, Rebuttals, and Rehashes

One final note on the publication process: If you publish enough, you are likely to be subjected to critiques, rebuttals, and so on, and your first temptation will almost certainly be to expose the errors and poor scholarship of your critics. Don't. Our journals are littered with series of comments, rebuttals, and counterrebuttals that do little more than make the authors look foolish and quarrelsome. I have never seen an important issue resolved in exchanges of this sort, but I have seen many reputations go down the drain as a result of intemperate charges and countercharges. You have little to gain and much to lose by responding in print to critiques of your work, no matter how unfair they seem to you.

One of the highest forms of praise you can receive is to have your work criticized in a major journal. This means that someone has read your work, thought about it, and convinced an editor that your ideas and findings matter enough to deserve further attention. Accept the praise and get on with your life. There is an old Hollywood saying: I don't care what they say about me, as long as they spell my name right. This really is a healthy perspective. The next time you see a journal article titled "Comment on . . . ," hope that the comment is about you, and make sure they spell your name right!

Note

1. The other major motivation for publication is probably simple force of habit. Once you have been doing this for 10 or 12 years, it is hard to think of *not* publishing.

14 Revising and Resubmitting

AUTHOR EMOTIONS, EDITOR ROLES, AND THE VALUE OF DIALOGUE

J. Keith Murnighan

I was appointed associate editor of *Administrative Science Quarterly* (*ASQ*) on April 1, 1994 (I always thought that the choice of that date was particularly appropriate). This was the only administrative position I had ever desired, so when Steve Barley called to offer me the position, I said yes even before I really knew what was involved.

One of the major reasons Steve appointed me was to try to broaden the appeal of the journal. *ASQ* is a sociologically oriented journal; as I am an experimental social psychologist, at least by training, Steve hoped that my appointment would signal that *ASQ* was open to micro as well as macro papers and that we would seriously consider experiments. This shift in emphasis, however, meant that my manuscript load was less than that of the other editors; it has increased slowly.

All editors look forward to getting good manuscripts—without them, journals would be in

tremendous trouble. So we are absolutely delighted when a good manuscript arrives, it gets good reviews, and we can send a positive letter back to the author. Even a good paper, however, will typically get a "revise and resubmit" decision, especially because, at *ASQ*, it is reviewed by three reviewers who have been chosen because they take different approaches to the same topic. Although a revise-and-resubmit decision should be seen by authors as very good news—most papers do not get such a positive decision—it is still something less (much less?) than what many authors hope for when they submit their work.

In this chapter, I describe the editorial process surrounding a good paper that was submitted to *ASQ* in the summer of 1995. All three reviewers were positive about the paper; each recommended either a revise and resubmit or a provisional acceptance, with one predicting that a successful revision was fairly likely, one predicting that it was a near certainty, and one checking off both of these categories. This combination of reactions was very positive, more positive than that accorded any other paper I had handled in the year and a half I had been associate editor.

Ironically, however, the authors reacted to the reviews as if we were asking them to swallow a bitter pill: They were not very happy, at first, about the feedback the reviewers and I had provided. This chapter displays many of those reactions verbatim. Because I have had a long friendship with one of the authors, they have allowed me to share information from their reviews, my decision letter, and a series of e-mail interchanges we had right after they received the reviews and just before they began their revisions. This chapter shows how, even with the most positive of reviews, authors can feel that editors and reviewers are attacking their work, their scholarship, and their self-image. This reaction is typical: We are all pretty tender when it comes to our own work. We are even more tender when our research gets rejected. I'll touch on that in this chapter as well, from my own personal experience as an author who submitted a paper to *ASQ* during this same period.

The Reviews and
the Decision Letter

The authors submitted their paper on August 17, 1995; it was received by the *ASQ* office on August 21. I received the paper and assigned it to three reviewers on August 29. I read the paper with considerable interest. It focused on a topic that I had conducted some research on years ago. More importantly, it was interesting to read, the study was competently conducted, and the paper had the potential to make researchers and practitioners rethink an established stream of research. As a result, I selected three reviewers whom I respected very much: They are all critical, constructive, accomplished scholars. One is currently active in this area of research; two are active in related areas. Of the latter two, one is particularly meticulous: I could trust that he would not let one word go unturned without questioning whether it was exactly right. The other has a tremendously broad point of view on work in our field. As a trio, I

expected that the reviewers would be thorough, competent, and constructive. If the paper was as good as I thought it was, they would help make it better. At the same time, if my reading had been influenced by the fact that one of the authors was a friend, they would take my blinders off very quickly.

The first reviewer, who worked in the field and might not have appreciated the authors' different approach, was very positive.[1] She started her one-and-a-half-page, single-spaced review by saying:

> I liked this paper. I liked the clear lively writing. I liked the short sentences. I liked the multimethod approach. I liked the solid field legwork. I liked the topic. In fact, just about the only thing I didn't much like were the conclusions and inferences. Let me make my case and see if I can persuade the authors to shift their pitch a bit.

She followed with three paragraphs that raised a series of questions, focused on a central issue in the paper, and made a series of recommendations. She concluded her comments to the authors by saying, "But it is a very nice piece of work!" On the *ASQ* reviewer form, for my eyes only, she suggested that I provisionally accept the paper subject to "minor but significant" revisions and indicated that a successful revision was a near certainty.

The second reviewer started by saying:

> Overall: I think this is a terrific paper. It was interesting, fresh, fun to read, and relevant to real world issues. It reflects a tremendous amount of work and a rich understanding of an intriguing company. This paper does a great job of shaking up the stodge of traditional literature on [this topic], and that alone makes a valuable contribution to the field.

In the second paragraph, this reviewer went on:

> That said, the paper needs some conceptual work, and the writing needs some clarifying. The methods section needs fleshing out. Some of the constructs and terms need to be sharpened.

She added six single-spaced pages of specific comments on sentences, paragraphs, ideas, and claims, and raised questions she couldn't answer from this version of the manuscript. On our reviewer form, she suggested that I offer the authors the chance to revise and resubmit the paper and that a revision was either fairly likely or nearly certain to be successful.

The third reviewer started with a summary of the paper's topic and approach. He then wrote: "The manuscript has the potential to stimulate a variety of new streams of research on [the general topic]. However, as currently written, it is weakened by three critical flaws." After outlining these issues, he concluded this section of his review by saying, "Fortunately, none of these three weaknesses is fatal. All they require is revision, although what I am requesting is a *major* rewrite." He ended his four-page, single-spaced review with 23 separate points. He recommended a revise-and-resubmit decision and judged that a successful revision would be fairly likely.

These reviews came in very quickly, arriving on September 13, 18, and 25. I received the last review on September 28 and wrote my decision letter that day and the next. The *ASQ* office mailed our feedback to the authors on October 2; they received it on October 9. The total time elapsed since the author's original mailing was 53 days, 19 of which were taken up by transit within the U.S. and Canadian postal systems.

Despite a tone that was not uniformly positive, these constituted a very favorable set of reviews. They rivaled the most positive reviews I have ever received on papers I have handled at *ASQ* or on my own work. This illustrates that even the most positive of reviews is bound to have something negative in it; possibly this is the nature of the beast.

The reviews were also remarkably thorough, which made my editorial decision very easy: I offered the authors the opportunity to revise and resubmit their paper. In writing my decision letter, I wanted to be as clear as I could be about what we wanted the authors to do. As a result, my letter was six pages long. I told the authors that I would reiterate some of the reviewers' comments, but that I hoped this was a small price to pay for increased clarity.

After acknowledging that we had received three reviews of their paper, I started the letter by saying:

The reviewers and I were all intrigued by your paper: The topic, and your treatment of

it, is both interesting and important. Your new twist on what many might think is a dead issue is particularly noteworthy. While we all had concerns about various aspects of your paper, we also felt that you could handle them in a serious, substantive revision. As a result, I am happy to offer you the opportunity to revise and resubmit your paper.

I could be wrong, but I thought this was a very positive first paragraph.

After a paragraph in which I expressed my appreciation for the unusually fine reviews, I outlined four general issues that I hoped the authors would address: the paper's theoretical contributions, the authors' methods and approaches to their research project, how they characterized the related literature in the area, and the limitations of their study. Then, because this was a revise-and-resubmit decision, I included 24 minor comments to help the authors polish their revision.

I started the last page of the letter by saying:

As you can see, the reviewers and I enjoyed your work and recognized its considerable promise. We would all like to see you deal with the issues that we have raised in a revision. I am happy to work with you as you revise your manuscript, to clarify any of my comments or expand on them, and to help in any way I can.

I asked the authors to notify the *ASQ* office if they planned to write a revision and when we might expect to receive it. I told them that they did not have to respond to every reviewer comment, but that a summary of the major changes would be helpful, and that if they did not respond to a reviewer suggestion, they should tell us why.

I started the final paragraph by saying that if they had any questions they should call me at my office, and provided my phone number. Finally, I wrote:

Thank you for submitting this interesting manuscript to *ASQ*. You have clearly invested a lot in this work. I truly hope that you will go the extra mile to make this paper all that it can be. I look forward to seeing it in the near future.

I ended the letter with "Sincerely" and my signature.

The Authors' Reactions

I think that these were tremendous reviews: They were positive and very constructive. I also tried to be very encouraging in my decision letter. How successful were we in stimulating the authors to undertake a substantial revision in line with our suggestions? A series of electronic mail interchanges between me and the lead author reveal how their emotions rose and fell over time and how they planned to proceed with the paper.

On October 11, two days after receiving the reviews, the senior author wrote:

> I got the reviews and am moving to the point where I can almost think about them. Most of it looks doable, but I'll almost certainly have a question or two. I am tempted to ask some now, but I'd better process a bit more deeply. I am, to be frank, discouraged about some of the comments, but I'll get over it. My coauthor is shocked.

Here we see the kind of pain that Susan Ashford describes in her outstanding essay on publishing in this volume (Chapter 12). It is also clear that the author is experienced enough to know that he needs to contain his reactions so that he can respond not only to his emotions but also to the substance of the reviews.

I replied that I agreed that everything suggested by the reviewers was doable, and that I was sorry that his coauthor was shocked. I asked whether this was due to the extensiveness of the comments or to the possibility that they were nasty (which I didn't see). I also expressed the hope that we had not discouraged him. The senior author replied that his coauthor "was shocked because he had never seen *ASQ* reviews; this is his first submission. It is a good lesson. I keep telling him, 'This is as good as it gets.' " The junior author undoubtedly benefited tremendously from the senior author's experience. The senior author could make sure that they did not make the same mistake Susan Ashford and her colleagues made—which she also describes in her chapter—that is, getting a revise-and-resubmit decision with long reviews and thinking that they couldn't satisfy the editors and the reviewers. I also think that, in this case, the senior author's responsibilities as a mentor helped him temper his own emotional

reactions. But there is much more information on this in his later messages.

That same day, October 12, I received another message:

> I am recovering quickly. I read the comments again this morning and I agree that they are doable and quite reasonable for the most part. I think the shock was partly the volume and partly the inevitable "You are ruining my perfect baby." Well, I agree my baby ain't so perfect. . . . Also, now that I am getting beyond the volume, I realize that I've never had three reviewers and an editor who are all on my side, all trying to make the paper better.

The image of a paper being one's child, and a perfect one at that, is a metaphor that I expect many authors use. The author also noted that the accommodation process had begun: He was beginning to see the value of the reviews, even though he, too, was affected by the volume of our comments.

I wrote the author on October 16, on another topic, and asked if he would "give me some feedback as an editor. I get it all too rarely, and I always finish my letters thinking that they still leave something to be desired." He replied the next day:

> My problem is that my initial reaction to reviews—any reviews—is so strong that it isn't fair to use them as an indicator of the quality of your letter. Now, every time I read your letter, it seems more reasonable. I'll read it again and give you another reaction, but at this point, my hunch is that your letter is fine, but my coping skills are not.

Frankly, I disagree: His coping skills are excellent, especially given the strength of his (normal) emotional reactions. Although it took time for his angry emotions to subside, he knew from the start that they would, and he was willing to wait for them to go away before he reacted rashly.

Editors as Authors

Ironically, on October 27, a coauthor and I received a letter from *ASQ* rejecting one of our papers, a revision of our initial submission. Now the shoe was on the other foot, and, short-sighted as I am, I took the decision personally and was quite upset about the reviews. (Note: This was a rejection of a revise and resubmit, rather than an invitation to revise. As such, it was doubly painful.) I wrote to my friend, the author of the paper we are discussing in this chapter, to vent a few frustrations. My message included such phrases as "disgusting," "picked nits," "more than casually misinterpreted our measures and our data," and "stupid." I was not displeased by the editor's decision letter—only by the reviews. As I write this chapter, a month has gone by and my emotional reactions have not subsided.

My friend wrote back that day, saying, "I am sorry about the rejection. They suck. I am glad that you got upset at the associate editor and reviewers—signs of continuing fire in the belly." He also came back to his own *ASQ* submission, which I have been describing in detail:

> I'll soon get to the revision. I may need to check out one part of my revision strategy with you before I go forward. Most of it is pretty straightforward; as I read it more closely, I realize how good your letter is, muting some of the unreasonable and inconsistent suggestions and emphasizing the reasonable and consistent ones.

Two observations are in order here. First, any negativity in a review will lead to its being perceived as unreasonable; if this is the nature of the review beast, it's no wonder we are always angry at reviewers. Second, it was nice to hear that my decision letter was constructive.

On November 6, I received a long message:

> We are starting to work on the revision. Enough time has passed that I can read the reviews and respond in a more or less rational fashion. I think we can address the major concerns in an acceptable fashion, but I want to make clear what we plan to do.

Note the importance of time in the author's conceptualization of the process.

Proposals on how the authors would respond to the four main issues in the paper followed. The first, on the paper's theoretical contribution, was longest. The first two sentences indi-cated that they agreed that there was room for improvement. Their fourth sentence started with the words "Please note" and began to make their side of the case. The authors took a strong but perfectly appropriate stand to emphasize what their paper is and what it isn't. From my perspective, this is extremely important: It shows that they have a clear idea about what they want to do with their paper and it makes it easy for me to suggest that they describe their paper in just these terms, succinctly and forcefully.

The authors continued to make their case. Three subsequent sentences started with "We believe," and four with either "Please note" or "Note." At the same time, they peppered their plans with a series of "We will" and "We prom-ise" sentences, especially when they addressed issues concerning their methods, how they had characterized the literature, and the limitations of their study. They expressed a serious concern that they wouldn't be able to satisfy one of the reviewers, who "didn't get (or didn't accept) our main point." Ironically, this was the re-viewer who was most positive about the paper and had suggested a provisional acceptance of the initial submission.

They closed their five-page letter by again noting what their paper does and doesn't do. They used the word "purpose" three times, high-lighting their paper's intent. They indicated what they couldn't do in the paper. The senior author closed with the following:

> Finally, in reading the reviews, I'm a bit wor-ried that we are being pressed to make this paper one that will be all things to all people. I suspect that you understand these pres-sures; many of your suggestions appear to be intended to help us manage them. But I want to make clear that if we try to do everything the reviewers ask, we will have an impossible task before us.

I responded on November 8 (I had been out of town November 4-7), "I appreciate your let-ter about your paper. In almost every way, I agree with your plans and your approach to the revision. But let me outline my reactions a bit more specifically." In the rest of my two-page letter, I asked them to "be explicit about what you can and can't say about" the phenomenon, told them that "I don't think you will have trouble convincing reviewer no. 1," reinforced their plan to show how their approach differed from previous approaches in the area, reiterated a request to present some propositions at the end of their paper (which they suggested they might not be able to fulfill), and tried to clarify the central thrust of the paper and how I thought it could make the most impact. Also, I told them:

> I agree that the reviewers and I were implicitly asking you to make this paper all things to all people. I think we are all idealists, especially when we see how much impact a paper might have. . . . I don't think we have asked you to do an impossible task, although it might feel that way. Instead, we have asked you to consider a series of suggestions, some of which may be inconsistent, but all of which were presented with the idea that, together, they might make the paper almost everything to almost everyone. There will still be some limitations to the paper when you finish it—this is true of all papers. But by walking several tightropes simultaneously, you can come close to accomplishing a multitude of big objectives. You can't completely take away readers' "but they didn't do this" reactions. What you can do is push them to appreciate a new approach and some neat new ideas even after they've raised any of the "buts" they might be able to find in the corners of your paper.
>
> Finally, no matter how much you tone down the paper, you will get some people to react. Absolutely. Hopefully. That is just what you want. But you want them to react to your ideas and your suggestions rather than to your labels of their work. . . .
>
> I hope all this is clear. You are on the right track in your plans for revising the paper. I know there will be some agonizing during the rewriting process, but I also hope it will be fun. I sure look forward to seeing it.

The senior author replied the next day: "We are on the same wavelength. We will get to the painful business of revising text as soon as we can." He went on to describe how they agreed with my characterization of the overall thrust of the paper, in some detail. He ended by saying:

> Well, I'm starting to have some fun thinking about how this paper will be improved as a

result of the revisions. This means that I've moved from believing that, in order to get the paper published, I will have to "mutilate" my masterpiece to believing that the paper will get stronger as a result of the review process. It always takes me time to make this transition. We will be in touch if we have any questions, but I think that we know what to do and feel confident that we are on the same wavelength with you.

As often happens, especially with holidays intervening, it took the authors some time finally to knuckle down to the actual task of doing their revision. On January 2, I received another e-mail—a fitting end to a real emotional upheaval (but an end, I think, only because the paper's prospects are so good).

> Well, I am finally moving on this thing. I did the introduction today. It went pretty quickly once I started, but I am writing to make sure that you won't be surprised by a longer paper. . . . The reviews now seem so civilized— are you sure they haven't changed since I first read them?

Papers, Reviewers, and Editors

The extended interchange depicted above was incredibly important—for the paper, for the authors, and for me as an editor. It is just the kind of dialogue that the other editors at *ASQ* and I would like to have with all authors who are working on revisions.[2] We don't want any misunderstandings about what we are looking for; we want to share a vision for the paper with the authors. If we can agree on how a paper can be improved, then it is likely to become a much better paper, which is something we all are hoping for.

These messages also show how authors' reactions to reviews of their work move from angry, negative emotions to a mix of emotions and reason and even the possibility that the work of revision might be fun. It took these authors about a month to make this transition, and it was another couple of months before all of the negative emotions had finally dissipated. Their messages suggest that they might have had a much harder time revising if they had tried to push things any faster.

Paper Metaphors

The senior author's metaphors for their paper—a perfect baby and a masterpiece—are probably common ways of describing the products of one's labors. For an academic, the desire to write a paper means that you must pour yourself into the task, taking an idea or two and pushing it as far as you can to see what you can make of it. It is a personal, emotional endeavor that, one hopes, includes both logic and creativity. When we finish a paper, we often share it with friends, hoping that they will say good things about it, even if we tell them to be brutal in their comments. I think everyone dreams of writing papers that will cause readers to think we are absolutely brilliant. Thinking of our papers as personal tours de force is a natural element in this process.

With my own papers, I try to use a different metaphor, one that makes reviews a little easier to take.[3] As I enjoy cooking, I try to think of my papers as recipes: They are my best attempt to concoct something absolutely delicious. I tinker with them, revise them, add something here or there to perk them up. Then I try them on friends, hoping that they'll be appreciative. To extend the metaphor, the ultimate test is to submit a recipe to a cooking contest. If the recipe wins a prize, that's great. If it comes back with a suggestion that will make the dish taste better, that's not as good, but it still improves future eating experiences. Also, if the suggestion doesn't make the dish taste better—at least to me—then I don't have to change it. It still might win next year's contest.

The review process for papers is similar: If the reviews are helpful and constructive and they contribute to making the paper better, it's great—not as good as an immediate acceptance, but still a very positive result. In the end, it means that the reviewers are helping me make my paper better. In fact, it is probably the only way my papers and I have been pushed so far; nonanonymous comments are almost necessarily less critical. In the end, tough reviewers improve papers, and better papers make authors look like better scholars. I know this has been true for me many times.

I have always felt that a long, constructive review is priceless: It may seem negative when it first arrives, but it forces me to reconsider many if not all of the issues in the paper. Although long reviews mean more work, they also mean that a thoughtful reader has read my paper with great care. This is something we should all hope for. Long reviews should be seen as reasons for rejoicing, especially if they come with opportunities to resubmit.

Another example amplifies this point. A colleague and I once had a paper accepted as is—with no requirements to change anything. Although the acceptance was good news, the lack of substantive commentary led us to work incredibly hard to make sure that we didn't publish something we would regret later. Because we both had or would soon have tenure, we realized that we were facing the "publish and perish" rather than the "publish or perish" problem, which Kevin Murphy also describes in his chapter in this volume: We might have published something that we could never change and never live down. This was a terrifying thought, one that has made me even more appreciative of thorough reviews.

Although they are a necessary evil, reviews can be tremendously constructive: They can open your eyes to things that you hadn't even considered in your work. Applying metaphors to their work that allow them to see feedback as constructive, or having review-reading rituals such as the one Susan Ashford describes in Chapter 12, can also give authors opportunities to make real progress with their papers.

From an editor's perspective, a reviewer's major role is to screen papers so that poor research and/or poor theory do not find their way into our journals. In contrast, most people think of editors as gatekeepers. This role, however, is truly overrated. Most of the time, multiple reviews are consistent. When three reviewers make similar recommendations, the editor doesn't need to make a decision; it's already been made. Only in rare instances do editors actually have to exert decision control; thus reviewers themselves are actually the primary gatekeepers.[4]

The more typical role of the editor is to act as the author's friend. Steve Barley has made this explicit at *ASQ*. In deliberations over the past year, he formulated a series of guidelines for our editors. He wrote:

> Editors play a unique role vis-à-vis the author, a role quite distinct from that of a reviewer. Whereas the reviewer's job is to be critical in

order to protect the field from shoddy scholarship, the editor's job is to ensure that feedback can be heard. Whereas reviewers can traffic in the details of the paper, editors must articulate larger gestalts, especially broad strategies for revision. Whereas reviewers have the luxury of aligning themselves with the field, editors must orient themselves simultaneously to the journal and the author. The last alignment is critical: The editor is the only person in the review process who can afford to function as the author's friend. Although other journals may not perceive this as an aspect of the editor's persona, at *ASQ* it is.

In addition, because top journals accept only 10%-20% of the papers they receive, most of an editor's decision letters do not encourage resubmission. Although it is self-serving to say this, I also think we really do act as our authors' true friends, friends authors need when we decline to accept their papers. If we accepted papers that shouldn't be accepted, we would not be protecting authors from publishing works that, in the end, they don't really want to have in academia's archives. In other words, we can help save authors from the "publish and perish" problem. We can also try, as best we can, to help them toward revising their work so that it will eventually be published in other journals (and thus assist them in avoiding the "publish or perish" problem).

When we get good papers that generate good reviews and revise-and-resubmit decisions, we bend over backward to give authors as much help as we can with their revisions. We want to be able to accept these papers. We hate having to say no to authors who have gone through the enormous trouble to make major changes to their work. As is clear from this chapter, starting a dialogue with authors as they work on their revisions is something we are very happy to do—and that should lead to more positive outcomes for everyone. All editors may not want to get involved in these dialogues, but we

certainly do at *ASQ*; this is something authors should consider trying whenever they get revise-and-resubmit decisions.

In sum, the road from submitting a paper to having it finally published is one that is littered with emotion. It feels great to complete the first draft. It feels just as good to have a paper that's finally ready to be submitted to a journal. Then, regardless of the nature of the reviews, receiving them is a real downer. It takes time to get over this negative hump, but then it's possible to see how the reviews might actually help improve your work. When you get a revise-and-resubmit decision, you have started a continuing relationship with the editor, one that you can work on together. At *ASQ* and probably at other journals as well, it is both appropriate and important to make sure that you and the editor see the revision process and its goal in the same way. Scholarship in the social sciences only infrequently depends on isolated, individual action. Instead, it is and should be based on a series of constructive interactions, from the beginning to the end of the process. Putting a positive spin on the process, even on tough, anonymous reviews, will help you persevere and achieve as much as you possibly can with your work. It will make you a much happier and more productive author. It also makes for happier editors.

Notes

1. I flipped a coin to determine whether I would use male or female pronouns for each of the reviewers. In fact, one is female and two are male.

2. It goes almost without saying that it would be impossible for editors to engage in such dialogues with authors of papers that have not received invitations to resubmit.

3. Rejections, as noted earlier, are *never* easy to take.

4. As editors, we do choose the reviewers, so, in an indirect sense, we are still gatekeepers.

Working With Doctoral Students

My heroes are emerging and pushy, models of enthusiasm with new ideas and approaches. They bring new vigor, sometimes with rigor (but in its absence, that can be taught), and light to established topics. Some even bring new topics to the field.

Larry L. Cummings (p. 151)

I see part of my role as an academic as helping to produce the next generation of scholars.

Susan J. Ashford (p. 154)

The key characteristics of working with doctoral students are the diversity of relationships and the uniqueness of each dyadic pair.

Linn Van Dyne (p. 159)

In looking back on our relationships, we recognized that it was often one of our students—and not one of us—who made the first move with respect to initiating a collaboration

Roderick M. Kramer and Joanne Martin (p. 167)

Most academics can recall their experiences with one or a few key people during their time of apprenticeship en route to a graduate degree (often a PhD). Some others are currently in the midst of collaborative relationships as advisers or as advisees making their way through a doctoral program. Each dyadic pair is probably unique (as Linn Van Dyne observes), and there likely are many different styles and philosophies of mentoring among contemporary academics who serve as advisers to doctoral students. In this section, Cummings, Ashford, and Kramer and Martin all provide information about their own approaches to the advising role. However, it seems important that all of us, as advisers, develop our own frameworks or sets of guidelines that implicitly or explicitly inform the approaches that we take to the role.

Kramer and Martin note the importance of the psychological contract between the adviser and the advisee as a hedge against harmful extremes for both parties: "Setting clear and somewhat conservative expectations is often best—as long as it is coupled with a willingness to modify the contract as experience working together accumulates" (p. 171). They recount an unfortunate experience with one promising graduate student:

> She was so smart and eager, and I was so sure everything would work out well. Also, I was uncomfortable with discussing an explicit contract. It seemed unnecessarily formal, and I worried that it would undermine the more egalitarian, friendly, "we're in this together" mood I wanted to establish. So the student was left with the impression that she would be a coauthor—not only on our experimental article, but on everything I wrote on a particular subject. This came back later to haunt me. (pp. 171-172)

Larry Cummings discusses a number of specifics that go into the orientation he has with doctoral students. He makes some distinctions in his style of engagement depending on factors such as the student's progress in the PhD program: "Am I dealing with a rookie, a postprelim wondering student, a dissertation beginner, or a neck-deep dissertation swimmer?" (p. 148). Kramer and Martin also observe the importance of dealing with the stage a student has reached intellectually and emotionally as he or she makes progress toward the completion of the degree. They discuss issues of appropriate psychological and social distances and the importance of timing the development of the relationship in its early, middle, and closing stages. They

also note that the intensity of relationships between professors and doctoral students, as well as the availability of academics as advisers, can diminish as academics progress in their careers and become caught up in their own personal circumstances.

Working with doctoral students can produce positive benefits for both parties. Susan Ashford, reflecting on her experiences with Larry Cummings as her adviser, notes: "He saw more in me than I saw in myself at that time. Therefore, I attempted more than I thought I was capable of doing. I also strove hard to meet his expectations and, by so doing, developed work habits that served me well throughout my early career years" (p. 155). Kramer and Martin cite a case where one of them was drawn into an advising role and into a research area by a persistent and artful student:

> "Would you be willing," he asked, "to read just one article on the subject?" I agreed reluctantly. . . . I did read it, and the next day he came in just briefly, to exchange it for an even more intriguing article. Every day for several weeks, this process of exchanging papers went on. . . . After a while, my behavior told me that supervising this dissertation was just what I wanted to do. Now, years later, most of my research is on the topic he introduced me to. (p. 170)

The nature of the mentoring relationship in academia appears to be a much more reciprocal and responsive one than is the case in business. Linn Van Dyne, who was also one of Larry Cummings's advisees, makes this point and adds that mentoring in academia emphasizes "socialization into a profession that transcends organizational boundaries" (p. 160). In academic settings, no two experiences are quite the same, in part because the emphasis is, or ought to be, on training students to develop their unique abilities and skills to discover their own research programs.

There are few explicit guidelines for becoming an adviser to a doctoral student; it seems to be mostly a case of trial and error. We typically model ourselves on our own mentors if we have had successful experiences. Although this can be a potentially useful place to start, it can prove misleading. As Kramer and Martin observe:

> Both of us started out as new assistant professors by trying to re-create the relationships we had with our mentors. Both of us regarded those relationships with great fondness because they not only helped us become scholars, but led to terrific friendships.... Over time, we learned that we were not as good at being like them as we had hoped. Our collaborations have worked better as we have tried to evolve our own styles. (p. 173)

The experiences reported by Kramer and Martin and by Ashford also attest to the unique and memorable emotional elements of these relationships. For the adviser and the student involved, such relationships are rarely simply predictable, transactional exchanges. As a former student of Kramer and Martin put it after reading an initial draft of their chapter:

> My experience of our relationship was not one of "being managed" or of being part of a predictable stage sequence, but of talking about the meaning of life and Woody Allen while running the dish [a jogging trail], talking about ideas and cognition over Thai food, as well as struggling over experimental design, theses revisions, and paper reviews. (p. 167)

Beyond the Research Agenda

Virtually all the focus in these chapters on working with doctoral students is on the research link. This has been and continues to be the central task of advisers. We think another critical role for mentors is to help their students develop teaching skills. It is not necessary, in our opinion, that the mentor be the (only) teacher role model for a student, although working with doctoral students is a very important teaching activity through which values and techniques about teaching are inevitably communicated. Advisers can provide encouragement and moral support for students as they learn to teach. They also can help their students to find ways to integrate or balance this activity with research and other tasks they will carry out subsequently as professionals in academic institutions.

Another important task of academic advisers in their relationships with doctoral students is to model the type of "good citizen" behaviors that contribute to productive and harmonious lives in university communities comprising other academics and professionals, administrators, students, and support staff. Universities, particularly public ones, are currently under a great deal of pressure to justify the expense of their contributions to society. When the academic ego manifests itself as arrogance, intolerance, and total self-absorption, it can blind scholars to the limits of their own work and to the needs of others in the university community. Insensitivity to fundamental human dignity in dealing with others can handicap the potential of academics to contribute constructively to the well-being of this community. Doctoral students are the future generation of academics and professionals in our field. Advisers can play an important role in sensitizing their students to this important issue.

15 The Development of Doctoral Students

SUBSTANTIVE AND EMOTIONAL PERSPECTIVES

Larry L. Cummings

The original initiative to prepare this essay was provided by an invitation from three of the Academy of Management's divisions to present my thoughts, experiences, and feelings about the development of doctoral students. I thank the OB, OMT, and OD Divisions, and Walt Nord and Art Brief in particular, for that invitation.

What I am about to present is, in part, based on that Academy presentation in August 1993. It is also, in part, based on a 1986 paper published in the *Organizational Behavior Teaching Review*. It was there that I developed the theme of the heroic nature of doctoral student behavior in my development as a teacher. I want to thank Susan Ashford for important and stimulating inputs to what I have to say here. I would also like to acknowledge the important influence of 54 other PhD students I have advised since 1964 at Indiana University, the University of Wisconsin, the University of British Columbia, Northwestern University, and the University of Minnesota.

Philosophy of Involvement

I believe that all good PhD advisers have philosophies that underlie their involvement with their students. These philosophies differ across professors and are sometimes latent, never achieving articulation. My philosophy of involvement contains the six components that I describe in turn below.[1]

First, involvement can take multiple forms and multiple levels; I see it as pluralistic. Second, I see and feel these forms and levels, from minimum to maximum involvement, as follows:

- Giving *technical* answers and advice
- Assisting in *intellectual guidance* concerning formulating and specifying a research question, hypotheses, designs, and analyses
- Giving *support* and *affirmation* when appropriate on intellectual issues
- Being a *personal friend* to a student when the student needs personal advice or a friendly

147

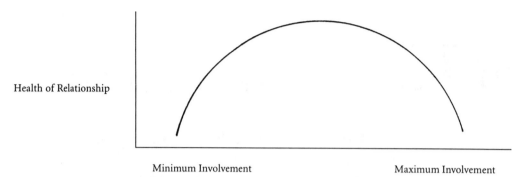

Figure 15.1. Health of Relationship and Level of Involvement

listener on emotional, value, and interpersonal issues

- *Sponsoring* the student to those in public arenas, particularly outside of our home university
- Accepting the *personal friendship* offered by the student to me
- *Controlling* the student, intellectually and emotionally
- *Psychologically owning* the student ("This student is *mine*—keep away")

The third component of my philosophy focuses on the healthiness of the relationship. I believe there is likely a curvilinear relation between these degrees of involvement and the health of the student-adviser and, later in the career cycle, the colleague-colleague relationship. I would depict this as shown in Figure 15.1. I believe the health of the relationship is reflected in and can be indicated by symptoms such as mutual comfort, respect, productiveness, maturity, and longevity.

The fourth dimension of my philosophy involves my intentionally *differentiating* among students. This process of differentiation produces differing styles of relating by me and usually by the student, depending on the following:

- The *student's mood,* particularly his or her mood associated with maturity in dealing with authority (I try to avoid being the target of latent aggression felt toward earlier authority figures; if it cannot be avoided, then we deal with it explicitly as a mutual problem), the student's intellectual *interests,*

the intellectual *capacities* of the student, and the degree of *initiative* taken by the student.

- My *own moods* (see Cummings, 1992) and other *commitments.* I explicitly ask myself if I can handle another relationship with grace, calmness, thoroughness, and caring.
- The stage of the *student's progress* in the institutionalized program of becoming a PhD. Am I dealing with a rookie, a postprelim wondering student, a dissertation beginner, or a neck-deep dissertation swimmer?
- The amount and form of *intellectual and emotional support* the student is receiving from my faculty colleagues. Is the student blessed with resources or in deep need?

I believe the fifth component of my philosophy reflects an interaction of four forces that should influence the roles I play. These four forces are as follows:

- What are the *facts* of the discipline that I should be held accountable for tending?
- What are the research and communication *skills* I should teach?
- What professional *behaviors* (e.g., colleagueship) should I teach and attempt to model?
- What *personal values, standards, and beliefs* should I exhibit because I am committed to them in action?

I see these four forces as interacting to form and shape my style of involvement as shown in Figure 15.2.

Finally, I believe that any personal philosophy of acting as an adviser, mentor, or in any

Facts of the Discipline   Professional Behaviors

Professorial Role

Skills of the Discipline   Personal Values, Standards,
                                                   and Beliefs

Figure 15.2. Forces Influencing the Professorial Role

other human context should contain a consciousness about one's pitfalls, vulnerabilities,
and weaknesses. In the context of working with
PhD students, my greatest potential weakness
is frustration, even occasional anger, when a
student does not accept and/or appreciate my
efforts and commitment.

These elements (the student, me, and developmental dimensions) seem to flow into a strategy
of involvement as depicted in Figure 15.3.

Questions and Challenges

The following questions were generated by
Professor Walter Nord and other colleagues as a
framework for the 1993 National Academy of
Management presentation. I, along with several
others, was asked to respond to them in terms of
my experience and behavior. I use the questions
here as a framework for illustrating and articulating the philosophy I have just described.

Question or Challenge 1:
What behaviors have you found
most helpful (and least helpful) in
working with PhD students?

- Most helpful
  1. patience
  2. diagnosis
  3. appropriate and careful timing of my ex-
     pectations
  4. managing the students' expectations
  5. knowing what resources are available all
     around the campus, not just in my depart-
     ment

6. honoring and respecting the student's intellectual interests, particularly if I see some
   passion for these interests and ideas within
   the student
- Least helpful
  1. premature judgments made by me of students
  2. assuming that I will get feedback directly
     from the students without inquiry or moni-
     toring by me

Question or Challenge 2:
Do I differentiate my strategies of
development for individual students?

The answer to this is a definite yes. The challenge is to work the following three components into a specific strategy for each student. I
diagnose my abilities, the student's characteristics,
and the dimensions of development most needed
by the student. From that I select what appears
to be an optimum degree of involvement, as
described earlier. The three components of the
model are as follows:

1. The student
2. Me
3. Dimensions for development

Question or Challenge 3:
What tips would you offer
students in working with faculty
and potential mentors?

- Be prepared—don't bluff.
- Be politely demanding.

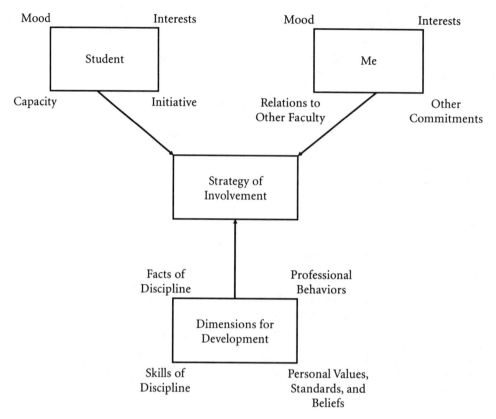

Figure 15.3. Elements Leading to a Strategy of Involvement

- Remember that the faculty person is going through stages with you just as you are going through stages within your program. Both are organic, dynamic scenarios.

Question or Challenge 4: What are the most important components of a PhD student's education?

- Learning to trust and affirm what he or she already senses or even knows. The student needs to learn not to be afraid to allow those intuitions and insights to emerge from discussion and development.

- For the first 2 or 3 years of the PhD program, focusing on what I call "carpentry" (the facts and skills of the discipline). There are two components to be mastered during this time: the basic knowledge of the field and the research methods, statistics, and analytic tools needed to conduct good research.

Question or Challenge 5: What have been the most difficult situations I have found myself in with PhD students?

- Losing respect for the intellectual integrity of a student who attempted to use faked data in his dissertation—he was dropped from the program.

- Having to fail a student of a respected colleague on his oral examinations because of a combination of lack of preparation and incorrect answers by the student to my questions.

- Loss of personal respect for a student who betrayed agreed-upon personal values.

**Question or Challenge 6:
How does one handle the challenges
of disengagement as the student
prepares to leave the program?**

- First, talk about it with the student—openly. Are there unsettled issues?
- Plan explicit guidelines for publishing from the dissertation. For example, my guidelines are that the first, probably the best, and maybe the only paper be sole authored by the student. If there is to be an additional paper, I would like to coauthor, as second author.
- Encourage the student to continue to expand his or her network beyond me and other peers and colleagues at the home institution.
- Get involved with another student before the graduating student leaves. This helps one to transfer a portion of one's energy in a positive direction and eases the "letting go" of one's best students.

Closing

Students have been, and continue to be, the most important part of my professional life and satisfactions. Some have become close personal friends. The best have always been my heroes. I would like to close by quoting from the 1986 piece I mentioned above.

My heroes are emerging and pushy, models of enthusiasm with new ideas and approaches. They bring new vigor, sometimes with rigor (but in its absence, that can be taught), and light to established topics. Some even bring new topics to the field. They encourage me, some even force me (otherwise I lose face) to consider new topics and to defend my reasons for requesting (even forcing) them to go through dated literature on established topics. My heroes stimulate, start, ignite my intellectual curiosity and critical capacities. Occasionally, but not too often, and even then primarily on methodological issues, do they teach me anything. That contribution would be significant. It is to these heroes that I turn when I need new food for thought, controversy, questioning and encouragement (usually through their behaviors rather than words) to undertake yet another new research topic. To me, they are heroic because:

1. they start things in me;
2. they are pleasant when I am active, alert, intellectually exciting: yet, they can be distant, even punishing, when my mind seems dead and my thinking and expression unimpressive;
3. they ask so little of me in return, and
4. they frequently are not aware of these extremely beneficial consequences of their acts; i.e., they go about the task of keeping a mid-career scholar interesting, stimulated and as pleasant as possible without expectation of direct reward for those acts. (Cummings, 1986)

Note

1. I acknowledge that the philosophy may shift, in usually small increments. Each new student brings new challenges, problems, and insights.

References

Cummings, L. L. (1986). Heroes, mentors and the development of teaching and scholarship. *Organizational Behavior Teaching Review, 10*(3), 60-65.

Cummings, L. L. (1992). Calling, disciplines, and attempts at listening. In A. G. Bedeian (Ed.), *Management laureates* (Vol. 1, pp. 237-266). Greenwich, CT: JAI.

16 Working With Doctoral Students

REFLECTIONS ON DOCTORAL WORK PAST AND PRESENT

Susan J. Ashford

This essay stems from a 1993 Academy of Management preconference symposium on working with doctoral students for which I was a panelist. As a member of that panel, I was asked to reflect on my experiences as a doctoral student with my adviser, Larry Cummings, and discuss how I was beginning to translate what I learned into my own recent work with doctoral students.

First, a little history. My doctoral education was shaped primarily by Larry Cummings, Jeanne Brett, and Joe Moag. Larry Cummings was my adviser at Northwestern University from 1979 to 1983, with a year of that being long distance, as he was in residence at the University of Wisconsin. I graduated from Northwestern in 1983 and took a faculty position at the Tuck School at Dartmouth College, an institution that does not grant doctoral degrees. I was at Tuck for 8 years. During that time, I worked with a couple of my psychology colleagues' doctoral students,

but only informally. I basically developed my entire work style without interaction with doctoral students. My real experience in working with doctoral students began in 1991, when I was recruited to the University of Michigan. Thus, if these reflections on my experiences offer useful advice to anyone, it will probably be for those just starting out on the adventure of doctoral student training. I offer these "lessons" with much modesty; I still have much to learn in this area.

It might be appropriate to start with why I wanted to move to a place that had a doctoral program, a major reason for my move from Dartmouth to Michigan. As most doctoral students would, I found it nearly inconceivable when I began my career that I would be at an institution without a doctoral program. Like most of us, I wanted to work at a place that was just like the place that produced me. At Tuck, however, not knowing what I was missing, I found that I didn't miss doctoral students particularly. I was able to do my work, find excellent research assistants, and collaborate with colleagues from other institutions. I missed the idea of participating in doctoral student development, however. In part this desire stemmed from an identity issue—I see part of my role as an academic as helping to produce the next generation of scholars. In part, it represented a desire for a different mix of activities from those available at an institution without a doctoral program. Doctoral students provide a unique source of stimulation and challenge for faculty members. Selfishly, I wanted both. I have discovered, however, that the reality is far more complicated than I had anticipated—there is stimulation and challenge, to be sure, but also new demands that are tough to meet, complaints, and new questions. My goal in this essay is to share some of these.

Reflections

As is true for most of us, my doctoral education was a vivid experience. The faculty who shaped my education, the student colleagues with whom I shared the experience, the physical setting, and my internal reactions are all burned into my memory. Not surprisingly, then, I have many memories of my work with my adviser. These memories might be a good place to start. My hope is that if I reflect on both these memories and my current struggle to put the lessons they suggest into practice in a way that feels comfortable for me, some useful insights might result. I will thus begin each segment of this essay with a memory of my relationship with Larry.

Empathy

For a few years, Larry Cummings was one of the most important people in my life. What he thought of me and how he reacted to my work mattered a great deal. This was true not so much because of the power he had over me (though clearly his power was, as an adviser's is for all doctoral students, considerable), but because of what he represented: He was someone who was what I wanted to be. He was an important figure in my development. To this day I

have him in my head. I find that statements that he made (probably quite casually) play back in my mind at the oddest times when I am doing my work.

And yet I have no sense that I am such a figure in the lives of my doctoral students (indeed, it is hard to imagine). Herein may lie the first lesson derivable from this jog down memory lane: Realize what you may represent to your doctoral students. Be aware that your influence is powerful in informal and social settings as well as in classroom settings. In short, have empathy for what they might be experiencing and how they see the world. This doesn't mean that you must always be sympathetic toward them (sometimes tough love is appropriate), but rather that you should have empathy—devote conscious attention toward being aware of their points of view. For example, I remember being very upset over a comment that for Larry might have been offhand. I remember trying to psych out the various messages contained in the Organizational Behavior Department faculty's behavior at social gatherings. Yet in my present situation, I am seldom explicitly conscious of my behavior in such settings. This insight is probably old hat to those of you who have done this for a while, but it was an important realization for me. I need both to be more self-aware and to have more empathy for what the doctoral students are experiencing. Having that awareness, I can then take more considered action.

Emotions

A second and quite vivid memory is the following: On several occasions, Larry got excited about my ideas (and other people's ideas as well). It wasn't just that he liked them, he got excited about them. He jumped up and down, went to the blackboard, kept bringing the ideas up in conversation, and kept thinking of extensions. For me and my colleagues of that time, this was incredibly flattering. That we could have ideas that would be that exciting to someone so, well, *big* meant a great deal to us.

For me, the lesson offered by this memory is the following: There is much content to be taught to and learned by doctoral students, but the emotional is important too. Doctoral students don't always know what they know—they don't always recognize insights. By your excitement, you guide them. Your emotional tone is read for its meaning.

Once I became aware of this, I realized that I have no idea of the effects I have on my doctoral students. I do know that on many occasions I am too wrapped up in my own life to show genuine excitement for their ideas. If they are reading my emotional tone for its meaning, they must be very confused! I need to work on the clarity and consistency of my messages, to make the emotions match the content.

Having been on the faculty side of this relationship for a few years now, it is clear to me that emotions are important in the other direction as well. And herein might be a lesson for PhD students. I was a very enthusiastic doctoral student. I think that my student colleagues at that time and I realized that there was a selection process going on. We felt that our job was to entice faculty with our good ideas so that they would want to work with us. As the field is all about enticing people to our ideas anyway, this wasn't a bad way to start. From my current vantage point, I can now see what fun this must have been for Larry. Enthusiasm, spirit, and willingness to work hard are attractive to faculty members, as are expressions of appreciation. It is disconcerting to work with doctoral students who don't express emotions—you feel you've done some great thing for them and they look as if you've asked them to take up worm collecting. Negativity is a downer. The emotional aspects of this whole enterprise are important—on both sides.

Expectations

Perhaps the most vivid memories doctoral students have about their advisers concern their expectations. Larry had extremely high expectations of me (and all his students, from what I could tell) and enforced them rigorously. He expected a lot and, at that time, was not particularly tolerant of a student's need to have a life too, if that life got in the way of task accomplishment. He enforced his expectations through expressions of disappointment and general all-around surliness if I didn't come through. This was a man of whom people were afraid; I know I was at times.

In reflecting on my experience, however, it is clear to me that Larry's high expectations have

played a very important role in my career. First, he saw more in me than I saw in myself at that time. Therefore, I attempted more than I thought I was capable of doing. I also strove hard to meet his expectations and, by so doing, developed work habits that served me well throughout my early career years. Although, unlike Larry, I did take a vacation before I had been on the job for nine years (in fact, I took one every year), like Larry, I worked nights and weekends in those early years. Finally, I internalized his expectations. I won't send a paper out until it reaches a certain level; I expect a certain level of production from myself each year; and so forth. It is my experience that the professional world is somewhat cruel, and the journal/publishing process particularly so. I have found that those doctoral years of being pushed and tested by fire have been particularly useful to me. I don't begrudge them. I think there is a lesson here regarding the level of standards to which we should hold our PhD students—I think high standards are helpful to students in the long run.

Larry's high standards did have their fallout, however. First, I didn't feel comfortable sharing personal things with Larry until after I received my PhD. For example, I somehow failed to mention to Larry that I would be taking a 4-week honeymoon until *after* my dissertation defense! Larry and I have become much better friends since I completed the PhD program. Perhaps this is as it should be. Second, I had to know myself well and know when to turn off my striving to meet his expectations. For example, it was my impression that Larry wanted me to take a job at a school that would not have been comfortable for me—I chose not to go. For students without this modicum of strength, their careers can become their advisers' careers all over again—not an attractive outcome.

When I observe myself with Michigan's current doctoral students, I find that I am much less tough than Larry was with me. I am not sure why that is, but I don't always think it is right. The world these students will face is only tougher than the world I faced when I emerged with my PhD in 1983. It will reward them only for excellence, not for trying hard. So why do I have trouble being tough? One answer lies in my growing realization (as I develop my style with doctoral students) that Larry must have paid some costs for his approach. Tough love may produce remarkable outputs, but people don't necessarily love you for putting them through it. Living without love (appreciation, fellowship) is painful. It is perhaps to avoid this pain that I (and others) do not adopt this style completely. I hope that I am developing a style that is softer on students in earlier stages than in later stages, softer on emerging ideas than on later conceptual and empirical development of those ideas, and softer on the spoken word (e.g., discussions in my office) than on the written word. It could be, however, that I just seem inconsistent. This is an issue that I will continue to struggle with as I work to find a style that is comfortable for me. It is one that I see my colleagues, even those more senior, struggle with as well.

Colleagueship

Larry treated students at Northwestern as colleagues—not all the time, but enough to make it noticeable and rewarding. He solicited our opinions, professional to professional. He introduced us to people at the Academy meetings. He created opportunities for us to go to dinner with people we admired in the profession.

Larry and I worked together on projects with deadlines. It was here that I gained my most memorable and useful learning. The craft of our profession cannot be taught through the verbal or written word alone. Its subtleties and its contingent nature need to be experienced again and again to be understood. Thus the most powerful lessons that I learned from Larry were learned in the heat of battle (e.g., to get a paper out) rather than in the calm environment of a PhD course. This lesson has been directly transferable into my emerging work with doctoral students. I have collected data with them, written with them, and met with them in seemingly endless preparation for these tasks. I have found these interactions stimulating and challenging (e.g., they expect you to know the answers to a variety of impromptu questions for which you have no time to prepare), and they are also a lot of fun. I am convinced that it is in these interactions that the most teaching and learning occurs between faculty and doctoral students.

Personal Investment

Larry made a personal investment in me as an emerging scholar. He did so in numerous ways, but the greatest impact he achieved came from his willingness to interact with my writing deeply and in a timely manner. He read my work over and over again, giving me detailed feedback each time. Nothing was more useful. The turnaround for his feedback was usually a day or a weekend, never more than a week. He didn't do this just for me, but for all students, "his" and others. This was incredibly valuable. Somehow, Larry and the other faculty at Northwestern made us feel that we were at the center of their universe. I don't know how they did it. They had very high MBA teaching pressures and high-powered executive education demands, but somehow all of the students felt as if those activities were peripheral to their real task, which was teaching us.

It is clear to me that I don't always convey this kind of impression to my students at Michigan, nor do all of my colleagues (from my observations). Our world is so pressured, so overdetermined, that we are always coming loose at the seams. Our students know it. They know when they are being squeezed in. What I tell my students now is that I may not be able to meet to socialize (e.g., over lunch), but I will interact with their writing. I learned from my interactions with Larry that writing is (or should be) the core activity for doctoral students, and I make dealing with their writing a priority. I will turn drafts around to PhD students with feedback as quickly as I can, and my comments will be thorough. Just how the Northwestern faculty created the environment they did at the time of my doctoral program still remains a mystery, though at the time it was almost unnoticeable to me. My few years at Michigan have given me a healthy respect for the task. My strategy for handling it has been to pick the aspect of the task that I consider most important (the writing/feedback process) and to do that well.

It seems to me that it is most important for faculty members to make personal investments in their students. For some this might take the form of offering lots of social support; for others, it might be tangible help in networking. What is important is that one make a personal investment. This is no easy task. As mentioned above, I generally feel as if I am two steps behind with my PhD students, that I could do better by them. Given the nature of doctoral students' learning task (apprenticeship), they need our time, and lots of it. And yet, given how universities and business schools are set up, they are sometimes the last in line to get our time. Reward systems barely take into account doctoral teaching, and the everyday informal rewards of our culture are not as supportive of doctoral teaching as they might be. For example, at my university, MBA teaching evaluations are published in the student newspaper (which is read by all of my colleagues); doctoral teaching evaluations are not. There are awards given for excellence in MBA teaching, but none for work with PhDs. The MBAs work on fast cycle-time tasks that are extremely demanding, whereas the doctorals work on longer cycle-time tasks and are much more reticent. To pull time away from highly visible and informally rewarded MBA teaching to work with doctoral students requires an inner desire to do so—a sense that it is right and important. I have that sense, and I see it being swamped by the immediate and vocal demands of the system. As such, I feel as though I am constantly trying to catch up on my work with my doctoral students, always apologizing to them for delays. Others must have figured out how to work these trade-offs

better than I have. I can only offer them here as a source of unexpected frustration.

A final comment: In talking about this issue with some of the Michigan PhD students, I have begun to see clearly how different they are from one another. Their needs are different, as are their strengths and weaknesses. There probably is no universal formula or recipe for working with doctoral students. Rather, it is in the development of individual relationships *around tasks* that these needs can be spoken to. It is also striking to me that it generally takes only one. As many of my student colleagues and I look back on our careers at Northwestern, it is clear that it wasn't the whole department that invested in us, but one person (I was lucky and had the support and careful guidance of Larry Cummings *and* Jeanne Brett). As faculty members, I think it is our job to be explicit in our minds about our level of commitment to various students. It is also important that we *do* commit to one or two. The future of our field would seem to depend on our meeting not only the current market test (determined primarily through MBA and executive teaching) but also a future market test (determined by the quality of the scholarship that we and our "offspring" produce in the future). For students, this observation suggests that finding that one person with whom you are in sync is most critical; the rest is gravy.

17 Mentoring Relationships

A COMPARISON OF EXPERIENCES IN BUSINESS AND ACADEMIA

Linn Van Dyne

This essay began as my part of a panel discussion presented at a 1993 preconference session of the Academy of Management. The session was titled "Working With Doctoral Students," and it included presentations by five other faculty members, with an emphasis on each individual's personal experiences of working with doctoral students. At the time of the presentation, I had just defended my dissertation and had not yet started my new job as an assistant professor at Michigan State University. I did not have any personal experience working with doctoral students as a faculty member. So, I asked myself, What could I contribute to the panel discussion that might be unique? I did not want to presume to speak for doctoral students in general, because I believe (based on personal experience and observation) that the key characteristics of working with doctoral students are the diversity of relationships and the uniqueness of each dyadic pair.

As I continued to think about what I could contribute to the panel discussion, I found myself comparing my mentor-mentee experiences in academia with those that I had previously experienced in the business world. I concluded that this comparison might be interesting to others and that my experiences might stimulate insights among "second-career" students and faculty who were working with such students.

In order to put my comments in perspective, I offer the following information on my background. Before I entered the PhD program at the University of Minnesota, I had worked for several different business organizations for more than 15 years in positions of increasing responsibility as a human resources executive. Thus my PhD student years were the beginning of a second career. Why did I choose to change careers? My primary motivation was to increase the amount of intellectual stimulation in my life. In addition, my work experience had led

159

me to generate a number of research questions. I was curious about why some employees were willing to take initiative and speak up with constructive recommendations for change, whereas others simply accepted the status quo. Over the years, based on my work experiences with managers and employees in four different organizations as well as ongoing conversations with senior executives of many different organizations, I had developed the belief that in changing environments, organizational performance is enhanced when employees exercise initiative and when they are willing to take the risks of challenging standard operating procedures and suggesting new approaches. I wanted to research this proposed relationship and gain a better understanding of what individual and situational factors lead to initiating behaviors in the work place.

As a graduate student, I worked with a number of mentors and benefited in different ways from each relationship. I include Hal Angle, Larry Cummings, Chris Earley, Judi Parks, and Jon Pierce as key mentors who contributed significantly to my development. I learned from each of these special individuals. Some of what I learned concerns behaviors that I want to replicate, whereas other lessons concern behaviors that I hope I never exhibit. There were high points and low points in each relationship, and as each evolved into more distant interaction, I felt a sense of loss and separation. Typically, I found myself wishing that the closeness and excitement that represented the "best of times" could continue. Nevertheless, I realized that the changes represented rites of passage.

The following comments are based on my personal experiences in *informal* mentoring relationships. I use the concept of informal mentoring to describe close and intense personal relationships between individuals with hierarchical differences in status where the interaction involves career guidance, emotional support, and loyalty. In these relationships, one individual is more senior and the other is more junior in terms of experience in a particular job, profession, or organization. I focus on informal mentoring relationships that develop spontaneously, without formal organizational support or encouragement, in order to differentiate these types of experiences from more formal, organizationally sanctioned relationships.

When I first began this comparison, my thoughts centered on the *differences* between mentoring in business and mentoring in academia. After several months, however, I found myself emphasizing the similarities as well as the differences. The organization of this essay follows the same progression. First, I focus on the differences; second, I consider the similarities.

Differences Between Business and Academia

In general, three key differences emerge when I review my personal experiences with informal mentoring relationships. First, in business settings, most mentor relationships focus on socialization into fairly well defined roles in the organization. In contrast, in academic settings, mentor relationships seem more personal. The emphasis is not on helping a protégé fit into a predefined role in a specific organization, but on socialization into a profession that transcends organizational boundaries. There are exceptions to these generalizations. Clearly, some socialization of doctoral students focuses on specific departments and institutions. Similarly, there are professional roles in business settings where new recruits are socialized simultaneously into organizational roles and professional roles. Nevertheless, my observations in both settings suggest that the typical mentoring role in business emphasizes helping an individual adjust to the organization's expectations. In academic settings, the best mentors develop their students and socialize them into the academic profession.

For example, in one business organization everyone joked about how a particular vice president was able to clone administrative assistants. Even though there was fairly high turnover in the job, the incumbents were extremely loyal to the vice president and seemed more similar to each other than different. In this business setting, the emphasis was on fitting in and doing the job as it had been done in the past. In contrast, I did not observe any obvious patterns in the relationships between faculty and students in my PhD program. Instead, faculty members seemed to work with a wide variety of students, on a wide variety of topics.

The emphasis in universities on professional socialization rather than institutional socialization leads to additional contrasts between business and academic mentoring relationships. One of the key objectives of most doctoral programs is training future scholars to develop their own research programs. In general, the typical job content of an academic position is more variable and more idiosyncratic than the job content of a typical position in a business organization. Thus I believe that the best mentors in academia help their students discover and develop their own research interests. Even though students can become coauthors faster when they work with faculty on existing research projects, it is also important for students to generate their own research ideas. In some situations, faculty may need to help students examine their past experiences in order to identify research questions that have personal relevance to the students and will have lasting interest for them.

Accordingly, a successful mentor in academia must listen to the student—both what is said and what is not said—in an attempt to facilitate clarification of the student's interests. Additionally, mentors can play a significant role in helping students transform their general interests into researchable questions that can be examined within theoretical frameworks. The driving force thus emerges from within the individual student, and not from the mentor. An ideal mentor draws out what is already in the student; he or she does not impose a research agenda on the student.

Every dyadic relationship is unique, whether it exists in a business setting or an academic setting. Nevertheless, the emphasis in doctoral student training on developing student ideas necessitates a more reciprocal and responsive relationship than that between mentor and mentee in business, where the content of the role is defined by the organization and one of the key contributions of the mentor is to assist the individual in fitting into organizational roles.

Second, although promotions are institutionalized in both settings, the timing of transitions in academia (particularly those involving doctoral students) is more predictable than the timing of transitions in business. In academia there is a well-established pattern of transition after 4-5 years from the role of PhD student to the role of assistant professor. This transition usually involves a physical move, such that the mentor and mentee are no longer in close physical proximity. This transition is predictable and more or less unavoidable. In contrast, in business settings, the duration of a proximate, informal mentor-mentee relationships is open-ended. The timing of promotions and transfers is unpredictable, because individuals are promoted or transferred based on business needs. These needs fluctuate over time and often are based on external economic factors. In business there often is little warning of disruptive changes in proximity for mentors and mentees. If a vice president decides to transfer a general manager, this may happen suddenly and somewhat unpredictably. Thus transitions in mentoring relationships in business are more abrupt and less predictable.

Something that happened to me early in my career serves as an illustration of the open-ended nature of business mentor-mentee relationships. I was working for an upwardly mobile individual who had invested significantly in my development. At one of our periodic career planning/progress review meetings, this individual "warned" me that I most likely would not be able to complete all the projects that we had just outlined in detail because a reorganization "might" occur and I "might" be getting new responsibilities. I was left with a general feeling that my job would be changing and that my mentor would be assuming a new and more distant role, but no one knew exactly when things would change or how they would be different. Similarly, several years later, an associate of mine commented that he never knew how long it would be until the next reorganization would force him to find a new junior associate to develop. From his perspective, the only things constant in the job were change and the inability to predict the timing of change.

A third difference between mentoring in academia and mentoring in business involves the cycling of relationships that is built into the structure of the system. Just as the transition from doctoral student to assistant professor is predictable, so is the matriculation of new PhD students that could benefit from mentoring relationships. Thus the system constantly renews itself, as more senior students progress through doctoral programs and are replaced by new students. This contrasts with business, where entry into jobs, exit from jobs, and replacement with new hires is generally not standardized. In addition, many business organizations that in the past have traditionally hired, trained, and

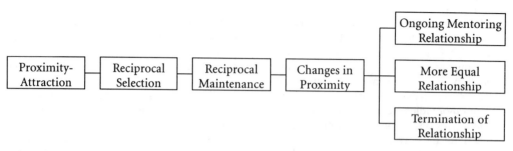

Figure 17.1. Critical Characteristics of Informal Mentoring Relationships

socialized new entrants in cohorts now have de-emphasized large recruiting programs based on downsizing and cost-containment practices.

I have observed two contrasting faculty responses to this "flow" of doctoral students through the educational system. Informal mentoring requires personal commitment, involvement, time, and attention from faculty members. The flow of students through the system makes significant demands on faculty and ensures that mentoring relationships change over time. Some faculty members seem to view doctoral students as a renewable resource subject to constant and predictable changes. These mentors are excited about each new cohort of PhD students as a source of new and exciting *potential* relationships that might be mutually stimulating and rewarding. From this perspective, mentoring doctoral students provides faculty with exposure to constantly changing interests and opportunities. On the other hand, not all faculty members actively engage in mentoring. Some seem to avoid mentoring doctoral students; perhaps they feel it is not worth the investment. Perhaps the demands of mentoring seem too high given the relatively short duration of the proximal relationship.

Similarities Between Business and Academia

Although my initial thoughts about mentoring in business and academia concentrated on the differences between the two settings, reflection over a longer period of time has led me to concentrate more on the similarities. This change in emphasis is based on my analysis of specific mentor-mentee relationships that I have experienced and observed in both set-

tings. The preliminary model depicted in Figure 17.1 summarizes my view of the characteristics of *informal* mentoring relationships that are critical in both business and academia. I describe the elements of this model in turn below.

Proximity-attraction. From my perspective, informal mentoring in both business and academia begins with physical proximity and a developing awareness of similar interests. These shared interests can include work and nonwork domains and are based on face-to-face personal interaction.

Reciprocal selection. Regardless of setting, if both individuals recognize their mutual interests, the possibility of reciprocal selection occurs. In other words, an informal mentor-mentee relationship will develop *only* if both individuals are attracted to each other and both are willing to invest in the relationship. Unlike formal mentoring relationships, where the organization provides structure and encourages the development of a supportive relationship, an informal mentoring relationship requires the active interest and participation of both partners. If only one person is interested or there is a significant imbalance in the degree of interest or willingness to interact, the two individuals are unlikely to develop a mentor-mentee relationship.

Thus the emergence of an informal mentoring relationship is based on reciprocal selection. It is not a simple function of the mentor "picking" the mentee and then developing him or her. Likewise, it is not a simple function of the mentee seeking out a mentor and becoming available for development. If selection is not mutual, problems will develop. For example, if a more senior individual aggressively attempts to provide mentoring to a more junior individual and this attention and development is not wanted, the mentoring efforts will be viewed as interference and attempts to control. Similarly, if a more junior individual aggressively attempts to obtain the support of a more senior individual when the senior individual prefers to avoid this type of involvement, attempts to develop a mentoring relationship will be viewed as manipulative.

Reciprocal maintenance. In business settings and in academic settings, an informal mentor-mentee relationship cannot be maintained unless both mentor and mentee actually invest time and energy in the relationship on an ongoing basis. This suggests that shared interests and willingness to invest must be followed by actual behavioral investment. Although both partners need not make precisely equal investments in the short run, mutual and reciprocal investment is required for a continuing and healthy relationship with benefits to both parties.

Changes in proximity. Finally, although the timing and predictability of changes in proximity may differ between academia and business, transitions involving changes in proximity occur in both settings. The proximity that allows recognition of shared interests, development of the relationship, and maintenance of the relationship can rarely be continued indefinitely. Changes in proximity are almost inevitable in both settings. PhD students graduate and move to other institutions. Employees in business organizations are promoted, transferred, or hired by new organizations.

In some cases, changes in proximity act as a catalyst for development of the relationship. Although contact is not as convenient with more distal relationships, reciprocal commitment to a continuing relationship can facilitate personal growth for both mentor and mentee. After changes in proximity, some mentoring relationships retain the senior/junior distinctions, whereas others evolve into relationships characterized more by equality. In other cases, changes in proximity lead to the dissolution of the relationship.

These transitions can be difficult for both mentor and mentee. The very closeness and personal nature of the relationship can make these changes in proximity challenging, regardless of whether the setting is business or academia.

Summary

In this essay I have pointed out three significant differences that I have observed between mentoring relationships in business and academia. First, mentoring in business often tends to emphasize socialization of the individual to "fit" into a preexisting organizational role, whereas mentoring in academia tends to emphasize socialization of the individual into the profession, with a focus on developing the research ideas of the individual. Thus mentoring in academia can be more personal, more idiosyncratic, and more reciprocal than mentoring in business.

Second, the timing of transitions in academia is more predictable than that in business, given the fairly standardized movement from being a doctoral student to becoming an assistant professor. In business, transitions are often externally initiated and based on business needs. Thus the timing of changes in the proximity of mentor-mentee relationships in business can be less predictable than in academia.

Third, informal mentoring in academia involves a constant flow of PhD students through the system. Healthy PhD programs continually admit students and graduate students. Faculty, accordingly, have recurring opportunities to develop mentoring relationships with a variety of students over time.

Finally, I have proposed a preliminary model of informal mentoring processes based on my perceptions of the similarities between mentoring relationships in business and academia. I hope that these observations of the similarities and differences are interesting and also helpful to readers who are involved in mentoring relationships where the student has significant prior work experience.

18 Transitions and Turning Points in Faculty-Doctoral Student Relationships

Roderick M. Kramer
Joanne Martin

There is an old nursery rhyme about a little girl: When she was good, she was very, very good, and when she was bad, she was horrid. Collaborative relationships between faculty members and doctoral students can also be very good or they can be—not so good. When good, they enrich the scholarly life enormously, enhancing the intellectual growth of both faculty and students. When they are bad, they can consume a great deal of time and emotional energy, sometimes even leaving psychological residue that clouds future relationships. In this chapter, we describe high points—and low points—in our collaborations. We try to make explicit the lessons we have drawn from those collaborations, extracting in equal measure from those we feel were successful and those we feel were unsuccessful. We try to analyze how the good collaborations became good, and why the bad ones, which began with the same high expectations, soured.

In keeping with the broader theme of this volume—namely, exploration of the rhythms of academic life—we focus much of our discussion on the rhythms we have experienced in our collaborative relationships. As with any close personal associations, these relationships have seldom remained in stasis for any length of

AUTHORS' NOTE: We thank all of the students with whom we have worked for what they have taught us, especially Robert Bies, Michael Boehm, Jerry Davis, Kim Elsbach, Martha Feldman, Lisa Goldman, Benjamin Hanna, Kathy Knopoff, Barbara Levitt, Debra Meyerson, Elizabeth Newton, Pamela Pommerenke, Melanie Powers, Darryl Roberts, Maureen Scully, Caren Siehl, Sim Sitkin, Suzanne Stout, Mark Weiner, Alan Wilkins, and Stephanie Woerner. We also want to thank our teachers, who endured us as students and who are the finest mentors we can imagine: Marilynn Brewer, David Messick, Chuck McClintock, Tom Pettigrew, and Shelley Taylor. Several of these people have given us comments on and quotes for this essay. We are especially grateful for the frank, extensive feedback offered by Ben Hanna and Deb Meyerson.

time. Instead, either they continue to develop and mature or they stagnate and wither, sometimes without our fully realizing it at the time. Progress in our relationships has seldom been linear and constant, nor has regression been constant. Instead, our relationships have been characterized by ebbs and flows. Accordingly, being able to recognize the signs of transition, and the opportunities these turning points present, is among the most crucial skills necessary to successful collaboration.

＼ These transitions and turning points are embedded, of course, within broader passages in the working and personal lives of both students and faculty members. The life of a professor is punctuated by both predictable and unpredictable phases and hurdles, such as learning to teach, coming up for tenure, meeting a daunting array of professional obligations, and coping with work-related burnout of various kinds. Superimposed on these comparatively mundane academic matters are challenges related to family, health, dual careers, and personal self-renewal.

Students confront a host of no less challenging issues. On the professional front, they are expected to learn the fundamental skills needed to conduct independent and significant scholarly work, pass qualifying exams, and establish working relationships with one or more faculty members. They must learn how to subordinate (at least temporarily) their own interests to another person's research agenda (if for no other reason than mere economic survival), and at the same time develop their own independent perspectives. On the personal front, they are often struggling with romantic relationships or young marriages, often in unfamiliar cities or towns, trying to meet a variety of economic burdens, and trying to maintain outside interests.

Before embarking on writing this chapter, we surveyed a number of scholarly musings about the challenges and vagaries of collaboration, in the hope of finding a "guiding metaphor" that might help us in our efforts to make sense, retrospectively, of our collaborative experiences. We examined work on the psychology of flow, because at times our best collaborative relationships have seemed punctuated by moments of intense and satisfying flow. For a time, we viewed the collaborative process through a negotiation lens, because it was clear that bargaining processes—explicit and tacit, effec-

tive and ineffective—have also shaped how our collaborative relationships have evolved. And we thought about the roles of power and social influence in the collaborative process. We also scoured previous work on managing academic relationships and were struck by how often such musings remain silent about faculty members' needs to integrate the academic challenges they confront, such as managing the march toward tenure, with the unfolding of other aspects of their lives: maintaining relationships, making decisions about childbearing, and so on. The life of the student, and the role the student plays in shaping a professor's life, has received even less attention. In short, there has been little discussion of the juggling of career and personal lives that in fact has played such a large role in our collaborations.

Recognizing such embeddedness—and appreciating the silence about it—we concentrate in this chapter mostly on managing these important transitions and turning points more successfully: knowing when to push, when to pull back, when to stop, and so on. To be successful and viable in the long term, the relationship between a faculty member and a student must evolve—and, therefore, must build within itself the capacity to evolve, to transform itself in response to the changing circumstances it will confront. Those in the relationship must not only recognize turning points and transitions, but must use them creatively to accomplish these various goals. Regardless of who notices the need first, for both faculty member and student this requires both perceptiveness (recognizing it is time for a change) and behavioral skill (managing the transition or turning point smoothly).

Intent and Scope of the Chapter

We should probably say something at the outset about the intent and scope of this chapter. In this short space we cannot address all of the issues that are relevant to faculty-student relationships. For example, we do not discuss such concrete issues as advising students on their course work, helping them deal with failed field exams, or developing their skills as instructors. Rather, we focus on the dynamics of collaborative research projects. We discuss the difficulties of starting, sustaining, and energizing these intense, fragile, but enormously important partnerships. We discuss how such relationships sometimes progress toward more intense personal collaborations and sometimes become more limited relationships that can nonetheless enrich the working lives of both individuals.

In our first draft of this chapter, we initially emphasized, quite naturally perhaps, our role as architects of our collaborations. Because the faculty member possesses the benefits of both role-conferred power and greater experience, we thought it was self-evident that he or she has a special responsibility and role in managing the collaborative process. Thus we attempted to articulate some of the general principles that we have found useful in managing these important but often far from easy relationships.

We still believe that faculty members have important responsibilities in this regard. However, in looking back on our relationships, we recognized that it was often one of our students—and not one of us—who made the first move with respect to initiating a collaboration. And it was often one of our students who was first to recognize that the relationship was overdue for a change of some sort. On more than one occasion, it was a particular student's ability to perceive an opportunity for transition that prompted change in the relationship. And it was the student's skill in managing that transition with interpersonal grace, without unduly upsetting our delicate (in)sensitivities, that contributed to a successful resolution.

Realizing this, we decided early on in the composition of this chapter to seek out and incorporate insights and observations from our former students. In our first draft, we tried to figure out what we had done right, which of our actions at least did no harm, and what we had done that was clearly wrong. However, recognizing that one of us suffers from a persistent and uncontrollable tendency to see all in a rosy light, whereas the other tends to revisit past mistakes with a finely tuned capacity for worry, chagrin, or guilt, we thought it might be helpful to provide some counterpoints to our views on these matters. We therefore asked a few of our mentors and our past and present students to read the first draft and to add, with the requisite amount of cynicism and a hefty dose of frankness, their perspectives on the types of events we recounted. Their remarks on earlier ver-

sions of this chapter made us radically rethink its content. For example, our first draft emphasized phases in transition points in a faculty member-student relationship, focusing on instrumental rather than emotional concerns. One student, who has had a close working relationship with both of us, was offended by the tone of our first draft:

Yes, relationships can be managed and certainly have stages and qualities that can be reduced to rational analysis, neat stages, boundaries, managing communication, "keeping healthy distance." . . . But my experiences with either of you were nothing like what you described. . . . Beyond the predictable developmental challenges, the human relationships are absent in your treatment. . . . You may have experienced it differently, but I treated and thought of you as a friend, as well as an adviser, from the get go. My experience of our relationship was not one of "being managed" or of being part of a predictable stage sequence, but of talking about the meaning of life and Woody Allen while running the dish [a jogging trail], talking about ideas and cognition over Thai food, as well as struggling over experimental design, theses revisions, and paper reviews. . . . The experience of relationship, in my experience, if they are rich, are filled with emotion—positive and negative. In my mind, this human, affective part of relationships qualifies a faculty-adviser link as a relationship and distinguishes it from a collaboration or "interdependency." Yet these experiences or parts of the relationship are completely absent in your paper. Anyhow, all this should say I felt pretty alienated by the highly rational and intentional tone of your paper.

We hope this revised version of the chapter overcomes some of our reticence to speak of the emotional aspects of our relationships with students. However, to be honest, as we have struggled to combine child care, dual-career marriages, and more-than-full-time careers, we regret that we now have little time for Thai dinners with students and, we fear, less inclination to invest the time it takes to build emotional, as well as instrumental, relationships with students.

Of course, with many students an instrumental relationship is all that either party desires. This diversity of experiences and needs makes it difficult to write a chapter that covers a full range of student-adviser relationships. As one student described this issue:

How different students will enter and engage with this text is itself a function of our very different and incomparable relationships. . . . The position from which a current student enters and reads the text is completely different from the position a past student would take. The place from which someone with a relatively deep relationship would enter is completely different from the way someone with a new or purely instrumental relationship would engage.

We have responded to this difficulty by writing a chapter that describes a spectrum of student-faculty relationships, ranging from the personal to the distant. We intend this analysis to be descriptive rather than prescriptive, although in spite of our best efforts, we sometimes admittedly slip into prescriptive phrasing. The chapter is not intended as a "how-to" guide or an "instructor's manual," leaving the impression that we've "figured it out." Rather, we hope that the combination of detailed descriptions of events we have regarded as milestones in our relationships, our interpretations as faculty members of those events, and our mentors' and students' additions will give the reader enough information to decide what we have done well and where we might have made avoidable mistakes. We view the chapter as a combination of exhortation and cautionary tale. We feel that we—and we suspect others—often fail to enjoy all of the benefits that are possible in collaborations. Often with good intentions and seemingly sound motives, we have found ourselves holding back. Thus this chapter is intended as exhortation in terms of encouraging both faculty members and students to explore their relationships—and, we hope, push them further. Yet the chapter can also be regarded as a cautionary tale in terms of raising awareness of the potential pitfalls that can plague such relationships, especially when boundaries are prematurely crossed or relationships drift in wrong directions. Transitions can be mismanaged and opportunities for growth bungled.

In writing this chapter, we found that our own memories of our lives as graduate students intruded often. We feel fortunate in having had outstanding relations with our advisers. We remember what it was like to be students, and we have tried to write this essay as exhortation and cautionary tale for students too—in many ways, managing a collaborative relationship successfully is of even greater importance for them, because so much rides on the outcome.

Recognizing the Rhythms— and Managing the Blues— of the Collaborative Relationship

Unit of Analysis

Although it is natural enough to start by thinking about the unique role the faculty member plays in managing the collaborative process, the relationship itself becomes a very useful unit of analysis. In our view, it is the collaboration or partnership that is or isn't dysfunctional, not necessarily the participants as individuals. It is possible, for example, for both partners, each in his or her own way, to be performing quite well. However, because of lack of fit or coordination, the whole becomes less than the sum of the parts; synergy is lost. Thus both partners can independently be quite skilled, quite bright, and quite competent, yet together they can make a disastrously poor collaboration.

Structure and Process

Because of the high degree of interdependence that characterizes collaboration, the extent to which a given collaboration works or doesn't work depends upon numerous decisions made by each of the partners: who will be the right collaborator; what project will maximize joint talents and engage respective interests; what kind of structure will best bring those talents and interests to fruition; how much will each partner lead and defer; when are the best times to improvise and to stop; and how to part company gracefully when the relationship is over. When all of these decisions are made well, the result is fluid and fun. Several elements seem critical to good decisions.

Choosing the Right Collaborator

Good collaborations, like good marriages, probably aren't made in heaven, but they aren't forged entirely out of whole earth either. For that reason, both of us tend to be pretty careful in making decisions about with whom to work. We say no more often than yes. In the beginning, both of us failed to be selective enough. For example, one of us had an "open-door policy" on collaborations:

When I was a new assistant professor, I felt you should never turn anyone away. I viewed it as an obligation to agree to work with anyone interested in working with me—and I believed there was always something we could find to do together. Now, I say no quite often, and for reasons that I believe make sense for both individuals. For a collaborative relationship to work well, a lot of ingredients have to be in place. For me, intelligence or even interest in a topic isn't enough. I look for a lot of passion and energy, because that's how I like to feel about my work. I like a person who has trouble sitting still when talking about his or her research. I look for evidence of a burning desire, a "fire in the belly."

Also, I like people who laugh and see humor in their day-to-day victories and defeats. I like people who've knocked around a bit in life. For me, the relationship has to be fun, and if it isn't fun in the beginning, we probably aren't going to connect in a very deep or profound way.

And I try to be honest about my dislikes also. I shy away from people who are overly critical or negative. I like a student who reads someone else's work and talks about what is good in it—I like people who see the glass as more than half full rather than somewhat empty. I remember one new student who came in after a talk by a prominent visiting professor, and her comment was, "I really admired her book, but I was disappointed in her talk—she dresses really frumpy." It was a minor comment, but one of many that came out in that conversation that convinced me this person probably wasn't for me.

In addition to wanting to enjoy the process myself, I really want the students who work with me to have a great experience. Thus I want them to select me for reasons that seem right to them. For this reason, I try hard to be myself in our first get-togethers, so that they have a realistic preview of what working together will be like. I try to be candid about how I work, so that they can make an intelligent decision.

Selection is especially important, because I've come to realize that I don't need or want many students working with me in an assembly-line fashion, churning out studies. There are experimentalists who like that style of research, and for them it works well. I prefer a more intimate relationship.

For me, being selective isn't being arrogant. It's appreciating the fact that time is short for both student and faculty. There are also nontrivial opportunity costs to saying yes. And there are—or can be—significant side effects to failed collaborations. Thus I tend to be careful about the kinds of relationships that I enter into in my research.

When we began as assistant professors, our dance cards were a bit empty. We were not, as our economist friends might put it, in demand. We were therefore overjoyed when the first doctoral students stopped by to look us over as potential advisers. One of us recalls:

I was talking on the telephone with my former faculty adviser, and I announced with glee, "Only a week on the job and already two students have come by asking me to be their thesis adviser!" "Well," she cautioned, "I certainly hope you didn't agree without first checking with your faculty colleagues. You know, those two students may be problem students that no one else wants to work with. Never say yes right away."

Who to Choose

We (like many other new assistant professors) were eager to invest lots of time with students whose ages and interests were still relatively close to our own. Conventional wisdom urges faculty (especially those without tenure) to focus energy on students who are known to be competent and who have research interests close to their own. This way, whatever projects are chosen, they will directly or indirectly feed into their own publication records. Like most rules, this one has exceptions and is worth breaking on occasion. In fact, we break it more often the older we get: The longer we have remained professors, the more attractive students with dissimilar interests have become to us. They offer intellectual stimulation, the chance to broaden our research interests, and a challenging kind of synergy, the benefits of which often don't become evident for some time.

Even early in one's career, working with a student with dissimilar interests might be a good idea:

> One student knocked on my door soon after I started work as an assistant professor. He wanted me to supervise his dissertation on a topic I had never heard of. I wasn't even sure what it was, so I explained, "I'm an experimental social psychologist who does research in a completely different area. I'm sorry, but I don't know enough even to read your dissertation, let alone be your adviser." "Would you be willing," he asked, "to read just one article on the subject?" I agreed reluctantly. He pulled a paper from his briefcase and left it on the corner of my desk. It did look interesting, I did read it, and the next day he came in just briefly, to exchange it for an even more intriguing article. Every day for several weeks, this process of exchanging papers went on. I noticed that whenever I had a moment free, I chose to read the "irrelevant" papers on his topic, while the new manuscripts in my own area of interest were piling up, ignored and untouched. After a while, my behavior told me that supervising this dissertation was just what I wanted to do. Now, years later, most of my research is on the topic he introduced me to.

The benefits offered by such students are particularly important as your reputation becomes more established and students seek you out for what you've been, not what you are now or what you want to be. Students who pick you because of work they've read about are sometimes selecting someone who no longer exists, because your interests and tastes have moved on. It is better when you can select students who will help you become what you want to be.

Of course, differences in research interests and personal styles are not always complementary. Relationships predicated on difference and diversity can be fraught with peril, for both the faculty member and the student. Given the difficulties of managing dissimilar relationships, most faculty members find it's best to have a mixture (over time, if not at once) of students who are similar and dissimilar to themselves.

How to Choose

Both of us have found it useful to make these decisions, at least in part, based on unobtrusive observations. For example, we listen to students' comments at colloquia and seminars, and we listen to what other faculty and other students say about them. One us makes it a point to visit students' offices to see what books are on their shelves and how they organize their desks. We might take a walk to the bookstore with a student and get a feel for the kinds of topics he or she likes to think about and how he or she thinks about them. There are no surefire rules for making sensible selections—everyone develops his or her own unique approaches to buying cars and finding mates—but having rules helps, and knowing what you are looking for and what works for you is important.

Students should also be encouraged to think about the trade-offs associated with a given relationship. It can seem—and be—risky for a student to choose to work with a new assistant professor who is not a known quantity and may not have the prestige or job market connections of a more senior faculty member. On the other hand, some of our students seem to prefer new assistant professors. As one student described it:

> The joy of working with my adviser when he was brand new was that we, as graduate students, were able to set the norms, or at least mutually set them—this we did not experience with more established faculty members. I remember being thrown off a bit by how open he was to meeting whenever. As a graduate student, I appreciated it. . . . I think I was his first graduate student and I feel lucky, because we were friends from the start. Now he realizes he must set boundaries.

Thus there are advantages to having a newly minted adviser, and students can enlist the help of more senior faculty by asking them to be members of dissertation reading committees. In choosing a primary adviser, seniority may be less important than personal rapport and intellectual fit.

Why Selection Matters

As these various arguments suggest, it is important for both faculty and students to choose each other with deliberation, rather than just accept the first partnership suggested. One reason the selection process is so important is that students deserve a deep commitment on our part. Students' time, energy, and opportunity costs are substantial. They have only 4 or 5 years to establish a basis for launching a career. If you don't think working with them is going to make a difference, our advice is: Don't.

There is another reason to be selective, and it is more subtle. In our experience, the process of mentoring changes not only the mentee but also the mentor; the influence is reciprocal. Thus the faculty member is influenced by the student in profound and easy-to-underestimate ways. Now when we contemplate working with given students, we try to anticipate how the relationships might unfold. Although we ask ourselves whether a pooling of our talents and backgrounds is likely to produce interesting and important work, we also ask whether it will produce an enjoyable collaboration.

A final observation about selection: If you find that all of your collaborations are failing or ending up on a sour note, then it is obviously time to run some diagnostics. But if you find that they are all "working"—well, congratulations. You may have the selection problem solved. However, it is also possible that you are being too careful. You might want to ask yourself if you are you leaving enough room for surprises and challenges.

Structuring the Collaboration

Once you've made a commitment to work with someone, the next step is to choose a project and, within that project, a set of tasks for the student to do.

Pace

We both started out, as new advisers, with very high expectations; we had visions of Watson and Crick and the double helix in front of our eyes. We assumed that every student would become a valued and equal coauthor, participating in all phases of a project, and becoming a personal friend to boot. We firmly expected that the student starting to work with us today would someday be a colleague at another university with whom we would enjoy fond memories and strong ties that would endure. This has sometimes happened for both of us, and these special relationships remain among the most rewarding aspects of our careers. Nevertheless, such fine outcomes cannot be guaranteed, even in the best of circumstances. Now we enter relationships more guardedly. We let these relationships develop in carefully graduated stages. Although our aspirations remain high, we often start out assuming less; we set more moderate goals. The tenor of the initial stages of a relationship is, "Let's take a few steps together and see what happens."

The Psychological Contract

We also try to be clear about our expectations and to become clearer about their expectations. To do so, we try to establish a psychological contract with a student, one that specifies, for example, how much work will be required to earn coauthorship status. The psychological contract concerns the mutual expectations, goals, norms, and so on that will govern and shape the relationship. Setting the relationship on contractual terms can be uncomfortable, because it highlights the inequalities that inevitably color new faculty-student relationships. It also can appear unseemly to talk in explicitly exchange-based terms so early in a relationship, when it is fragile and still forming—it's like talking about a prenuptial agreement on a first date. Yet our experience is that setting clear and somewhat conservative expectations is often best—as long as it is coupled with a willingness to modify the contract as experience working together accumulates.

Avoiding the discomfort surrounding negotiating clear expectations can be costly down the road. It was discomfort in doing so that led one of us to skip this crucial phase with one promising doctoral student:

> She was so smart and eager, and I was so sure everything would work out well. Also, I was uncomfortable with discussing an explicit

contract. It seemed unnecessarily formal, and I worried that it would undermine the more egalitarian, friendly, "we're in this together" mood I wanted to establish. So the student was left with the impression that she would be a coauthor—not only on our experimental article, but on everything I wrote on a particular subject. This came back later to haunt me.

After we designed the experiment and collected the data, the student offered to write the first draft of our coauthored paper. I agreed. When her draft arrived on my desk, it was so poor that I never even tried to teach her to write. I thought it would be quicker and better if I wrote it myself. I was nearing my first review after 3 years as an assistant professor and, to be frank, I needed publications sooner rather than later.

This was a mistake—for both of us. Most important, she needed to learn to write in an academic style. I should have taken the time to show her why the draft was poor and I should have worked with her on the rewrites, even if it meant many drafts. The damage to me did not surface until a year or so later, when I was invited to write a review chapter on the same topic area. The chapter was to include, among other things, a summary of the experiments I had done with this student. She thought I would ask her to be a coauthor, and when I did not, she asked why. The truth was that I did not want to coauthor the chapter with her. A review chapter is mainly a writing task—not her strength. Rather than telling her this, which I should have found the courage to do, I just said that the book editor had asked for only faculty-level contributors. Without telling me, she went directly to the editor and asked him if he would let her be my coauthor. As I had never asked him about having her as a coauthor, this was awkward for him and embarrassing for me. We finally got it all straightened out (with the student being coauthor on an empirical paper but not the broader review chapter), but the student and I never worked together again—a promising relationship gone bad, and it was my fault.

This tale has many morals. It takes a lot of time to teach even a good student how to develop theory, design studies, and write papers.

We can teach doctoral students just the "easy" tasks (like running subjects and administering questionnaires), in which case they are helping us at minimal investment of our time, but when we do they don't learn what they need to know to become independent researchers later. To be effective, a faculty member has to be willing to confront poor performance and invest the time it takes to allow improvement to occur.

One of us uses the psychological contract as a device for helping both faculty member and student to assess where they are in the relationship and whether they are progressing:

> Every 3 months or so—at some logical point, such as at the end of a quarter—I make it a point to take the student to lunch or dinner. We use the time to catch up on what we've accomplished, but also to pull back the microscope a bit and assess where are we going: Are we really making good progress? Should we be going faster or slowing down? Should I be encouraging the student to seek out other professors with whom he or she might work?

Finally, as expectations change, it is essential to revisit the terms of the initial contract, so that progress (or lack of it) can be honestly assessed and new goals and expectations established. In our view, this periodic reassessment and recalibration is critical for healthy and productive collaboration. The psychological contract should be a living, fluid agreement. It should be open to renegotiation, to expansion or contraction, as history and circumstances dictate.

Framing the Relationship

The first few meetings with a doctoral student are crucial. Almost invariably, the faculty member sets the tone and pace; this is usually appropriate, unless the student is unusually mature, experienced in research, hardworking, and self-starting. Both partners should disclose their expectations about the kind of relationship it will be (for example, the degree of informality), the tasks to be done, and the timing and quality of what will be produced. Sometimes there are tacit agendas that may or may not need to be brought out into the open. Norms need to be set early in the relationship. For example, time demands often need clarifying and negotiating. If one of you has a tight schedule, the other's showing up late can cause inconvenience. The faculty member needs to be made aware of the demands on the student's time (midterms, a child's illness), and adjustments should be negotiated explicitly. The faculty member needs to make his or her degree of accessibility evident. If norms around this and other matters are not established firmly, undiscussed disappointments can needlessly balloon into a spoiled relationship.

The Importance of Small Wins

A useful way of thinking about the relationship is that it should be structured so as to produce fairly reliable and regular small wins.

I continually try to decompose tasks into small chunks that allow "small wins." For example, rather than have a student write a paper by doing the introduction first, I have him or her start with the methods section. Then we move to the results section. Finally, we might move to the introduction, where the theory is laid out, or the discussion section, where the student has to pull it all together. The goal in all of this is to allow the student to experience a string of small victories in the writing process. I believe these small wins, over time, really add up. They not only increase the student's confidence, but, just as important in my view, they give him or her pleasurable experiences that ultimately get associated with the research process. They also help the student recognize the often gradual, incremental progress associated with research projects. Too often, I have seen students get fearful, risk averse, and even paralyzed because they tried to write a "grand theory" introduction before doing anything else.

By starting modestly, with carefully bounded tasks, we think we gain a lot: Any later expansion of those boundaries seems like progress and development, whereas starting too ambitiously and having later to pull back inevitably seems, especially to the student, like failure or retreat.

The Shadow of the Past

One of our mentors observed that faculty-student relationships sometimes recapitulate past conflicts that students have in other parts of their lives or with other professors:

Because the stakes are so high, dissertations magnify conflicts in the rest of a student's life; any habitual way of relating to authority or stress can get magnified. Perfectly enchanting people can do peculiar and unexpected things—for example, becoming very obsessive or even belligerent.

Incidents from our own pasts can be misused as well. For example, both of us started out as new assistant professors by trying to re-create the relationships we had with our mentors. Both of us regarded those relationships with great fondness because they not only helped us become scholars, but led to terrific friendships. In retrospect, our advisers seemed to have done everything right (although, curiously, neither of us remembered having this perception at the time we were graduate students). Over time, we learned that we were not as good at being like them as we had hoped. Our collaborations have worked better as we have tried to evolve our own styles.

Faculty members can also suffer from a tendency to overgeneralize from earlier relationships with other students. Especially if a relationship was unusually good or particularly bad, it is easy to draw too many lessons from it. One way to get around this problem is to try working sometimes with students who seem almost the opposite of what might appear to be the ideal student with whom you should work. For example, one of us tends to dislike overly aggressive and demanding collaborators. However, when a particularly smart—but aggressive and demanding—student came along, the chance was taken—and it led to a productive (even if somewhat challenging) collaboration.

Sustaining the Collaboration

Getting off to a good start is important, but in the long run it is more difficult to keep a relationship exciting and vital, especially given distractions and demands on one's time and

attention. Sustaining a good research collaboration requires attention to a variety of issues,
including managing the focus of the relationship, dealing with stumbling blocks, and managing the psychological distance or intimacy
between the partners.

Avoiding Drift

One of the important issues in managing
relationships is the problem of drift—gradual,
unintended transitions that go largely unno-
ticed early on in the relationship. One source of
drift is a failure to maintain a task focus in the
research relationship. The graduate student needs
publications and so does the professor, especially if untenured, yet it is easy for research
meetings to be consumed by small talk. Small
talk makes the relationship fun and provides a
useful lubricant, but, if carried too far, it can
divert the relationship. For instance, one of us
was too willing to discuss problems in a student's personal life, and this drift crept into the
relationship unintentionally:

This student had a great deal going on in her
personal life, including adjusting to a new
baby, in-laws visiting, a husband seeking work,
and so on. In the beginning, I felt as if it were
part of my duties as adviser to help the student learn to juggle the load. Over time,
however, our research meetings became consumed by talk about such matters. A simple
inquiry regarding the status of some data
analyses would lead to a 10-minute account
of the unexpected obstacles that kept the
student from getting to it over the weekend:
relatives coming to visit, baking a cake for a
graduate student's birthday party. All of these
were legitimate, and I felt it inappropriate to
criticize the student. Over time, however, I
realized the student's attention span was a
recurring problem. She was too easily distracted and not able to stay on task. Once I
realized this, I completely stopped reinforcing digressions in our meetings. I explicitly
directed attention and discussion toward the
task at hand. The relationship felt less friendly,
but the work progressed. She experienced
the change in my behavior as a withdrawal
of support and loss of interest.

Impasses and Researcher's Block

It helps both partners to know that most
doctoral students, at some time during their
graduate years, come to a discouraging halt. At
Stanford we call the third year of our organizational behavior program the "black hole," because so many of the students go through a time
in which they make no apparent progress. This
occurs shortly after they complete their course
work and qualifying exams, and suddenly the
task shifts from imposed deadlines and requirements to the self-imposed requirements of finding a dissertation topic, structuring the design
and execution of the independent work, and so
on. During this period, not only does the finished prospectus fail to surface, even a title for
a prospectus fails to arrive. Students disappear
from sight. Depression sets in.

One reason students disappear into a morass
of seeming inactivity is that they have set their
expectations excruciatingly high. It is as if they
are saying to themselves, "Now after all those
years of exposing the foibles and fatal flaws of
the most famous research in the field, my dissertation will be better than all those that have
come before. It will avoid all the major problems with research in this field and stand as a
beacon for future students for decades." Sometimes, to students, it seems as if faculty are the
ones with the excruciatingly high expectations:

I remember well a student who coped, showing great strength of character, with a severe
case of black hole disease. He just couldn't
come up with a dissertation idea. We tried
writing one-paragraph abstracts of different
theses. We tried writing different titles. We
tried noun phrases (topics he was interested
in) and then adding verbs to make these
nouns into hypotheses. Many tries later, he
still wasn't happy (for good reason). Then he
went to talk to another faculty member, one
who was known for his wit and broad intellectual interests. That afternoon, the student
knocked on my door; they had come up with
a strange idea that at first seemed unrelated
to his interests. But when that noun phrase
was matched with a few verbs, transformed
into a paragraph, and then into an abstract—
suddenly it turned into a prospectus. To this
student's credit, he hit gold—on the twenty-
fifth try!

One of our mentors had a commonsense perspective on these issues:

> Some people endow the thesis with more importance than it deserves—seeing it as a culmination of a life's work: a little silly at the age of 26. Some students plan their careers up to the point of the dissertation, but have no clear plans for afterward. Often, they are the same students who benefit when a school has a 5-year limit. A thesis should be a stepping-stone along a path, as opposed to an endpoint.

Another mentor had a useful remedy: She never let a dissertation consume all of a student's time or attention. She treated the dissertation study as yet another study in a portfolio of ongoing projects. If it didn't bear fruit, one or more of the other studies would. Having multiple projects not only limited the amount of time a student could ruminate about the dissertation, it always necessarily put it into perspective—an important study, but only one of many he or she would do in the course of a long research career.

Faculty enter black holes of their own as well. One of us still goes through five or so "stew days" before finding the ability to draft a new paper. During these stew days, no words get written, there are severe doubts about writing anything ever again—certainly not this paper, which will undoubtedly be worthless. Then the doubts clear (or at least are put aside) and the words start to come. No matter how long we remain in this business, the creative process seems to have its own idiosyncratic pace, and no "method" can prevent times of apparent stagnation.

Framing these seemingly fallow periods is important. Times of apparent inactivity are an unavoidable part of the research process for both students and faculty. If the impasse comes immediately after a period of intense work on another project, especially one that has just achieved closure, then it can be regarded as a well-earned "refractory period." Times of apparent impasse and stalemate can be constructive as well: They may represent periods of "fertile void," where ideas are germinating. Lack of progress in a given direction can be diagnostic that the direction, for that student at least, is not worthwhile; it may reflect lack of true interest.

A delay, however, is not a full and permanent stop—5 days is not 5 months. If a stalled student needs a jump start, a different faculty adviser, a book in another field, or a threat of trouble should get him or her moving again. Here's where the small-wins approach works quite well—we encourage our students to make steady progress: If unable to fix the theory, work on the methods section; if the results aren't making sense, work on the figures and tables; even typing the title page, acknowledgments, and references can get a stalled student moving again.

Maintaining a Healthy Distance

Although our relationships have almost always been initiated with the mutual expectation that strong and enduring collaborations might evolve, we find it important to remain mindful of the fact that such partnerships are born in a severely evaluative, hierarchical context. Typically, they are played out on a national or international stage where one of the actors is more senior and may be better known than the other (at least at first). Often the more senior partner is expected to provide the intellectual structure and guidance, yet in such a way that the student learns to think independently and feels empowered rather than dependent—a tricky task.

There's a scene in an old Marx Brothers film where Groucho is dancing with a woman who is quite taken with him. As they whirl around the dance floor, she keeps beseeching him to come closer. Finally, when he is as close as he can get, he says, "If I come any closer, I'll be on the other side of you." Getting too close, so that the boundary between adviser and friend blurs, can be a serious problem.

The issue of appropriate psychological and social distance relates closely, we believe, to the short-term productivity—and long-term success—of the relationship. One of us started out as an assistant professor thinking that providing psychological and social support was the most important aspect of being a good mentor. As noted above, however, this can lead to an insidious and destructive conversion of the relationship into a kind of therapeutic friendship.

Ultimately, of course, the intensity of friendship within a student-faculty relationship varies, depending on the needs and time available to each person. This issue must be carefully worked out, and revisited periodically, with each student.

Timing

As noted earlier, both of us view the evolution of the relationship between student and faculty member into a lifelong collegial association as a highly desirable goal. Accomplishing this goal, however, requires a sensitivity to the question, at each stage in a relationship, What is the right distance to maintain with this person at this time? Timing is important because moving too quickly can establish an intimacy that later has to be renegotiated, leading to a sense of failure or withdrawal. At the same time, failure to achieve dissolution of the boundary or to move the relationship to a more intimate level when the time is right may stall the relationship.

As the relationship progresses, unspoken questions arise, such as, Who's going to lead now and how much? Am I deferring too little or much? Such questions should be asked often, at least privately. The answer to these questions change from one time to another. Some students will move from being thanked in a footnote on the first paper to the position of second author on the next publication. Advanced students may be ready to do independent work, perhaps with a faculty member as a second author. Sooner or later, the faculty member should become an adviser on an independent student research project—one for which the faculty member takes and deserves no authorship credit.

One sign that a change is called for may take the form of indications that the relationship is going well and is on solid ground. But if the relationship isn't going well, or if it seems stalled, "testing the limits" and experimenting with something different may be called for as well. These moves toward independence are never a clear progression. Steps forward are often followed by regressions. Tacit moves and countermoves shape evolving expectations, influencing how well each person will behave and respond. Improvisation can happen. Improvi-

sation and risk taking by both partners should be encouraged. This is another area where consciously being alert to opportunities for small wins can play a role.

Importance of Clear Communication

Clear communication plays an obvious role in effective collaborations. At the same time, there are many psychological and social barriers to clear and honest communication. We naturally tend to censor ourselves, mute criticism, deflect attention away from sensitive areas. All of these inhibitions and difficulties are magnified in the context of a relationship that, by its very nature, is evaluative and characterized by asymmetry in power.

One of us took a sabbatical shortly before coming up for tenure:

I knew I would be gone for a year. I was looking forward to getting away. The student I was working with was working on her dissertation. I didn't want her to feel abandoned, so I emphasized that, although I would be gone, I would be readily available by phone whenever she needed me. This student was also dealing with a new baby. She seemed to be enjoying tremendously the experience of being a mother. I felt strongly committed to not imposing my own expectations on her— this was a great period in her life and, frankly, I felt the dissertation was less important than her enjoying her child. Thus I assumed she was excited about having no explicit demands or expectations placed on this year in her life. I tried very conscientiously to leave her alone. I felt it had gone well, but when I came back after my sabbatical, I realized she had made very little real progress on her work. She blamed me for her lack of progress, feeling I had been too lenient with her. She told me I should have pushed her harder. I told her I would do that in the future—and did. At the time, I felt she was right. Perhaps some students need—or think they need—a stern external taskmaster. Filling this role for them may be helpful, at least in the short-term. Yet, to this day, I remain ambivalent about this experience—the academic life is one that requires self-imposed discipline. No one hangs around outside your door asking when your next paper is going to be ready. If you can't do it yourself, perhaps someone else shouldn't make you.

Clear communication has to work both ways. We cannot expect our students to be honest and forthright if we are not as well. Accordingly, sometimes it helps to tell students about our own habits and faults. For example:

Over time, I came to realize that I have an extremely short attention span. There are too many topics in which I am interested. And I have a strong philosophy that each day has to be exciting. So, if an idea grabs me, I drop what I am doing and play with it. If I see a book I want to read, I start reading it. I operate with an assumption that any given day might be my last—so each day has to have at least a little pleasure in it.

As a result, when I was starting out, my research plans often seemed to change almost weekly as I went from one interest to another. The students working with me paid dearly for this; one week we would design an experiment on one topic and the very next week I would want to tinker with an entirely different project. On the one hand, I think this is good. I think it's useful to be experimenting with ideas and thinking all of the time about generating different directions for your work. I also think it's important to walk away from ideas that aren't worth pursuing or where interest has lagged. But I also realize that this made it extremely hard for my students to know what to really respond to. Over time, some of them probably grew discouraged trying to work with me.

Recognizing these trade-offs, I have learned to lengthen my attention span. Most important, I don't get students involved with projects in the early stages. Instead, I involve them only in projects for which my commitment is strong and focused.

Also, I tell them they can hit me over the head when I frustrate them too much.

Forms of Miscommunication

It is not only easy for misperceptions and misunderstandings to develop, it is easy for either one or both parties to fail to appreciate the extent to which they are getting out of hand. One of the biggest sources of trouble is the tendency, understandable but deadly, of sometimes not saying enough of what we really mean. With the help of our students, we have assembled Table 18.1, which summarizes some of the more obvious instances of situations in which we say one thing and mean another.

Managing Miscommunication

The points listed in Table 18.1 are, of course, expressed in exaggerated terms. For each, however, there is an underlying kernel of truth that we regard as quite serious. Perhaps most important, when the discrepancy between what we are thinking and what we are saying becomes too great, we construe that as a symptom that the relationship has become problematic. When we find ourselves holding back, we have learned to ask ourselves: Why aren't we saying what we are thinking? Are there problems of trust? Are we too concerned about hurting feelings?

We have also found that, if we are having these problems and concerns, the chances are good the student is as well. Misperceptions tend to be reciprocal, thus raising the issue often brings relief for both and injects a note of hopefulness into the relationship. This can actually create a wonderful opportunity to move the relationship toward a deeper, more honest level. If both individuals in the collaboration engage in regular preemptive or prophylactic reality checks, it is easier to keep misperceptions and misunderstandings small.

Trust

Trust provides an important buffer in collaborative relationships. It adds resilience to a relationship by enabling the parties to weather the shocks, both endogenous and exogenous, that inevitably permeate it. One of us likes to think of trust as a reservoir or bank account that we can draw on. The image is useful because it reminds us that building trust is an active process that requires measured steps and continual effort.

One way to build trust is through "strategic" self-disclosures. As the person in a position of relative power, the faculty member can try to

TABLE 18.1 How We Miscommunicate

What We Say	What We Really Mean
I understand why this is late.	No I don't.
Take your time.	Do it now.
Call me if you have any questions.	Try to find me.
The ideas are good.	The methods stink.
Interesting methods.	The ideas stink.
The results are interesting.	The theory is terrible.
This is a good first draft.	This really needs a lot of work.
You might want to do a literature search.	This study was done about 100 years ago.
I'm looking forward to reading this latest draft of your dissertation.	How many is that, anyway?
This is really a nice piece of independent, scholarly work.	Gee, I wish I were a coauthor.
I could use your help analyzing these data.	I can't make heads or tails out of this mess.
I think we are getting close to a final draft.	You've got a long way to go.
You might want to think through some of the implications.	Why haven't you done so?
I'm glad you brought me up to date on your dissertation.	Where have you been since September 1987?
That's a reasonable interpretation of these data.	It's a lot better than mine.

What Students Say	What They Really Mean
Here's my draft; it's still a little rough.	I wrote it last night.
Do you happen to know anything about this topic?	Give me the citations so I don't have to do a literature search.
What do you think of the theory?	The results stink.
What do you think of the data?	The theory stinks.
That's a good point that I didn't think of.	I have no idea what you're talking about.
That's a *really* good point.	You have no idea what I'm talking about.
These are really good suggestions.	What a pain.
Then I transformed the data using acceptable multivariate techniques.	I got rid of the outliers.
Support for the main hypotheses was weak.	Support was nonexistent.
I misunderstood your comment.	I thought we agreed on this.
I guess I didn't reason that way.	If you think it through, it doesn't make sense.
I guess I wasn't clear about . . .	Didn't you read it?
If you sign off so I can just file it, I'll make the changes right away.	See you same time next year.

model the process by making measured, graduated self-disclosures. In the beginning of a relationship, we focus on the work at hand and try to project an image of confidence and control over the research process. Over time, as we get to know the students better, and they get to know us, we increasingly try to involve our students in broader dialogues about trade-offs, ambiguities, and subjective decisions. We also increasingly involve students in candid discussions about what we view as the politics and pragmatics of the academic world: how to think about selection of a research topic that is based on current interests and enthusiasms; how to respond to unfair referee reports in the review process.

Both of us read Jeffrey Pfeffer's *Managing With Power* and had something close to an epiphany. We had always focused very diligently on doing good research, but we underestimated the importance of promoting our work and our ideas. Now, although we want our students to have a positive, "kinder, gentler" view of academia, we also want them to understand the way things work. We want them to be more effective.

Managing Endings:
Learning to Know When It's Over

Much of our analysis up to this point has implicitly, if not always explicitly, implied that the collaborative relationship resembles—or should resemble—other forms of close personal relationships. If that is the case, it is reasonable to raise questions about separation, divorce, and moving on.

Divorce

We think the "divorce rate" in collaborations is sometimes too low; students and faculty often remain in relationships far longer than they should (we also think they remain in the wrong programs too long, but that is another chapter). The academic life is too short, the opportunity costs too high, and the risk of psychological damage too great to justify enduring in a damaging relationship.

It is important to evaluate when endings are near because the punctuation of time and the "socially expected durations" of relationships in academic life are, in many respects, no more sensible than the punctuation of time and the expected durations of relations in other spheres of our personal and social lives. A doctoral student's career typically lasts 4-5 years in a given institution—but that may not be the best life span for any given relationship. Thus knowing when to end a relationship is just as important as knowing when to begin one. One reason it is sometimes hard to recognize when the time has come to move on is that there are many barriers to exit: Both faculty member and student may worry about the reputational costs of relationship failure; both may feel they have too much invested to quit; and there is always the hope that the relationship can be turned around, especially with more effort. We have found it useful to keep reminding ourselves that the ending of a relationship is seldom as catastrophic to the other's ego as one imagines. In fact, it often turns out the other party has been entertaining the same thoughts.

To some degree, this critical stage in the evaluation of a relationship is helped by the trust that has evolved out of the frank exchanges and periodic evaluations that have been ongoing in the relationship since its inception. This is when early investments in communication and understanding really pay off: Both parties can feel comfortable raising their doubts and expressing their longings about moving on.

One of us has developed a mental strategy for assessing when the time to exit the relationship may be at hand:

I periodically apply a "hedonic barometer" to all of my relationships. Am I having fun? Am I enjoying this? Do I look forward to seeing this person? Asking these questions helps me in several ways. First, it helps me become aware of sunk costs and escalation of commitment. Also, it directs my attention to possible problems, such as drift and breakdowns in communication. Things should be enjoyable (not always, but on average). If it isn't fun, and the work is not progressing well, it's time to consider other possibilities.

Managing the Exit

Of course, not all endings reflect problems. Sometimes, the termination of a collaborative relationship reflects a "graduation" in the true sense of the word: The student has learned and is ready to move on. When it becomes necessary, we believe it is important to do everything possible to ensure that the exit is graceful. The tricks here are to recognize when to bail out and to know how to do so with grace, so neither party is hurt. Sometimes a temporary exit, if handled well by both parties, can provide breathing space and permit a reentry to an improved relationship. As one of our students describes this kind of experience:

While I was struggling to develop a prospectus (my black hole period), my adviser was playing the "tough, caring" mentor, trying to set up small wins, but at the same time holding me to some very demanding standards and timeliness. I often felt frustrated and at times psychologically "beaten up" after meetings. I was not delivering on expectations, so, understandably, our frustrations with each other mounted because we really wanted it to work; by then we had a lot invested in our relationship. Fortunately, our relationship was solid enough for us to admit that I needed to be working closely with someone else for a while. So I did. It freed me up and helped me make progress. I later returned to my adviser and, I think, our relationship was much stronger after this break.

Not all exits are temporary, of course, but a graceful exit is always a better outcome, if it can be achieved. And after graduation, an adviser needs to recognize—explicitly—that a student is no longer a student. One of our students marked this change by a reversal of roles:

> Although we had already transitioned quite a bit by this time, I saw my adviser's request for comments on her book manuscript as a real opportunity to give back and add value to her work as she for so long had done to me, and, in so doing, take our relationship to a new place. This placed some of the responsibility for the relationship with the student, which in my mind is essential. I can't imagine a successful relationship managed by only one of the parties in the relationship.

Concluding Remarks

In writing this chapter, we have had an opportunity to revisit many of our past relationships, with the advantage of hindsight and in some instances with the passage of considerable time. In doing so, we have come to appreciate how distinctive each relationship has been, with its unique rhythms and distinctive developmental phases. Each of the relationships we've had with our students has been one of a kind—

not just because the students were different, but because we were different as well. For this reason, when we reviewed this chapter from a reader's perspective, we felt rather critical of what we had written. We don't know if our experiences will be useful or relevant in shaping others' thoughts about their relationships; we are not even sure how well they will apply to our future relationships. We hope that by explicating some of the rules that have guided our management of our collaborative relationships, readers might be stimulated—or provoked—into searching for their own. Indeed, one of the students we asked to read our first draft told us, "You've got it all wrong." In a way, we hope so. We hope there are still surprises awaiting us and things we've missed.

Writing this chapter has also led us to realize how much we want to resist thinking in terms of influence strategies, rules, prescriptions, and so on. We prefer, whenever possible, improvisation and spontaneity. But we also recognize that improvisation and the appearance of spontaneity often depend upon effortful reflection about technique and process, and steady practice and rehearsal. In this regard, we have come to believe that a good collaborative relationship, like any close personal relationship, requires a fine balance between careful and honest analysis, improvisation and consistency, experimentation and tried-and-true methods, reasoned action and intuition. In the final analysis, it is probably useful to resist being too analytic or prescriptive about one's relationships. As the Gryphon said to Alice, "The adventures first . . . explanations take such a dreadful time."

Getting Tenure

Of course, it's getting better now that I have tenure—I no longer feel I have to spend every *free moment writing.*

faculty member quoted by Marilyn E. Gist (p. 185)

In some ways the experience of working toward tenure, at least in North American academic institutions, is like the pain associated with severe toothache. Its presence is felt at almost every moment that we have it, but after the toothache has gone, the pain becomes a memory we might talk about, although the acute emotions that accompanied the pain cannot be as easily recalled. The period leading up to the tenure decision typically demands our full attention, particularly when the standards set are very high. The situation can be a real pressure cooker—one is both in advanced training mode and facing high expectations that one produce high-quality research and/or be a first-rate teacher.

The time frame within which one is expected to create a portfolio of excellent performances is typically quite short (5-7 years), and the demands on one's time are many and varied, extending beyond those required to teach and do research. There is no equivalent institutional or professional pressure placed on an academic after a positive tenure decision. At the very least,

with tenure the uncertainty of employment disappears. Subsequent hurdles, such as promotion to full professor status, can be declined, or the timing of such decisions can be managed by the candidate. Such choices are not available to the pre-tenured professional, unless he or she chooses to leave an institution and start the clock again. Consequently, decisions as to which institutions to join, how they will behave, and what tasks they will emphasize are important for scholars to address as they start their academic journeys.

There are also important personal and emotional issues confronted along the way to the tenure decision. What does one gain and what does one lose by pursuing a particular tenure-seeking strategy? What are the benefits and costs to the institution, to the profession? How much attention should one give to an instrumental pursuit of tenure versus following one's creative urges? Are the two approaches incompatible?

In her essay in this section, Marilyn Gist provides some cogent insights on the tenure process. She advises persons making their selection decisions to look carefully at the espoused and actual norms of hiring institutions. Are they focusing on cosmopolitan norms, hiring academics to perform on professional criteria, that is, activities "concerned with professional development in the field at large—gaining visibility and respect among a wide community of scholars" (p. 186)? Are they hiring academics in terms of local norms, to help them to "respond to local concerns and mission pressures" (p. 186)? If one aspires to a cosmopolitan career and in particular to making a significant research contribution to the field, then a decision to join a more locally oriented institution will likely result in a discouraging experience. The same is likely to be true if there is a lack of fit the other way.

Making good decisions about which institutions to join can be even more complicated for women and for people of color. For these individuals, the signals they receive and the expectations they face from hiring institutions can be mixed. As Toni King points out in her essay here, high demands are often made by institutions and professions on women, particularly women of color, to be very visible and active in the community, while they are also expected to perform at the same very high level as researchers. She notes: "After 2 years, I began to experience burnout. I attribute this to intense involvement in the following activities: Mentoring and counseling . . . serving on countless and ever-increasing committees . . . being discovered as a 'new' black professional" (p. 194). King had precious little time to develop and maintain a research agenda, despite her need to do this to become tenured in her school.

Looking beyond the issue of selecting a "good fit" institution, Marilyn Gist provides a comprehensive set of ideas for preparing for the tenure decision, particularly when one is pursuing primarily a research career in a compatible organization. She describes the need to structure one's time, to plan strategically, and to set proximal goals for achieving tenure. "Part of an academic's development during pretenure years is learning to balance what's urgent with *all* of what's important" (p. 191). She provides a sense of the persistence, the single-mindedness and discipline, that tends to be associated with the drive for tenure. She acknowledges the sacrifices: "The price one pays for tenure is typically several years of one's life spent *working*—to the exclusion of almost everything else" (p. 191). In her account of the pretenure years, Toni King captures the anxieties individuals feel as their tenure decisions approach (her tenure decision will be made in 1996).

Once one has been awarded tenure, it becomes important to take stock of one's progress and to establish some strategies for the next phase in one's career. Marilyn Gist accurately describes a positive tenure decision as one after which the individual is "trusted with . . . academic freedom indefinitely" (p. 192).

Of course, not all of those who apply for tenure receive it. Being denied tenured at a given university is not necessarily the death knell of an individual academic career. Most people do get tenure, but they may have to make at least one move in the course of their pretenure careers before this happens. Clearly, it is less disruptive to make such a move when one begins to see that a particular person-organization fit is not working out, before a tenure decision is to be made. There are benefits to be gleaned from moving on constructively. If one is patient and persistent, and if one adopts the long view of one's career and contributions, then one may be able to reduce or deal constructively with some of the pressures typically experienced in the pretenure years. Much of the problem can be reduced to "fit failure" rather than achievement failure. We think it is essential that institutions send signals to junior academics about their progress as researchers and teachers early and clearly enough that their likelihood of being tenured can be discerned well before the decision point has been reached. When there is genuine dialogue among a junior academic, his or her colleagues, and the administration, the experience of working toward tenure should lead the academic to the outcomes that Gist mentions: internal validation of his or her own competence, respect from others in the field, and a recognition of the freedom to try new things.

19 Getting Tenure

Marilyn E. Gist

During the interview for my first job in academe, I met with one faculty member who had recently earned tenure. He was well regarded by his colleagues, and junior enough that I was eager to hear how he liked the place. Although his remarks were positive, they included a qualifier I found disturbing: "Of course, it's getting better now that I have tenure—I no longer feel I have to spend *every* free moment writing." I wondered what sort of workaholism this implied, and felt confident that I would never relate to that feeling. That confidence was jeopardized a couple of months later, as I neared the end of my dissertation. I chanced upon a favorite professor from another department, and he asked how things were coming along. I mentioned how close to the end I was and how excited I felt about having landed a job at a strong school for the coming fall. Perhaps I sounded too elated for his taste, or perhaps he was really trying to be helpful, but his response certainly flattened my enthusiasm: "Just remember, the light you see at the end of the tunnel is another locomotive!" As if those two events weren't enough, a third brought the lesson home. Two months into that first job, I caught my

reflection in a mirror and realized suddenly that something internal didn't match what I saw on the outside. The person at whom I was looking had earned a PhD and a faculty position. Her students called her "doctor" and turned to her for expertise. Her colleagues did the same and expressed optimism about her scholarly career. But I didn't *feel* much like a scholar. Burdened with new beginnings, I felt rather lost. A mountain lay awaiting my climb and I was unsure where to begin.

It's easier now to look back on these moments and sort accuracy from sensitivity, potential from accomplishment. However, the incidents themselves illustrate an important point. Although there are marker events in careers, phrases such as *getting tenure* create the perception that careers are composed of a set of discrete points (e.g., getting the doctorate, taking a tenure-track position, getting tenure, making full professor). In truth, a career is a continuum of professional development; marker events merely indicate phases of transition in the ongoing process of acquiring and utilizing knowledge and skills. Thus, in thinking about getting tenure, it is important to think not only about

185

the outcomes that should be in evidence for a positive tenure decision, but also about the process—the ongoing skill development—that leads to the outcomes desired.

The Outcomes

As a starting point in discussing outcome requirements, it is worth noting that higher education is an industry—a marketplace like many others, in which services (and those who provide them) are bought and sold at varying prices. To ask what it takes to get tenure is a bit like asking what a car costs. The answer depends heavily on the brand name and features of the car. Similarly, colleges and universities respond to local concerns and mission pressures, even as they are part of the larger industry of higher education. Thus, the first issue one must reckon with in getting tenure is that there are both local norms and national norms about what should be accomplished by the point of tenure review. National norms are concerned with professional development in the field at large—gaining visibility and respect among a wide community of scholars. Ideally, the two norms are compatible; if so, success in the local environment implies national success, providing faculty with maximum career opportunities. When the norms are in conflict, it is important that one deliberate carefully about which path to take. In this chapter I adopt the perspective of national norms, assuming that the reader can identify divergence in local perspectives and choose what is best for him or her.

Scholarly Achievement

Because tenure decisions typically incorporate evaluations from senior scholars outside the local university, national norms are important. The three outcomes most widely discussed in tenure decisions are scholarship, teaching effectiveness, and organizational citizenship. Although the emphases on each of these, as well as the specific criteria used to gauge progress, vary from school to school, national norms tend to prioritize these outcomes in the order mentioned. This is partly because the mission of most universities involves creating, as well as transmitting, knowledge. Research is the means by which knowledge is generated to fill textbooks and lectures.

However, there are other reasons research has such high priority. One is the widespread belief (which appears to have some merit) that scholarly effectiveness requires mastery of higher-order skills than those required for teaching. Another is that junior faculty have the most current, broad-based training in the field. They may be more likely to contribute fresh ideas and perspectives through research than are faculty who have advanced specific research programs but, in the process of specialization, lost contact with a broader array of topics. This "freshness" factor is a significant resource, and its greatest potential is achieved only when research is conducted and published.

Finally, the junior faculty years are part of the continuum of development. Fresh research training, even coupled with participation in some research as a doctoral student, is an indicator of potential. After tenure, when we look back at where we started, most of us are amazed at how much we have learned about research and writing. The marker event of tenure coincides with a stage of development that is no longer characterized mainly as potential but as potential augmented by substantial accomplishment. Ideally, the research accomplishment reflects mastery in developing, managing, and publishing results from an independent research program. If this is not accomplished during the junior years, the prognosis is not good that the tenure candidate will later generate knowledge through research and contribute to that part of the university's mission.

Thus, outside reviewers may be most concerned with evidence of national visibility in research. To an extent, junior academics gain visibility by presenting work at conferences; however, reviewers place greater reliance on publishing. Three general criteria are commonly used in assessing the effectiveness of scholarly research: quality, independence, and impact.

Quality

In general, research quality is gauged in terms of theoretical and methodological rigor. The quality criterion reflects the question, Is this person's work well done? As outside reviewers may differ in their evaluations of an individual's work, heavy reliance is placed on *whether* the work has been published and *where*. Some journals are more "prestigious" than others because they have stronger review boards, more selective standards for publication, and wider readership and respect among leading scholars in the field. Work that is published in these journals is often considered superior to work published elsewhere, because it has survived rather rigorous peer examination. In general, faculty members whose tenure packages show multiple publications in "top journals" will be reviewed more favorably than those whose work has not achieved this placement.

I once heard a junior scholar remark, "It's better to give them a line on the vita worth arguing about than not to have the line on the vita at all." This may be true at the margin because tenure evaluations consider the broad pattern of publications. If the majority of one's work is gauged to be of high quality, occasional lines "worth arguing about" might be acceptable. However, if used as a dominant strategy, this may produce a record whose overall quality is weak.

Many factors contribute to whether or not particular work is publishable in leading journals, and I will discuss some of the process issues later in this chapter. However, the time to consider quality is in the design phase itself. Often, junior scholars remark, "I've an idea for a study that may not make it in a top journal, but I can probably get it published somewhere." Considering that time is limited during the junior faculty years, it's worth asking whether such a study might be strengthened with more forethought. If it is developed carefully and targeted for a good journal but doesn't make it there, it can then be aimed at other outlets.

Similarly, journals have different audiences and objectives; these affect the likelihood of a study's relevance and should be considered in the design phase. Studies that have only one feasible outlet among top journals are riskier than those with several strong possibilities. A good rule of thumb is to plan research, if at all possible, so that it addresses issues of theoretical interest, sample, and/or task in ways that will make two or three strong outlets for publication possible. Then, if the manuscript fails at one, it may be revised (with weaknesses corrected) and submitted to another strong journal. Relatedly, each manuscript needs to be crafted for relevance to the targeted journal. Although the basic research issue may be appropriate for multiple audiences, the paper needs to be positioned carefully in the literature according to the theoretical concerns of interest to each audience.

Independence

In evaluating pretenure performance, a second concern is independence in research. This criterion reflects the question, Can *this* person conceptualize research projects and manage all phases of them? One proxy that is used in assessing independence is the proportion of publications that are solo authored. However, because joint-authored work is quite common, reviewers also look at the order of authors. Work for which one is first author is assumed to indicate leadership, whereas secondary authorship is less clear. As with quality, independence is gauged from the dominant pattern. Records in which first or solo authorship predominates inspire more confidence than those in which leadership is rare. Similarly, joint publications with a range of people, particularly if they are students or colleagues not associated with one's employing or degree-granting institutions, inspire more confidence than records dominated by the same collaborators or by those who have some stake in one's success.

Reviewers also may consider the correlation between leadership attempts and quality of journal outlet. A fair amount of first- and solo-authored work at top journals is preferred. A few secondary-authored publications at leading journals, with most first-authored work being less prominently placed, may indicate difficulty in conducting independent research of high quality.

Impact

The impact of research refers to its contribution to the knowledge base in the field. Assuming the work has been well placed, the criterion of impact reflects the questions, So what? or, What difference have these publications made? Evaluators are concerned with whether the "body of knowledge" produced during the pretenure years is significant enough to provide the individual visibility as a scholar. One proxy for impact is quantity, because a high volume of work is likely to be more visible than very little. However, as one senior colleague mentioned, "You have to publish three articles on a topic before people associate your name with it." Beyond name recognition, programmatic work has more impact because it goes deeper: Several publications on any topic are likely to contribute more to the field at large than the same number of publications spread out over different topics. Programmatic work also may contribute more to the individual's own scholarly development by providing deeper immersion in relevant literature, more astute conceptualization of ideas on topic(s), and mastery of a range of research skills needed to study the topic(s) well.

Other factors worth considering that relate to impact include the significance or importance of the work. This is partly related to quality, because the most important criterion for acceptance or rejection of manuscripts at leading journals is the significance of the contribution to the field. However, some tenure reviews also favor work that contributes theoretical or methodological innovation over work that is incremental, or work that has applied relevance over work that is limited to the esoteric interests of a small group of scholars. Thus, although quantity contributes to impact, programmatic work that breaks new ground or addresses important applied concerns may increase impact even more.

Some proxies used for assessing impact are the outside reviews of the tenure package itself (including sample work), the extent to which the work is being cited by other researchers (based, e.g., on the *Social Science Citation Index*), work published as the lead article in a top journal, success in securing funding for the research, and spin-off among practitioners from the knowledge generated. Because it is hard to leap tall buildings in a single bound, some schools utilize longer pretenure periods (e.g., 9 years) so that they can gauge impact more accurately. Those using shorter periods (e.g., 5 years) expect proportionately less impact and appear to weight quality and leadership more heavily; still, evidence of positive impact is impressive.

Teaching Effectiveness

Most universities use student evaluations as one measure of teaching effectiveness. Increasingly, student ratings are being augmented by various peer assessments, such as classroom observation and review of course syllabi and exams.

However, flexibility in teaching also may be a factor. Faculty who teach well at only one level may not be viewed as favorably as those who can teach well in several programs. In business schools, MBA programs are highly visible, and strong performance in core classes is typically beneficial. However, because few faculty enjoy teaching, or teach equally well, at all levels, individuals may earn positive overall evaluations on teaching by being able to teach well in several electives or across three or more programs (i.e., undergraduate, master's, doctoral, or executive master's degree programs or public nondegree programs).

Further, teaching is subjected less to national norms than local ones in tenure decisions. Some schools use a compensatory model in which classroom excellence can offset less-than-stellar research performance. At others, these factors are noncompensatory. Also, the range of teaching effectiveness that is considered acceptable for tenure is wider at some schools than that used in evaluating scholarship. Although this may be changing, a mediocre teaching record coupled with excellence in research has often been more favorably reviewed in the past than a mediocre research record coupled with outstanding teaching.

Organizational Citizenship

This category is often referred to as *service*, and it encompasses service to the department or school, the university, the field, and/or the community at large. Most institutions try to protect junior faculty from heavy service obligations in order to further scholarship. Accordingly, although tenure reviews welcome evidence of wide-ranging service, they typically stress research and teaching more heavily.

Participation on committees, attendance at meetings, presence in one's office, and a willingness to supervise students are generally expected. Membership on editorial review boards and participation at national conferences help. Again, local norms may be more relevant to citizenship than national ones. This is also an area in which the two may conflict, should local expectations for service interfere significantly with achieving the level of research productivity that is valued in the field at large.

The Process

Most junior faculty arrive with some sense that the outcomes described above will be important in getting tenure. Despite good intentions, many quickly become immersed in the demands of the new job and end the first year feeling distressed at how quickly it has flown and how little research they accomplished. Those who succeed with tenure grow in two process areas: structuring time and managing progress.

Structuring Time

Perhaps the greatest single challenge in getting tenure is that of imposing structure on a demanding yet largely unstructured job. The autonomy an individual has in an academic position is at once part of its greatest joy and its greatest frustration. When I was a student, I recall one professor saying, "I wake up and am at my desk by 7:00 in the morning. On many days, the whole day stretches before me with no externally imposed structure. It's hard to decide how to best use the time and hard to stay focused so that I do what I *need* to do. No one really monitors that closely, and if I don't come in to the office, I can go the entire day not talking to anyone. It can be a very isolated existence."

The challenge is to cope with more than a day; most universities provide 5 to 9 years of unstructured time before tenure reviews are conducted. Still, the period between conceiving a research idea and getting an article published in a leading journal can easily be 3 years, given all the steps in between. When one considers the volume and quality of research productivity required, as well as norms for teaching and service, it is no surprise that some faculty are caught short. Strategic planning and proximal

goal setting can be useful methods for structuring this mass of time.

Strategic Planning

First, it is important to think strategically about time: Review the outcome requirements and clarify goals for tenure review. A classic question that most people have early on is, How much does it take? For scholarly productivity, how many publications of what type are expected? For teaching, what range of teaching ratings are expected in what kinds of courses? Few people are willing to commit on these issues, but by questioning several faculty members in the local environment, one can derive the mean expectations and gain a sense for the variance. It also helps to ask people outside one's institution about the norms in their environments (particularly schools that are considered to be "peer" institutions) and to consider the records of other individuals who have achieved tenure recently. These data will (a) provide normative comparisons between one's institution and others, (b) clarify the probable expectations of outside reviewers at different types of schools, and (c) help one to set promising strategic goals.

Because it is difficult to predict research outcomes with certainty, it helps to strategize a tenure record that will be stronger than needed for success. This leaves room for miscalculations: a study with ambiguous findings, a planned publication that gets rejected from the targeted journal, another that is detained in the review process for longer than expected. Mishaps are common, but tenure reviews, like professors, offer little grace for "last-minute" crises.

It helps to assess one's assets and liabilities early in the process and to plan how to strengthen weaknesses. Some new faculty members begin with masses of data they gathered as students. For such individuals it may be best to begin writing, not designing new work. Doctoral programs often emphasize research proposals in content courses, so it may be most natural to think of new ideas and new designs for studies. However, as a colleague of mine once remarked, "Ideas are cheap." He meant this in the sense that there is a very long way between an idea and a publication. Nearly half the time spent in getting most papers published is expended on what is required *after* the data are collected. Starting new studies instead of writing up existing data may not be a wise use of time early on. Particularly when one is adjusting to the demands of a new job, design and data collection work may detract energy from writing, so that a couple of years pass with no publications. An individual who has data and focuses on writing initially will probably publish earlier and will find that his or her subsequent research is stronger and more programmatic as a result of lessons learned in the review process.

By contrast, if one has few data, one may find it helpful to identify resources that can maximize the research strategy. One resource may involve collaborating with doctoral students, who can contribute time on relatively simple tasks (data collection, guided analysis), freeing one to concentrate on more difficult aspects of the research (significant theoretical questions, complex design issues, writing). Similarly, one should pursue funding. This may provide resources that the local environment cannot, such as money for research assistants, summer support, release time from teaching, and direct research costs.

Proximal Goal Setting

Once one has established some overall goals, it helps to break these down in a time line, setting short-range targets, or proximal goals, for each year. However, as one colleague has noted, "It takes time to get the machinery in motion." Part of this requires thinking about the processes involved and finding ways to measure progress long before outcomes are clear. For example, one can track progress toward each stage of a project: design, data collection, analysis, first and subsequent drafts, draft sent out to colleagues for comment, final draft submitted to journal, revision(s) requested and completed, final acceptance.

It helps to set challenging goals, but goals must also be realistic. I learned that it was useless to think I was working on a dozen projects at once. Perhaps I had a dozen in my head, but there were far fewer that I could move forward consistently, from one stage to the next, in any given year. Once realistic goals are set, getting the machinery in motion involves synchronizing work on multiple projects. Every project has downtime (e.g., waiting for journal reviews to come back), and that time can be used for other

purposes if one has planned well. It is also helpful to use conference deadlines as part of the machine; for example, annual calls for papers can be important for moving work toward a first draft, regardless of whether it is later accepted for presentation.

Finally, it is useful to set a process goal to keep a fixed number of manuscripts under review at all times. As papers progress in the review process, this means that other work has to be readied to fill the pipeline when something is accepted. This helps ensure a continual flow of publications.

The methods described above may seem mechanical, but they can help impose structure on the unstructured mass of time available to the pretenure academic. Further, the evidence on goal setting is compelling—goals direct attention and increase effort. They may enhance discipline when it is lacking from externally imposed deadlines.

Managing Progress

Control

Once goals are set, it helps to exercise high control over daily, weekly, and monthly schedules, to see that they are met. An operational definition of control in this case involves how much one allows one's schedule to be interrupted by nonessential requests and expectations. Those who take their plans seriously and understand the importance of continual progress will find that they must say no, politely, to a range of requests. Certainly there are times to yield, but, at tenure review, one is accountable for how well one has used one's time. And although I'm loath to admit it, during the last few years before tenure, I *did* feel as if I had to spend every free moment writing!

Above, in discussing the structuring of time, I used research productivity as an example; similar planning must be done for teaching and service activities. With these factored in, control of time is even more important. Teaching and service not only consume time, they break the week up into blocks that make finding time for research progress even harder. Further, they carry a sense of urgency that can derail scholarly activity. For example, one must prepare for classes before they meet, so this work feels very important. However, research progress, although appearing to have more flexibility, actually may have less. Because it is difficult to sense how time is running out on research, one may spend more time on "urgent" activities than one would otherwise. Part of an academic's development during pretenure years is learning to balance what's urgent with *all* of what's important. Typically, one has to *make* time for research. An important indicator to watch is whether one is making regular progress on research goals or whether week after week is being consumed by other demands so that research activity is neglected.

Persistence

During my first year as a faculty member, a senior colleague advised me that persistence is nine-tenths of success. Although others might debate the proportion, there is no doubt that persistence is important. Few people achieve tenure without experiencing failure along the way: courses they worked at diligently that received lower ratings than they felt they deserved, manuscripts they felt would move the field that were rejected by leading journals, brilliant revisions to papers that received yet more requests for substantial revision.

The difference between success and failure is often in how one interprets and handles rejection. I once watched as a colleague was presented with an award for outstanding scholarship throughout his career. During his acceptance speech, he described how much acclaim he had received for his most renowned article: an award and heavy citation by other scholars. He went on to tell how this article was published by the seventh journal to which it was submitted—but only after he had received six prior rejections and had revised it substantially before each subsequent submission. That's persistence. Rejection comes to most of us, and it is hard for everyone. It helps to take it in stride, persist in improving the work, and try, try again.

The Price and Rewards

The foregoing review of what it takes to get tenure may make the required outcomes and process seem daunting, but it *is* doable, as many success cases show. Still, it is worth reviewing what the struggle for tenure takes (and perhaps costs) on a personal level and the benefits that come with success. Each person's experiences will be unique, but some common themes are described below.

Time and Emotional Challenges

The norms for tenure at major research institutions require significant productivity and offer little grace time for catching up if one falls behind. In turn, the price one pays for tenure is typically several years of one's life spent *working*—to the exclusion of almost everything else. As imbalanced as this seems, it parallels the process of development in several other professional fields (e.g., making partner in a law firm, completing internship and residency to become a practicing doctor). In other words, the junior years of professional development are often taxing; those who intend to succeed find they must make a multiyear intensive investment beyond graduate school training. Whether this is worth it is always a personal decision. There are significant rewards for the effort (described later) and some emotional adjustments along the way.

Most of us enter the junior faculty years with a sense of achievement based in having earned a doctorate and much enthusiasm about being a faculty member. These feelings often give way to dismay as time flies by and so much remains to be done. As one person put it, "Fear of failure is a great motivator!" It is one thing to consider tenure in the abstract; it is quite another when the process and result become very personal. Anxiety tends to increase each year as the moment of truth approaches and continues until the final result arrives. Some degree of anxiety affects almost everyone, regardless of how strong his or her tenure package looks. It is amplified by stories of others who seemed exceptionally qualified but who were denied tenure somewhere for unclear reasons. The potential loss of a job is simply hard to ignore, and it is difficult to have absolute confidence in a favorable outcome when one's own turn comes for review.

On the other hand, preparing and submitting a tenure package forces one to reflect intensively on what one has achieved. Assuming one has produced well, pretenure anxiety is counterbalanced by a sense of deserving (and expecting) a favorable outcome. Yet this mixture of feelings—both anxiety and self-respect—is what may make the moment of finally getting tenure feel surprisingly anticlimactic. As described by one of my predecessors, "getting" tenure felt like *not* getting hit over the head. The real rewards are typically realized less at the moment tenure is awarded than more gradually over the next few years. As a marker event, tenure denotes a stage of transformation whose meaning is clarified by hindsight. The changes occur in substantive professional skill and post-tenure self-image and direction.

Substantive Skill Gains by Tenure

Along the path to tenure, if one structures one's time and manages one's progress well, one masters a significant amount of content knowledge and skill in research and teaching. Indeed, many academics feel they learned as much during their junior faculty years as they did during their doctoral programs. This is perhaps the most important transformation that tenure marks. To a great extent, the process of conducting research becomes the classroom after graduation. The peer review process for manuscripts forces us to read literature we have overlooked, integrate ideas with concepts from domains we had not considered, clarify our thinking where it is fuzzy, improve our skill at quantitative analyses, understand contributions and limitations of our work that we had not anticipated, and articulate ideas in writing with greater precision. While we improve in all of these with experience, the review process forges an intimacy between scholar and work. This intimacy typically adds value not only to our papers themselves, but to our own knowledge. In turn, we often find synergy between the knowledge developed through research and our classroom teaching.

So, despite the structural and motivational challenges involved in getting tenure, the process yields strong *professional* rewards. The work itself is much easier by the time one achieves tenure; one has mastered the challenges and one's confidence is higher. But there is even stronger gratification in watching a research program unfold and take wing, in watching teaching effectiveness grow, and in finding one-self amid a national community that offers exciting new avenues for contribution.

Personal Gains From Tenure

Apart from adjustments in title and income, tenure brings three other rewards. The first is that tenure occasions *internal validation and adjustment in self-image*. It begins with a sense of genuine pride that emerges as one pulls one's package together for review. Many of us realize during this time that we have learned a tremendous amount since graduation, that we have indeed accomplished a lot, and that we are not so junior anymore. Also, publications often gain increasing visibility within 2-3 years after they appear in print. Thus one's pretenure scholarly contributions continue to gain recognition in the field *after* tenure. As more calls and letters come in over time, one recognizes more clearly the value to the field of the body of knowledge one has created by the point of tenure. This not only increases the pride felt in one's own contribution, but helps clarify the reasons behind national norms for scholarly productivity that apply to tenure reviews.

Second, tenure permits *more freedom in activity*: flexibility to attempt riskier projects, to explore new topics, or to seek more balance between work and personal life. Time pressures rarely ease after tenure, but stronger skills enable one to work more efficiently; thus the freedom to explore and manage time more to one's liking is perhaps the greatest reward of earning tenure.

Finally, getting tenure brings more respect from colleagues—*external validation*. On a local level, this may be apparent with senior colleagues outside one's own department, or as one gradually assumes a larger role in institutional governance. On a national level, it is often manifest in opportunities for wider service to the field. Similarly, there are psychic rewards in knowing that those in positions of decision power, both internally and externally, feel that one has learned to manage one's time well, has built strong skills, and has contributed significantly in research, teaching, and service—enough to be trusted with this academic freedom indefinitely.

20 Rounding Corners

AN AFRICAN AMERICAN FEMALE
SCHOLAR'S PRETENURE EXPERIENCES

Toni C. King

The pretenure phase of career represents for me a period of establishing competence within my field of organizational behavior. Beyond establishing competence, I feel a strong need to establish a niche within the field with which I am comfortable, build competencies within this niche, and become known to others as a legitimate scholar vis-à-vis these specific areas of competence. With respect to teaching, I want to form meaningful relationships with students and to feel that I am developing a unique style as an educator. Within my local/departmental community, my goal is to have a voice that contributes to the community as a whole. A significant part of this contribution is an active role in support of diversity and in resisting organizational structures and group or individual behaviors that foster racism, sexism, or classism. These goals, desires, needs, and motivations have shaped and are shaping my experiences in the years prior to tenure.

My Personal and Professional Background

I graduated from Case Western Reserve University with a PhD in organizational behavior. Prior to this, I obtained a bachelor of arts degree in psychology and a master's degree in guidance and counseling. During the time that I attended Case Western Reserve University, the Department of Organizational Behavior was a tight-knit community of students and faculty. As such, it was fraught with tensions, growing pains, and the inevitable group issues of competition, power, and racial and gender diversity, to name a few. In addition, there was a great deal of creativity and collaboration. Students were strongly encouraged by faculty to follow our energy in engaging in research and practice.

I was strongly influenced by Professor Donald M. Wolfe. He reinforced for me the thinking that human development underlies all learning.

More than anything else, he showed me by his close attention to my growth that the more I could integrate what was currently significant in my life with my education, the richer my learning would be.

The Pretenure Years

As I reflect on these pretenure years, my memories of seeking employment are most alive. As a means of discussing what the pretenure phase has been like for me, I will describe some of my experiences in interviewing and selecting positions within academic institutions. Because these activities involve a focus of energy from the job candidate as well as the organization, many levels of attention are involved. During the two job searches that I undertook, one after leaving my doctoral program and one after I had experienced my first full-time academic job, I made a number of connections between my values and my personal/professional needs and goals. These connections allowed me to achieve some sense of "completion" in terms of professional identity. I feel that this sense of creating an identity within the academy is a significant component of the pretenure phase.

My First Job Search

During my first job search, I was closing the door to financial strain, the concerns of family and friends that I might never be gainfully employed, and other lower-order needs for food and shelter (Maslow, 1970). During this first job search I also needed to redeem myself as "able" to contribute to a meaningful community of others. As an African American female, my identity is integrally linked to an Africentric values system. This cultural system emphasizes interdependence and a consciousness of the community as a whole; congruence among thought, verbalization, and action; and acknowledgment of such quasi-rational processes as intuition and spirituality (Mbiti, 1970).

Specifically, I have been socialized to "uplift the race" and "give something back" to the black community. It came as no surprise to colleagues, friends, and family that I accepted my first full-time tenure-track position at a

historically black college in the South. This was also my first job offer.

In that first job, I taught my first large lecture class (70 students), Introduction to Business, as well as upper-division courses in organizational behavior and courses in organization theory. After 2 years in this position, I began to experience burnout. I attribute this to intense involvement in the following activities:

- Mentoring and counseling first-generation-to-attend-college students with myriad family pressures and demands
- Grading huge numbers of papers
- Providing extensive tutorials to students—themselves "playing catch-up" after poor and inadequate high school experiences
- Serving on countless and ever-increasing committees to establish programs "quickly" so as to remain competitive with predominantly white universities
- Being discovered as a "new" black professional in the larger polycultural environment and thus being sought after to participate on public agency boards and as a speaker, discussant, panelist, or volunteer
- Being sought out by my colleagues to discuss "issues" deriving from their personal/social/political experiences at the university

I began to experience fatigue and a number of stress-related physical symptoms. Consequently, I began to seek ways to limit my participation in informal community activities, such as listening to my colleagues' "problems." I found it extremely difficult to limit participation on committees and felt subtly sanctioned when I declined requests for my participation on voluntary projects. At other times I felt clearly pressured to take committee assignments.

Despite these pressures, I vowed that I would not fall prey to the stereotypical pattern of female academics, whose boundaries of participation are perceived as so permeable that they are forever solicited to respond to colleagues and community while losing sight of research and writing agendas. Hence I pumped time into staying on top of these multiple commitments and hoarded weekends for writing. I chose not to teach during summers, and this time away from teaching responsibilities and university service commitments was an added blessing.

Still, a combination of internal anxieties and external pressures compelled me toward further involvement. I feared that my worth in the job market had been compromised by my having chosen employment at a predominantly black college that was battling to meet standards set by the national accreditation board for schools of business. I also had fears about how I would be viewed on subsequent interviews—fresh from my experiences at a black college—touting my research agenda on the career lives and social support networks of black women. I asked myself questions such as, Where are my dominant-culture badges of honor and legitimation? Where are my timely research topics that prove my ability to engage in mainstream research? I feared that even my fears were invalid, silly, a dimension of the "paranoia" attributed to blacks by whites.

With enthusiasm, I steeped myself in activities intended to counter my perceived "image." I attended and presented papers at meetings of the Academy of Management and other professional associations. I sustained a subcontractual trainer association with a well-known diversity consulting firm and also procured periodic freelance organizational consulting assignments. I was honored to be invited to assume a board member role for an international professional organization, the activities of which I not only benefited from, but valued and respected.

It became clearer and clearer to me, however, that my increasingly complex research agenda was not being supported at my current institution, owing to mixed organizational messages and norms. Although university officials indicated that research was important, the reality was that teaching and committee obligations were all-consuming. Once this became obvious, I began to seek other employment.

My Second Job Search

My second opportunity to engage in interviewing for positions was quite enlightening. This time, I thought it wise to have more than one interview. The interview process taught me much about the environment and culture of "the academy." Moreover, during this series of interviews, I myself was "somewhere different."

I had grown professionally and was financially secure. No longer pursued by collection agencies, I was secure in the knowledge that I could put my airfare on a charge account (and even pay the bill while waiting to be reimbursed for interview travel).

After more than a half dozen formal interviews, I had several viable offers to consider. My self-esteem and identity as a scholar had begun to stabilize. The interviews gave me concrete (versus fantasized) data about how I was perceived by university departments in my field. Further, I had selected these universities based on personally established criteria for rating their observable or stated commitments as follows:

1. Values and emphasis on both teaching and research
2. Values with respect to diversity of students and faculty
3. Clarity about boundaries and expectations for junior faculty committee involvements
4. Values with respect to collegiality and professional development opportunities and support
5. Clarity and congruence of the stated mission of the school/division with actual programs and practices
6. Instincts, chemistry, or the feeling that people were generally happy there—especially junior faculty, women, and minorities

During the process of interviewing, many of my previous concerns were confirmed. Others were not, and new concerns relating to my identity arose. I became clearer and more centered in my value commitments. I did experience interviews in which my employment at a predominantly black college was seen to be a "curiosity," a mere anomaly in my career path, perhaps an "error" in career planning or a "stopping-off point." Yet at least a few interviews took place at schools struggling to retain or reapply for national accreditation whose faculty appeared genuinely interested in my description of my current employers' dilemmas in meeting and sustaining those rigorous criteria.

At times I was patronized by some faculty I spoke to for developing a research agenda focusing on minority career experiences. However, the general response was energized interest in the findings and the quality of the research design as well as the future implications for building a long-term research agenda. I was as much heartened by this response as I was shaken by disconfirming comments such as, "Of course, if you come here, we'll help you establish some more solid research interests" and "Perhaps after you've gotten one or two publications from your dissertation, you can work with one of us to develop a more realistic agenda. We'll get you set up to publish your work." This last concern may have had some validity (Cox & Nkomo, 1990) in terms of enhancing my tenurability at a particular university, but the discussion felt premature and disconfirmed the importance of the work I was currently engaged in.

In addition to the subtle devaluing I have described, I observed these organizations' systemic and communal needs to have a member of a racial minority on the school faculty. Many schools of business were struggling to hire and retain severely underrepresented female faculty. I would, in essence, be a "twofer"—a female faculty member who was also black, or vice versa, depending on the particular void a given school might be experiencing. In such cases I was welcomed with open arms. At times, the arms of the institution were socially healthy. That is, organization members were conscious of and able to inquire about their responses to me vis-à-vis explicit and thoughtful diversity values and goals. At other times, the organization's overall dysfunction and unaddressed emotional issues and unconscious needs in relation to race, ethnicity, and gender provided enough red flags to warn me that a problematic environment would await me (Dumas, 1979).

In situations I determined to be "more healthy," faculty members, beginning with the department chair, were able to "own" the desire to have racial minorities as part of their faculty community. This was a valued goal, pursued in the context of other organizational and departmental goals, as opposed to an overwhelming need to abate the organization's or department's history of inaction concerning diversity, abuse of affirmative action policies, or poorly defined and operationalized diversity goals. In healthier systems, someone often asked—by the end of the second day—how I thought I might fare as a black woman there. Such a question was appropriately included and integrated in discussions reflecting a general interest in and

sometimes growing excitement about my credentials, previous experience, teaching style and philosophy, research interests and approaches, and overall personhood.

In contrast were the denigrating experiences of feeling a part of some coded (though obvious) barter system in which adding a minority gained the individuals and the team additional points on a scorecard. Here, individuals became overly explicit about the "need" for "a" black faculty member to work with "our diversity issues." The midrange of this continuum included a mix of reactions, including interviews where the words *black* and *female* were avoided or barely whispered as well as those in which these words came up at all-too-frequent intervals and out of context.

I emerged from this montage of experiences with an interest in three universities that were expressing similar interest in me. Each valued both research and teaching, with the perspective that "if you don't excel at research, but carry your weight with a few quality publications and are a good teacher, you'll do well here. But if you're an excellent researcher, yet mediocre as a teacher, you probably will not do well or fit here."

I utilized the criteria mentioned above and ultimately made a choice. My decision was made on all levels—rational, emotional, and intuitive. I accepted employment in the Human Development Division of the School of Education at the State University of New York at Binghamton. Although there was some concern on the part of my colleagues and mentors that I might be reducing my employability within a school of business in the long term, such consideration did not outweigh the pluses offered by this new job opportunity. I felt this position would offer me enhanced freedom to create courses I had always wanted to teach and to expand upon my interests in multiculturalism, the role of race and gender in career experiences, group dynamics, and the integration of adult development and organizational behavior.

Still, this was not an easy choice. I had invested much in my identity as a professor of management—specifically organizational behavior. I would not make more money in this position than in my previous one. I would have to build for myself the bridge between my identity as a professor of management and my identity as a professor of human development. Yet it felt right.

My Current Academic Position

Once again, in this new position a struggle for balance ensued. The pulls on my time and energy came from many directions. As an inter-disciplinary division, this small group of eight full-time faculty members represented a diverse range of disciplines and specializations, including counseling and human services, criminal justice, organizational behavior, peace studies, and adult development, with an emphasis that included women's development and women and work. I was fortunate enough to have one new colleague in the area of organizational behav-ior. Aside from this common ground, we all brought our differences in pedagogy, inquiry, group facilitation, and discipline-related values and styles to each faculty decision-making situ-ation. We valued congruence between division and school mission and actual practice. Such values prompted us to hold frequent and lengthy meetings to achieve relative consensus regard-ing mission, values, goals, and how these could be continually translated into the curriculum in ways responsive to our students.

In addition, the department's mission to meet the needs of a diverse student body placed me in a never-ending cycle of being asked to respond to multiple constituents. African American women students and other women students of color, white women students, nontraditional students, white male students who experienced themselves as disenfranchised or marginal, African American male students and other male students of color, lesbian and gay students, and differently abled students looked to me as an ally and advocate for their personal experiences within the university as well as for organized group activities on the campus. The additional demands I experienced from students, the university community, and the larger local community again conspired to strip me of time for research and writing.

Slowly, I have begun to gain mastery and competence with respect to when to say no, how to say no, and when to commit due to my own sense of individual or communal purpose or due to such pragmatic needs as being per-ceived as a valued colleague and team player. Although far from living a balanced life with respect to work demands, I am learning how to enjoy much of the work. Below, I summarize some of the lessons I have learned from the experiences described above:

- Through research presentations, required as a component of the interview process, I learned that the integration of qualitative and quan-titative data employed in my research was perceived to be stimulating, and that my (experiential) research design and findings were considered provocative. This seemed to be true even when I was later encouraged to abandon the current agenda in order to "grow professionally."

- I have accepted the idea that I am well quali-fied. I have learned that my experiences in the throes of teaching a broad array of Afri-can American students and economically dis-advantaged Euro-American students,[1] vary-ing greatly in the quality of their college preparation and degree of dominant-cul-ture professional socialization, have given me excellent preparation for working with diverse student bodies. I am particularly pre-pared to work with adult students. Such stu-dents vary widely in background, previous career and professional socialization, and length of time out of school. They too have complex educational, familial, organizational, and adult developmental needs.

- I have begun to see that what I feared to be paranoia was merely my attunement to the intuitive—a trait therapists now associate with the functional adaptation of ethnic or racially oppressed group members (Sue & Sue, 1990). This characteristic reflects a sen-sitivity to metadynamics created by the or-ganization's (or society's) culture that has implications for the racial minority mem-ber's life.

- I have learned unequivocally that I need to be seen as a whole person, including my African American femaleness, but not to the exclusion of other dimensions of self. I have learned that I was seeking organizational congruence—a school or department that had thoughtfully approached its cultural val-ues and was consciously engaged in acting on them.

Completion

After accepting my second tenure-track po-sition, I realized that I had rounded another corner in my personal/professional growth. This cycle gave me a sense of completion of professional identity in the field of organizational behavior begun during my doctoral student years. For me the real message of "completion" is a sense of what I have to offer the field of organizational behavior. Perhaps it is only then that one can begin in earnest. Here are some of the lessons marking the corners that I rounded:

- I now feel even more strongly that the rigorous, though rewarding, experience of research and publishing is too central to academic work to be based on external approval rather than on my intrinsic desire to generate knowledge about a topic in which I am keenly interested.

- I am continually learning to wear many masks—that is, to stagger my involvements, to make trade-offs with respect to what will yield higher outcomes in terms of visibility, teaching effectiveness, or research. Sometimes, achieving a goal in one area means less-than-optimal performance in another— at least temporarily.

- I am beginning to "play" more fully in my work. I am learning to negotiate the academic environment from a more integrated sense of personal clarity and to align professional performance with internal requirements for self-actualization.

- Interestingly, in addition to becoming familiar with archetypes of wisdom, I am becoming more comfortable in my identification with the notion of the "fool's child." This archetypal image refers to a naive, foolish, or carefree way of being in the world based on trust that things will somehow work out for the best.

Hope

Hope is salient to me because this corner I have rounded is anchored in my own hopes and visions. It includes a deepening of my professionalism through becoming a child again in the work. Indeed, it is these childlike dreams that replace the heroic images of flawless performance. Rediscovery of the inner child is becoming for me an antidote to role overload, stultification, and rigidity. I now find that I have a strong urge to follow my energy, despite the risks and uncertain rewards of pursuing new directions.

I am continuing to persist in my inquiry about what I genuinely enjoy doing, and I am engaging in proactive behaviors to propose and develop such activities. I am beginning to clarify what organizational arrangements I want to challenge. I recently took a serious look at how healthy the pace of my work was and began to question the personal sacrifices this pace had demanded. I asked myself what I needed to change in order to sustain myself in this career over the long term. I have examined and confronted in detail (and continue to examine and confront) painful realities about what I do and do not do well and the conditions under which I work best. I am developing an insistence on pursuing those things that energize me.

I am still seeking the "path with a heart"; there are many corners yet to round. I end with a beginning:

> Anything is one of a million paths [un camino entre cantidades de caminos]. Therefore, you must always keep in mind that a path is only a path. If you feel you should not follow it you must not stay with it under any conditions. . . . Look at every path closely and deliberately. Try it as many times as you think necessary. Then ask yourself and yourself alone one question. . . . Does this path have a heart? If it does, the path is good; if it doesn't, it is of no use. Both paths lead nowhere; but one has a heart and the other doesn't. (Castañeda, 1968, p. 105)

Note

1. The student population of this historically black state university comprised predominantly African Americans. Euro-American students and students from other ethnic minorities were recruited in accordance with affirmative action and diversity goals.

References

Castañeda, C. (1968). The teachings of Don Juan. Berkeley: University of California Press.
Cox, T., & Nkomo, S. M. (1990). Invisible men and women: A status report on race as a variable in

organization behavior research. *Journal of Organizational Behavior, 11,* 419-431.

Dumas, R. G. (1979). Dilemmas of black females in leadership. *Journal of Personality and Social Systems, 2,* 3-14.

Maslow, A. (1970). *Motivation and personality* (2nd ed.). New York: Harper & Row.

Mbiti, J. S. (1970). *African religions and philosophy.* Garden City, NY: Anchor.

Sue, D. W., & Sue, D. (1990). *Counseling the culturally different: Theory and practice* (2nd ed.). New York: John Wiley.

Pause Point 1:
Integration of Work and Nonwork Lives

Harmony is produced when both work and love are given voice simultaneously.

James P. Walsh (p. 204)

I think it is critical that we create spaces in our lives in which we are invited to step back, in the company of others, and look at our "balancing acts" in some way, and be vulnerable to each other and the moment.

Marcy Crary (p. 217)

Academic life can be very fulfilling. It can also induce frustration, disappointments, and burnout. Over time, an academic career, like careers in many other professions (such as law and medicine), can produce a portfolio of contributions and accomplishments accompanied by growth in more personal arenas. It can also reflect a life of success in one arena (e.g., the professional) and failure in another (e.g., personal), or diminished creativity and performance in both arenas.

There are many reasons one or another of these various outcomes can occur to individual scholars, yet the physical, psychological, and spiritual conditions of people in our field are rarely addressed in any open and systematic way. We think it makes sense to reexamine periodically who we are as academics and as partners, parents,

and members of our various communities. Is what we are doing professionally and/or personally the best use of our time and energy? Should we be doing more of some things and less of others? Do we (should we) have some kind of a strategy or game plan for where we are heading in our research, in our teaching, in our lives? How are we dealing with success? With failure? Are we investing sufficiently in ourselves and in others? Do we experience what we are doing as satisfying or are we off balance? How long have we felt as we do now, and is this something we should address or adjust? We urge the academic community to legitimate the value of some form of shared reflection, to acknowledge that it is useful to step back from the rhythms of our academic lives from time to time, to examine, as Crary suggests, how we are faring as human beings. We don't seem to have many shared stories about what it is we do to be productive and to have happy lives. Nor is there much published material about academic life that might help us begin to understand how and why things can go wrong professionally and personally, or what we might do to redress imbalances. In two chapters later in this book, André Delbecq and Meryl Reis Louis discuss their experiences in making major changes in their professional and personal lives after sabbatical years of exploration. For most of our academic lives, however, we are intensively involved in performing our various professional roles. A long retreat, such as a sabbatical, is available only occasionally; we need to take our pulses on a regular basis. We need to give ourselves opportunities to respond and to adjust to feedback that affirms or challenges the way we are living.

Many of the contributors to this volume implicitly acknowledge this need to stop and reflect. Others write explicitly about finding ways to interweave the threads of their personal and professional lives effectively. Their stories form the bases for the sections we call "pause points." These sections are devoted to ongoing issues of balance and adjustment of one form or another in an academic's life.

James Walsh, in our first pause piece, expresses a strong belief in the importance of intertwining love and work, and in the wisdom of doing this one's own way. Much of the texture and meaning of that blend is captured rather vividly and candidly by Marcy Crary in the second piece in this section. She brings to the surface many personal dimensions of an academic's life, as scholar, spouse, colleague, and friend. The chronicle of her life as a professional, making transitions from being single to being married, to being a parent, all the while

progressing as a scholar, conveys a sense of how academics juggle priorities and deal with the tensions and trade-offs associated with having to perform competently in many spheres. Crary's story is primarily oriented to the issues and struggles that can be associated with a strong commitment to being a mother while maintaining an identity as a productive academic. When her priorities became distorted by her responsibilities at work, Crary reacted to the discomfort she felt by taking the initiative to change this orientation. She was fortunate to have a sympathetic dean who helped her to establish a different work schedule, and she went to a part-time arrangement at Bentley. Although this may not be the desired resolution for every scholar as parent, it speaks to the creativity and competence of both Crary and her dean. Her story also illuminates the emotional and intellectual struggles that academics face and must address when they do not fit the traditional model of devoting their entire beings to the professional (and generally to the research-oriented) life. Most available descriptions of the successful academic presume that he or she is someone for whom everything other than attention to a professional life is taken care of. We note the comment of the chaired professor to Jim Walsh and his wife at the start of their careers: "I defy you to name me a very accomplished person in our field who isn't either divorced or living with a completely selfless and invisible spouse" (pp. 204-205).

The contents of this volume suggest that academics have a greater variety of choices and experiences than this statement suggests. Although the intense demands of an academic career do impose high costs on scholars, Crary draws attention to the importance of relationships and support group activities as ways to maintain the rhythms of one's life.

21

Thoughts on Integrating Work and Personal Life (and the Limits of Advice)

James P. Walsh

Without work all life goes rotten.

Albert Camus

Take away love and our earth is a tomb.

Robert Browning

The basic requirements of human existence are work and love.

Sigmund Freud

Peter Frost and Susan Taylor asked me to share my views about the integration of work and personal life. As a veteran of a number of conversations about this issue in various Academy of Management doctoral student and junior faculty consortia, I reflexively said yes. I discovered that my initial enthusiasm for this task waned, however, as the time came to put my thoughts on paper. I think my shifting reactions to this task may be as informative as any observations I might generate, and so I would like to share these reactions, as well as a few thoughts about work and love, in this chapter.

My first reaction was, "Why me?" Being blessed with a strong ego, it did not take me long to

answer that question! I have juggled the demands of work and family for years. I have been happily married to another academician in our field for more than 10 years; we are raising three wonderful children together. It was easy for me to conclude that I have a fine personal life. As I looked at my work life, I realized that I am blessed there as well. My work feels more like a calling to me than a job. My wife and I are also fortunate to be tenured at one of the finest universities in the world. In the end, I wondered how Peter and Susan knew I had such a terrific life. Nonetheless, I concurred with their judgment and set out to discuss the secrets of my "success."

AUTHOR'S NOTE: I would like to thank my family for their love and Lance Sandelands for our conversations about this particular piece of work.

I took my own bait. I went to my favorite coffee shop and began to develop a list of prescriptions for others to follow in my footsteps: Find the perfect spouse, work hard/play hard, find great day care, and so on and so on. It was a list of self-aggrandizing aphorisms. I was quickly embarrassed. I realized that any success my wife and I might enjoy could also be related to our parents' selfless efforts to raise us. I also knew that our professional success could be traced to both the graduate education we received at Northwestern and the institutional support we have been fortunate to receive from Dartmouth and Michigan. I was a victim of my self-serving attribution biases. As a social scientist, I knew that understanding any "success" I may enjoy would require me to monitor my hubris and humility and then try to untangle the dispositional and situational contributions to this success. Recognizing the enormity and complexity of this task, and then wondering about the external validity of any "lessons" I might be able to distill from this exercise, I had my second basic reaction to this assignment: I thought the entire premise behind Peter and Susan's request was ridiculous.

Something has gone awry in America in recent years. We are living in the Age of Advice. A trip to my local bookstore illustrated the magnitude of this problem. The shelves are filled with guidebooks purporting to tell us how to conduct our personal and professional lives. There are manuals that will tell you how to meet someone of the opposite sex (Rabin, 1993), how to love (Hendricks & Hendricks, 1990), how to make love (Hooper, 1992), how to stay married (Barnes & Barnes, 1993), and how to get remarried if you cannot (Belovitch, 1987). Professionally, we are told how to get a job (Bolles, 1994) and then how to keep a job in turbulent times (Hirsch, 1987). Closer to home, we find no shortage of advice about how to write a dissertation (Davis & Parker, 1979), get research funding (Bauer, 1988), publish (Cummings & Frost, 1995; Frost & Stablein, 1992), teach (Christensen, Garvin, & Sweet, 1991), and handle our many professional roles (Zanna & Darley, 1987). We seem to have lost the ability to live our own lives.

Plato once said that the unexamined life is not worth living. Certainly, all of these manuals and guidebooks are offered in the spirit of helping people examine and, so, better live their lives. Having said that, I would like to add a caution: A prescribed life is not a lived life. To live a life prescribed by someone else (no matter how titled or accomplished) is to deny one's own existence. It is up to each of us to chart his or her own destiny. It is in this light that I am reluctant to add to the chorus of those who are telling us all how to live. Rather than offer any advice about how to live, I have decided I will modestly offer two thoughts about how *not* to live.

First, consider the quotations from Camus, Browning, and Freud at the opening of this essay. I wholeheartedly agree with all three sentiments. When we discuss work and love, we are talking about the human condition. And although we may love our work and work at love, the two are entwined in deeper and more subtle ways to give form and meaning to our lives. Rohrlich (1980) points out that work is about order, mastery, the future, and our minds; love is about freedom, submission, the present, and our feelings. As a result, work and love combine to create a harmony of opposites that defines us.

My first thought, then, is that this harmony is produced when both work and love are given voice simultaneously, not sequentially. I sometimes hear people say that graduate school and the first job are a time for total dedication to one's work. A chaired professor mentioned to me upon our arrival at Dartmouth that there were tenure-track and non-tenure-track houses in the area. The tenure-track houses were nondescript houses within walking distance of the library, computer center, and office. In his mind, non-tenure-track houses were the wonderful kinds of houses on large tracts of land that can be found only in northern New England. As someone who was enjoying life in one of these wonderful homes, he seemed to be signaling that life begins after tenure. I disagree. If there is such a thing as a work/life balance sheet, it is to be totaled daily, and not upon entering the grave.

My second thought is that one should beware making either work or love an obsession. To continue with the harmony metaphor, a harmony is created when two voices sing simultaneously and with equal vitality. I still remember a comment a chaired professor in our field made to my wife and me as we were getting ready to begin our careers. He said, "I defy you to name me a very accomplished person in our field who isn't either divorced or living with a completely selfless and invisible spouse." True or not, his point was a dark and ominous one. He seemed to believe that, ultimately, you have to make a choice between work and love. Again, I disagree. Remember Freud: "The basic requirements of human existence are work *and* love." Believing that one must preclude the other sets a person up for a life filled with tragedy.

In the end, I have no ready prescriptions for how to integrate work and personal life. All I can say is that our lives are defined by a harmony of work and love. Harmony is created as the two are sung together with equal passion. What song you choose to sing is your own business.

References

Barnes, R., & Barnes, R. (1993). *Rock-solid marriage.* Dallas: Word.

Bauer, D. G. (1988). *The "how to" grants manual.* New York: Collier Macmillan.

Belovitch, J. (1987). *Making re-marriage work.* Lexington, MA: Lexington.

Bolles, R. N. (1994). *The 1994 what color is your parachute.* Berkeley, CA: Ten Speed.

Christensen, C. R., Garvin, D. A., & Sweet, A. (1991). *Education for judgment.* Boston: Harvard Business School Press.

Cummings, L. L., & Frost, P. J. (Eds.). (1995). *Publishing in the organizational sciences* (2nd ed.). Thousand Oaks, CA: Sage.

Davis, G. B., & Parker, C. A. (1979). *Writing the doctoral dissertation: A systematic approach.* New York: Barron's Educational Series.

Frost, P. J., & Stablein, R. (Eds.). (1992). *Doing exemplary research.* Newbury Park, CA: Sage.

Hendricks, G., & Hendricks, K. (1990). *Conscious loving.* New York: Bantam.

Hirsch, P. (1987). *Pack your own parachute.* Reading, MA: Addison-Wesley.

Hooper, A. (1992). *The ultimate sex book.* New York: Dorling Kindersley.

Rabin, S. (1993). *How to attract anyone, anytime, anyplace: The smart guide to flirting.* Garden City Park, NY: Avery.

Rohrlich, J. P. (1980). *Work and love: The crucial balance.* New York: Harmony.

Zanna, M. P., & Darley, J. M. (1987). *The compleat academic.* New York: Random House.

22 Holding It All Together

Marcy Crary

I am married, an associate professor, and have a 5-year-old daughter, a 23-year-old stepson, and a 25-year-old stepdaughter. In this essay, I want to outline the way in which my life as a scholar, wife, mother, colleague, friend, and so on has unfolded over the past several years and how the roles I inhabit and the things I try to accomplish create both stressors and opportunities for me to come into new understandings of myself and my world. I will go into a lot of concrete details about my current life structure here because this is the only way I know to describe the rhythms of my life at the moment.

My story is best begun through a recounting of one day of parenting and working in my life. This is not a representative day—it's just one of my days.

A Day

Wake up to feel Mary Lauran (M.L.), our 5-year-old, getting into our bed at 5:30 a.m.

Too tired, and can't see clock, so can't object to her being there so early. She says her stomach is bothering her and her head is spinning. I say something like, "Oh, that's not good!" Put my arm around her to cuddle while we all snooze. But now I'm worried about what to do if she is sick today. Have to go to the Diversity and Faculty Development Action Team meetings this morning. It's critical; but Tim, my husband, is teaching today—can't get him to stay home with M.L. Maybe I could take her to the meeting.

I watch M.L. throw her blanket over Tim's eyes two different times. Not sure it's on purpose or not. But Tim's not responding. I think he is wisely not giving her any signals that he's awake. Then I get worried and to make sure he's alive I touch him. He's alive. Good. I try to go back to snoozing again, but M.L. is moving her legs around a lot and keeps bumping me. But at least she's not talking, so some half snoozing is still possible.

AUTHOR'S NOTE: I would like to thank Peter Frost and Susan Taylor for their feedback on this chapter. I would also like to thank the following folks for their comments and thoughtful conversations about this piece: Fernando Bartolome, Polly Bunting, Lynda Detterman, Lois Feldman, Tim Hall, Diane Kellogg, Kathy Kram, Vicki LaFarge, Meryl Louis, Duncan Spelman, Bill Torbert, Barbara Walker, and Don Wolfe.

Tim gets out of the bed and M.L. gets up and turns cartoons on and gets into Tim's space to watch them with her blankie. Tim and I talk a little bit about possible strategies for the day. I move in to cuddle with M.L. and to feel her forehead. Not sure she has fever.

I get up. Make M.L.'s bed, pull up her shades, turn off her night-light. Pick out some clothes for her and iron them. M.L. says she is hungry. Good sign. She seems to have more energy now. Get her some cereal and milk, cider. Get my shower, get dressed.

M.L. hasn't asked to stay home. I go and check her forehead and decide to take her temperature. She asks if she can go to school and says she feels better. I'm relieved that she wants to go to school. She doesn't have a fever, so I guess she can go. I say to myself, "She just has a cold."

I wonder if I should call her friend Katie's mother. Katie is supposed to come home with M.L. after extended day. Maybe I should call and tell her M.L. has a cold. But M.L. has been looking forward to this so much, maybe I should just let things go and see what happens.

I go downstairs. Tim has made the coffee, but now he's upstairs rummaging around at his desk. I set the table and do M.L.'s lunch. I start to have my breakfast. Nibbles the cat meows. I tell M.L. Nibbles is downstairs. She loves to see him in the morning and play with him upstairs in our room. I'm not sure Nibbles loves it as much as she does, but this morning I am watching to see if M.L. has the energy to do her Nibbles thing. She does. She comes downstairs and takes Nibbles up to hold him hostage in our bedroom. Judgment: She can't be all that sick.

I finish eating my breakfast with Tim. Tim goes to the office. I go upstairs to get M.L. going. She is eager to go to school. We get her dressed. I persuade her to let Nibbles out of the room, because he is meowing now.

I walk M.L. to school and drop her off. She seems okay. I say goodbye. It's 8:50 and I have to get to my office before the 9:45 meeting. I hurriedly walk home (my exercise for the day) and get my things from the house and drive to school, thinking of the agenda for the meeting.

Into my office, start to slightly depile the center part of my desk. Get mail out of my box, check for messages. Say hi to administrative assistants. See Duncan and talk with him for a few minutes about the meeting and how we should set it up.

Go to the Diversity and Faculty Development Action Team meeting. Intense dynamics. Finish that and start meeting in my office with Lynda and Duncan about next steps in diversity work. I get a phone call. It's the nurse at M.L.'s school. M.L. is in her office and has a temperature of 101.3. I say I'll be right there. Duncan suggests he and Lynda go to meet in his office. I walk out with them, so sorry I can't be part of the conversation, blurt out the two things I think we should be doing, and charge off to the car.

While driving I'm thinking about M.L. and realize I'm not panicking, that I'm glad to be free to go pick her up right away, that I'm not feeling guilty about her being in the nurse's office, but then I begin to wonder how she is feeling about all of this. Maybe I should have stayed home with her with the suspicion that she was coming down with something, but we made that decision together—she wanted to go to school. I'm so glad to be going to see her.

I pick M.L. up, talk to the nurse, take M.L. home. Put her back on our bed, give her some Tylenol, turn on TV. I bring her some juice and fruit and sit with her for a while. Go downstairs and get her some noodles she has requested. Begin to make phone calls to Action Team members to schedule next meeting and debrief today's. Rest of afternoon is spent off and on the phone, interspersed with moments with M.L., who is seeming more spunky now with Tylenol in her system. She is tired of cartoons, so we do puzzles together. We go to the grocery store to get more Tylenol and other needed supplies.

Get home. Unload groceries. M.L. playing in the living room. I'm on the phone again, working on the meeting setup. Talk with Brenda about the meeting today, the emotional reactions to the faculty retreat, getting her feedback about the process, what needs to be done. There is so much feeling about this diversity work, things are heating up. This is a critical time— how are we going to handle people's fury about these issues? What should I be doing?

It's dinnertime. I get M.L. her dinner, talking with her about various things. Tim is not due back until later cause of late-afternoon and evening engagements. Maybe Phil will be coming home with him. Should I make the bed up there? But Tim didn't seem absolutely sure Phil was staying here. Maybe I'll wait.

Get M.L. up to tub. Lynda returns my call to give me a report on gist of their meeting re tomorrow's meeting. M.L. is calling from the tub. I tell her to wait, I'm on the phone. We continue. Second request from M.L. and I hold her off once again. Third request and now I'm feeling like I have to go—wish I could talk more. Say goodbye. Didn't get to do the talking I wanted to do with Lynda.

Get M.L. out of the tub. Get her into bed. Select some books with her. Read with her, cuddling together. Turn off light. She asks if I'll lie with her a little. I do and in 4 minutes she is snoring (I've never heard her snore before, it's such a little snore! I'll have to tell her that tomorrow, imitating her, she'll like that). Get out from the covers. Close the door just the right amount.

Go downstairs, eat dinner, watch some of *MacNeil/Lehrer*. Can't handle it, so read colleague's paper he asked for feedback on while I have leftover beef stew. Go upstairs, wondering how to be constructive in my feedback to him.

Go to desk to write notes on how I'm feeling about the diversity work at Bentley so far. But then remember I need to do minutes for the New Rep Theatre; our board meeting is next week. But then what I really need to do is to make more headway on the "integrating work and life" piece for Frost and Taylor's book. Put the computer on and load the "Marcy" file. It's 8:30. So I begin.

Phone rings. It's my stepdaughter—we talk about her plans for next weekend. Then back to the writing.

I work more on the computer. In writing about diversity issues I think of a colleague who left Bentley. Put in a call to touch base with him. Try to check out whether he still considers the possibility of coming back to Bentley at some point. Relieved to hear it's still on his screen. Back to the writing.

Tim comes home around 9:00. I sit and talk with him a little and give him a copy of "My Day" hot off the press. I'm smiling—it feels satisfying to attempt to capture images of a kaleidoscope using words on paper. It is an impossible task, of course, but at least I have something to offer to the universe.

A First Look at This Day: Central Themes

Looking back on this day, what do I see? From my perspective, it seems to have "worked." There were no major conflicts or crises. I was able to keep all the balls in the air. I was able to shift my attention back and forth between work and family responsibilities in accommodation to what was being presented in the moment. (It's like navigating through a visual field in which the figure and ground are constantly in play with each other.)

But if I hadn't had that meeting to attend, I would probably have insisted that M.L. stay home, just to be on the safe side. I had to balance the importance of my work activity in relation to my concerns about her health. Having said this, I see that in this day my professional concerns were a strong determinant in my decision making. If M.L. had wanted to stay home, I would have had to perform a different calculus, but I took advantage of her wish not to stay home in deciding to go to work.

I also see that I frame the balancing process as one in which I am the one in charge of accommodating unexpected demands. I make the assumption that it is up to me to choreograph the day. But if I were teaching, would we assume this is up to Tim? This would most likely depend on the significance of his other work commitments on a given day. Needless to say, this is a complex calculus—this balancing of professional and parent roles between the two of us. How we each feel about a given decision or the process of our decision making has a significant impact on both our selves and our relationship. The day described above is not at all representative of the kinds of days we have—there are now days when Tim is the primary parent while I teach or attend meetings. But it is my experience that I carry a sense of having more responsibility for the moment-to-moment care of M.L. than Tim does. I know he does not worry as much as I do.

The day appears very fragmented. Events occur in very short time frames and involve many different relationships and activities across my home and work domains and my professional and parenting roles. I care deeply about each of the people and activities involved in this day. I am able to move in and out of the different spaces with some grace. But I also know this sense of fragmentation has its costs in the quality of my thinking and my ability to center and ground myself. I am too much a short-order cook, too little a chef.

The Larger Context: Current Personal Investments

To portray more adequately the way I have been "fitting in" work with other aspects of my life, I think it will be useful for me to describe the full set of investments in my current life structure. It is made up of the following "contexts" of roles, relationships, activities, and responsibilities:

1. *My ongoing relationships with Tim, M.L., my stepchildren, my parents, my sisters and brothers, my friends, and my neighbors.* The telephone keeps me connected in many of these relationships.

2. *My professional work.* This includes my roles and responsibilities as a tenured associate professor and colleague at Bentley College. At present, I have a part-time teaching arrangement there with a one-course/semester (the diversity course) load. I have had significant involvement with the formation of Bentley's diversity change agenda as a member of the Diversity Steering Committee there and am currently chairing the Faculty Development Action Team, which is exploring ways of creating strategies for faculty development around issues of diversity. I have just become a member of a cross-disciplinary Bentley team that is participating in the American Association of Colleges and Universities networking project on diversity in the curriculum and faculty development. External to Bentley, I have been a founding member of a local Diversity Practitioners' Consortium, which includes corporate, academic, nonprofit, and community organizations. I also have ongoing involvement in professional associations (e.g., the Organizational Behavior Teaching Society), and I serve as a reviewer for the *Journal of Manage-*

ment Education and *Case Research Journal.* Finally, I have many writing projects—this part of my professional work has been most negatively affected by my parenting role. I have simply done very little writing. I have started a number of writing projects, but they all seem to slide to a back burner after a period of time. At work, my attention tends to go to course work and connections with colleagues in the process. At home, the small everyday tasks—like going to the grocery store, buying M.L. new pajamas, going to the dry cleaner's—take precedence over my writing work; they give me the satisfaction of accomplishing something simple and concrete. But these tasks are immensely unsatisfying to my larger hunger for writing out my ideas about adult development and intimacy at work and sharing ideas about experiential diversity teaching. These undone projects can weigh heavily on my spirits at times.

3. *Ongoing professional development work for myself.* This includes involvement in a monthly study group at the Clinical Development Institute focused on the use of constructive developmental perspectives in examining one's own theory and practices. I regularly present issues/dilemmas from my own work life at these sessions. I am also a participant in Bill Isaac's MIT Boston Urban Dialogue Project, which involves bimonthly meetings using the dialogue process based on David Bohm's thinking, and a member of a seminar group on "diversity and dispute resolution," which meets monthly at Harvard Project on Negotiation to discuss each other's work. I have presented material on the diversity change project at Bentley to this group.

4. *Community work.* I have been on the board of directors of a local professional theater company for the past 7 years. This has involved a number of different roles over the years—functioning as a clerk for the board, doing long-range planning, designing retreats, and tending to board development. I am also involved in M.L.'s school. This kind of work varies: Last year I was the head of the Parent-Teachers Committee at M.L.'s preschool, but this year, as she has moved to the local public school, I have yet to become very involved—in part because of the increase in responsibilities at Bentley around the diversity work, but also

because the school system seems overwhelming to me in its size and complexity. It's hard to know how I can add value to its current workings. I'm satisfied to be a "room parent" for her kindergarten class for now.

The Historical Context: How I Got From There to Here

Personal Background

From the "family" side of my life, certainly getting married, becoming a stepmother, and having a child have had powerful influences in the shape of this "time" for me. The introduction of these new family roles has altered the structure of professional work in my current life structure. Internally, it has created new challenges for me as I have attempted to manage the increased psychological complexity of this arrangement for myself.

How I have constructed these work and family roles has certainly been influenced by my own socialization within my family of origin. My mother's choice to stay at home and be a full-time mom with five kids has also undoubtedly shaped my attitudes, beliefs, and feelings about my role as a parent. I think some of the conflicts I feel about my role as a working mother are probably based on my choosing a road different from my mother's. But she also had regular volunteer jobs and was always reading books on the philosophy of science and quoting Plato to us. So my choice to go the academic route may have been inspired by her work as an independent scholar.

My father played the role of the full-time breadwinner in our family as a lawyer in New York City, and also was a very active member of a number of nonprofit boards over the years. When I was a child, much of his work was invisible to me, given his 2-hour commute into and out of the city each day. What was more visible to me was his love of sports, particularly skiing and tennis. He encouraged my siblings and I to take ourselves seriously in play. To this day I experience tennis as a context in which to play out what I name as the more male side of myself—the direct, assertive, competitive, focused part of myself—aspects I sometimes associate with my professional self.

I was also "brought up" by my experiences in the 1960s and 1970s, as I came of age in a place and time where there was strong public challenging of those in "authority" and young women were actively questioning society's design of gender roles for ourselves.

I graduated from college in 1972 with little idea of what I wanted to do, while many of my women friends were going on to law and medical schools. I got a job working with Jerome Kagan at Harvard as a research assistant for a comparative study of home-care and day-care children. I stayed at this job for 2 years, and during that time I attended a number of workshops on group dynamics and took a lab course in basic human interaction in 1974 with Don Wolfe. He introduced me to the field of organizational behavior and told me about the doctoral program at Case Western Reserve. In the fall of 1975, I went to Case to join the Organizational Behavior Department and study for a PhD in organizational behavior. I worked on a number of consulting and research projects there, the most central one being a study of midlife transitions with Don Wolfe and a number of other colleagues. My dissertation, *Patterns of Life Structure: Person-Environment Designs and Their Impact on Adult Lives* (Crary, 1982), came out of this study. My work with Don and others at CWRU was a very deep, rich immersion into the interdisciplinary field of organizational behavior, including the theories and practice of experiential learning, systems theory, and adult and organizational development.

In the fall of 1981, I moved back to Boston and took a position at Bentley College.

Previously Occupied Adult Life Structure

I had one kind of work/life balance when I was single, living in Cambridge in my own pad, feeling empowered as a professional woman, feeling a sense of my ascending into my "career," reaching out to professional organizations, getting networked, beginning to take on responsibilities in these organizations, getting articles published, and working toward tenure.

I was intensely engaged with constructing my identity as a professional woman. Most of my waking hours seemed focused on my professional development in one way or another.

Even my tennis playing felt connected to my professional self: Could I hold my own on the court? Playing was a forum in which I could test my focusing and visualization skills, feel comfortable with my own aggression, stay in active competition with my opponent, and not wimp out. My friendships with other women professionals were very important to me. I loved the feeling of being free and independent.

After a few years of this kind of single's life, however, I found myself wanting something more. I remember driving in my car and looking up into the sky and saying out loud, "Okay, I'm ready to meet someone." To make a long story short, 5 years into my job at Bentley, I got married and moved to the suburbs, adding two significant new identities to my life: wife and stepmom. In 1987 I received tenure at Bentley.

Additions: Marriage, Parenting, Community, and So On

M.L. was born in May 1988. By coincidence, I was scheduled to go on sabbatical in the 1988-1989 academic year, so in M.L.'s first year I based myself at home with her. At the same time I was also beginning a research project on intimacy at work. I worked a few days of the week in my study or went out for interviews with managers in several local organizations. Three days a week we had an au pair take care of M.L. at home from 10:00 to 3:00.

When I was due to return to Bentley after my sabbatical, we decided to put M.L. in family day care 4 days a week, from 9:00 to 4:00. At this point M.L. was 16 months old. Either Tim or I would stay home with her on Wednesdays, her non-day-care day. We stayed with this arrangement for the next 2 years. When M.L. turned 3, we switched her to a preschool, which she attended for the next 2 years. Now M.L. is 5 and in kindergarten at our local elementary school.

But after returning from my sabbatical to full-time teaching at Bentley, I continued to feel off balance, finding it difficult to leave M.L. each day at Josephine's home (even though Josephine was extremely competent as a day-care provider). I worried about how well I was doing as a mom, whether this was the right thing for M.L. I was struck by how adult-oriented our life as a family was, servicing the schedules of the adults' work organizations and

our duties there, as we fit our time with M.L. into the remaining slots. Was this okay with me?

I came to find that the answer for me was *no*. On a typical morning, after dropping M.L. off I would be irritable: I would feel bad about dropping her off, irritated with Bentley and with the requests others made of me, and disconnected from everyone; I would feel no peace inside, no sense of leisure, or smooth flowing time. I didn't know who I could talk with, I didn't know how to figure out what was going on and what M.L. needed. I felt very off balance. At the same time, my work at Bentley was becoming much more interesting to me. My growing involvement with diversity issues in and out of the classroom was becoming a valuable source of both personal and professional development.

In the spring of 1991 I finally decided to approach the dean of faculty to ask for a part-time work schedule. This came after months of agonizing about whether or not I should do this. The dean made it very easy for me to make this shift in my contract on a temporary basis. I felt an enormous sense of relief after working this out for the next year. I would be teaching just one course a semester.

In the fall of 1991 I became very involved with M.L.'s new preschool class, going on field trips with them regularly and getting to know the teachers and staff. It was delightful to be immersed in the worlds of a bunch of 3- and 4-year-olds. That winter, a lot of conflicts began to surface at M.L.'s school, and I became very active in trying to address some of the issues being raised by the school's director. In December, the director resigned, and parents became involved in the hiring of a new director and in working with the founder and president of the board around her leadership style.

In the spring of 1992 I was asked to become the president of the Parent-Teachers Committee. This was a wonderful opportunity to both practice my organizational development craft and be connected to the backstage of one of M.L.'s special places—a very nice integration, indeed.

As a result of this new work/parenting arrangement, I felt myself more able to be present in M.L.'s life. This is illustrated by the following entry from my journal, written after a walk M.L. and I took in March when she was 4 years old:

A walk with M.L. into the Cabot woods on an almost cold rainy spring afternoon. We went in search of signs of spring, or as M.L. would say, "to see what we can see." There is a special delight I take in wandering in the woods with her. I spent so much of my childhood in the woods, it's somehow poignant to be there with her. We mushed into the swampy pools, looking for frog eggs Edye had described to us—the eggs they had found when walking there with Chris, Jamen, and Joey so many years ago. We tromped up and down wooded hills, pushing branches away from our eyes. We found the chimney of the house that once held the valley on its own. Walking ahead of me, doing singing/talking with herself, much like Winnie the Pooh . . . , I heard M.L. saying, "There are no monsters in the woods." Earlier she had asked whether I thought there might be wolves in here.

I stood M.L. up on square rock posts that marked the edge of the wooded path and we played a statue game, four times on four different posts. We stomped down a cattail in the center of the wet, reedy swamp, and bent down to see what the little brown seeds were that we had seen earlier but hadn't investigated. M.L. counted out four to take home to Dad. A few steps later she discovered that they were gone from her hand so we made a few back steps to recapture them from the brown bed of leaves and reeds. I suggested that she close her hand around them. She walked more cautiously then, watching her fisted hand as we went.

M.L. suggested we gather some rocks, so she bent to do that and then carried them to the edge of the field where she had sighted a stone wall and threw them over the edge. That done, we walked back to the car, the spring walk in the woods now over.

This description of a walk with M.L. represents one of the things that I find so powerfully compelling about witnessing her childhood—it allows me to weave my connections to childhood spaces into what she and I find to share together. It wakes me up and freshens my perspective on the world, pulling me out of what at times can feel like a life "on automatic pilot." And it seems to me that I would have been less apt to be present for M.L. in this experience if I were feeling more torn about professional responsibilities I was not attending to in making the choice to take that midday walk with her

on a weekday. By unloading some of my professional work commitments, I hoped to lessen my internal strife and be more available as an active participant in M.L.'s days.

The Challenge of Holding It All Together

So, overall, how am I "integrating" my "professional" work with the rest of my life? Put simply, since M.L. entered our lives, I have found myself wanting to redesign my work commitments around my time with her. Parenting has become the leading part of my life structure.

The challenge of "integrating" seems to me to be one of being able to hold adequately within my life space, in some harmonious whole, the different kinds of investments and commitments (to relationships, work) that deeply engage and stimulate me, and make a contribution to the world in some fashion. However, the act of holding them all together within my life structure seems to require continuous calibration, questioning of time, energy, and payback across these different contexts. It also requires working in sync with Tim's and M.L.'s schedules. The more flexible Tim can be with his commitments, the easier it is for me to maintain my outside-of-the-home work commitments, relationships, and activities (and I'm sure the reverse is true as well). So, in effect, the quality of the integration of the different pieces of my life (i.e., the extent to which they are not in significant conflict with each other) is very much in interaction with the choreography of Tim's and M.L.'s lives. In addition, my relationships with Tim, M.L., my stepchildren, and the rest of my family are critical ground for how the rest of my life feels in a given moment. When things are difficult with these relationships, this may affect my sense of well-being within all the other contexts.

Psychological Tyrannies

The holding together of all my different investments entails an internal monitoring of myself and how I am doing—it is in this internal process that I am most challenged. There are days, even weeks, in which I feel like I'm in a "permanent" state of disequilibrium with myself, with a sense that my investments are at odds with each other. In these kinds of off-balance moments I often can turn against myself and doubt my competence, capabilities, and intelligence. They are moments in which I am operating with a strong critic within me, spewing doubts about myself. Maintaining my own self-esteem becomes a challenge.

The particular psychological tyrannies that I can fall prey to while navigating through my days affect my sense of internal balance in the following ways:

1. *There are many moments when I doubt my own professional competence.* I compare myself to any number of my colleagues and can feel much less capable of managing any number of the tasks we all have been trained for, whether writing, teaching, leading a workshop, or consulting. It's also possible to suffer in the comparison of my output professionally with that of other friends of mine who are also parents, but who devote greater parts of their days to their professional work than I do. I end up wondering if working part-time has eroded my own professional self-identity—if in some sense these aspects of myself have become less real to me in my own constructions of who I am in this world. The challenge seems to be in making this okay for myself.

2. *I can become absorbed in worrying about how others are perceiving me.* Do they also see me as less competent or as less professional in making the choices I am making? (Within my more mature adult self I know this is hogwash—I say to myself, "Aren't these really your projected feelings, Marcy? Why do you care what others think of your choices? It's your life! Maybe this is all about your dissatisfaction with what you are choosing.") And am I making the choices that I really want to make? I think these wonderings are part of my struggle to feel of value, to have some recognition or feedback that I am adding value to my places of work. It feels as if I am overly dependent on others to reassure me that I do contribute, that I am okay.

3. *At times, I doubt how good a job I am doing as a parent.* Being a parent is fraught with uncertainties. There are many moment-to-moment "crises" to manage and then judge oneself on. I find it very easy to worry about M.L. in all

kinds of ways. In managing our balancing acts as a family, there are some days in which I am very grumpy and easy to anger. I worry about how this affects us all, particularly M.L.

4. *I worry about my mental competence.* One of the fears I carry about myself (and that everyone who knows me well has heard about many times) is that I am losing my mind, literally—that I have the beginning symptoms of Alzheimer's or the like. In more rational moments I diagnose my sense of mindlessness as a stress symptom and tell myself I need more exercise, that I should get back to meditating, and so on. At times I am very easily distracted and am very often during the day holding several concerns or issues in my mind. This affects my ability to attend fully to others at times—to focus and listen to where they are. This in turn affects how I feel about myself and my own effectiveness in connecting with others and/or thinking deeply about anything.

In sum, my attempts to keep a sense of balance between my professional and parenting roles sometimes generate a lot of internal stress. This is the cost of this kind of choreography for me personally.

My Identity Shift: Disequilibrium

In getting married and having a child, I experienced a whole new set of vulnerabilities as I faced a new and larger constellation of roles and identities: mother, stepmother, wife, sibling, daughter, neighbor, professor, colleague, friend. I wanted to do right by all of these relationships, and I needed them to be there for me in a new way, though I wasn't sure what that way was.

Looking back now, I realize I had no idea what the experience of becoming a parent would be like—how it would challenge my ability to center, ground myself, and how it would challenge the construction of my professional work commitments. As much as I can recall, I went into becoming a mom pretty naive about the emotional terrain that comes with this job, particularly as it has evolved within the context of my other roles, responsibilities, and activities. The sense of having more events and people I had to do right by was all a part of my feeling less in control of my living and its qualities. I felt reduced to a reactive, passive strategy in dealing with the complexity of my newly populated family life and all that it evoked for me emotionally. In one of my postbirth calls to my mother, I was telling her how emotional I felt, how often I felt like crying, and she said, "Now that you have a child, there will always be tears behind your eyes." She was right. I have more tears than I ever had before.

My heightened sense of dependence on and interdependence with others kept me off balance. I felt as if I was being asked to redraw, relocate, redesign the boundaries of my self. The independence that I had so proudly crafted for myself as a professional woman seemed to be under assault. And I didn't trust myself or the world enough to let go of this self-image. I remember having fears that this was what happened to the Stepford wives—they got married, had children, and then were forever fixed in the roles their society had crafted for them. In the process, they lost their selves and any power to make their own choices. Who is in control of my life? Who makes the "rules" for how to live it?

One of the entries in the journal I kept during my sabbatical in 1988, when M.L. was 6 months old, reflects the disequilibrium I felt during my first years as a new mom:

I have felt under siege in some fashion. . . . I'm not sure by what or whom. . . . But I find myself having to pay extra attention to what I am doing—as if I were on some drug that was constantly taking myself away from myself. Every act becomes an effort of exerting conscious control over my seeing, my feeling, my getting, hearing, walking, picking up.

I am also struck by how others hold power over how I am evaluating myself at any given moment. My future students, my Chairman, VP of faculty, the readers of my sabbatical report. . . . I hand them a power I won't keep for myself. Why? Their viewings of my activities occupy me, not giving me room for my own fresh spontaneous being in the moment. I feel obliged to them. . . . I owe them something. I cannot have these moments to myself really.

I think to myself—I am the carved and less the carver. I wish for the opposite. How extraordinary that I have objectively this time "free"—but I have subjectively imprisoned myself within a jail constructed from cells I have previously occupied.

Looking back at the past 6 years, I can see that I have been negotiating a very significant transition for myself—a transition in the kind of life structure I inhabit and the taking on of the new identities that accompany it. Regaining and keeping a sense of balance and personal well-being has required a lot of support from others.

Sources of Support and Guidance

My relationship with Tim is critical ground for much of what happens in my current life structure. Our abilities to hang in there with each other in figuring out our family dynamics (e.g., our choices, our feelings of anger, resentment, jealousies) and to reach a loving space together after navigating through this rough terrain are prerequisite to our making it all work for our family. What supported me after M.L. was born was the growing realization that our relationship is loving, robust, and yielding enough to incorporate darker emotions, and that we are good at listening to and respecting each other's thoughts and feelings.

I have also depended upon my parents as well as my siblings and their families as emotional anchors in my new family life. Having M.L. in my life, I felt a new need to reconnect to my family. I wanted to share the joys and angst of having a new little one with them. Their joining in with us to love M.L. seemed to create a new piece of family web for us all. It also made me feel less lonely in some way.

There are a number of relationships I have at Bentley and elsewhere that are absolutely critical underpinnings to my well-being. They are friendships in which I can share my moment-to-moment concerns and always feel welcomed in doing so. They offer a context in which I can weave together the fragments of my concerns and issues and feel more whole as a result. All my different identities seem welcome in these friendships. As one of my colleagues there, Duncan has played a special role in my link to Bentley. One of the risks of going part-time for me was that of becoming somewhat isolated from my colleagues and less connected to the college as a result. Because I have done so much collaborative work with Duncan, our relationship has provided a critical transition space in my movements back and forth from home to work. Being able to talk about what was happening at home with him made it easier to enter into work. And because so much of our work is together, I can more easily be marginal or absent at any given time (e.g., because of M.L.'s being sick) if he is able to cover for me (in our team-taught course, in the change project, and so on).

I remember that, early on in my new mothering role, I felt very concerned that I might have less to give in my close friendships because of my submersion in this new family constellation, in which I was struggling to keep a sense of myself together. I feared what would happen to our friendships now that I was caught into this new emotional web and feeling so focused on myself and my struggle. I was afraid my friends would feel that I was deserting them, and that they in turn might distance themselves from me. There were a few friendships that I did lose in this transition, in fact; we couldn't make the adjustments to accommodate each other.

Sonia, my longtime therapist/buddy, helped me construct an image of myself as a mother and professional woman, and helped me understand that this is just a different way of bringing up a child—that children come into life in all kinds of different circumstances, and this is what M.L. has. It is not better or worse, it is just different and part of reality. I think this work with Sonia has helped me to let go of my image of Mother as how my mom did it when my siblings and I were young. Sonia supported the importance of professional work to me, helping me keep attached to it and not let it go, which I was tempted to do many times as a way of trying to get rid of the complexity of my commitments. But each time I considered this, I realized that there was something about my work at Bentley that I loved. And this came even more true as I began to work on issues of diversity in my professional life.

My involvement with the Clinical Development Institute group, an ongoing study/seminar group focused on the application of constructive-developmental theory, gave me a context for exploring my own decision making about going part-time. The members of this group helped to create a space that made it easier for

me to think about the kinds of "demands" I was experiencing at home and at Bentley and to sort through what was important for me in making this kind of transition for myself, my family, and Bentley. I felt I was allowed a perspective on myself and my own struggles that was less punishing than the images I had internalized from my upbringing about the "right" way of being a mother, a colleague, an employee, a wife.

There were certain professional buddies with whom I did not have a lot of regular contact, but just knowing that we were connected in some special way somehow reassured me that I had not lost contact with certain aspects of myself and my interests that I could not activate in my current life. The Organizational Behavior Teaching Conference has been an important personal and professional home for me in this transition time. For the past 5 years, various members of our diversity teaching team have used this conference as a place to discuss our teaching and personal dilemmas with colleagues from other schools. I experience OBTC as a place where I am my most effective self—where I experience the fewest self-doubts and feel the most grounded, personally and professionally.

Lessons Learned

Through all this I have learned many things. First, I've learned that, though there are a lot of ragged edges in the current structure as I live it for myself, I carry a quiet belief that these times are learning times, grounding for new understandings of myself and the world. I tell myself that I must be patient, but at the same time I would feel impatience to get going with my work in the world. Writing this essay has actually been helpful as a means of getting some perspective on the kinds of psychological challenges I have experienced in the past few years. Naming the tyrannies has made them seem less powerful. And, as friends have read the various drafts of this work, I have increasingly felt joined by other women, in particular, who have said that they have shared many of the feelings I have described.

Second, I've learned that I have been spending the past few years trying to get to know myself within a new set of identities and to find a new balance with some measure of autonomy and differentiation from all my significant others. I have grown much more attentive to how I respond to others' expectations, needs, and directions. In fact, I feel less the carved and more the carver these days. This chapter is part of the carving.

Third, I've learned that this is a solitary journey is some sense—that I have to make own choices, follow my own heart, find my own voice. I can't rely too heavily on others' charting of their waters in navigating my own. There are no "directions in the box."

Fourth, I've learned that, at the same time, while I seek a stronger, more differentiated sense of myself, my relationships are my treasures. I feel profoundly dependent on them to teach me about myself and the world, and to keep me company in managing the differences that are always emerging between us.

I started this essay by saying to myself that I was going to describe how I have experienced the development of my identity/role as a mom in relation to my professional work. A few writing sessions later, however, I went back to read the letter Peter and Susan had sent to their chapter authors and reread the section describing the "contributor's task." The first item on the list was "to consider the circumstances that brought me to this point in my professional life." Rereading this, I realized that the focus in my thinking/writing so far had centered on my role as a parent and how I had accommodated my work life to it. That is, I wasn't saying, "This story is about how I have experienced the development of my professional work in the context of my commitments as a mom." Rather, it was reversed: My role as mom was figure and my work life background. Very little of the passion I feel about my work around diversity issues is present in this telling of my story.

As I near the end of my storytelling, I realize that the figure is more complex now—more of the background has seemed to join it. I'm more aware of how all the pieces are there and important to me. It is as if the telling of the story has hatched a new gestalt of myself and my life—for the moment, anyway.

Postwriting Thoughts

It's my guess that a number of the things I have described about my experiences are not "generalizable" to others. I'm coming to see that I have certain life themes that are apt to be triggered in times when I experience disequilibrium—such as self-doubt or a preoccupation with the view of others—that may not be the same themes that haunt others in their times of adult transitions.

So what "lessons" might I offer others who are anticipating or starting identity transitions similar to mine? I have shared some very personal things about my life in this story. I wanted to talk about how it feels to me to be in a struggle to "hold it all together" while managing new identities within the context of an increasingly complex life structure. And in doing so, I feel as though I have, in part, dared others to follow—not to disclose just for the sake of disclosing, but at least to take some perspective on what it is we have in common and what it is we feel the need to hide from each other as we work to manage our "personal" and "professional" identities and the transitions they undergo. For instance, in sharing earlier drafts of this chapter with other working mothers at Bentley, and in return hearing of their concerns, I have felt as if we were coming out of the closet in some fashion with each other. By sharing our otherwise undervoiced anxieties, concerns, and angers, we were giving testimony to the complexities of our lives outside of our boundaries of "work." And for the moment it felt like we were transforming our workplace into a more vibrant, personal domain by doing a little unwrapping of our professional identities for each other. I remember smiling and laughing a lot. These conversations, in effect, helped me to "cohere" my work/family identities and experiences, and made my world seem a little less fractured in the moment.

I think it is critical that we create spaces in our lives in which we are invited to step back, in the company of others, and look at our "balancing acts" in some way, and be vulnerable to each other and the moment. In making our "tyrannies" more public and discussable to ourselves and others, we might hope to move to a place in which we have more of a hold on them than they have on us. To observe and reflect on them is in some part to alter our relationships to them.

I think the developmental challenge of this kind of life transition is to evolve the capacity to right oneself within the context of newly wrought identities and life structure design. I expect that this requires working to create an internal gyroscope that will help to keep one's sense of self level and intact while one negotiates the currents of a more turbulent life space. My guess is that the creation of this increased capacity of the self to orient from within is enhanced by the sharing of one's story with others.

Reference

Crary, L. M. (1982). *Patterns of life structure: Person-environment designs and their impact on adult lives.* Unpublished doctoral dissertation, Case Western Reserve University.

III

Middle Rhythms
Traditional Paths

Working Collaboratively

Working with other people in intensive ways has always been part of our academic lives.

C. R. Hinings and Royston Greenwood (p. 225)

Our collaboration began serendipitously. We did not start with a rational assessment that we ought to work together. In fact, our divergent research interests made us a somewhat unlikely team. Rather, the catalyst for this collaboration was our shared emotional reaction to what we perceived to be strong, established norms about how one ought to think about research and work with doctoral students.

Jane E. Dutton, Jean M. Bartunek, and Connie J. G. Gersick (p. 241)

What had been two duos (Arja and Jerry; Arja and Päivi) was now a trio. The trio's marching orders were to plan for two national doctoral seminars (composed of a gaggle of Finnish business administration students from all over the country). . . . Conducting the seminars was very stimulating for us and reinforced our feelings as a successful team. What had been two successful duos was now a successful trio.

James G. (Jerry) Hunt, Arja Ropo, and Päivi Eriksson (p. 250)

Professional collaborations are a critical part of the lives of many academics. There are undoubtedly several explanations for this. First, collaborations bring complementary knowledge bases and skill sets to research endeavors, providing the synergistic potential for higher-quality products. Second, these relationships enable academics to bounce their ideas and tentative conclusions off others who are also excited about particular lines of work and thus replenish their motivation and commitment to their research voices. Third, the highly specialized nature of academic work often yields products that can be competently evaluated by only a small number of subject-matter experts. Thus collaborations provide a mechanism through which academics can receive critical feedback on their work in progress from trusted sources. Finally, the solitary nature of the academic life frequently makes it a relatively lonely one in the absence of collaborations that can provide enjoyable personal interactions as well as critical research products. This is particularly true in the early rhythms, pretenure stage, when the publication task is often hardest and the pressure to establish one's research reputation the greatest.

In this section we examine the nature of three professional collaborations that differ on a number of important dimensions, yet show some surprising similarities. The first collaboration is between two male colleagues employed at the same university, Bob Hinings and Royston Greenwood. Their professional relationship, born out of a fortuitous funding opportunity for changing organizational structures in government municipalities in England, has lasted for more than 22 years, spanning two different countries (Great Britain and Canada) and yielding numerous articles, books, and research grants.

Beginning for very instrumental reasons—including the availability of an outstanding funding source for research on a topic in which they were both interested—the origin of Hinings and Greenwood's collaboration was based on their belief that they possessed complementary knowledge bases and skill sets, and thus that they could staff a very effective research team. As the opening quotation above from their chapter indicates, both researchers had strong models of effective collaborations to draw on from their early research experiences. These models enabled them to create a physical and psychological environment for successful collaboration right from the beginning of their first joint project. After working together for a time, their initial beliefs about complementarity of knowledge and skills were borne out, but equally as important, they discovered that the complementarity extended to their personal styles and interests as well. In their words: "Our differences in style still exist. At a recent meeting, Royston was still pushing hard for more productivity. At the same meeting, Bob was saying there is only so much we can do, we can't do all these things at once, don't be too hard on others" (p. 235). Over time, they have learned to capitalize on their differences in the structural allocation of both work tasks and writing responsibilities and, as their careers have progressed, to increase the efficiency with which they can carry out growing teaching and administrative responsibilities. This increased efficiency has in turn maximized their research productivity in the face of heavier role demands for teaching and service.

Note, however, that Hinings and Greenwood are careful to acknowledge their similarities (e.g., in their interests in sports, and in literature and music). They well recognize the contribution of these similarities to their personal enjoyment of the relationship.

Unlike many collaborations, virtually all of Hinings and Greenwood's work together has occurred while they have been employed at the same university. A shared physical location has enabled them to use time together for research while they have been engaged in other professional activities, such as executive teaching, and to use one another for feedback on other independent projects, such as planning course curricula or dealing with administrative matters. Thus the logistics of their relationship have been easier to manage than are those of many academic collaborators. Although in today's multimedia world physical distance no longer need deter productive working relationships, we suspect it does impact the sheer amount of interaction that occurs between collaborators and, thereby, the intensity of their relationships.

Hinings and Greenwood are clearly quite pleased with the professional and personal outcomes of their collaboration. In fact, they found themselves collaborating again after stating their intentions to go their separate ways upon moving to the University of Alberta. As they describe it:

> After about 6 months of this, we found that we were still talking to each other about research issues. The relationship continued to be an easy one, interpersonally, and one that seemed to produce a fair number of ideas about research projects and papers. We came to the conclusion that our collaboration had been fun and fruitful, and it made no sense not to work together. (pp. 231-232)

At this point, having mastered the intricacies and dynamics of managing the collaborative process, their team seems destined to last forever. As Hinings and Greenwood put it: "So, our working together continues, with no particular end in sight; we enjoy it too much for that. Here's to the next 22 years!" (p. 236).

The second collaborative team presented here differs from the first on several dimensions. It is a recently formed relationship, now moving into its third year, among three female academics who reside at great geographic distances from one another: Jane Dutton (Ann Arbor, Michigan), Jean Bartunek (Boston), and Connie Gersick (Los Angeles). The Dutton-Bartunek-Gersick collaboration began fortuitously, as the quote from their chapter above indicates, after the three women served as panelists for a doctoral consortium at the Academy of Management. They recognized strong similarities in their views about research ideas and working with doctoral students while confirming expected divergences between their views and those of the other panelists. The discovery that they shared views with others in the field whom they admired and respected was comforting but also stimulated their interests in understanding the basis for their shared set of values, one they suspected might be related to gender. Thus Dutton, Bartunek, and Gersick's collaboration began as their attempt to learn more about the basis of their shared views, rather than to undertake a specific research project, as did the Hinings-Greenwood relationship. Further, at the time of their first collaboration, each had already experienced a fair amount of career success that brought "more responsibility to lead and fewer options merely to observe" (p. 242), yet each had some misgivings about what this meant. In their own words: "Looking back, it seems that we started this collaboration partly as a way to work on our own development together—not just as a vehicle for writing a paper or becoming friends" (p. 242).

From its beginning, the Dutton-Bartunek-Gersick relationship has emphasized the interpersonal aspects of collaboration. Yet, over time, these women's shared conversations have spawned a shared professional interest in the meaning of relationships in professional life and a research study of the professional relationships experienced by male and female academics in business schools. In a reciprocal way, the research process and early findings from the project have subsequently strengthened the interpersonal aspects of their collaboration, as well as those of other professional relationships that were examined in the data collection stages of project. Like Hinings and Greenwood, Dutton, Bartunek, and Gersick are quite pleased with the outcomes of their collaboration. Their personal relationships are very enjoyable and their findings have, in a sense, legitimated collegial relationships as an important aspect of professional development, thereby confirming their own feelings and experiences and also encouraging others who have reached similar conclusions to acknowledge them openly.

The third collaboration presented in this section is a relationship that bridges cultures, career stages, and gender. It is a collaboration among an American researcher, Jerry Hunt, a male in late middle career, and two Finnish colleagues, Arja Ropo and Päivi Eriksson, females in their early career rhythms. This three-way collaboration was born out of two dyadic relationships, with Arja serving as the connecting link. Like the relationship among Dutton, Bartunek, and Gersick, it is still in its early stages, specifically in its first year, and operates across large geographic differences, primarily through the use of electronic media, with occasional exchange visits. Like the other relationships discussed in this section, the Hunt, Ropo, and Eriksson collaboration seems to fulfill a variety of needs for its participants—a unique professional synergy that has begun to yield tangible research products, enjoyable personal re-

lationships, and shared professional activities outside of research (e.g., teaching). Unlike the other two, however, this third collaboration must manage tensions brought about by differences in the participants' career stages and in the academic systems of their two countries. After reading their contribution, one suspects that although the management of these tensions requires continuing effort, the differences underlying them are an important source of the relationship's reward potential for all parties.

In combination, it appears that collaborations that persist for any length of time must yield two types of products: a research achievement that is valued by the parties and enjoyable interpersonal interaction. As Hinings and Greenwood observe:

> For collaboration to continue as long as ours has, there have to be successful outcomes, which are of two kinds. First, there have to be academic outcomes, publications that not only make some minimal impact on the field, but that we see as stronger than anything we could do individually. Second, there have to be personal outcomes, enjoyment in working together. We have experienced both of these. (p. 234)

For Dutton, Bartunek, and Gersick's collaboration, the interpersonal and the professional aspects are tightly interwoven. As they note:

> This research project is genuinely enjoyable to all three of us. However, its generative nature also complicates things. The project is jam-packed with feeling. The weaving of the personal and the professional means that we know each other more closely than we might if this were a strictly "professional" relationship. The enhanced vulnerability means that there is an enhanced sense of responsibility to care for one another. The caring is important work;

it is also sometimes draining. But awareness that this work is generative makes us feel good. It helps us to see the project as productive in a way that we don't usually see. It also feels genuine and real. (p. 246)

Now it is time to let the parties speak about these components in their own relationships.

23 Working Together

C. R. Hinings
Royston Greenwood

Working with other people in intensive ways has always been part of our academic lives. Bob began as part of the Aston team, and the experience was a very positive one (for descriptions of the workings of the Aston team, see Pugh, 1988; Pugh & Hickson, 1976; Pugh & Hinings, 1977). This was followed by the strategic contingencies theory of power team (for thoughts on the workings of the Alberta team, see Hickson, 1988), a team to study church structures and career patterns, and, in 1972, the beginnings of collaboration with Royston. Royston started his career in the very collegial atmosphere of the Institute of Local Government Studies (ILGS), University of Birmingham, working with John Stewart on issues of management in British local government. A pattern of working collaboratively was laid down at the outset of our academic lives.

Since 1973, we have worked together around one dominant theme enshrined in two major research programs. The theme is change and stability in organizations: Why is it that some organizations embrace change and others resist it? What produces change and stability? The first research program, which began in 1973 and lasted until 1982, investigated attempts to transform the management of municipalities in Britain. It was carried out at the Institute of Local Government Studies, University of Birmingham. The second major program began in 1985 at the University of Alberta and is continuing. It centers on management and change in professional service firms, with an emphasis on accounting and law. Over our 22 years of collaboration, we have become committed to long-term, longitudinal, programmatic research that is firmly rooted in understanding the sector or industry in which we are working. It has been a journey during which we have learned to work together, gained a better understanding of each other's strengths and weaknesses, changed in our collaboration, and produced a number of publications together and with others. Working together has been a significant experience; it would not have continued for so long if it had not been.

In this chapter we explore our 22 years of collaboration, which have taken place in two different universities and on two continents.

Included in our account are discussions of how we got started, the dynamics of partnership and collaboration, and the lessons we have learned. The account is personal, but we attempt to highlight what we think is general.

Getting Started

In 1972, Bob was teaching organization theory at the University of Aston. Across town, Royston taught public administration in the Institute of Local Government Studies at the University of Birmingham. Royston decided to attend Bob's course as a way of learning more about organization theory, as he had begun to do research on the management of municipal governments. During the course, Royston mentioned that a major functional and geographic reorganization of municipalities in England and Wales was to occur on April 1, 1974; that a central component of the reorganization was an anticipated transformation of management structures and processes of the 422 individual organizations; and that ILGS was to be awarded a major research grant to study the change. Would Hinings be interested in taking part? The upshot was that Bob moved to the University of Birmingham to head up a research team that eventually comprised himself, Royston, Stewart Ranson, and Kieron Walsh. The team stayed together until 1978. The research continued until 1982 and culminated in a book, *The Dynamics of Strategic Change* (Hinings & Greenwood, 1988).

Why did Royston ask Bob to collaborate, and why did Bob say yes? Royston was looking for a reasonably experienced collaborator, someone who, he hoped, had both theoretical and empirical interests. The Aston papers in *Administrative Science Quarterly* had been out for 3 or 4 years and were gaining recognition (Pugh, Hickson, & Hinings, 1969; Pugh, Hickson, Hinings, & Turner, 1968, 1969). The first product of the Alberta power work had been published (Hickson, Hinings, Lee, Schneck, & Pennings, 1971), and a further paper was in the pipeline (Hinings, Hickson, Pennings, & Schneck, 1974). Attending Bob's course gave Royston additional confidence that maybe Bob had something to offer.

Bob was attracted by the possibility of studying major structural changes at a time when the academic study of change was quite unusual. The fact that the research grant was already in place was a further attraction. The grant allowed four people to be appointed as full-time researchers for 4 years. This was so attractive that Bob gave up tenure at Aston to move to a contract at Birmingham. Having previously spent a number of years at the University of Birmingham, Bob was familiar with the territory, which was also a positive factor.

The Environment for Collaborative Research

David Hickson (1988) has examined the environment for team research, and suggests that time and money are critical: "Researchers with longer-term aspirations need enough time to fully think out what they are to do, before they are diverted into composing further proposals for funds, or into precipitate fieldwork because they dare not delay it any longer" (p. 149).

There are institutional differences between the United Kingdom and North America that are important in promoting team research. In the United Kingdom, research grants are often used to fund full-time researchers, *not* part-time student involvement or PhD dissertations. This does not mean that teaching is not done by such people—it is. But the prime job requirement is research, and teaching is generally very limited. Being a full-time research officer is an accepted alternative to the PhD route to a tenure-track appointment.

The research experiences both of us had been exposed to had been in focused program research—that is, research designed to go on indefinitely around a major theme, regardless of the particular funding period, with the research program our main or only research activity. Collaboration was around a research program that was the major activity and priority for everyone involved—a real task group, with an indefinite life. Involvement in this kind of research has been a good and successful experience for both of us.

A further factor that helped our collaboration was ILGS itself. The Institute of Local Government Studies was set up in the mid-1960s as a management development and research organization for the public sector. The impending changes in the functions and structures of local government produced a need for new research as a support for management development activity. So there was support for large-scale, programmatic research that could be carried out only on a collaborative basis.

At this stage, then, we had established that there was a significant research opportunity; that, *prima facie,* there were good reasons to collaborate; and that ILGS would be a supportive environment. Both of us had positive experiences of previous collaboration and believed that it was the only way to do significant research with a long-term focus. However, the dynamics of the relationship had to be worked out.

The Dynamics of Partnership and Collaboration

One necessary component of a work relationship is complementarity of interests and skills; another is the active management of that complementarity. Our collaboration started with perceived complementarity of skills. We then had to discover whether what we perceived was real and, if real, whether our interpersonal relationship meant that those skills could be harnessed. This is not just a matter of affinity, but also of management. There have to be successful outcomes from cooperation for it to continue; partnership has to "add value" to the academic product. Of course, a 22-year relationship is not static. Interests, skills, interpersonal relationships, and outcomes change over the years. The contexts in which one works change. We will attempt here to show how these changes occurred in the various aspects of our collaboration.

Complementarity of Interests and Skills

Hickson (1988) argues about team-based, long-term research that "effective research requires heterogeneity on a basic homogeneity. It requires argument but not dispute, variety but not confusion, novelty but not strangeness" (p. 148). The initial complementarity of interests and skills was real for us, and based on a very clear complementarity of *difference.* Royston was trained as a political scientist/economist and had developed an interest in municipali-

ties. He had a *substantive* interest in British local government. Bob was trained as a sociologist/social anthropologist, and through the 1960s he had concentrated on organizational and industrial sociology. His interest lay in large-scale comparative analysis of organizations. Royston had an incredibly detailed knowledge of the operation of local government generally, and of many individual municipalities in particular. Bob knew nothing about local government; his strengths were in his knowledge of organizational sociology and in his experiences of a wide range of different kinds of organizations. Bob was a reasonably competent quantitative methodologist; Royston was much more qualitatively oriented. What these differences presented was a dovetailing and the basis for some kind of division of labor.

But there were also complementarities that were based on *similarities* around the nature of the research process, which came from our experiences in single-minded, programmatic research work. We both believed that significant theoretical and empirical contributions were more likely to come from teams, because teams have different interests, skills, and strengths to draw upon. We also believed that research had to be programmatic; that is, the focus was on major issues, with a long-term orientation going beyond any particular funding period.

So different interests, skills, and knowledge, together with a common commitment to the nature of research and a method of working, provided a strong initial base. It was apparent that our perceptions of how we could work together were based in reality. But any collaboration over a particular piece of research is also a process of learning, technically and personally. Working together on the local government research did not leave us unchanged. Over time, there was a convergence of our interests.

We believe that in order to do good organizational research it is necessary to build a deep understanding of the organizations one is studying. So Bob had to get up to speed on British local government. Royston was an excellent tutor in this. In the process, Bob went beyond the level of understanding he needed to do research to a genuine interest in the organizational issues facing local government; he became interested in municipalities for their own sake. This transition is important for the programmatic, long-term nature of the research. It is difficult to sustain such research unless the subjects themselves are intrinsically interesting. It is impossible to spend 10 years of one's life studying something in which one doesn't become involved in some significant way. And it was impossible to survive in ILGS without a genuine interest in the issues facing local government.

Royston's interest in, and knowledge of, organization theory grew apace. He had published on the organization of local authorities (Greenwood & Stewart, 1971, 1973); now was his opportunity to immerse himself in the literature on organizations. This process happened very quickly, and not only did Royston become knowledgeable about organization theory, he developed a strong interest in it.

Between 1972 and 1975, there was a beneficial convergence in interests and knowledge between us. For collaboration to grow, and to continue over a long period, there has to be some basic consensus of view about research and scholarship. Although we thought we had that, it was only in the process of working together that we really discovered whether this was true. The process of acquiring each other's interests and knowledge confirmed our basic similarities of outlook. These similarities amounted to an agreement on values and methods of working at a general level. This does not mean that there was a cloning process—far from it. There were, and are, enough similarities and enough differences that creative disagreements arise within a common framework of approach.

By the mid-1970s there was a convergence in our interests around a set of themes that have provided the bedrock for our collaboration ever since. The major theoretical theme was, and continues to be, the analysis of organizational change and stability. Within this, there are slight differences in emphasis, with Royston being particularly interested in change in organizational archetypes (see Greenwood & Hinings, 1993) and Bob in the internal dynamics of change (see Hinings, Brown, & Greenwood, 1991). The second theme is a commitment to understanding organizations within a sectoral or institutional context (Child, 1988). Bob came to this somewhat slowly with his initial belief in a research strategy that emphasized broad organizational comparisons. But the 10-year project on change in municipalities showed him how important it is to understand how a sector evolves over time.

Royston came to this theme more naturally because of his involvement with ILGS.

The third theme is a commitment to longitudinal work that is designed to evolve over time. The evolution aspect is important both conceptually and empirically. It came out initially in the local government work, but has also been important in our work together at the University of Alberta on professional service firms. The Change in Local Government project was designed in 1972 and initially funded for 4 years. The Aston program, together with the work of Burns and Stalker (1961), Hall (1963), Woodward (1965), Perrow (1967), Lawrence and Lorsch (1968), and Hage and Aiken (1969), had set an agenda of understanding the relationship of organization structure to context. In 1972, John Child had published his seminal paper on strategic choice, which began to turn attention to power and interpretation in the development of organizational structures.

The local government project was fixed initially in contingency theory, but with the beginnings of a critique. The first papers were very clearly contingency theory focused (Greenwood, Hinings, & Ranson, 1975; Hinings, Greenwood, & Ranson, 1975). By the late 1970s and early 1980s, it was increasingly difficult to see where contingency theory figured (Greenwood, Hinings, & Ranson, 1977; Walsh, Hinings, Ranson, & Greenwood, 1981). The major theoretical paper that came out of this work (Ranson, Hinings, & Greenwood, 1980) was an attempt to deal with the structure/agency debate through Giddens's (1979) ideas of structuration and a more comprehensive approach to strategic choice through the concepts of interpretive schemes, interests, and power. By the time the book appeared (Hinings & Greenwood, 1988), the concepts of archetype, tracks, and capability had been added.

Research programs that go on longer than 3 or 4 years run into new conceptual developments that they have to take into account in a way that cross-sectional research does not. We became increasingly aware of this as our research stretched on into the late 1970s and early 1980s, and it is now a principle of our collaboration that long-term, programmatic research will require conceptual and empirical adjustment as it develops. The focus of our attention had to change, and data collection had to reflect this. The initial empirical emphasis was on structural changes, but as the reorganization progressed, we focused more and more on systems of decision making and human resource management.

These three themes of organizational change, the importance of the sectoral or institutional context, and longitudinal work that is designed to evolve over time have continued as the basis for our collaboration since we came to the University of Alberta. Since 1985, we have focused on studying professional service firms. The research program has no end point, the conceptual frameworks and theoretical approaches continue to evolve, and the circumstances in which those firms operate have changed significantly since we first began our research 9 years ago.

Managing Collaboration

Both Pugh (1988) and Hickson (1988), when discussing the Aston program and the Alberta/ Bradford research, emphasize the need to manage the process of collaboration actively. Working together is matter of management as well as affinity. Long-term partnership, collaboration, and teamwork have to be based on some element of those involved liking, respecting, and trusting each other. In the process of working with others on a task, we discover how far we like and respect those with whom we work and whether or not we can trust them, and the process of working together can be managed positively to help produce desirable interpersonal outcomes. As we worked together on developing the research program on organizational change in local government, we discovered that the supposed complementarity of our interests and skills was real. Our agreement on the nature of the research process and the importance of the topic of organizational change was particularly significant. It provided that basic homogeneity within which the initial heterogeneity of interests, knowledge, and skills could be given play. Early on, we found that we could work together without much friction.

Personal Styles

An important element in working together, which is related to liking, respect, and trust, is that of personal style. Working together as long and as intensively as we have involves understanding our personal similarities and differences. These are mainly differences that provide an important complementarity that comes out in our methods of working.

Royston is direct in manner and at times blunt and confrontational. He gets to the heart of things very quickly, challenges positions, and requires convincing about the validity of a position. (Some would say that this is typical behavior in the part of England that he comes from, Yorkshire—Yorkshire people have a reputation for bluntness.) Royston's great strengths come out in his enthusiasm, commitment, and directness. Bob's style is more conciliatory and conflict avoiding. He likes to see the positive aspects of any position and situation, long after there is nothing positive to be seen. He can take a long time to come to a conclusion, and even then it is only tentative. His strengths are in his abilities to see value in most things and to summarize positions.

These differences come out most strongly when we work in a larger team rather than only with each other. Only about 3 of our 22 years of collaboration have been just the two of us working together; the other 19 years have involved others. In those 22 years we have coauthored 31 publications (books, book chapters, journal articles, and monographs), 21 of which have involved one or more others.

In the local government work, Royston was always pushing for more effort, more commitment, more writing, more of everything. He did this by challenging all of us at our regular research meetings, demanding to know what we had actually done in the past few days, and pointing out that we had not implemented what had been agreed. Team members may get uncomfortable and defensive when confronted so bluntly, even in a supportive environment. Bob acted as conciliator and mediator in these situations, particularly between Royston and Stewart Ranson. He looked for ways of showing that things were not as bad as Royston suggested and that they could be rescued anyway. He found compromises by "rewriting" priorities and goals.

We found ourselves able to work with our differences and unite them. Exactly why and how this occurred, neither of us is really sure. It might be better to ask our other collaborators to give their views. Certainly, for us, our differences in temperament and style have been positive. We come back to Hickson's (1988) point that they are differences within an agreed-upon general approach to research and scholarship.

Principles of Collaboration

Our initial collaboration and ways of working were heavily influenced by Bob's experience on the Aston and Alberta research projects. The principles were as follows: First, research was to be the major commitment of each team member, not just the major *research* commitment; second, everyone was to participate in all aspects of the research, and any formal division of labor was to be minimal and agreed upon by the team; third, the researchers were to be together physically, with a room in common; and fourth, there was to be active "personnel management" of the team. Platt (1976), in her investigation of research styles, says, "In a few cases research directors had conscious policies on social matters; the extreme case I came across was [the Aston project]. It was very much a total system. One had to ask the group . . . about doing anything, had to be totally involved in the group. . . . The group did seem to show remarkable cohesion, despite the usual intellectual stresses and differences" (pp. 138-139).

It was this model that was adopted. The general experience of ILGS in both management development and research was that it had to be done in teams that "lived together" at work. Because we were all funded on a full-time basis for the research, the issue of major commitment was directly dealt with. Teaching came in a distant second, and no one was engaged in administration for the first 2 years of the project.

The second component of complete participation was also readily achievable. Royston and Bob had discussed the nature of the project in general terms during 1972-1973, but nothing detailed had been done. It was only when Royston, Bob, and Stewart got together at the University of Birmingham in September 1973 that real work began on the project. From then on, everyone participated in theory building, concept formation, sample selection, interview and questionnaire design, analysis, and writing. It was a matter of principle in the collaboration that the only specialization would be in caseload. The complete participation principle is important

in building trust, respect, and a common understanding. It cemented the possibility of collaboration for Bob and Royston.

The third component of having a room in common was also put in place and, again, was important in cementing collaboration. Such an arrangement produces constant contact, so that research issues are always under discussion, not just in three or four formal meetings a week. Perhaps more important, in the early stages it gave each of us access to the whole lives of the others. It became established and expected practice to read each other's mail and to know about each other's activities outside the project. When, after the first 2 years, teaching and administrative demands began to build, they had to be discussed within the group. Stewart developed a strong interest in educational administration and found himself being questioned by Royston about the extent to which he should follow this. Bob pointed out the ways in which this could be advantageous for the research.

The issue of being together has another aspect to it that we have found important over the years. Working together on all elements of the research has involved us in a lot of traveling together to research sites, conferences, and so on. Up to 3 hours on British Rail, or 4 hours on Air Canada, provided time during which we were able to both work and get to know each other better. A number of the papers we have written were sketched out on journeys such as these. The outline for one *Academy of Management Journal* article (Greenwood & Hinings, 1993) was done on a flight from Toronto to Edmonton as we returned from a fieldwork trip. A *Political Studies* article (Greenwood et al., 1977) was developed and partially written while we were spending a few days in rural England, teaching together at a management development program.

The fourth component, active "personnel management" of the team, has both technical and sociopolitical aspects. Technically, it means ensuring that things get done, that meetings are arranged, that decisions are followed on, and so on. At first in the local government project this was primarily Bob's responsibility, because of his role as senior investigator. But the interests and skills of the other participants, together with the inclusive mode of working, meant that they also ensured coordination and direction happened. Particularly important, and difficult, is ensuring that what happens at meetings is written up and circulated—we are not talking about minutes, but about the discussion of concepts, theories, methods, and measurements. There is a major interaction here with time. When collaboration takes place on a project where all members are giving the majority of their time to it, then these tasks get done; when the project is one among many, then things are more problematic. Royston was especially able to become more and more involved in the technical aspects of management, with his tendency to be output focused.

The sociopolitical aspect of the personnel management of the team is that of managing team development. On the Aston project, Bob had learned from the way in which Derek Pugh saw this aspect of team management as extremely important. Derek believed that our knowledge in organizational behavior could be drawn upon in our own team building. The extent to which researchers in collaborative relationships *do not* draw on their organizational behavior disciplinary expertise in their own working relationships continues to surprise us.

In the local government project, we started off as a team of three. We had to find a way of working that was enjoyable and productive. Bob's style—seeing value in most things, the ability to summarize positions, and a general conciliatory way of working—contributed positive attributes for team building. Royston's strength of being task oriented meant that we didn't get too bogged down in process discussions and took the unproductive edge off Bob's penchant for conflict avoidance. Stewart Ranson shared some of Royston's more confrontational style, and throughout the research, Bob had the task of ensuring that in team meetings Royston and Stewart gave each other enough room to make their respective points. There were times when they engaged in arguments that really did have a strong basis of agreement underlying them, and Bob was able to point this out on many occasions.

Of course, a team that is properly developed continues to evolve and change; it is a matter of continuous learning. Over time, our collaboration changed, with Royston taking on a larger and larger role in managing team processes. But the basic difference of Royston, in general, being more output focused and Bob, in general, being more process focused has remained. We

think of these processes as sociopolitical because they involve dealing with differences as well as similarities, differences that may be based on divergence of discipline, experience, goals, career stage, status, and so on.

The Changing Nature of Collaboration

Both of us regard the time that we spent on the local government project as an ideal—something, perhaps, that can occur only in particular institutional contexts and at particular career stages. Since we left Britain for Alberta, the structure of our collaboration has changed because of those institutional and career changes. Before outlining those, however, we feel it is necessary to say something about how we arrived at the University of Alberta.

Royston, unusually even for the British scene, had done his bachelor's, master's, and doctorate at the University of Birmingham, becoming a full-time research officer and then tenure-track faculty member before completing his PhD. Bob suggested that Royston should get some wider experience. By 1980, our collaboration was at a point where we were working together only on the final products of the local government research, and we did not have any plans for further cooperation. When Bob was asked by the then chair of the Department of Organizational Analysis at the University of Alberta whether he knew of anyone who might be interested in a position, Bob mentioned Royston. To Royston he suggested the tactic of offering to go for a 2-year visiting period.

The upshot was that Royston went to the University of Alberta, taking up his appointment in July 1982. In the final stages of working out the agreement, in 1981, Bob was asked if he would be interested in going to the University of Alberta. His initial answer was no, but, in a completely independent set of negotiations, he did eventually accept an appointment that began on January 1, 1983. We both saw our arrival at the University of Alberta as coincidental and decided that we both wanted to go our own ways. Bob became involved in research on Olympic sports organizations and Royston, who wanted to move away from the public sector, threw himself into work on private sector organizations.

After about 6 months of this, we found that we were still talking to each other about research issues. The relationship continued to be an easy one, interpersonally, and one that seemed to produce a fair number of ideas about research projects and papers. We came to the conclusion that our collaboration had been fun and fruitful, and it made no sense not to work together. We then began to design a research program based on extending the ideas and analysis from the local government research. We were looking for organizations that would be interesting from the point of view of change, and we wanted to exclude the public sector. John Brown introduced us to accounting firms as a possible site, and in 1985 we began work on accounting firms.

What has happened to our collaboration over the past decade? How have institutional and career changes altered it? Pugh (1988, pp. 129-130) describes three traditional research formats. The first of these, which he asserts is the most common, he calls the "kindergarten" approach. Research is essentially about individual training and development leading to a teaching position. As he puts it, "Researchers are mostly young, without the necessary knowledge, experience or status to teach with authority, and they do research until they have grown up to be big and strong enough to be an adult and thus to teach" (p. 129). The second he calls the "Riviera" approach, where teachers who become stale renew themselves through sabbaticals so that they can become better teachers. The third approach, according to Pugh, is how all academics do research. We are sure that many will recognize his description: "After they have done their lectures, tutorials and marking, seen individual students, participated in their professional association's activities, they will also do their research, perhaps on Thursday afternoons from 3:30 till 6 o'clock" (p. 130). Because the implicit concept is that research can be taken up and put down as and when necessary, Pugh calls this approach "academic knitting."

Pugh contrasts these approaches with the commitment of resources (time and people, particularly) needed to carry out large-scale, programmatic research. All of our research had been carried out under the conditions that Pugh regards as necessary for programmatic research, and our first aim was to reproduce these conditions in Alberta. However, in Canada there is no structure or tradition of having full-time researchers in organization theory who are not students. Research is done by faculty members

with part-time student assistance and the aid of PhD students obtaining dissertations from some part of the project. In Pugh's terms, research is a mixture of his three types: kindergarten through the PhD, Riviera through the sabbatical, and academic knitting for most of us.

We found that even when we put a full-time research officer into our research grant applications and got the money, there just wasn't anyone around to take the position. The impact of this was to push us back onto our own resources and collaboration. Because of the difficulty (or impossibility) of building up a full-time research-oriented team we have, in a sense, collaborated more closely than before. During our first decade, others were *always* involved. The new structure of our collaboration means that others are *usually* involved. Our current team is made up of four senior people: John Brown, David Cooper, Royston Greenwood, and Bob Hinings.

We have also found it difficult to involve PhD students directly in our own research. We have brought the British social science model with us and have positively encouraged students to "do their own thing." It is only in the past 3 years that we have become comfortable with this approach as a possible way of achieving some of our own general research goals. And we have found it virtually impossible to use part-time research help from students whose interests lie elsewhere. Part of this represents our own inability to adapt the nature of our collaboration. Although it has become more and more difficult to maintain the continuous, committed collaboration with a long-term, programmatic focus, we still behave on the basis that this is the ideal to which we should aspire and anything less is a form of failure (and, of course, frustration). From time to time our coffee and lunchtime conversations are centered on how we can solve some of the problems of cooperating in this way.

Career Changes and Collaboration

Perhaps an even more important factor in changing the nature of our collaboration has been that of the differences in our careers in the 1980s and 1990s compared with the 1960s and 1970s. One of the reasons we both contemplated leaving ILGS in the early 1980s was because of increasing administrative and teaching responsibilities. Moving to a "regular" department as an ordinary professor at least promised a decrease in administrative activities. Although these assumptions about teaching and administrative responsibilities were true in the short run, the fact of academic seniority has strong effects. As one becomes more and more senior, there are simply more and more demands on one's time. Not only are they there, they are expected by one's colleagues. The Faculty of Business at the University of Alberta has been on a 20-year (successful) journey to raise its academic profile. Only one path is to do research and publish in a direct sense. So when invitations come to edit a journal, edit a special issue, be a member of a panel at a national conference, review research proposals for national granting bodies, speak to local groups of businesspersons, and so on, these are seen as important, and administrators use them as evaluation criteria for senior faculty members.

Similarly, when one is approached about major administrative responsibilities, such as being department chair or PhD program director, or sitting on committees, it is generally expected that one will say yes. Senior faculty who have established research track records are not meant to protect themselves from wider responsibilities in order to continue with that research. Nor do they necessarily want to. So we both found ourselves increasingly involved in the department, faculty, university, and professional associations because we were asked, because we wanted to be, and because it was expected.

As a result, *by our ideal standards,* our ability to collaborate on the same kind of intensive level was cut back. Of course, in an institutional environment where intensive collaboration is not the norm, others don't see it this way. Around the faculty we are sometimes known as the Bobbsey Twins or Tweedledee and Tweedledum because we spend so much time together. Although the work on professional service firms is our *primary* research focus, we each have one other substantial research area that involves collaboration with others but not with each other. We both have substantial teaching responsibilities, although in this area our collaboration has grown since we came to the University of Alberta. We jointly design and deliver organizational theory courses and executive development courses. We also have major administrative responsibilities in the faculty and university.

In the process of taking on this range of activities over the past 10 years, we have come to recognize some of the other differences between us that we can turn to our advantage. It makes sense in our collaboration for Royston to do more administration and less teaching, and for Bob to reverse this. Royston is an efficient administrator, able to sort the wheat from the chaff. Bob tends to worry over every minor detail. The result is that Bob takes longer over administrative issues than does Royston. For teaching, the reverse is true. Royston has to review and rewrite every lecture he has given every time he gives it, putting in large amounts of time and energy. Bob takes much less time in review and is more prepared to wing it if pushed. In the past 7 or 8 years we have been very conscious of these differences and have attempted to work with them in managing our collaboration.

Our other collaborators on the professional service firm research are also senior, with additional major responsibilities (one is an associate dean; the other edits a major journal), so the management of the team is more difficult. The reasons are both technical and sociopolitical. Technically, it becomes difficult to schedule meetings to discuss research progress. Also, our research program currently involves fieldwork in Toronto, Calgary, Vancouver, Montreal, New York, London, Amsterdam, and Brussels. We have a principle that, where possible, interviews are carried out by two people. Thus scheduling fieldwork for these four people can be challenging.

Sociopolitically, there is the issue of working with an agreed-upon conceptual framework. Our approach has always been to have a well-worked-out conceptual and methodological framework, even when changes have to take place in that framework from time to time. And we came into the study of professional service firms from our work on archetypes, tracks, and the dynamics of change, seeing those firms as an empirical site for developing and extending that framework. Thus we had a clear theory and set of concepts that had been part of our lives for many years. Our two new collaborators had not been "socialized" into that approach.

This is a variant of what Hickson (1988) and Pugh (1988) call "the second-generation effect," which happens when members join a team that already has a clear view of where it is going and what it is doing. The new members don't have the same opportunity to contribute to all phases of the research and therefore feel ownership. This is not quite our situation on the professional service firm research, because the other members of the team, being senior and tenured, have their own views and make their own contributions about research directions. Because of our own many years of working together, we (Bob and Royston) have a whole series of taken-for-granted approaches to research, theoretically and methodologically, that our coworkers do not necessarily share. This, again, brings to the fore issues of team development and management, but without the time and resources to do what was done at Aston, Alberta, and ILGS.

Successful Outcomes

For collaboration to continue as long as ours has, there have to be successful outcomes, which are of two kinds. First, there have to be academic outcomes, publications that not only make some minimal impact on the field, but that we see as stronger than anything we could do individually. Second, there have to be personal outcomes, enjoyment in working together. We have experienced both of these.

Our collaboration has produced a reasonable stream of publications in areas that we think are important. They have appeared in journals in organization theory, public administration, and political science, including leading ones in both North America and the United Kingdom. There is no doubt in our minds that these publications are better than anything we could have produced individually. This is because we are drawing on, and putting together, different skills and interests, and having to debate with each other (and our other collaborators) about the direction, shape, purpose, and content of each publication. The collaboration also tends to lead to more adventurous research and writing. Again, our style differences come out here. Bob tends to start with a "stream of consciousness" draft, which is immediately handed off to Royston for extensive pruning, focusing, and reorganizing. Debates about the purpose of the paper come from this. Royston likes to get things really nailed down before

handing them over, and Bob finds himself asking to see a draft, which Royston resists by saying that it is not quite ready and needs one more revision. We have both learned to expect these differing responses; they are part of our understanding of each other.

Outcomes, of course, occur across time, and the literature on team building suggests that there have to be positive outcomes early on in the process. At the personal level, we discovered immediately that we could interact and enjoy each other's company. An important event happened in 1973 at the major public administration conference in Britain. Royston had been an active member for some time, and he organized matters so that Bob presented a keynote paper that outlined an organizational approach to understanding local government, something that was very unusual at the time. The discussant on the paper was one of the doyens of public administration in the United Kingdom. His comments could be summarized as, "This might be interesting, but it certainly isn't public administration." This had two positive effects that enhanced our collaboration: One was that it united us against a common enemy; the other was that it convinced us that we had a mission to reform British public administration through organization theory.

There were then three publications that were important in showing that we could reach top journals in the various fields we hoped to influence. One was an early analysis of local government data that appeared in two parts in *Public Administration* (Greenwood et al., 1975; Hinings et al., 1975), the leading journal of its kind in Britain. The second was a research note on centralization that was accepted by *Administrative Science Quarterly* (Greenwood & Hinings, 1976). The third, and most important from our point of view, was a paper in *Political Studies* (Greenwood et al., 1977), one of the two leading political science journals in Britain. So we were able to produce papers that were acceptable to leading journals and that developed our thinking.

Coming to Canada meant something of a refocusing for publication, in two senses. First, we had to aim more consciously at North American journals, because they are given a heavy emphasis in the faculty evaluation process. They have a different style and approach compared with most British journals, a style that doesn't always fit our predilections too well. Indeed our first joint work from the University of Alberta was still aimed at British journals; it is only since 1990 that we have published regularly in North American outlets (Cooper, Greenwood, Hinings, & Brown, 1993; Greenwood & Hinings, 1993; Greenwood, Hinings, & Brown, 1990, 1994). Second, in North America books seem to have very little standing in the academic community, a marked difference from Britain. In fact, we spent much of 1983-1986 working on *The Dynamics of Strategic Change* (Hinings & Greenwood, 1988), which we thought was a critically important statement. We were asked by a senior faculty member, "How many *ASQ* articles is *The Dynamics of Strategic Change* worth?" Bob said five, and Royston said that he had seriously undervalued the book!

Over time, the personal outcomes of enjoying working together have become more important to us. In academe, one has a great deal of choice regarding with whom one works, so perpetuating a relationship over a long period of time means that there is enjoyment. A telling fact here is that when we came to Alberta we expected to go our separate ways but found that we spent a great deal of time talking to each other about research issues. Perhaps over time we have become more and more like each other— a thought that scares both of us! Again, the issue of difference within a generally similar outlook about academic life is important here.

Two other aspects of personal enjoyment are worth mentioning. One is that we have increasingly collaborated on teaching and administrative activities, and here there is no doubt that Royston takes the lead. This working together arose from our doing research together, and primarily because we gain enjoyment from the give and take of debate and see better products as a result. The second aspect is that we have nonwork interests in common, and always have. One is a strong interest in sports, especially soccer in Britain and hockey in Canada (baseball, football, and basketball don't figure in our conversations). This has always provided a basis for conversation, as it did in Britain, where Stewart Ranson was a rabid soccer fan. We also have fairly similar interests in literature and music. All of this has given us a basis for an ongoing relationship. But—and this is a big and to some a surprising *but*—we very rarely socialize outside the university. Our nonwork lives are very separate and different and always have been (Royston is one of the most successful coaches of girls' soccer in Alberta; Bob's interests are centered on his local Anglican church and extended family). The extent of our getting together socially tends to be having dinner together with our wives maybe twice a year.

Lessons Learned

So what, if anything, can be learned from this highly personalized account? Perhaps it is worth reiterating a few key points; we hope that they don't sound too banal.

Floyd, Schroeder, and Finn (1994), in examining collaborative research, have produced a typology of relationships based on the dimensions of power balance (equal/unequal) and motivation (social/productivity). For example, if the power balance is unequal and the motivation is productivity, then the relationship will be burdened with the liability of feelings of exploitation and the possibility of withdrawal from the relationship. This has never been true of our collaboration. We made definite attempts to equalize power and to emphasize both the social and productivity aspects of our collaboration. In Floyd et al.'s terms, our relationship would be *both* collegial (equal power and a social emphasis) and meritorious (equal power and a productivity emphasis). The differences in our styles and personalities lead Royston to emphasize productivity and Bob the social, but neither in a conflictual way.

Our differences in style still exist. At a recent meeting, Royston was still pushing hard for more productivity. At the same meeting, Bob was saying there is only so much we can do, we can't do all these things at once, don't be too hard on others. *Plus ça change.* The balance between these approaches is very important, however, as it tends to keep us on track.

We both resist regarding the continual balancing of major research responsibilities, major teaching responsibilities, and major administrative responsibilities as ideally normal. We think it is important to strive for something that is often difficult to achieve. We have actually experienced what we regard as ideal, and for relatively long periods of our careers. Our collaborations with others before we met were positive, so we were disposed to regard working together in a favorable light. The fact that our interests, skills, dispositions, and styles blended together fast and then reinforced the partnership and the academic outcomes gave us further positive feedback. Hickson (1988) enunciates a team-building principle, "that a minimum base for a viable team is two research-minded, full-time, fully committed members right from the beginning. They can hold on to the aims even if others are subjected to competing pressures, and in the last resort they can ensure continuity even if all goes awry" (p. 139). We feel that was the basis for most of the first 10 years of our collaboration.

Two further points are worth restating. One is that probably no collaboration can continue for any length of time without active management at both technical and social levels. This is basic organizational behavior. Differences have to be dealt with; in our case, Royston is better at ensuring that differences are surfaced, and Bob is better at ensuring they are resolved. Work has to be monitored, anxieties dealt with.

Second, the nature, positives, and negatives of collaboration will change over time, particularly as careers develop. The early stages of a career tend to allow the greatest concentration on research. As our careers developed, more administrative and professional responsibilities came our way. A major effect of this was to reduce our genuine research time, but the base of collaboration that we had established during the 1970s meant that our productivity declined less than we think it would have had we worked alone. Also, the strength of our research collaboration led to strong collaboration in many of these new areas of involvement.

So, our working together continues, with no particular end in sight; we enjoy it too much for that. Here's to the next 22 years!

References

Burns, T., & Stalker, G. M. (1961). *The management of innovation.* London: Tavistock.

Child, J. (1972). Organization structure, environment and performance: The role of strategic choice. *Sociology, 6,* 1-22.

Child, J. (1988). Organizations in their sectors. *Organization Studies, 9,* 13-19.

Cooper, D. J., Greenwood, R., Hinings, C. R., & Brown, J. L. (1993). Biggest is best? Strategic assumptions and actions in the Canadian audit industry. *Canadian Journal of Administrative Sciences, 10,* 308-321.

Floyd, S. W., Schroeder, D. M., & Finn, D. M. (1994). "Only if I'm first author": Conflict over credit in management scholarship. *Academy of Management Journal, 37,* 734-747.

Giddens, A. (1979). *Central problems in social theory.* London: Macmillan.

Greenwood, R., & Hinings, C. R. (1976). Centralization revisited. *Administrative Science Quarterly, 21,* 151-155.

Greenwood, R., & Hinings, C. R. (1993). Understanding strategic change: The contribution of archetypes. *Academy of Management Journal, 36,* 1052-1081.

Greenwood, R., Hinings, C. R., & Brown, J. L. (1990). P^2 form: Strategic management in the professional service firm. *Academy of Management Journal, 33,* 725-755.

Greenwood, R., Hinings, C. R., & Brown, J. L. (1994). Merging professional service firms. *Organization Science, 5,* 239-257.

Greenwood, R., Hinings, C. R., & Ranson, S. (1975). Contingency theory and the organization of local authorities: Part 1. Differentiation and integration. *Public Administration, 53,* 1-23.

Greenwood, R., Hinings, C. R., & Ranson, S. (1977). The politics of the budgetary process. *Political Studies, 25,* 25-47.

Greenwood, R., & Stewart, J. D. (1971). *Corporate planning in English local government.* London: Charles Knight.

Greenwood, R., & Stewart, J. D. (1973). Towards a typology of English local authorities. *Political Studies, 21,* 64-69.

Hage, J., & Aiken, M. (1969). Routine technology, social structure and organizational goals. *Administrative Science Quarterly, 14,* 366-376.

Hall, R. H. (1963). The concept of bureaucracy: An empirical assessment. *American Journal of Sociology, 69,* 32-40.

Hickson, D. J. (1988). Ruminations on munificence and scarcity in research. In A. Bryman (Ed.), *Doing research in organizations.* London: Routledge.

Hickson, D. J., Hinings, C. R., Lee, C. A., Schneck, R. E., & Pennings, J. M. (1971). A strategic contingencies theory of intraorganizational power. *Administrative Science Quarterly, 16,* 216-229.

Hinings, C. R., Brown, J. L., & Greenwood, R. (1991). Change in an autonomous professional organization. *Journal of Management Studies, 28,* 375-393.

Hinings, C. R., & Greenwood, R. (1988). *The dynamics of strategic change.* Oxford: Basil Blackwell.

Hinings, C. R., Greenwood, R., & Ranson, S. (1975). Contingency theory and the organization of local authorities: Part 2. Contingencies and structure. *Public Administration, 53,* 169-220.

Hinings, C. R., Hickson, D. J., Pennings, J. M., & Schneck, R. E. (1974). Structural conditions of intra-organizational power. *Administrative Science Quarterly, 19,* 22-44.

Lawrence, P., & Lorsch, J. (1968). *Organization and environment*. Cambridge, MA: Harvard University Press.

Perrow, C. (1967). A framework for the comparative analysis of organizations. *American Sociological Review, 32,* 194-208.

Platt, J. (1976). *Realities of social research*. New York: John Wiley.

Pugh, D. S. (1988). The Aston research programme. In A. Bryman (Ed.). *Doing research in organizations*. London: Routledge.

Pugh, D. S., & Hickson, D. J. (Eds.). (1976). *Organization structure in its context: The Aston programme*. Farnborough, UK: Lexington.

Pugh, D. S., Hickson, D. J., & Hinings, C. R. (1969). An empirical taxonomy of work organizations. *Administrative Science Quarterly, 14,* 115-126.

Pugh, D. S., Hickson, D. J., Hinings, C. R., & Turner, C. (1968). Dimensions of organization structure. *Administrative Science Quarterly, 13,* 65-105.

Pugh, D. S., Hickson, D. J., Hinings, C. R., & Turner, C. (1969). The context of organization structures. *Administrative Science Quarterly, 14,* 91-114.

Pugh, D. S., & Hinings, C. R. (Eds.). (1977). *Organization structure: Extensions and replications*. Farnborough, UK: Lexington.

Ranson, S. R., Hinings, C. R., & Greenwood, R. (1980). The structuring of organization structures. *Administrative Science Quarterly, 25,* 1-17.

Walsh, K. M., Hinings, C. R., Ranson, S., & Greenwood, R. (1981). Power and advantage in organizations. *Organization Studies, 2,* 131-152.

Woodward, J. (1965). *Industrial organization: Theory and practice*. London: Oxford University Press.

24 Growing a Personal, Professional Collaboration

Jane E. Dutton

Jean M. Bartunek

Connie J. G. Gersick

Prologue

This is not a "how-to" account of research collaboration. Rather, we intend this essay to be one story of an evolving research collaboration among three women. We focus here on issues that are not often discussed in either doctoral student training or accounts of how collaborative work is done.

The three of us are working on a study about the meaning of relationships in academics' professional lives. This topic is new to each of us, and our research is still developing. We are also relatively new at working together. Our collaboration is different from any we have experienced in the past, and we are still finding our way. The chance to write about our experience here presents us with some special opportuni-

ties. By reflecting on our own collaboration, we hope to understand our research topic better. This chapter is also our first occasion for writing together formally, and—because this is a relationship we enjoy—it gives us an excuse to have some fun.

We describe below four different aspects of our collaboration as it has developed so far: its roots, its rhythms, its routines or ways of doing, and, finally, reactions—the reactions we have had to it and reactions some others have had to our work up to this point. We talk about these four aspects with a special focus on how this work connects the personal and the professional aspects of our lives. We use our individual voices as well as our joint voice, in order to capture the similarities and the differences in our aspirations for the work and our experi-

AUTHORS' NOTE: We would like to express our appreciation to the colleagues who provided us with valuable feedback on earlier drafts of this essay. We have decided not to name these colleagues explicitly, but we extend a special thanks to them.

ences of it. We hope that, by examining this collaboration, we can increase our ability to re-create its positive aspects in other professional relationships. We also hope our description will help readers to sense both the rich professional possibilities of collaboration and the personal sustenance that our experience and description celebrate.

Because we live in cities that are geographically separated, a good deal of our collaboration has been carried out through conference calls (augmented more and more frequently by e-mail). A few months after we began our regular conference calls, we started tape-recording them and having them transcribed. We have drawn heavily on those transcripts in preparing this chapter.

Roots

In 1992 we were "distant professional colleagues," although we had read each other's work, appreciated the styles and content of each other's research, and had met. Despite the brevity of our contact with one another, we had formed distinctive impressions.

Jean: I admired both Connie's and Jane's work, and, in fact, had been a reviewer for some of it. Jane's paper with Janet Dukerich on homelessness (Dutton & Dukerich, 1991) had evoked complex emotional reactions in me. In addition, I had often taught Connie's model of time and transition in work terms (Gersick, 1988) in my classes, and found it quite provocative for my students.

Jane: Jean's work (Bartunek, 1984) affected me as a doctoral student. I especially liked her work because it took things that I thought were sacred and turned them topsy-turvy. Connie's work does the same thing for me. However, I didn't get exposed to Connie's work until later in my career. Before I met Connie and Jean personally, I had been around lots of other people who had talked about them very positively. I felt as though I knew them through other people.

Connie: Before the three of us started talking, I had done just one coauthored paper (Gersick & Hackman, 1990). I was getting tired

of going it alone so much, and was looking hesitantly for a way to try collaborating more. I knew Jane and Jean only from reading each of their papers and seeing each give conference presentations, but I admired their skills and identified with the values I saw in their work. I imagined each of them would be a wonderful partner.

Several points stand out about the impressions we had of one another prior to the time we began collaborating. First, even though our individual work was very different, we shared a strong, positive set of work-related and personal impressions of each other. So we began this collaboration with a sense of trust in the relationship and optimism that something good would result from it. Second, despite some familiarity and connections with one another's work, we had had limited, if any, direct personal contact with each other. Thus part of what drew us into collaboration when the opportunity presented itself was the chance to get to know one another. We thought this would be fun, especially in contrast to the many other pulls and drains on our time. In the first year of the collaboration, Jean began a new role as department chair at Boston College at a time when BC was beginning a PhD program in organizational studies. During this same year, Jane was program chair for the Organization and Management Theory Division of the Academy of Management. Connie had intense teaching responsibilities during the fall, and she and her family moved to a new house during the late spring.

We probably would have stayed distant admirers of each other's work except that someone put us together on a panel at the Organization Behavior/Organization Development and Change/Organization and Management Theory Doctoral Consortium at the 1992 meeting of the Academy of Management. We were part of a session in which presenters were asked to address the issue of "how to ask the right [research] questions and find interesting answers." Each of us rejected the implied assumptions of this topic, that a set of "right" research questions exists and that some people can or should tell others how to find them. Jean talked about the importance of relationships in doing research. Connie used the design of her doctoral classes to talk about creating a context in which doctoral students can develop interesting questions and find valid answers. Jane talked about ways one could search out "interesting enough" questions by finding one's personal connection to theory.

After we gave our talks, we had an opportunity to remark in person to each other about how similar our perspectives seemed, especially in taking a nurturing and nonhierarchical stance vis-à-vis doctoral students and participants in research projects in which we were involved. It was also striking that we used ourselves and our own research in very personal ways to discuss our ideas about helping others find interesting research questions. We felt our comments reflected a feminine reaction and voice, and we acknowledged the comfort that we experienced hearing this voice expressed by individuals we admired.

Acknowledgment that we were using a gendered "voice" did not come easily. We have not published articles on women's issues, nor would we describe ourselves as having feminist academic identities. However, the chance to hear each other speak in the consortium sparked an interest in us all to explore further the general issue of how, as women, we work with doctoral students, using the idea of nurturing as central in our exploration. After returning home, Jane wrote letters to the other two of us, suggesting that we have a conference call to explore whether there was interest in taking the conversation further and eventually putting our perspectives in writing. We each had different expectations and concerns about this small step toward collaboration:

Jane: I remember being scared and excited about sending the letters to Connie and Jean. I was scared because I worried about committing the act of saying, "Let's have a conversation." What if we had nothing to say to each other? What if, in getting closer on this project, Connie and Jean, whom I really admired professionally, did not like me personally? What if we started something and I could not deliver?

Jean: I was excited and flattered that Jane sent the letters to Connie and me inviting the collaboration, though I already felt quite overwhelmed with my upcoming workload. I secretly hoped that no viable research project would emerge until my work life calmed down, and decided that, initially at least, I would just enjoy the conversation.

Connie: I thought, if not now, when? I had been wanting to try something new, and Jane's invitation appeared to be a perfect opportunity. I roamed between grandiose fantasies and doubts about how we would click, what we might actually produce together, and whether I could be a good research team player.

We all decided we wanted to talk and work together. Once we were able to find an initial time to connect, we started scheduling conference calls about once every 3 or 4 weeks.

Reflections

Our collaboration began serendipitously. We did not start with a rational assessment that we ought to work together. In fact, our divergent research interests made us a somewhat unlikely team. Rather, the catalyst for this collaboration was our shared emotional reaction to what we perceived to be strong, established norms about how one ought to think about research and work with doctoral students. Prior to our presentations, each of us thought her own beliefs were private and unique, and perhaps somewhat strange. Hearing other women we respected professionally express familiar views was enabling and reassuring. For example, notes from our November 10, 1992, conversation illustrate the sense of relief and excitement produced when we shared our common experiences (this was before we started tape-recording).

One of us talked about the importance of having these conversations among ourselves at this point in time in her career. She described having a sense of reaching the top of a ladder and she feels like she has no map of where to go. The feelings are a mix of discomfort with what one is supposed to do or not do and what one is supposed to know and not supposed to know. She went on to say that as women we are discovering more that there is a disjuncture between what we have been told and what we really think. The other two listeners resonated strongly to this point. We all talked about different episodes of when we felt fraudulent, Jean in the context of consulting, Jane in the context of giving a presentation to university donors, and Connie in the context of teaching.

Looking back, it seems that we started this collaboration partly as a way to work on our own development together—not just as a vehicle for writing a paper or becoming friends. Each of us was embarking on a major new career stage. Jean and Jane became department chairs (Jane at the end of the second year of our collaboration); Connie got tenure and finally bought a home after years of (noncommittal) renting. Our status as provisional, junior members of academe was over.

As we entered the senior ranks, we all found ourselves with more responsibility to lead and fewer options merely to observe. At that point, discrepancies between who we really were and who "the field" wanted us to be became more serious. Each of us, individually, reacted strongly against speaking at the doctoral consortium to support a norm about research that violated her real feelings about her work. Each of us was ready to take a small risk, to try to legitimate another point of view for the students.

There was a real sense of strength and relief that came from the recognition that we were at similar places in terms of our misgivings; there was also excitement about discussing what this career really means. Thus the collaboration was initiated with a clear sense of possibility. At the same time, it was scary to voice some of our feelings to people we didn't know well but who we hoped would like us and support our efforts to become more authentically ourselves at work.

As we talked, we discovered that we shared many career dilemmas, although Jean has been in the field longest and has a slightly different experience from Connie or Jane. It was surprising to learn from each other that we share some similar doubts and concerns about career commitment and our desires and/or capabilities to deliver on the "amped-up" standards that go hand in hand with being tenured professors. In addition, we find ourselves increasingly approached to help female graduate students and female faculty, and have mixed feelings about our abilities to do anything that will really help. We use our conversations to vent anger and frustration at the impossibility of doing all that

we are asked to do at the level of quality to which we aspire.

Thus an important dimension of our collaboration, from the start, has been a sense that we share career success, and that this leads to some challenging and sometimes difficult experiences for us. Although our success is certainly gratifying, it is also accompanied by some ambivalence and self-doubt about the changes it has brought. We share a need to talk about what roles we want, what roles we can play authentically, and what roles we need to rewrite as women in the academic establishment.

Rhythms

Our collaboration is connected to the personal side of our professional lives. This personal dimension has given sustenance to the collaboration, but it has also subjected it to the rhythms imposed by personal and professional crises and challenges confronting each of us. For example, during the period of Jane's intense involvement in the program for the Organization and Management Theory Division, she wondered if we should continue our conversations at all, as she did not have time to do anything other than simply talk. We decided to continue anyway, and had some very fruitful discussions that laid the groundwork for the research in which we ultimately became involved.

Up at least until the time of this writing, in the fall of 1994, the collaboration has usually been sufficiently ill defined and without clear deadlines that we have been able to adjust our expectations to meet what each of us is capable of delivering at the time. We have found that we have been able to trade off taking responsibility for different parts of our project, and that usually one of us has time to work on a particular aspect even if the others do not.

The Research Project

In the summer of 1993, a little less than a year after we began conversing, our conversations turned to the actual conduct of joint research. The original focus and goal of our discussions had been to write something about nurturing doctoral students. However, our telephone conversations led us beyond this topic; we became interested in the relational side of work in general. The issues we had discussed in our phone conversations, and in fact the nature of those conversations, were the main source of our decision to pursue this topic, because it was very different from the topics about which any of us had previously conducted research or written. We had begun to see relationships as a side of professional experience that is typically invisible and undervalued, not usually noted in discussions of academic work lives.

As an attempt at joint research, we committed ourselves to learn more about the meanings of relationships in professional life by conducting a study of the professional relationships experienced by male and female academics in business schools. We wanted to study a context we understood and with which we had a professional connection, and we wanted to study it in a relational way. It appeared to us that the best way to do this was through interviews with business school faculty members that would enable us to learn in some depth about their interpersonal relationships with colleagues. We tried to accomplish this by designing an interview schedule that would enable respondents to tell us about relationships that were significant as part of their professional lives, to tell us some of the history of the relationships, and to tell us stories about events that symbolized the relationships.

When summer arrived and our teaching obligations ended, we had weekly phone calls to work out the details of our interview protocols. We each conducted several pilot interviews, not only with colleagues, but also with each other. We wanted to be able to appreciate the experiences of those we would be interviewing.

During the summer we began to conduct the interviews; these were completed during the 1993-1994 academic year. The interviews involved engaging with colleagues at our own schools and other schools in our local areas. All three of us found that collecting data for this project altered our attachments to our workplaces. For example, the interviews served as introductions to individuals we did not know well in our own workplaces. Because the interviews often elicited stories that were painful or joyful for study participants, they provided an opportunity for us to connect meaningfully with former "strangers." After each interview, we

recorded our reactions. Here are two excerpts that illustrate how the interviews affected us:

> I identified a lot with what was said, but also felt that I've been more fortunate. This person sounded almost tormented. Some of what was said made me angry at the academic establishment.

> This person I just talked to I've known since she was here, but I haven't known her very well. My reactions to the interview are very positive. Afterwards we talked a fair amount, and she was asking me if I was able to balance my life. I told her it's been harder and harder ever since I was promoted. . . . This conversation felt good. It felt like it's going to create a connection between the two of us.

The interviews gave us an opportunity to appreciate the variety—both within and across universities—in our colleagues' experiences of professional life. We came away from the transcripts with a much more complex and vivid sense of the pleasures and hardships, rewards and disappointments, generosity and meanness that can be part of academic life.

At the time of this writing, we have completed the interviews and begun an extensive process of analyzing them. Connie took the lead in organizing a symposium on relationships in organizations for the Academy of Management 1994 meeting, at which we presented a paper on our work. In that paper, based on our analysis of our data to this point, we addressed two questions: What types of relationships do people talk about as part of their professional lives? What are some underlying themes in the descriptions of the relationships? We talked about the fact that the majority of relationships the people we interviewed discussed were relationships largely restricted to the work domain (relationships that Rawlins, 1992, calls "agentic"). A smaller number spoke of relationships that include and transcend the workplace (what Rawlins calls "communal"). Moreover, the types of themes described in stories about the relationships differed between men and women. Men were more likely to talk about agentic relationships and about receiving resources from others that fostered their career success. Women were more likely to talk about receiving non-career-related help, about difficult

relationships with superiors, and about participating in communal relationships that transcend the workplace. The interviews made it
evident that, for our interviewees, the relational
experiences of men and women at work are
quite different. They also made it evident that
our own relationship is a communal one that
includes, but goes well beyond, our formal work.

Reflections

Our collaboration contains substantial flexibility, with each of us able to increase or decrease her involvement as schedules allow. For
example, Jane took the lead in creating this
chapter, Jean took the lead in preparing our
convention presentation, and Connie is taking
the lead in analyzing our data.

This flexibility is possible, in part, because
we all have tenure. Instrumental, career-cen-
tered goals are not prominent for us in determining when and about what we have con-
versed or the process of our work together.
Instead, more expressive goals of getting to know
one another have played an important role in
how this collaboration has evolved.

The changes in rhythms and demands of this
collaboration, over busy and less busy times,
and over more and less stressful times, have
been aided by our conscious attention to each
other's expectations of the collaboration. We
spend a portion of each conversation realigning
expectations to make sure we can deliver to
each other on implicit or explicit promises of
work.

The collaboration also has a sense of life and
growth to it because of its reflective quality. Our
own relationship as collaborators is strongly
intertwined with the subject of the research
that we are trying to conduct, and helps us gain
insight into our central research question. Similarly, by sharing how relationships with others
inform our own professional experiences, we
deepen the bases for our own friendship. Thus,
in this collaboration, there has been relatively
little separation between the personal (i.e., getting to know each other as friends) and the
professional (i.e., coming to understand and
writing about professional relationships in academic life) dimensions of our lives.

Routines

Over time, as part of our collaboration, we
are evolving a repertoire of "ways of doing" or
research routines, part of the structure that
keeps the collaboration growing. As social scientists, we know that articulating the patterns
in our behavior together can help explain how
it works and how it affects us. As creators of the
work, we believe we are evolving ways of doing
in this collaboration that help us fuse the personal with the professional sides of ourselves.
We have been influenced and inspired by Lynn
Brown and Carole Gilligan's (1992) account of
their own search for a way to "do psychology"
that takes seriously the relationships the researchers have with each other and with the
individuals whom they are studying (see also
David Berg and Ken Smith's *The Self in Social
Inquiry*, 1988). We will share a few examples of
the practices we use that illustrate this type of
collaboration.

Personal Attention

We came together based on similar experience, but we could not begin the research project
until we had developed personal connections
with each other. We developed these connections in ways that allowed us to pay attention to
each other's concerns. A special project perhaps
best illustrates the importance of personal attention. Jean initiated this undertaking when
she sent Jane and Connie copies of the prose
poem "Girl," by Jamaica Kincaid (1985). This
poem has been discussed by Peggy McIntosh
(1989) and used by a group of teachers Jean had
been studying (Bartunek, Lacey, & Wood, 1992;
Wood & Lacey, 1991) as a model for creating
stories of their own. Jean suggested that the
three of us similarly use it as a model for prose
poems we would write and share about ourselves, both to open up other dimensions of
ourselves and to build trust. (We attach the text
of "Girl" as an appendix to this chapter.) The
poems we wrote and read to each other evoked
several observations that give a sense of how
listening to each other affected us. This is an
excerpt from our notes on this phone call:

> The messages in our poems were often ad-
> monishing and represented a lot of "shoulds."

There was also a blending or sort of an easy flow between work and nonwork types of concerns. In substance, the messages were flowing, seamless, and sensical both to ourselves and also to each other. We were also struck by how difficult it was to know who we were in the context of all these "shoulds." "I don't know what I want because I don't know who I am." And we also talked about how nurturing is more complex than we had anticipated, especially in academic settings that include political dimensions.

Pilot Interviews With Each Other

The pilot interviews we conducted with each other in preparation for our study were rich and revealing, uncovering dimensions of our individual experiences we had not previously shared. From these interviews we learned much more about how each other thought about relationships and connected them to professional experience. These relationships were data. They were also additional sources of sustenance from one another. The deepening of our personal connection helped remove barriers in our own communication, which we hope improves the quality of our data collection and analysis.

The Study

The interviews we have conducted with the research participants have had effects similar to those from our interviews with each other. Several study participants have sought us out afterward to ask about the study or just to talk about topics they wouldn't have thought to discuss with us before. Thus the interviews have been personally and professionally meaningful. Rather than designing a way of collecting data that tried to downplay the personal and relationship sides of respondents' lives, we have created a design that brings relationships center stage.

Reactions

Our involvement in this research project has evoked several reactions in ourselves and others that are an important part of the story of our collaboration. In particular, the project has

been generative. We have been stunned and delighted by the life-giving, relationship-building quality of the project to us and to our relationships with colleagues who had been only distant connections in the past. Some of them have become partners in the creation of this research product and process.

Our project has also proved generative to Pam, the person who has transcribed many of the tapes of our phone conversations. She told Jane about how much listening to the tapes had affected her. Pam first spoke to us from the perspective of trying to make helpful suggestions about how to coordinate our different word processing systems.[1] Having heard us complain about and try to coordinate our technology in our taped phone conversations, she made useful suggestions to "lighten our burden." In further conversations with Jane, she conveyed how surprised she was at the difficulty we had talking about our own experiences in a gendered way and how we struggled to convey accurately the experiences of our study participants. As Pam stated it, "You are women of privilege, and you experience your jobs in this way?" Pam's initiative in conveying how the transcription process affected her made her part of, as opposed to outside of, the research. Jane has begun a separate research project with Pam that builds off of her interest in women in organizations.

Finally, our work has generated expectations and reactions from others that are different from the reactions we have encountered in our other work. In most cases the interaction is positive and full of hope, as if our participation in this project will generate something of value intellectually and personally. One example comes from an e-mail message that one of us received from a doctoral student after attending our academy symposium: "I wanted to tell you how much I enjoyed the symposium. . . . I am so glad you had the courage to talk about these issues in a session. I think it is important to get them out in the open. I really appreciated it."

On the other hand, some colleagues expressed concern about the first draft of this chapter. One told us, "The chapter shouldn't be written as though your relationship is a coffee klatch." Another expressed concern that the chapter had no sharp edges—"it just doesn't grab you by the throat." But we have decided to let this essay generate images of a coffee klatch and let that be okay. Sometimes our collaboration is a klatch—it involves conversation without the coffee. We also decided that we are satisfied that there are no sharp and hard edges here (with the exception of the technological ones). This chapter is intended to have soft spots and round edges.

Reflections

This research project is genuinely enjoyable to all three of us. However, its generative nature also complicates things. The project is jam-packed with feeling. The weaving of the personal and the professional means that we know each other more closely than we might if this were a strictly "professional" relationship. The enhanced vulnerability means that there is an enhanced sense of responsibility to care for one another. The caring is important work; it is also sometimes draining. But awareness that this work is generative makes us feel good. It helps us to see the project as productive in a way that we don't usually see. It also feels genuine and real.

We close with an excerpt from a conversation we had a year ago, when we were trying to decide how writing this chapter felt and how we should respond to critical reactions to our first draft:

There's not a disconnect between what we're writing and how we're writing it and what I feel. Oftentimes there's a disconnect. You know, "I have to write it this way, although I might feel this way." Or something like that. So it seems really, no, I had fun. It was a blast!" . . .

[Laughter] It's just so incredibly amazing, because, what I felt—and this just gives more of my emotional reaction to this—what I felt like is that finally I can let my guard down. We were letting our collective guard down. It felt safe, because I was with people who I respected professionally, and I felt, you know, increasingly personally close to.

But I, I don't want to make it more professional. To me that's what's so wonderful. This is not like any collaboration that I've ever had.

Appendix

"Girl"

by Jamaica Kincaid [2]

Wash the white clothes on Monday and put them on the stone heap; wash the color clothes on Tuesday and put them on the clothesline to dry; don't walk barehead in the hot sun; cook pumpkin fitters in very hot sweet oil; soak your little cloths right after you take them off; when buying cotton to make yourself a nice blouse, be sure that it doesn't have gum on it, because that way it won't hold up well after a wash; soak salt fish overnight before you cook it; is it true that you sing benna in Sunday school?; always eat your food in such a way that it won't turn someone else's stomach; on Sundays try to walk like a lady and not like the slut you are so bent on becoming; don't sing benna in Sunday school; you mustn't speak to wharf-rat boys, not even to give directions; don't eat fruits on the street— flies will follow you; *but I don't sing benna on Sundays at all and never in Sunday school;* this is how to sew on a button; this is how to make a buttonhole for the button you have just sewed on; this is how to hem a dress when you see the hem coming down and so to prevent you from looking like the slut I know you are so bent on becoming; this is how you iron your father's khaki pants so that they don't have a crease; this is how you grow okra—far from the house, because okra tree harbors red ants; when you are growing dasheen, make sure it gets plenty of water or else it makes your throat itch when you are eating it; this is how you sweep a corner; this is how you sweep a whole house; this is how you sweep a yard; this is how you smile to someone you don't like too much; this is how you smile to someone you don't like at all; this is how you smile to someone you like completely; this is how you set a table for tea; this is how you set a table for dinner; this is how you set a table for dinner with an important guest; this is how you set a table for lunch; this is how you set a table for breakfast; this is how to behave in the presence of men who don't know you very well, and this way they won't recognize immediately the slut I have warned you against becoming; be sure to wash every day, even if it is with your

own spit; don't squat down to play marbles—
you are not a boy, you know; don't pick people's
flowers—you might catch something; don't
throw stones at blackbirds, because it might not
be a blackbird at all; this is how to make a bread
pudding; this is how to make doukona; this is
how to make pepper pot; this is how to make a
good medicine for a cold; this is how to make a
good medicine to throw away a child before it
becomes a child; this is how to catch a fish; this
is how to throw back a fish you don't like, and
that way something bad won't fall on you; this
is how to bully a man; this is how a man bullies
you; this is how to love a man, and if this doesn't
work there are other ways, and if they don't
work don't feel too bad about giving up; this is
how to spit up in the air if you feel like it, and
this is how to move quick so that it doesn't fall
on you; this is how to make ends meet; always
squeeze bread to make sure it's fresh; *but what
if the baker won't let me feel the bread?;* you mean
to say that after all that you are really going to
be the kind of woman who the baker won't let
near the bread?

Notes

1. Jean uses Microsoft Word on a Macintosh, Connie
uses WordStar on an IBM, Jane's secretary uses Word for
Windows, and, until recently, Jane used WordPerfect on
the IBM. Although the interpersonal aspects of our
collaboration have been smooth, the technological ones
have been fraught with complications. Jane just learned
Word, which helps a bit.

2. Used by permission.

References

Bartunek, J. (1984). Changing interpretive schemes and
organizational restructuring: The example of a religious order. *Administrative Science Quarterly, 29,*
355-372.

Bartunek, J., Lacey, C. A., & Wood, D. R. (1992). Social
cognition in organizational change: An insider-outsider approach. *Journal of Applied Behavioral Science, 28,* 204-223.

Berg, D. N., & Smith, K. K. (Eds.). (1988). *The self in
social inquiry.* Newbury Park, CA: Sage.

Brown, L., & Gilligan, C. (1992). *Meeting at the crossroads.* Cambridge, MA: Harvard University Press.

Dutton, J., & Dukerich, J. (1991). Keeping an eye on the
mirror: Image and identity in organizational adaptation. *Academy of Management Journal, 34,* 517-
554.

Gersick, C. J. G. (1988). Time and transition in work
teams: Toward a new model of group development.
Academy of Management Journal, 31, 9-41.

Gersick, C. J. G., & Hackman, J. R. (1990). Habitual
routines in task performing groups. *Organizational
Behavior and Human Decision Processes, 47,* 65-97.

Kincaid, J. (1985). *At the bottom of the river.* New York:
Vintage.

McIntosh, P. (1989). *Feeling like a fraud: Part two* (Work
in Progress No. 37). Wellesley, MA: Stone Center.

Rawlins, W. (1992). *Friendship matters.* New York: Aldine de Gruyter.

Wood, D. R., & Lacey, C. A. (1991). A tale of teachers.
NWSA Journal, 3, 414-421.

The Doctoral Student
by Amy L. Kenworthy

Who am I?

I am a student working for a doctorate of philosophy in the science of management
I am a woman.
I am a partner, sister, daughter, friend.
I am confused.

I have passion. I feel alive. I feel lost and cold and barren.
I once knew why I was here
Now I wonder.

Who am I looking at?
What am I studying?
Am I really learning about chi-squared, alpha, beta, and gamma?
What about the children who can't even A, B, or G in "our" alphabet?

I think about my passion—about the people in the streets—
about my friend John who is my lifelong educator, mentor, and friend.
John is homeless; he has passion.
He knows more than statistics will ever teach me.

I think about my impact on the world, what I want to do, and who I will become.

I think about myself. Am I simply a GMAT score or am I passion? Am I the 99% statistic or am I
a woman who loves, cries, rejoices, and feels about others?

I know that through my confusion will come knowledge.
I know I must tap into the passion if I want to survive.
I know my challenge is to create a world for myself in academia where I can share
my passion and create lasting knowledge.

I know that I can make a difference if I don't forget who I am.

Note: Used by permission. This poem by Amy Kenworthy, a first year doctoral student in Organization Behavior at the University of North Carolina at Chapel Hill, was written in response to the chapter by Jane Dutton, Connie Gersick, and Jean Bartunek.

25 Three Voices Reflecting on Scholarly Career Journeys With International Collaboration

James G. (Jerry) Hunt
Arja Ropo
Päivi Eriksson

Prelude

This is a narrative about scholarly career journeys that emphasize different aspects of international collaboration. It is told in three voices—two from a small but highly developed country (Finland) and one from the United States. Each voice is different and describes different aspects of international collaboration. Jerry's journey is about emphasizing international scholarship while operating primarily within the so-called U.S. publication system, with its well-established norms. Arja's journey is about balancing a scholarly route versus a service route where the former has a heavily international flavor and the latter has a local or national emphasis. Päivi's journey involves conflicts between national and international objectives and preferences in scholarly terms.

The three of us have a history of collaboration as duos, across time and with varying intensity, and more recently have collaborated as a trio on this chapter and other projects. The narrative starts with a triggering mechanism—our involvement in two Finnish doctoral seminars, which caused us to reflect deeply on our different career experiences. We then present our own journey descriptions in our different voices, and these deep reflections lead to a "ruminations" section. Writing this final section has been helpful for us; we hope that reading it will be helpful for others.

The Trigger

There were the three of us (Arja, Jerry, and Päivi), grouped around the PC in Arja's spa-

cious office in a new, virtually all-white building at the University of Tampere. Only a day or
two before, Jerry had arrived in Helsinki from
Lubbock, Texas, and was driven to Tampere by
Arja and her husband, Eero. Jerry was in Finland for the summer, largely because of Arja's
influence with Finnish funding agencies.

What had been two duos (Arja and Jerry;
Arja and Päivi) was now a trio. The trio's marching orders were to plan for two national doctoral seminars (composed of a gaggle of Finnish business administration students from all
over the country), the initial seminar to be
conducted within a few days. Jerry and Arja had
worked together closely (with visits back and
forth) and had become increasingly close colleagues and friends over the previous 5 years.
Arja and Päivi were best friends and colleagues
who had received master's and licentiate (post-
master's, predoctorate) degrees from the University of Tampere. Arja had then completed
her doctorate at Tampere and Päivi did her
work at the Helsinki School of Economics and
Business Administration.

National doctoral seminars were increasingly
being used to provide "more bang for the Finnish higher education Finnmark." The two upcoming ones differed substantially from the
usual national symposia in their emphasis on
active discussion, team papers, and team presentations from the students, as well as our planned
videotaping of the proceedings, with follow-up
playback in Jerry's office.

Our planning on these and the content aspects of each seminar (organizational change
and scholarly publishing, respectively) went very
smoothly, and we felt that our trio was coming
together very nicely indeed. An underlying tension throughout the planning was how the individually oriented Finnish students would handle these seminars.

Conducting the seminars was very stimulating for us and reinforced our feelings as a successful team. What had been two successful
duos was now a successful trio. Student responses indicated that the seminars had gone
even better than we might have expected. The
normally reticent, individually oriented Finnish students had reacted enthusiastically to the
team-oriented activities, with an interesting combined U.S. and Finnish flavor.

As (what we were now calling) our dynamic
trio met to plan and evaluate the seminar sessions, the planning and discussion process in-
exorably pushed us to reflect deeply on our own
careers. We engaged in much retrospective and
future sensemaking and soul-searching. Jerry
was at a very different stage in his career journey from those of Arja and Päivi (late middle
compared with beginning and early middle).
Even Arja and Päivi, who had graduated only
about year apart, had rather different career
rhythms. All of this reinforced some anticipated
informal career planning discussions that the
three of us had wanted to do.

Our reflections were extended as we worked
together on other projects throughout the summer of Jerry's visit and as we prepared this piece
for Peter and Susan's book. That preparation
was done via fax and Internet, and made us
really wish we could meet face-to-face again.
Even so, this non-face-to-face mode of communication has come to form the cornerstone
of much of our collaboration with each other
and with other scholarly communities.

All the reflecting and soul-searching described
above led us to look at our career rhythms as
being part of journeys whose destinations are
something to strive for but are never reached.
We articulate these journeys with three sharply
distinct voices. We present below the voices of
each of the trio members, not only for the
insights they provide us, but for any insights
our readers may find in them as well.

Jerry's Voice

I am the senior one among us; my postdoctoral career goes back nearly 30 years. I have
been a tenured full professor since 1973 and
have held a chaired professorship since 1984. I
started at Southern Illinois University, Carbondale, and moved to Texas Tech as department
chair in 1981. As previously mentioned, I might
be considered to be in the late middle career
stage. Besides a scholarly interest in leadership,
wherever that takes me, one of my other interests is in the sociology of academe, from both
scholarly and personal standpoints.

I first developed a scholarly curiosity about
overseas treatments of leadership in the late
1970s. In 1980, I was able to spend a semester
at the University of Aston in Birmingham, England, and while there, I worked with Dian-
Marie Hosking, who has become increasingly

well known for her leadership work. Besides Dian, there were very few Europeans with serious interest in the scholarly study of leadership. Indeed, she and I worked very hard to locate what interest there was, and this was reflected in leadership symposia volumes that I coedited in the 1980s. I knew just enough about leadership developments outside North America to be dangerous.

At about this same time, I became acquainted with Timo Santalainen, a high-ranking Finnish banking official with a doctorate who also was an adjunct professor at the Helsinki School. He was visiting at Carbondale, and some time later he spent a year at Texas Tech. It was he who initially invited me to Finland. Given my continuing interest in developments outside the United States, I was eager to go, and in 1989 we finally worked things out for a short visit. There, as I took part in a series of symposia, I met Arja, who was well into her dissertation on leadership and change. I found her work on the processes involved in leadership and organizational change in the recently deregulated Finnish banking industry to be fascinating. This was my first exposure to grounded theory in leadership and I was hooked, even though my own training and research were built around survey approaches and sophisticated statistical analyses.

The connecting point between the two approaches was treatment of leadership as embedded within organizations. I served as what is called an *opponent* in the Finnish system, where for Arja's dissertation defense I grilled her before a very large public audience, for as long as I chose (up to four hours). For my part, this procedure and the traditional celebrations following Arja's successful defense formed a collegial and friendship bond that led us to follow up on her dissertation work. The dissertation seemed to provide a way of bringing together the strong traditional U.S. interest in leadership with the broader organizational and contextual interests of Europeans. The Finnish higher education system encouraged and supported travel and extended stays outside the country, and Arja and her family were able to spend a summer and a later follow-up year in Lubbock.

We submitted articles based on her dissertation to the *Academy of Management Journal* and *Organization Science* and had our hopes raised, only to have them dashed after a great deal of revision effort. This rejection caused us to think seriously about what it was we were trying to do and how we were going about it. We concluded, basically, that there were too many innovative notions packed into the same piece that made it both too long and too complex. First, there was a substantive innovation effort: to describe and reconceptualize leadership as a multiple-level organizational phenomenon with spiral configurations across time. Second, our grounded theory methodology was relatively unusual in leadership papers at the time, and our detailed reporting made the manuscript difficult, long, cumbersome, and not always clear.

We determined from this that we needed to write simpler, more highly focused papers. Ultimately, we refocused and reconceptualized some of the data and have now had successful work published in areas such as entrepreneurship (Ropo & Hunt, in press), higher education (Hunt & Ropo, in press), and even a leadership process examination of the decade-long tenure of General Motors former chair and CEO Roger Smith (Hunt & Ropo, 1995). Concurrently, a Texas Tech doctoral student completed a dissertation based heavily on Arja's dissertation work and the student, along with my colleague Kim Boal and I, are struggling mightily to get an acceptable revision published in a major journal. All of this is simply to point out that Arja's original work has had an impact in rather unexpected ways. Through all of this, Arja became very familiar with the U.S. publication system and I became impressed with the increasing difficulty of getting pieces, especially nontraditional pieces, published in major U.S. journal outlets.

We both saw our relationship as a uniquely synergistic one and frequently discussed why this might be so. We concluded that personality, interests, and international factors seemed to be intertwined. We came to trust each other implicitly; everything was in the open, and there were no power games. We had similar senses of humor and similar underlying values concerning work, and so on. Internationally, our experiences were very different but very complementary. Arja questioned mainstream thinking and pushed the innovation envelope (something emphasized throughout her doctoral studies)—for her, these were inherent in scholarly work.

Though dramatically different from Arja in scholarly background, training, and career stage, I basically valued innovation. As Arja and I worked together, our complementary personalities, international orientations, and constructive differences in research approaches came together in unique ways. This working together has not always been painless or easy, but it has been very satisfying. Given this synergy, we had talked many times about my spending a semester in Finland. Arja was able to get the funds held for my summer visit, which involved the previously discussed national doctoral seminars as well as the completion of some of our earlier work and initiation of new projects.

As far as my career rhythms are concerned, these collaborations will make no difference in tenure or promotion. Also, given the current cutbacks in financial support for higher education in Texas, even very successful collaborations are likely to have only minimal merit-raise impact. What these kinds of collaborations can do for me is teach me about new aspects of leadership through work with international colleagues and, I hope, broaden the community of scholars aware of my own work. Maybe this will encourage, in some small way, more integration of U.S. and European work. In any case, these collaborations have certainly provided me with an additional set of colleagues with whom it is a pleasure to associate, in what for me is still an exotic part of the world.

Arja's Voice

I am a female associate professor of management at the School of Business Administration at the University of Tampere in Finland. I am married to an education scholar, and we have two children. For the past 2 years I have been "acting" full professor because the position opened up after an older scholar retired. The placement process is still pending (after $2\frac{1}{2}$ years). Along with that, I have served as the director of the business school for the past 3 years. To understand some of the rhythms involved in my past and future scholarly career journey, one needs to know that I got my doctorate in 1989.

I feel that my career has fallen into a "competency trap," a term used by Levinthal and March (1993) in discussing the "myopia of learn-

ing." In fact, I have used two different routes to end up trapped: the *scholarly route* and the *service route*. Some contextual aspects, such as the reward and promotion system in the Finnish higher education system, recent resource cuts, and the university survival games described below, have mediated and accelerated the trapping process. Shortly I'll fill in some details, but first I will describe what my scholarly route looks like.

Very early in my scholarly career, when I was still working on my licentiate and doctoral degrees, I was exposed to international challenges in the form of workshops in Brussels, Stuttgart, and other European cities. My research adviser, Professor Risto Tainio, encouraged me to step outside national borders and meet the challenges of a broader context. In the mid-1980s I studied for a year in Pittsburgh, Pennsylvania, where, among other things, I attended Ralph Kilmann's doctoral seminars. That's where I first encountered the U.S. standards of presenting papers and communicating my own research ideas. It was a hands-on experience that was reinforced later when I started working with Jerry. However, before I began to work with Jerry, I visited the United States a few times. Each time I was fortunate enough to discuss my research interests with well-known organizational scholars in high-profile schools. At that time, I naively thought that scholarly wisdom was contagious: All one needed to do was keep hanging out with the right people. Later I found out about the blood, sweat, and tears side of the business as well.

External reviewers are used for doctoral dissertations in my country, and in recent years, more and more of the reviewers have been foreign scholars (further encouraging the crossing of cultural borders). Because my research topic was leadership, Jerry Hunt, as a well-known leadership scholar, was considered eminently qualified to evaluate the scholarly contribution in my work. Obviously he saw some potential in it, because ever since we have been working together on different projects: conference papers, joint presentations, publications, organization of national and international workshops, and the like.

Working closely with an already well-known scholar has had its highlights and its dark side. Jerry's vast experience in scholarly projects has almost overwhelmed me. I have concretely felt the "Matthew effect" described by Hunt and Blair (1987), in which those with much receive much and those with little receive little, or what little they currently have is taken away. My name, when teamed with Jerry's name, has often been downplayed or even deleted on some occasions. I have been rather sensitive about this. It seems that the name of an unknown scholar from another part of the world who is hardly identifiable to anyone, male or female, collaborating with a well-known scholar is easy for some editors and conference organizers to overlook.

Each time I have gone through the same steps: First, I notice that I have been overlooked (what Jerry and I have come to call the "Rodney Dangerfield, I don't get no respect" syndrome). Second, I feel hurt. Third, I tell myself to go for it! I deserve some respect here also. Fourth, I talk to Jerry about the problem. Sometimes he has not noticed the deletion of my name in a conference program or something similar. Most often, Jerry makes an extra effort to relate to me as a colleague, not as a patronizing mentor. Fifth, Jerry takes action by calling the editor or conference organizer to express our concern. Sometimes my name appears in an appendix (that nobody reads) or is simply omitted from a conference program.

I feel rather ambivalent about these occasions. On the one hand, I do not want to be remembered as a troublemaker or an aggressive feminist. On the other hand, I have done my fair share in our joint projects and should be credited for that accordingly. Little by little, I have become more thick-skinned in this respect and now consider my scholarly contribution to be as taken for granted as Jerry's.

The brightest highlights of our collaboration have been found in the almost endless brainstorming sessions we have had in which the contradictions between our backgrounds and personal preferences in doing research have led to innovative ideas and eventual papers. Jerry's more linear thinking and my grounded theory type of case study, processual methodology, with nonlinear circles and spirals, have kept our joint work very dynamic. This dynamism and being on the edge has not, however, paved the way for the kind of scholarship we desire if one simply counts the number of articles so far accepted in the better-known U.S. journals. A part of my scholarly trap is that Jerry and I feel that we are doing the right thing, and that our work has the

potential for innovative theory development. However, we are still working to present our very different material so that it meets the criteria of these journal outlets. I am learning to persevere!

It also is very important to note that the fact that English is not my native language is an extra hurdle to my becoming a scholar recognized outside Finland. Having English as my second language, I feel that native English-speaking scholars have a big advantage in having their work known. For me, teaming up with people like Jerry has been necessary, but again not painless. How would you feel if you constantly encountered the joke that "your English is better than my Finnish" (after studying English 6 years at school and 3 years at the university)? This shows the difficulty of mastering English well enough to meet scholarly publication standards.

I have made some choices, partly unconsciously, that have restricted my progress in an international scholarly career. First, I have not played by traditional objectivist rules. Instead, I have been an opportunist when engaging in processual case studies that are very time- and labor-intensive, hard to report, and often too complex to be published in the journals to which we have submitted them.

Second, teaming up closely with U.S. scholars has attuned me to the "U.S. model" of scholarship, although I do not want to conform to U.S.-based leadership approaches. Ever since our initial contact, Jerry and I have had a vision of mutual contribution. We definitely have something to say to the community of leadership scholars. My contribution is to encourage some insights into leadership by providing fundamentally different conceptual views and a different methodological orientation. I think Jerry and I are "using" each other as vehicles for making innovations in the leadership field. All the while, I have stood against "importing" U.S. models of leadership into my country.

Third, with my background, making a scholarly breakthrough would call for, beyond a genius message and an angel's touch in writing (a touch in English, at that), a total commitment to research, with no interruptions from any other side of human life—that is, self-centered egoism. I am not sure if I am up to such total commitment or even would like to be.

Finally, I feel that my scholarly route, the way I have approached it, has led me into a trap because I got a head start and know that I am doing the right thing by moving in the directions described above. However, in that context, it will call for a big stretch to be as successful as I would like. Having recently worked with people other than Jerry and related more to European and Scandinavian organization scholars, I have come to see the possibility of becoming a member of a research community that is culturally closer to mine and focuses more specifically on my interests. I will continue working with Jerry and hope to be part of a research community that is close to our mutual interests.

The service route is still another aspect of my competency trap. It is typical in my country for people to receive all their degrees at the same university. Gradually, one ends up being a faculty member at the same school. Having this kind of background myself, over many years I have developed a deep commitment to the common good of my school. The business school at the University of Tampere is small, some 35 full-time faculty members and about 15 researchers and other staff. This means that once you get your doctorate, you are hooked. I had been at the school long enough and worked on different projects reasonably well without irritating too many, so that I eventually was picked for more responsible tasks, whether I wanted them or not.

The directorship of the Tampere business school carries a 3-year term that rotates among subject areas (accounting and finance, management, marketing, private law). In addition, the director must be a member of the school council. In my case, all the pieces came together in January 1992, 2 years after I received my doctorate. Despite my arguing that I was not the right person because I was leaving for the United States within 6 months to work with Jerry, I was chosen as director of the business school.

One might think it a piece of cake to head a small school like this, but for several reasons, my term has not been easy. First, funding was cut by 20% and a threatened merger with another business school in another city forced us to develop a working partnership with the University of Technology in our city. Second, there were growing concerns about teaching and research quality in the overall higher education system, and evaluation approaches needed to be developed. Also, a national-level act or governance system (equivalent to an accreditation

system defining the structure of business studies nationwide) was under renewal, and I was chosen for the group to do the job. Third, when schools and departments became profit centers, responsibility for creating and staying within budgets was laid on directors and department heads. Besides all the above tasks, I had my usual teaching load, plus doctoral students to advise. Here, teaching became a sideline in my work. Fortunately, I was able to give my students interesting insights into managing a professional organization in a bureaucratic system that strives for more dynamism—and I got good course evaluations.

When I came back from the United States in 1993, work morale was extremely low. People had given up. Fortunately, we had a sizable body of young and more senior scholars on board, my friend and colleague Päivi among them. We started working intensively to revamp the outdated management curriculum. Later (after 1½ years), it turned out that we showed the way for the other subject area groups to engage in the same type of process.

Simultaneously, a joint project for all of us was to start thinking strategically: how to position our school among other business schools, to find out our strengths (the weaknesses were obvious) and develop a vision for the future. Committing people and redefining the vision collaboratively turned out to be a very time-consuming and stressful process. My days were full of meetings, either at the school or in the university, in town or out of town.

In completing my term as director, the accomplishments are clear; because of our strategy work, the Ministry of Education is not on our case anymore. Instead, we have received some extra resources to reinforce the Tampere Management Network. To improve our financial status, some long-term agreements have been made to compensate us for continuing education, and some other external fund-raising efforts have been successful. As a high point of an even longer-term effort that intensified quite recently, the city of Tampere finally announced that it will cover the costs for a new full professorship for the next 4 years in an area that is critical in our strategic vision. These innovative starts are the results of true joint efforts between and among our faculty members and some external stakeholders. I am especially happy about the dynamic spirit and the positive atmosphere that we have continued to enjoy.

The trap in the service route is that the more one works, the more one gets new tasks—and the less time one has for scholarly work. Also, the psychic rewards in service work are more immediate in a system where the pay is the same regardless of performance. Scholarly activity can help with travel money and grants, and teaching is becoming increasingly more recognized, but it is all too easy to forget that when the chips are down and professorships are being filled, it is scholarly achievements that count.

I can see two ultimate routes out of my competency trap. The first is for me to make exclusive, either/or choices. That looks like a pretty narrow route, where I would need to harness my knowledge and skills for only one purpose in life. The second route would be to split my career into periods that can contribute to each other. For example, my practitioner experience may shed some light on scholarly problems concerning how to manage professional service organizations—the current core of our business school focus on service management. Taking the second route would call for self-discipline and control to avoid dropping too much either in abstract scholarly work or in service. Here, good scholarly networks with people like Jerry and Päivi would be very helpful. Also, I would need to accept the contradictions of academic life. That may mean recognizing the different expectations that I can reasonably have toward myself while being engaged in either scholarly or service tasks. However, totally disengaging those two would mean abstracting an aspiring scholar from life and denying her the potential of eventually achieving scholarly innovations.

Päivi's Voice

I am a junior academic compared with my coauthors, Jerry and Arja. I see myself as being in the late beginning or early middle career stage. As I write this, I am a full-time researcher and am completing a year at the Center for Corporate Strategy and Change led by Professor Andrew Pettigrew at the Warwick Business School in England. My husband is a medical doctor, and we have two daughters.

My university education in the 1980s took place in an era of increasing enthusiasm toward internationalization in Finland. I had previously developed an interest in foreign countries and languages during my early school years. One of the advantages of choosing to take my doctoral degree at the Helsinki School was that there my research supervisers were internationally oriented; they had good contacts with the international research community and encouraged their students to attend workshops, seminars, and tutorials in Europe and in the United States. Therefore, my orientation toward an international scholarly community was an easy decision. Of course, in addition to my personal plans and objectives, the possibility of making this decision was influenced by other issues, such as the interests and preferences of my family. The support of my husband and children has been invaluable; they have always been eager to live abroad and to collect new experiences as a trade-off for a more secure life in Finland.

Reinforcing our introduction to this chapter, from my perspective, an academic career is indeed a journey. For me, using the journey metaphor highlights two important issues that we three coauthors look at from three different angles. One picture is no more right than the other; all are just different pieces of the whole (or three voices describing our journeys). Therefore, the journeys and destinations can look very different from U.S. and non-U.S. points of view, for example.

First, for me, there are several ways of making the journey, depending on one's cultural and national background and the characteristics of the educational and evaluation systems to which one has been exposed. For example, a journey can emphasize national or international aspects or service versus scholarly aspects. This implies that, although it helps to list the ingredients of an "optimal" career journey (such as publications in international journals), many of us (particularly outside the U.S. system) find it difficult to combine these ingredients with the values and objectives we have in our national academic work.

Second, a journey is a combination of more or less rational intentions and decisions and forces enabling and constraining these decisions, such as one's personality, ambitions, experiences, and family circumstances. In comparison to Arja's story, I feel that I have been more in control of my own choices. I have developed close contacts with more than one national business school. This has given me the opportunity to choose among different types of values and preferences—for example, the Helsinki School is more scholarship oriented, whereas Tampere is more service oriented.

Although I do not feel trapped like Arja, I do recognize the importance of the issues she discusses. At the same time, in my own work, I have faced some of the scholarly versus service dilemmas she mentions. However, the difference in our emphasis is that I have stressed a scholarly orientation as opposed to a service orientation earlier in my career. Let us now look at my journey in more detail.

After finishing my doctoral studies at the Helsinki School, I thought that it would be useful to work abroad for a year to be able to broaden my perspective and skills concerning the international aspects of academic life. Luckily, my family was prepared to follow me. Considering my work, I had three specific objectives. First, I wanted to learn about the practice of research work outside Finland. Second, I was hoping to make contacts with foreign researchers in my topic area. Finally, I wanted to improve my English, so that I could be as confident as possible in using a language other than Finnish.

With the help of the contacts of my research supervisors, I got the opportunity to work at the Scandinavian Consortium for Organizational Research (SCANCOR), led by Professor Jim March at Stanford University. The year at Stanford was very interesting and valuable, both for my family and for me, in terms of work and social life. However, that year also made me see very concretely the differences between U.S. and Finnish (also European, in a more general sense) research orientations. In Finland, some of my research colleagues had become involved in longitudinal case studies and qualitative research methods, combined with an interest in the impact of the contextual factors on business in Finland. I also had taken this approach in my dissertation: a historical case study emphasizing the managerial processes involved in the product mix changes in one Finnish case during 40 years. For my colleagues and me, trying to understand aspects of business deeply embedded in the Finnish society and its historical development (or any other context) was a valu-

able goal. Many of us also were specializing in studying certain industries or sectors.

However, it was rather difficult to find academics at Stanford who had carried out this type of research or, if they had, who would have been interested in sharing their thoughts with a novice in the field. One conclusion I drew from that year was that I was too inexperienced and not established enough to be able to benefit fully from what Stanford could offer.

At Stanford, I was struck by the overall competitiveness and efficiency of the U.S. system. One major difference, compared with Finland, is the very defined focus of research topics and the relatively narrow but exhaustive expertise of academic scholars in their own fields. In Finland, there are so few of us that to be successful nationally one usually needs to have broad knowledge across several topic areas. The advice given to me in Finland after I finished my dissertation was to abandon the topic area of my thesis completely and start working in a new area, optimally one as different as possible in terms of substance, methods, and research design.

I did not take this advice seriously, but continued to work within the topic area of my dissertation and developed new interests only after 2 or 3 years. The result was that, nationally, my research work and my expertise did not cover as many fields as emphasized by the Finnish evaluation system. In other contexts (particularly from the U.S. perspective), my approach is still not considered well defined and focused enough. Is it possible to resolve this dilemma by simultaneously working harder to become more narrowly focused within a specific field of research and to develop wider expertise on several topic areas, research designs, and methodological approaches? I still do not have the answer.

Despite increasing globalization, Finland (like other countries) is still a unique society in terms of its own culture, traditions, and practices. Thus the distances between local and national and between national and international aspects of academic life persist, in both positive and less positive terms. When we wish to broaden the orientation of our work, we need to change our working language (most often to English) and usually be prepared to work abroad for both short and longer periods of time. These steps, particularly if one takes them before one has established a strong position within the Finnish academic world, may distance one from the Finnish system in many ways.

After my year at Stanford, I returned to the University of Tampere, where I had taken my master's and licentiate degrees. There I worked as "acting" full professor for a year (the same chair that Arja mentioned). That year taught me much about the various aspects of the Finnish system: the huge load of administrative responsibilities and the time constraints of considering research work in the context of a small business school with only one chair in each discipline. The differences among the various routes within academic life (the service route and the scholarly route, for example) and the possible traps in considering exclusive choices between these routes became very obvious to me during that year.

For us Finns, the service route has typically been locally or nationally oriented (although it may also cross cultural borders, particularly later in one's career). Traditionally, the service route has been a respected way of making a career within Finnish academic circles. In contrast to Arja, I have managed to be more persistent in avoiding the service route; I have accomplished this by "being on the move" during the past 6 years (or perhaps the other faculty members have seen my lack of talent in that area?).

During this time, I have been working with 1- to 3-year contracts in three countries and in four different business schools. Despite this, I have managed to develop continuing cooperation with some national and international researchers (for which I thank fax machines and the Internet). In contrast to Arja, I have worked mostly with European scholars (instead of U.S. scholars). I feel this gives me more freedom in terms of what we consider useful and interesting research (as I see these scholars' interests as more attuned to mine) and in terms of where we try to publish our research.

In the beginning of my career, the decision to follow the scholarly route exclusively and to combine that with an international orientation seemed to be right for me. However, it meant ignoring many local and national career aspects and expectations. Later, I have faced the situation where, besides experiencing many of the same problems in publishing as Arja and many other Finns, I still lack extensive experience and the rewards of the service route. Considering my wish to work in Finland, at least for now, I have since realized the need somehow to combine these two routes. Thus I also have developed an interest in and deep appreciation for service work. This is mostly because of my positive experiences in working together with Arja in our department at the University of Tampere during the recent crisis period she has described above.

Despite increasing awareness of the problems in combining different aspects of academic work, I am still very satisfied with my decision to give more emphasis to an international scholarly route during the earlier years of my career. I feel that at this stage it might be easier for me (because of established research contacts, for example) to continue this orientation, even though I could use more time in local and national service work in the future.

Finally, my conclusion is that my career journey, with its mix of ambitions, is as complex as life itself—and what else could it be? Coming from a small and, from the U.S. perspective, peripheral country, with a wish to develop a career that is respected both nationally and internationally, one needs to be ready to make many compromises and to live with contradictory expectations and evaluation systems. Perhaps this is exactly the point that makes our work interesting and worth the effort.

Ruminations

It seems to us that international collaboration is becoming more and more ubiquitous. It is now increasingly common even in areas such as leadership—at one time viewed as almost a peculiarly American research area. It also is becoming increasingly common in the United States in virtually all fields, as the so-called global management imperative (Schermerhorn, Hunt, & Osborn, 1994) spreads its impact even into scholarly areas. At the same time, small but highly developed nations, such as Finland, have encouraged such collaboration for some time and in many ways, as have numerous other countries throughout the world.

Ubiquitous as international collaboration is, our individual discussions above suggest that there is no single way to embark on scholarly career journeys involving such collaboration.

Arja's journey, with its close collaboration (but with her own unique contributions) with a U.S. scholar and its early emphasis on a wide range of service activities, is one form. Päivi's is another, where she has deliberately sought out extended stays with colleagues in other countries. These stays have involved a heavy, indeed virtually exclusive, research emphasis, with no consistent teaching or service. And although Päivi has had an extended visit at SCANCOR in the United States, most of her work has been with European colleagues. Jerry's journey has taken still another form, where, using an already established career base, he has most recently collaborated closely with Finnish scholars, especially Arja, while still maintaining contact with others in Switzerland, the United Kingdom, and the Netherlands.

The above discussion also illustrates a second point, namely, that international collaboration can be developed at different career stages and thus can have different impacts, careerwise. For example, Arja developed her collaboration very early and then struggled with how to reconcile that with increasingly strong service demands. Most recently, she has been concerned with broadening her collaborative efforts, maintaining her previous collaboration with Jerry, and still keeping her hand in service activities, but at a lower intensity. Throughout, it has been a given that she maintain a strong teaching presence. In contrast, Päivi, who has been out of school almost as long as Arja, had both relatively broad and deep collaborative research efforts at the very beginning of her career. However, she has had little in the way of service or teaching responsibilities. Finally, Jerry developed his international collaboration much later in his career, and it has been a far less central activity for him than it has been for either of his Finnish colleagues.

A third related point is that international collaboration takes different forms and is of differing intensity across scholarly careers. Arja's and Päivi's levels of collaboration have been very intense very early—Arja's then dropped back with service and is now increasing again and broadening. For Päivi, we might expect its intensity to lessen as she attempts to integrate

service and teaching. Jerry's international collaborative intensity has waxed and waned and changed direction since it started in the early 1980s, and is likely to continue at a high level into the future. For Arja and Päivi, we would expect even more change in intensity as they spin out the much longer remaining segments of their careers.

Finally, we touch on the relationships between scholarly career progress and international collaboration. Although such collaboration is increasingly commonplace, it still seems to be possible, at least in the United States (with its strongly developed system and norms), to build a successful career without it. That is probably less likely to be the case in countries outside the United States. Nevertheless, there is not currently a one-to-one relationship between international collaboration and a scholarly career. However, we are convinced that this relationship will become more direct in the future, as the global imperative makes international collaboration not only ubiquitous, but increasingly important.

References

Hunt, J. G., & Blair, J. D. (1987). Content, process and the "Matthew effect" among management academics. *Yearly Review of Management of the Journal of Management, 13,* 191-210.

Hunt, J. G., & Ropo, A. (1995). Multi-level leadership: Grounded theory and mainstream theory applied to the case of General Motors. *Leadership Quarterly, 6,* 379-412.

Hunt, J. G., & Ropo, A. (in press). Systems motivation, leadership, and teaching in an innovative academic setting. In J. G. Bess (Ed.), *Teaching well and liking it: The motivation of faculty in higher education.* Baltimore: Johns Hopkins University Press.

Levinthal, D. A., & March, J. G. (1993). The myopia of learning. *Strategic Management Journal, 14,* 95-112.

Ropo, A., & Hunt, J. G. (in press). Entrepreneurial processes as virtuous and vicious spirals in a changing opportunity structure: A paradoxical perspective. *Entrepreneurship Theory and Practice.*

Schermerhorn, J. R., Jr., Hunt, J. G., & Osborn, R. N. (1994). *Managing organizational behavior* (5th ed.). New York: John Wiley.

Becoming a Reviewer

As I look back at literally hundreds of reviews, what is most clear is that the audience for the reviews—the audience in my mind, of course—has changed quite substantially. Where I once wrote for editors, I now write for authors. . . . In part, the audience has changed because I have grown more secure and more confident in my ability to write a good review. In part also, however, the audience has changed because I have grown more caring about the objectives of my reviews.

Elaine Romanelli (p. 264)

I believe that, on the average, most authors spend their valuable time, energy, and resources to work on things that they are committed to and consider valuable. The reviewer's task is to appreciate authors' efforts and lend a sympathetic ear to what they want to say. This is our collective responsibility. The role of a reviewer, as a critic and adviser at the same time, is to fulfill this collective obligation.

Huseyin Leblebici (p. 273)

My observations of activist reviewers suggest that they enact a more humane, emotionally satisfying, and intellectually challenging role than reviewers who follow the approach of the first and second umpires. They enact this role by building reputations with journal editors for doing constructive, developmental reviews. Editors often start sending activist reviewers papers that seem especially likely to benefit from their efforts. When this happens, activist reviewers find themselves working on papers that improve more during the review process, that these papers are more likely to be published, and, that irrespective of the ultimate publication decisions, authors get more valuable feedback.

Alan D. Meyer (p. 278)

The process of reviewing for professional journals has a formative influence on the lives of most academics. As researchers who have their work reviewed by others, academics must cope with the frustration, anger, and embarrassment of having research that is highly reflective of their time, effort, and creativity, at worst, rejected or, at best, thoroughly critiqued. Regardless of the ultimate outcome, reading a reviewer's comments is usually an upending experience that stimulates uniquely ritualistic ways of coping (see Chapters 12, 14, and 30 in this volume, by Ashford, Murnighan, and Sutton, respectively; see also the chapters on reviewing in Cummings & Frost, 1995). Yet few researchers would deny (unless asked just after receiving reviews) the importance of the review process for strengthening the depth and soundness of research contributions to the organizational sciences. These outcomes are the results of the developmental role of reviewers, one that is likely to be less apparent to authors than the evaluative function, but that is equally significant in its effects on the field.

The review process affects academics in still another way when they are invited to serve as reviewers who evaluate the work of others. Receiving such an invitation is usually a heady event, symbolizing a rite of passage from novice researcher to the status of one who has acquired a sufficient knowledge base, methodological competence, and big-picture perspective on the organizational sciences to critique and evaluate the work of others. However, the acceptance of such an invitation also symbolizes that an academic is willing to devote considerable time and effort toward having an impact on the field by improving the work of others, rather than investing in it through his or her own research stream. Thus reviewing moves an academic further along the generative continuum, increasing his or her responsibility for the work of others.

Fortunately, for the field and for individual academics, most reviewers concurrently wear author and reviewer hats. The experience of receiving reviews on their own work from others typically serves as a powerful and often painful reminder that reviewers are not engaged in a mechanical process of evaluation and development. Instead, they are participants in a series of intense conversations between reviewers, authors, and editors. These conversations have real-world implications for the egos, careers, and lives of all involved, as well as for the development of the academic discipline. As a result, most reviewers struggle to find the boundaries of their role within the publication process; such struggles are vividly reflected in the opening quotations.

In this section, three academics—Elaine Romanelli, Huseyin Leblebici, and Alan Meyer—reflect on the reviewing process as they have come to view it after many years of high involvement (i.e., simultaneous membership on several editorial committees). Their comments show many similarities in their views. For example, all note the huge time demands associated with reviewing, particularly when one holds an activist definition of the task, and the need to complete the task as efficiently as possible in order to satisfy their other role demands. As Huseyin Leblebici comments after describing a particular review process, "After 7 hours of concentrated effort, it is not possible to avoid pondering whether or not it was worth it" (p. 272). Similarly, Alan Meyer notes, "However, as a reviewer assumes an activist role, the time and energy he or she devotes to each manuscript are almost certain to increase. Working with authors, particularly less experienced ones, to develop their work into publishable papers is time-consuming and emotionally involving. One must be careful to invest effort where it is most apt to yield a return" (p. 278).

All three reviewers display strong concern for the human element in the review process, a concern that is undoubtedly strengthened by their own experiences as authors. They are clearly aware of the negative effects that thoughtless or tactless reviews can have on authors' egos and self-esteem, and they advocate reviewer-author dialogues that convey constructive criticism without destroying an author's sense of self-worth. Their intent is to motivate authors to strengthen their research products. As Elaine Romanelli reports:

> But not so fast. I learned some hard new lessons about reviewing when, during my first year as a junior faculty member, I got some reviews on a paper of my own. I will never forget Reviewer 2, who called my hypotheses "vapid and inane." Those words set the tone for virtually every comment in the review. . . .
>
> I also vowed never to be callous in my comments to authors. I had learned too well how debilitating it is to contend with a hostile reviewer. It takes a lot of time to be angry and hurt. (pp. 265, 266)

A third common element in these essays concerns the reviewers' struggles to find the boundaries of their developmental role. A central issue in this arena is how much of an activist perspective researchers should take in challenging authors to raise their research to the highest possible level. Is the reviewer's task simply to make a judgment call about a paper's acceptability for publication in its current form? Is it to improve the paper as much as possible within the parameters of the existing framework, by tightening linkages to theory, strengthening methodology, reinterpreting findings, and clarifying ambiguities in language? Or is it, in some cases, to help authors write papers that go far beyond their current conceptualizations of the issues?

Each of the contributors here provides his or her own view of these boundaries, and each notes the evolution of that view over time as his or her reviewing experi-

ence increased. Some clearly feel that it is acceptable to push an author to write a different paper from that originally submitted, one that goes considerably further in developing theory or integrating different literature. Alan Meyer advocates the activist role, noting:

> When I submitted a paper of my own to *ASQ*, it was assigned to an associate editor, Jerry Salancik, who . . . took an interventionist approach. Jerry saw in my paper a more ambitious article and a more important contribution than I did. With the reviewers' help, he pushed me to find that paper and write it. . . . The prospect of offering this sort of assistance to other authors revived my fading enthusiasm for reviewing. (p. 278)

Elaine Romanelli expresses greater reservations about the activist role in developing papers:

> A few years ago, at an editorial board meeting, this [senior] colleague called into question what he considered the pervasive practice among reviewers of asking an author to write the paper that the reviewer would have written. Guilty, I thought. It is not the reviewer's job to describe the perfect paper the author might write. It is arrogant of a reviewer to believe that he or she could know enough, or even read enough, to do competently all the research authors have tackled. The only real job of the reviewer is to show authors how they might have done their identified research better. (p. 266)

Finally, all three authors comment on how much their own views of the reviewing process (and, indirectly, the conscientiousness with which they undertake the task) have been shaped by the reviewing behaviors of respected colleagues in the field. These comments suggest that reviewing is another professional skill that is best learned through observation of other master scholars performing the task. As Huseyin Leblebici reveals:

> Gerald R. Salancik and Richard L. Daft probably influenced my writing style the most. As a colleague in the same institution for a long time, I had the opportunity to observe especially Jerry in action. His deep commitment to helping guide authors made a lasting impression on my own style of reviewing. I had seen him spend long hours at his computer, trying to write detailed, constructive reviews for even those manuscripts that were rejected by the reviewers. His sense of duty was always apparent, both in his idea that every manuscript deserves reviewing and in his diligence in carefully articulating the reasons for his decisions. (p. 272)

In combination, these three essays provide an insightful view of the review process and the reviewer's task. As Huseyin Leblebici notes, by diminishing, even a bit, the "black box" image of reviewing that many authors have, we may also reduce their suspicions regarding the process and thereby enhance their motivation to respond constructively.

Reference

Cummings, L. L., & Frost, P. J. (Eds.). (1995). *Publishing in the organizational sciences* (2nd ed.). Thousand Oaks, CA: Sage.

26 Becoming a Reviewer

LESSONS SOMEWHAT PAINFULLY LEARNED

Elaine Romanelli

As I begin this essay, there are three manuscripts sitting on my desk awaiting review. One is already late, and I am feeling guilty. Two are due within the next week, and I am feeling pressured. Editors' protestations notwithstanding, I know that new manuscripts will arrive within a week or two of my returning these. I am also dimly aware of several manuscripts under revision that will probably return to my desk for second review sometime in the near future. In more than 10 years of reviewing now, it seems that there have been only a few short periods when I have not had at least one manuscript to review. It strikes me, then, that one of the most basic challenges of reviewing is handling the ubiquitous deadline. The question I have struggled with during all that time is how to write a good review efficiently.

What does *efficiency* mean? It means that the review is begun and completed in a relatively short period. There are many ways to do this. One way that I have heard espoused by many colleagues is for the reviewer just to start writing comments, section by section, paragraph by paragraph, as many as are needed, until the entire manuscript has been addressed. For this method, only one thorough reading is required. Another way, also frequently espoused, is to skim the manuscript quickly, making notes about important problems or questions until two or three, or some number deemed sufficient by the reviewer, have been found. The reviewer can then simply write up these few central problems and recommend revision or rejection depending on the severity of the problems. In those rare cases when the reviewer finds few or no major problems, he or she can note this fact, point out a few major contributions, and recommend acceptance.

I believe that there are positive aspects to both these approaches. The first is certainly thorough.

AUTHOR'S NOTE: This essay first appeared in *Publishing in the Organizational Sciences* (2nd ed.), edited by L. L. Cummings and Peter J. Frost (Sage Publications, 1995).

The author will be treated to a detailed exposition of virtually every question and issue that occurred to the reviewer. The second is probably very effective for gatekeeping for the journal. Manuscripts that exhibit a few basic problems need revision. Manuscripts that exhibit more than a few probably merit rejection, because the likelihood of successful revision tends to be low. I don't believe, however, that either approach satisfies an objective of writing a *good* review efficiently. In my experience (and I have tried all the ways), the first approach is comprehensive, but fails to clarify key problems that the author should address. The second approach is satisfactory for evaluation and probably points out some of the central difficulties, but fails to provide constructive help.

So what is a good review? Today, I think there are some rather straightforward answers to this question, all of which, I must acknowledge, are well presented in the major journals' "instructions to reviewers." A good review clearly identifies key contributions and problems in the manuscript. A good review provides constructive suggestions to the author for improving the manuscript. A good review provides consistent support for a recommendation to the editor about the disposition of the manuscript, and does so without necessarily revealing the recommendation. Unfortunately, although these objectives are straightforward, and I have always understood them in my mind, they have not been easy to achieve in a practical sense. Nobody taught me how to spot key contributions quickly. Nobody taught me the difference between constructive criticism—although it seems like I remember something from fifth grade on this—and just an elaborated list of a paper's deficiencies. Like too many aspects of an academic's job, the good review can be described, but the lessons for writing one are left to individual experimentation, self-doubt, and random conclusions.

It has been an interesting task, in contemplating this essay, to consider what I have learned about reviewing, and when I have learned it. In keeping with the motivations for this book, I think the best way I can tell the story of my learning is through the personal "passages" I have experienced. As I look back at literally hundreds of reviews, what is most clear is that the audience for the reviews—the audience in my mind, of course—has changed quite sub-

stantially. Where I once wrote for editors, I now write for authors. More on that below. In part, the audience has changed because I have grown more secure and more confident in my ability to write a good review. In part also, however, the audience has changed because I have grown more caring about the objectives of my reviews. The following sections identify the changes in the audiences and describe the lessons that have promoted the changes.

First Reviews:
Writing for Editors

I received my first manuscript to review when I was still a doctoral student. I felt both honored and challenged by the assignment. I had no published papers, only one book chapter accepted, and just a few conference presentations. Like most academics in the early stages of their careers, I had dreams of becoming a well-known and well-respected member of my profession. As I observed my mentors, I saw that they spent rather large amounts of time reviewing manuscripts. They were proud of being invited to serve as members of editorial boards of top-tier journals. As I scanned the lists of names on editorial boards, I saw that they comprised a lot of famous people whose names I also saw as authors of articles in the journals. Reviewing, apparently, was a route to status. I wanted to become a reviewer.

Thus when I got that first manuscript—and I am a little embarrassed to say this—before ever reading a word, I had only one objective: to get a second manuscript. Who gets manuscripts, of course, is controlled by editors. I had to figure out how to write a review that would impress the editor. In truth, I hadn't a clue. I thought I had to show that I was up on my literature, and that I knew the relevant research questions. I thought I should demonstrate competence at research methods. No fatal flaw should get by me. In keeping with the "instructions to reviewers to take into account clarity of writing," I supposed I should also help the authors to write more clearly. Thus I set out to comment, having read the paper maybe once, on virtually every aspect of the manuscript.

Needless to say, efficiency was nowhere on my mind (I didn't know then that it would be a problem to worry about). I spent at least a week worrying about the review and writing it, all the while ignoring the dissertation proposal I was supposed to be writing. I looked up and read many of the paper's important references. That first review was more than eight single-spaced pages long, organized according to sub-headings used by the author. I patiently explained problems in each of the sections and, with some pedantry, described how the author could do better. I didn't know then, and I don't know now, who that author was, but I hereby offer an apology.

As I look back at the review (yes, I still have it), I think maybe the only objective it met was thoroughness. At least the editor got plenty of fuel for the rejection that the paper received. The review was highly evaluative. Although I offered many suggestions for improvement, I don't believe the author got much constructive help for a revision. Mainly, I criticized.

A few months later, I received that second manuscript to review—and then I got a third, and a fourth. Apparently, I was now a reviewer. I followed much the same procedures as before in reviewing the new manuscripts, but two things seemed wrong. First, I was beginning to notice, and feel frustrated, that reviewing took an awful lot of time. I was reading a lot of articles—authors' references—that had little to do with my own research, and the reading didn't seem to be helping much with the reviewing anyway. I was also beginning to notice that editors were only once in a while mentioning my reviews in their letters to the authors. It is a strange fact of reviewing that the only feedback a reviewer ever gets directly on an individual review is the editor's letter to the author. How come my comments weren't guiding the editor's decisions and instructions?

I thought that maybe my reviews weren't sufficiently to the point. Almost certainly, this was true. Perhaps my reviews should focus more directly on the major problems in the manuscript. Maybe I should just concentrate on the central problems of the manuscript, so that the editor would have clear issues (that I had identified) to point to in the decision letter.

My reviews got shorter. I adopted the approach of identifying and discussing a few key problems. My reviews were finished more quickly. I didn't have to read papers in detail, and I didn't have to write comments on every issue that the papers addressed. I guess the real truth

is that I didn't have to bother helping authors to write better papers. As we all know from grading students' papers, evaluating is easier than explaining. For a while, it seemed that I had learned how to review efficiently. Simple gatekeeping was the ticket.

Later Reviews: Writing for Myself (or, The Paper I Would Have Written)

But not so fast. I learned some hard new lessons about reviewing when, during my first year as a junior faculty member, I got some reviews on a paper of my own. I will never forget Reviewer 2, who called my hypotheses "vapid and inane." Those words set the tone for virtually every comment in the review. The review was evaluative in the extreme, and constructive not at all. Once I was done cursing the reviewer for meanness, cowardice, and stupidity—not necessarily in that order—I was left to revise the paper so as to convince a reviewer who was on record for plain hostility toward my work. I was angry that I would have to respond to this reviewer in a tone that was "appreciative" for help that had not been given. I didn't know how to begin.

The other reviewers were more helpful. Reviewer 1 praised the study's basic research question. This was a very useful focusing device. Through that reviewer's restatement of my objectives, I could see what main line of argument my paper should follow. I was able to initiate the revision easily just by jettisoning all the extraneous discussion and fascinating nuances that were intelligible, in retrospect, only to me. Reviewer 3 liked the data, but pointed out ways in which they might be better analyzed. This reviewer, too, worked hard at linking the analyses to the questions of principal interest. These reviewers showed me how to revise the paper.

Somewhere about this time, I had a conversation with a senior colleague who was then an associate editor for a top-tier journal. He talked about writing, reviewing, and editing. He suggested that the best papers—that is, those that advanced understanding of organizations and got cited a lot—were those that had mainly only one good idea to present and clarify. I thought this was useful advice for me as a writer; maybe it wasn't such a good idea to integrate *all* the literature and solve quite all the empirical problems every time I wrote a paper. I decided that it was also a good guideline for me as a reviewer. Other reviewers had helped me to see what was interesting and important in my own work. Here was a positive contribution that I too could make. From that point forward, and to this day, my reviews always begin with a short statement of what the useful contribution of the paper might be.

I also vowed never to be callous in my comments to authors. I had learned too well how debilitating it is to contend with a hostile reviewer. It takes a lot of time to be angry and hurt. If I was not so "vapid and inane"—yes, it still rankles—as Reviewer 2 thought, then maybe I owed commensurate credit to the authors I was reviewing. I was pleased to see recently, in the "instructions to reviewers" of one top journal, *Administrative Science Quarterly*, some specific admonishments against scornful or dismissive remarks. The editors point out that the damage of a rude review extends well beyond just the author's hurt feelings. Authors who are too cavalierly dismissed or insulted may be reluctant to submit to the journal again, and some of those authors may someday write very good papers.

So I set out to be positive in my tone and helpful in my suggestions for improvement. One important thing I discovered quickly was that I changed my mind more often about a manuscript. Sometimes, especially for papers that seemed poor on first reading, when I tried to state their central contributions, I discovered new value. Sometimes a recommendation for rejection became a recommendation for revision. Maybe this is only a halo effect from my efforts to write the contribution. Nevertheless, it seems good to err on the side of supposing that the author has something to say.

Of course, this positive reviewing also opened up three new traps for me to fall into. First, there was growing disparity between the positive tone I was taking with the authors and the often negative evaluations I was presenting to the editors. I found myself writing long letters to editors, trying to bridge the gaps. Second, increasingly it seemed that I was spending vast amounts of time (and paper) explaining to authors just exactly how I thought they should revise their papers. Finally, none of this was very efficient. The reviews were getting very long again, and I was expending rather a lot of creative energy on other people's papers.

I don't know that I've ever solved the first problem satisfactorily. I still write letters to the editors, though they are shorter. I still worry, especially when I get a revision to review, that authors haven't fully "heard" my requests for major revision. Perhaps it is true that the tension between evaluation and constructive help cannot be completely resolved. One small solution I have hit upon is to close the review with a restatement of what I like about the paper, but also a summary of the revisions I think will be required. Mainly, however, I still leave it as the editor's job to communicate the likelihood of successful revision, assuming that revision is the decision.

For the second problem, another senior colleague provided much useful help. A few years ago, at an editorial board meeting, this colleague called into question what he considered the pervasive practice among reviewers of asking an author to write the paper that the reviewer would have written. Guilty, I thought. It is not the reviewer's job to describe the perfect paper the author might write. It is arrogant of a reviewer to believe that he or she could know enough, or even read enough, to do competently all the research authors have tackled. The only real job of the reviewer is to show authors how they might have done their identified research better.

My reviews got shorter again. They also got quicker.

Current Reviews: Writing for Authors

I began this essay by talking about efficiency and the career concerns that dominated my early reviews. Although it seems obvious that neither efficiency nor career should drive the reviewing process, I believe that both, in subtle but powerful ways, do direct the objectives of reviewers. At least this has been true for me. I would like to close this essay by talking about what efficiency means to me today, and also about how some career changes have affected my reviewing processes.

Efficiency seems a mundane and possibly even a dangerous place to begin an essay on reviewing. On the mundane side, I do not suppose that what I have written is particularly new or insightful for any experienced reviewer. Certainly there are reviewers who have learned these lessons faster and better than I have. On the dangerous side, it would be wrong to convey that efficiency alone is an appropriate objective for reviewing. Efficiency is only a plain flat need for those of us who review frequently.

Efficiency became a silent objective in my reviewing because I seemed always to be struggling to meet deadlines. As you can see from the opening paragraph of this essay, I still struggle with deadlines, but in a different sort of way. Ten years ago, the deadlines were tough because when I began a review I never knew how long it would take to complete. The process was wholly unstructured. Today, when I approach a review, I know that it will be done in just a few hours' time. Deadlines are a problem only because I tend to procrastinate.

I hope it is clear that the keys to this hard-won efficiency are focus and collegiality. Focus saves time because it leads the reviewer to direct comments toward fundamental problems that need to be fixed and away from extraneous issues. For example, if the data overall are inappropriate for the research question, additional amounts of effort don't need to be spent explaining problems with measurement. If the author has made major errors in describing the arguments of other theorists, then the hypotheses that are premised on the errors don't have to be criticized explicitly. The reviewer may wish to offer a brief comment or two about improvements in measures, or describe how hypotheses might change if theories are properly presented, but great detail is unnecessary. The rule of thumb that I use goes as follows: If revisions to improve the fundamental problems in the paper would clearly eliminate associated problems, I spend little time on the associated problems.

Note that I think this is also fair to the author. Nothing annoys me more, as a writer, than a reviewer who nitpicks his or her way through every detail of a manuscript after already calling for "a complete overhaul." Not only may I have to respond to all those comments, even though they may no longer be relevant, I feel somewhat humiliated. I would like a reviewer to give me a little credit, and a little room to revise my paper myself.

This brings me to collegiality: Collegiality saves time because it helps a reviewer to assume that the author is a competent professional who can probably revise a paper given some general good guidelines. Less detail about minor problems can mean more focus on the broad strokes that most revisions require. If the author can successfully address the large problems, the details can be handled in the second review. The details will always change in a revision, so why spend time in the first round identifying them all? It is not efficient and, in the end, it is not helpful.

Career changes also have led me to greater focus and collegiality in my reviews. Today, I think it is a little funny how concerned I was, 10 years ago, about getting that second manuscript to review. Little did I know that demand for reviewers is so great that reasonable intelligence and general familiarity with the basic questions and methods of our field are about all that is required. But perhaps my ignorance was a good thing. My desire to impress an editor, first to get a second manuscript and later to be the reviewer who gets cited in the editor's letter, led me to care a great deal about the quality of my review. I am uncomfortable, however, that impressing the editor may not the best objective for producing a helpful review for the author.

Eventually, I was invited to serve on an editorial board. This was a very nice reward for what had been, by then, several years of hard reviewing work. Of course, it also increased my workload, and efficiency became even more important. My attitudes also began to evolve. For a while, I was concerned with justifying the confidence that had been placed in me by the board membership. I wanted the editors to know that they'd made a good decision. Over time, however, as I became more and more secure about my abilities and my credentials as a reviewer, slowly, slowly, I stopped worrying about impressing the editors.

Today, I am a member of three editorial boards, and I have been a member of two more. Although I still feel honored to be invited, the achievement has lost just a bit of its excitement. In some funny way, I don't really care anymore whether I get papers to review. It goes without saying, but I'll say it anyway: Reviewing is a service that we provide to our profession and to our colleagues—a service, not a rung on a career ladder. Maybe learning this deep down is the final stage of becoming a reviewer.

27 The Act of Reviewing and Being a Reviewer

Huseyin Leblebici

It is a Friday noon, 2 weeks before the end of the fall semester. I go to check my mail and find several letters and a thick, wide envelope. I know from experience that it contains a manuscript to be reviewed. I know this because review manuscripts usually arrive near the end of the week and near the end of the semester. For some odd reason, I get my review requests during the second half of the week. They also arrive more frequently at certain points in the academic calendar—the beginning of the fall, when people finally complete their summer projects, or at the middle of the spring semester, when academicians submit their year-end activity reports. There are certainly particular rhythms to all aspects of academic life.

I dutifully open the envelope, look for the due date, and record it on my calendar. I approach every manuscript I receive with some apprehension. It could be a wonderful piece that can make me appreciate my colleagues'

ingenuity or a dreadful text that can make me lose all patience. Whatever its quality, however, it puts new demands on my time and energy. I now need to find a free afternoon or an evening to do the first reading of the paper. I scan the title, the abstract, and the references to see if I am familiar with the topic. Reviewers are always given the option to return manuscripts if they believe they cannot complete their reviews within the 3 to 4 weeks usually allotted. It is always tempting and sometimes wise to return manuscripts, but in this case, I know the editor personally and also know that such an act will cause an undesirable complication in the journal's schedule. Moreover, the topic is interesting and I may learn something.

A week later, on a Thursday evening, I am sitting in my favorite coffee shop and lamenting the fact that I missed my own deadline to finish reading the paper. I had to prepare final exams, and revisions on a paper of my own are not

AUTHOR'S NOTE: This short essay is dedicated to the memory of Louis R. Pondy, who helped me appreciate the idea of reviewing as participating in our collective conversation.

269

going as planned. When one faces regular reviewing tasks, time management becomes a must.
It takes me at least two separate reading of a
manuscript before I am ready to write a review,
and another 2 hours to do the actual writing;
unless I manage my time well, it is very easy to
miss the journal's deadline. Thus postponing
the inevitable is in no one's best interest.

The Review Process

I read the first 11 pages of the manuscript.
The introduction is interesting, but I cannot
locate the essential question the authors are
asking. Two more pages later, I find a set of
questions, but they are not really related to the
one I personally constructed. I read the first 10
pages again to understand the essence of the
paper. I always feel that the first responsibility
of a reviewer is to have a good overall understanding of a paper's fundamental objective
and to communicate this understanding at the
beginning of the review. This not only helps the
editorial process but informs the authors as to
what the reviewer understood from their text.
If there is a misunderstanding, it is at least
obvious from the beginning.

At the beginning of my reviewing career, I
used to consider my role to be one of providing
a long list of specific comments. The result
usually was a cryptic text with little coherence
of its own. These reviews may have been useful
for the authors, but they were probably not
valuable to editors. Such lists did not identify
the critical issues in the papers reviewed; moreover, they failed to show what I understood
from the papers. I was able to realize my mistakes when I got the opportunity to read other
reviewers' comments on the same manuscripts.
For someone new, as I was, receiving all the
reviews when the review process was over was
an important learning opportunity. The reviews
and the editor's letter to the author were useful
reference points; they allowed me to see how
much my own review contributed to the editor's judgment. Seeing how others approached
the same manuscripts, organized their thoughts,
and provided feedback to authors was the most
important experience I had in learning to improve my reviewing skills.

The manuscript I have in hand now is, fortunately, an empirical study rather than a conceptual or theoretical piece. In my experience,
as well as that of my colleagues with whom I've
discussed this, theoretical manuscripts are always more difficult to evaluate, comment on,
and write reviews for. Empirical pieces provide
a more predictable outline and narrative structure. One can more easily evaluate specific issues, such as the relationship between the theoretical ideas and the hypotheses, the validity
and reliability of measures, and the suitability
of the method and statistical techniques for the
question at hand. It is also much easier to provide concrete suggestions and point out specific weaknesses, if there are any. Theoretical
pieces, on the other hand, require the reviewer
to engage in more concentrated reading to sort
out the critical elements. Furthermore, the reviewer's judgment may be influenced more by
the way the paper is written than purely by its
content.

My initial difficulty with the theoretical part
of the manuscript is eased after I go over the
hypotheses and the measurements. It is clear
that the front end of the paper is overly dense
and requires a new structure. This is one of the
most common problems encountered by reviewers. As several editors I have worked for
have suggested, most manuscripts get rejected
because of their theoretical construction rather
than because of their design or empirical analyses. I scribble several more notes in the margins
and decide that I need to go back to the beginning of the paper in my second reading. At
about 11 p.m. I am finally done with the first
reading; I have made a lot of notes that will
direct my second reading and my subsequent
evaluation of the paper.

A week later, I am getting anxious to complete the review and decide to take a break from
reading the term papers I had assigned to my
class. I decide to leave the office and go to the
coffee shop, the one place I can hide out at busy
times of the semester; only a few people know
how to contact me there. The second reading of
a paper is usually a more intense activity than
the first reading; it demands concentration and
may require some homework beforehand. In
every manuscript there are ideas, techniques,
and references with which a reviewer may not
be completely familiar. The same is true for this
manuscript. The authors use a multinomial lo-
git for the statistical analyses, but their dependent variable is composed of three ordered cate-

gories. I consult my statistics books to find out if the standard multinomial procedure is suitable under these conditions.

The Reviewer's Yardsticks

In analyzing and evaluating a paper, relevance and rigor are the two critical yardsticks suggested by editors and reviewers. These are, however, highly generalized concepts, and must be made concrete. In place of these yardsticks, I use three criteria that may relate to these more general issues of evaluation. The first is what I call *external consistency*. Is the paper consistent with and built upon existing knowledge? This question usually translates to whether or not the paper includes relevant concepts and references and is asking questions that are pertinent for this area of research. This does not mean, however, that the author has to accept the received wisdom and not question its validity; rather, he or she should be willing to go beyond established ideas. The author should not simply use existing knowledge to build a straw man of these views. The author's arguments should identify critical issues and questions in such a way that the contribution of the manuscript is readily apparent. The second criterion is *internal consistency*. Does the manuscript contain internal contradictions? Are the theoretical propositions or empirical hypotheses derivable from the paper's theoretical argument or conceptual model? This translates into the logical and empirical rigor of the author's thinking. The third criterion I use is probably the most personal: Do I find the paper exciting and worth reading? Do I agree with the author's assessment of the questions and the answers he or she offers?

I should confess here that my criteria did not evolve out of vacuum, but are the products of my cumulative experience in working for a variety of editors, especially the ones who guided the editorial policies of *Administrative Science Quarterly* for the past 15 years. From the time of my first review for Louis R. Pondy, when he was an associate editor of *ASQ,* and in reviewing for his successors, I have learned that a research paper has to do more than report on a competent piece of research—it should help the reader reach a new level of understanding. Among the editors who have influenced my

thinking most is Gerald R. Salancik. I probably did more reviews for him when he was the coeditor of *ASQ* than any other editor of any other journal. I always found in his letters to the authors critical insights that influenced my thinking.

The more I reread the paper, the more questions and comments are filling the margins of the manuscript's pages. On a separate sheet, I try to organize these comments into some meaningful order. As I come to the end of the paper, it is becoming clear that the authors use diverse literatures but fail to integrate them fully. This leads me to the conclusion that either they end up with a straw man argument or I am not fully convinced of their logic. I suddenly become suspicious that my own personal biases on the topic may be influencing my judgment. Maybe my overly critical evaluation of the paper stems from the fact that the questions raised in the manuscript are not really interesting to me. Can I offer an alternative set of questions? But this creates the ultimate dilemma for a reviewer. Many authors' most severe criticism of the review process is that most reviewers supply suggestions for the papers the reviewers would like to write instead of evaluating the authors' papers on their own merits. I think this is a fair criticism. I try to concentrate on the paper itself and accept the questions the authors ask as relevant. I decide that my review should concentrate on their questions rather than mine. Already feeling tired from 2 hours of concentrated work, I finish my coffee and go back to reading term papers.

It is now Tuesday afternoon—I have to write the review now or I will be embarrassingly late. I open my word processor, knowing that this is going to take at least another 2 hours of work. I first organize my notes again and try to integrate them. For the actual writing of a review, there are at least two critical issues. First, the review should be as complete as possible. It should summarize the fundamental ideas and the way the reviewer understands them, and should be specific in criticisms, suggestions, and praise. These conditions are necessary to help guide the editor as well as the authors. The second issue is style. Most editors suggest that a review should be written in a tone that implies a decision of revise and resubmit. Except perhaps in extreme circumstances, the style of a review should be constructive rather than destructive.

Another style consideration is that a review should address issues in the manuscript rather than the manuscript's authors. Every piece of writing, of course, exposes the author, and any research an individual conducts is partly a personal statement. The reviewer, however, cannot take advantage of this situation to criticize the author's intelligence, knowledge, or scientific capabilities. In other words, the reviewer's first duty is to write the kind of review he or she would like to receive on one of his or her own manuscripts.

Gerald R. Salancik and Richard L. Daft probably influenced my writing style the most. As a colleague in the same institution for a long time, I had the opportunity to observe especially Jerry in action. His deep commitment to helping guide authors made a lasting impression on my own style of reviewing. I had seen him spend long hours at his computer, trying to write detailed, constructive reviews for even those manuscripts that were rejected by the reviewers. His sense of duty was always apparent, both in his idea that every manuscript deserves reviewing and in his diligence in carefully articulating the reasons for his decisions.

Finally, as a regular reviewer, I also learned that one needs to develop a rough template that can be used for a variety of manuscripts. This is not simply a timesaving device—the template I use helps me to organize my thoughts and to avoid missing critical elements of a review. The template does not need to be more than a rudimentary outline or structured list of issues to be addressed. When a reviewer works without such a template, his or her reviews can become nothing more than lists of page numbers and comments, without much convincing argument or content.

The Reviewer's Role

I finally finish writing the review. It is about two singe-spaced pages of text, about average length for one of my reviews, excluding the comments to the editor. Most review requests include an evaluation form covering items such as the publishability of the manuscript and its technical and theoretical adequacy. It is very easy and tempting to be noncommittal and pick the midpoints on these scales, but I don't think this strategy is very helpful for editors. By the end of a review process, a reviewer should be able to develop a fair appraisal of the paper and should report that appraisal. This is always a judgment call, and a reviewer's sincere opinion should be as unequivocal as possible. I mark the space for "major revision" on the form and give a satisfactory mark for the paper's technical adequacy. In my comments to the editor, I reiterate my points in the review that the manuscript should have a more streamlined theoretical focus and that a lot of its unnecessary complexity should be eliminated.

Even though I am satisfied with my review, one nagging issue is still unresolved. Is this a paper the readers of this particular journal will find interesting to read, or would an alternative journal be a better outlet? This is not really an issue a reviewer should ponder specifically for every manuscript; such decisions should ultimately be left to authors and editors. But in this case, I feel that the manuscript may be exposed to a more interested, or wider, audience if it is submitted to another journal. I finally decide to include a couple of sentences about this issue in my comments to the editor.

I print a draft of the review and read it one more time to check for grammatical errors and ambiguous expressions. This step may not be necessary for someone else, but in my case, as English is not my first language, I am always compelled to check my prose. At the beginning of my reviewing career, I used to ask my wife, who is a linguist, to edit my writing. Now neither she nor I has the time to enjoy such a luxury. I also feel more confident of my proficiency and have a lower level of anxiety about writing in a language other than my native tongue of Turkish.

At last, I am done with this review. It is in its envelope and ready to be mailed. After 7 hours of concentrated effort, it is not possible to avoid pondering whether or not it was worth it. I have always believed in the metaphor used by the late Louis R. Pondy, that research and publication are like participating in an intense conversation, and the more public the conversation is, the more effective it will be. The review process is probably the least public part of this conversation. First of all, in most cases reviewers are anonymous, and second, their reviews are available only to the authors and journal editors. Such a structure immediately leads to suspicion, criticism of gatekeeping, and accusations that journals publish only those manuscripts that support the received wisdom. Given the diversity of opinions, methods, and theories in our fields, these may not be sound criticisms, but they still bother me. I believe that, on the average, most authors spend their valuable time, energy, and resources to work on things that they are committed to and consider valuable. The reviewer's task is to appreciate authors' efforts and lend a sympathetic ear to what they want to say. This is our collective responsibility. The role of a reviewer, as a critic and adviser at the same time, is to fulfill this collective obligation.

Reviewing is a voluntary act. Each time I face a difficult paper, as this one has been, I ask the same question: Why have I kept doing it for the past 15 years? At the beginning, I participated in reviewing because it provided me with a feeling of relevance and of being needed; I felt that my expertise was valued. Being asked to review a manuscript is a signal that one's opinion counts in our collective conversation. Now, however, I feel that the most important personal reward of being asked to review a manuscript is the learning opportunity it offers. As students of our respective areas of specialization, we reviewers get a firsthand chance to learn from our colleagues' efforts—their successes and their failures. Reviewing gives us the opportunity to read manuscripts in a more intense and careful manner than we might otherwise. But the reward of being a diligent and conscientious reviewer may also be seen as unique punishment—more manuscripts to review. As I am putting my latest review in the mail, I check my mailbox. Through the glass door I see, mixed in with other mail, two thick, wide envelopes and intuitively know . . .

28 Balls, Strikes, and Collisions on the Base Path

RUMINATIONS OF A VETERAN REVIEWER

Alan D. Meyer

The story goes that three umpires disagreed about the task of calling balls and strikes. The first one said, "I calls them as they is." The second one said, "I calls them as I sees them." The third and cleverest umpire said, "They ain't nothin 'till I calls them."

Simons, 1976, quoted in Weick, 1979

The task of reviewing papers submitted for publication in scholarly journals has often been likened to the task of officiating in an athletic competition. Reviewers are termed "referees," and the leading academic journals that employ them are known colloquially as "refereed journals." Publishing is the principal "game" played in academic circles, and analogies to baseball are especially popular. Editors and reviewers make "judgment calls" (McGrath, 1982). When authors submit their work, those fortunate enough to avoid "striking out" often talk about getting a journal "hit."

In the big leagues of academic publication, the umpire squad consists of a journal's editorial board and ad hoc reviewers. While serving two terms on the boards of *Administrative Science Quarterly* and the *Academy of Management Journal*, I have made well over 200 judgment calls about papers submitted for possible publication. I have learned that the editorial review process is largely a process of sensemaking (Weick, 1979), the primary outputs of which are suggestions about how papers might be improved and explanations about why they cannot be published.

AUTHOR'S NOTE: I thank Nancy Meyer and Jim Terborg for their helpful comments, and Jan Beyer, John Freeman, Mike Hitt, Rick Mowday, Bill Starbuck, and Karl Weick for teaching and supporting the practice of activist reviewing. This essay first appeared in *Publishing in the Organizational Sciences* (2nd ed.), edited by L. L. Cummings and Peter J. Frost (Sage Publications, 1995).

The three different approaches to sensemaking taken by Simons's apocryphal umpires provide a useful framework for thinking about how a reviewer might approach the task of evaluating manuscripts:

1. The first umpire treats each ball pitched toward home plate as an unequivocal event. A pitch lies either within or outside the strike zone when it passes the plate. The umpire is an objective observer, and his or her task is limited to making the appropriate call. The umpire has no part in creating the event; indeed, any capable umpire would have made the same call.

2. The second umpire sees pitches as ambiguous events and umpiring as an exercise in judgment. Pitches near the boundaries of the strike zone are sufficiently equivocal that an umpire's eyesight, values, and idiosyncratic biases influence the call. The second umpire understands that the role played by sensory perceptions makes the umpire a participant in the event.

3. The third umpire maintains that a pitch has no fixed ontological identity. It becomes a ball or a strike only through the pronouncement of the umpire—as influenced by the ball's trajectory, the batter's behavior, and the umpire's beliefs. Note that the umpire now has become a coproducer of the event.

"I Calls Them as They Is"

When I was asked in 1981 to review my first manuscript for an academic journal, I approached the task somewhat as the first umpire handles pitches. I set out to determine whether the paper's arguments were logical enough and the methods rigorous enough to justify publication. I saw the reviewer as a gatekeeper charged with enforcing high standards, ensuring fairness, protecting readers from fraud, and generally guarding the profession's status and the scholarly journal's reputation (Nord, 1985). The comments that I wrote to the author of that first manuscript reflect three characteristics common to reviewers who follow in the first umpire's footsteps:

1. The tone of my commentary was highly impersonal. Although the feedback form instructed me to write "comments for the author(s)," I consistently referred to him/her/them in the third person: "On page 6, the author claims that . . . ." In fact, in several passages I wrote as though the paper had no author: "This manuscript argues that . . . ."

2. Most of my comments were evaluative and critical. I listed earlier studies "with which the author is apparently unfamiliar," I identified "problems in how this study was designed," and I characterized certain interpretations as "going beyond the data."

3. Most of my verbs were passive. Using passive phrasing in discussing the manuscript suggests that instead of seeing the paper as at an intermediate stage in an ongoing process, I saw it as a final product. Passive verbs gave my commentary a static quality. (I may have adopted passive phrasing partly because I was an assistant professor trying to emulate an academic writing style. But whatever the reason, the effect was to cast the research report under review as a fixed product rather than an evolving process.)

For the next year or so, I continued reviewing papers using the first umpire's model. I saw the peer review process as a cornerstone of the scientific process. Reviewing seemed a great honor and a grave responsibility. Gaining confidence in my own judgment, I enlarged my focus from simply evaluating a paper's logical and technical rigor to judging its overall contribution to the field. I worked hard on reviews, and when I ran into unfamiliar methods or incomprehensible concepts, I had feelings of inadequacy and guilt. After reviewing about 20 manuscripts on an ad hoc basis, I was invited to join the editorial boards of *ASQ* and *AMJ*.

"I Calls Them as I Sees Them"

As an editorial board member, my reviewing workload grew rapidly, and my approach gravitated toward that of the second umpire. I changed my approach for several reasons. One impetus was a growing interest in the philosophy and sociology of social science. My faith in positivistic inquiry was shaken when I read Schutz

(1967), Husserl (1931), Habermas (1971, 1973), and Burrell and Morgan (1979); the implications of their ideas for academic publication are spelled out in *The Structure of Scientific Revolutions* (Kuhn, 1962) and *Publishing in the Organizational Sciences* (Cummings & Frost, 1985). Rather than serving exclusively as forums for scientific communication, academic journals are apparently used by some authors as vehicles for building their reputations, castigated by others as bastions of elitism, and usurped by university personnel committees as tools for evaluation.

Another impetus for change came from the direct feedback set up by journal editors' practice of mailing me copies of commentaries written by each of a manuscript's anonymous reviewers, along with a copy of the editor's decision letter to the author. I was surprised to see how often we reviewers disagreed, focused on entirely different issues, and offered inconsistent recommendations to authors. I found this feedback most enlightening, for, as Pondy (1985) has noted, "the norms of reviewing are passed down from generation to generation in a subterranean exchange between author and reviewers, almost entirely hidden from public view" (p. 211).

I came to recognize that the review process in the social sciences is more subjective and political than that in the physical sciences (Pfeffer, Leong, & Strehl, 1977), and that actors' positions in social networks play a far greater role. I saw that any differences between "enforcing high standards" and "screening out innovation" were subtle and ideological. I was unsettled by Morgan's (1985) suggestion that publication decisions may be "dominated by the interests and subjective decisions of editors and reviewers who are involved in an elaborate and sometimes unconscious game of control conducted under the guise of objectivity" (p. 63).

A third reason I changed my approach to reviewing was that I too was an aspiring author. Reviewers' overreactions to what I saw as insignificant errors in my own papers made me angry, and some of their criticisms stung bitterly. Sometimes I felt discouraged and disillusioned, and it was unsettling to realize that my reviews of others' work were undoubtedly evoking similar waves of doubt, anger, and disappointment.

As my perspective on reviewing moved toward the second umpire's approach to umpiring, I adopted different criteria in evaluating manuscripts and changed my approach in writing comments to authors:

1. Instead of representing my comments as the output of some mechanical metering device set to register ratings of a paper's rigor and significance, I decided to write like a human reader responding to a human author. To personalize my comments, I started writing exclusively in the first and second person: "On page 4 you say that resource scarcities motivate vertical integration . . . ."

2. To acknowledge my role in interpreting manuscripts, I began reporting my own feelings and reactions to the arguments offered: "I liked your explanation of prospect theory, but your discussion of commitment confused me." (Back when I made "objective" calls, like the first umpire, I would have attributed any confusion experienced to a lack of clarity inherent in the manuscript.)

3. I approached manuscripts as processes in which I participated. To one author I wrote, "In revising, you need to convince me that these two constructs are different." To another I said, "Before I can recommend your paper to my colleagues, you must . . . ."

4. Recalling my own overreactions to reviewers' criticisms, I tried to curtail authors' defensive reactions to my criticisms by invoking readers' needs instead of listing authors' shortcomings and failures: "*ASQ* readers have come to expect authors to ground their arguments in theory and tie them into the current social science literature." To another author I wrote, "Readers who are unfamiliar with institutional theory may have trouble following this discussion."

Making minor adjustments of this sort probably made me a better reviewer. At least these changes let me feel that my behavior was reasonably consistent with my changing beliefs about social science research. But they didn't address a more basic problem. To this point, I had reviewed only a few manuscripts displaying careful scholarship, developing innovative methods, or offering creative interpretations. I was getting tired of plodding through turgid prose, illogical arguments, and poorly described methods. I tried not to think about how few of the manuscripts I was working on would be published, and not to dwell on authors' likely reactions to my recommendations. Reviewing was turning into a thankless, joyless task.

Nevertheless, I knew that the reviewing process sometimes takes a more positive turn. Two senior colleagues, Paul Nystrom and Bill Starbuck, were editing the *Handbook of Organizational Design,* and I found that they were using a more active, interventionist, and developmental approach than mine. Of course, editing invited chapters and reviewing blind submissions are different tasks. However, when I submitted a paper of my own to *ASQ,* it was assigned to an associate editor, Jerry Salancik, who also took an interventionist approach. Jerry saw in my paper a more ambitious article and a more important contribution than I did. With the reviewers' help, he pushed me to find that paper and write it (Meyer, 1982). The prospect of offering this sort of assistance to other authors revived my fading enthusiasm for reviewing.

"They Ain't Nothin' 'Till I Calls Them"

The third umpire is probably singled out as "the cleverest umpire" because only he or she fully appreciated an umpire's potentially pivotal role in controlling the flow of a ball game. A reviewer who sees similar potential in the game of publishing can create opportunities to move beyond the gatekeeper role to become a coach, mentor, advocate, or even "defense attorney" representing an author's interests (Pondy, 1985). From my backstage vantage point as a board member, I started studying reviewers whom I call "activists," hoping to learn how they go about helping authors flesh out promising insights, remediate seemingly "fatal" flaws, and exploit serendipitous findings.

My observations of activist reviewers suggest that they enact a more humane, emotionally satisfying, and intellectually challenging role than reviewers who follow the approach of the first and second umpires. They enact this role by building reputations with journal editors for doing constructive, developmental reviews. Editors often start sending activist reviewers papers that seem especially likely to benefit from their efforts. When this happens, activist reviewers find themselves working on papers that improve more during the review process, that these papers are more likely to be published, and, that,

irrespective of the ultimate publication decisions, authors get more valuable feedback.

However, as a reviewer assumes an activist role, the time and energy he or she devotes to each manuscript are almost certain to increase. Working with authors, particularly less experienced ones, to develop their work into publishable papers is time-consuming and emotionally involving. One must be careful to invest effort where it is most apt to yield a return. I would estimate that about 1 manuscript in 10 has substantial unrealized potential for development. Manuscripts especially likely to benefit include those that try to build theory, combine different perspectives, open up new lines of inquiry, or develop innovative methodologies.

Even the third umpire probably would acknowledge that not every pitch has the same chance of being called a strike—some go into the dirt and bounce across the plate. Likewise, not every submission has the same chance of being called a publishable paper. Some research questions just aren't worth asking, some data sets contain no useful information, and some papers are so far off the mark that no amount of developmental work can save them. Developmental reviewing is necessarily a joint venture among author, reviewer, and editor. However, some authors seem to be more interested in publishing than in what gets published. They see little value in developmental reviews and are not responsive to them.

Activist reviewing also places additional demands on journal editors by requiring them to become more deeply involved in the evaluation of manuscripts. One reason for this is that activist reviewers can fall victim to escalating commitment (Staw, 1981). Advocacy often comes at the expense of objectivity, and the editor may need to intervene to sort things out. Some journal editors consciously assign beginning authors' manuscripts to developmentally inclined reviewers. In fact, certain manuscripts were identified in one editor's cover letters to activist reviewers as possible "diamonds in the rough."

Developmental reviewing is not widespread. Cummings, Frost, and Vakil (1985) identify two dimensions of reviewing style, the "coach" and the "critic." Coaches are reviewers who offer encouragement, identify strengths, instruct authors about how to improve, and explain reasons for their recommendations. Critics are reviewers who evaluate merits, identify flaws, and censure improper methods. Cummings and his colleagues content analyzed 162 reviews of manuscripts sent to *AMJ* and found that "clearly, most reviewers score relatively high on the critic dimension while scoring relatively low on the coach dimension" (p. 479). Pondy (1985) explains the predominance of the critical approach as follows: "Our present corps of reviewers have been trained and conditioned in a prosecution mentality, in large part through observing how their own manuscripts have been treated by an earlier generation of reviewers" (p. 211).

The activist reviewers that I admire are not afflicted with Pollyannaism. They are not uncritical optimists who invariably recommend inviting authors to revise and resubmit. Indeed, to be genuinely constructive, developmental comments must be based upon an incisive critique of the work. The best activist reviewers don't pull their punches. But after telling an author that they don't see his or her work as ready for publication, they go on to spell out specific changes that could close the gap. The feasibility of combining critical and developmental roles is supported by Cummings et al.'s (1985) finding that the coach and critic dimensions are not mutually exclusive. In fact, they report that in writing comments to authors, reviewers scoring highest on the sum of both dimensions were significantly more thorough, attentive to technical detail, methodologically oriented, and substantive.

My observations of activist reviewers' comments to authors point to several common characteristics:

1. Activist reviewers' comments are candid and lengthy. They start with forthright criticism and proceed to recommend changes. Their stance is interventionist. Activist reviewers often refer authors to exemplars in the published literature. Sometimes they propose alternative strategies for revision for authors to consider.

2. Activist reviewers challenge authors to specify the purposes, outcomes, and contributions of their research. "Why did you write this paper?" they ask. "What did you learn, and what does it mean?"

3. Activist reviewers coach authors in expository writing. They think about how papers are structured, asking, "Does the argument unfold in a logical way?" and "Does it carry the naive reader

along?" They often suggest consolidating related concepts, recommend resequencing of ideas, and offer specific plans for reorganizing arguments.

4. Activist reviewers tend to be champions of theoretical and methodological pluralism. They can see value in different perspectives, and they often urge authors to combine methods.

5. Activist reviewers are particularly sensitive to the alignment between stages in the research process. They ask, "Does the literature review adequately justify the hypotheses? Is the analytic model consistent with the conceptual model? Do the results as interpreted inform the underlying research question?"

I think my observations of activist reviewers have started to pay off. Some of my attempts to emulate this approach have had positive results. I hope I've helped a few authors express their ideas more clearly, educe more robust measures from their data, and see more interesting implications in their results. On several occasions, I have suggested wholesale reorganization that authors then used to salvage incoherent arguments or to lay to rest another reviewer's seemingly insurmountable objections.

Now and then—out of the tedium of routinized, ritualized manuscript review cycles—a bona fide high-performing system emerges. On five occasions, I have seen a seriously deficient or highly preliminary paper somehow pique the reviewers' interest and trigger a set of especially thoughtful and constructive comments. Usually the reviewers' objections appear irreconcilable and their demands seem impossible, but instead of giving up, the author rises to the occasion—perhaps by inventing a brilliant analytic strategy that answers a reviewer's concern or by laboriously collecting new data that remedy a fatal flaw. When the revision is resubmitted, the author's unexpected improvements delight and energize the reviewers, eliciting creative ideas for further sharpening the analyses, extending the argument, and enlarging the contribution.

It is an exhilarating and oddly aesthetically pleasing experience when a distributed network made up of blind reviewers linked to an anonymous author by a harried journal editor jells in this way. The review process becomes self-reinforcing and takes on the feel of a peak experience. I have noticed that the authors who elicit these unusually constructive review processes are generally young researchers. Among my personal sample of five "peak" reviewing processes, two were studies reporting the authors' doctoral dissertations. Two others were the work of recently hired assistant professors. The articles that resulted often won prizes and established their authors' reputations. Weick (1992) remarks that young ethnographers seem to get better data than older ones, and he speculates that this may be because they are less threatening to informants. My observations suggest that inexperience may also confer advantages in the review process. Perhaps new authors' manuscripts evoke constructive reviews by subtly signaling their creators' naïveté.

How Authors Can Turn Umpires Into Coaches

My ruminations on reviewing suggest that authors can take steps to encourage developmental reviews and, at the same time, increase the odds that their work will be accepted for publication. I offer these recommendations to authors interested in doing so:

1. Do not submit your paper prematurely. Use your colleagues as a sounding board. Volunteer to give a colloquium, listen to people's reactions, and use them to sharpen your thinking. When you finish a first draft, circulate it and invite criticism. Treat each and every misinterpretation of your writing as evidence that you've failed to communicate clearly. A good rule of thumb is to push your paper through at least two major revisions before submitting it. (When I've followed this rule, my publication "batting average" has been 1,000—when I haven't, I've been far less successful.)

2. Make your paper user-friendly. The introduction should answer a first-time reader's questions (What's the central research problem? Why is it important?). Foreshadow the paper's outcome and contribution (If I keep reading, what will I learn?). Provide enough information about your sample, measures, and instruments to enable the reviewer to understand exactly what you did and found. Having to

guess irritates reviewers and distracts their attention from your argument.

3. Be compulsive about craftsmanship. Your manuscript is the reviewer's only contact with your study. If it is not well crafted, reviewers are likely to make attributions about the integrity of the whole research project. Typos, missing citations, and errors in calculations all suggest that you may not care about quality.

4. No reviewer is ever wrong. Reviewers may be careless, bullheaded, or mean-spirited, but not wrong. It is self-destructive to assume otherwise. Never go one-on-one with a reviewer. (I am amazed by how often authors defend their manuscripts by lashing out at reviewers.) Ben Schneider (1985) comments, "Trying to publish in refereed journals is not a path to positive feedback" (p. 239). (If you want positive feedback, I recommend getting a dog—my golden retriever neutralized reviewers' unkind barbs for more than 13 years, and he also forced me to get regular exercise.)

5. The best way to appreciate the preceding recommendation is to become a reviewer yourself. The program chairs of the Academy of Management's national and regional meetings are constantly on the lookout for reviewers. Journal editors routinely use ad hoc reviewers. Write and volunteer to review, identifying your areas of expertise.

Journal editors also can help turn umpires into coaches. Editors can encourage developmental reviewing by recruiting activist reviewers, assigning them promising manuscripts, and monitoring the ensuing exchanges. Editorial policies can also help institutionalize development. For instance, *Organization Science* now requires each author submitting a paper to include a 50-word statement justifying how and why the paper is appropriate for publication. This statement is forwarded to reviewers. Should the manuscript be published, the journal requires the editor who accepted it to introduce the paper to readers *personally*, explaining why he or she recommends it to them. These are small interventions, but they encourage authors, reviewers, and editors alike to focus their attention on the contributions of the research. This is an important cognitive shift, because the established norms of reviewing direct everyone's attention to shortcomings and flaws. Attending to what's right about a paper instead of what's wrong is an important first step toward development.

Conclusion

I have taken a controversial stance in this essay by advocating an activist style of reviewing. Some editors discourage activism. Some reviewers see it as unseemly interference. Some authors regard it as highhanded meddling in their intellectual property. Some radicals may see activist reviewing as a means of exerting social and professional control.

Activist reviewing certainly carries risks. H. G. Wells once remarked, "No passion in the world is equal to the passion to alter someone else's draft." I once got carried away and offended a respected colleague. Envisioning a "far better paper" than the manuscript he had submitted, I suggested a complete recasting of the theory and data. I could hardly wait to see the revision. My enthusiasm for the project was dashed, however, when the author abruptly withdrew his paper from further consideration at that journal. My colleague later explained that although he found my ideas for revising "insightful and most interesting," that was not the paper he had set out to write. He felt that I had tried to "hijack" his research.

Since then, I have taken pains to present any recommendations for significant changes as ideas offered for an author's consideration, not as conditions for a favorable recommendation. Authors invest their egos in their writing, and reviewers need to remember this. When an editor once asked Henry James to cut just three lines from a 5,000-word article, he did so and then noted, "I have performed the necessary butchery. Here is the bleeding corpse."

Not every manuscript is a candidate for activist reviewing. In some cases, the potential contribution is well developed. In others, the potential is absent or minimal. But when the conditions are right, activist reviewing can catalyze significant advances in social scientific theory and research.

Peter Vail once said, "A .350 hitter isn't just a .350 hitter. Typically, he's a .350 hitter in *context*." Reviewers who know when to move beyond their roles as critics and gatekeepers to

become coaches help create a context that can make the difference between a home run and just another long foul ball.

References

Burrell, G., & Morgan, G. (1979). *Sociological paradigms and organizational analysis*. London: Heinemann.

Cummings, L. L., & Frost, P. J. (Eds.). (1985). *Publishing in the organizational sciences*. Homewood, IL: Irwin.

Cummings, L. L., Frost, P. J., & Vakil, T. F. (1985). The manuscript review process: A view from the inside on coaches, critics, and special cases. In L. L. Cummings & P. J. Frost (Eds.), *Publishing in the organizational sciences* (pp. 469-508). Homewood, IL: Irwin.

Habermas, J. (1971). *Knowledge and human interests* (J. J. Shapiro, Trans.). Boston: Beacon.

Habermas, J. (1973). *Theory and practice* (J. Viertel, Trans.). Boston: Beacon.

Husserl, E. (1931). *Ideas: General introduction to pure phenomenology*. London: Allen & Unwin.

Kuhn, T. S. (1962). *The structure of scientific revolutions*. Chicago: University of Chicago Press.

McGrath, J. E. (1982). Introduction. In J. E. McGrath, J. Martin, & R. A. Kulka (Eds.), *Judgment calls in research*. Beverly Hills, CA: Sage.

Meyer, A. D. (1982). Adapting to environmental jolts. *Administrative Science Quarterly, 27*, 515-537.

Morgan, G. (1985). Journals and the control of knowledge: A critical perspective. In L. L. Cummings & P. J. Frost (Eds.), *Publishing in the organizational sciences* (pp. 63-75). Homewood, IL: Irwin.

Nord, W. R. (1985). Looking at ourselves as we look at others: An exploration of the publication system for organization research. In L. L. Cummings & P. J. Frost (Eds.), *Publishing in the organizational sciences* (pp. 76-88). Homewood, IL: Irwin.

Pfeffer, J., Leong, A., & Strehl, K. (1977). Paradigm development and particularism: Journal publication in three scientific disciplines. *Social Forces, 55*, 938-951.

Pondy, L. R. (1985). The reviewer as defense attorney. In L. L. Cummings & P. J. Frost (Eds.), *Publishing in the organizational sciences* (pp. 210-219). Homewood, IL: Irwin.

Schneider, B. (1985). Some propositions about getting research published. In L. L. Cummings & P. J. Frost (Eds.), *Publishing in the organizational sciences* (pp. 238-248). Homewood, IL: Irwin.

Schutz, A. (1967). *The phenomenology of the social world*. Evanston, IL: Northwestern University Press.

Simons, W. H. (1976). *Persuasion*. Reading, MA: Addison-Wesley.

Staw, B. M. (1981). Knee-deep in the Big Muddy: A study of escalating commitment to a chosen course

of action. *Organizational Behavior and Human Per-*
formance, 16, 27-45.
Weick, K. E. (1979). *The social psychology of organizing*
(2nd ed.). Reading, MA: Addison-Wesley.

Weick, K. E. (1992). Jolts as a synopsis of organizational
studies. In P. J. Frost & R. Stablein (Eds.), *Doing*
exemplary organizational research (pp. 99-104). Newbury Park, CA: Sage.

Becoming a Journal Editor

My vision for *AMJ* was that it would eventually publish the most significant empirical research in management in a way that would be accessible to members of the different specialties represented in the divisions of the Academy. I wanted *AMJ* to be must reading for all researchers in management and related disciplines.

Janice M. Beyer (p. 291)

I hope I've done a good job typing this parade of decision letters. I've made mistakes. I've sat on papers too long because I couldn't figure out what to say about them. I've given authors advice that I later decided was wrong. I've written decision letters that I later realized were confusing. . . . I think that I've done other things well. I think my letters are usually constructive and specific. I think I've learned how to make good use of the cast of reviewers who evaluate papers for *ASQ*. I think I was right to urge Karl Weick to submit his lovely paper "The Collapse of Sensemaking in Organizations: The Mann Gulch Disaster." . . . I learn something new every time I read it.

Robert I. Sutton (p. 302)

Few individuals play a more central role in the dissemination of new knowledge in a discipline than do the editors of its most prestigious journals. In this section, Jan Beyer, past editor of the *Academy of Management Journal*, and Bob Sutton, past associate editor of *Administrative Science Quarterly*, write about their experiences preparing for, accepting, and enacting these influential but demanding roles.

The extensive preparation and qualifications that both Beyer and Sutton pos-sessed at the time of their selection speaks highly of the rigor of the editorial selection process in our field. As Beyer tells us, "Looking back, I can see that there was never a time from before I began graduate work until I was asked to become editor of *AMJ* that I was not exposed to and thinking about publishing and editing" (p. 290). Similarly, Bob Sutton reveals how much he learned about the editorial process just from his experiences as an author:

The most important lessons I learned in graduate school, however, were from the papers that my coauthors and I submitted to journals, not from classes. . . . I decided during my first year at Michigan to make the process of writing and submitting papers to refereed journals the primary element of my doctoral education. . . .

I arrived [as an assistant professor] at Stanford with enough skill to publish in top organizational behavior journals like the *Academy of Management Journal, Academy of Management Review, Administrative Science Quarterly,* and *Organization Science* on a regular basis. (pp. 300, 301)

As the quotations that open this introduction indicate, both authors assumed their editorial responsibilities with the desire to make unique contributions during their terms of office. Beyer discusses the desire to change *AMJ* by broadening its response to different methodologies, specifying journal standards in written statements accessible to potential submitters, changing the journal format, and speeding up the time between submission and author notification. Similarly, Sutton identifies his concern for "good writing" characterized by strong logic, limited jargon, and straightforward sentences, and illustrates his activism in pushing authors to "tell clear, interesting, and well-integrated conceptual stories" (p. 303) with their published papers. Neither claims to have fully achieved her or his goals, but both could see the journals moving closer to their ideals during their terms of office. These signs undoubtedly served as welcome rewards for the large quantities of time and effort invested.

Because editors are privy to the backstage reality of the scholarly publishing process in a way that few others can claim, it is gratifying to find strong consensus between Beyer's and Sutton's views of reviewers. Both praise the competence, fairness, and diligence of a cadre of reviewers

who worked with them in carrying out the review and publication process. Jan Beyer notes, "I have fond feelings for every single member of my editorial board. They served me and their field well and wisely" (p. 297). Similarly, Bob Sutton comments on his initial skepticism about authors' motivation to improve their work and how their responsiveness later caused him to change his views:

Before my stint as associate editor, I believed that most authors were more concerned with getting their work published than with doing the best possible work. I thought that most authors would seek to do as little work as possible when making revisions, and that once their papers were accepted for publication, they would really start slacking off. I assumed that, because of the reward structure of our occupation, most authors would be concerned mostly with getting more papers listed on their vitae, not with producing the best possible work. Again, I underestimated my colleagues. I've noticed that, if anything, the closer their papers get to publication, the more concerned most authors become about each nuance. (p. 303)

Both authors are clearly proud of the contributions they made to the field during their editorships. However, neither seems to doubt the wisdom of limiting editors' terms of office. At the end of 3 years as *ASQ*'s associate editor, Bob Sutton's longing descriptions of the three in-progress manuscripts of his own sitting on his desk contrast sharply with his almost resentful references to the full week of *ASQ* editing work that requires completion. As a result, the reader has little doubt about the choice he will ultimately make when deciding whether to remain on the job for another year. It is interesting that Bob apparently intuitively felt and acted out the rhythms of his future decision long before he was able to articulate them to himself. His own deliberations continued for more than 6 months longer. As he relates in his essay:

> I was more interested in doing my own work than in reading and commenting on work done by others. After spending a week in November writing rejection letters to some of my best friends (including two rejection letters to one person I especially like and admire), I decided to resign. I wrote a resignation letter just before Thanksgiving. I handed Steve Barley the letter and told him to "take this job and shove it." It was a delightful moment, and I've never regretted it. (p. 307)

In a similar vein, Jan Beyer says simply, "When my 3-year term as editor was up, I had no regrets. I was tired. . . . I was glad to get back to my professorial pursuits. But I was also glad I had taken the once-in-a-lifetime opportunity to be an editor—and I still am" (p. 297). These two accounts vividly portray the rhythms involved in becoming a journal editor.

29 Becoming a Journal Editor

Janice M. Beyer

I was working at home when the phone call came. It was Bob Duncan, and he began his conversation with what seemed like a rather extended set of remarks about duty to the field and to our colleagues. I didn't listen very carefully because my mind was racing. Why was he calling? What was he leading up to? Then I thought I knew—he wanted to ask me to run for the Board of Governors of the Academy. But why the big windup? It couldn't be that much work. Then he said words I was not expecting— editor of the *Academy of Management Journal*. I was astounded. Me? I don't think I asked him any questions. In the end I pulled myself together enough to say that I would think about it and get back to him.

Then the soul-searching began. Why me? I felt rather junior in the field. His call came in the spring of 1984; I had finished my PhD work in 1973. I had served only one term on the *AMJ* editorial board. I was happy and very busy doing research with Harry Trice. We had a lot of projects under way, a book on culture planned, and an excellent data set we had just begun to publish from. Surely I could not continue to do research at the same pace if I accepted the edi-

torship. Which was more important to the field? I knew the editorship would affect many different people in the field. Was it more important than my own research? Then the honor of being asked hit me. Tom Mahoney and members of the Board of Governors must trust me and my judgment.[1] What could be a greater honor than to be trusted to make decisions that would affect so many careers and possibly the future directions of the field?

My next thought was to call Harry and talk to him about it. We had begun our relationship as research collaborators and fellow divorcées during my final year of PhD work at Cornell. Soon the relationship had developed into love, and we married. We had been in a commuting marriage between Ithaca and Buffalo for almost 10 years when Bob Duncan made that call. I don't remember what I said to Harry, but I do remember that he said I couldn't turn it down. He said it was the opportunity of a lifetime and urged me to accept. I was still somewhat unsure, and so we discussed the issue again and again during our daily phone calls over the next weeks.

The day after Bob Duncan called, I went to see my dean, Joe Alutto. By then I realized that

I would need some institutional support if I were to accept. He was pleased and encouraging, but very businesslike. He asked me to work up a budget of what I would need. I didn't yet know, so I started calling up past editors and asking them what arrangements they had made and what they advised. Everyone was very helpful, and all gave me one piece of advice: Don't take the job unless you get some time off from teaching. I began to get an idea of the scope of the job—the actual duties, the large number of submissions yearly, the past polices of *AMJ* and the Academy.

On the basis of the advice I had received, I prepared a budget and presented it to Joe. SUNY at Buffalo was not a rich school, so I tried to be conservative. For example, I asked for only a part-time secretary. Joe approved the budget and encouraged me to accept the editorship. I still was uncertain. Being the first woman editor of *AMJ* was a big responsibility. Would I, as a woman, be watched more closely and viewed more critically than a male editor? Would my performance reflect well or badly on women academics in general? In the end, I accepted. Harry was right—I couldn't turn down an honor like this; such an opportunity might never come again.

My mother and my daughters, Claire and Andrea, were the next to know. They were all pleased for me, and my children apparently soon told their father, Tom Lodahl, for when I next talked to him by phone, he made a thoughtful comment. He said: "I'm not surprised. You've been preparing for this your whole life." He was right, but I had not been thinking that way. I now began to reflect on what I had learned that would be useful and realized it amounted to a lot. I began to feel more confident and ready for the job I had taken on.

The Preparation Path

An Early Role Model

Sometime during grammar school, I decided I wanted to become a journalist. No wonder— the only college-educated person among my relatives was one of my mother's younger sisters, my Aunt Margaret, and she was a reporter and later art critic for the *Milwaukee Sentinel*

while I was growing up. I had a lot of contact with her because she had been widowed in World War II and lived during this period at my grandmother's house, where I ate lunch on school days and often hung around after school. Also, she and her little girl, Mary, frequently joined my family for Sunday dinner and whatever subsequent outings or activities we had planned.

As I grew older, I often helped to care for Mary, especially when Margaret wanted someone to bring Mary downtown to join her for dinner. These trips exposed me to the *Sentinel* offices, the Press Club downstairs, and the people Margaret worked with or met socially in connection with her job. Among the things that impressed me were that all of the women reporters and editors wore hats while working at their desks. It was just like what I had seen in the movies. The newspaper looked like a glamorous and important place to work.

Practicing

When I reached high school, I had the opportunity to begin to practice being a journalist. From the beginning of my freshman year in high school, I worked for the student paper, eventually becoming business manager and then editor in chief. I also took all of the writing and journalism courses I could. In addition, I helped to found and later headed a Junior Achievement company that prepared a youth page for the *Sentinel*'s Sunday edition. I enjoyed all of these activities immensely. I liked writing. I liked working with people to produce printed pages. I reveled in the finished product. How accomplished I felt! So, after graduation from high school, I worked as a copy girl for the *Milwaukee Sentinel* for two summers. I didn't get to write anything for publication, but I learned a lot about newspaper operations and ethos from working there. My duties took me into the print shops, the photography department, the library, and the press room; my desk was in the center of the action in the city room, next to the city editor's desk. From all of these activities, intended as preparation for my eventual career, I learned about printing, editing, photography, layout, and all the other elements of publishing.

By the time I entered the University of Wisconsin, I had decided to combine my interests in journalism and music to become a newspaper music critic. I majored in music history and theory, and began working on the student newspaper almost immediately. By the end of my freshman year I was music critic, one of the five daily news editors, and co-magazine editor for the *Daily Cardinal*. In my junior year, as soon as I was able, I took the basic newswriting course. After my instructor, an editor for one of the local papers, told me I didn't need any more newswriting courses, I branched out into radio and television production courses. As a part of these courses, I wrote the afternoon news on Saturdays for the local NBC affiliate and operated a television camera when the local PBS station went on the air.

Detours

I was following a very straight and rational path to my desired career until I fell in love. In those days, people who fell in love got married, so that's what I did. During final exams at the end of my sophomore year, I dated Tom Lodahl for the first time. We were soon engaged, and we got married before our senior year. By graduation I was expecting our first child. Shortly thereafter, we moved to Berkeley, so that Tom could enter the PhD program there in psychology. I tried to get writing jobs at newspapers and TV stations in the area, but the best I could do without full-time experience was a job as a bookkeeper at a minor radio and TV station.

By the time Tom completed his PhD work 3 years later, I had lost interest in journalism as a career. By then I had spent many hours in the company of graduate students, vicariously participated in Tom's graduate studies, and longed to go to graduate school myself. My aspirations now were that I could teach in a college or university someday. So, after we moved to the Boston area for Tom's first professional job at MIT, I tried graduate work at Brandeis in musicology, my undergraduate field. It soon became evident to me, if not my professors, that I lacked both the talent and the passion for music that such a career would demand. In any case, it was time we had another child; Claire was already 4 years old. So I again deferred my career plans and became pregnant.

Two years after our second daughter, Andrea, was born, we moved to Ithaca, New York, when Tom took a job at Cornell University. A

year later, when Andrea began nursery school, I decided to look for a part-time job in writing or editing. I ended up working as an editor in Cornell's electrical engineering school, where I not only edited research reports, but supervised their publication. I enjoyed the work and being on campus again, but editing reports of research that I really didn't understand was not what I wanted to do with the rest of my life. Meanwhile, Tom had become editor of the *Administrative Science Quarterly* and was busy building the circulation and quality of that journal. I listened with great interest to everything he told me and helped to entertain his editorial board members at professional meetings.

My Turn

As soon as Andrea was in first grade, I began graduate work in organizational behavior at the Industrial and Labor Relations School at Cornell. My initial goals were modest—to get an MS degree and assist others on their funded research projects. After a paper drawn from my master's thesis was accepted for publication (Lodahl & Gordon, 1972), all of my academic friends urged me to pursue a PhD. With some trepidation but a lot of eagerness, I took their advice. My initial reluctance to pursue the PhD stemmed from a nepotism rule and hiring norms at Cornell. If I did earn a PhD, I could not be hired in the business school because that was where my husband worked. I could not be hired by the ILR School, because it had a policy of not hiring its own graduates. I was pursuing a PhD at this point primarily because of my interest in doing research, so I didn't consider teaching at any of the small colleges around Ithaca. Moving didn't seem a possibility, because everyone in the family liked living in Ithaca.

When I modified my plans to pursue a PhD, my vision of my future career changed only a little: Instead of assisting others in their research, I would try to win research grants so I could pursue my own research. This was another kind of career that some spouses of faculty we knew were following. My new plans didn't last long, however. The summer after I passed my comprehensive exams, Tom decided to end our marriage. Suddenly I had to confront what had been rather casual plans for a satellite career and convert them into building a breadwinning, full-fledged career. It wasn't easy to do, given my emotional situation, but I wrote and defended my dissertation over the next 8 months. That spring I accepted a position as an assistant professor at the School of Management at the State University of New York at Buffalo. Circumstances had propelled me into reaching my career goal—I would finally be a professor.

What I Picked Up Along the Way

Looking back, I can see that there was never a time from before I began graduate work until I was asked to become editor of *AMJ* that I was not exposed to and thinking about publishing and editing. From my work as an editor in electrical engineering and from my many years of work on school papers, I was familiar with editorial practices and many of the technical details of printing and publishing. From my close contact with Tom Lodahl during his two stints as editor of *ASQ*, and from observing Karl Weick's later editorship, I had a very good idea of how much work goes into being an editor and what levers can be used to change things. From my subsequent experience on the editorial boards of *ASQ* and *AMJ*, and in reviewing for other journals, I had observed the differences among excellent, good, and bad reviews; gained a very good feel for the criteria that reviewers and editors use to make their evaluations of the worth of research papers; and sharpened my standards for what I personally thought deserved publication. From working closely with Karl Weick in editing a special issue of *ASQ* (Beyer, 1982-1983), I had acquired confidence in my judgment about what was worth publishing.

My general development as a scholar had, of course, also prepared me to take on the editorship in various ways. From carrying out research activities, especially those done jointly with Harry Trice, I had learned about a wide range of research techniques and new bodies of literature, gained experience with fieldwork, and developed confidence in my scientific reasoning. From my good and bad experiences as an author who submitted to a wide range of journals, I had developed strong personal views about how the review process should and should not work. My research on science and universi-

ties had reinforced my view that journals are vital and central to the scientific/academic enterprise. In one of my studies I had also observed wide variations in journal policies and practices and thus was exposed to the possibilities of how differently journals could be managed (Beyer, 1978).

Tom's comment was right. I had been preparing for being an editor much, if not all, of my life.

Planning My Editorship

Listening to Advice

Soon after the announcement that I would be the next editor of *AMJ*, various people sought me out to offer a few words of advice. I listened especially to those who had been editors themselves. At this point, I probably remember only the advice I actually tried to follow. Larry Cummings advised me to do what I wanted—it would be so much work that I deserved to be pleased with the end product. John Slocum advised me to name an editorial board early and to be careful to balance the board with persons representing all divisions in the Academy. He also tried to reassure me by telling me what a tough lady I am. I wasn't sure I liked being thought of as tough, but I didn't tell him so because I thought he meant it as a compliment, and I knew editors had to make tough decisions. Tom Mahoney suggested that I name someone to assist me with reviewing the statistics and methods used in articles. Several people suggested that, like the editor of *ASQ*, I should have other editors to help me. Someone, I don't remember who, commented to me during the Academy meetings that I should change the format and typeface used in the *Journal*, because the current format was not attractive.

Karl Weick gave me the most challenging advice. He suggested that I spend a lot of time thinking about and writing an editorial for the first issue of my editorship. He said that it would be important for me to communicate my values, and that the signals I sent could determine what happened during my whole editorship. This was both thoughtful and scary advice. Naturally, I followed it, worried a lot about what I was going to write, and in the process decided what I wanted to accomplish as editor.

Setting Goals

It went without saying that I wanted to improve the *Journal,* but how? I began reading issues of *AMJ* more critically than I ever had before to decide where there was the most room for improvement. I soon decided that four things could be improved: the clarity and liveliness of the writing, the theoretical development in articles, the explanation of methods, and the presentation of sufficient data to permit meta-analysis. I also had the impression that *AMJ* had the reputation of not being receptive to qualitative research. I didn't know what the facts were, but wanted to send clear signals that would change that impression, if others shared it, because I believed qualitative research was becoming more important and prevalent in management fields.

On the other hand, there were several features of *AMJ* that I saw as distinct competitive advantages that should be continued. First and foremost was that all Academy members received the *Journal* as part of their membership. It also had a substantial list of library and other subscribers. Clearly, articles published in *AMJ* enjoyed a large potential readership. Second was that *AMJ* already had a very good reputation; in the field of organizations it was usually ranked second in quality behind *ASQ.* Third was that *AMJ* had a reputation for prompt reviews, whereas *ASQ* had a reputation for long, drawn-out review processes. Fourth, I learned that *AMJ* was not burdened by tight financial restrictions. Although I was expected to adhere to a budget, the Academy officers viewed the Academy's journals as among the most significant services to members, and the Academy's financial condition was good enough that it could afford to give its editors some leeway. I did not have to worry, for example, about exactly how many tables, figures, or pages I published in an issue.

As a sociologist, I was familiar with the *American Sociological Review,* which I now saw as a model in some ways for what *AMJ* could become. *ASR* was generally recognized as the premier journal in sociology. It published the most important and pathbreaking articles in all sub-

fields of sociology. Like *ASR, AMJ* was published by a professional association and went to all of the association's members.[2] My vision for *AMJ* was that it would eventually publish the most significant empirical research in management in a way that would be accessible to members of the different specialties represented in the divisions of the Academy. I wanted *AMJ* to be must reading for all researchers in management and related disciplines.

Deciding What to Keep and What to Change

From talking to past *AMJ* editors, especially John Slocum, I learned about some of the *Journal's* traditions. One was that almost all articles were sent out for review; providing reviews to submitters, especially those who were Academy members, was seen as a service to the Academy membership. Another was that, despite the lack of pressure on editors' budgets, all officers of the Academy were expected to be frugal managers. It was a matter of pride to run a tight ship. Other matters that amounted to traditions were the physical appearance of the *Journal,* the inclusion of research notes, and a prohibition against any person's serving on the editorial boards of more than one of the Academy's journals. I could readily accept all of these traditions except the one concerning the appearance of the *Journal.* After the now-anonymous person had commented on *AMJ's* appearance, I had looked critically at its printed pages and decided that the page format could definitely be improved.

Dealing with the *Journal's* appearance, however, required expertise I did not have. So I sought out a small firm that designed publications and contracted its services to design a new page format. I got samples of typefaces and chose one that I thought was both attractive and clear—especially in the way numerals and mathematical symbols were designed. I worked closely with the designers, and early in the process they advised me also to change the *Journal's* cover. I then commissioned the layout artist at the *Journal's* printing firm to work up several new cover designs. I visited typesetting firms, gave them the new layout, and asked them for samples of how they would set up pages. On the basis of their sample pages and prices, I chose a new typesetting firm. I decided to continue with the same printers and, so as to continue some traditional aspects of the *Journal's* appearance, to use the same paper stock for the cover and pages as had been used in the past, with the same colors on the covers of the various issues throughout the year.

I next turned to the issue of improving the writing. If I wanted *AMJ* to become must reading for all scholars in management, articles had to be interesting and readable. I began to read past issues more critically and, having been a copy editor myself, soon came to the conclusion that better copyediting could improve the appeal and readership of the *Journal*. I began looking for a new copy editor in Buffalo and in Ithaca. I tried three candidates out by having them edit several old manuscripts that had already been published; on the basis of their performance, I decided on Seph Weene, who is still the *Journal* copy editor.

Aspirations for the Review Process

As I worked to realize my initial goals, I began to form other aspirations for my editorship. From my own experiences as an author, I knew that reviews can be very helpful, but that not all are. Some are unclear, some are ill informed, some try to impose reviewers' ideas on authors, and some are downright nasty and destructive. I decided not only that I would try to encourage constructive reviews, but that I would monitor the tone and content of reviews closely, so that I would know which reviewers were helpful and which were not. I would then know which reviewers to use in the future.

Perhaps the most frequent complaint I had always heard about journals was that the review process takes too long. As an author, I hated long, drawn-out review processes, especially when they can end up as rejections anyway—a double insult. I had been urging Karl Weick for years to make the accept/reject decision on *ASQ* submissions on the first revision. I would try to implement this idea at *AMJ*. I saw benefits in such a policy for everyone involved. The authors would know, one way or the other, sooner. Quicker rejections would make for quicker resubmissions elsewhere. Quicker acceptances would mean that authors had more time available for other writing and research. Fewer revi-

sions would mean fewer resubmissions, which would mean less work for the *Journal* staff, the editorial board, and other reviewers.

Reorganizing the Editorial Process

The more I got involved in the many decisions I faced as editor-to-be, the more I was grateful for the 6 months the Academy wisely gives its editors before they have to assume their full duties. Another crucial event during this period was a visit I made to Tom Mahoney at Vanderbilt to learn about how he had set up his office in order to run the *Journal*. This visit was invaluable; I was able to see how he processed manuscripts and to get his advice on how I might restructure the editorial process. From him and others, I learned how rapidly the number of submissions to *AMJ* had been growing, and I became convinced that adding some kind of subeditors might be a good idea.

Different people had different ideas about where I would need help and how I should restructure the editorial process. The plan I ended up following was built upon one Harry Trice told me had been used at *Social Problems*. I decided I would use consulting editors in the fields in which I lacked specific expertise but had many submissions—organizational behavior, strategy, and human resource management. I would try to structure the ways in which we worked together so that no delays were introduced into the review process. Finally, to assure uniformity of quality and equity across subfields, I would use the consulting editors in an advisory capacity, reserving for myself the final decisions. At that point, I had no idea who I should ask to be consulting editors, so I decided to choose from among the members of my editorial board, on the basis of the quality of their reviews.

Choosing an Editorial Board

Another big set of decisions I had to make early on was who to invite to be members of my editorial board. I received some self-nominations and agreed to try out those persons as reviewers, but did not name any to the board without a trial period. From my discussions with John Slocum, I had developed a sense of wanting to broaden participation in *AMJ*. At the same time, I wanted excellent and prompt reviewers. I finally decided that the best way to send a signal of wide participation was to continue a minimal number of members from the current board to the new board. From my calculations on the number of reviews likely to be needed over the course of a year, I figured I would need a board of about 50 members. I would have plenty of room to name new people to the board, and could further widen participation by using many different ad hoc reviewers. I also decided to continue members on the basis of when they had joined the board. I would ask only those who had served one 3-year term or less to continue. I didn't rush to fill up the editorial board immediately, however. I took my time, so that I could select people I had tried out as ad hoc reviewers and whose abilities and inclinations as reviewers I judged to be exceptionally good.

Another concern was to avoid overloading my board members, so that they would be able to return reviews promptly. The prevailing *AMJ* norm of two manuscripts a month seemed a heavy workload, but was necessary because of the large number of submissions.[3] I therefore looked for new members of the editorial board by first eliminating people who were already on two or more journal boards. I would try to select and develop a new group of reviewers who were not already overburdened. I asked a student assistant to make photocopies of all of the current editorial board listings in the leading management journals. We then made file cards with all of the individuals' names and the boards they served on for my later reference. I then started browsing through the leading journals, looking for authors who had recently published strong articles. When I located authors whose work I admired, I checked to see if they were already serving on more than one editorial board. Those who were not became candidates for my board. Most of the new members I asked to join my editorial board initially were chosen in this way.

Setting Targets

After I learned that *AMJ* was getting about 250 new submissions yearly, I began to work out estimates of how many reviews that number of submissions would require yearly under varying sets of assumptions. To make these estimates, I needed to decide the number of reviewers I would use on each submission. I decided to use two when the article had a relatively narrow focus in terms of topic and methodology, and three when the article drew on a wider set of ideas and methods. To calculate the total reviewing workload, I also needed to estimate how many additional reviews would be needed when revised articles were resubmitted; this obviously depended on what percentage of authors was encouraged to revise and resubmit. It soon became obvious that a loose resubmission policy—say around 50%—would entail a crushing number of additional reviews. I decided such a loose resubmission policy made no sense when I could publish only about 10% of the submissions unless the standards and size of the journal changed drastically.

From these calculations I reached a tentative decision, which I ended up following throughout my editorship—namely, to encourage revisions on around 20-25% of first submissions and to reject the remainder. I felt it was fairer to both authors and reviewers to try to make most rejection decisions on the first submission. Rejected articles could then be submitted to other journals without long delays.

I so firmly believed in the benefits this policy would bring to authors that I always processed the manuscripts on which all reviewers recommended rejection before those that had more mixed reviews. I didn't always follow those recommendations, but I did read over the articles and reviews first, and, if my decision was to reject, made sure the letter was sent out as promptly as possible.

Making It Work

The first challenge in executing my plans came during the initial meeting of my chosen editorial board at the 1994 Academy meetings. Other challenges included the potentially fateful first editorial, how to signal the changes I hoped to make in the first issue, and how to adjust if some of my plans didn't work out the way I envisioned. As it turned out, the biggest challenge was one I didn't fully anticipate—all the things that happened to delay getting out the first issue.

The First Editorial Board Meeting

I gave a lot of thought to what messages I wanted to send to board members during our first meeting. I prepared a detailed outline of points I wanted to make that I followed during the actual meeting and later mailed to members of the board who had missed the meeting. Perhaps the most important message I wanted to convey was that, because *AMJ* is an empirical journal, our primary criterion in reviewing papers should be the worth of the data collected. If a paper was based on data that, in their judgment, were of value to the field, we would work with the author to develop the paper for publication. We might not always succeed in developing all such papers to our publication standards, but I felt we should try when the data reported could make an important empirical contribution. If the paper ended up also making a theoretical contribution, we would publish it as an article. If the contribution of the research was mostly empirical—for example, it mainly confirmed well-established theory—we would publish it as a research note.

I also wanted to emphasize the importance of tying empirical work to theory. In my outline for the meeting, I put it this way:

> Let's encourage strong conceptual and theoretical development. We probably need to help some authors sort out the theoretical importance of their findings and ideas. Not in an imperialistic way, but in an appreciative, helpful way. If *AMJ* is going to be more useful and cited, the relation of empirical findings to the rest of both the theoretical and empirical literatures must be made evident. We must try to help develop more theoretical cumulativeness in empirical results.

In effect, I urged board members to cultivate an appreciation for both new ideas and the data people collected. It was easy to be critical of a submitted paper and harder to appreciate what had potential and could be developed.

I also said that, if they felt an article should be rejected, it was their responsibility to justify that decision with sufficient specific and clear comments to the author. I said I would be guided more by their comments than by their ratings, but that they probably did not need to write equally long sets of comments for articles they felt should be rejected as for articles they felt were worth an encouragement to revise and resubmit. I also urged the board members to be polite and to hold any reviews they had written in anger or disgust for at least 24 hours, and then edit out any nastiness that might have crept in. I reminded them that it was bad enough to have an article rejected without being insulted besides.

Another important message concerned the promptness of their reviews. I urged them to be prompt, pointing out how this was an important competitive advantage. As I recall, the new board members responded positively to my ideas, and we had a lively discussion about our aims and how we would try to achieve them.

Sending Signals

There were two important documents to write for the first issue to be published under my editorship: my editorial and a new style guide. As Karl Weick had pointed out, these would set the tone for my editorship. The signals sent by that first editorial were, I hoped, for a significant but not radical change. Although I had many changes in mind, they were reforms designed to revitalize and improve the journal while maintaining many of the traditions already established. In the beginning of the editorial I set forth a rather modest aim: "to publish the best research that is submitted" (Beyer, 1985, p. 5). I had decided not to follow the practices of other journals that sought out papers on certain topics and then published them in special issues. *AMJ* had such a large number of submissions that I felt special issues would be unfair to the many regular submitters seeking to have their work published there. Also, as a student of the sociology of science, I was skeptical about whether the field as a whole benefited when editors encouraged some research topics and not others. Who is wise enough to know the direction research should be taking?

My second stated aim was "to assist authors to present their research in a way that makes it accessible, interesting, and scientifically useful to the entire membership of the Academy and other management scholars, both now and in the future." The third was to "encourage authors to consider and discuss the usefulness of their research to the practice of management" (Beyer,

1985, p. 5). I then set forth a series of expectations of what should be reported about the methods employed in articles submitted, including fuller descriptions than typical in most journals of the populations studied, sampling procedures, measurements used, and relationships between researchers and subjects. Without such information, I felt, research results could not be accurately interpreted or used to guide subsequent research. I also added the requirement that all papers must report basic statistics that could be used for future meta-analyses. Finally, I urged authors to "discuss their research findings in terms of their implications for practice" (Beyer, 1985, p. 5).

During my editorship, I took all of these admonitions seriously. When papers did not follow all of the guidelines set forth in this editorial, the omissions did not affect my initial decisions about publishability, but the authors were asked to add the information in revisions.

The new style guide reinforced these requirements and also presented a new, simplified format for references. When I had sought advice from an expert on the issue of the reference format, his immediate response was, "Not that terrible APA format!"[4] Because I also saw the APA format, with its parentheses and periods, as unnecessarily cumbersome, this remark gave me the courage to advance a format that was similar but had simpler punctuation.

Another signal I deliberately sent was made possible by the early submission of a strong qualitative article that was rather quickly revised and accepted. I decided to use this article (Harris & Sutton, 1986) to send the signal that *AMJ* was now receptive to qualitative research methods by placing it as the lead article in the first issue of articles that had been accepted under my editorship. Because Tom Mahoney had left me with the customary backlog of accepted articles for four issues, this signal was delayed for a year, but I think it did have the desired effect, for I subsequently received and published other important qualitative papers. As of this writing, several of the papers that have won the yearly *AMJ* Best Paper Award have been based on qualitative data.

As my editorship progressed, I continued to seek ways to send signals to the field about my aspirations for the *Journal*. The chief way I did this was to attend every single professional meeting to which I was invited to talk about the *Journal*. In this way I was able to reach a sizable audience face-to-face. I was amazed at how much interest there was in what editors think and how many people were eager to see their editors and talk to them in person. In one of the talks I gave, I compared the role of editor to that of shaman. This is how I had begun to feel—as if I was expected to do magic.

Unexpected Hurdles

Because all of the articles in my first issue in 1985 had been accepted by Tom Mahoney, all I had to do was supervise any final revisions of the papers, their copyediting, and the actual printing, binding, and circulation process. I had the additional advantage of a very experienced production editor, Barbara Miner, to help with the latter portions of the process. Because I was pretty familiar with the publication process myself and had made my decisions about format and had chosen the typesetting and printing firms long in advance, I did not anticipate any great difficulties in getting the issue out. Just to be on the safe side, however, I set conservative deadlines. I was lucky I did.

The first obstacle was relatively small—the SUNY at Buffalo Management School was slated to move from the old campus to its new building on the new campus in January 1985, between semesters. By that time, the articles for the March issue would be typeset, and we would be in the middle stage of production corrections from galleys and layout of the pages. After that would come the final stages of printing, binding, and circulation. The move was expected to entail all office files' being inaccessible for about a week. That seemed manageable—and it was. However, the infamous Buffalo weather intervened. A big blizzard hit, the president closed the university, and the carpet layers could not get into the new management building to do their work. This delayed our move into the new building by about another week.

After the delay, everything was going along satisfactorily until a week or so later, when the snow melted. I lived in a housing development built on a flood plain, and it soon became evident that I might not be able to leave the development by car. So I packed up my personal things and needed papers and moved to a hotel—I would let nothing delay my first issue!

How could I possibly know that a domestic quarrel was going to lead to the shooting of a key employee at the firm that did the typesetting and layout of the journal pages? Fortunately, no one was killed, but the incident, which involved the accidental shooting of two struggling parents by a minor child, affected not only the mother, who was shot in the leg and therefore unavailable for work, but also her sister, who supervised the firm's layout work. Under the circumstances, it would have been churlish to put additional pressure on the small typesetting firm that I had hired. So I sat tight and waited, and the delay was relatively short.

After all of these hurdles and the more usual obstacles were surmounted, my first issue finally came out. It wasn't the first week in March, but it was still mid-March and, unless there were further delays in the mails, most Academy members would get the issue before the month was over. I had made it. My first issue was out.

There were other hurdles ahead: the resignation of the production editor, the move to New York University when I accepted a job there, many replacements of secretaries and other assistants. But I had learned, to a degree, to take such things in stride. None of the later hurdles would seem quite so big as the ones I had to get over for that first issue.

Monitoring Performance

One of the most important decisions that editors, like other managers, must make concerns what they need to measure and watch as indicators of their performance. *AMJ* editors had traditionally monitored and reported to the Academy Board of Governors the time elapsed between submissions and the return of decision letters as well as how long reviewers took to return reviews after they received manuscripts. I set up a system to collect these measures and added some other measures that I thought would help me manage.

One of these concerned the revision rate, which I decided to monitor closely and regularly. As discussed earlier, I had set a target of 20%-25% revisions—in part as a strategy for keeping the workload within bounds, but also because I felt it was more considerate of authors than having a bigger pool of revised manuscripts and having to reject a substantial proportion of them. As it turned out, I did not have to intervene to keep the revision rate low—rather, I had to intervene to keep it high enough. If I had used a majority rule in following the suggestions of my reviewers, I would have encouraged a much lower percentage of revisions than I did. I soon discerned this pattern and initially decided to encourage revision if even one reviewer saw promise in a paper. I reasoned that the reviewer could be right, and I was concerned about avoiding Type II error if I could.[5] Even with this liberal policy, the revision proportion sometimes fell below 20%. I would then call up my consulting editors and urge them to loosen up a bit by looking more closely at papers that did not evoke enthusiasm because their merit was unclear—usually because of poor presentation of ideas, data, or both. I, in effect, asked them to look for diamonds in the rough. We found a few by looking.

Another area I monitored closely was the quality of reviews. I tried to grade each review after I had read it, and recorded my grade on the sheets that were kept on each reviewer's assignments. These grades enabled me to decide who to ask to be my consulting editors and who to ask to join the board as I expanded it. The grades were, of course, very subjective and tended to reflect the degree to which I felt reviewers were constructive, thorough, clear, and appreciative of new ideas and approaches. Reviews that I felt were rude, careless or superficial, hard to understand, or narrow-minded were graded negatively. Reviews that contained actual mistakes or serious misinterpretations received very negative grades.

In monitoring turnaround times, I followed the same practices as my predecessors—sending a reminder on the day a review was due if it was not received, and following up with a phone call from my secretary a week later. Very late reviews usually prompted a personal telephone call from me. A few reviewers were too busy with other career demands to meet my stringent expectations and left the board. A few others resigned for other reasons. On the whole, however, I held on to my board members very well and was (and still am) very proud of their constructive reviews and good judgment. My favorable assessments of them were confirmed when many of them were soon asked to join other editorial boards, but my aim of keeping them from being overloaded was thus somewhat defeated.

Looking Back

As I reflect on what happened while I was editor of *AMJ*, I feel that I was able to realize most of my aspirations for the *Journal*. I think the quality and reputation of the *Journal* continued to improve, and I have been gratified by the degree to which some of the policies I set have been continued by my successors. The fact that a substantial number of qualitative articles have appeared in *AMJ* and have been greeted with appreciation by many within the field pleases me. The *Journal* seems both more readable and more catholic in what it publishes than it used to be. I was not able to realize every aspiration I had, however—for example, I found that many more articles than I expected required more than one revision before I could make a firm accept/reject decision.

One feeling stands out. Being editor of *AMJ* was the most gratifying period of my professional life. I felt I was doing important work, and I had the best people in the field helping me. It was very satisfying to be the first to publish the work of outstanding young scholars and to see members of the editorial board advance in their careers, perhaps helped by what they had learned as reviewers. It was humbling to see how much research was being done and how much the standards for what constituted acceptable empirical work were going up.

I have fond feelings for every single member of my editorial board. They served me and their field well and wisely. I feel immense gratitude to my consulting editors—Rick Mowday, Manny London, and Carl Zeithaml—for their diligence, unfailing courtesy, and good judgment. I feel grateful for a supportive and friendly Board of Governors and departmental colleagues who never gave me a hard time and seemed to appreciate my efforts. Above all, I feel fortunate to have had an opportunity to work with so many bright and talented authors to develop their ideas. When my 3-year term as editor was up, I

had no regrets. I was tired. My style of being editor was very demanding and had left me little time for other professional activities, so I was glad to get back to my professorial pursuits. But I was also glad I had taken the once-in-a-lifetime opportunity to be an editor—and I still am.

Notes

1. Tom Mahoney was then editor of *AMJ*.
2. This is no longer true; *ASR* is now but one in a long list of journals from which ASA members can choose to subscribe.
3. I rejected the alternative of naming a huge board because I felt large size could detract from cohesion and dilute my ability to influence members' reviewing practices.
4. He was referring to the format used in the publications of the American Psychological Association, which has been adopted by other publishers as well—coincidentally, the format used in this volume.
5. This is another issue I raised in the first editorial board meeting by asking board members to be equally concerned with both Type I (publishing what might not be "true") and Type II error (not publishing what might be "true").

References

Beyer, J. M. (1978). Editorial policies and practices among leading journals in four scientific fields. *Sociological Quarterly, 19*, 68-88.

Beyer, J. M. (Ed.). (1982-1983, December-March). Utilization of organizational research [Special issue]. *Administrative Science Quarterly, 27-28*.

Beyer, J. M. (1985). From the editor. *Academy of Management Journal, 28*, 5-8.

Harris, S., & Sutton, R. (1986). Functions of parting ceremonies in dying organizations. *Academy of Management Journal, 29*, 5-30.

Lodahl, J. B., & Gordon, G. (1972). The structure of scientific fields and the functioning of university graduate departments. *American Sociological Review, 37*, 57-72.

30 Work as a Parade of Decision Letters

PLEASURES AND BURDENS OF BEING AN ASSOCIATE EDITOR AT THE *ADMINISTRATIVE SCIENCE QUARTERLY*

Robert I. Sutton

My development as an organizational scholar has been shaped most strongly by the review process. I began writing my first journal article as a psychology undergraduate at the University of California, Berkeley. Looking back, I can see that this article resulted from a nearly random set of events. My classes had convinced me that psychological research was an important, intriguing, and somewhat mysterious activity. This blend of excitement and ignorance meant that I had a strong interest in doing research and a weak notion of what I wanted to do research about. I wandered around Berkeley's Psychology Department for several months, asking any faculty member or doctoral student I could corner if he or she needed help with

research. No one wanted help until I meet a Denise Rousseau, then a doctoral student in industrial and organizational psychology at Berkeley. Denise was nice to me, expressed excitement about guiding my research (rather than assigning me grunt work on one of her projects), and gently pushed me toward a project that matched her research interests.

Denise gave me advice about how to design a study and helped me write up the resulting paper on the link between dependence on a parent organization and managerial autonomy. We finished this paper around the time that I moved to the University of Michigan, where Denise was a new faculty member and I a new doctoral student in the Organizational Psychol-

AUTHOR'S NOTE: I would like to thank Keith Murnighan for his insightful comments. This essay was prepared while I was a fellow at the Center for Advanced Study in the Behavioral Sciences. I am grateful for financial assistance provided by the Hewlett-Packard Corporation and the National Science Foundation (SBR-9022192).

ogy Program. The *Journal of Applied Psychology* probably made a mistake by publishing the paper (Sutton & Rousseau, 1979). Denise did a nice job reviewing the literature in the introduction, but my lack of training meant that the paper was plagued by methodological flaws, such as a tiny yet wildly varied sample of organizations, poor measures, and a vague link between theory and data.

Nonetheless, I learned a key lesson from the review process. *JAP*'s editor, Chuck Hulin, complained that the paper was poorly written. He urged us to read Strunk and White's *Elements of Style* (1979) and then to make repairs. My first reaction was to kick the furniture and cuss. My second reaction was to show the paper to my girlfriend (and now wife), Marina Park, who had won writing contests in high school and been an English major in college. I expected her to support my hostility toward the obviously misguided editor who had made these absurd complaints. Instead, Marina told me she was amazed that there was any chance that a prestigious journal would want to publish the paper. She found that it was plagued by poor logic, incomprehensible jargon, and convoluted sentences. Marina also complained that we rarely used the active voice. She first made me read *Elements of Style,* then she sat with me for several days and helped rewrite almost every sentence in the paper.

This experience during my first semester in graduate school caused me to become obsessed with the writing in my papers. I still drive coauthors crazy with my picky comments. When Rick Mowday and I wrote an *Annual Review of Psychology* chapter a few years ago (Mowday & Sutton, 1993), he couldn't believe that I kept asking for "one more week" to fiddle with every sentence. I make so many comments about writing style to *ASQ* authors that our managing editor, Linda Pike, jokes that I start doing her copyediting work before a paper reaches her desk. And I sometimes recommend that authors read *Elements of Style* before revising their papers, just as Hulin did to me.

The Review Process as My Best Teacher in Graduate School

I learned wonderful lessons from the faculty and students in my doctoral program. My ad-

viser, Bob Kahn, was mighty busy but still took time to give me good advice. Bob was also a wonderful role model, because he viewed writing as the most important part of his job and viewed other parts as necessary evils or pleasant distractions. Richard Hackman visited Michigan for just a year, but he gave me more feedback during that year than any other faculty member did during my 5 years at Michigan. Richard delivered good advice in a loud and cynical tone that somehow conveyed that he cared about me. I once walked into Richard's office and told him I was going to become a population ecologist. He said something like: "Congratulations, Sutton. You have just thrown away your promising career as an organizational psychologist to become a third-rate sociologist." He was right—I would have been a lousy population ecologist.

The most important lessons I learned in graduate school, however, were from the papers that my coauthors and I submitted to journals, not from classes. My experience with the *Journal of Applied Psychology* taught me that, although I needed to understand something about theory and research methods, the skills I needed to publish papers were only loosely related to what I could learn in the classroom. Similar to other crafts, publishing in refereed journals entails learning subtle and difficult-to-articulate skills that can be acquired only by doing it, rather than by reading, watching, or hearing about it. I decided during my first year at Michigan to make the process of writing and submitting papers to refereed journals the primary element of my doctoral education. I still went to classes, read the literature, went to seminars, and spent a lot of time talking to fellow doctoral students about research, but I tried to use these lessons as stepping-stones to help me write whatever papers I was working on, not as ends in themselves.

I wrote papers mostly with other doctoral students. After the *JAP* paper with Denise, I published four articles in refereed journals on the basis of work prior to my dissertation research, along with three book chapters. Bob Kahn was the only faculty member among my seven coauthors on these papers. I also wrote at least two other papers that were submitted for publication, but never saw the light of day. Except for two of the book chapters, each of these papers was first submitted to a more prestigious outlet than that in which it was ultimately published, if it was published at all.

I am glad that most of these papers were eventually published in respectable outlets. More important, however, were the lessons I learned from the dozen or so rejection letters and supporting reviews, from the five or six sets of reviews requesting revision, and from the conversations that I had with faculty and students about such feedback. Two sets of reviews were especially instructive. Howard Aldrich, then an associate editor at *ASQ*, wrote a detailed letter in a warm tone explaining that my paper with Larry Ford on problem-solving adequacy in hospital subunits could not be published. He noted that the hypotheses were poorly motivated; the links between theory and data were tenuous; the predictor, mediating, and dependent variables all seemed to be measuring the same concept rather than different concepts; and the observed relationships were hard to interpret because they were probably inflated by correlated measurement error. These comments helped us to repair the paper so that it could be published in *Human Relations* (Sutton & Ford, 1982) and provided an important early lesson that it would be difficult to publish papers where correlated measurement error appeared to be a problem.

Jerry Salancik, who I followed as associate editor at *ASQ*, rejected a paper that Bob Kahn and I had written on prediction, understanding, and control as antidotes to job stress. This lesson was instructive for several reasons. First, I noticed that the usually serene Bob Kahn got even madder about the rejection than I did. Second, I realized that Bob's considerable prestige was no buffer against rejection. Third, and finally, Salancik's rejection letter taught me that a good review of the literature is not enough to justify publication in a first-tier journal. Authors need to use past literature as a springboard for new and well-developed ideas. I was glad that this paper was ultimately published in a respectable handbook (Sutton & Kahn, 1987). Again, however, the lessons I learned from the negative feedback proved to be more important in the long run. For example, when Anat Rafaeli and I began developing a stream of research on expressed emotion several years later, we struggled to add original twists so that our theory papers might be published in first-tier journals.

Dealing With the Review Process as an Assistant Professor

These early lessons from the review process made it easier for me to make the transition from graduate student to assistant professor at Stanford. I arrived at Stanford with enough skill to publish in top organizational behavior journals like the *Academy of Management Journal, Academy of Management Review, Administrative Science Quarterly,* and *Organization Science* on a regular basis. I still cussed editors and reviewers on the days their comments arrived, I still routinely disagreed with their advice, and I still held (often irrational) grudges against editors who rejected my work or made me take out or mutilate parts that I loved. Yet I also realized that the review process was my most important teacher. And I was working with wonderful coauthors, such as Anat Rafaeli and Tom D'Aunno, who helped me learn these lessons.

For example, thoughtful and detailed comments from Jan Beyer at *AMJ* taught me how to develop the logical flow of my arguments. She constantly found places in my papers where there was no apparent link between one sentence and the next. Dick Daft served as the initial associate editor on my dissertation paper on organizational death at *ASQ* (Sutton, 1987). He taught me that, although qualitative papers are different in many ways from quantitative papers, the introduction still needed to provide a conceptual and empirical motivation for conducting the study. Rick Mowday, who followed Jan Beyer at *AMJ*, taught me how to develop stronger links between theory and data. I couldn't even bring myself to kick the furniture and swear at him (which remain my standard responses to rejection letters) when he rejected one paper because he did such a good job of showing me that the data had little to do with the theory. Jerry Salancik at *ASQ* wrote some of the most painful letters I received. I was especially upset by one letter in which he identified four incompletely developed themes in a paper on bill collectors. I was irritated by his insistence that I discard three of the four themes and write about the remaining one in depth. But he was right; the paper became much better as a result (see Sutton, 1991). This experience taught me that, even if a data set contains numerous interesting conceptual issues, I can probably tell only one conceptual story adequately in the space of a journal article.

I also worked actively as a reviewer for the journals where I had submitted articles for publication, especially *AMJ, AMR,* and *ASQ.* I enjoyed writing reviews because they were, next to trying to write articles and get them published, the most enlightening part of my postdoctoral education. I took special pleasure from the two occasions when I worked hard on papers that later each won the award for the best paper published in a given year in the *Academy of Management Journal.*

By 1990, several friends, including Jane Dutton, Keith Murnighan, and Anat Rafaeli, had suggested that I was likely to be asked to serve as a journal editor. Keith repeatedly suggested that I was the logical successor to Jerry Salancik at *ASQ* when he decided to step down. I responded to their comments by saying that I wasn't likely to be asked and, even if I was asked, I wasn't sure I'd take the job, because it would interfere with my research. But I was being disingenuous. I secretly wanted to be an editor quite badly. I thought I could learn a lot from such a role. I also thought I could do a good job because I am a product of the review process.

In late 1990, I told Marina that I hoped to become an associate editor at *ASQ,* because I think it is the best journal in my field. *ASQ* is known for its exacting review process. It publishes only 22 to 24 papers in a typical year, and everyone involved in the review process—editors, reviewers, and copy editors—puts authors through the toughest gauntlet to be found among organizational research journals. I have received more rejection letters from *ASQ* than from any other journal. *ASQ* even rejected a paper of mine that later won the award for the best paper *AMJ* published in 1988 (Sutton & Rafaeli, 1988). The two papers of mine that *AMJ* did publish required the most massive, distressing, and instructive revisions I have completed during my career (Sutton, 1987, 1991).

Life as an *ASQ* Editor

ASQ editor John Freeman called me in early 1991 to ask if I would like to follow Jerry Salancik as an associate editor at the journal. John said that the job would entail assigning reviewers and writing decision letters for papers using psychological theory, for other "micro" papers, for culture papers, and for qualitative papers. John also indicated that I would serve as *ASQ*'s "strange master"—that is, he would assign unusual papers to me. I accepted John's offer immediately, telling him that I was honored and would rather do this job than any other in the field.

It is now April 1994, and I've had this job for more than 3 years. It has transformed how I spend much of my time. From my early days in graduate school, I've spent about 50% of my work time pounding away at a keyboard. I work best when I can write for long periods without interruption. I hid at home in my study before Marina and I had children. In recent years, I've hidden in an office that I rent away from campus. I type slowly, using two fingers and rarely breaking 20 words a minute. But I am persistent, and my favorite part of my job is sitting alone, crafting sentences and paragraphs, and trying to make them fit together.

Before becoming an editor, I spent most of this typing time on my own papers. Now, however, depending on my *ASQ* load, I spend 25%-75% of my typing time writing letters about other people's work. As the title of this chapter suggests, I've shifted a big portion of my typing time from working on my own, slow-moving, parade of manuscripts to working on a somewhat faster-moving parade of decision letters about other people's work.

I hope I've done a good job typing this parade of decision letters. I've made mistakes. I've sat on papers too long because I couldn't figure out what to say about them. I've given authors advice that I later decided was wrong. I've written decision letters that I later realized were confusing. And one paper that I rejected still haunts me. I fretted over it for over a month before writing a rejection letter. It just appeared in another journal and I'm still not sure if I made the right decision.

I think that I've done other things well. I think my letters are usually constructive and specific. I think I've learned how to make good use of the cast of reviewers who evaluate papers for *ASQ.* I think I was right to urge Karl Weick to submit his lovely paper "The Collapse of Sensemaking in Organizations: The Mann Gulch Disaster" (1993). This paper received what Linda Pike described as the most positive reviews of any paper she has seen during the decade or so she has been managing editor at *ASQ*. I learn something new every time I read it. I am also proud of the help I gave to Barker (1993) in developing his case study of self-managing teams and to Cooper, Dyck, and Frohlich (1992) in developing their experimental paper on gainsharing. Both papers tell clear, interesting, and well-integrated conceptual stories, partly because I pressed the authors so hard to make them better.

It isn't my place to evaluate my performance as an associate editor. That judgment is best made by reviewers, readers, other editors at *ASQ*, and, especially, the authors who submit manuscripts to *ASQ*. But I can tell you about the pleasures I've enjoyed and the burdens that have distressed me during my first 3 years as associate editor, especially those that have surprised me.

The unexpected pleasures have come from the review process itself. I was excited about becoming an *ASQ* editor, but I came to the job with strong and unflattering beliefs about the intentions and actions of both reviewers and authors. Those beliefs have largely been proven wrong. First, I believed that most reviewers did not take their responsibilities seriously; I believed they were slow, irrationally biased, out to reward their friends and punish their enemies, and nasty. I could cite a few examples of reviewers I've used at *ASQ* that fit these negative stereotypes, but such problems occur far less often than I expected. They occur less often partly because all *ASQ* editors—especially managing editor Linda Pike—do what we can to reduce the harm caused by such reviewers. We sometimes edit reviews or decide not to use them. When we find that a reviewer performs poorly on a regular basis, we stop sending him or her manuscripts to evaluate. But these efforts to weed out the small percentage of poor reviews and reviewers don't fully explain the high quality of the average *ASQ* review. The number of consistently excellent reviewers continues to surprise and impress me. Reviewers such as Patricia Adler, Max Bazerman, Jennifer Chatman, Mark Fichman, Connie Gersick, John Jermier, Rick Mowday, Maggie Neale, Brian Pentland, Jeff Pfeffer, and Marlene Turner routinely delight me with their fast, thoughtful, and kind evaluations. The most impressive *ASQ* reviewer I've worked with is John Wagner from Michigan State. He is always one of the fastest of the

several hundred reviewers we use each year. He routinely reads the original sources cited by authors (sometimes reading a new book to write a review). Then he often gently points out how the authors' interpretations seem to be at odds with what he found in the original sources. John is such a broad intellectual that he can make informed comments on many different methods, including survey research, analyses of archived data, meta-analysis of published studies, laboratory experiments, and qualitative research. His conceptual range is equally broad. My admiration for John does not mean that he and I always agree. He did not agree with my decision to publish at least one paper on which he served as a reviewer. I accepted it partly because the other two reviewers recommended that it be published, but I also felt comfortable accepting the paper because it had improved so much as a result of John's insightful comments.

Second, before my stint as associate editor, I believed that most authors were more concerned with getting their work published than with doing the best possible work. I thought that most authors would seek to do as little work as possible when making revisions, and that once their papers were accepted for publication, they would really start slacking off. I assumed that, because of the reward structure of our occupation, most authors would be concerned mostly with getting more papers listed on their vitae, not with producing the best possible work. Again, I underestimated my colleagues. I've noticed that, if anything, the closer their papers get to publication, the more concerned most authors become about each nuance. *ASQ* publishes many papers that are based on dissertations. I've noticed that these junior authors will take a great deal of time to make sure that even the smallest details are right. Perhaps this is because these are usually among their first publications or because they have worked so long and hard on their dissertations. I was most cynical about experienced and established authors. I assumed that senior people would be most resistant to suggestions because they would see themselves as having skills and prestige similar to or higher than those making the suggestions. I also thought that once the pressure to develop a respectable pile of publications was absent, authors wouldn't feel the same pressures that untenured faculty do to make sure that each published paper is as strong as possible. Again, I was wrong. There are the usual exceptions, of course, but if anything, I've found that more established authors—such as Keith Murnighan, Charles O'Reilly, Barry Staw, and Karl Weick—are usually more willing than less established authors to make improvements beyond those needed to produce acceptance letters.

Karl Weick is, by any measure, among the most prestigious organizational scholars, and he is remarkably responsive to suggestions. As I noted earlier, his paper on the collapse of sensemaking received the most positive initial reviews of any paper that I have handled. Yet the version that was published in *ASQ* is much better than the version that was provisionally accepted, largely because Karl was so responsive to suggestions. He was pleasant and humble throughout the process, and always seemed concerned only with making the paper as strong as possible.

Similarly, a fairly experienced author recently submitted a paper so strong that the reviewers suggested that only modest revisions would be needed before it could be published. However, he called me to say he was going to take an extra 6 months or so to code a large additional batch of data, so that his findings would be more convincing. I pointed out to him that, although one reviewer had noted that more data would make his findings more persuasive, no one had suggested that more data were required before the paper could be published. The author responded that he wanted to code more data because, otherwise, he would not be able to take pride in having done his best work after the paper was published.

I've seen a similar level of concern and care by other experienced authors who have submitted papers to *ASQ*. Keith Murnighan, who is one of these careful authors, once told me that I had reached a point in my career where I had passed from the "publish or perish" to the "publish and perish" stage. He explained that I'd shown that I could publish enough papers; the challenge for the rest of my career would be to publish papers good enough to improve, or at least not harm, my reputation. Keith's interesting argument may explain why established scholars continue to be concerned about the quality of their work.

In contrast to these pleasant surprises about the quality of the work done by both *ASQ* reviewers and authors, this role has been a bur-den to me in several ways. As I expected when I took the job, the worst part of being an editor is the time it takes from writing my own papers. I've written between 75 and 100 decision letters each year I've been at *ASQ*. This is trivial compared with the 500 or so letters that Rick Mowday and Jan Beyer wrote each year as *AMJ* editors. I have no idea how either of them maintained this pace for 3 years and still managed to write such high-quality letters. But even my comparably small load has reduced my productivity.

Right now, as I look around my office, there is a small pile of four folders with *ASQ* manuscripts and complete sets of reviews; I need to write a decision letter for each. I've looked through each folder closely enough to know that none of these papers can be rejected quickly, in less than about 2 hours. I read every paper submitted to *ASQ*, even when all three reviewers agree that it is best rejected. But I rarely overturn the reviewers' decision when there is a high level of consensus. As a result, when they all agree that a paper shouldn't be published, I don't read it as closely as I would read a paper that might be publishable or that has mixed reviews. When there is consensus that a paper shouldn't be revised and resubmitted, I don't need to write a detailed letter explaining what needs to be done before it can be published or to help the author sort out conflicting reviews. But when there is a lack of consensus or when there is much agreement that a paper should be published, I spend a lot of time with it. All four of the papers sitting on my desk right now have received mixed reviews, and there seems to be a reasonable chance that each of them will be worthy of a revise-and-resubmit decision. As a result, it will take me between 4 and 8 hours to write a decision letter for each one.

This backlog, which is fairly typical of the 3 years I've worked for *ASQ*, means that I will lose a week of writing time to the other piles in my office during the next 2 or 3 weeks. I have learned always to do at least an hour or two of my own work every day, no matter how many decision letters I need to write, otherwise my work stalls completely. The size of the *ASQ* pile varies, but it is always there, subtracting hours from my own papers. For example, to my left, there are piles of materials for a long theory paper that Charlie Galunic and I are trying to write on the impact of intense public scrutiny on leaders and organizations. We have a long and confused draft that is more than a year old. If I hadn't had the constant load of decision letters to write during the past year, I suspect this paper would have been repaired and submitted for publication by now.

Also to my left is a smaller pile for a paper on clients as sources of enjoyment for service employees, an empirical study of hairstylists. I wrote the first draft during Christmas break, about 3 months ago. Before I was an *ASQ* editor, I would have devoted all my writing time during the break to my own papers, but I could work on this draft only half of each day because I had a pile of about 10 *ASQ* papers to get through. As a result, the draft wasn't quite as strong as I had hoped it would be by the end of the break. And since then, I've repeatedly broken promises to coauthor Randi Cohen about when I would complete the changes it needs before we can submit it for publication. I need a week to concentrate on just that paper, but I wonder when my *ASQ* pile will shrink enough for that to be possible.

Finally, to my right is a pile of readings for a paper that Jim March and I have been talking about that will advocate that organizational research should use performance as an independent variable more often and as a dependent variable less often. I am excited about this paper. We have had some wonderful conversations about it and have outlined what seems to be a compelling argument. But there is no way to tell if the paper will be any good without writing it first. I am now almost 2 months behind on my promise to draft the first 10 or 15 pages. Again, I wonder when my *ASQ* pile will get small enough so that I can get to this paper.

The press of the *ASQ* job has not only affected the hours that I spend pounding away at the keyboard. I've been surprised to find that it affects where my thoughts wander during those times that I have to reflect, fantasize, and fret about my work. I didn't realize how much I worked on my research during such odd moments until I took the *ASQ* job. Before I was an editor, I used the times when I exercised, drove, or sat through boring seminars mostly to think about the papers that I was trying to write. I recall, for example, that when I was doing a massive revision of my dissertation paper on organizational death for *ASQ,* I would use a 45-minute run each day to help resolve problems I couldn't fix at the keyboard. Often at the

end of a run I'd be excited about the idea I'd developed to repair the part of the paper that I was stuck on. I'd go straight to my study and immediately start scribbling notes or fiddling with the manuscript to see if my new idea was any good.

I still spend some of this time thinking about my own work, but it seems that I now spend at least half of such time fretting about other people's work. For example, several weeks ago I was trying to make some progress on an outline for the performance paper with Jim March. I went for a row (I sometimes use a rowing shell for exercise) with the intention of thinking about a conceptual mechanism we were wrestling with for part of the paper. Once I started rowing, however, I couldn't stop thinking about a promising but disorganized paper submitted to *ASQ* that had received mixed reviews. By the end of the row, I had some new ideas about how the paper could be revised and had decided that, although two of the three reviewers recommended that it be rejected outright, there was hope for the paper and that an invitation to revise it was in order. As a result, rather than going back to the outline for my own paper, I spent the next 3 or 4 hours writing a decision letter.

I once talked to Jerry Salancik about this focus-of-attention problem. He told me that being associate editor at *ASQ* had a similar effect on him. He said that he went for long walks to think about the manuscripts he was handling, and would often compose decision letters in his head as he walked along. It made me feel better to hear that my behavior wasn't much different from Jerry's, but I wish I could start thinking about other people's work less and start thinking about my own work more.

Should I Stay or Should I Go?

My current term as *ASQ* associate editor ends in September 1994. Steve Barley, who recently followed John Freeman as our editor, asked me to continue at *ASQ* for at least another year. As of this moment (April 1994), I have not decided whether to accept his invitation or to enjoy my sabbatical next year without the burden of the *ASQ* pile on my desk. I've been fretting about this decision a lot lately. My thoughts keep turning to a comment about critics made by author

John Updike, who has won the Pulitzer Prize and the National Book Award. He said something like, Criticism is to writing as hugging the shore is to sailing in the deep blue sea. Updike reminds me that giving advice about writing is less draining, less risky, and less interesting than trying to do it. He reminds me that I often experience moments of joy or despair when I am writing my own papers, but I rarely experience these strong feelings when I am writing decision letters. As a result, beyond the negative effects on my productivity and thinking time, I worry that another year or more at *ASQ* will mean that I am condemning myself to hundreds of relatively dull hours that I can avoid by just saying, "No, thanks" to Steve Barley.

Yet, despite this fretting, I am leaning toward accepting Steve's invitation. Jeff Pfeffer once joked that I would never willingly quit being an *ASQ* associate editor because I'd get "Potomac fever": Just like politicians in Washington, D.C., I'd be unwilling to give up the power that goes with the position. I hope this isn't why I am thinking about staying on at *ASQ* for another year or so. Jeff's argument is amusing, but I think it is wrong, because the amount of power that an *ASQ* associate editor has is very small. I have accepted fewer than 10 articles in each of the years I've worked at *ASQ*. Not only is this a small number of papers, but each is likely to be read by no more than a few hundred people.

I am likely to stay on for several other reasons. The first is that Steve Barley and Linda Pike have asked me to do so. I've suggested numerous able replacements for me, but they keep insisting that they want me to stay. I find this flattering, and I feel bad about letting down these two good friends, even though I know the journal wouldn't suffer from my departure. Another reason I'm likely to stay is that I am pleased with the wise changes that Steve is making in the philosophy and operation of the journal. He has increased the size of the editorial board by about 25% and the number of *ASQ* associate editors from two to four. Marshall Meyer and I have been joined in recent months by Christine Oliver and Keith Murnighan. Steve has made these changes to encourage authors to submit papers on a broader range of subjects, to appeal to a broader range of readers, and to speed the review process. John Freeman did a good job leading *ASQ*, but the changes Steve has made seem as if they will make the journal even stronger. I am worried that, if I do quit, I will miss the chance to be part of these exciting changes.

The final (and most selfish) reason I am likely to stay is that the recent changes in procedures and in *ASQ* editors will probably reduce my workload, perhaps by as much as 50%. Steve has been sending back to authors a higher percentage of papers that are inappropriate for publication in *ASQ* instead of leaving this task to the associate editors. He has also begun to handle some of the qualitative papers submitted to *ASQ*, which reduces my workload. Finally, and most important, Steve recently appointed Keith Murnighan as a fourth associate editor. Keith has done wonderful field research, but he is best known as a prolific and well-respected experimental psychologist. We hope that his presence will encourage authors to submit more experiments to *ASQ*. In addition, Keith was also appointed to ease my workload, and it seems that he will reduce it. Keith has been on the job just over a month as of this writing, but he is already handling several psychological papers that would otherwise have been sent my way.

I hope that the changes will allow me to continue working as an *ASQ* editor, but to do so for fewer hours a week. I am waiting to see if the anticipated results of the changes do occur, or if I am just fooling myself. I want to write more of my own papers, submit them to more refereed journals, and learn more lessons from the reviews I get during the next 3 years than I have during the past 3 years. If I do quit this job, however, I will miss the less exciting but equally enlightening vantage point on the review process that I've enjoyed as an associate editor at *ASQ*. I will miss working with the reviewers, authors, and other editors who devote so much effort to developing good papers for *ASQ*. I will especially miss working with Linda Pike, who has a remarkable ability to improve the writing and the logic in the papers that *ASQ* publishes. These scholars have taught me hundreds of lessons about research methods, theory, writing, and ethics that I would never have learned if I had not spent the past 3 years working on a parade of decision letters for the *Administrative Science Quarterly*.

Postscript: July 1995

The first draft of this paper was written in April 1994. I was so excited about the changes that were happening at *ASQ* that I had decided to sign up for another 3-year term at *ASQ* in July 1994. This was a mistake. By November 1994 it was clear that I had lost the ability to put *ASQ* work ahead of my own writing and research. Steve Barley showed me data indicating that I had degenerated from being the *ASQ* editor who gave the most rapid feedback to authors to being the editor who gave the slowest feedback. I was more interested in doing my own work than in reading and commenting on work done by others. After spending a week in November writing rejection letters to some of my best friends (including two rejection letters to one person I especially like and admire), I decided to resign. I wrote a resignation letter just before Thanksgiving. I handed Steve Barley the letter and told him to "take this job and shove it." It was a delightful moment, and I've never regretted it. I've had a more productive and enjoyable sabbatical as a result. Dan Brass replaced me as associate editor at *ASQ*—a splendid choice. Dan is an accomplished researcher and has been one of *ASQ*'s most insightful and fastest reviewers. I should have resigned in September 1994. More accurately, based on the statistics that Steve showed me, I resigned in May 1994, but I didn't have the courtesy to tell myself or anyone else.

References

Barker, J. R. (1993). Tightening the iron cage: Concertive control in self-managing teams. *Administrative Science Quarterly, 38,* 408-437.

Cooper, C., Dyck, B., & Frohlich, N. (1992). Improving the effectiveness of gainsharing: The role of fairness and participation. *Administrative Science Quarterly, 37,* 471-490.

Mowday, R. T., & Sutton, R. I. (1993). Organizational behavior: Linking individuals and groups to organizational contexts. *Annual Review of Psychology, 44,* 195-229.

Strunk, W., Jr. & White, E. B. (1979). *The elements of style* (3rd ed.). New York: Macmillan.

Sutton, R. I. (1987). The process of organizational death: Disbanding and reconnecting. *Administrative Science Quarterly, 32,* 542-569.

Sutton, R. I. (1991). Maintaining norms about expressed emotions: The case of bill collectors. *Administrative Science Quarterly, 36,* 245-268.

Sutton, R. I., & Ford, L. H. (1982). Problem-solving adequacy in hospital subunits. *Human Relations, 35,* 675-701.

Sutton, R. I., & Kahn, R. L. (1987). Prediction, understanding and control as antidotes to organizational stress. In J. Lorsch (Ed.), *Handbook of organizational behavior* (pp. 272-285). Englewood Cliffs, NJ: Prentice Hall.

Sutton, R. I., & Rafaeli, A. (1988). Untangling the relationship between displayed emotions and organizational sales: The case of convenience stores. *Academy of Management Journal, 31,* 461-487.

Sutton, R. I., & Rousseau, D. M. (1979). Structure, technology, and dependence on a parent organization: Organizational and environmental correlates of individual responses. *Journal of Applied Psychology, 64,* 675-687.

Weick, K. (1993). The collapse of sensemaking in organizations: The Mann Gulch disaster. *Administrative Science Quarterly, 38,* 628-652.

Becoming a Department Chair
and an Administrator

As I said earlier, there are few books or guidelines available on the role of department chairman. From my perspective, serving as chairman has been a full and challenging way to learn—about individual faculty members, about myself, and about how difficult it is to apply much of what we teach. . . . For me, the notion of learning to be more of a buffer, facilitator, and guide has been valuable and is something that I can apply even when I become a "real" professor again.

Nancy K. Napier (p. 319)

Driving home the other night, I had a sudden revelation: I am a hygiene factor. It's tempting to say that this job is invisible, but it isn't. It is invisible only when things go well; when things go poorly, disaster looms large. . . . The name [hygiene factor] derives from the analogy of physicians' washing their hands before treating patients—the practice prevents illness, but it doesn't cause health. Maybe this is why Herzberg posits that "supervision" is a hygiene factor—he is drawing on his own experience with department chairs.

Cynthia V. Fukami (p. 322)

Academic culture is so powerfully antiadministration, antihierarchy, and anti-authority that even an undisciplined, spontaneous, and self-disclosing person like me has to learn to accept the insistence of faculty members that while I am in the role of academic vice president I cannot just be me. . . . If you are still ready, after all of this, to jump into (or continue in) administration, my best wishes. I know a fascinating opportunity that should be available soon after you read this. And from the faculty role I will once again be in, I'll be glad to help you, once I get my teaching schedule right.

Allan R. Cohen (pp. 325, 331)

Feelings of extreme disdain for bureaucracy, administrators, and administrative tasks may be the most collectively socialized response across the academic population. Although most academics purport no desire, and certainly no ambition, to be involved in administration, they nevertheless demand a great deal from those who run their universities. They speak loudly and frequently about the type of assistance they must have from the administration (department, school, and university) in order to get their own work done effectively. Because most refuse to accept administrators who lack fairly stringent academic credentials, it is logical to conclude that at some point many academics *must* assume administrative roles and perform them well if our universities are to function effectively. This observation, however, is not one that seems to be shared by many full-time academics.

The contributors whose chapters appear in this section examine their own paths as academic administrators; two of the authors are department chairs, and one is an academic vice president. To be certain, there are differences of degree in these roles, with the department chairs more appropriately classified as boundary spanners, falling somewhere in between the academic role and the administrative one. Nevertheless, there are many similarities in the three accounts concerning why academics venture into administrative roles, the rewards associated with such paths, and the qualities and prior experience that seem to prepare them to be successful in such journeys. The synergy that results from their similarities and their differences is what caused us to place these three accounts within the same section.

Turning first to the role of department chair, Nancy Napier and Cynthia Fukami speak openly and, at times, humorously about the boundary-spanning nature of the position; for example, Napier speaks of the job as "at times harrowing and always frustrating" (pp. 313-314), and Fukami calls it a "part-time job with full-time responsibilities" (p. 322). Like Allan Cohen, our academic vice president, they report that they had little initial ambition for their administrative positions. Rather, they were called or drafted into service by the needs of their units. Napier seems to experience more rewards from her position than does Fukami, who (jokingly, we believe) classifies herself in her job as chair as a hygiene factor and compares her management task to herding cats. In our experience, the high frustration of department chairs is fairly widespread. Although it must be partially attributed to their boundary-spanning role, we suspect a significant portion of the variance might also be explained by the fact that few receive any type of training for the role before undertaking it. Nevertheless, both Napier and Fukami report having learned some important truths from their experiences, including the often limited practical applicability of the management and leadership theories they teach and greater appreciation for the "practicing manager" students who often question the validity of these theories in the classroom. Like the journal editors who shared their experiences in the preceding chapters, both Napier and Fukami are looking forward to returning to their academic roles full-time. We suspect, however, that they will not return untouched, a conclusion consistent with their statements that virtually all faculty members should have some experience as department chairs for a period. Whether they admit it or not, Napier and Fukami seem likely to reemerge as faculty members who display greater tolerance and respect for the foibles and performance of those who remain in administrative positions. We are confident that such understanding makes our universities better places to learn and work. Frankly, we have mixed feelings about the suitability of all faculty members for the department chair role; nevertheless, we too wish that such transitions, although temporary, were more widespread.

Allan Cohen, the academic vice president in this group, made a greater leap along the administrative continuum than Napier and Fukami in accepting his position. His move was a discrete one, "from partisan bystander to enmeshed advocate" (p. 328), and at times it is clear that he feels this keenly—for instance, when former colleagues say to him, in essence, as one did, "When we talk you are not Allan Cohen, you are the vice president" (p. 325). Yet although Cohen certainly did not volunteer for his current position, his transition was probably more predestined than those of our two department chairs. Certainly it was encouraged by a number of factors in Cohen's history as an academic, including an early and continuing interest in educational reform; a pragmatic, rather than theoretical, bent; a bias toward action; consulting experience working beside other leaders; and the development of an institutional perspective.

Despite significantly higher costs (80-hour workweeks, small pay increases and a loss of consulting opportunities, the formalization of collegial relationships), compared with those associated with the position of department chair, in many ways Cohen is much less frustrated by his position than are Napier and Fukami. We suspect the explanation lies in its greater reward potential—the opportunity, as he puts it, "to change management education dramatically" (p. 328). Few academics will ever have such an opportunity, and one senses that many might find it more appealing than they would ever admit. Nevertheless,

Cohen's essay clearly articulates that the road of an administrator is not an easy one, with little appreciation from faculty members and a lot of resistance to the inevitable threats that change brings to their autonomy, convenience, and comfort. The only reason to take on such a challenge, Cohen concludes, is that "you have a compelling educational vision and believe that there is a chance to accomplish it. . . . Without a compelling personal vision that you can translate into an organizational vision, there is almost no hope of getting individualistic and quasi-autonomous faculty to work together" (p. 329).

Cohen is by now quite clear about the length of his commitment; he anticipates a full-time return to academic life around the time this volume is published. Again, however, there can be no doubt that the individual who reassumes his academic role at the end of this administrative experience will be quite different from the person who became academic vice president of Babson College 3 years ago. Further, we suggest that all academic units involved—university, college, and department—will most certainly be the better for his foray into academic administration. In these times, when virtually all universities are experiencing great turbulence in their external and internal environments, it seems shortsighted for academics to expect that such problems can be resolved by others while they continue to devote time and effort to other pursuits, e.g., teaching, research, and professional service. We believe that more and more faculty will be called upon to serve brief but intense stints in administrative positions in order to protect those academic freedoms they hold most dear. Furthermore, we expect that in the long term, such assignments will benefit all parties concerned.

31 Alice in Academia

THE DEPARTMENT CHAIRMAN ROLE FROM BOTH SIDES OF THE MIRROR

Nancy K. Napier

I never knew how hard it could be to choose a name. When I had the opportunity to assume the task of overseeing my department 3 years ago, one of the first issues that arose was what I should be "called." It was astonishing to me that the members of my department (all of whom happened to be male), as well as the secretarial staff and students, felt called on to offer or reject titles. What "we" should put on the front door was a topic of conversation for several days, taking much longer than the 30 seconds I had taken to decide.

Many argued that *chairman* is sexist and outdated. The more progressive among the faculty and student ranks insisted that *chairperson* and *chairwoman* are the modern and politically cor-

rect terms, although to me, both seem too long and awkward. Others argued for the more "neutral" term *chair* (something I sit on). Still others cautioned against calling me the *head* of the department, because in navy parlance, a head is a latrine. In the end, I settled for *chairman,* for its simplicity and familiarity to the "outside" (i.e., business) world. That was my first lesson in how hard it is to please many people.

After such a daunting start, I wondered whether I would ever learn to live gracefully with my dozen male department members. Like most of us, I did not count moving into administration among my goals. I succeeded a dearly loved chairman who became associate dean and then dean; he was a hard act to follow. It has been at times harrowing

AUTHOR'S NOTE: I shared some of these ideas at the 1992 Western Academy of Management Doctoral/Junior Faculty Workshop in Spokane, Washington. Thanks to Kim Boal for asking me to participate in the workshop; to John Bigelow, H. S. Napier, and Bill Wines for their insights on earlier versions of this chapter; and to Kathleen Anderson for her patience and good humor, even on the ninth (tenth?) revision. A slightly different version of this chapter was previously published in the *Journal of Management Inquiry,* Vol. 2, No. 3, September 1993.

and always frustrating, but after nearly 3 years, I've learned more than I expected; I would like to pass on a little of that knowledge.

My focus here is to present some ideas that may be of particular help to new faculty members—or to doctoral students hoping to become faculty members. These are the ones who may have little idea what to expect from a chairman when they join a department. Furthermore, in this essay I focus on what a chairman does *inside* the department, rather than the chairman's role in dealing with external issues. Finally, these thoughts are tied to what a chairman can do to help faculty members in their traditional roles as teachers and researchers, as well as individuals who otherwise serve the college or university. Another essay might address how these traditional roles may need to change in the future.

I view the relationship between a department chairman and (junior) faculty members as an exchange; I will present my thoughts in such a framework. Below are general and gentle thoughts on what I think junior faculty members can expect from their chairmen and what chairmen can expect from faculty members. I draw on my own experience rather than on research and writing (of which there is almost none) about the job. I've quizzed counterparts in the job and found no single way to do it. Thus the following ideas are truly personal reflections, particularly as the job affects the more junior members of a department.

What Can You Expect From Your Chairman?

Faculty members have a right to ask and should consider what their relationship can be with their department chairmen. After serving in the job for 3 years, I'm beginning to define the role I think I should play for individual faculty members and for the department as a whole. My thoughts may be particularly useful for junior faculty as they consider how they want to interact with their chairmen. A chairman should play at least three roles for a junior faculty member: buffer, facilitator, and guide.

Buffer

As a chairman, I see one of my key roles as that of buffer for junior faculty members. I try

to protect them from administrative tasks (committees, task forces, students), from what I consider to be potentially harmful information, and, to some extent, from themselves.

Administrative Buffer

Administrative tasks drain time from anyone involved in them. Because time is one of the key resources of a junior (or any) faculty member, I try hard to protect my junior department members from excessive assignments on committees, in particular. In meetings between department chairmen and the dean, there is frequently a need for "volunteers" for various committees (e.g., Graduate Policy, Undergraduate Policy, Tenure and Promotion, Dean Evaluation, Faculty Senate). The chairmen usually talk about which members of their departments are in their early career stages and should refrain from taking on committee duties. Rarely are requests to exclude junior faculty from demanding committees disregarded.

The more difficult situations for the faculty member arise when the individual is asked directly for help (e.g., to put together a proposal, oversee an internship) and he or she is reluctant or unwilling to refrain from giving time. In such cases, junior faculty members have the right, I think, to refuse a request and use the chairman as the reason (e.g., "She asked me to focus more on my research this year"). If a faculty member is uncomfortable doing this, I ask that he tell me about the request and, if we decide it is inappropriate, I can "say no" for him. Although I offer this "service," a number of our faculty members nevertheless often jump into various commitments. Again, I figure they can make their own decisions; if they want help or buffering, however, I am ready to assist.

Information Buffer

In times of chaos (and what university is not facing such times these days?), it is easy to become mired in concerns about what will happen—to the university, the college, the department, individuals. Spending too much time seeking information and speculating about outcomes can drain valuable time from faculty members. As a chairman, I try to pass along accurate and useful information to faculty members rather than stimulate the always-vibrant rumor mill. As a result, I sometimes withhold information or "repackage" it for certain people.

The last academic year was a roller coaster for us. We hired a new dean from business (a former portfolio manager, based in Boston), our university president was fired by the State Board of Education, and our well-regarded associate dean became seriously ill—all by mid-November. Especially in the weeks following the new dean's arrival, some junior faculty members were beside themselves. The dean had tossed out ideas (taken seriously by too many people) ranging from dissolving departments to finding a way to terminate tenured faculty members who "weren't performing." Such rumblings caught many faculty members by surprise (thinking we had cagily hired an "outside dean" whose sole job would be to find additional resources). As a result, I found some junior faculty members frazzled and unable to concentrate on work. They took fragments of "deanspeak" and carried them to their most unreasonable outcomes. They worried that they'd have no jobs, no careers—you name it.

After several days, I finally started saying, "Let me do the worrying. If you need to start a job search, I'll tell you in enough time for you to get your curriculum vitae ready." Although one could say this was a paternalistic (maternalistic?) approach, it seemed to have a calming effect.

I also buffer individuals from information that I feel might do more harm than good, particularly if it concerns an isolated incident. For example, students frequently complain to me about professors. If I receive one complaint about someone and I have reason to question the validity of the claim, I tend not to report it immediately to the professor. I feel strongly about this, particularly if I know the professor is going through some difficult personal times. Rather than pass along a single student complaint, I might make more of an effort to ask the faculty member how he feels his classes are going and offer suggestions for ways to improve that are along the lines of the student comments.

If I hear several complaints, however, I take them to the professor and discuss with him what might be going on. Even then, I weigh whether I should convey the (usually negative) passion that might have come through from

students. Similarly, colleagues sometimes talk to me about other colleagues. Unless I get a distinct pattern of comments (good or bad), I tend to buffer the professor from talk that I think might be unfair to that person.

Buffer From Self

Sometimes faculty members need to be protected from themselves. Typically, this occurs when a junior faculty member wants to take on what I would consider to be too many obligations. Before I became chairman, I watched one professor who really needed such a buffer. In his first year, he decided that to become visible in the community (as a way to have research doors opened to him) and the university (as a way to "get to know people"), he should join several professional associations and committees. Indeed, he soon became well-known around town and the university, but he was also swamped with many commitments that took time away from teaching and research. He spent the next 2 years extricating himself from several obligations that were "nice," but that had little payoff for him.

Even though a chairman should help to buffer people from their own enthusiasm, how a faculty member chooses to spend time is ultimately his or her decision. When I was planning class scheduling for fall semester, one new faculty member insisted that he wanted to teach a new course as well as one he had been planning to teach (neither of the courses has multiple sections). Because we each teach three classes each semester, most people want only two preparations. I explained that, to fulfill his teaching obligation, he would end up teaching three *different* courses if I granted his request. I tried hard to suggest that perhaps this was not a good use of his time in his early years. He was determined, however, and after thinking about it for a while, he decided to do three different courses. His decision stands. Thus I found that I am not always successful, even when I try to buffer faculty members from themselves.

Facilitator

Watching faculty members develop their teaching and research skills is the best part of being a department chairman. When the frustrating parts of the job get me down—signing student add/drop slips, deciding whether courses will transfer from another university to ours, listening to one more complaint about salary inequities that I can do nothing about—I draw on (limited) financial and other resources to assist faculty members in meeting the needs they may have, so that they can do a better job in the classroom or in their research. It helps to keep the job in perspective.

Teaching Facilitator

I try to help with teaching in several ways. One of the most important things I can do for faculty members, but perhaps particularly important for junior faculty members seeking blocks of research and writing time, is to work with them in planning the teaching schedules. In our college, scheduling is more an art than a science; we try to "give people what they want" in their schedules. This can make the chairman's life very frustrating, but it gives faculty members more flexibility in planning their work.

I try to assign people the courses they want to teach. Although we must cover certain required courses, we have a range of electives and upper-level courses that many people like to teach. This often involves negotiation among faculty members ("If you let him teach this in the fall, you can go back to it in the spring"), and sometimes I must find an adjunct professor to teach a course that no one is available to teach, but I believe it is worth the effort.

Help in teaching sometimes involves things as specific as finding the right classroom. Last semester, a professor who uses group exercises in his courses was upset that a lecture course in information systems had been scheduled in what he regarded as the "Management Department's" classroom. The room has movable tables and chairs, can be sectioned off for negotiation exercises, and happens to be next door to the department. I arranged with the chairman in Information Systems to shuffle rooms and classes so that this professor could have access to the room he wanted, and everyone seemed satisfied.

Other ways to facilitate teaching include offering help with grading (for large-section courses) and finding money to buy or rent equipment, videotapes, or databases needed for particular classes. Sometimes, the best way to support teaching is just to listen. When faculty members need an ear—to try out thoughts on course content, grading, use of projects—I want to be ready. This role often emerges when a faculty member is concerned about a class problem. For example, last year a professor believed that two students had cheated on an exam and take-home work. It was soon clear to me the professor had a plan for how to approach the issue, but just needed to confirm it by talking about it. By listening and asking a few questions to assess how thoroughly and fairly the professor had investigated the situation, I tried to facilitate the professor's teaching rather than tell him what to do.

A final way in which a chairman can aid faculty members' teaching is by giving them a chance to teach special-topic courses. In the past several years, at least half of my department members have had the chance to teach elective courses they wanted to offer. Given our tight resources and the need to staff many required courses, it has been a struggle, but, again, I see facilitating such opportunities for teaching as an important part of our quality of work life.

Research Facilitator

A chairman can also support faculty members by finding ways to encourage and promote research. Arranging for student help (e.g., graduate assistants [GAs], research interns) is one of the most important ways of doing this. I fight hard at the beginning of the academic year to obtain GA help. My faculty members usually assure me that there is no way they can ever accomplish what they want to do on the limited GA time they are allocated. Oddly enough, I typically discover that midway through the semester, the GAs frequently have little to do. My advice to junior faculty members is to use their assigned GA time wisely, so I can argue the benefits gained from those hours of student help. It makes my life easier the next time I fight for more assistance.

In an effort to provide research time for faculty members, I try to make available a reasonable amount of course release time. I try to offer release time to junior faculty members when they join the university and consider it again every 2 years or so if their productivity continues. Ours is a school with limited resources and a lot of required courses to teach. The budget is never adequate, but I've worked to use it to offer faculty members the time they need to improve their teaching ability and to pursue research.

Summer financial support has become an expected part of many university compensation packages for new faculty members. In our school, faculty members compete for a pool of summer fellowship stipends. Currently, we are able to fund about half of the research applicants. By encouraging faculty members to apply for support and helping them with their proposals, I also try to facilitate their research efforts by helping them "buy time."

Sometimes faculty members need additional funds—to pay for mail surveys or to travel to overseas conferences, for example—that are beyond the scope of the normal department budget. I try to facilitate their efforts to get funding by steering them in the direction of internal funding sources. For instance, we have a college research pool that can fund small efforts (up to a few hundred dollars). A university pool will also support research efforts, as long as the college matches the funds. Sometimes our dean is willing to fund special activities out of his discretionary funds. Helping faculty members prepare their proposals to secure some of this money—even going to the dean of the business school, if necessary—is a task that falls within my role as research facilitator.

I also try to keep faculty members informed about external funding sources when I hear about them. I receive requests for proposals from various groups and habitually post them or show them to particular faculty members who may be interested. With the cutbacks in resources at all universities in recent years, it is imperative that all department chairmen become more knowledgeable about getting external funding.

A final way in which I try to facilitate research, particularly for junior faculty members, is by introducing them to contacts they might find helpful in the academic and business worlds. Introducing faculty members to others at conferences, suggesting people they might call or write to regarding research topics, and offering them chances to review papers or be discussants at conferences are all ways to help them build their own networks. Much of the research our faculty members do requires organizational sites, and we are fortunate that a number of major facilities exist close by (e.g., Boise Cascade, J. R. Simplot Co., Hewlett-Packard, Ore-Ida, Morrison-Knudsen); several Fortune 500 firms have their headquarters in Boise. Introducing our faculty members to individuals associated with these firms is another way to help them carry out their research and service commitments to the community.

Guide

The final role of the chairman is that of guide for faculty members who want or need guidance. I think of guiding in two ways. In my canoeing days, I guided by sitting in the back and making small changes in the paddle position to steer the canoe in one direction or another. When I came ashore, I guided by forging ahead through brush and woods.

Junior faculty members may need guidance on such diverse topics as how to fit into the department, how to understand policy on research or teaching, and how to do the necessary tasks to qualify for tenure or promotion. Every department has norms, ranging from how often faculty members are expected to hold office hours to what is considered a reasonable workload for students. I try to help faculty members decipher the expectations and put them into a context that is workable for them. Usually, I try to do this through the "canoe steering" approach rather than by the "forging ahead" method. I recently had a complaint from a graduate assistant who felt that a faculty member's expectations were unreasonable. After talking with the student and consulting with the director of the MBA programs, who also oversees the GA program, I met with the faculty member. When he understood the student's concerns, he was able to come up with a more reasonable (for the student) work request.

A more direct form of guidance is to offer suggestions on research or teaching, sometimes even when one has not been asked. One faculty member has a long list of publications in his publishing record, but the articles have appeared primarily in journals that are practitioner oriented or are not widely read in academic circles. He also conducts research in areas that are outside the mainstream of his field. In my most recent evaluation meeting with this individual, I felt obliged to suggest that he conduct at least some of his future research in areas more central to the field and that he set his publishing sights on more challenging (i.e., lower acceptance rate) journals.

I further try to guide by acting as a counselor, if need be. Several department members have gone through difficult personal experiences during the past 3 years. Often, the best way I can help is by listening and offering opinions only when asked. I've listened to people talk about concerns about their family members and friends, their health, their successes and failures. I'm flattered to provide an ear for those who need one. Even so, I find it important to encourage people to get beyond their personal travails and concentrate on doing the tasks they need to do to succeed at our university. Thus there is a fine balance to be struck between being a counselor or listener and being a "nudger," encouraging people to do their work.

Finally, I try to guide by modeling behavior I value. I work hard on my own teaching and research, figuring I cannot ask others to perform certain activities if I do not.

What I Expect From Faculty Members

Although the exchange between faculty members and chairman should be primarily weighted toward what the chairman can do to make life better for department members, like all good relationships, it should not be only one-way. I count on faculty members to uphold their end of our relationship. Although fewer in number than my obligations to them, the requests I have of faculty members are, to me, quite significant and fundamental.

Help, When I Ask

I try hard to limit the direct requests I make of faculty members. When I do make requests, they tend to be service oriented (e.g., concerning committee service or working with students). I try to view each request from the perspective of the faculty member and determine what benefits it may have for that person. In other words, I try not to make requests that represent gains for me or the department at the expense of lost time, energy, or resources to faculty members. My requests should concern matters that will benefit faculty members in terms of learning; gaining visibility throughout the college, university, and community; or contributing in some way to their research or teaching.

This past year, I asked a new department member to sit on the dean's Evaluation Committee. It was a short-term assignment (three meetings), gave him an opportunity to work with some of the key players in the business school, and was a chance for him to learn more about what he could expect from a dean. I asked another member to work with a graduate student who wanted to do an independent study project. That faculty member subsequently invited the student to be a guest speaker in class and will likely continue to work with him in developing a business idea. I asked another of our junior faculty members to take charge of organizing an invitation to bring a keynote speaker to campus. The task gave the faculty member a chance to help choose the speaker, spend some time with one of the field's top people, and gain some visibility around the university as one of the organizers.

Time for the Rest of My Professional Life

My greatest fear in becoming chairman was (and continues to be) that I would cease to be an effective researcher and teacher. Because of the need to be around the office and because I must carry out various administrative duties, I spend less time on research and writing than I like. Because of the course time release, I spend fewer hours in the classroom. I worry about my personal skills becoming rusty, and I miss the excitement of teaching classes.

For me, one of the joys of being a professor has been having control over my time. The chairman job wrenches that control away from me every day. So far, I have fought it. My solution, and one that my faculty members have graciously learned to live with, is to "disappear" for certain periods during the week. Usually, I stay home some portion of the week to do "my" work. This keeps me sane, allows me to jump back refreshed into the fracas at school, and permits me to keep my hand in scholarly activities. Indeed, it has become a luxury to have the time to think, learn, read, and write. So, when I disappear, I am implicitly asking, or rather demanding, that my faculty members respect my need to remain part of the scholarly world.

Good-Faith Effort on the Faculty Members' Part

Despite all the attempts I make to buffer, facilitate, and guide, faculty members will succeed or fail on their own. If I make the effort to help, I expect them to make serious efforts to succeed. We hire in good faith, the best we can find, fully expecting our faculty members to be promoted, to be granted tenure, and to have long productive lives as members of the university. I expect a serious effort from each member in return.

One of the surprises of this job was learning that not everyone is as self-disciplined and motivated as I expected. I have tried participative management and found it does not always work. I looked for good-faith effort and was disappointed when it was not forthcoming. I am dismayed, for example, when a faculty member fails, for some reason, to provide the best experience possible for students. When a faculty member teaches a course, I expect respect for students, integrity, and excellence in that effort. When I sense that things are not progressing as they should be, I have the responsibility to say so, and I expect a faculty member to, at a minimum, acknowledge the concern and take action if appropriate.

We all expect faculty members to make their best showing in the classroom, in their research, and in their service activities. If they fall short in their efforts or choose to follow a different path, that is their right. Ideally, separation should occur as a faculty member's choice and not by default. Nevertheless, I am learning that in some situations, firmer guidance and more diligent monitoring may be called for. I dislike this, but I feel it is my responsibility as chairman.

Respect for Support Staff

Finally, perhaps because I am blessed with the world's best secretary and support staff, I feel very strongly about the importance of faculty members' demonstrating respect for them.

One of the reasons I agreed to take the job as chairman was the honest willingness of our secretary to "train" me. As the source of our department's institutional memory, she has helped me through decisions in situations she has seen before but I have not. She relieves me of most of the routine work of department administration and provides a welcome and refreshingly objective perspective. She thinks for me and for herself, takes initiative, and warns me of potential or actual problems, with students and with faculty members. She manages our work-study students, is a liaison with adjunct faculty members, and solves a thousand problems, from tracking down frustratingly elusive books to advising hopelessly confused students about their scheduling problems.

Because of her contribution to making the department run smoothly, I try to protect her. When faculty members take undue advantage of her good nature and willingness to assist them, I try to become her buffer. Not many, but more than enough, still try to give her exams to type and copy for 200 students the day before they are needed. Others have asked her to type conference papers on the day they must be sent out by overnight courier. Such requests are unacceptable.

As a member of the faculty, I try to remember—and encourage others to remember—that our own support staff, the secretaries in other departments, the staff in the registrar's office, the computer technicians, and the librarians, to mention only a few, are all critical elements in making our working lives more pleasant. Thus I insist that we respect those who help us do our jobs.

Conclusion

As I said earlier, there are few books or guidelines available on the role of department chairman. From my perspective, serving as chairman has been a full and challenging way to learn—about individual faculty members, about myself, and about how difficult it is to apply much of what we teach. I make mistakes daily, and I have appreciated the willingness of my department members to live with them and me as we move along. For me, the notion of learning to be more of a buffer, facilitator, and guide has been valuable and is something that I can apply even when I become a "real" professor again.

32 Herding Cats Part Deux

THE HYGIENE FACTOR

Cynthia V. Fukami

If you're ever feeling too full of yourself, I've found the cure. Be a department chair. I'll bet there is an opportunity available in your neighborhood. There's nothing like being responsible for others for bringing you down to your knees. In my recent life, I have felt like a responsibility magnet. Perhaps it is my stage of life development (read: middle age), or perhaps it is a simple confluence of events: tenure, serving as a member and then chairing the board of directors of the Organizational Behavior Teaching Society, parenthood. Nonetheless, the past 6 years or so have been marked by an ongoing requirement that I be responsible—not just for myself, but for others. Mind you, I'm quite capable and unconcerned about the prospect of being responsible for myself. But responsibility for others, that comes harder. After all, I am a child of the sixties.

And then I crossed the final frontier of responsibility in October 1991, when I was appointed chair of my department. "Read my lips," I had said—many times—"I will never be a department chair. Never." I had spoken with authority. Why would any rational person take on this task? Why, indeed? I had begun my research career by asking a similar question. Why do people become committed to something they clearly don't want, let alone when that commitment is irrational? I was born to be a faculty member. I love to teach. The chair is "relieved" of teaching duty. I love to do research. The chair has little time for such luxuries. Was this the best use of me as a resource for my department? Absolutely not. And yet, here I am, knee-deep in the Big Muddy (with homage to Barry Staw), 32 months later (and counting), with about as much credibility as George Bush was ascribed for statements regarding his lips.

In my earlier paper (Fukami, 1993) I wrote about the experience of being chair, written roughly 16 months into the job, I was frazzled. Well-meaning friends and colleagues had given me sound advice. "Think about what you want to accomplish in the job," they had said. "Set some goals for yourself." I did set a goal. It was my only goal. I wanted to survive. As I had in my doctoral program, I told myself that being chair was a bounded experience. It had a term, an ending. I could hold my nose and run until the term expired. I didn't have the fear that I would bring the institution to a crashing halt, as I had when I held a responsible position in OBTS. Departments don't crash—chairs crash. I had observed a number of these crashes. One of my friends had developed a condition in which he turned beet red. The longer he was chair, the more often he turned red, and the longer he stayed red. At the end, he was red. Another of my friends was a calm man, a quiet man. I knew he was about to crash when his temper grew shorter than his attention span. Another one of my friends told me that he had fewer and fewer colleagues interested in going to lunch with him. Eventually, he didn't want to go to lunch with anybody either. I didn't want to meet with that fate.

Exactly why I was "convinced" is beyond the scope of this essay. But agree to serve I did, in spite of the fears, in spite of the irrationality of it. And, hold on to your hats, I have come to the conclusion that everybody ought to sit in this chair at some point in his or her academic career. Does misery love company? Yes, but there is more. Does it make one appreciate what a good deal one has as a simple, tenured faculty member? To be sure. In essence, this is a low-win assignment. After all, it is a part-time job with full-time responsibilities. I'm still expected to teach well and to produce scholarly output, while at the same time managing a fairly challenging task.

Driving home the other night, I had a sudden revelation: I am a hygiene factor. It's tempting to say that this job is invisible, but it isn't. It is invisible only when things go well; when things go poorly, disaster looms large. As Fred Herzberg has pointed out, there are some parts of a job that, when absent, produce disappointment and lack of motivation. If present, however, they cause "no dissatisfaction." Happiness and fulfillment don't follow, just the absence of dissatisfaction. Herzberg calls these "hygiene factors." The name derives from the analogy of physicians' washing their hands before treating patients—the practice prevents illness, but it doesn't cause health. Maybe this is why Herzberg posits that "supervision" is a hygiene fac-

tor—he is drawing on his own experience with department chairs.

So that's the key to being a department chair who survives—the hygiene factor. The best one can hope for is to cause no dissatisfaction. This is now my quest—to do no harm. That's not such a bad aspiration. Isn't that what medical doctors vow in the Hippocratic oath?

Following this revelation, and somewhat unexpectedly, I realized that I have learned valuable lessons while sitting in this chair. On the chance that you may someday answer the call yourself, I share these lessons with you; I call them my "10 Lessons for Herding Cats Hygienically":

1. *We take good administrators for granted, and are probably too harsh on poor ones.* Some people are born with a knack for organization and for keeping track of many tiny details. Some people acquire these skills. Some people take care of business better than others. Some listen better. Some just don't have a clue. It's hard enough for them to keep track of themselves, let alone a set of others. Notice that I attribute these very difficult positive behaviors to luck, not effort. As attributional bias suggests, we blame people for mistakes, but don't give them credit for success. Unfortunately, when people are good administrators, we punish them with greater burdens instead of developing these skills in others. In my view, anybody who is willing to try out this role deserves some slack. Those who are good at it deserve more than our thanks—they deserve to be left alone for a while.

2. *It's easier to complain than it is to fix what's wrong.* The downside of listening to your constituents is that you hear many complaints. Worse than that, once you are chair, you can't complain to the chair anymore. I walk the halls looking for someone to complain to. Usually, other chairs and deans are the only ones with sympathetic ears, but they often expect you listen to them, too! Fixing things takes a lot of resources, planning ahead, and energy. These commodities are in short supply in my life.

3. *There is something to symbolic management.* Jeff Pfeffer wasn't kidding when he opened our eyes to the symbolic side of manage-

ment. The academic world is fraught with symbols, rituals, rites of passage, and myths. It is critical that the chair embrace these cultural artifacts in managing professors. For example, I am an associate professor in a department with four full professors. The fact that I serve as chair takes on interesting meaning in this context. If I don't manage with this in mind, I make big mistakes. Don't ever discount the role of process in managing academics.

4. *It's far too easy to slip into Theory X/high-control mode.* Last year, I had my first close call with budget concerns. We had some unexpected travel expenses at the end of the fiscal year, and we were in danger of running a modest deficit. I took this opportunity to look at all the line items for cost-saving opportunities and sent out a two-page memo to my colleagues that discussed such things as the relative merits of 2-day mail versus overnight mail, overnight mail versus faxing, and copying options. Several weeks later, I received a travel reimbursement form to sign and remarked to a colleague that I didn't recall the traveler mentioning this upcoming travel to me. "She was probably afraid," he replied. In my earnest attempt to save money, I had quickly regressed into a Theory X manager. This wasn't pretty. Since then, I have tried to apply more "high-commitment" concepts into my management style. We try to enact as much policy as possible in a consensual manner. Rather than being responsible for everybody, I'd rather have people feel responsible for themselves. Besides, I don't have to be the only one to make the decisions.

5. *Lamaze breathing techniques work for more situations than giving birth.* Breathe deeply. Calm yourself. Count to 10. Patience, patience, patience. Here's one of the advantages of being a woman—Lamaze training. My biggest mistakes and personal disappointments have occurred when I let my anger at particular situations talk before I put my training to work. These situations are personally stressful to me as it is. When they worsen because of my own stupidity, it is even more stressful. Regular exercise has been important for me because (a) it gets me out of the office, (b) it makes me feel stronger, and (c) I do it for me. Just like the stress experts say!

6. *Communication is a daily challenge.* This is so cliché—but it is still true. You get so caught up in the flurry of daily activities that you stop paying attention. You know things, so you assume others know the same things—but they don't. And what's more, they rely on you to tell them. But this also goes both ways. You can easily fall into the trap of believing you always have to have the answer. More times than you can believe, one of your colleagues will have the idea or the information you seek. Turnabout is fair play. By far the most difficult communication issue for me is how much to divulge and how much to keep private. It's the nature of the business that some confidential information is passed to the chair that shouldn't be passed on to others. Of course, this is seen as the most valuable information for the rumor mill. Being open and honest, gaining people's trust, and keeping confidences are really very difficult goals to keep in balance.

7. *There is something to be said for setting your goals higher than simple survival.* Surviving means getting from one day to the next. Although this is a fine accomplishment in itself, it also means that you let the day-to-day minutiae get to you. It's important to move forward, if only in one small area. Above all, be true to yourself. The term of chair will someday expire, but you will still have to look at yourself in the mirror.

8. *Keep your sense of humor.* Eventually, if my earlier predictions hold true, your sense of humor may be your only friend. Hold on to it for dear life.

9. *The lower the stakes, the more heated the battle.* This certainly is the heart of academic symbolism. Somehow, we approach the big issues differently. We put aside smaller grievances and work well together to enact good decisions. But those small issues will get you every time—maybe because you don't prepare for them; maybe because this is one of life's little jokes. Interestingly, Tom Peters wrote about the pitfalls of "the little things" when he was still a relatively unknown consultant.

10. *Delegation and division of labor make sense.*
Directly before my appointment, my predecessor as chair and our entire department
created a unique design. We analyzed all the
tasks associated with the chair and sorted
them into three roles: chair, coordinator of
research, and coordinator of teaching. We
then elected an individual to each of these
positions. In our department, the chair is
given three course releases, so we determined that one course release would be
given to each role incumbent. From the
dean's office came a mildly surprising reaction to our restructuring—the dean was
not particularly enthusiastic. The design
would be tolerated, but the chair would be
held ultimately responsible for all activities. This reaction makes sense from a too-
many-cooks point of view, and so I have been
careful to coordinate the work of the coordinators. At times, I regret having traded one of
my only benefits (the course releases) away,
but most of the time I'm glad to have the
additional support and relief from all responsibility, and I gain great pleasure from
being in the classroom. I have heard of at
least one other department with a similar
division of labor. I think this type of system
makes a lot of sense in a basically team-based
consensual structure.

In a word, being a department chair has been
humbling. And the 12 years of Catholic schooling I endured taught me that there is some
blessing in humility. For one thing, if we academics are going to continue to govern ourselves, the system requires each of us step up to
the plate from time to time. For another, as I
teach and research in management issues, I will
never again cover the material as I have in the
past. I can truly relate to my students' dilemmas
as practicing managers. On the bottom line, I
have developed a great deal of respect for many
of my colleagues—those who have taken their
turn at bat in being administrators (those of
whom I used to ask naively, "What could you
possibly be doing this for?"), and those in my
own department who serve silently, who serve
willingly, who do what it takes because it's the
right thing to do, not because it "counts."

Other than that, there's always Lesson 11:
Strive to be a cat again. I never anticipated
being in this chair. I don't see this as my future.
I was born to be a "simple" professor. I watch
with jealousy when administrators leave office
in my college. I am angry when they smile. At
least I don't have to worry about being irre-
placeable. Is anybody listening?

Reference

Fukami, C. V. (1993). On being an irrational manager,
or the art of herding cats. *Journal of Management
Inquiry, 2*, 305-306.

33 Becoming an Administrator

THE EDUCATION OF AN EDUCATOR

Allan R. Cohen

One of my favorite books when I was a graduate student in organizational behavior was Carl Rogers's classic, *On Becoming a Person*. When Peter Frost and Susan Taylor suggested the title for this chapter, it reminded me of Rogers, and immediately evoked the temptation to subtitle the chapter "On Becoming a Nonperson." Academic culture is so powerfully antiadministration, antihierarchy, and antiauthority that even an undisciplined, spontaneous, and self-disclosing person like me has to learn to accept the insistence of faculty members that while I am in the role of academic vice president I cannot just be me. The role carries such potent expectations that no amount of goodwill, cajoling, or attempts to break the mold in which I have been cast allows me to escape the insistence that, as one faculty member put it, "When we talk you are not Allan Cohen, you are the vice president."

Although this constraint is for me the most difficult part of being an administrator, it certainly makes a major contribution to one of my two objectives in accepting the responsibilities: creating a crucible in which to learn more about leadership and organizational change. The living laboratory in which I am a participant-observer is renewing my respect for leaders/managers/administrators and helping me to understand in my (increasingly weary) bones the phenomenology of leading change in conditions of uncertainty, anxiety, and ambiguity.

I did not, however, agree to inflict myself on my colleagues (nor did I agree to the excruciating pleasures of 80-hour workweeks) just to learn at everyone's expense. The desire to transform management education and the glimmer of the possibility that at Babson we could just conceivably pull it off were the dominant attractions, and will serve as the external themes for this analysis of my odyssey from a happy, autonomous, committed, and productive faculty member to an overworked, overcommitted, harried, and (every so often) productive administrator.

One of Carl Rogers's most potent lines is, "What is most personal is most general," and this matches the view of literature I learned as an undergraduate. Though there are numerous idiosyncrasies in the story I am about to tell, and probably a lot that can't be duplicated, in the second part of this essay I will build generalizations from the particulars in the hope that something might resonate for others in very different situations.

A Brief History of My Life as a Faculty Member

After completing MBA study, I spent a year writing teaching cases in the Philippines, simultaneously receiving fieldwork credit in Harvard's doctoral program. Having fallen in love with India while traveling home, I was delighted to find that after a year of course work, I could join a team of three doctoral students and one professor to help start the Indian Institute of Management in Ahmedabad.

For 2 wonderful years I was involved with all aspects of building a business school, from developing teaching materials to recruiting and developing faculty, establishing policies, inventing a curriculum, creating a culture, and wrestling with organizational politics. Heady stuff for a person 25-27 years old!

As a result of having to think about what kind of management education to create from scratch in India (and a propensity to enjoy iconoclasm and its results), by the time I started my first faculty position after finishing the DBA, I was unusually opinionated and partisan about the shortcomings and needs of higher education, especially management education. I was probably insufferably arrogant, and for a number of years my certainty about how to transform education fell on deaf ears—or perhaps helped to close them. I wanted to eliminate functional courses and reconfigure them to follow systems theory, bring interpersonal education into the curriculum, introduce experiential work into many courses, and other such wild ideas that took 25 years to become legitimate.

I took my first faculty job at the University of New Hampshire in 1966; I stayed there until 1982. I initially went to New Hampshire for a year to wait for the job at Harvard Business School that I had been offered; a few months into the first year, I realized while teaching a career choice case that I did not want to join the

Harvard faculty. The establishment climate had never been to my liking, and only when in a young, developing business school did I see that I could be happier away from HBS. I liked being at a place where I could help shape the school, the curriculum, and the organizational behavior courses.

After a year at UNH, I spent the summer in NTL's Applied Behavioral Science Internship Program, learning T-group technology and more about interventions to support change. Not only did my excitement about experiential learning get accelerated, but I learned a great deal about myself and the impacts of my interpersonal style. The themes that began there, having to do with the power of focusing on others' issues rather than on whether they saw me as smart, and the problems caused by appearing invulnerable, have woven throughout my life, and reappear regularly in my life as an administrator.

Having attended two great teaching schools, Amherst and HBS, and being comfortable with audiences, teaching came naturally to me. I found a great deal of pleasure in creating classroom experiences that challenged students with complex organizational and personal dilemmas, and was well received from the beginning. I brought case method skills mixed with the commitment to a more experiential style, and began experimenting with group methods over the next 10 years. In collaboration with my UNH colleagues, this resulted in the development of a textbook and teaching methodology for the introductory organizational behavior course. It was a heady period, during which we invented the "classroom as organization" model, did some exciting organizational consulting, and made enough noise to become recognized as one of the better organizational behavior groups. It didn't hurt that the field was young and that we were at a place that was underadministered, so that we could experiment freely.

I wasn't such a natural researcher, however. It had taken me several years to get started, mostly because the anthropological observation methods I preferred were slow to unfold and rather against the increasingly statistical grain of the field. My thesis, which was built around eight complex case studies, didn't easily translate into spin-off articles. But a semester spent at the Institute of Social Studies in the Hague, on behalf of UNH, created an opportunity to convert my out-of-the-mainstream dissertation on Indian family business to a book, and the textbook project became a place where I could use everything I knew in a creative way. Inventing what I hoped would be the definitive teaching-oriented text became an obsession, and in the process I found my writing voice. Most of my scholarly activity since then has been built from my fieldwork as a consultant or teacher, providing a synergy that has let me bring together theory, practice, and conceptualization. I decided that I would write only what I wanted to say, mostly to practitioner audiences (including writing about teaching methods to faculty), and never worried about whether what I was doing was tenurable or academically respectable. Fortunately, both UNH and Babson have valued what I have done; had they not, I might well have become a full-time consultant, though I never wanted to do that.

I left UNH and moved to Babson only because my wife's commuting to the Boston area was hard on our young family, but quickly found that my pleasure in institution building was welcomed there too. From the beginning of my academic career in India, I have wanted to be at the center of the action, although I have always preferred to do it by achieving informal influence through sheer force of ideas and energy. Before becoming academic VP, I had only two formal administrative experiences, as MBA program director for 5 years at UNH and as Management Division chair for 3 years at Babson. But I believe I was as influential from my faculty role as I ever was in these essentially advisory roles that carried little formal power.

At Babson, my stint as chairperson ended when I was selected to be the first recipient of a rotating-term chair. Earlier, on a sabbatical, I had written a book on leadership with my colleague David Bradford of Stanford Business School. The chair's conditions gave us the opportunity to complete a second book together, *Influence Without Authority*. I had fewer teaching responsibilities (though I was having great fun developing and teaching a negotiations course), more writing time, the chance to teach a seminar on teaching, and a nice kind of recognition. Thus serving on the search committee to find a VP of academic affairs was an opportunity to help the college, and, feeling considerable gratitude for having been granted a chair, I gladly joined. Had I realized what would happen, I'm not sure I would have agreed.

The Academic Vice Presidency at Babson

At the time of the search, Babson was at an interesting juncture in its history. It had been in a 15- to 20-year period of movement from a 3-year institute to a serious academic institution. A new president, Bill Glavin, formerly vice chairman of Xerox, had led a strategic planning process that resulted in very high aspirations: to become recognized as a world leader in management education, dedicated to educating leaders who can initiate, manage, and implement change. The aspirations far exceeded Babson's resources, but management education everywhere was under attack, and many of us saw a glimmer of opportunity to accelerate Babson's reputation if we could take a number of bold steps, including radical curriculum reform. I had played a part in creating the plan, chairing a team on "management education in the twenty-first century," and was excited about the possibilities. Thus it wasn't much of a leap for me to be enthusiastically selling candidates on the wonderful opportunity at Babson to transform management education. We had an exciting plan, a decisive and energetic president, a rising reputation, a new and successful executive education center, a strong teaching faculty, a new decentralized faculty governance plan that could enable educational innovation rather than bog it down, and an emerging critical mass of faculty and others who wanted dramatic change.

The VP job at Babson, however, was an unusual hybrid. At a university, the position would be dean of the business school. But Babson also teaches liberal arts and sciences, to balance general with professional education. Thus the VP had to be educated broadly enough to be credible to nonbusiness faculty. Universities have academic VPs, but at Babson the job is far more hands-on and also contains the dean of faculty role. Thus the VP needed to have university-type administrative skill, but had to understand management education well enough to lead a business school. The universe of people with the right mix was small to start with—the incumbent VP had taken the job from his faculty position and search committee role when 5 years previously a search had been unable to land an external candidate—and was complicated by another structural factor. Faculty members qualified to be acceptable in this job tended to have a mix of academic prowess and mana-gerial/consulting experience that gave them satis-fying and lucrative careers as faculty members. Their consulting opportunities and rates made it difficult for Babson to pay enough to make the lack of autonomy inherent in the VP job worth doing. Several good candidates withdrew when they realized this.

Although I had been asked several times if I was interested in the job, I too had refused even to consider it, because I was very happy with my faculty life. But I trapped myself, because the harder it was to find a candidate both suitable and willing, the more glowingly I described the job. When it became clear that we couldn't find an external candidate for the next academic year, I reluctantly offered to defer my upcoming sabbatical and fill in for a year while we contin-ued searching. This was not a carefully planned career move; indeed, it was neither a planned nor, from my perspective, a desirable move, but I thought the college had positive momentum and I dreaded the idea that we could lose it through lack of academic leadership. There wouldn't be many more chances in my remain-ing work life to change management education dramatically. I told the president I would do the job for no more than a year, but only if I could run with it and act as if I had it for life. He was delighted at the terms.

A year later, the search was still coming up empty, and I was hooked. I could see that we were not finding anyone, and I was even more committed to the changes we were making, considering, or needing. Furthermore, there were some unexpected pleasures in the job: The presi-dent, with whom I had no more than a passing acquaintance when I started, turned out to be an extraordinarily stimulating boss whom I could respect, learn from, and enjoy. My colleagues on the president's "cabinet" were talented and sup-portive and committed to the college as much as to their own areas. I was discovering places where I could help encourage the development and sub-sequent approval of the radically new MBA cur-riculum I deeply believed in, and I had a sense of the kinds of changes needed to provide the appro-priate infrastructure for the future. I agreed to stay on for another 3-4 years, which was what I believed would be needed. Only occasionally did I think about the entrapment process just de-scribed—under which I had moved from parti-san bystander to enmeshed advocate.

The reader will by now have noticed the ele-ments that probably overdetermined my his-torical, unplanned drift into academic admini-stration. From the beginning of my career, I was interested in educational reform, was more prag-matic and conceptual than theoretical, was biased toward action, had as my professional interests subjects that are the stuff of administration—teams, leadership, influence, and change—worked with a variety of leaders in my consult-ing, had done a number of tasks that helped me gain institutional perspective, and was in a rare academic situation where significant change was possible and under way. Perhaps the more puz-zling question is what took me so long to get here.

Potential Lessons

Based on the vantage point of 5 years as an administrator, I have reached some conclusions that may be helpful to others:

1. Administering/managing/leading is diffi-cult work that most academics barely see, let alone recognize as valuable. When I described the coaching, mentoring role of department chairs to one faculty group, a senior professor responded scornfully, "Well, if *that's* all you expect from chairs [and do not insist they be educational visionaries], virtually any intelligent person can do it." Both the tone and the opinion are com-mon; many faculty members neither re-spect nor believe in the management proc-ess, do not see it as challenging, and notice it only when managers do something "wrong." Thus if the reference group from which you get your identity is primarily faculty, there is danger in hoping for appreciation of the daily work. There may be sympathy for the long hours, but the important work going on often will be invisible, as infrared light is to the human eye (and what faculty can't see can burn you).

2. Not only is the core of administrative work inherently undervalued, but the nature of leading change, especially in an era of tight-ening economics, is that you will automat-ically be asking faculty members to do things that are inconvenient or uncomfortable

for them, inconsistent with their socialization and probably the profession's—if not the organization's—reward system, an interference to their autonomy, and incompatible with their strengths. It is thus inevitable that academic administrators are seldom loved or overtly appreciated. If that's what you want, you'll be looking for love in all the wrong places.

3. If recognition and affection are unlikely, then the only time to venture into administration is when you have a compelling educational vision and believe that there is a chance to accomplish it. The hours are longer and the money, if a net increase at all, isn't enough to compensate for the aggravation; potential for major accomplishment is the only motive that makes it all worthwhile. Furthermore, without a compelling personal vision that you can translate into an organizational vision, there is almost no hope of getting individualistic and quasi-autonomous faculty to work together. The centrifugal forces are otherwise too great.

4. There is a paradox for administrators, given the centrality of vision for change and the inherent resistance likely: Without fundamental belief in your own capacities and adequacy, it would be hard to get through a week, yet it takes a strong person to be willing to admit mistakes and learn from them. Without both strength and willingness to learn, administrative life can be torture. Only the strong can take criticism, examine it, and decide, when appropriate, to change behavior. I don't know how to get this kind of confidence, although it is possible that it can be forged only in the crucible of action, failure, learning, and new action that succeeds, but without a fair amount going in, survival in the role is unlikely. This is even more true in a period of rapid change, which is inescapably the current state of academia.

5. The satisfactions of managing are even more indirect than those of teaching. If you want direct, personal observation of progress, managing numbers of people is too remote, too slow to be rewarding. Although direct coaching is possible and desirable, and can be satisfying if the person or group

is responsive, many of the best things managers do only reframe the conditions that eventually lead to new behavior. For example, I have spent more than $1\frac{1}{2}$ years redoing with deans and chairs the so-called faculty load system at Babson. We can now better take into account teaching that isn't in entire course chunks, scholarly activity, and service to the college. The system needs refinement, and many of those who helped develop it still aren't committed to it or don't know how to respond to faculty attempts to beat the system. There is sniping, avoidance, and petty picking at the model. Yet I believe that, over time, there will be many important benefits from the new system. It will promote meaningful planning for overburdened faculty and stimulate healthy discussion between chairs and individual faculty members. It will provide data that will help demonstrate when we need more faculty and when we need to make performance expectations clearer. Best of all, it will facilitate more differentiated activities for individual faculty members, making very different mixes of teaching, scholarship, and service legitimate and valued. Although all of this has been said, few besides me really see or believe it, yet I am convinced it will be helpful in the years to come. But I won't be present during the positive individual chair-faculty discussions; I have to take pleasure in the (hoped-for) long-term potential. There's nothing wrong with that, but it's definitely different from the immediacy of helping a student learn how to solve a knotty problem.

6. The wonderful parts of academic administration include using resources to enable individual and group faculty accomplishment, breaking logjams through timely intervention, shaping long-term direction, and supporting changes initiated by the many inventive and dedicated others on campus. Awarding tenure and promotions feels wonderful; coaching others through conflict or into new opportunities is deeply satisfying. But sometimes it is necessary to enforce an unpopular decision to ensure equity, stop a faculty member from ripping off the school, use threats and punishment, raise the dead(wood), make very

hard trade-offs among competing good ideas, and force a nice but underperforming person to leave. There's heat in any managerial kitchen, and standing it is part of the job.

7. My observations of managers in companies have led me to the conclusion that one of the core managerial challenges is to determine when to drive from above and when to allow/encourage bubbling up from below. It is remarkable how often managers get this wrong, directing when they should be listening or waiting for others to take the initiative when bold clarity is required. This is even more complicated for academic managers, as faculty so readily complain, sometimes in the same sentence, about administrative wrongheadedness and lack of leadership/vision. What they often mean is, "I want to see leadership vision that I'll know is right because it matches my own." As I have tried to suggest, faculty are at best ambivalent about power and powerful people. They value both autonomy and community, but are more keenly aware of the costs to their autonomy of institutional commitment than they are of the benefits. Left to their own devices, they may well choose to avoid the conflicts inherent in educational reform and focus on legitimate solo work, even while missing collaborative work. Yet, pushed from above toward programmatic cooperation, they easily can feel that illegitimate pressure is being created.

There is delicate art in sensing when to coax and when to coast, when to articulate a goal or vision or process and when to wait for the spark to strike others. Because no one gets it right every time, a willingness to monitor and adjust constantly is essential. This probably is counter to the strong faculty tradition of studying ideas for a long time before acting, so faculty contemplating becoming administrators need to reflect on their own capacities to act before all the data are in, then act again with new but insufficient data.

8. Although a bias toward action is necessary, there are times when doing nothing is a more than adequate response. This is particularly difficult for me, because I take every request/suggestion/inquiry seriously, and too readily believe that a response of some kind is an important chance to validate the initiator or reinforce some goal. Having the soul of a teacher makes me want to convert every last person on every issue, no matter how insignificant. Yet many things just vanish if pondered (or, perhaps more accurately, are allowed to disappear into the piles of "future reading/future action" documents that grow exponentially in any administrator's office). The problem is, it is difficult to know which is which.

Time management experts say that if something is really important, it will come back, but I don't find that helpful. Trivial things sometimes come back often, when pushed by a particularly insistent party, whereas tiny initiatives are sometimes critical symbolic tests to see whether anyone up there is listening. Until some more experienced administrator comes along with more useful guidelines, my suggestion is just to be alert to the reality that things aren't always what they seem.

9. There are two reasons for accepting the reality of illusion: (a) One's position in an organization shapes what one perceives (where you sit determines where you stand) and (b) the first version of any incident or relationship difficulty will always be utterly convincing—until you hear the other party's version, which would have been just as convincing had you heard it first. Sociology teaches that position shapes perspective, but in the relatively flat and self-governing world of academia, it is easy to overlook the potency of position. Despite being someone who had long been interested in larger issues, I was nevertheless surprised by this. For example, as a faculty member I put no less effort than did any of my colleagues into thinking about how to get a favorable teaching schedule. As VP, I have to think about the need to spread courses throughout the day and week and how to afford the course releases all faculty covet. Chairs rightly worry about how many courses should be covered by part-timers, as does the VP, but the 1:5 cost ratio of the part-time to full-time faculty member requires attention—as does the need to maintain quality. These differing perspectives

set up fascinating dynamics, as each party worries about different things and therefore sees differing parts of the elephant.

The second aspect of learning to live with differing versions of reality requires no more than a strong caveat: Never, ever, no matter how reasonable it sounds, assume that the first person who tells you about another person has a monopoly on the "true story." There is inevitably another side(s) that is equally reasonable from the perspective of that person(s). Few people believe they are doing "evil," despite the multitudes ready to accuse others of it!

10. Compared to the life of a faculty member, there is a very different rhythm to administrative life. Although every faculty member has to deal with the open-endedness of mastering fields that grow faster than the capacity to learn, the ebb and flow of the academic year allows satisfying endings. The intensity of exhausting end-of-semester grading is over in a few long days, and there is a natural release that lasts for several weeks. Summers are generally much slower and self-paced. Administrative work, however, is endless. Projects or task forces may end, but the implementation demands continue. Disgruntled, upset, or entrepreneurial faculty know no season, and they need attention whenever they appear. Other constituencies demand responses: chairs, deans, potential recruits, students, parents, alumni, administrative colleagues, donors. The list is endless and far more extensive than the usual interactors with faculty members. An administrator had better like "dealing with people," or the relentless crush of needy—and fascinating—humanity can seem like dripping water torture. Incidentally, although many aspects of dealing with faculty can be problematic, I am absolutely certain of one thing: If you don't fundamentally like faculty and their foibles, you should *not* become an academic administrator!

This wonderful quote from Bernie Brillstein, a theatrical manager talking about actors and actresses, applies very well to managing faculty: "You have to know how to listen to talent, you have to know how vulnerable they are, you have to know how to put up with their strengths and weaknesses and with their craziness, which makes some of them geniuses" (*New York Times,* February 20, 1994).

Perhaps another conclusion is in order. Based on my own experience, and my observations of others, it is at the least critical and imperative to have a spouse, friend, or colleague—better yet, all three—with whom you can talk freely. Too much goes on for you to hold in all of your reactions, and strange behavior can result if you try to go it alone. Without my wife and some special friends and colleagues, I could not have sustained the pace or what little effectiveness I have had. At the least, their willingness to let me bounce my ideas and frustrations off them has kept me in the fray and helped me avoid unplanned blowups.

Anticipating my return to faculty life isn't easy. I doubt that I will be able to go back to the faculty without taking the institutional perspective along. As much as I'm sure my eventual successor won't get it quite right, I'll never be able to be unsympathetic to the complexities of the role, and I *will* seek opportunities to be helpful, to move the college forward, because I have spent a lot of hours and sweat on making Babson even more the kind of institution in which I want to be a faculty member. One of the wonders of academic organizations is that opportunities for faculty members to succeed also help the institution's reputation, access to funds, and supply of interesting students. Thus many of the individual's and the organization's interests overlap. I'll keep seeking those areas of overlap, both in and out of the classroom. And, of course, I'll try to use what I've learned about leadership and change in my teaching about those slippery, subtle, and central subjects.

If you are still ready, after all of this, to jump into (or continue in) administration, my best wishes. I know a fascinating opportunity that will be available sometime after you read this. And from the faculty role I will once again be in, I'll be glad to help you, once I get my teaching schedule right.

Becoming a Full Professor

New full professors must struggle to figure out their place in the system. Everyone assumes that we know what we are doing, but this is another case of a conspiracy of silence. Few are willing to admit the ambiguity, and this may result in the poor utilization of a valuable resource.

Ray V. Montagno (p. 338)

All in all, full professorship seems to offer about as clear a shot at self-actualization as anyone is ever likely to get. To the extent that the transition to full professor has caused some restlessness on my part, it has largely been the result of my having so many options and not enough time to pursue them all well. One can imagine a whole lot worse set of problems than that.

Sara L. Rynes (p. 347)

It is an interesting reflection on academic life that the achievement of full professor status is simultaneously a liberating and disconcerting experience for many individuals. What is it about becoming a full professor that causes folks first to revel in their freedom and then to chafe against it? In this section, two full professors who have held that role for about 3 years at the time of writing, Ray Montagno and Sara Rynes, respond to this question. Montagno begins with the revelation that had his first career as a mechanical engineer not been rudely interrupted by the Vietnam War, he would likely be a manager in the factory where he worked prior to enlisting rather than a full professor today. Thus he reminds us that his reactions to the life of a full professor are based on comparisons with a standard held by relatively few academics, the life of a plant manager in today's hypercompetitive world.

In Montagno's view, becoming a full professor provided him with greater opportunities to choose among administrative, governance, consulting, and teaching roles than he had previously experienced. Although the researcher role continues to remain an option, he notes that the external pressure to pursue it pales in the face of the additional roles vying for his attention. He also proposes a hypothesis, developed by a colleague who is also a recent full professor, that the nature of an academic's socialization during graduate training and his or her treatment while moving through the promotion and tenure system will be significant determinants of the role choices that individual makes after attaining full professor status and of the way he or she enacts the chosen roles. Specifically, Montagno suggests that the higher an individual's socialized expectations about levels of career success and the greater the number of hoops he or she was forced to jump through on the way to full professor, the more disenchantment and alienation can be expected with the change to full professor status.

Sara Rynes echoes this view of extensive role options, noting that the sheer number of roles available to her as a full professor partially account for the tensions she experienced during the role transition. Unlike Montagno, she focuses more on her personal reactions to this transition. Looking back, Rynes is now able to recognize that many of the options made available to her as a full professor differed from her previous role requirements by involving increased responsibility for others— high-level service commitments, doctoral student mentoring, and so on. Furthermore, these options became available at a time when similar changes were taking place in her family situation. Thus it is not surprising that tension inevitably resulted between her high standards for excellence as an individual contributor in research and her new (additional) role demands of greater responsibility for others. She concludes that more realistic expectations about the extent of the transition required would have helped her deal with some of the anxieties she experienced along the way to full professor. This conclusion, in turn, suggests that books

such as this one may be useful tools for helping other academics cope with similar transitions.

In combination, Montagno's and Rynes's essays depict the transition to full professor as a process, rather than an event. Their experiences cast doubt on the notion that one can expect to become a full professor as soon as one receives the promotion notification letter. The choices that academics confront after achieving full professor status emphasize the importance of striving for deeper insights about what one wants to do and be, in the face of considerable freedom to decide. These authors' experiences with their full professor roles also suggest that organizational efforts might wisely be devoted to the identification of early career experiences and later career paths that subsequently prove satisfying for both the individual and the institution. Yet, despite experiencing some unsettling feelings during their ascent to the position of full professor, both authors carefully remind us that few other occupations provide their incumbents with such freedom; few permit them to make, adjust, and readjust their decisions about the appropriateness of different work roles to the extent that is possible in the academic career. In short, few others—perhaps none—offer such prime opportunities for self-actualization. This realization leads both authors to conclude that we academics must take greater responsibility for determining and enacting our own destinies. As Montagno puts it, we may "serve ourselves and others more effectively by appreciating what we are about than by reacting to what we perceive the system is doing to us" (p. 340). We expect that this reminder may prove equally valuable for academics at virtually all stages of their career progression.

34 On Becoming a Professor

Ray V. Montagno

Beginnings

The word *becoming* in the title of this essay implies that if someone is now a full professor, he or she must have been something else before. It seems reasonable, then, that before you can understand where someone is at present, you need to know something of that person's history. Toward that end, I provide a bit of my history below; following this, I will attempt to examine some of the realities of professorship as they have affected me.

I have been a full professor for 3 years at a university that attempts to balance teaching and scholarly activities. Both effective teaching and scholarly research are required for movement through the system, but the definitions of these elements often resemble moving targets.

An observation about the academic setting will serve as an introduction to my personal route to professorship: There are no big, noisy machines in university buildings. This may seem both obvious and silly at the same time, but for me, it has always been the source of some career tension. Let me explain. My father, due to a set of circumstances that I'm sure I couldn't begin to understand, never completed high school. Through good fortune, a high level of ability and a considerable amount of hard work, he managed to become the chief engineer for a small manufacturing company not long after World War II. Saturday work was common for him, and I had the opportunity to accompany him to work on many Saturdays as I was growing up.

The plant was usually not operating during these visits, and if I was not helping him in some repair task, I was left free to wander about the premises. I was driving a forklift when I was 10 (I'm not sure what OSHA would think of that today). In retrospect, I know the plant was probably not large, but my recalled image of it is one of an immense space with thousands of incredibly mysterious places to explore.

My first two summers in college, I worked in the machine shop of the plant, and I was actually socialized into factory life. My undergraduate degree is in mechanical engineering, which fit well with my fondness for machines and factories. My first job was with a manufacturing company, and my fate seemed sealed—I was going to be around big, noisy machines for the rest of my life. Unfortunately, the Vietnam War would interrupt that path, and some time later I ended up as a sales representative for the firm. Having no training or inclination toward sales, I chose graduate school in industrial psychology as an alternative. Throughout my studies, I always intended to return to the "factory floor." Academic life, however, had an allure that was hard to resist. Now, 20 years later, I occasionally find myself thinking, "What if?"

With my history and my position as professor of management, I often wonder if I could actually manage a manufacturing facility in this highly competitive world. My boyhood fantasies aside, it is a question that stays in the back of my mind. This is not to suggest that I do not appreciate and enjoy my current status. In fact, in my current position I get to work with people in manufacturing settings, but it is not quite the same. Perhaps I have overglamorized the idea of work in the "real world," but my experiences give me a grounding to judge my current life position.

This brief history has, of course, left out entirely any discussion of my academic career. There have been significant and important influences in my academic pursuits that have provided me with both direction and the motivation to flourish in the academic environment in which I now exist. Probably the most significant of these influences was my graduate work at Purdue University. My years there set the tone for my academic career expectations. In conversations with my current colleagues, I find that this socialization process appears to be a well-established role for doctoral programs. Some programs, I'm sure, do it better than others, but the results are basically the same. Career expectations are implanted quite firmly by the doctoral candidate process.

What were some of those expectations? How did they change along the way? What does the future hold with respect to someone in an academic career? A professor at Purdue once said to me that one should be careful about criticizing the tenure system in universities, because one will have tenure a lot longer than one will be without tenure. Today, I can attest to the fact that the perceptions of the outsider are often quite different from the realities of the insider.

I will attempt to identify some of my expectations and place them in the perspective of experience. Probably the most attractive thing to me about academic life was the flexibility and freedom it presents to pursue questions and ideas driven primarily by my own interests and idiosyncrasies. The primary constraint on this pursuit is the publishability of these ideas, but my observation has been that this is a rather weak limiter. A second expectation I had was that my participation in the academy would somehow contribute to making society, in general, better. This rather lofty expectation is somewhat ill defined and even more difficult to assess.

A simple analysis of my expectations reveals the underlying American cultural value of individualism. It is interesting that candidates for faculty positions rarely talk about meeting the needs of the department or the university to which they are applying. The process almost always consists of the candidate stating his or her goals and needs and the department deciding whether or not this person fits the department's profile. It's as if a freshly minted PhD somehow has every aspect of his or her career mapped out, and it's a "take me as I am or don't take me" situation. It is conceivable (assuming good basic skills) that candidates would be better served entering the job search process with the attitude that they are flexible and will adjust to meet the needs of the employing institution.

This in not to suggest that academic freedom and personal interest are not important, but the new academic probably needs more help in establishing a career than is typically provided in today's institutions. I have often wondered why there are so many cynical older professors. Is it intellectual arrogance (they don't appreciate me for how smart I really am) or the result of poor career management by the university?

It is clear that career management for faculty is a poorly developed practice in most universities—but I will reflect on this a bit later. My point here is that an individual's expectations are often based on the socialization process he or she has undergone in the doctorate-granting institution. Clearly, most academic jobs are in schools that have different roles and expectations for faculty from the ones in which these new faculty created their visions of the academic life. Failure to have expectations met is a well-developed area of job satisfaction research.

From a personal perspective, I have to report that, overall, I am quite satisfied with the course of events in my own career, but the question of disenchantment stays with me. There are others who began their careers with me who seem quite unhappy for one reason or another. Some of the more common reasons for unhappiness are that their teaching loads are too great, they haven't received enough recognition for particular research efforts, and, most commonly, the university service work they provide is not appreciated and rewarded. The ironic part of this situation is that most of the unhappy people end up in about the same position as the happy people. Their salaries are not too different, and they all usually end up getting promoted to professor.

The Promotion and Tenure System

Most universities operate with a promotion and tenure system, which is a surrogate for a career management system. Having recently completed the last hurdle in this system, I would like to comment on some of my impressions of the system and its effectiveness. This is not intended to be a comprehensive analysis of the process, but will cover some reactions to specific aspects of the process as it affects the individual, the university, and the larger community of scholars. The question of effectiveness of the promotion and tenure (P&T) process must be redefined for each of the different interest groups.

Does the P&T system serve the individual? The easy answer is that for those who make it through the system, it works. A colleague (also recently promoted to professor) once suggested that a person's behavior after going through the system may be a result of his or her experience with it. My own experience has been positive, and I think this reflects a somewhat effective application of the system at my university. Feedback is regular, the rules are relatively clear, and people are rarely surprised by the negative decisions that result from the deliberations of the members of the committee.

This is not to suggest that everyone is happy with the system. Particular components of the system over which individuals feel they have little control are a constant source of contention. The best example is teaching evaluations. What role should these play? At our institution, a person with poor teaching evaluations cannot be promoted, despite good research performance. This is especially troublesome for those who have marginal performance as measured

by teaching evaluations. Substantial changes in an individual's evaluations are possible, but difficult to facilitate on a regular basis. The system does not regularly provide either tools or options for individuals either to change or compensate for poor teaching evaluations. In the end, the question comes down to this: Will someone with less-than-outstanding teaching ratings be an associate professor forever?

On the other hand, individuals can and do regularly adjust their research activities in response to pressures from the system. Research productivity is perceived to be largely under the individual's control and more subject to focused effort.

This distinction between teaching and research may be a source of some of the disenchantment alluded to before. Most faculty are led to believe in grad school that their careers will hinge on research, and having an unexpected obstacle like teaching evaluations arise may sow the seeds of long-term mistrust of the whole system. The impact of the existing system is often anxiety producing for most and punitive for some, and in the end, usually does not serve a developmental role for the individual.

Does the system serve the needs of the university? This is a complex question that certainly has been debated long and hard in academe. Again, the short answer is that it works well for most faculty but not for all. All universities are plagued with deadwood. The existing system offers some controls, but with inconsistent standards across departments, the university must manage by expressing its hope that the system is producing the high-quality faculty it desires.

Would a different system produce less deadwood and higher quality or merely a different class of individuals who have learned to play a game with different rules and in the end contribute as much to the institution as under the current system? It is unlikely that the system is open to substantial change at this point in time, but experimentation might be healthy.

The last part of the equation is, Does the system contribute to the broader community of scholars? My personal reaction to this question is that P&T systems are probably irrelevant to the larger audience. The leadership of academic and professional organizations, for example, is made up of high achievers. These are individuals for whom the P&T process was probably an annoyance at worst. For the rest, membership may be seen as an obligation, and most of their activities are primarily local or regional and of little consequence to the academic elite.

My conclusion, after going through the process, is that P&T should be seen as a developmental tool rather than as an obstacle to career growth. Unfortunately, it is the latter more often than it is the former. New faculty need to be hired with openly stated expectations of contribution, and the P&T system should be used to help the individual and the university achieve their respective and complementary goals.

Post-P&T Life

Recalling the caveat of my PhD adviser, I must now look at that period of my career that will be the longest—fully tenured, fully promoted. Most of my experience has been in one institution. I now find myself fourth in seniority in a department of 15. What is my role now?

I consider myself a loyal member of the organization. As I have become better-known around campus, I have found myself invited to serve on a number of permanent and ad hoc university committees. Similarly, I have developed a bit of a reputation for group facilitation and now get asked to assist various department and administrative groups in planning meetings and the like. The dean of my college has asked me to chair our internal committee on internationalization. I also serve on a number of departmental committees. Additionally, I serve on several boards and committees for civic and economic development groups. The result of all this has been an unwitting, but significant, change in the focus of my academic life.

I used to believe that television was going to be the downfall of Western society. I now, however, believe that our downfall will be "busyness." This seems to be a common state in many areas of life. Ask someone a simple question like "How are you doing?" and almost invariably he or she will say, "Busy."

Now, in one sense, this is better than having nothing to do, but one wonders if this is a good space for academic pursuits. The development and integration of knowledge is not a hurried process. I once envisioned full professorship as a time when I would be able to pursue ideas and questions at a more relaxed pace, without the pressures of each year's annual review to concern me. I find quite the opposite to be true, however. More people are making more demands on my time than ever before, and the prospect of pursuing an interesting and complex research project seems quite remote.

I must add that consulting activities are part of this mix as well. Lengthy association with one institution brings with it the opportunity to become known in the area's business community, creating rewarding experiences there, also. The net result of this is that I have witnessed a metamorphosis in my career that has been by and large unplanned and unexpected.

Roles of Professorship

From the perspective of becoming a full professor, are there new roles and expectations? Is there a real change that brings with it new responsibilities? Part of the problem with this question is that it is a further example of the poor job the P&T system does in career development. New full professors must struggle to figure out their place in the system. Everyone assumes that we know what we are doing, but this is another case of a conspiracy of silence. Few are willing to admit the ambiguity, and this may result in the poor utilization of a valuable resource.

The comment of my colleague who suggested that a person's response to promotion may be a function of his or her experience with the process leads to several observations. Individuals who feel that their promotions have been based on a process of achievement of reasonable but difficult standards may take a more proactive view of their new status. On the other hand, individuals who struggle throughout the process, always needing just one more publication or needing to raise their teaching evaluations by two-tenths of a point, may view promotion as an opportunity to withdraw from what has been perceived as an oppressive system. Their role becomes one of reaction and avoidance.

In a sense, then, what it took to get there determines what someone does when he or she arrives. There are any number of roles that are possible. No one person can perform all of them, but at some level each needs to be performed, and it seems reasonable that those in the professor ranks should be the ones to assume responsibility for these roles. Most of the suggestions below, of course, reflect my own academic experience at an institution that does not offer a PhD in my college. Other institutions with other missions may have a different mix of roles.

Mentor

As suggested before, the traditional P&T system does little to develop faculty. Further, university department administrators are generally not well prepared to manage the career development process. This is not to say they are not well-intentioned, but career management is a function that requires preparation and understanding of career growth and change. The senior professoriat has a potential leadership role in this process. A mentor system in which mentors are prepared with appropriate training could be an effective strategy for creating and maintaining an excellent faculty. This would require an appropriate reward system and an administrative commitment, but most of all it would require a cadre of professors who see this as an appropriate role for themselves.

The real trick with a mentor system would be to avoid the evaluator role. Trusting, positive relationships need to be established in which the experience of mentors can be used to facilitate growth in new faculty members rather than merely provide them with a set of strategies for coping with the system.

Maintainer

A second, related, role is that of ensuring the integrity of the P&T system as a measure of performance and not a tool of arbitrary control. The colleague I mentioned earlier has taken on such a role. Two difficult promotion cases have come up since his promotion, and in both cases I have been extremely impressed with his patience and fairness in dealing with what at times became very emotional issues. His assumption of this role of maintaining integrity was instrumental in preventing unnecessary conflict. Although this role isn't for everyone, it is a necessary one. It would be much easier merely to say, "I've got mine, now you fend for yourself."

University Server

A choice for many, after they have achieved professor status, is to spend more time on service to their departments, colleges, and universities. Although some of this activity is necessary for the effective maintenance of the institution, there is a risk that these activities can become self-perpetuating and at the same time less relevant. Preoccupation with such activities can be an easy excuse for not continuing the more rigorous work of scholarship.

Another level of leadership is needed within universities today. As universities become more complex, there is a tendency to move toward a more professional management class within the university administration. Traditional faculty governance systems seem less able to cope with the pressures facing their institutions. A potential new role for professors is to serve in an advisory capacity to senior administrators. To be effective, this would require both judgment and discretion, as well as acceptance by administrators of the legitimacy of this role for professors.

Scholar

Is there a change for the professor in terms of contribution to his or her academic field? It is well-known that in many academic disciplines the quantity of scholarly production diminishes for individuals who have become senior members of their departments. Is this good or bad? As with most value-laden questions, the answer is not clear-cut. If the person has assumed a role of leadership in his or her field and is contributing to the facilitation of the creation and/or dissemination of knowledge, then a reduction in productivity may be quite appropriate.

Certainly there are those who continue to publish and create at very high levels throughout their careers, but this is probably not the path for everyone. We would need a lot more journals if that were the case. The issue is one of continuing contribution to the academic endeavor, not the number of publications.

Teacher

One role that does not change appreciably with promotion is that of teacher. For those of us for whom undergraduate- and master's-level teaching is a primary activity, the task of continuing to be effective as a teacher after achieving full professor status is a difficult one. As I observe younger faculty who seem to have a natural rapport with students, I wonder if I'm as approachable and open to students as I once was. Is age a barrier that will continue to make this task more difficult? I once heard an older faculty member say, "I never want to become a boring old professor." Well, I don't either. I feel this is my biggest challenge. I know that I can find numerous other valuable activities of both a scholarly and service nature in which I can make contributions.

How to keep the edge in the classroom will be the biggest challenge for me personally, and I suspect the same is so for many others who have progressed through the academic ranks. Age brings with it changing relationships with students. Students can relate to young faculty members as "peers," but those of us with a little gray must seek a different form of identification with students. We may have to work at making our wisdom and experience both relevant and accessible to them.

Other Roles

There are certainly many other roles that could be identified, involving such areas as public and community service, or applications of knowledge through industry. Those, however, are more discretionary than the roles mentioned above. The task facing the new professor is one of choice. You can choose to be passive in this arena, which may lead either to your doing nothing or to letting others make choices for you, or you can look at the array of possibilities and be proactive in choosing a path that leads to continued growth and contribution.

Conclusion and Lessons

The biggest issue for me today is how to sort through the choices I have before me. Many of the options I have seem both interesting and rewarding. Unfortunately, I cannot do them all, lest I fall prey to the busyness syndrome and probably do nothing very well. The decisions are more difficult than I expected. Some of the choices seem to represent an abandonment of scholarship in favor of administrative work. Is this a problem? I know I feel a sense of ambivalence about this situation, but I have yet to resolve my dilemma.

I see new roles that are needed within the university. It will take energy to implement them. Although I feel I could influence their creation, I'm not sure I want to divert that energy from other activities.

Are there some things that I would have done differently that would help me now? Is there some inspiring advice I can give that may save someone else from struggling through ambiguous waters? There are three strategies that I believe should be effective. The first is to work with others as much as possible. This often requires that you act in a proactive fashion—for instance, invite others to work with you; not only is it more fun, but it will help you maintain perspective. Second, don't say no too often. Although maintaining focus is important for success, saying no may keep you from opportunities with rewarding payoffs. Finally, and this sounds almost too trite for inclusion here, it is critical to maintain some sense of dignity and humor about the whole endeavor. Few faculty die from job-related stress, and we would probably serve ourselves and others more effectively by appreciating what we are about than by reacting to what we perceive the system is doing to us.

In the end, being a professor is not what I expected. Life is more complicated, demands are increasing, and answers are difficult to discern, but the journey is exciting and challenging.

35 Becoming a Full Professor

Sara L. Rynes

> At around 40, when he reaches the top rung of his early adult ladder, a man has
> to reappraise the ladder itself. It is not just a matter of evaluating how well he has
> done within the current definitions of success and failure. He has to question the
> basic meanings of success and failure, and the value of the ladder itself.
>
> *D. J. Levinson,* The Seasons of a Man's Life, *1978*

When I first became a full professor, I expected very little in the way of a transition. Looking back, the main things I expected were a slight reduction in my drive to produce research and an increase in leisure time and family activities. In short, I expected life to go on pretty much as before, but with a little less pressure and a little more time for family and self. I certainly had the feeling that with not only tenure, but full professorship, I would feel much freer to do what *I* wanted to do than at any point in the past.

However, 3½ years into full professorship, I am surprised at the degree of personal overload I feel and the amount of effort I devote to thinking about how to manage my life. At least one part of my prediction has come to pass: My research productivity has slowed somewhat. But I am not really sure that this downside development has been compensated for by increased leisure or family time, and I certainly do not feel much reduction in pressure or stress. As I write, these continue to be the central issues in my life.

In the end, I have concluded that a number of factors (some self-imposed, others not) have created additional work in my life since I became a full professor. These additional demands are pressing up against more limited personal stamina, higher aspirations for the personal side of my life, and a reluctance to reduce my personal quality standards in almost any area of life (except, perhaps, housecleaning). I have come to view this combination as untenable in the long run, and I am currently thinking about how to increase the efficiency of what I do, reduce the number of things I do, or reduce at least some of my personal standards. I cannot, at this point, imagine reducing my expectations for more family involvement or personal time.

What follows is a description of some of the areas in which I have noticed changes since I became a full professor. Some of these changes, such as increased time spent in service activities, are probably direct results of my becoming a full professor. Others, such as changes in teaching,

AUTHOR'S NOTE: I would like to thank Herb Heneman, Judy Olian, Jennifer Rynes, and Paul Weller for helpful comments on earlier versions of this essay.

mentoring, and research, have had more varied origins.

Finding New Research Interests

By the time I became a full professor, I had become tired of the areas in which I had previously pursued research. At that point, I had spent 10 years studying organizational recruitment, individual job search, compensation administration, and, to a lesser extent, the careers of engineers. My interest in these topics was increasingly waning, and I found myself thinking wistfully about people such as Ed Locke or Frank Schmidt, who have made contributions to very important topics for many years without any apparent loss of enthusiasm.

More generally, I was beginning to feel less enthusiastic about the entire field of human resource management. In the 10 years I'd been teaching by the time I became a full professor, I had seen many changes in the way real organizations carry out their activities, but few differences in the content of what we, as academicians, were studying. I was also becoming frustrated at being told by managers in evening or executive MBA programs that the material in our textbooks was not useful to them, or that our textbook solutions "just don't work" in real life (for a discussion of similar issues, see Longenecker, Sims, & Gioia, 1987).

So for the past 3 years I have been investing in learning about other areas of management. Happily, the decision to study other areas has begun to inject new enthusiasm into my research life (or, more accurately, my research *plans*). To date, few of my ideas have been put to paper because I have been unable to find the time to start up entirely new research streams. But at least I am reenergized and ready to squeeze new work into the odd moments when I have time to write. I have spent the past few years feeling anxious about my reduced research productivity, but I am finally to the point where I can visualize the potential returns to my investment in new learning. Lately, I have been trying much harder to find more time to write again.

Changes in Teaching

I can't recall thinking much about anticipated changes in teaching upon reaching full professorship. However, I believe that at some level, I expected teaching to require somewhat less effort than in earlier years. My assumptions were that I would be doing fewer new course preparations and that I would have worked out all the bugs in my old classes by now.

These assumptions have both turned out to be incorrect. The fact is that I have never devoted more time to teaching than I do now. Not only have I continued to develop new courses, I have also continued to modify old courses each time I teach them. In addition, I have greatly changed the types of assignments and examinations I give in all but my highest-enrollment courses. These new assignments have generally moved in the direction of integrative simulations or mini-consulting projects, which are seen as more valuable learning experiences by students but also require substantially more of my time for initial development, ongoing student support, and evaluation and feedback.

Why am I doing this, particularly given that what I would really like for myself at work is more time to conduct research? I am not really sure, but a number of partial explanations come to mind. First, students in our college attach very little credibility to "objective" examinations in behavioral areas, and they have been quite vocal in expressing their preferences. Given the important role of student opinions in highly publicized business school rankings, my colleagues and I have certainly felt pressure to respond to student preferences regarding teaching and learning.

In addition, I have now read a considerable amount of literature on the perceived weaknesses of today's college graduates. Survey after survey shows that these graduates are thought to be weakest in oral and written communication skills, teamwork, and complex problem solving. Because such skills are probably best developed and evaluated through integrative applications or project work, I have moved toward making mini-consulting projects and elaborate simulation questions major aspects of my class requirements.

As I write, I still have mixed feelings about spending so much time on teaching, coaching, and assessment. On the one hand, it is clear that the students feel they are getting a more useful education by applying classroom principles to real, multifaceted projects. In addition, some of the work produced in this way has been absolutely outstanding. On the other hand, designing and evaluating these projects is enormously time-consuming, and not all students rise to the occasion. Therefore, on balance, I am not sure whether the average overall return to such efforts (in terms of student learning) is worth the huge expenditure of effort on my part. I plan to continue active monitoring of this issue into the future.

Mentoring of Graduate Students

I have always felt that I have done a fair amount of student mentoring. Although I have never been closely involved with large numbers of students at any given time, there have always been a small number of students with whom I have had reasonably broad relationships involving more than purely academic issues. At this point, however, the scope of my mentoring activities is clearly expanding. Until now, I have chaired a considerable number of master's committees and sat on a number of doctoral committees, but have chaired only two dissertation committees. This is changing. For the first time, I am heavily involved in advising doctoral students, and it appears that I am now about to get involved in chairing several dissertation committees at once.

I regard PhD-level mentoring as a very serious responsibility. Frankly, I am a little awed by the extent to which doctoral students are hungry for career advice and by the amount of weight they attach to the suggestions they receive. Thinking back, I realize that I did much the same thing at that stage. So I am trying to grow into this role, and I find myself hoping I don't give much bad advice in the process.

I am strongly motivated to do a good job at this, in part because I received such excellent mentoring myself as a graduate student. My graduate school mentors (Don Schwab and Herb Heneman) have made invaluable contributions to my career and have remained strong friends and trusted advisers to this day. I am also motivated because it appears that both getting and keeping jobs in academia will continue to grow more difficult for new graduates. For these reasons, the mentoring role is increasing in importance, and I anticipate that it will take up a larger proportion of my time in future.

Increased Demands for Service

The aspect of full professorship that is probably most salient to those who have not yet reached it is the reduced external pressure to publish. However, the aspect that may be most salient to those who *have* reached it is the escalation of expectations for a variety of nonresearch contributions.

Perhaps the most common form that increased service expectations take is that of requests for committee work, particularly at levels beyond one's own department. Other expectations (or opportunities, depending on your perspective) may include requests for public speaking, outreach, and fund-raising; presentations to legislative or oversight bodies; nighttime, weekend, and off-campus teaching; and facilitation of student outreach and placement.

Prior to becoming a full professor, I had felt that the most reasonable approach to distributing service requirements would be to allocate more obligations to people who are no longer active researchers. I now believe this was a somewhat naive position, predicated on the assumption that most committee work is unimportant and can be entrusted to anyone. Although this is undoubtedly sometimes true, I have been surprised in recent years to discover how many committees are charged with making decisions on important, difficult issues that require highly committed and effective members for resolution. Also, I believe that, like hiring and tenure standards, service requirements are likely to increase at *all* academic levels due to declining full-time enrollments, reductions in public funding for higher education, increasing legislative oversight, and increasing challenges in student placement.

For these reasons, I have found myself putting more time into service than I expected a few years back. Although I certainly do not say yes to all requests for service, I acquiesce a bit more often than I want to. I suspect this is true of most professors, who probably find it difficult to get excited about additional meetings and report-writing obligations, but who nevertheless feel the pull of social obligations and organizational commitment.

In any event, my appreciation has grown for those who take on considerable service loads, and I do feel a sense of duty to carry my load. All the same, I sometimes find myself thinking,

"The 8 hours I just spent in those meetings are 8 hours that could have been applied directly to my research instead." In addition, my colleagues and I have all been in administrators' offices where the bookcases are lined with dusty, unopened committee reports. So I am now thinking much more explicitly about how much overall service is appropriate, what kinds of service are most important, and which committees best fit my particular skills and interests.

Keeping Up With Change

Whatever the general public might think, professors are not isolated from the phenomenal pace at which knowledge, technology, and work methods are changing. In fact, unless one has been pursuing focused self-development, one is likely to feel at least partially "obsolete" in a number of areas at the point of reaching full professorship. Three areas in particular come to mind: research methods, technology, and content areas outside one's own research domain.

In my own case, my ability to keep up in these areas has been constrained not only by the competing demands already mentioned, but by the considerable amount of journal reviewing that I do. Because much of what is sent to reviewers is based on their research strengths, being on review boards tends to reinforce one's knowledge in one's own areas while taking time away from broader learning. Thus I have been able to keep up in such areas as compensation and recruitment, but have fallen behind in such areas as motivation and organizational development. Therefore, at the end of my current board terms I will be reconsidering the balance I want to strike between the narrow, detailed reading required in reviewing and the more general reading that leads to broader knowledge.

In the other two areas of change, research methodologies and technology, I must admit to pursuing largely "just-in-time" methods for keeping up. That is, with few exceptions, I have delved into new technologies and new methodologies only at those points when I actually needed to use them. Still, even with this externally driven approach, I am amazed at how technologically different my work is today compared with 10 years ago. At that time, I was not using word processing, electronic mail, voice mail, or fax machines. Now, with prodding from the technological capabilities available in our new academic building, I plan to conduct computer-based statistical process control analyses in real time, right before my students' eyes. In addition, I plan to begin conducting research using computerized group decision support systems. That feels like quite a bit of change for someone who has essentially been dragged into the technological age.

Ideally, I would like to establish habits that are a bit more proactive with respect to self-development in areas that are prone to obsolescence. The obstacles to making progress in this particular area seem to be, in very busy times, the press of the moment and, in less busy times, the growing desire for leisure and non-work-related activities.

Increasing Physical Constraints: Full Professorship Meets Middle Age

I hit full professorship at a point when a great deal was happening in my life. Within the preceding year, my mother had died, my father had had a stroke, I had married for the second time, and I had a new baby. In addition, because my new marriage had produced a dual-career situation, I was out on the road interviewing for new positions within 8 weeks of my son's birth.

Another thing I thought about a lot when I became a full professor was that I was rapidly approaching the age at which my mother had developed her first cancer. I also began to think about the health of other people I knew in academia; among my best friends in the field, I counted people who had had heart attacks, organ transplants, renal dialysis, cancers, circulatory problems, and serious problems with alcohol. Most of these people were approximately 10 years older than me, and, in the absence of any preventive steps, I saw myself headed in the same direction.

Every one of those people advised me to place a higher priority on my health than on my job and to think more about my personal life than my professional life. So in the summer of my thirty-ninth year, I found myself going from physician to physician, checking out every bodily system to find out where I stood in terms of personal health. From these checkups, I learned that I have one bad knee and one bad ear, but no other problems of consequence (at least so far).

Nevertheless, I have changed my lifestyle considerably over the past few years with respect to alcohol consumption, smoking, fat intake, and the types of exercise I pursue (e.g., less jarring aerobics, more weight lifting and stretching). I think a lot about my parents, who always looked forward to retirement but never really had the opportunity to enjoy it.

The biggest physical change I have noticed over the past few years is the need for more sleep. Even if I wanted to, I could probably no longer pull an all-nighter to meet a deadline. When I am tired, I get irritable and can do only light cognitive work. The need for more rest acts as a very real constraint on my accomplishing all I would like to do. Increasingly, sleep is winning out over other activities. This causes me frustration in the short term, but I now view it as necessary for the long haul. Besides, when I am really tired, I no longer have much choice about whether I'll sleep—I just do!

Achieving Personal Balance

The question of balance is probably the most central one in my life at this time. Like most professionals with families, I find it difficult to find enough time simultaneously for work, family, and self. The amount of time I spend around other people at work has increased the value (as well as the scarcity) of time for myself. I think of "alone time" as essential to my health and well-being, but find it hard to acquire.

Nevertheless, despite my obvious yearning for more personal and family time, I still consider myself to be fairly work-heavy in personal orientation. (Note: Upon reading this, my daughter placed an exclamation point after the phrase "fairly work-heavy." Apparently, I have not yet satisfactorily resolved the issue of balance.)

I remember George Carlin (who has had several heart attacks) saying that because his office was in his home, he never felt that he was in the right place: If he was with his family he felt he should be working, if he was working, he felt he should be with his family. I have similar problems with the separation of work and family. Most of the year, I spend my life like George Carlin: thinking about home when I'm at work,

thinking about work when I'm hiking with my family, and so on.

However, I have found one way to attain true leisure successfully: by scheduling blocks of time to be away from both work and home. The arrangement I have made with myself is that when I go on vacation, I take no work. Happily, that decision has effectively removed the temptation to slip into work-related thinking while on vacation. It has also influenced my decision not to pursue international human resource management seriously as a topic of research; international travel is something I have decided to reserve for pure pleasure.

So I have found one highly successful way to achieve leisure and time for rebuilding, but I would be happy to find some additional, less extreme methods as well. Right now, exercising, playing the piano, meditating, and reading are the most satisfying ways I have found to relax for short periods of time. Still, I must make an active commitment to *make* the time—a commitment that somehow seems easier to make between semesters than during the heat of midterm.

The rub in the balancing act between work and nonwork activities is that the aspect of work that suffers most from increased leisure, family time, and sleep is my research. Because the other types of work activities tend to have externally imposed timetables, the thing that slips away is research. Thus I feel the need to make more deliberate choices about my use of time in the future.

Final Thoughts

I began this essay by saying that the transition to full professor has not provided the sense of relief and relaxation I expected. My original diagnosis of the problem was that I had failed to anticipate the shift to full professor as any kind of transition at all. As a result, I had spent little time developing an explicit master plan for change, although I did make a number of ad hoc adjustments in my approach to both work and family life.

Upon rereading this essay several months later, however, I had a different kind of thought. Specifically, I was struck by my statement that I had expected the transition to full professor to be accompanied by a reduction in my "drive" to produce research. In retrospect, I see that this has not happened; although *external* expectations for research productivity have probably been reduced, my internal expectations are as high as ever. I continue to struggle with whether it is realistic, or desirable, to continue with such high research expectations, given all the other demands and opportunities in my life. Because I increasingly suspect that it may not be, I am also pondering the question of how one goes about modifying those expectations in a way that does not feel like copping out.

In trying to deal with these issues, I have found several sources of support and guidance. First, I get a tremendous amount of emotional support from peers (mostly academics, but not all) who are also close friends. Because they are for the most part struggling with similar issues, they give me the sense that what I am going through is "normal," and not the result of poor planning, irresponsibility, or inefficiency.

Second, I have always sought advice from people I admire who are somewhat older than myself. These people are mentors in the fullest sense of the word: trusted guides in *all* aspects of life, not just career matters. In fact, I have noticed that the older I become, the more I seek the company and advice of these "full-life" people. Taking closer note of what I admire in other people has become a major impetus for looking more closely at questions of balance and long-term objectives in my own life.

Third, I have long had a habit of reading books that, by relating the experiences of others, cause me to reflect on my own life and the directions it is taking. Most memorable in this regard are biographies, autobiographies, and memoirs (e.g., Lindbergh, 1955; Radner, 1989; Steinem, 1992), books on social trends (e.g., Schor, 1992), and various books on career and life stages. In this last group, for example, I have read Levinson's *The Seasons of a Man's Life* (1978) several times; Gail Sheehy's *Passages* (1984) and *The Silent Passage* (1991); and Elisabeth Kübler-Ross's *On Death and Dying* (1970). These books serve several functions for me. First, like peers and mentors, they confirm that I am not alone in my worries or frustrations. Second, they allow me to think about things in complete privacy. Third, in contrast to my interactions with peers and mentors, the *books* set the agenda for contemplation. In this way, topics that I (or my friends) might never have considered are more likely to surface.

In fact, in preparation for writing this essay, I reread *Seasons of a Man's Life* as well as some additional material on career stages (e.g., Dalton, Thompson, & Price, 1977). My reading caused me to realize that what I have been going through since becoming a full professor is probably more accurately viewed as a particular (academic) manifestation of broader midlife and career transitions. Specifically, I experienced my first 3 years of full professorship from the ages of 37 to 40. This period corresponds with the beginning of the classic midlife transition phase, during which people contemplate all sorts of things as they realize they are moving into the second half (the *last* half) of their lives. It also corresponds to the ages when, according to Dalton and his colleagues, most people move out of the "individual contributor" stage toward the mentoring and sponsoring stages. These general patterns fit quite closely with some of the seemingly spontaneous actions I have taken in recent years, such as my innovations in the classroom, my willingness to take on more graduate students, and my search for research areas that are more personally meaningful to me (but riskier in terms of publishability).

Perhaps the most comforting thing to me as I reread these books at this point in time is their reminder of just how difficult it is for *many* people to move from the individual contributor stage of life to stages marked by greater social and institutional commitment. Moving away from individual contributions (in my own case, research) involves real risks and potential losses (for example, of technical proficiency or external visibility). This helps me to understand why it has been so hard for me to reduce my personal standards for research.

On the other hand, these same descriptions of life and career stages suggest that the people who are generally most valued in later life are those who rise to the challenge of taking on additional roles. This conforms to my own personal experience of coming more and more to value people with multidimensional lives, those who make diverse contributions. It may also explain why I feel the pull of institutionally oriented activities at the same time that I bemoan the toll they take on my role as individual contributor or researcher.

In short, I think that although I have already made the *formal* transition to full professor, I am still in the process of making some other, more encompassing, life transitions. If that is correct, then people who enter full professorship at different points in their lives may well find that much of what has been causing so much angst in my own life has already been resolved in theirs.

In closing, I would like to make some positive comments about academic life, at all stages up to this point. In the end, I have come to believe that there are three very important advantages to academic life. One is that, more than in almost any other occupation, one has the freedom to incorporate issues that are personally exciting into the mainstream of one's work. Second, one can experiment with a large number of different activities and continually adjust the balance among them. For example, one can take on a "little more" consulting, adopt a "slightly different" research stream, or test one's leadership in an important committee before committing to a departmental chairmanship. In this way, academics can continue to grow, but at an acceptable level of personal risk. Finally, although good academics work long hours, there is enough flexibility in those hours to incorporate a good measure of one's own personal preferences, aspirations, and commitments.

All in all, full professorship seems to offer about as clear a shot at self-actualization as anyone is ever likely to get. To the extent that the transition to full professor has caused some restlessness on my part, it has largely been the result of my having so many options and not enough time to pursue them all well. One can imagine a whole lot worse set of problems than that.

References

Dalton, G. W., Thompson, P. H., & Price, R. L. (1977, Summer). The four stages of professional careers: A new look at performance by professionals. *Organizational Dynamics*, pp. 19-42.

Kübler-Ross, E. (1970). *On death and dying.* New York: Simon & Schuster.

Levinson, D. J. (1978). *The seasons of a man's life.* New York: Ballantine.

Lindbergh, A. M. (1955). *Gift from the sea.* New York: Pantheon.

Longenecker, C. O., Sims, H. P., & Gioia, D. A. (1987). Behind the mask: The politics of employee appraisal. *Academy of Management Executive, 1,* 183-193.

Radner, G. (1989). *It's always something.* New York: Avon.

Schor, J. B. (1992). *The overworked American: The unexpected decline of leisure.* New York: Basic Books.

Sheehy, G. (1984). *Passages.* New York: Bantam.

Sheehy, G. (1991). *The silent passage: Menopause.* New York: Pocket Books.

Steinem, G. (1992). *Revolution from within: A book of self-esteem.* Boston: Little, Brown.

Pause Point 2:
The Overenriched Work Life

Unfortunately, external markers of success—which reflect the satisfaction of others regarding our performances—may not translate readily into feelings of personal satisfaction. Searching for more and better ways to work efficiently is, I think, a strategy built on the implicit assumption that accomplishing more will lead to more recognition from others and, therefore, more personal satisfaction. This logic is flawed, however.

Susan E. Jackson (p. 354)

As we mentioned in Pause Point 1, these sections are devoted to essays that examine the ways academics deal with recurring sets of rhythms they encounter, albeit in different forms, throughout the life span, such as balancing work and nonwork activities or coping with an overenriched work life. The phrase *pause point* in the titles of these sections conveys our belief that we academics must periodically slow down the pace of our lives for brief periods, reassess our success in putting "first things first," and respond in ways likely to move us closer to the lives we desire. We have come to call these adjustments "retuning on the run." In this pause point we focus on a recurring theme in the lives of many academics: dealing with the overenriched work life.

Increasing opportunities to choose their own work tasks and work situations, the topic of much discussion in the preceding section on becoming a full professor, constitute a powerful catch-22 for many academics. They often find that the better established and more respected one becomes in the profession, the more tasks one is asked to undertake within the local institution, professional associations, and society in general. In combination, high external expectations of the academic's performance and the individual's even higher personal expectations for his or her own achievement provide most of the ingredients for a turbocharged work life that just "keeps on going." Unfortunately, as reported in the early job design research (see Katz, 1980), even the most challenging and exciting task is likely to mutate into sheer drudgery by the twenty-fifth repetition. Individuals caught in this quandary are likely to find themselves working constantly, doing a variety of "exciting" things that are, on the whole, less and less satisfying.

In the following chapter, Susan Jackson (full professor, current editor of *AMJ*, past chair of the Organizational Behavior Division of the National Academy of Management, and prolific author and researcher) relates her own experiences with managing the overenriched work life. Susan identifies two primary strategies for dealing with this issue—workload management and self-management—while noting that they differ in objectives and associated methods. Workload management, in Jackson's view, is best achieved through an avoidance strategy: "Perhaps the simplest way to cope with too much work is to avoid *getting* too much work. . . . Thus, long before Nancy Reagan would popularize the phrase, I started to suspect that 'just say no' could be a nearly magical cure-all for stress and job overload" (pp. 351-352). She warns, however, that this tactic is no longer as simple to implement as it once was— "People who ask for your time have learned how to respond to those of us who try to just say no" (p. 352)—and goes on to identify some of the tricks "they" use to change the intended no to an eventual yes. In Jackson's opinion, academics can deal with

the increased sophistication of those striving to get others to increase their workloads only through familiarity with commonly used tactics and enhanced skill at just saying no, developed through practice.

Jackson's second strategy, self-management, may be the more important one over the long term for "dealing with" as opposed to "coping with" the overenriched work life. Here, Jackson, like Montagno and Rynes in the previous section, suggests that a bit of introspection and enhanced self-knowledge may prove invaluable. "I can elevate my satisfaction by setting my own priorities and by making commitments to tasks that are consistent with those priorities. I can also elevate my satisfaction by placing greater value on the tasks at which I excel and less value on tasks at which I am less proficient" (p. 354). For those of us who frequently find our responsibilities pushing at, if not truly exceeding, the boundaries of our capabilities, such advice seems well worth heeding and quite necessary for the "retuning on the run" theme of these pause point sections.

Reference

Katz, R. (1980). Time and work: Toward an integrative perspective. In B. M. Staw & L. L. Cummings (Eds.), *Research in organizational behavior* (Vol. 2, pp. 81-128). Greenwich, CT: JAI.

36 Dealing With the Overenriched Work Life

Susan E. Jackson

Several years ago, when I was doing research on the topics of job stress and burnout, I occasionally received calls from newspaper reporters and practitioners in organizations asking me to speak about stress management. Hearing myself say things like, "We don't really know a great deal about which stress management techniques work well" and "You might want to call someone who conducts time management workshops," I should have known that this was a topic to learn more about. Each of us should probably go to one those workshops. Unfortunately, I never did. Instead, I've been learning about time and stress management the slow way—through experience. When the editors of this volume asked me to write about "the overenriched work life," I found I had the chance to record what I've learned about getting work done during the past several years, when I've often felt I had too much work to do.

Before describing some of the lessons I think I've learned, a caveat is required: Readers should realize that I do not consider myself to be any more of an expert about this topic now than I was a decade ago. I have, however, given the question considerably more thought during the intervening years. Two tactics for dealing with the overenriched work life now seem apparent to me: workload management and self-management. These two tactics are helpful in accomplishing two different objectives, and should never be confused.

Workload Management

Just Say No!

Perhaps the simplest way to cope with too much work is to avoid *getting* too much work. Some of my most vivid memories from graduate school are of an overworked adviser. At that time, he was at about the same stage in his career as I am now. He clearly had too much to do. Why else would he be in his office for 12 to 14 hours on weekdays and weekends? Surely it was not just to set a good example for the students. Once or twice I expressed concern about how all the work might affect his health. His answer was simply, "I just haven't learned to say no." Thus, long before Nancy Reagan would popularize the phrase, I started to suspect that "just say no" could be a nearly magical cure-all for stress and job overload.

Just say no. It sounds simple. So simple, in fact, that little *learning* should be necessary. But learning does seem to be necessary, and I am still learning. Learning is necessary because people who ask for your time have learned how to respond to those of us who try to just say no. Some of the tricks they use are as follows:

- *Flattery.* This usually is the first offensive move. Through flattery, the person asking for your help will convince you that *you* really are the best person for the time-consuming task. Those who are good at this will convince you that if anyone else does the job, the world just won't be in quite as good shape as if you had said yes to the request. Given how seldom most of us hear flattery, especially in our work lives, this is a tough first lesson. I was a slow learner—it took me about 8 years to both recognize and learn not to respond to flattery. (Of course, there is a downside to learning this lesson: Showing that you can resist flattery extinguishes the behavior, so be prepared to experience some flattery-withdrawal symptoms.)

- *Long lead time.* This is a common second move. After you resist the flattery, the person will explain that you have many months before the work is to be done. How can you say you won't have time to attend a half-day meeting to be held 18 months from now? Do you really have so much to do that you can't prepare a chapter that isn't due for 2 years? Be careful with this one. It's important to realize that any deadline you are given is just an opening bid. You may say, "I know it's hard to believe, but I couldn't even think about finding the time until at least [6 months after the person says it's needed]." The reply? "Oh, of course I understand how busy you are. We can work around your schedule." If you already have expressed interest in the task, you are now trapped.

- *Small task.* A long lead time plus a small request is still a deadly combination. "The committee's work won't start until next year, and there will be only two or three meetings." "You won't have to write much, just give your reactions." "I don't really expect

much from you as my sponsor when I visit next year—it's really just a formality."

- *You're in control.* Those who are most skilled at extracting other people's time have learned to hand you the noose: "You can write on any topic you want." "Feel free to involve a coauthor." "What's most interesting to you?" "We want the committee to structure this in whatever way they feel will have the most impact." "Take as much time as you need— just tell me when I can expect it." These are devious words.

- *It may be your only opportunity.* This is not something one often hears stated explicitly, but it is easy to self-administer a dose of this thinking as an additive to an unusual or seemingly prestigious activity.

Learning to just say no is a good starting point for anyone feeling overenriched, but it is just the beginning. It helps put boundaries on the length of your required workday and keeps anxiety levels below the boiling point. But simply learning the skill is not enough. As with any skill, you should practice to keep in shape. Make it a point to practice regularly on small requests, so that when the bigger requests come along, you can just say no effortlessly. And be sure to reinforce your learning with rewards. When the day of that conference you decided not to attend finally comes along, take an extra hour or two to enjoy a leisurely lunch, play some tennis, visit an exhibit, spend time with a friend, or work on that research project you're really interested in! After all, aren't these the reasons you worked so hard to just say no?

Watch Out for Monkeys

Just say no is a phrase I try to keep in mind in order to manage my interactions with well-intentioned colleagues who are working on various projects that require input from others. It is a phrase to use when you are feeling tempted to get involved in a project that will ultimately yield positive recognition and/or intellectual stimulation. In other words, it is a phrase that can help you avoid creating an overenriched work life.

When I was discussing the "just say no" strategy with a colleague recently, he asked if I meant "Keep the monkey off your back." This is a time management phrase, the meaning of which is that you need to be alert to situations in which others want to make you take responsibility for dealing with their constraints or shortcomings—quite a different type of situation from those I've referred to above. The generic "keep the monkey off your back" situation involves someone asking you to make an exception to your normal or planned activity. The trick is to determine whether agreeing to the request amounts to being suckered (you're an easy mark) or being flexible (you're willing to make reasonable accommodation). There are no easy rules to follow, but many opportunities to learn. If you like to think of yourself as flexible, chances are you also wrestle with monkeys that someone else really should be wrestling.

The most frequent and irritating monkey-business situations I encounter involve *rearranging* scheduled meetings. To me, agreeing to a meeting time is equivalent to making a contract. The expectation is that all parties take responsibility for scheduling other activities in a way that ensures they will be available for the meeting. Some of us take such contracts seriously; others act as if they include a disclaimer that reads, "Party X and Party Y [you, the flexible one] jointly agree to these arrangements, assuming nothing else comes up for Party X. In such circumstances, Party Y agrees to whatever adjustments are necessary to ensure that Party X is not inconvenienced by this agreement." (You may recognize this as the last line of the Hippocratic oath, which guides the behavior of most members of the U.S. medical community.)

Is there a way to avoid carrying other people's monkeys? The first step is learning to recognize these situations. If you are having a conversation and it becomes apparent that the other person has "a problem" to resolve, visualize a monkey on the other person's back. Now your objective is to help the person resolve the problem while keeping your eye on that monkey. As you work out a way to resolve the problem, don't get too friendly with the monkey, because if you do, he will view your outstretched hand as a limb to be used to climb onto your back.

Job Unenrichment
(a.k.a. "Swiss Cheese Your ETs")

With the onset of the industrial age a century ago, job simplification spread throughout the workplace and was, we often teach, a destructive and demotivating force. Massive, daunting tasks were dissected to reveal thousands of tiny, easy tasks that required little if any thought or skill to perform. Like a hole in a block of Swiss cheese, a small task is difficult to appreciate if it is all you experience. At 10:00 a.m., I hear myself lecturing to my students, telling them about the dozens of studies that document the virtues of job enrichment. Give workers a whole block of cheese—don't condemn them to focus on just one of the empty holes! Then at noon, I sit with a manuscript that has just been submitted for review. After doing only the small and intentionally routinized task of assigning topic codes, which serve as input for the next small step of manuscript processing, assigning reviewers, I am pleased to hand it back to Lou, the office manager for the *Academy of Management Review*, for the next step of processing. It's paradoxical that I would never consider trading my work life for a life on an assembly line, yet the only way I can deal with an (over)enriched work life is by disassembling my work into small pieces.

Most days, I take great satisfaction in crossing off a few small items on my "to do" list—even if I have added a greater number of new items. Of course, the real incentive is knowing that a few times a year I will have the satisfaction of crossing off one final small item that is the last step in the completion of a big item (e.g., the first, second, or perhaps final draft of a paper is in the mail!). At some abstract intellectual level, it is the enriched tasks (ETs) that provide motivation for the long-term commitment to productivity in an academic setting. But at a behavioral level, day in and day out, it is much easier to find energy to do little tasks: returning phone calls and e-mail, preparing for a class, grading papers, reviewing manuscripts, meeting with students, ordering books, registering for conferences, and so on, and so on. Some of these tasks sound almost as meaningless as the holes in Swiss cheese, but small tasks have many virtues. When you have only 5 minutes before your next appointment, you can squeeze one out. When your energy is low, you can nevertheless tap into your reserves to take care of one or two small items. Thus you can start large projects even when you have only enough time and energy for small tasks. Completing a series of related small tasks creates the momentum needed for larger projects.

Managing Yourself

There are, of course, many other suggestions about workload management that I could offer here. Indeed, time management is a staple topic in the self-help industry, so "new" advice books can be found regularly at your local bookstore. For those who believe that inefficiency is their major problem, such books may be worth the investment. I suspect, however, that most people reading this chapter already know how to manage their time reasonably well. At a minimum, you have probably made it through an undergraduate curriculum with flying colors. Perhaps you also have completed a doctoral degree, worked successfully in at least one employment setting, and managed to have a life besides. Such accomplishments would be nearly impossible for anyone who is truly unable to cope successfully with overload situations. To the contrary, your success to date probably indicates that you thrive under overload conditions.

Unfortunately, external markers of success—which reflect the satisfaction of others regarding our performances—may not translate readily into feelings of personal satisfaction. Searching for more and better ways to work efficiently is, I think, a strategy built on the implicit assumption that accomplishing more will lead to more recognition from others and, therefore, more personal satisfaction. This logic is flawed, however. There are, after all, human limits to how much one can accomplish—incremental gains in efficiency and its associated rewards (internal as well as external ones) become harder to achieve as one becomes more efficient and productive. Readers who think visually can imagine efficiency gains plotted as an asymptotic curve that eventually levels out to a flat horizontal line. Human satisfaction, or at least the desire for increases in satisfaction, is probably unconstrained, however. In the world we like to imagine, our satisfaction graph shows a continual upward trajectory. This little thought experiment clearly predicts that frustration is the most likely consequence of continual striving for efficiency gains as the route to personal satisfaction. And, to the extent that the approval of others depends on ever-increasing productivity, it also predicts frustration for anyone who is dependent on such approval for personal satisfaction.

How can such a dilemma be resolved? Someone much wiser (i.e., older!) than me may be able to tell you the ultimate solution. For now, my solution is to be my own "satisfaction generator." What this amounts to is reminding myself several times a week that I create my own reality, including my own (dis)satisfaction. Anyone who doesn't experience "failure" is condemned to a very conservative existence, right? A little failure here and there simply reflects a healthy acceptance of risk. I can elevate my satisfaction by setting my own priorities and by making commitments to tasks that are consistent with those priorities. I can also elevate my satisfaction by placing greater value on the tasks at which I excel and less value on tasks at which I am less proficient. After all, is anyone out there really

a truly inspiring teacher,

personable colleague,

and helpful mentor to junior faculty,

who actively serves the profession

and builds the home institution

while still finding time to write beautifully creative theoretical pieces

and to conduct flawless research

that is destined to be relevant,

now and forever,

to scientists seeking understanding

and to practitioners seeking solutions,

backed by megabuck funding

and the resources of the best university in the world,

which is pleased to see a research process that makes transparent the individual's independent contribution

while revealing the interpersonal skills of our team player,

whose inspiration comes from hard knocks and successes accumulated over years of high-prestige consulting or line-manager experience

in an international setting,

which makes it possible to live in laptop luxury

surrounded by a loving and productive family

and lifelong friends

who take pride in the community's appreciation of our superhero's selfless volunteer work, not to mention those special talents that help the home team beat the local competition,

even on those occasional days when a wild party cuts into our superhero's usual 8 hour sleep?

If you know such a person, as a professional courtesy, keep this information to yourself. Without knowing such people, the rest of us can cope with our modestly overenriched work lives by keeping in perspective which of many possible accomplishments are truly important to our own satisfaction.

IV

Middle Rhythms

Nontraditional Paths

Working as a Consultant

Although not born to consulting, I did have some flair for the work. In high school, for instance, I sold shoes, and in college I hawked magazines. Besides skills at selling (which is not to say marketing, positioning, networking, and such), I also got comfortable and reasonably skillful at diagnosing problems in organizations, helping people understand their situations, and at planning and implementing change—all acquired under the mantle of "action research."

Philip H. Mirvis (p. 362)

I know my consulting is enhanced by my academic ties. I don't see the two as incompatible, as many of my colleagues do. . . . If anything, I have learned more that continues to inform my career choices and deliberations from my consulting work than from almost anything else.

Mary Ann Von Glinow (p. 375)

Virtually all academics in the organizational sciences encounter opportunities to consult. Most, lured by some combination of supplementary income, the chance to make a difference in organizational settings, and the opportunity to increase their credibility in the classroom, accept at least a few invitations. However, an unmistakable tension arises when those who are trained to think conceptually, talk abstractly, and build new knowledge slowly, rigorously, and cumulatively work with others whose work settings demand a diametrically opposite set of characteristics. Conflict also frequently arises "back at the ranch," where colleagues usually disagree on the value of consulting in the academic model and send conflicting signals about the effects of exceeding informal thresholds for consulting activities on performance evaluations, promotion decisions, and scholarly reputations.

In this section, two academics with extensive consulting experience provide their views of the skill requirements, costs, benefits, and tensions that accompany consulting. Phil Mirvis is a former professor turned consultant. His quotation at the beginning of this introduction illustrates the candidness—about attitudes, characteristics, and interests—that made his departure from the academic world and subsequent move into full-time consulting almost inevitable. At the same time, Mirvis is equally forthcoming in relating the feelings of identity loss, institutional anomie, career path ambiguity, and financial uncertainty that such a move brought to his life:

Making this sort of transition may not seem such a big deal. . . . However, a change in self-identity is more freighted. . . . The investment in training, anticipatory and actual socialization into a profession, reinforcement through the rites and rewards of passages, plus the continuous detailing of one's self-picture all make contemplation of a career change rather scary. (p. 362)

Nevertheless, a career change is exactly what Phil undertook, working through the self-image difficulties and the dilemma of being unable to conduct research in the traditional sense while consulting. As he puts it: "Yet even those high-minded clients who aspire for theirs to become learning organizations tend to shy away from extensive analysis of their own assumptions and blanch at the idea that you cannot expect things to turn out right" (p. 364). Persevering, Mirvis found his niche—helping organizations to hear, face, and, ultimately, attempt to change the multitude of "truths" that members or other constituents tell about their current functioning. As he notes: "There is little akin to 'refreezing' in today's world, but, in the best of cases, this kind of consult teaches clients about helping themselves and speaks to Argyris's final criterion of effective interventions: 'psychological commitment' to change" (p. 365).

Mary Ann Von Glinow blazed her path into consulting while she was a university professor with ongoing academic responsibilities. Not surprisingly, she has observed firsthand the academic reaction when the consultant returns home to colleagues who may have little appreciation of the importance of such activities. Yet Von Glinow feels strongly that she has experienced reciprocal benefits from her participation in both the consulting and academic arenas, as the quote at the opening of this introduction indicates.

Speaking openly of the chasm between academics who consult and those who do not, Von Glinow doubts the need for or utility of such extreme separatism. As she puts it, "I try not to bifurcate issues into camps—rigor versus relevance, for example. Both are important, and I try to maintain that emphasis throughout my academic and consulting lives" (p. 375). Her essay contains several lessons, acquired from her experiences as a consultant, that those considering such a path in their career journeys should find quite informative. However, she also recognizes the difficulty of forays into the consulting world as an academic, and notes the importance of working with master consultants in the development of her own skills.

Regardless of consulting skills, expertise, and the status of one's academic affiliation, in Von Glinow's opinion, corporate consulting opportunities are far from gender-blind. Women, as a group, she believes, typically find such entry more difficult than do men. As a result, she urges women who are considering the consulting path to seek out female mentors to assist them in developing necessary skills and entrée connections, although she acknowledges the scarcity of female mentors from which to choose.

Although they speak from somewhat different vantage points, both Mirvis and Von Glinow paint intriguing pictures of the academic as a consultant. Together, they make a strong argument for moving beyond existing stereotypes—both those concerning the "right" path for academics to follow and those concerning academics bringing little value to organizations—to a more flexible view. Such a stance would place consulting in the context of one more path in the rhythms of an academic's life, a path with its own unique set of costs and benefits and requiring introspection and self-management skills to pursue. Perhaps Phil Mirvis expresses this best:

> For a time, anyway, consulting will be what I do along with a lot of other stuff. When I last talked to Karl Weick, he did a bit of career counseling and asked me whether I truly saw myself as a consultant and would want that on my gravestone. "No," I replied. "I'd wish it to read: 'Here Lies Philip Harold Mirvis, A Curious Fellow.' " (p. 367)

37 Midlife as a Consultant

Philip H. Mirvis

I ended my professorial career in much the way I started it: fired with enthusiasm.[1] The president and provost at Boston University did not favor my work, politics, or manner; nor did it help matters when I called the head of the university's committee a "pinhead" when I was asked to dot i's and cross t's in my tenure dossier. Looking back, I'm glad to be out of the place (and they rid of me!), but it was angering and deflating at the time (7 years ago).

If truth be told, I would not have given me tenure either. Oh, my scholarship was fine, teaching innovative, and service, discounting churlishness, a step above acceptable. The problem was that, somewhere along the way, I lost the professor's vocation. Generation X MBA students, desperately seeking high-paying jobs, helped quell the fire, as did faculty meetings where the "community of scholars" discoursed about grade inflation, excessive use of the copier, and other aspects of the decline of Western civilization. That I had spent 5 years studying cynicism was another factor: I took on the persona, and life at the university, as in business and society in the 1980s, came into sharper focus through the cynic's lens. Yet losing my

vocation is not wholly attributable to my employer, or even to my own increasingly jaundiced way of looking at things: Choices made along the way hinted at other destinations.

For instance, in my preprofessorial college years, I used to sleep through classes and haunt late-night movie houses. The academic topics that caught my interest involved hands-on research: sifting australopithecine shards or earning sociology credits by observing Alcoholics Anonymous meetings. I also enjoyed shutting the campus down on May Day—even more so after learning why—and did a stint as a volunteer in the McGovern campaign. After graduation, I hitchhiked around the country and worked in state government in Ohio, where my job was to show it would be "cost-effective" to free workers from oppression.[2] This hardly equates with a "dream" to become a classroom professor, but it reveals the curiosity that leads one on to further study and counterdependence that often gets you into trouble.[3]

In graduate school I was immersed in the research craft, training under Edward Lawler and Stan Seashore, and spending an average of 100 or so days a year "out in the field." By the

361

time I graduated, schools of management had started hiring liberal arts types to improve their research records, and they had the only jobs available. So I signed on at the Management School at Boston U, hoping to fly the school colors, and soon got into a brouhaha with peers and administrators over credentialing ROTC students, never got comfortable with dressing up for classes, and thereupon moved myself over to an applied research center on campus.

There I could conduct field research and dress like a slob without having to worry about "face time" or attend to "departmental housekeeping." Over time, and this is more telling, my busyness had me beg off admission committee assignments, discussions of the MBA curricula, and even the doctoral student seminar. I guess I was more curious about life in organizations than life in the classroom, more taken with the issues (ideas on empowerment and collaboration were making headway), and more apt to feel I could make a difference working with companies rather than against the tide in my university. So I began to put my energies into energizing managers and workers rather than my colleagues and students.

I was fired just as my wife was graduating with a PhD, and she got an offer from American University. So we looked at our options, fought and wept, looked into each other's eyes (hers were brighter), and moved to the Washington, D.C., area. She was now the professor and I was reborn as a consultant, or, like others who stumble into the field, more or less unemployed.

A New Identity: The Consultant's Calling?

Nurses seldom hold up bawling babies for proud parents to exclaim: Look, a consultant![4] Such prognostication is usually reserved for future doctors, inventors, beauty queens, athletes, or professors. Although not born to consulting, I did have some flair for the work. In high school, for instance, I sold shoes, and in college I hawked magazines. Besides skills at selling (which is not to say marketing, positioning, networking, and such), I also got comfortable and reasonably skillful at diagnosing problems in organizations, helping people understand their situations, and at planning and implementing change—all acquired under the man-

tle of "action research." As a professor, I did plenty of this, learned a bit of business-speak, and gained a modest reputation as a good "thinker" about organizational change. But aren't consultants supposed to be doers?

Making this sort of transition may not seem such a big deal. After all, the typical American changes employers 10 times during his or her work life, and nowadays increasing numbers are self-employed (U.S. Bureau of Labor Statistics, 1989). On the practical end, purchase of a copier and fax machine went smoothly, and setting up a home office in the former back kitchen of our farmhouse meant scrubbing 80 years of fried-chicken grease off the walls but was otherwise uneventful. However, a change in self-identity is more freighted. Seymour Sarason (1977) contends that many midcareer professionals are imbued with a one life/one career perspective. The investment in training, anticipatory and actual socialization into a profession, reinforcement through the rites and rewards of passages, plus the continuous detailing of one's self-picture all make contemplation of a career change rather scary. My own emerging sense of aging and foreclosed options (such as pitching for the Red Sox), financial insecurity, and somewhat shattered self-confidence from being fired made the idea of "starting over" even more threatening.

Accompanying this midlife and career transition were months of depression, lameness in my left leg, tongue-lashings of my wife, and general bitchiness. No doubt some of this had to do with losing my job, moving to a new city, missing my friends, and feeling envy over my wife's delight in her new post.[5] Lacking a professional identity was also a factor.[6] So I read about loss, disengagement, hanging on, and letting go, and concentrated more on "being" than on "doing" (Bowlby, 1950-1980; Bridges, 1980; Hudson, 1991; Tannenbaum & Hanna, 1985). I also did some "body therapy" for the purposes of self-centering and some searching for my soul with old friends.

My men's "support group" helped me find it. When David Brown first put a bunch of us together, he envisioned us exchanging views, like Freud's group in Vienna. Although the "Brookline Circle" is our formal designation, I think of us more as the "Mystic Knights of Marginality" (in honor of Amos 'n' Andy). Few of the group members (originally Lee Bolman,

Barry Oshry, Dave, and me; later Tim Hall, Bill Kahn, and Todd Jick) do mainstream academic work, and all of us are more or less marginal to institutions. Anyway, the group, after listening patiently to moaning, complaints about emasculation, and stereotyping, advised me to deal with dislocation (Get a life!), talked me through my anger (It's not your wife, it's you!!), and beat me up about my self-limiting picture of consulting (We all do it; are we all assholes too?).

As the Zen saying goes, when garbled: Understanding is no substitute for participating. To get on with my new work and ease my anxiety, I envisioned myself making a lateral career move: using the same sort of skills, just operating from a different base. Interestingly, rereading articles from the early days of organizational development (Bennis and Beckhard called it an educational strategy) let me continue to see myself as something of a "teacher" (Have Knowledge, Will Travel—Fax Mirvis) and reawakened in me a bit of the old revolutionary fervor (to free the masses, make things right, and change the world!) that initially attracted me to the field.[7] I then began to network to "reality test" my notions and see how they might play in practice.

Up to this point, my role model was Ed Lawler, who continues to intermix research and consulting from an academic center. Searching for some nonacademic exemplars, I talked with David Nadler, who runs an upscale consulting firm in midtown Manhattan. Hats off to him, but the idea of leasing a downtown office, hiring staff, putting together a brochure, fretting over logos, and pitching my wares in corporate boardrooms was too much to contemplate when my vistas were acres of farmland and my marketing plan was to throw up a shingle. More to the point, he was approaching the work like a businessman. Conversations with Michael Maccoby and Daniel Yankelovich reassured me that it was feasible to run a solo practice, network with others to do projects and process data, and still retain my academic interests while making a living as a consultant.

There remained the matters of what to call myself and what to put on my business card. Rebirths often involve renaming. First I tried out "psychologist" (Yankelovich); that is what my graduate degree said, and it fit my bearded self-image. However, queries about my couch necessitated lots of explaining and I found myself dissembling at parties when probed about Freud's shortcomings or my own views on codependency, and utterly at a loss when asked about the treatment of somebody's symptoms. When I explained that I was a consultant and worked with organizations (not people?), partygoers would either change the subject or shrink away. I tried to face this straight on and put the rather rakish "p.c." on my card (Maccoby). In Washington, this made me a political consultant, and elsewhere it was read as an unsubtle announcement of my correctness. Finally, I settled on calling myself an "independent researcher and consultant," which said everything and nothing—in short, it was an apt description.

A couple of great clients, in turn, helped me to ease into the work. I consulted with Ben & Jerry's as the founders strove to put their ideals into their organization, and then with M. Scott Peck, whose Foundation for Community Encouragement gathered together clergy, doctors, lawyers, healers, businesspeople, and some honest-to-goodness mystics to teach community-building skills through public workshops and private consultations. Ex post cynicism, my leg healed and my spirits were restored; my practice was enlivened by retreats featuring rope courses, woodworking, chanting, and mask making; my wife's career success became more of a pleasure; and my client work was largely helpful, instructive, and therapeutic for them and for me. Yet to the extent consulting was to be my calling, who was I kidding putting research first on my business card?

Consulting/Research Conundrums

Stanley Seashore taught me in graduate school about the dilemmas between "research" and "action" in an academic role.[8] They are trickier still in consulting assignments.[9] For instance, in the research enterprise, the protocol is to work from hypotheses, conduct careful experiments, come to tentative conclusions, and identify areas for further research. In a consulting venture, by comparison, the primary concern of clients is "deliverables." With a collusive wink by me, the tasks as defined are to dig up facts, propose doable recommendations, make good things happen, and minimize collateral damage. Over the course of a consult, this can-do emphasis turns hunches into truths and gives suggestions the air of tested solutions. And problems that crop up come as a surprise—with blame attached to management, Murphy, or Mirvis, depending on whom you ask.

Now, everyone knows this is nonsense—and no way to learn how to learn about change. Yet even those high-minded clients who aspire for theirs to become learning organizations tend to shy away from extensive analysis of their own assumptions and blanch at the idea that you cannot expect things to turn out right.[10] I try to be true to the work by having clients draw their own maps of organizational dynamics, think through the ins and outs of interventions, and assess thoughtfully the downside results of change. But the practical press is such that the theorizing behind action is often simplistic, contingency planning is sloppy, and reflections on results are marred by finger-pointing or, on occasion, unseemly grasps for glory. Mea culpa.

Needless to say, this kind of action research does not approximate the rigor found in controlled studies and, frankly, subordinates careful conceptualization and conclusion drawing to the pragmatics of getting something accomplished. It also means that my writings about change increasingly consist of case studies and retrospective reflections made scientific sounding by questionnaire data and an unsubstantiable chart or two about changes in productivity, turnover, or blood pressure rates. On the one hand, it is heartening that qualitative data and storytelling now pass for research in academic books and even journals. On the other, it is humbling when, upon meeting a newly minted researcher at an Academy of Management meeting, she remarks, "Oh yeah, you *used* to do good research."

Finding My Niche

Fortunately and not, there is less of a consensus about what makes for good consulting. Ben Cohen, for example, handed me a wizard's hat at our first meeting, and an hour later he and other members of the Ben & Jerry's board were setting fire to their personal vision statements in a ritual of transformation.[11] Needless to say, I was never mentored into consulting but take to heart Chris Argyris's (1970) points on the importance of "valid data" and the "authority of knowledge" when intervening in an organization. Pyrotechnics can be part of the show, but I see myself as a sort of seer in consultations who emphasizes truth telling and "discussing the undiscussable" (Argyris, 1985). Of course, there are many different truths in organizations—in boardrooms, back rooms, and bathrooms, as well as at sales sites and on factory floors—and my job is to make these varied truths known and help the client system understand what is behind them. Analogies to movies like *Rashomon,* in which it is clear a murder has been committed but there are different stories about who wielded the knife, illuminate this "social construction" of reality (Berger & Luckmann, 1967).

In practice, this means creating a story about current organizational dynamics that makes different versions of murderous events credible. It is all brought to life in my practice when different interests—say, two parties to a merger, or a boss and middle managers, or farmers and environmentalists—share their versions and play out the future implications. Usually, some combination of understanding, shame over past practices, and horror over the prophetic consequences serves to "unfreeze" the situation. A measure of collective catharsis—involving tears, gallows humor, and righteous indignation—in turn readies people for change. Clients, using different images, say that this sort of storytelling "lets us walk in each other's shoes," or "establishes a level set," or simply "opens up lines of communication."

My onstage role is to orchestrate the storytelling, make interpretive comments, police the process, and, where appropriate, push ahead an action agenda. Meanwhile, backstage I might urge the bosses to listen or to speak their own truth, advocate for unheard voices, appeal to instincts—moral and material—and in other ways keep discussions moving along. Lest it seem that it is all "talk therapy," I also encourage clients to set sail, climb rocks, make masks, put on skits, and join in other manner of "play therapy" that opens up perspectives, creates common experiences, and reminds them that body and spirit are connected to the intellect.

Now, this sounds a lot like "old" organizational development with some newfangled features—funny how the longest journey is the one back to yourself.[12] The new stuff here is to be found in the "dialogue" techniques being studied at MIT and elsewhere, in methods of "appreciative inquiry" practiced at Case Western Reserve and by Bill Torbert, and in community-building workshops wherein people reach a state of "emptiness" and thence open themselves to others and to spirit. Its applications in "large group" interventions, as reported in a special edition of the *Journal of Applied Behavioral Science,* in the "future searches" of Marvin Weisbord and others, and even in the Workout program at General Electric put me squarely in the middle of something going on.[13] There is little akin to "refreezing" in today's world, but, in the best of cases, this kind of consult teaches clients about helping themselves and speaks to Argyris's final criterion of effective interventions: "psychological commitment" to change.

A Boundaryless Career?

The left leg hurts again; this time it's the foot. I'm crabby with my wife and fed up with farm chores. It seems my midlife and career "transition" continues and makes it hard for me to know where I am headed. Triangulation may help: From one angle, I seem to be traveling a "boundaryless career." This kind of career entails regular movement from project to project, into and out of work groups, and across organizations, whether voluntarily or not. As it unfolds, however, the moves are not necessarily upward: Many are lateral, some are downward, and there can be times of under- or unemployment plus lots of retraining. In this way, a boundaryless career involves several cycles of "starting over," and people "age" within each career stage (Hall & Mirvis, 1994). Looked at from another angle, mortality lurks; I'm starting to look back as much as forward, and I have loads of responsibilities—financial and familial. Thus, although I may be young in my new career as a consultant, I am aging chronologically and in terms of life's developmental agenda.[14]

There is plenty of good advice available on maneuvering through different ages and stages and plotting a life and career course. Frederick Hudson (1991), for instance, advises those who lead cyclical lives to look to "process" as much as "progress" and to commit to leisure and health along with work. In terms of employability, Tim Hall says that one needs higher-order "generalist" skills to cope with the demands

of many different kinds of assignments and a high level of adaptability to withstand the psychic toll.[15] Yet, as with most people, to the extent that these are my strengths, they are also my weaknesses.

To illustrate, when it comes to work, my interests remain broad and varied: developing surveys, observation methods, and accounting schemes to assess life in organizations; conducting studies of the workforce and workplace; consulting in start-ups, mergers, and reorganizations; facilitating team building, town meetings, and dispute resolutions; plus a bit of work with a baseball team, a grocery store, and the AARP. Being a generalist makes it comparatively easy to pursue these diverse interests and move from setting to setting. But it also makes it difficult to earn a living and keep track of what I do.

Most top-drawer teachers and researchers, for instance, are both expert *and* known to be expert in one subject or another. The same is true of consultants: If you want to build market recognition, ensure an income stream, and attract a following, you specialize. I have not, and so do not—have followers, a steady income, or a market identity. Furthermore, I have not mastered any subject, industry, or situation, meaning I have to learn quick, talk fast, and deflect details. The upshot is that my work seems very fragmentary—a patchwork of projects, papers, and plane trips—and is spread over desk piles, in computer files, and through a stream of phone messages from people whose names and reasons for calling me I have trouble remembering. On good days, I fancy myself something of a Renaissance man. More often, I'm like a gadfly and have to content myself with the moniker of raconteur.

Material Matters

One fanciful way to do what you want is to get others to work for you—for example, by running your own firm and hiring help. Much as I might dream of someday being an "institution builder," I don't want the responsibility or demands now and am pretty sure I could not do it very well anyway (If you can't do, teach—and if you can't teach, consult). This means that I collaborate with other marginal types, like Amy Sales and Dennis Ross, who are wonderful people but do not cotton to the idea of being my "staff." It's hard to manage large projects when your firm is you. So I occasionally team up with fellow professionals who run or work in consulting firms, like Toni Lucia at Manus or Mitch Marks at Delta, but they are busy and our socializing is done in flight. With no institutional home, I am like the freelancer who wonders, Where is my kingdom?

I've handled this over the years by investing myself in client organizations and making good friendships in them. I've even styled myself as a "relationship" consultant. In my two longest-lasting relationships, however, changes in top leadership severed my ties to the companies. Oh, I felt my work would still make a contribution, but my identification with the old regimes made me suspect with the new ones. I've not found it easy to handle the loss of these valued clients. Lately I've worked with clients who hire consultants as a matter of course. Here I have looked for love, but they have wanted only services for hire. Hence the specter of prostitution has begun to haunt me.

Which brings up money: Big-time consultants charge anywhere from $5,000 to $10,000 a day. Bigger bucks come with a bigger name, expertise in the hard side of business, and/or well-heeled clients that don't care about fees. I do a lot of work with nonprofits, small outfits, and, as in the case of Ben & Jerry's, clients with relatively "flat" pay scales. Add to this that I'm hardly a household name and my work is relatively soft, and you can better understand why I'm concerned about cash flow. Lest this sound like selfless service, I'm open to a bonanza. I had one client (a New York bank) object to my proposed fee. As I started to lower it, my contact explained that they paid other consultants much more and had to at least bring me "up to scale." I didn't mind. I do mind, however, that I see subtle changes in my demeanor in the cases where I'm paid what seems to me to be a lot of money. I'm not talking about dress: I've outgrown my hang-ups over suits and ties, partly because my issues (e.g., dress) can get in the way of helping people address their issues. What I am talking about is conscience.

To elaborate, I no longer blanch at the idea of layoffs or look aghast when a manager talks about the need to fire so-and-so. I also partake in manly talk about end runs, trench warfare, and screwing somebody when this is the corpo-

rate vernacular, and yield to painful decisions when, short of cruelty, the ends seem to justify the means.[16] I am not troubled (just defensive!) when armchair sociologists criticize the likes of me for "selling out" from their perches in business schools. Frankly, I like many of the businesspeople I meet and respect how they moralize and agonize over actions that have hurtful consequences. But I do worry that I most often talk and act like a tough-minded manager when I'm paid well and work with them. It should not be surprising that, after finishing a day of this kind of consulting, I rush home, put on jeans, chase after my wife, and check out the budget. Ooh, aah, ugh.

One rationalization, and it's not a pretty one, is that consulting in big business buys me free time and allows me to pursue my "nonwork" life. I have time to go skating with my two older daughters, to go to gym class with my youngest, and to chop wood, take naps, and read novels. I also go on adventures, visit museums, and goof off periodically. Sure, I had time for all of this when I was working at a university, but I seldom took the time. Now I do. This is more than a trade-off of time against money. It is also a matter of aging: Taylor Cox marvels that I "carve out" time from my work to be with my kids, to exercise and recreate, even to introspect. I marvel at how he finds the time to be with his family, to pursue his ministry, and to call me just to talk. We are both coming to recognize that "work" is not quite so important to us anymore. Other facets of life seem to matter more and more.[17]

My Career as a Not-So Eccentric Predicate

I remember well reading Karl Weick's 1974 paper *Careers as Eccentric Predicates,* and have since heeded his advice to "make yourself up as you go along." The meaning of my current work will, to use his words, require "articulation post factum":

- *Work and family:* consulting with the Work and Family Institute of Boston University to learn more about the impact of work on parents and families and what it means to operate a "family-friendly" organization

- *Spirituality:* member of the board of directors of the Foundation for Community Encouragement (Being around so many loving people has helped to heal my cynicism and opened my heart to new possibilities.)
- *Environmentalism:* going green gradually, learning loads about the natural environment, boning up on industrial ecology, and beginning consulting in this general area
- *Globalism:* traveling abroad once or twice a year to look around and learn; studying issues of global competitiveness and wanting to know more about the potential of global cooperation

To an extent, all of these subjects are "hot" nowadays, and I'm merely joining the crowd. But they also seem to be the sorts of things that fortysomethings turn to when "making it" becomes less important and generativity starts to matter (Erikson, 1959; see also Jacques, 1965). Sure, I have inklings of death; I'm also concerned about the world I'll leave to my kids. This makes my current doings not so eccentric after all.

I expect to continue searching for the center of me, and I hold on to the hope of finding what Herbert Shepard (1984) calls the "path with a heart." For a time, anyway, consulting will be what I do along with a lot of other stuff. When I last talked to Karl Weick, he did a bit of career counseling and asked me whether I truly saw myself as a consultant and would want that on my gravestone. "No," I replied. "I'd wish it to read: 'Here Lies Philip Harold Mirvis, A Curious Fellow.'"

Notes

1. This line has been attributed to Clark Kerr, professor of industrial relations, who used it to describe his departure as chancellor of Berkeley.

2. One's generation can have a profound effect on one's personal identity and career choices. For more on people from my era, see Gerber, Wolff, Klores, and Brown (1989); Jones (1986); and Leinberger and Tucker (1991).

3. Levinson (1978) has found that young men's dreams of adult life shape the ways they form their occupations during their late 20s and early 30s.

4. Although it is highly questionable whether or not career interests are inherited (see Grotevant, Scarr, & Weinberg, 1978), there is considerable evidence that

children's parenting, adolescent experiences, and high school activities shape their occupational choices (see Vaillant, 1977).

5. According to measures of life stress occasioned by change, I was near legal death. See Selye (1978) and Williams (1989) on the corrosive effects of cynicism.

6. Marris (1974) writes about the loss of loved ones, but generalizes this point: "The fundamental crisis of bereavement arises, not from the loss of others, but from the loss of self. . . . Life becomes unmanageable because it has become meaningless" (pp. 32-33, 38).

7. The importance of revisioning core values seems crucial to "self-renewal" (see Hudson, 1991; Kegan, 1982). On early organizational development, see Beckhard (1969) and Bennis (1969).

8. The substantive dilemmas between research and action involve trade-offs between the design of controlled experiments and practicalities of introducing change in an organization. It is difficult, for example, to define the actual intervention when so many changes are happening simultaneously and to construct control groups when none really match and nobody wants to be left out. Furthermore, the so-called subject pool constantly changes, extraneous events intermingle with planned activities, and conclusions about what happened are open to varied interpretations. Still, most action researchers muddle through as best they can, and the more academically minded at least keep research at the forefront of their efforts. (See Mirvis & Seashore, 1979.)

9. For instance, many clients come to me with the expectation that my job, first and foremost, is to serve their needs. Now this expectation is creeping into universities, where students are called customers rather than raw material and professors sign up businesses into research partnerships where, for $10,000 or so, executives can influence research agendas, yak over theory, and schmooze with faculty. By comparison, the serve-us ethic is well established in consulting, where clients typically spend more, may not necessarily care about advancing science, and often don't want a partner. They mostly want problems fixed and things to get better. Of course, researcher/consultants don't have to work with practical-minded clients and can insist that every consult involve a rigorous research design and thoroughgoing measurement. I'm keen on change, however, and attracted to crises, craziness, and clients with a missionary zeal. This means that I, like my clients, have a bias for action and will compromise research elegance for the sake of making change.

But I do have standards. When people seek help from doctors, therapists, clergy, and lawyers, they have some inkling that these professionals are bound by a code of ethics. But in a preprofessional field like organizational consulting, it is a revelation to clients that certain codes make sense. Still, I have not had much trouble getting clients to assent that all who participate in a project need to be briefed on its scope and need to give their voluntary, informed consent. Most readily agree, too, that diagnostic data shall be confidential—not identified with any one individual—though they will often ask, "What did so-and-so say?" and attribute comments to, say, Gerry, Mary, or Fred because "we've heard that before."

There is also typically some friction about publication. I insist on being able to publish my findings and assure clients that, if desired, their identities will be disguised. Some don't like the idea in principle, and those who say, "No problem" often expect to look good in print—as one of the "excellent" or "100 Best." Agreement to publish is, for me, a go/no-go decision. But where I waffle is in recognition that key people in an organization will find themselves in my articles and books or that others will learn something juicy about their firm. What this means is that in publications I often slide over seamy, but otherwise pertinent, information about back stabbing, illegalities, who's sleeping with whom, and other such stuff that often has a lot to do with the course of change and surely makes for a better read. Nonetheless, in at least two cases, writings about the goings-on in companies have made me something of a persona non grata on-site.

10. See Mirvis & Berg, 1977; Senge, 1990.

11. See Mirvis, 1991; for more on these kinds of interventions, see Egri & Frost, 1991.

12. In some respects, this journey back to the roots is being followed by the field of organization development (see Mirvis, 1988, 1990).

13. Stent (1972) contends that although many ideas are ahead of their time, they are being developed, independently, in many different fields. On new forms of intervention, see discussion by Senge (1990) on dialogue; on the Workout program, see Cooperrider and Srivastva (1987), Torbert (1981), Bunker and Alban (1992), Weisbord (1992), and Tichy and Sherman (1993).

14. Levinson (1978) sees development in the "middle years" as involving reconciliation of various polarities: young/old, destruction/construction, masculine/feminine, and attachment/separation. For a different view, see Gilligan (1982).

15. See Hall & Associates, 1986.

16. See Alinsky, 1971.

17. On the shifting importance of work, see Bardwick (1978, 1986). For examples of how people re-sort their priorities, see Hyatt (1990).

References

Alinsky, S. D. (1971). *Rules for radicals*. New York: Random House.

Argyris, C. (1970). *Intervention theory and method: A behavioral science view*. Reading, MA: Addison-Wesley.

Argyris, C. (1985). *Strategy, change, and defensive routines*. Cambridge, MA: Ballinger.

Bardwick, J. M. (1978). Middle age and a sense of the future. *Merrill-Palmer Quarterly, 24*(2), 129-138.

Bardwick, J. M. (1986). *The plateauing trap: How to avoid it in your career . . . and your life*. New York: AMACOM.

Beckhard, R. (1969). *Organization development: Strategies and models*. Reading, MA: Addison-Wesley.

Bennis, W. G. (1969). *Organization development: Its nature, origins, and prospects*. Reading, MA: Addison-Wesley.

Berger, P. L., & Luckmann, T. (1967). *The social construction of reality: A treatise in the sociology of knowledge*. Garden City, NY: Doubleday.

Bowlby, J. (1958-1980). *Attachment and loss* (Vols. 1-3). New York: Basic Books.

Bridges, W. (1980). *Transitions: Making sense of life's changes*. Reading, MA: Addison-Wesley.

Bunker, B. B., & Alban, B. T. (Eds.). (1992). Large group interventions [Special issue]. *Journal of Applied Behavioral Science, 28*(4).

Cooperrider, D., & Srivastva, S. (1987). Appreciative inquiry in organization life. In R. W. Woodman & W. A. Pasmore (Eds.), *Research in organizational change and development* (Vol. 1). Greenwich, CT: JAI.

Egri, C. P., & Frost, P. J. (1991). Shamanism and change: Bringing back the magic in organizational transformation. In R. W. Woodman & W. A. Pasmore (Eds.), *Research in organizational change and development* (Vol. 5). Greenwich, CT: JAI.

Erikson, E. (1959). *Identity and the life cycle*. New York: International Universities Press.

Gerber, J., Wolff, J., Klores, W., & Brown, G. (1989). *Lifetrends: The future of baby boomers and other aging Americans*. New York: Macmillan.

Gilligan, C. (1982). *In a different voice: Psychological theory and women's development*. Cambridge, MA: Harvard University Press.

Grotevant, H. D., Scarr, S., & Weinberg, R. A. (1978, March). Are career interests inheritable? *Psychology Today*, pp. 88, 90.

Hall, D. T., & Associates. (1986). *Career development in organizations*. San Francisco: Jossey-Bass.

Hall, D. T., & Mirvis, P. H. (1994). Careers as lifelong learning. In A. Howard (Ed.), *The changing nature of work*. San Francisco: Jossey-Bass.

Hudson, F. M. (1991). *The adult years: Mastering the art of self-renewal*. San Francisco: Jossey-Bass.

Hyatt, C. (1990). *Shifting gears: How to master career change and find the work that's right for you*. New York: Fireside.

Jacques, E. (1965). Death and the mid-life crisis. *International Journal of Psychoanalysis, 46*, 502-514.

Jones, L. (1986). *Great expectations: America and the baby boom generation*. New York: Ballantine.

Kegan, R. (1982). *The evolving self: Problem and process in human development*. Cambridge, MA: Harvard University Press.

Leinberger, P., & Tucker, B. (1991). *The new individualists: The generation after The organization man*. New York: HarperCollins.

Levinson, D. J. (1978). *The seasons of a man's life*. New York: Ballantine.

Marris, P. (1974). *Loss and change*. London: Routledge & Kegan Paul.

Mirvis, P. H. (1988). Organization development: Part I. An evolutionary perspective. In R. W. Woodman & W. A. Pasmore (Eds.), *Research in organizational change and development* (Vol. 2). Greenwich, CT: JAI.

Mirvis, P. H. (1990). Organization development: Part II. A revolutionary perspective. In R. W. Woodman & W. A. Pasmore (Eds.), *Research in organizational change and development* (Vol. 4). Greenwich, CT: JAI.

Mirvis, P. H. (1991). Ben & Jerry's: Team development intervention (A and B). In A. Glassman & T. Cummings (Eds.), *Cases in organization development*. Homewood, IL: Irwin.

Mirvis, P. H., & Berg, D. N. (Eds.). (1977). *Failures in organization development and change*. New York: Wiley Interscience.

Mirvis, P. H., & Seashore, S. E. (1979). Being ethical in organizatonal research. *American Psychologist, 34,* 766-788.

Sarason, S. (1977). *Work, aging, and social change*. New York: Free Press.

Selye, H. (1978). *The stress of life* (2nd ed.). New York: McGraw-Hill.

Senge, P. M. (1990). *The fifth discipline: The art and practice of the learning organization*. Garden City, NY: Doubleday/Currency.

Shepard, H. A. (1984). On the realization of human potential: A path with a heart. In M. B. Arthur, L. Bailyn, D. J. Levinson, & H. A. Shepard, *Working with careers: Understanding what we apply and applying what we understand*. New York: Columbia University, Graduate School of Business.

Stent, G. S. (1972, December). Prematurity and uniqueness in scientific discovery. *Scientific American, 227,* 84-93.

Tannenbaum, R., & Hanna, R. (1985). Holding on, letting go, and moving on. In R. Tannenbaum, N. Margulies, & F. Massarik (Eds.), *Human systems development: New perspectives on people and organizations*. San Francisco: Jossey-Bass.

Tichy, N., & Sherman, S. (1993). *Control your destiny or someone else will: How Jack Welch is making General Electric the world's most competitive company*. New York: Doubleday/Currency.

Torbert, W. (1981). Empirical, behavioral, theoretical, and attentional skills necessary for collaborative inquiry. In R. Reason & J. Rowan (Eds.), *Human inquiry: A sourcebook of new paradigm research*. New York: John Wiley.

U.S. Bureau of Labor Statistics. (1989, Summer). *Occupational Outlook Quarterly*.

Vaillant, G. E. (1977). *Adaptation to life*. Boston: Little, Brown.

Weick, K. E. (1974, October 11-12). *Careers as eccentric predicates*. Paper presented at the annual meeting of the Society of Experimental Social Psychology, Champaign-Urbana, IL.

Weisbord, M. R. (Ed.). (1992). *Discovering common ground: How future search conferences bring people together to achieve breakthrough innovation, empowerment, shared vision, and collaborative action*. San Francisco: Berrett-Koehler.

Williams, R. C. (1989). *The trusting heart: Great news about type A behavior*. New York: Random House.

38 Working as a Consultant

ACADEMIC IMPRIMATUR OR TABOO?

Mary Ann Von Glinow

Consulting has always been a taboo topic for those of us reared in traditional research universities. I went to Ohio State, and my degree was very research focused. In fact, when I graduated with my PhD in 1978, I had five articles already out or soon to be out in refereed journals, and not a stitch of consulting work. In fact, none of my professors at OSU had done much consulting. Consulting was always portrayed as "selling out." And so it was that I came to value and be socialized into the academic rigors of research.

After I arrived at the University of Southern California, where I observed a very different set of norms around consulting, I still didn't think much about the "C word." After all, I had to publish and do research in order to get tenure. I was counseled into staying as far away as possible from the consulting opportunities that would come my way. Well, perhaps it was because of my gender, my age, or my specialty, but no opportunities seemed to come my way, so de facto the decision was made. Nevertheless, we

junior faculty whispered about all the senior faculty members who were "never around," or "out doing consulting," as though it were something to be hushed up. Mostly, we rationalized it in that USC was very "applied" in its research emphasis, so many of those "consultants" were probably doing applied research.

Tenure came and so did the academic imprimatur. I, and others, however, began to question the legitimacy that some of our work had for the "real world" and began teaching in more executive education programs, at USC and elsewhere. Over time, I came to enjoy that venue quite a bit, although I found it often frustrating, sometimes humiliating, and always challenging. My telling largely male audiences made up of individuals with considerable years of experience how to "manage" seemed to catalyze strange reactions. I never seemed to get offers to "consult" with their firms, even though many of my male colleagues did. Over time, I learned to push back with my executive group, and that was when I was finally asked to "consult" to a

371

few of them. In other words, if I challenged their position (never denying their experience) and tried to offer alternate interpretations, I found the dialogue beneficial and it often caused the executives to question their own views. Sometimes that resulted in additional dialogue with particular executives, and a few times it resulted in consulting assignments. Now, this wasn't an overnight process; indeed, it took many years, and my male counterparts were off consulting regularly by then, or so it appeared.

Being a woman didn't help. As I mentioned, most of the executive education classes were dominated by men, and early on I found myself being challenged on "not having met a payroll"—as a substitute for other, less flattering attributions due to my gender. Of course, I hadn't "met a payroll," but then neither had my male colleagues, and even some of the senior faculty. I always felt that my gender put me at a distinct disadvantage in executive education. Now, many years later, there are still venues in which I feel gender makes a difference, and most women are asked constantly to prove themselves more than men, all other things being equal in terms of content.

So, here it was, the mid-1980s, and I had my first consulting assignment. Actually, it wasn't my first, as I had occasionally accompanied more senior faculty members, such as Mike Driver, on research/consulting work with various client organizations. It was my first solo, however, and it was exciting! I prepared much as one would research an article, but the clear link to me was that I had the expertise and they needed the help. The message from my doctoral student days was that "a *good consultant* works him- or herself out of a job quickly," and so I did. Whereas it was relatively easy for me to enter a firm for the explicit purpose of doing "applied research," it was still difficult for me to wear my "consulting hat" because I did so little consulting. Time went on, and I observed a bifurcation in my department: The researchers occupied one side (this included some new junior faculty as well as a few senior faculty who didn't spend time consulting), and consultants and those who didn't engage actively in research occupied the other. What complicated this neat configuration was that some consultants were world-renowned scholars who had decided that they no longer bought into the "traditional" writing-for-publication thing. I had

many conversations with several of these colleagues over a long period of time, and whereas our academic rigor taught us to add value to our knowledge base, these scholars felt that our knowledge could be enhanced by our getting closer to our organizational brethren. Ian Mitroff taught me that lesson, and other subscribers included Warren Bennis and Jim O'Toole. However, there was still the question of how, if not through consulting. Meanwhile, one of our colleagues, Bill Davidson, was being whisked away by corporate jets to consult to numerous corporate titans. I remember a remark made by then-chair Barry Leskin about Bill's consulting: "It's pretty heady stuff to be asked to do consulting to the chairman of the board, and to be brought to headquarters by their corporate jet. Most faculty criticize consulting until they're asked to do it, and *then* they do it gladly. It's the ones who haven't been asked to consult who bitch the loudest about consultants." That stuck. I often wondered about how *I* would feel were I asked to do that. That was several years ago, and in the interim, I got my chance.

The circumstance that propelled me headfirst into consulting was General Electric's Workout initiative in 1988-1989. The person who was most responsible for this shift was, ironically, my husband, Steve Kerr. Steve had been tapped by G.E. to head up the Workout project on the West Coast, specifically, G.E.'s Nuclear Energy Group, and he assembled a group of tall, impressive men whose collective experience in consulting was formidable: Aside from himself, there was Harry Bernhard, an ex-IBMer who developed IBM's executive education programs, with more than 25 years' experience; and Barry Leskin, a former head of human resources for Natomas and Sun Company, with considerable consulting experience. And then there was me. I had much to learn from these experts, and so I did. Harry, Barry, and Steve continue to be instrumental in my consulting growth and experience today, but back in 1988 I couldn't have imagined just how much this experience would change my life.

I recently came across one of the Managerial Consultation's newsletters (Academy of Management), and in it is a special section devoted to academic and practitioner consulting practice. As I perused the newsletter, I saw many of my heroes expounding on the topic of consulting, and I read this with considerable interest.

I wasn't a "certified management consultant," an organizational development practitioner, or a consulting psychologist, and I'm not a true "practitioner consultant," according to Ken Mackenzie's definition. I also hope I'm not the type of consultant with just another set of students, a type Mackenzie says reminds him of "a fist plunged into a bucket of water, and then withdrawn. The hand gets wet, there is a little less water in the bucket, and the contents of the bucket do not change." Although I love the metaphor, it's that attribution that gets consulting and consultants their bad name. I guess I fit into the "academic consultant" category, because my home is in academe and I now do consulting. While not consciously cultivating any particular approach, I've found that falling back on my "content expertise" is largely the reason I'm asked to consult; however, when it comes to working with organizations going through their versions of G.E.'s Workout, or culture change, I'm asked to coach or facilitate because I have good process skills. I have consciously cultivated these skills since 1988, and continue to do so through ample opportunities.

I have a few observations, too, that I would like to share with my colleagues. In some sense, these are lessons I've learned in approaching consulting from a perspective different from that of my OD colleagues. My perspective has been molded by my feminist views and by my years of teaching and writing in several areas: international management, "women in management," and human resource management. I have drawn a lot from these areas that has helped inform my consulting nowadays. The topics of international and women's issues don't fit neatly into the same sentence, but I see them as closely aligned. I have charted over the years the percentage of corporate officers and members of boards of directors who are women in the Fortune 500, Fortune Service 500, and the largest health care institutions in the United States. Currently, women fill less than 10% of those positions, across the board, which tells me that I will most often be working with and consulting to men, generally speaking. My international work has taken me to several large multinational enterprises around the globe, and mostly these are dominated by males. There are rarely women expatriates who run the show, worldwide, and in many parts of the world, women still retain second-class citizenship in terms of business prowess. Therefore, the human resources policies and practices of global enterprises are largely responses to male figureheads developed largely for male-dominated management groups. With rare exceptions, I don't see many women consulting to these corporate titans. Women seem to consult most often to human resources professionals, and unless they have some technical expertise that they can parlay into high-level consultation, they do not seem to penetrate the senior levels in terms of consulting expertise. That irks me. There are, of course, notable exceptions—Rosabeth Kanter, my friend and collaborator, being one—but by and large, even a prestigious university affiliation is necessary, but not sufficient. The sufficiency criterion is met when the individual has a skill that few people have and the client organization is in need of that skill.

Therefore, my lessons learned are predicated on my experiences, what has worked and what hasn't, despite good intentions and efforts. The consulting I have done over the past several years has been perhaps the biggest stretch for me, far bigger than I could have imagined in 1988 when Steve Kerr was assembling his G.E. Workout team, which I was to be a part of and continue to contribute to over the years. Some of these lessons are elaborated below.

Clients don't know what they want sometimes. They know that they have a problem, but sometimes they cannot see an easy solution to that problem. Every consultant knows that if there is a large problem, and everyone recognizes it to be a problem, and no one attempts to solve that problem, that problem is there for a reason—probably a very good reason. The consultant needs to understand why the problem hasn't been resolved, recognizing that political agendas may be at the root. In this time of expectations of political correctness, problems are occasionally masked as other than what they are; root causes may rarely be tackled. The *last* thing clients want to hear is that their problems are bigger than they thought. Diagnosis plays a key in this stage, and the wise consultant will remember who the client is in preparing his or her remarks. However, this doesn't mean soft-pedaling; most clients prefer to have a clear outside head help in the diagnosis and/or solution of their problems. In fact, one client recently said to me that she valued my contribution as an outsider more than she valued her inside consultant, but that the pairing was essential to maintain the integrity of the intervention.

Style makes a difference. Some clients cannot relate to certain styles. This is a gender-related issue, too, and this statement may get me into some trouble. I once had a Korean CEO tell me that I shouldn't be working, because I was taking a job away from one of my male colleagues. I now believe that for consulting work, expertise is necessary, but not sufficient. How one should go about delivering one's expertise has been an important learning process for me. Some clients appreciate a direct approach; some prefer a circuitous approach. However, regardless of the end result, the consultation process itself is very important; consultant and client must develop a rapport that will allow the client to "hear" what the consultant has to say. I've found that most male clients will listen carefully to me if we are in a small group or talking one-on-one, but that in large groups this is not always the case. I've also learned that if there are women at the top of the organization, the latter problem is less apt to occur.

In some non-Western cultures, consultants often need to take a circuitous approach in discussing problems with clients. I have found through my work in various Asian enterprises that a certain amount of indirectness may be desirable. Unless the purpose of the consultation is highly technical, and thus a direct answer is appropriate, I've discovered that consulting to many Asian leaders is like appreciating a rock garden. Sometimes, very little gets moved around, but the garden is quietly reconfigured.

The lessons to be learned regarding consultation style can be formidable. A consultant must learn to assess his or her own style in relation to the client's style, and must do so in real time.

Many clients don't have the time or the willingness to tackle problems integratively. From our years of studying organizational phenomena that undergo change, we academic consultants know that it's a systems world. I am reminded of an analogy drawn by Harry Bernhard, then at USC as an executive in residence. He described the senior business leader as the "big wheel" who makes a small change, which causes the midlevel folks to run around and around, while the people at the bottom are spinning off their axes to keep up. In such a context, the temptation is to offer vertical solutions to vertical problems. If marketing has a problem, the solution resides within marketing. However, if the goal is cycle-time reduction, or "valuing diversity," solutions tend to become more horizontal, or process focused. Core processes rarely stand alone; in fact, they may overlap many different units, issues, and problem solutions. The net result is that process issues are highly integrated with other process issues.

It is hard to step out of one problem area and observe the relationship that area has to other areas, but that is the consultant's responsibility. I recently consulted to a large Asian bank where the issue was performance appraisal. Of course, in human resources we know that appraisal is linked to compensation, training, and so on. No one in that bank was willing to tackle the spillover issues, however, and appraisal was isolated as a practice that needed fixing. A consultant always needs to remember who the client is, and usually attempts to meet the client where he or she is on a given issue; clearly, a consultant can run the risk of alienating a client by discussing integrative issues. However, I now feel that clients need to hear both sides: The problem can be encapsulated and dealt with as is, or it can be examined in its broader context. The other side of the coin is, as Ken Mackenzie so aptly notes, that "client problems almost never fit neatly into our academic specialties." I find that toy problems generally tend to fit the academic specialties, but more global problems have no generally accepted academic base of knowledge. Consultants need to think in process terms appropriate to the problems they are called upon to examine.

Using this integrative approach is contingent on two things: the ability of the consultant to offer a decent reengineering strategy and the ability/willingness of the client to accept this. Both are necessary. If the client has tunnel vision and works with a consultant who uses "silo, vertical, functional, or bin" terminology, an expansive process redesign probably is inappropriate. However, if the client is flexible and open to discussion of overlapping systems and processes, and the consultant is chosen to implement this, then an integrative approach will have greater likelihood of acceptability.

Connections (or guanxi) make a difference. No matter who you consult to, chances are there have been others there before you and there will be others after you. The good consultants I know keep track of who has been where, and doing what, charging what, and don't hesitate to call on their colleagues for advice. In fact, it is those people who are remarkable. When I think of outstanding consultants who keep abreast of what is happening in a variety of companies and industries, as well as current in their field of expertise, I realize that they are simply using their connections to augment their expertise. Connections can prove very helpful, and I equate these connections to a form of networking. It is far better to be involved in some form of network than none at all, particularly as pertains to consulting for client organizations. I was called in by a large aerospace organization for the sole purpose of overseeing a group of consultants. I know now that this opportunity came because of my prior connections to that organization, the rapport I had built with the key decision makers, and my staying connected through other networks. Most key decision makers in large organizations know full well which consultants their competitors are using, and have most likely worked with some of those consultants anyway. So, much as it is a systems world for problems, it seems that it is equally a systems world for consultants. I keep running across the same people in numerous situations and, over time, the connectivity among us has grown.

This leads me to the point where I am now in life. I have some wonderful academic colleagues and some wonderful consulting colleagues. The two groups overlap a bit, but not much. I suspect that my teaching and research are enhanced considerably by my consulting relationships with various multinational enterprises. I know my consulting is enhanced by my academic ties. I don't see the two as incompatible, as many of my colleagues do, perhaps because I am a full professor with tenure, not a doctoral student or a junior faculty member aiming for tenure. If anything, I have learned more that continues to inform my career choices and deliberations from my consulting work than from almost anything else. This is not to say that there isn't a tension—there is. But I believe that practice informs theory, and vice versa. I try not to bifurcate issues into camps—rigor versus relevance, for example. Both are important, and I try to maintain that emphasis throughout my academic and consulting lives. I have occasionally run across colleagues who

are extremely critical of consultants, and when they are in gatekeeper roles, I find myself trying to bridge both worlds. Such boundaries are becoming of less and less interest to me. I still encourage my junior colleagues to concentrate on research prior to tenure, but I also suggest that they broaden their experiences through consulting after that academic rite of passage.

I have had great mentors in my life, and they have helped me become established as a consultant. None of them is female, however, and I have missed that. I have worried long and hard about whether the problems I have had, and continue to have periodically, have stemmed from my gender or my style. It would have been nice to have been able to bounce ideas off a more seasoned female consultant. However, I have had other female colleagues and friends who have served that role. There are a number of us who talk and discuss issues regularly, and I value our exchange of views on issues into which I want to gain some insight. Some of my most exciting experiences in consulting have been those when I've worked with all-female teams. I would strongly encourage any young woman who wants to break into this field to seek a mentor who can provide guidance and support.

I see the value that we academic consultants add as twofold: First, we add value to clients because we continue to remain current in our respective fields of expertise (and we have the research publications to reflect that value added); second, we add value to our students (for grounding our comments more in reality), our respective faculties (for legitimating our institutional presence through our work), and our community (by offering our consulting skills to develop greater community awareness and by consulting to charity programs).

In summary, whereas I once thought that consultants were akin to used-car salesmen, I now see tremendous cachet associated with the consulting world. Some of the most creative minds in the field of organization science regularly consult and write. Their contributions to industry and to science are numerous and have had significant impacts. Having worked as a consultant for a few years now, I find the experience invigorating and enormously stimulating for personal growth. I hope to continue to do both scholarly research and consulting, to round out a career punctuated with many different rhythms.

Developing Innovative Teaching Materials

We had no interest in tagging along behind someone else's traditional text. We sought to create a stand-alone product, with its own style and identity. . . . We finally realized that an innovative book, written to support the video segments and create user-friendliness for students and instructors, did not compromise our vision. Once we made the decision to write a book with learning activities that supported and strengthened our video clips, we knew that it would be a very different project, like no other book available at the time.

Robert D. Marx (p. 385)

In particular, I believe that my enduring passion for the "skills" book stems from its innovative nature. Reflecting on how I have chosen to allocate my professional time over the past two decades, I am struck by how much I've enjoyed the role of "academic entrepreneur." In that sense, *Developing Management Skills* is most memorable because it is most typical

David A. Whetten (p. 391)

Teaching responsibilities consume at least half of the time of most academics, and probably more. They are also the source of some of our most immediate feedback and satisfaction. Yet, historically, teaching has received considerably less weight in performance evaluations and in academic promotion and tenure decisions than has research, a fact leading senior faculty to counsel junior ones against investing any more time and effort in their teaching than absolutely necessary. In the past, the message sent to junior faculty in the past about their investments in teaching has been quite clear: "Do not try to innovate or even do extremely well in the classroom until you have tenure. The payoff for such a strategy is extremely low. Perhaps after you have received tenure, there will be time to experiment with your teaching and with different methods of instruction. But for now, devote your time to your research."

Fortunately for our universities, our students, and the remaining part of the academic population, this message has always

been largely disregarded by a certain proportion of academics (our best guess is
about 8%). This small but elite group has
consistently devoted many "outside" hours
to innovation in the craft of teaching, from
curriculum to materials to instructional
methodologies. Although rarely receiving
meaningful recognition for their efforts,
they have been the predominant source of
innovation within the teaching arena. Furthermore, they performed this role long
before recent changes in the external environment began to raise the consciousness
of universities and faculty about the importance of high-quality teaching and
innovations.

This section examines the developmental actions of two such innovators and two
examples of their work. The authors, Bob
Marx, codeveloper and coauthor (with Peter
Frost and Todd Jick) of *Management Live!
The Video Book*, and Dave Whetten, coauthor
and developer (with Kim Cameron) of *Developing Management Skills*, provide sometimes all-too-vivid descriptions of their
struggles to create in the teaching arena. In
each case, the journey from idea to product was a long and arduous one, filled with
the need to convince colleagues and publishers that old models and methods were
incapable of servicing business education
in the future. As Bob Marx describes the
development of his project, "This portion
of the story is largely one of frustration,
false starts, mental stagnation, and occasional thoughts of terminating the entire
venture" (p. 384).

Notably, both authors praise the Organizational Behavior Teaching Society for legitimating their efforts by providing a forum
where like-minded scholars can convene,
share ideas, and provide feedback to one
another. David Whetten notes: "The merit
of the book project was further strengthened by the results of a poll of the OBTC
attendees. Asked to predict which of sev-

eral forms of instruction would be the
most popular in the next 5 to 10 years, this
group of highly committed teachers had
rated skill-based education number one"
(p. 393).

Both authors also praise the role played
by their idea champions in the publishing
world. Once convinced of the ideas' worth,
these champions went to bat for their projects time and time again to ensure that the
publishers' support continued until completion of the writing task. In Marx's words:

> Alison Reeves stood out among the editors
> we met because she was willing to gamble
> company time and resources on our un-
> tested video project. She was the one who
> contacted NBC (and later other networks
> and film studios) and negotiated the rights
> to our beloved Letterman clip, and she
> convinced her management team of our
> project's viability by playing the segment
> for them at sales meetings. More tradi-
> tional editors were not yet comfortable
> playing so close to the edge of publishing
> sanity. (p. 386)

Finally, both authors report that they
would have found their journeys impossible without the companionship and contributions of trusted coauthors. As Whetten notes:

> The decision to make this a joint venture
> proved to have important implications.
> First, it gave us an opportunity to test our
> ideas in more than one institutional envi-
> ronment. . . . Second, the fact that Kim and
> I are close friends with similar backgrounds
> and interests, as well as complementary
> skills and styles, has made our two decades
> of collaboration both enjoyable and pro-
> ductive. That "chemistry" was critical to
> the success of this project. (p. 394)

By the ends of their essays, the pride that
both Marx and Whetten feel in the contri-

bution of their models to the field has long outdistanced the significant obstacles they report encountering along the way. Further, the resulting products speak well of their efforts, having fundamentally changed the way many of us teach management today. Nevertheless, we offer a caveat to readers now considering such a career path: It is perhaps best not to dwell on the downside of these accounts, for both authors note that had they known then what they know now about the challenge of the journey, they might have been too intimidated to begin it!

39 Rhythms of an Academic Life

Robert D. Marx

In retrospect, it all seems obvious. We were three management professors who had discovered that students were bursting with ideas about leadership after watching a few minutes of Martin Luther King, Jr.'s "I Have A Dream" speech. We had noticed that a scene from the movie *Gung Ho,* in which a Japanese manager is struggling to get jeering U.S. autoworkers to begin their workday with Japanese-style jumping jacks, engaged students in a powerful discussion of cultural differences and how to manage change.

We were teachers who were dissatisfied with passive lecturing and wooden educational films. We had each recognized the powerful impact of brief, well-chosen video segments. When combined with a sequence of meaningful learning activities, these brief clips could make the classroom come alive. The story that follows chronicles the events that led from our realization about video segments to the completion of our efforts to write innovative text materials.

So let us press PLAY on the VCR and begin the story.

The Beginning

To innovate, according to Webster, means "to introduce as, or as if, new; to make changes, to do something in a new way." Writing innovative text materials, therefore, requires that one modify the standard, accepted, current form and/or content of existing texts and attempt to do something differently and, one hopes, better. It is important to acknowledge an internal bias held by most authors that their work is innovative. Even the most trivial changes from previously written works may be viewed as paradigm-breaking events. To put this matter to rest at the outset, let me state that my coauthors and I feel strongly that the way our book was written—with the videos as the beginning and the text written afterward—was innovative, that is, different. Whether our efforts meet a stricter criterion of innovation (i.e., new and improved) must be judged by the readers.

This story describes the development of one innovative project. It is a case study that emphasizes the chaotic, unpredictable and sometimes serendipitous evolution of an innovative idea into a real product that students and teachers can use.

The evolution of this project is a dramatic tale containing moments of creativity interspersed with weeks and months of frustration, writer's block, idea deprivation, and other maladies that afflict would-be innovative people. This is the story of our unique experience with innovation, but at the same time it exposes commonalities that can be of use to others embarking on innovative writing endeavors. The central characters are three coauthors, brought together by common interests, a supportive network, different strengths, and a common dissatisfaction with existing teaching materials.

It is my hope that readers will not view the details of the evolution of this innovative text project as guidelines to innovative text writing, but rather as the story of a set of shared experiences that will support and validate their own adventures in developing new text materials.

Although such projects differ in content and method, I believe that there are some affective similarities that are recognizable and probably well-known in the creative literature. First, there is likely to be a period of exhilaration when the creative spark is kindled. The beginning of the great idea, like the birth of a child, is filled with hopes, dreams, and emotions, together with some anxieties about what comes next. Soon to follow are the loneliness and self-doubt that come when it is hard to be sure whether one's ideas are innovative or simply out of touch with the mainstream. After the ideas have evolved, the arduous task of writing the book must begin. The excitement of idea generation gives way to the careful focus of writing and rewriting. Every word must add value and say what the author means. Each iteration refines the book closer to the vision of the authors. The final deadline approaches, and suddenly the project is complete and the book becomes a reality. Its personality and intelligence are there for the whole world to see. It is judgment day! The innovative ideas have become lines on a page that will be read with understanding and enthusiasm by a new generation of students. The thrill of taking a risk by doing something differently shares the emotional spotlight with the anxiety and hope that others will find the ideas to be creative and useful. Perhaps this is what skydivers feel as they plummet toward the earth, hoping they have packed their parachutes properly.

Management Live! The Video Book

I begin the telling of this story by fast-forwarding to the end of the videocassette, where we observe the 1991 publication of *Management Live! The Video Book* (Marx, Frost, & Jick, 1991) and its adoption in hundreds of management classrooms. As of mid-1994, a second edition of the book was in preparation, thus signaling that it is at least a modest commercial success in the eyes of the publisher.

Of course, in the 1990s, nearly all textbooks are accompanied by a rich array of video materials, including company cases, skill-building instruction, and timely news items from the world of management. What differentiates *Management Live! The Video Book* from these more traditional texts is that, whereas mainstream books offer video segments as ancillary materials, along with workbooks, instructor's manuals, test item banks, fax updates to the instructor, and more, *Management Live!* started with selected video segments—we intended the *book* to be the supportive material. A second important difference between *Management Live!* and traditional videos accompanying management texts is that our video segments, which make important points about management, were chosen from unusual and varied sources, including movies and television shows. Many of the videos available showing managers carrying out their daily tasks lack excitement and clarity or look too much like "educational films," and students tune them out. Our video selections are intended to capture the essence of management issues, and many do not even feature managers. Once we had selected the video segments, we then wrote accompanying chapters to support and emphasize the lessons inherent in the video clips. This necessitated our taking an innovative approach to writing the text material.

At the end of this saga, the finished product consisted of an 18-chapter text, an unusual instructor's manual, and a box of eight videocassettes, including six feature-length films, one cassette of Martin Luther King's "I Have a Dream" speech, and one cassette with 11 separate segments from television shows and other sources.

Let us now rewind to the beginning of this tale.

David Letterman Goes to the General Electric Building

In May 1987 at Bentley College in Waltham, Massachusetts, an idea began to take shape. What had hitherto been the separate experiments of three management faculty members fused into a shared vision of a novel way to teach our material. What happened in May 1987 was a product of the history and motivations of the three eventual coauthors and their coming together at the annual Organizational Behavior Teaching Conference. The planets were in the right alignment to spawn the start of *Management Live!*

One night several months before the May meeting at Bentley College, Todd Jick of Harvard University was videotaping NBC's *Late Night With David Letterman,* a comedy/talk show, when he noticed a segment that was very humorous and entertaining, yet it had, just beneath the playfulness, significant managerial/ organizational content. Briefly, when General Electric purchased RCA, which owned NBC, Letterman thought it would be interesting to meet his new employers by bringing a basket of fruit to the board of directors at General Electric's headquarters as a gesture of goodwill.

This vignette included many humorous moments, especially when Letterman was denied entry into the building because the G.E. security team refused to accept his letter requesting entry. Furthermore, the head security officer, upon encountering Letterman and his producer, refused to shake their hands. These "nonhandshakes" were captured on videotape and shown to Letterman's viewers as a glimpse of the official General Electric corporate handshake. (In slow motion, they appear even funnier, as the security officer's hand begins the natural handshake movement but jerks back at the last moment, as the man realizes that Letterman has invaded his turf and decides not to encourage him.)

Todd mailed a copy of this 6-minute clip to me at the University of Massachusetts. I had been using other video segments in class, and I found this one to have such a great impact on my students that I suggested that Todd and I present the clip at the annual Organizational Behavior Teaching Conference at Bentley College, where more than 300 teachers of management would be gathering to learn from one another and share their latest teaching ideas. We presented the video to more than 50 participants and then asked them how they might use it in their classrooms. The participants listed numerous topics and uses, and lively discussion followed.

One of the participants in that OBTC workshop was Peter Frost of the University of British Columbia. Peter had been using a great deal of film in his management classes and immediately recognized the impact of the brief Letterman clip. Later that evening, at the nightly informal gathering time specifically set aside by the OBTC for people to socialize and share ideas, Peter added the final ingredient to the creation of *Management Live! The Video Book.* He said, "We must do something with this!" His enthusiasm and entrepreneurial spirit helped all of us to believe that we were onto something that would appeal to other faculty and students in the same ways it had appealed to us, our students, and our colleagues at Bentley College in May 1987.

That was how *Management Live!* began. Todd recorded a video and sent it to me. I suggested it be presented at a conference of educators. Peter, after experiencing the impact of the clip, pressed for a way to continue developing the idea into a usable product. There was also the nurturing environment of the OBTC, which provided a forum for presenting the clip to our peers, a group of peers to support and critique our efforts, and a safe environment in which to talk about and explore our teaching in creative ways.

Three Authors Collaborating From Diverse Backgrounds

Stepping back in time before the beginning of this project, one would see three people with varied histories, backgrounds, and cultures from whom one might expect novel ways of looking at management education.

Peter Frost worked as a professional manager and consultant before turning to academia at the University of British Columbia. He grew up in South Africa, where films from North

America had a strong impact on his worldview during his formative years. Peter's discontent with traditional text material led to his supplementing class lectures with films that had implications for management and prompted him to coauthor an innovative book, *Organizational Reality*, now in its fourth edition (Frost, Mitchell, & Nord, 1992), which contains material from novels, nonfiction, and many nontraditional sources in order to engage students' interest in the real workings of organizations.

I joined the cast of *Management Live!* from my training as a clinical psychologist. In teaching my students to be effective therapists and good listeners, I used videotaped feedback extensively. I was heavily influenced by Allen Ivey at the University of Massachusetts, who introduced me to the idea of using famous interviewers on television to teach communication skills to students. A classic tape of Barbara Walters interviewing Elizabeth Taylor resulted in high student involvement and greater motivation among students to follow the principles that Walters utilized. I recognized that the familiar or entertaining video segment is a formidable teaching tool. When my interests shifted from depressed people to depressed industries, a whole new world of video opportunities lay ahead.

Todd Jick, the son of a rabbi, former disk jockey, anthropologist, and hi-tech video buff, was including numerous video clips in his organizational behavior course at the Harvard MBA program. As noted above, it was his VCR that was churning the night David Letterman made his trip to G.E. headquarters.

So there we were, three mavericks, bored with existing materials, stubborn, and persistent in our desire to parlay our joint dissatisfaction into a masterpiece. We came from different backgrounds, but we had a common interest in video and film. The ingredients for this tasty stew were assembled—little did we know how long it would have to cook.

It should be stated that for some, creative writing occurs in solitary, springing from inspiration, a clear vision one has while sitting on a mountaintop—a single person with a marvelous idea and the motivation and talent to carry the concept through to the end. For us, the process was completely collaborative. When we began this project we were already good friends and members of the board of directors of the Organizational Behavior Teaching Society. Part of our synergy was born out of our membership in this society, where creating together was a part of the culture. Our collaboration was also based on the fact that all of us had very busy schedules; we needed one another to keep the project alive. Many times during different phases of the creation of *Management Live!* one of us would shepherd the process along while the others were attending to other matters. One of us was always keeping this project atop his to-do list, and at certain moments, we all stepped up and worked together.

Two Years of Wandering: Innovation Meets the Reality of the Marketplace

As our tape winds on after the Bentley College meeting, the story slows down. There were to be long stretches when the creative process lay dormant, almost as if someone had pressed the PAUSE button.

This portion of the story is largely one of frustration, false starts, mental stagnation, and occasional thoughts of terminating the entire venture. After the enthusiastic beginning at Bentley College in 1987, when we decided that we were going to "do something with this" (the Letterman clip and others like it), numerous brainstorming sessions ensued. Some were held at restaurants during the Academy of Management annual meetings; others were carried out during long-distance telephone calls late at night, after all our "work" was done.

During this period of "wandering," which lasted nearly 2 years, we showed our infamous Letterman clip to many colleagues, students, publishers' representatives, consulting clients, and anyone else who would watch it. There was nearly unanimous agreement in appreciation of this kind of teaching modality. People enjoyed watching the clip, and it was clear that they learned from it. And yet, in spite of their approval and support of the idea of bringing such video segments to the mainstream management classroom, those who represented the marketplace presented a set of seemingly insurmountable hurdles: "These clips are great, but how can we sell them? Students don't have VCRs." "The clips are different, and they make a point very well, but the prices for permission to reproduce them are unbelievably high. We don't even know how and where to obtain them." "These clips are powerful! How about if we use a few of them as ancillary material for our best-selling 'principles of management' text?" "Your clips are entertaining and unique, but our editor isn't convinced that there is a market out there for them. After someone shows that this kind of product can sell, we'd love to talk."

This was sobering and somewhat discouraging feedback for us. All agreed that we had good ideas and great video clips, but we lacked a vehicle to drive this idea to market. We also lacked a product champion, someone from a publishing firm who shared our fervor for the impact of these video clips and would battle for our vision in the boardroom; someone who could move us from PAUSE to FAST FORWARD.

A Breakthrough

After nearly 2 years of intermittent brainstorming, with occasional time-outs to have babies, take sabbaticals, pay attention to other projects, and indulge in plain old procrastination, the clouds parted and our vision moved one big step closer to reality. We began to realize that the video clips, which we were so fond of using in the classroom, needed a book of materials that would form a context that would enhance their long-term impact on students. We recognized that the students didn't need to own the video clips, for most did not have VCRs on which to play them. They needed only to view the videos in class. Our video segments were exciting, but more was needed for them to be part of a substantive learning experience. We finally acknowledged that we needed a book of learning activities that introduced, supported, and followed up on the video segments; students could purchase the book, and instructors could receive the collection of videos free when they ordered the books for classes.

This was a critical realization. During the 2-year gestation period, we had sometimes felt very frustrated. In retrospect, we see that what saved us from giving up was the fact that the three of us got frustrated at different times. There was always at least one of the group proceeding with optimism. In an informal, nonplanned manner, one of us would always be running with the baton, as if in a relay race, calling publishers, searching for videos until he

was spent, and then the next person would take over with fresh enthusiasm. And yet the process seemed less like the inspiring conclusion of the film *Chariots of Fire* than like an extended siege of telephone tag.

It often felt as if we were in the shoes of Columbus, trying to launch our flotilla of new-age video segments toward an Old World publishing industry that kept telling us that the high costs of permissions and the uncharted waters of customer acceptance would keep our project in dry dock.

Single-Mindedness Almost Destroys Innovation

Ironically, part of our breakthrough came about because we realized that the video clips, as powerful as they were, need not be *incompatible* with the printed word, which we had viewed as traditional and dull. In our desire to "get beyond" books, we had rejected the useful aspects of that medium and somehow viewed the printed word as a minor part of our project. This left us little common ground with the publishers we hoped would support our venture. One publisher contributed to this overreaction on our part by suggesting that we create a workbook to accompany its best-selling textbook. We had no interest in tagging along behind someone else's traditional text. We sought to create a stand-alone product, with its own style and identity.

We refused to give in to this tagalong workbook notion! But we finally realized that an innovative book, written to support the video segments and create user-friendliness for students and instructors, did not compromise our vision. Once we made the decision to write a book with learning activities that supported and strengthened our video clips, we knew that it would be a very different project, like no other book available at the time. We were almost ready to write innovative text materials. The PLAY button was just waiting to be engaged.

Enter the Product Champion

Just about the time of our breakthrough, the idea of creating a book to support the videos, we met the heroine of this tale. Alison Reeves, a senior editor at Prentice Hall, was different, but—thankfully—in some of the same ways we were different. She was an editor with a keen visual perspective. She had just completed editing a top-selling management textbook and had selected paintings from modern and classical art to introduce each chapter in the text. At the time, Prentice Hall had just merged with Paramount, and there was a corporationwide initiative to merge the print and film media. (As of this writing in 1994, Paramount is owned by Viacom Corporation, which owns MTV. Can musical management videos be far behind?)

Alison Reeves stood out among the editors we met because she was willing to gamble company time and resources on our untested video project. She was the one who contacted NBC (and later other networks and film studios) and negotiated the rights to our beloved Letterman clip, and she convinced her management team of our project's viability by playing the segment for them at sales meetings. More traditional editors were not yet comfortable playing so close to the edge of publishing sanity. So, as we see it, Alison Reeves rode in on her white horse, carried the *Management Live!* banner into the corporate castle, and persuaded companies to give us the right to reproduce video segments for educational use only and for substantially lower permission fees than usual, thus making our project economically feasible.

The Work

With our ideas intact, a publisher secured, and a real budget and deadline in hand, it was time to give this book a structure and some words. In short, for our textbook writing to be as innovative as our video segments, we had to decide on a format that would facilitate smooth transitions from the printed word to the video clips and back. We had to decide on a structure that would fit our underlying values of emotional impact, unpredictability, freshness, student empowerment, ethics, activism, humor, and making a difference as a manager.

One magnificent spring day in 1990, we sat in Peter Frost's backyard in the beautiful city of Vancouver, British Columbia. We were joined by Fiona Crofton, then a doctoral student at Simon Frasier University. Fiona had a keen sense of what contemporary students wanted and

needed in their textbook materials, and her insightful contributions helped to keep us focused ahead on issues students would be facing a few years after they entered the job market and began to make important decisions.

Our task on that sunny day, with fruit and sandwiches on the picnic table, and daffodils in bloom in the garden, was to develop a set of learning activities that would constitute the structure of our book. It was to be a long day punctuated by a flood of ideas, some immediate unanimous agreements, a few major differences as to what was truly innovative and what was trendy or just plain silly, and several loose ends that never got fully resolved (and probably appear that way in the book).

In similar meetings over the next few weeks, we chose chapter content, created and titled learning activities, selected favorite video segments, and made writing assignments. This was one of the most intensively creative periods of the project. With a target date set for publication, there was no time for daydreaming. We had to make decisions about structure so that we could flesh out the chapters in a style that seemed consistent from chapter to chapter, yet retained a fresh, stand-alone quality.

The structure that emerged was to set the tone for the writing of the book. We chose seven learning activities that were designed to support and extend the impact of the video segment for each chapter. The titles of these activities reflect on the values of the text:

- "Ready for Class": This is a brief homework assignment to be completed prior to the class; it is designed to prepare the student for the video segment and related material (thus the title). "Ready for Class" (RFC) was a concept that we originally designed to be used in a large lecture class, where taking attendance was difficult. In one author's introductory management class, each class meeting included turning in the RFC assignment. Each RFC counted as a point toward an exam grade. So, for example, a 50-point test might include only 42 questions, with the remaining 8 points coming from completed RFC assignments, which could be turned in only during class sessions.

  Some RFCs are questionnaires, designed, for example, to identify the student's leadership style or most frequently used managerial role. Another asks the student to describe a job or project on which he or she felt highly motivated and one on which he or she experienced low motivation, and to describe the main factor accounting for the presence or absence of motivation on the job. Because RFCs are to be collected in each class session, we decided that the pages of the book should be perforated, so they could be easily torn out and handed in.

- "Textbook Tie-in": *Management Live!* was written to support lectures and textbooks, not to be an exhaustive, encyclopedic compendium of theories and research. Thus "Textbook Tie-in" introduces the main ideas and issues in each chapter, leaving the details to the discretion of the instructor and the textbook. (Our colleagues have sometimes referred to this portion of the book as "Management Lite!") The purpose of this user-friendly introduction, which often leads into a provocative video segment, is to motivate students to pursue more information.

- "Mirror Talk: Focusing on Me": This activity is designed to stimulate students' private self-reflection on each content area of management. We believe that students' understanding of their own attitudes, perceptions, and behaviors is an important prerequisite of their understanding the attitudes, perceptions, and behaviors of others. "Self-awareness in safety" is the goal of this portion of each chapter. For example, in the chapter on entrepreneurship, "Mirror Talk" contains a survey for students to complete to identify whether they have personality characteristics similar to those of successful entrepreneurs. Follow-up questions ask students to contemplate their scores and identify their strongest skills for entrepreneurial success, and also ask whether they want to pursue such a career. In the chapter on decision making, students identify how they would make decisions across a wide range of management problems and how these decision styles may serve as strengths or weaknesses in their management careers. Across all of the content areas, students are expected to understand their strengths and areas for further development as they move into the world of work.

- "Lights, Camera, Action: Management Live!" This portion of each chapter is the core of the book, the presentation of the video segment. "Lights" introduces students to the video by setting a context in which the video relates to the management topic (e.g., Martin Luther King's "I Have A Dream" speech contains numerous qualities considered to be indicative of effective leadership). "Camera" describes the video segment, the main characters, and the content of the video. "Action" instructs students on what they should observe while watching the video. For example, one video segment from the Tom Peters tape, *The Leadership Alliance,* shows Pat Carrigan, a GM parts plant manager, in action; students are asked to identify which of the eight management roles described by Robert Quinn in his book *Beyond Rational Management* (1988) Carrigan plays most heavily, and which she plays least frequently. We have found that giving students tasks to accomplish while watching the video results in their paying greater attention and in greater comprehension.

The title of the book, one of the last decisions made before going to press, came out of the title for the "Lights, Camera, Action" segment. Our publisher originally had the project listed as *Video Workbook on Management* (sounded boring to us). We played with numerous combinations of the words *video, management,* and *book,* and finally chose *Management Live! The Video Book* for its obvious connection to the zany *Saturday Night Live!* television show and *The Video Book,* clearly stating this is not a *work*book and it is *the* (one and only) video book. (The final title seemed a bit flashy to some nonmarketing faculty members, but we liked the sound of it.)

- "Making Connections: In Class Interactions": This activity is designed to prepare students for a workplace where teamwork will be an important skill. We wanted students to interact with their peers in every class session, and especially in large lectures classes, where learning is often too passive. Thus every chapter includes a brief group activity. Students in large classes are typically instructed to work in groups of three. (In a fixed-seat auditorium, this allows students to work with partners on either side of them.) In one such exercise, students are asked to compare the roles they selected as heavily used in the example concerning Pat Carrigan described above, reach a consensus, and report aloud to the class as a whole when the instructor debriefs the activity. We have found that peer pressure to be prepared for in-class interactions by doing the RFC assignments works well, and that most students prefer such active engagement to passive note taking.

- "Coming to Our Senses: Making a Difference": This activity requires students to examine how they will behave in their roles as managers and leaders to make a positive difference in their workplace and in society. Whether the awareness of today will translate into actions later on is yet to be seen, but the expectation of activism, equity, and ethical behavior is clear.

- "Dateline 21st Century": This is, perhaps, the least innovative aspect of this book, but it represents our attempt to include our favorite provocative readings from current sources (*Business Week, Fortune,* the *Wall Street Journal*) about the directions we feel management will be taking at the time when our students are in positions of leadership.

These seven portions of each chapter constitute what we feel is an innovative and substantive sequence of learning activities designed to augment the impact of the video clips that were the original reason for the book to be written.

We felt very satisfied with our work of that day. We had created an educationally responsible framework in which to offer our videos to educators and students. We had developed chapter sections that encourage preparation, interaction, and self-reflection, yet allow instructors still to be the focus of attention, using the videos and chapter sections as they feel appropriate to their teaching styles and class designs.

Finally, we never intended that the seven sections of each chapter must be covered in a rigid order. Some videos needed to be shown first, before any discussion took place, and others should not be shown until after some other exercise had occurred. So we decided to construct each chapter with the same seven sections, but to allow the order of the sections to

emerge as the chapters were being written. (Our editor, who was more comfortable with a predictable order of chapter design, hesitated at this, but eventually acceded to our demands for flexibility and freshness in each chapter.)

The Hard Work

Those creative spring meetings turned out to be very productive and resulted in a design for *Management Live!* that we thought would work. The truth of the matter was that not a single word had yet been written. Nearly 3 years of attention to this project, the 1987 meeting of the minds at Bentley, the ideas for the concept of the book, finding an editor, the development of the seven learning activities, and selection of our videos and chapters to be included in the book, left us with the hard work still to do. We still had to *write this book.*

Granted, given our carefully thought-out framework, our writing had a focus and style, but the feelings of innovation we experienced while designing a new kind of book shifted to a more focused kind of creative work, identifying and developing the right exercises, self-assessment tools, and reading assignments to fit chapter content. When it got down to actually writing the text materials, the tedium and detail of getting the references right, seeking permissions, writing numerous drafts, and making graphic/format decisions seemed to interrupt the creative energy that had fueled this endeavor from the beginning.

Our desire to make our project perfect conflicted with the editorial deadlines of the publishing machine at Prentice Hall, and compromises had to be made. The video material we wanted to use was not always available. Chapter sections had to be shortened. The hard work of writing this book consumed about 12 months, with three of us sharing the duties of writing 18 chapters.

At the End of the Cassette

In the summer of 1991, the first copies of *Management Live! The Video Book* appeared on this earth, in management educators' mailboxes, and later in classrooms across the country. So, once our creation was completed, how did we feel about it? Each of us was very proud of breaking new ground, introducing students to different kinds of video clips and a truly integrated learning experience involving video and text. We were proud of our insistence that ours be a stand-alone book and not a part of a shrink-wrapped package instructors received when they ordered the primary text. However, the perfectionists in us felt as if we could have done a lot better. Some tapes in the final product were our second choices, because out first choices were unavailable or too expensive. Some exercises were written too quickly, to meet impending deadlines. With a second edition now forthcoming, we will have the chance to study the feedback we have received from colleagues and students and to improve and refine what we see as imperfections.

As this cassette moves toward its own end point, I have some thoughts, questions, and a few suggestions to share with those who intend to write innovative text materials:

1. The Organizational Behavior Teaching Society was for us a vital source of support, constructive criticism, networking, and playfulness. One needs such a welcoming forum in which to share ideas undefensively. Colleagues such as Mark Maier, Steve Meisel, Larry Michaelsen, Sam Sitkin, and Lee Bolman provided video suggestions, case ideas, and their own brand of innovation and risk taking to inspire us during the difficult moments.

2. Making money was never the goal. We thought that our idea of introducing management educators to brief video segments from films and television was worth a major effort. Our permission costs were extremely high and cut substantially into royalties received. However, the goal was always to share our ideas and video experiments with our colleagues.

3. Writing innovative text materials may not be perceived by the academic community as a scholarly contribution. Writing a book like *Management Live!* was, in our biased opinion, a contribution to the methodology of management education and thus an intellectual contribution to the literature. At face value, however, the book may be viewed as an introductory-level presentation of management concepts that, despite its unorthodox mix of video and print, does not constitute a scholarly advance equivalent to publication in our field's top journals. Do not expect tenure or promotion decision makers at most universities to appreciate your cleverness as much as you do.

4. Strong passion for your new idea and your disappointment with existing text materials must be a core value as you embark on the innovative text writing path. It will be up to you to convince others that although your ideas may be ahead of their time, they are not weird; rather, they are an improvement over tried and true, but predictable and tired, formats. Then hope that Alison Reeves or someone like her can share your passion and convince hard-nosed publishing executives that your project should be turned into something tangible.

5. The definition of *innovation* changes rapidly. In the years since *The Video Book* concept was initiated, the world of publishing has changed dramatically. Whereas the video segment seemed innovative in 1987, laser disc, CD-ROM, and interactive video are all now cruising down the information superhighway. As we start work on the second edition of *Management Live!* we'll need to gather once again in the yard in Vancouver and hope that we can keep pace with changing technologies and cultural values. Can we maintain our niche of unorthodox videos and related learning activities? So far, no one has written anything similar to *Management Live!* However, we will need to choose fresh video segments that will capture the essence of issues that students and instructors will find timely and moving. We will also need to anticipate the future of electronics as we decide whether to expand our cassette package to laser disc and CD-ROM. Perhaps we will need help from a consultant on these matters.

6. Collaboration is an excellent process for expanding creative thoughts and bringing to the table several sets of contacts to help contribute ideas and eventually to buy the book. But among three busy coauthors there must be a project leader—either emergent or designated—to keep the project on course. In our case, one coauthor who was between babies, posttenure, and at a university that supported this type of scholarship took on the project leader role.

Writing innovative text materials will be different for you than it was for us. We hope that playing this chapter/cassette will offer you some solace during your moments of despair or frustration and that we can be a small part of your breakthrough times. In the absence of an innovative text writers' support group, perhaps our shared experiences can suffice.

References

Frost, P. J., Mitchell, V. F., & Nord, W. R. (1992). *Organizational reality: Reports from the firing line* (4th ed.). New York: HarperCollins.

Marx, R. D., Frost, P. J., & Jick, T. D. (1991). *Management live! The video book.* Englewood Cliffs, NJ: Prentice Hall.

Quinn, R. E. (1988). *Beyond rational management: Mastering the paradoxes and competing demands of higher performance.* San Francisco: Jossey-Bass.

40 Reflections on Championing an Innovation in Academe

THE CASE OF MANAGEMENT SKILL EDUCATION

David A. Whetten

If necessity is the mother of invention, serendipity must surely be the father.

Several months ago, I was asked by a young colleague what I would like to be remembered for as an academic. After some initial blustering about the fact that it was way too early in my career to be thinking about epitaphs, and that I wasn't sure that anything I had done merited remembering, I realized from my inquirer's earnest expression that I should take his question seriously. So, reluctantly, I responded, "Coauthoring the book *Developing Management Skills.*" That conversation came to mind when I was invited to write this chapter. I appreciate the opportunity to reflect further on what was for both of us a surprising answer. In particular, I believe that my enduring passion for the "skills" book stems from its innovative nature. Reflecting on how I have chosen to allocate my professional time over the past two decades, I am struck by how much I've enjoyed the role of "academic entrepreneur." In that sense, *Developing Management Skills* is most memorable because it is most typical.

A great deal of research has examined two key aspects of the innovation process: development and diffusion (Van de Ven, Angle, & Poole, 1989). It is widely believed that these phases, or cycles, of innovation require the coincidence of two critical factors: (a) an *opportunity* to innovate and (b) a perceived *need* for the innovation. It has been further noted that the rare cases in which these enabling conditions coincide depend as much on luck and timing as on hard work and good intentions. Following is my retrospective account of how these elements came together to produce what has become a reasonably successful educational innovation. At the beginning, there was little reason to believe that it would succeed. Looking back at the obstacles that had to be overcome, I am surprised that it did.

I'll begin this account by examining my opportunity to initiate a change in our introductory management course at the University of Illinois, and then proceed to examine its fortuitous match with an emerging agitation for change in the broader teaching profession. Throughout, the contributions of timing and luck will be evident.

An innovation opportunity requires two necessary conditions: (a) personal interest and commitment and (b) sustaining nurturance. I remember very clearly when my interest in management skill training was first piqued. While I was a college student at Brigham Young University, I attended a talk by Stephen R. Covey, who had recently returned from serving as a mission president in Ireland for the Mormon Church. At that time he was a faculty member in the Organizational Behavior Department and a very popular speaker on campus. Disappointed that I had not been able to attend any of his classes, I was eager to hear him speak. In listening to him relate his experiences as a supervisor of young missionaries and lay ecclesiastical leaders of small, struggling branches of the church, I found his observations about leadership development intriguing.

Soon after arriving in Ireland, he recognized a need for leadership training. Given his professional background, he proceeded to organize a series of workshops at the mission home on topics such as planning meetings, counseling members, and organizing activities. During these meetings he presented the relevant guidelines and discussed how they could be applied in a church leadership setting; he then sent the participants off with hearty expressions of confidence in their ability to improve.

Stephen was later dismayed when he visited the small, relatively isolated church units and observed almost no change. His initial reaction was to blame the learners: "Why don't they understand the importance of this material?" After further reflection, he realized that their failure to change was not due simply to a lack of understanding. In fact, he concluded that the root problem was not a lack of assimilation, but a lack of application. Based on this insight, Stephen redesigned his leadership training program to include role modeling and role playing, as well as on-site coaching. After a second round of training, followed by several months of intensive follow-up, he was gratified to observe substantial improvements in the skill levels of his mission leaders.

Stephen Covey's compelling distinction between teaching management principles and theo-

ries and facilitating the development of management skills faded into the recesses of my memory for nearly a decade. Actually, it was buried under a blizzard of new information and contrary perspectives, as I entered the doctoral program at Cornell, Leo Gruenfeld, Howard Aldrich, Karl Weick, and other able mentors worked hard to mold my normative commitment to "improve organizations" into a scientific capability to "understand organizations." Furthermore, my shaky start as an assistant professor at Illinois (it took me 3 years to publish my first major paper) kept me narrowly focused on accelerating my research productivity. It seemed like an eternity before my program of research reached the critical threshold of productivity necessary for the publication process to become self-sustaining.

Soon after receiving tenure, I had a discussion with Lou Pondy, a colleague, and David Boje, a graduate student, about their frustrations with BA 210, our large introductory undergraduate management class. They had been pioneering an experiential learning approach in which each section created an organization whose objective was to organize and manage the learning process. According to Lou and Dave, students found this approach more interesting than simply listening to lectures in a large hall, but they also complained about its lack of structure, focus, and relevance. Because Lou was taking on more administrative responsibilities in the department, he asked me if I would be interested in succeeding him as coordinator of BA 210. Given that my teaching experiences with undergraduate business students had not been particularly successful (especially given my hypersensitivity to the trade-offs between teaching preparation and data analysis time), the opportunity to swap instruction time for course development and TA supervision time was very attractive. In addition, my interest was quickened by the prospect of using this role to revisit my latent interest in skill development.

However, without institutional support, my personal commitment to change would have "died for lack of a second." In retrospect, the odds against my successfully using this seemingly routine faculty assignment as a hothouse for a significant academic innovation were extremely high. I was a junior faculty member in a research-oriented university during an era when contributions in the classroom mattered only at the margins. Consequently, there was no reason to expect that any teaching innovation, let alone a radical departure from current practice, would be viewed as legitimate and therefore worthy of the resources necessary to create a prototype that could be tested and eventually disseminated to other schools.

I believe that six critical factors accounted for the unlikely institutional support we received. First, one of the most important outcomes of this assignment was that it allowed me to account for my course and book preparation time as teaching and professional service, rather than as research. In retrospect, the fact that I could pursue the skills project in parallel with my research activities, rather than in competition with them, was probably the single most important source of institutional support—albeit unplanned and unrecognized support. I am convinced that absent this particular definition of "what it is" and "how to count it" my labor of love would have degenerated quickly into an exercise in futility. Second, the department was under considerable pressure to reduce the high level of dissatisfaction with one of our core undergraduate courses (800 students per semester). Third, my colleagues teaching the "OB electives" were concerned that in the past the "Intro to Management" course content (BA 210) had overlapped too much with their material. Fourth, Lou and Dave had already established a precedent for using BA 210 as an educational laboratory. Fifth, none of my colleagues was interested in taking on what appeared to be a high-risk/low-payoff assignment. The final factor was Lou Pondy's personal commitment and institutional role. Lou's support was particularly critical during the stage in the innovation process at which our project was most vulnerable to legitimacy-destroying criticism. As our course ratings improved, my confidence and dreams expanded accordingly. The major impediment to institutionalizing our fledgling enterprise was the lack of a supporting text. Because academic courses are largely defined by their accompanying texts, the institutionalization of a new course necessitates the development of a new text. However, in general, there is zero institutional support for a junior faculty member at a major university to write a textbook. Paradoxically, although the uniqueness of the proposed book constituted the greatest barrier to its publication, the legitimacy necessary to shield its development at Illinois stemmed from Lou Pondy's belief that our profession needed a radical alternative to current teaching practice.

Although Lou provided a protective shroud of legitimacy within my department, I still worried about what colleagues would think about my spending a lot of time on a project that had little scholarly merit in the Cornell/Illinois neighborhood of academe. (I never figured it would buy me any credits; the only question in my mind was how many it would cost me.) Therefore, I approached the first presentation of our ideas at the Organizational Behavior Teaching Conference in May 1980 with great apprehension. Indeed, that was a "coming out" experience, of sorts, for me. Given that the pain of my frustratingly slow start around the "getting published" track still dominated my short-term memory, I was especially concerned that the skills book project would be viewed as evidence that I was not a "serious" scholar—that my recent spate of publications was mere pandering for tenure. My apprehension was raised to the level of panic when I learned that Karl Weick was to be the discussant for my session at OBTC. Fortunately, during and following the session Karl expressed interest in, and support for, the skills project. Because he had been the editor of *Administrative Science Quarterly* as well as a former professor at Cornell, his thoughtful reassurance did much to assuage my apprehension. If, on the other hand, Karl had been highly critical of this project or of my participation in it, I probably would have gone back to Illinois and unplugged our experiment.

The merit of the book project was further strengthened by the results of a poll of the OBTC attendees. Asked to predict which of several forms of instruction would be the most popular in the next 5 to 10 years, this group of highly committed teachers rated skill-based education number one. This OBTC experience provided a much-needed affirmation of my personal commitment. I believe that this external validation also helped sustain Lou Pondy's nurturing support for a politically incorrect activity.

Even with the unusual protective umbrella of legitimacy afforded this project, I could never have completed the book on my own. As I recall, I first shared my interest in using BA 210 as a laboratory for developing a skills-based management course with Kim Cameron during one of our many late-night chats in our hotel room at an Academy of Management convention. As with many of these exchanges, there was an immediate resonance in our thinking. The decision to make this a joint venture proved to have important implications. First, it gave us an opportunity to test our ideas in more than one institutional environment—Kim had done some skill training at a small college prior to attending graduate school, and he was then at the University of Wisconsin; second, the fact that Kim and I are close friends with similar backgrounds and interests, as well as complementary skills and styles, has made our two decades of collaboration both enjoyable and productive. That "chemistry" was critical to the success of this project. We struggled for months (our editor would say years) to develop the "five-step skill development teaching model" and to select the right set of skills. These important decisions were the intellectual offspring of intense interaction, not isolated reflection. Fortunately, our long-standing relationship substantially reduced the transaction costs inherent in this type of collaboration. Third, during the period we were writing the book, Kim was working at a higher education research institute in Colorado. This setting provided indispensable writing time and secretarial support during the "crunch time" of meeting publication deadlines.

There wouldn't have been any deadlines to meet (read: miss) if it hadn't been for Jim Sittlington, business editor at Scott, Foresman. Four years lapsed between the inception of the idea and the publication of the book. During this period, we used custom-published collections of articles, cases, and exercises produced for us by GINN. A year or so into the project, we felt comfortable enough with our ideas to begin looking for a publisher. We sent proposals to every major book publisher, and all but one, Scott, Foresman, sent us rejections. (One editor told me, "Normally we look for an 80/20 proposal: 80% old material; 20% new material. Your project reverses those percentages, and that worries me.") During one of his get-acquainted visits to the Illinois campus (we were close to his Chicago office, so he visited often), Jim and I had lunch. He told me about his recent move from Irwin to Scott, Foresman and his accompanying interest in moving outside the traditional textbook mold. The fortuitous circumstances that brought Jim to Scott, Foresman and us to Jim's attention kept our brainchild from being stillborn.

The core of our proposal to Jim was a strong case for the need to publish a "skills" book. Against a backdrop of widespread criticism of existing teaching methods, we argued that our approach represented a logical, and much needed, alternative. It was clear to Jim (and to other editors) that there was discontent in the marketplace. Our task was to convince him that we had an alternative that would sell books. Whether Jim simply used our lengthy proposal to rationalize what he instinctively wanted to do anyway, or whether he would never have given us a contract without a compelling argument about the potential market for an untried product, doesn't really matter. What is clear is that our survey results, quotes from prominent scholars and business figures, and analysis of competing educational models made it easier for Jim to feel comfortable about this project and, just as important, made it easier for him to persuade his boss to bet on a long shot.

Serendipity continued to rescue us from despair. During a particularly difficult period of negotiations with our publishers, we learned that Scott, Foresman had acquired Goodyear's management text list, including the services of Lyman Porter, their consulting editor. In Lyman we found a kindred spirit, with clout. He served as a very effective mediator during several difficult discussions about content, format, design, price, and so forth. His contribution to forging a workable alliance between our idealistic convictions and Scott, Foresman's pragmatic concerns was indispensable.

Once we had a contract, Kim and I felt somewhat like the dog that finally caught a car. We now had to make good on our claim that we could translate our ideas into a system of instruction that would be implemented at other universities by professors who did not share either our zeal for, or our experience-based knowledge about, this nontraditional approach. Our discussions with colleagues had convinced us that gaining agreement on the need for change was the easy part. Students were bored with large lecture classes; the faculty teaching the OB electives complained that the introductory "management principles" texts were pirating most of the OB material; alumni and recruiters complained about how poorly equipped business students were for the changing demands of the workplace; scholars such as Henry Mintzberg and Jeff Pfeffer had raised tough intellectual questions about the validity of traditional management "principles" and the suitability of traditional teaching methods.

However, we also realized that gaining nodding acceptance for the need to change and incorporating a new approach into an established university curriculum were only moderately correlated. If our goal was to change how management was taught at other schools, then we had to do more than win a few converts at OBTC. Besides needing to make a case for skill training as a solution for a problem common to all campuses, we learned how difficult it is actually to change faculty routines and institutional policies and cultures.

Faculty members, like all other critters, resist changes in their routines. And the longer the routines have been practiced, the greater the resistance to change. Early on, we noticed that most of those who were excited about teaching behavioral skills were junior faculty. This meant that they were personally more pliable, but institutionally more vulnerable. Given the challenge of getting senior OB faculty either to change personally or to support the changes proposed by their younger colleagues, coupled with the related challenge of getting the economics, accounting, and finance faculty to acknowledge the value of teaching "soft skills," we began examining our "product design" choices from the perspective of our "customers" (these are strange concepts for organizational behavior folks).

For example, in the papers we published in *Exchange* (the predecessor to *Journal of Management Education*), we chose to present skill training as an amalgamated extension, rather than as a repudiation, of existing practices. Specifically, we argued that it brought together the best elements of the "principles of management," "experiential learning," and "behavioral science" approaches to teaching OB/management. In writing those papers, we also worried a great deal about how to present a persuasive case for the specific skills that should be taught. I remember discussing with Kim how to organize the results from our survey of several hundred managers into categories with familiar, legitimacy-conferring labels (e.g., "getting the most out of your people" was coded as "motivation").

Also, in our book design discussions with the editorial staff at Scott, Foresman, we found ourselves increasingly asking, "What will contribute to the book's (and, by inference, the approach's) academic credibility?" Not only did the chapter titles need to be familiar, but decisions about the size and "heft" of the book, the number, form, and location of the references, the cover design, the balance between the length of each chapter's "content" and its corresponding skill-building exercises, and so on, all needed to be evaluated against the standard "look and feel" of traditional, widely accepted, management texts.

Recognizing that faculty were more likely to use our book to teach management skills if they had answers to their questions about how much they would have to change their course designs, schedules, requirements, evaluation criteria, and so on, we included a great deal of material in the instructor's manual on how to design a skill-development course, including sample course outlines and schedules for various types of teaching environments (e.g., large lecture sessions, small-enrollment electives). Using the most frequently asked questions we heard in academic seminars and workshops on management skill training, we also included either reprinted or commissioned articles in the instructor's manual on topics such as using role plays as exams. In addition, we included in the transparency masters several slides containing survey results, organizing frameworks, and quotes from experts regarding the merits of a skill-building approach to help introduce (read: justify) the course to students and colleagues.

Although we devoted much time and attention to enhancing the legitimacy of the management skills approach and its accompanying text, the impact of our efforts paled in comparison to the benefits we reaped from the fortuitous publication of a number of supporting articles, books, and reports. One of these was a study published as *Management, Education, and Development,* coauthored by Lyman Porter and Lawrence McKibbon and commissioned by AACSB (the national accrediting association for business schools), which reported results from an extensive study of business leaders, management scholars, and students strongly encouraging business schools to strengthen their emphasis on behavioral skill development. The legitimacy that these reports bestowed on our nontraditional views significantly increased the willingness of faculty committees at other schools to create a curriculum slot for management skills education.

In retrospect, some of our most vexing challenges involved clarifying what our approach was not. In particular, our early feedback from colleagues indicated that we had to differentiate our approach from two others that were closely related and often confused: (a) behavior-modeling training in industry and (b) experiential learning exercises. In the late 1970s and early 1980s, behavior-modeling training became very popular in industry. In fact, several training firms, such as Zenger and Miller, specialized in producing videotapes for this arena. Our goal was to draw on this extensive base of experience while maintaining a distinction between the goals and philosophy of management "training" and the goals and philosophy of management "education." Consistently, we found that colleagues who were aware of behavior-modeling programs in industry would criticize what they characterized as "mindless mimicry" in those programs, and then proceed to paint our approach with the same anti-intellectual brush. No matter how hard we tried to say, "We're different," until we published an academically respectable textbook (remember, it took us 4 years to go from blueprint to finished product), we were continually frustrated by the harmful consequences of our confused identity. Although we had never considered using modeling tapes as the core of our instructional package, the need to avoid the academic stigma of being labeled a "training" program convinced us not to include them at all. Instead, we emphasized the importance of students' developing the "meta-skill" of adapting research-based behavioral guidelines to their unique personalities and situational circumstances. To reinforce this image of "the thinking person's choice" for developing management skills, we resisted editorial pressures to include "answers" for cases and exercises, we used conceptual models to organize the material in each chapter, and we grounded our behavioral guidelines in contemporary management theory and research.

Our second problem with mistaken identity involved being viewed as a throwback to the "fuzzy-headed experiential learning of the sixties." Several of the critiques of our early presentation dismissed our approach as a reincarnation of "touchy-feely" learning. They argued that students are poorly equipped to generate valid principles from their experiences, and even if they do stumble onto interesting insights during classroom exercises, they are ill equipped to generate real-world applications. Related concerns involved failing to teach students how to be intelligent consumers of OB theory and research, and losing prospective OB majors because they would conclude from this course that all our field has to offer is "fun and games."

To address these unfounded but persistent criticisms, we found it useful to distinguish between inductive and deductive learning approaches. Basically, we argued that our approach is primarily deductive (our focus is on application, not discovery), whereas the experiential learning model is pure induction. Instead of asking students to generalize principles from what they had learned, we started with principles derived from the organizational behavior literature that constituted what we considered the "best bets" for resolving conflicts, managing stress, conducting meetings, and so on. It is interesting that after years of defining (and defending) our approach as noninductive, we have begun to experiment with a more synthetic learning model that overlays alternating cycles of inductive and deductive learning processes onto our five-step skill development teaching model (Whetten & Clark, in press).

Thus far, I have outlined the process that led to the publication of our book and its adoption at other schools. The successful development and diffusion of our educational innovation represented the confluence of an opportunity to make changes in a single course at one university and a peaking demand for new approaches for teaching management within the broader educational environment. The final part of this retrospective account examines the challenges and frustrations of sustaining an institutionalized innovation.

As I am writing this chapter, the third edition of our book has arrived in our bookstore. Given the obstacles to our success, the fact that the sales of our book have increased nearly every year for a decade and that it is currently being used in a variety of educational settings in all 50 states and several other countries are still hard for us to comprehend. Qualitatively, this means that what was once referred to at Scott, Foresman as a "cult book" is now afforded major book status at HarperCollins (which bought Scott, Foresman several years ago).

This truly unexpected success has brought with it a new set of issues and challenges. Chief among these has been the emergence of clones. Although intellectually we know that "imitation is the sincerest form of flattery," emotionally we have found it difficult to separate the sales of "our book" from the success of "our approach." As long as there were no competitors, the adoption of our approach meant the adoption of our book. But once we started sharing the market with other books, these competing criteria of success (book versus approach) triggered feelings of ambivalence. On the one hand, given that our book continued to do well, increasing adoptions of competing books meant that the market was expanding—more people were accepting the management skills approach. On the other hand, the fact that others modified our basic model and used it to compete against us seemed somewhat unfair and even brazen. Furthermore, the fact that the senior author of our major competition is a close personal friend made these conflicting feelings especially troubling.

As we became caught up in the competition phase of our innovation's life cycle, I noticed a significant shift in my thinking. Whereas before I was worried about how to get colleagues to accept our approach, I found myself now focusing on "staying ahead of the competition." Instead of thinking about what would help adopters make the shift from "traditional teaching" to "skills teaching," Kim and I were invited to strategy sessions with our publishers to plan how the next edition could increase our market share. I remember flying home from one of these meetings in New York and feeling both satisfied that our fledgling enterprise had become a "market segment standard" and sad that our attention was shifting from our original, and to us very noble, goal of providing students and faculty with an alternative pedagogy to the more crass objective of staying ahead of the competition.

One of the practical implications of the introduction of competition was that conversations with other skills teachers became somewhat awkward. Even though I now feel quite comfortable "objectively" discussing the merits of our book and Bob Quinn's book, *Becoming a Master Manager,* and I have even recommended his as a better match in some settings, I've noticed that when individuals who are using another author's skills book engage me in a conversation at a conference, they are eager to share their enthusiasm about teaching skills but are obviously uncomfortable

if they inadvertently disclose that they're not using our book. On the other hand, if I'm approached by colleagues who are using our book, they typically disclose that information early in the conversation, as if, having passed a loyalty test, they will be able to have a more productive and informative discussion.

Through the tedium of two revision cycles, I have also developed a better appreciation for the challenge of sustaining a commitment to continuous improvement. It is a lot more fun to create than it is to modify and update. As a result, our major concern going into the third edition was getting the editor to pay others to do activities that Kim and I had jealously guarded before. The fact that it has taken us this long to "let go" reflects the intensity of our personal commitment to a scholarly product that for over a decade has been closely linked to our identities as scholars. It has served both as a vehicle for kindred spirits' identifying with us as champions of innovation in academe, and as a representation of many highly personal identity-instantiating experiences.

In conclusion, the emergence of the management skills development approach, and its accompanying text, illustrates much of the accepted wisdom about the innovation process—for example, the blending of internal opportunity and external need. On a more personal level, as I have reflected on these events that have spanned nearly two decades, I am struck by the unlikelihood of our success. It is natural for innovators to attribute their success to hard work and good judgment. In this case, it appears that perspicacity was less a factor than serendipity. The original idea was embedded in a talk by Stephen Covey; I was asked to take over a troubled course that no one else wanted; this opportunity came at a point in my career when I was motivated and able to pursue it; Kim and I brought highly compatible interests and complementary skills to the project; Lou Pondy was a very supportive department head during a critical period when my politically incorrect book-writing activities required a great deal of time; Karl Weick showed interest and gave support; Jim Sittlington made a "routine" office visit; the acquisition of Goodyear brought an "inside advocate" (Lyman Porter) into Scott, Foresman; the assignment of a new editor (Melissa Rosatti) "saved" the second edition; the publication of various professional reports endorsing the management skills development approach coincided with the publication of our first edition.

It is hard to prioritize the criticality of these myriad factors and conditions, but taken together they denote a highly precarious and fragile innovation process. Taking another line from Stephen Covey, not only would it have been impossible for us to "begin with [this] end in mind," but a knowledge of how unlikely this outcome was would probably have deterred us from ever starting. Clearly, our long-standing and substantial personal commitment to this innovation process is evidence that the passion of our hearts has overruled (many times) the calculations of our heads.

References

Van de Ven, A. H., Angle, H., & Poole, M. S. (1989). *Research on the management of innovation.* New York: Harper & Row.

Whetten, D. A., & Clark, S. C. (in press). An integrated model for teaching management skills. *Journal of Management Education.*

Working Inside the University

There is no question in my mind that even if I elect to retain the career frame as originally configured, my career picture has been enriched through these "reaching out" experiences. I have also enjoyed the opportunity to experience a realistic preview of a reshaped career structure, constructed from the planes of the original frame.

Judy D. Olian (p. 408)

Although socialized to "cosmopolitan" rather than "local" attitudes early in their graduate careers, most academics have at least some level of commitment to the institutions that employ them, and this tends to increase with their longevity on campus. Perhaps it is not surprising, then, that at midcareer many academics find themselves heavily involved in intracampus initiatives intended to increase their universities' effectiveness. Usually their involvement centers on activities to which they contribute unique knowledge and skills. What, then, is the nature of such internal service activities, and which academics find themselves more likely to heed such calls to action? What skills and abilities do they find particularly useful in carrying out their extended responsibilities? Subsequently, what happens to an academic's reward structure and career progression as a result of following a calling inside the university? In the following essay, Judy Olian, a full professor

and the project director of a large multidisciplinary teaching, research, and service project at the University of Maryland, relates her experiences with such a role.

At the beginning of the essay, Olian speaks openly about the attributes and motivations that caused her to venture into the director role:

I knew—now that I had the luxury of tenure—that I wanted to test alternative shapes of the frame that constituted "my career." Perhaps in the end I would elect to retain the frame in its original shape, but I was convinced that I first needed to test one or even several alternatives. (p. 402)

Nor are Olian's efforts independent of the importance that she places on the far-reaching goal of her project, implementing total quality management principles across the teaching, research, and service delivery functions of the university. As she puts it: "The program goals—changing *what* and *how* we deliver in academic, administrative, and service arenas—are not just values I buy into, they are a passion. I am absolutely convinced of the societal necessity of the project's goals, so it is not difficult for me to be its champion" (p. 405).

Those who work inside the university on special projects, even critically important ones that are highly consistent with their own values, typically discover that their responsibilities far outdistance their authority. Very quickly, they begin to use (or acquire, in some cases) the skill of influencing others without direct authority. In Olian's case this skill has proven an invaluable one, used on almost a daily basis, and she is clearly more than competent in this arena. Although unintentional, her description of exerting influence without power reinforces Susan Jackson's message in Chapter 36 about learning to "just say no" even to others quite skilled in getting one to say yes:

> All valuable members of the university community are overcommitted to projects that are near and dear to them. Just as I cannot afford to be seduced hook, line, and sinker into their projects, no matter how exciting,

they act to protect themselves from acquiescing to my pleas for their involvement in the IBM-TQ Project. Therein lies the challenge to me as a culture change agent. (p. 406)

Meanwhile, what are the institutional rewards for those academics who pursue sizable responsibilities outside the research arena? In another part of her essay, Olian speaks to this point directly: "There has been a cost to my research career. Clearly, the past 3 years have slowed down, though by no means halted, my research productivity. In an institution like mine, where research productivity is the single most important determinant of rewards and promotions, I have clearly paid the price in both domains" (p. 404). In the long term, however, Olian's choice to "break out from within" and follow a path consistent with her abilities and her heart appears to have served her well, for, as her postscript indicates, she is now associate dean of academic affairs at the College of Business and Management at the University of Maryland. Her new position seems likely to open yet more doors for still further experimentation, contributing another set of paths to her own career journey.

41 Breaking Out, Inside the University

Judy D. Olian

In my professional life, I occupy two primary roles. First, I am a management and organization professor in the Business School of my university, with a research focus in human resource management. I am also the director of the IBM-Total Quality (TQ) Project—a competitive award by the IBM Corporation to the university. The goals of the project are to promulgate total quality content and processes throughout our academic and administrative functions, with special emphasis on joint business-engineering curricula that teach TQ, using TQ pedagogical methods. The second hat I wear—that of project director—is inherently cross-functional, requiring creation of working partnerships across the university, as well as with business partners outside the university. Although there are complementary aspects to my roles as professor and project director, the roles also frequently compete.

The editors of this volume asked me to focus on my project director role—the one that requires me to straddle, and perhaps even destroy, walls inside the university. I will reconstruct briefly the chronology of events that led me into this particular career phase, as well as ruminate over the highs and lows of working within the university in the joint role of project director and professor. Specifically, I describe the critical phases in my personal evolution toward this role, the reasons for and against this particular form of university citizenship, and how these experiences have interacted with and changed the way I live my life as a professor. Finally, I speculate on the personal characteristics that explain my attraction to and selection into this administrative role, with the possibility that these features may be relevant to others considering similar functions within their universities. The reader will forgive me for approaching these issues from a decidedly self-centered perspective.

AUTHOR'S NOTE: I am indebted to Sara Rynes, with whom I have had a long and deeply enriching friendship. As she has done over many years, she read this piece too. In addition to her usual insights, this time she served as memory jogger, reminding me of some of the critical junctions in my personal and career journey, and as validating agent, testing the veracity of some of my recollections.

The Path Toward Breaking Out

After graduate school, my career pattern followed the traditional sequence. I finished my dissertation after I had already begun a tenure-track position, and then dived right into the tenure challenge. During that period I was lying low within the university—the usual committees, some outside activities in the profession, consulting, and some international speaking and travel. Nothing extraordinary. I had not relocated for a "real" sabbatical so—despite my relatively international upbringing (I was raised in several countries)—my adult life had become rather permanent, geographically confined, and quite narrowly focused. I realized that I was looking at another 30 years of a working career—would I want to be doing exactly the same thing for as long as I could foresee?

I was not sure of the answer, but I knew—now that I had the luxury of tenure—that I wanted to test alternative shapes of the frame that constituted "my career." Perhaps in the end I would elect to retain the frame in its original shape, but I was convinced that I first needed to test one or even several alternatives. Prior to graduate school, I had enjoyed a brief stint in a fast-paced administrative role in the Prime Minister's Office in Israel that required a lot of interpersonal interaction and problem solving. The pleasure of the adrenaline rush from the successful juggling of several crises and deadlines would sometimes come back to me. In my later academic life, perhaps because of these early work experiences, I was frequently visited with the self-assessment that some of my best skills remained untapped in my purist academic role. Moreover, when I was especially honest with myself I had to admit that among my peers, the package of talents and disposition that I brought into my academic role—though quite adequate—was not all that outstanding. In short, going back as far as graduate school, I had lust in my heart for "an other," another career direction.

As a new associate professor, I was invited to participate in an international trip with university faculty and administrators, one of whom was the provost of my university at the time. That trip was probably my first exposure to some of the issues addressed by upper-level university administrators. It also presented a new opportunity for me to interact at some length with faculty from other disciplines within my institution, and I was able to appreciate the meaning of a university community that transcends particular fields of expertise.

I look back on that event as an eye-opener to other possibilities for my life as a university professor. After that trip, I chatted a few times with the provost (who later was selected to become the university's president) to understand how he became a university administrator, what it was about his disposition and background that helped him in his job, and recommendations he would make to other faculty interested in expanding their roles into some form of administration. He, as well as several others, mentioned the American Council of Education (ACE) Fellowship as a way to learn about upper-level university administration. The ACE Fellowship is a 1-year program for midlevel university administrators and faculty that facilitates unusual access to all facets of the university's top management team and administrative issues.

The ACE Fellowship seemed like the best way to test my yearning for another career direction. The university nominated me for the fellowship, and the screening process forced me for the first time in my career to read up on higher education policy issues—another eye-opener. I spent 1990-1991 as an ACE fellow. I elected to do a "home" fellowship, at my own institution. Professionally, I thought I could "get down to business" more quickly than if I had gone to a brand-new environment—I already knew the president (who had just moved up from the provost position) and I thought I knew the institutional ropes, at least a little. Additionally, some of the negatives of staying in the same place were minimized because my university is quite large and I felt I could distance myself from almost all of the departmental business that might interfere with my necessary immersion in fellowship activities. In retrospect, I see that the one thing I did miss was extended exposure to a different university culture and community environment.

I worked in the president's office for a year as a fellow, and ended up staying there a second year as a special assistant to him. I had gone into his office to focus on everything I did *not* know, such as the politics of athletics in a Division I school, the challenges of running a physical plant for a 40,000-person university community, and the ins and outs of lobbying the state legislature. The president was agreeable to letting me learn about those things on my own time, but we struck a deal: He was interested in drawing on what he believed I *did* know something about—changing the university into a TQ culture.

I spent 2 years serving as the TQ agent for the top management team, helping the team learn about TQ and develop a TQ vision for the university, forging partnerships with business executives to serve as pro bono TQ consultants to the university, securing outside funding for TQ activities, compiling the campus TQ implementation plan as ex officio member of the campus planning committee, and launching several TQ pilot teams. Obviously, those 2 years were vastly different from my role as faculty member focused within a single college. The most notable differences surrounded the culture change activities I was spawning, as well as the range of university and corporate representatives with whom I associated.

Toward the end of the 2-year period, IBM launched a higher education TQ competition with a challenge to U.S. universities. The corporation's call was for more appropriately trained students who could add value to employers from day one, because of their TQ process skills and content knowledge and their business-engineering knowledge breadth. At the same time, IBM told universities that they had to be credible TQ role models in all aspects of their own service delivery.

With the help of the president, I pulled together a team of faculty and administrators from business, engineering, and computer sciences, and we worked on the proposal for several months. The proposal was successful. We were one of the eight awardees among almost 250 universities applying for the award, which meant that over a 5-year period we are to receive several million dollars from both IBM and university sources. As the proposal team leader, I evolved into the project director. In support of my role, I receive a summer grant, and I teach two rather than four courses a year. Other than that, I continue to perform the usual functions of a faculty member, including research, working with doctoral students, and professional and university service.

Life in the New Role

It has been more than 2 years since we received word of the award. We are now in the throes of implementing our loosely spun images of what sounded at the time of writing to be exciting and innovative, things we fantasized "might be doable" if we only had the money. Now we have the money, so it is delivery time, and I am fully accountable to IBM for the promises made earlier. IBM has made continuation of all TQ grants contingent upon accomplishment of the results promised for the first 2 years.

There have been quite a few successes, but there have also been challenges. For example, IBM pushed us into reducing cycle time and starting the new course sequence within 6 months of grant receipt. We managed that, despite the challenges within a university of getting four courses designed, approved, and in the schedule; we recruited and screened cohorts 1 and 2 of the program, and faculty delivered the first two courses through team teaching. We also built a state-of-the-art electronic classroom to facilitate TQ-based teaching and learning processes, and developed appropriate software. We have influenced extensive curriculum changes around TQ in both the College of Business and the College of Engineering, spawned research projects around TQ, and attracted additional outside funding.

There are also challenges, opportunities for improvement, and goals still waiting to be realized—sources of frustration to an impatient person like me. Several of our immediate customers (students and faculty) were not uniformly satisfied after our first pedagogical efforts, and the breadth of impact beyond the few TQ zealots is still limited. There are pockets of TQ initiatives across the university, but TQ is by no means routine or widespread. Remaining focused on the vital few priorities and keeping others energized are perennial challenges. As the initial excitement associated with new and "trendy" initiatives wears off and this effort becomes routine, it is harder to sustain the energy necessary to roll the boulder of change uphill. That has become the biggest hurdle for me personally, as well as for the process of institutional change.

Asking me to reflect on these experiences is like asking travelers to summarize a trip while they are still involved in sightseeing. Even travelers who have no tour guide and who have only general destination points will have already formed impressions—impressions that will certainly change as their journey continues, and change yet again when the trip is completed and they look back upon it through the snapshots of their memories. So, I am somewhere in the midst of my journey, and here are some impressions.

The Lows and Highs
of Breaking Out

Lack of rewards. Let's face it—there are a lot of good reasons *not* to bother with "service" in a research-oriented university. The reward structure, both internally as well as among one's professional peers, perceives these accomplishments at best benignly, and sometimes adversely. The kind of support that is needed in this type of collaborative project comes easily from a small number of colleagues who happen to be passionate about the project goals, but the vast number of people are already overcommitted to projects that pull them in other directions. With no hierarchical power and only some resources at my disposal, I end up spending most of my time cajoling, bargaining, explaining, and sometimes begging colleagues across the university to partake in this activity, which is, at best, in the second tier of their list of priorities. The challenge is even greater when the cross-disciplinary nature of the project is considered, and the cajoling is directed toward other colleges in which I have no track record and little knowledge of the pockets of receptivity among the faculty, and lack a continuing presence for follow-through and impact.

Loss of independence. There is no doubt that the broader the set of issues and people I deal with, the less control I have over my agenda and time. During the academic year, about 40-50% of my time is spent on the project, significantly more than is allocated through the official remuneration scheme. As a faculty member who has long reveled in the independence of my schedule and agenda, this has meant a very large, and sometimes painful, adjustment. I rarely have a

day that I can allocate fully to research or writing, and I look back with longing on those earlier periods. I frequently spend whole days between meetings and telephone calls dealing with mechanical coordination and PR issues, none of which bear any resemblance to heavy-duty academic or curriculum matters. But these activities are necessary if not critical to the continuing survival of the program activities and funding. Couple that with the total absence of hierarchical power to force change, and by now you are asking yourself whether any sane person would take on this kind of activity.

The inherent university-professor role conflict. There has been a cost to my research career. Clearly, the past 3 years have slowed down, though by no means halted, my research productivity. In an institution like mine, where research productivity is the single most important determinant of rewards and promotions, I have clearly paid the price in both domains. No matter how much lip service is paid to encouragement of organizational citizenship behaviors in a university, service—even outstanding service—is never afforded the same rewards as research. University colleagues argue that faculty make *conscious* choices about investment of time and efforts, knowing in advance that they will not receive the same rewards. If they do choose to commit extraordinarily to service projects, there are other rewards driving these behaviors, such as summer and teaching buyouts or public visibility. Research productivity is the currency for trading in the external market, and there is a market value assigned to such contributions. There is no market value to extraordinary internal service unless one becomes a full-time administrator, so the rational part of me cannot disagree with the university's reluctance to reward service.

Nevertheless, it does sometimes irk me that I have to fight to legitimize the value of my service contributions on a scale similar to research, especially because the internal (salary) rewards are the *only* tangible returns available for service contributions, whereas successful research pays off in *both* the internal (salary increases) and external (enhanced marketability) environments. However, in all honesty, I have to acknowledge that my decisions about how I invest my time reflect a tacit agreement with my colleagues—I choose to do what I like doing, in areas where I perceive my strengths. If I resented performing the service activities and suffering the opportunity costs of reduced research activities, I simply wouldn't do it. Certainly, there are some individuals who are better at juggling both roles without suffering losses on the research side. Ed Locke, chairman of my department and a contributor to this volume, is one of those unique people who can juggle both roles and still remain as prolific as ever. There are also people who are far superior at research. For them, the psychological costs of reduced productivity would be too painful, or their absence might actually impede research advances in their professional field.

Painful disappointments. Disappointments, and even failures, are part of a naturally evolving change process. There are some fortunate individuals with the fortitude to write these occurrences off as part of an expected uphill battle, but I am not such a person. These disappointments take a personal, sometimes emotional toll. I speak of disappointments when students are overtly critical of innovations that required tremendous personal and financial investments, when faculty vehemently dismiss any need for change in their pedagogical philosophy or delivery, when the scope of institutional change or leaders' personal engagement is far less ambitious than hoped for or even promised, and when the only medium for eliciting cooperation from skeptical colleagues is through mercenary promises of hard grant dollars.

These disappointments affect my outlook and behaviors only marginally, but they are real, and they come home with me. It would be entirely unrealistic to describe a change agent's role without acknowledging these inevitable, sometimes highly personal, setbacks.

Doing the right thing. Lest these negatives appear too discouraging, let me hasten to say that I am no glutton for punishment (at least not continuing punishment), and there are several compelling reasons to engage in these intrauniversity service activities, at least for me. First is the satisfaction of acting on my convictions, doing the right thing. The program goals—changing *what* and *how* we deliver in academic, administrative, and service arenas—are not just values I buy into, they are a passion. I am absolutely convinced of the societal necessity of the

project's goals, so it is not difficult for me to be its champion.

For example, I am convinced that employer requirements for cross-functionally trained graduates who are effective team members, computer fluent, and skilled in the "softer" side of management are here to stay. With those overarching developmental goals in mind, we are conducting massive curricula revisions in the Colleges of Engineering and Business. Our electronic classroom is an enabler of collaborative learning and multidirectional information sharing. It is linked to the information superhighway through teleconferencing capabilities, and already embodies Vice President Gore's vision of the classroom of the year 2000. Everything we are trying to do, in my mind, is in sync with where our society is headed or should be headed, so it's easy for me to maintain my enthusiasm!

Being part of a team. I also have the joy of working with a few close colleagues who are equally committed to these goals, and our mutual support is critical when the going gets rough. Although it's much easier to focus on the work remaining, celebrating periodic successes is a must, and it is sustaining until the next hurdle is overcome. Together, we remind ourselves of the fast successes we have achieved on the not-infrequent occasions when we hit a brick wall.

External visibility. Sometimes there is visibility that comes from playing a central role in a campus project. In the case of this project, there is greater external than internal university visibility. There are obvious pluses to the exposure, contacts made, invitations to participate in meetings and speaking engagements, and in my case exposure to private sector developments in TQ and interactive information technologies. Visibility also raises the stakes, meaning that missteps are no longer anonymous. Moreover, given that I am still primarily a professor, with the associated role expectations, these outreach activities compete with my core responsibilities and frequently dominate my time. Because these involvements are visible (including to my colleagues), they are interpreted as a conscious choice to invest my time in such engagements and, by default, not in other activities, such as research. This is a fair inference, and one that I have had to weigh against the returns of external visibility.

Straddling academic bunkers. Working within the university provides more subtle rewards. The network of colleagues I work with has grown larger and far more heterogeneous, and I have benefited from a more varied perspective on university issues. I interact with people from central administration in academic, budget, and fund-raising functions; some have an internal university focus, whereas others are sensitive primarily to public opinion or corporate funding priorities. Members of the IBM-TQ team are faculty from a variety of disciplines, with different dispositions and teaching, research, and service cultures. It is enlightening, and sometimes amusing, to float and test ideas among this motley crew of characters. Reaching consensus is a challenge, but invariably the diversity of approach and opinions has added to the quality of the decision process, and usually also to the end product. I have learned lessons from these discussions that I have been able to bring back to my group or college regarding alternative ways of thinking about or organizing issues.

I know whom to call for nonroutine requests or input. On many occasions I have had prior contact with these people, and we can interact as friendly acquaintances. In such a large organization as ours, tacit knowledge of this kind shortens cycle time dramatically, and may even facilitate results. The contacts I have outside the university are of similar benefit, and I sometimes act as a matchmaker for faculty colleagues. With these advantages comes the potential liability of too much of a good thing. I have to be very careful that familiarity with numerous colleagues and their task forces, committees, grants, and projects does not divert me from the vital few priorities I must realize. This is the problem I mentioned at the outset—in reverse. All valuable members of the university community are overcommitted to projects that are near and dear to them. Just as I cannot afford to be seduced hook, line, and sinker into their projects, no matter how exciting, they act to protect themselves from acquiescing to my pleas for their involvement in the IBM-TQ Project. Therein lies the challenge to me as a culture change agent.

A new avenue for research. I am lucky—and I have the university president's insistence to thank

for this—that my intrauniversity service activities are related in some fashion to my disciplinary interests. I have given university speeches and written about TQ; in fact I wrote one article with Sara Rynes—my friend and colleague from the University of Iowa—directly tying human resource management to TQ. I have some human resource and organizational behavior graduate students who have come to me *because* of my knowledge in TQ. Several future projects are spin-offs from my engagement in TQ. So, without reservation, I can say that my intrauniversity activities have spawned a whole new research interest, and my field experiences have lent new insights into, and some credibility to, what I have to say in this area. I must admit, however, that the synergy that occurred for me was a lucky (and unplanned) coincidence that, though not unique, may not always work for others. I say it is not unique because several other illustrations come to mind. Ben Schneider, a professor in our Industrial Psychology Department, has been active in the development and validation of the university's teacher evaluation instrument. He recently published an article relating these forms of customer service evaluations to his primary stream of research on service cultures. Susan Taylor, one of the two editors of this book, is responsible for a large study of the implementation of a performance appraisal system at this university. It ties nicely into her research interests and publications in the area of performance management. Marilyn Gist at the University of Washington has been actively involved in diversity issues at the university in addition to publishing work on the topic.

These types of synergies—between university activities and writing agenda—are a best-case result. There is an element of luck to such happy mergers (a potentially interesting, though burdensome, need on the part of the university), as well as an academic's openness to steering and stretching his or her research agenda around the available opportunity. These are not isolated opportunities in universities, and they frequently yield rewarding results, yet they do entail risk (the outcomes are entirely uncertain) and they require extra effort—at least in the creation phase.

Personal growth. There are both tangible and less tangible returns from working within the university. Over time, I have been—sometimes reluctantly—changing the way I behave, known in TQ as "walking the talk." As a person who thrives on last-minute "rejiggering" in classes, sometimes euphemistically known as making "just-in-time" adjustments, I am a lot better at responding to my customers' needs for fore-warning, planning, and preparation time. I now benefit greatly from the ongoing feedback provided by students in a variety of forms. I also try—to the extent possible—to facilitate opportunities for my students' cross-functional and field experiences, and to create a discipline among them for understanding their clients' needs. I am better—though far from perfect—in responding to my students' and colleagues' requests for input and feedback. And, I must apologetically admit, in all areas of my life I have become a demanding customer who insists on receiving top quality, a condition perhaps not uniformly appreciated by my service providers.

I am also changed as a member of the university's faculty body. I am less likely to be the professor I was, with blinders obscuring vision of any perspective other than that of my department or college. The larger good, or different way of operating, has an impact on the positions I take. I am also more engaged in university-wide activities, sitting on a fund-raising board, attending universitywide hearings on occasion, and caring about many issues affecting the general quality of life within the university community. I do worry, however, that with all of these additional interests and commitments, I may no longer have the luxury of sitting down for "shoot the breeze" sessions with my graduate students, or I may be overly time conscious in collegial exchanges with my peers. I enjoyed both of these activities, and find myself doing less of each.

Making Choices

How one embodies the role of university citizen reflects an implicit cost-benefit analysis of preferences and opportunities. The role of university bridge builder is not for everyone. It is for the person who can tolerate reduced research productivity, because, with rare exceptions, that is inevitable. It is for the person who enjoys the process of human interaction, nego-

tiation, and sometimes dissent, for whom team processes are not an emotional drain. It is for the person who can appreciate dispositional differences integral to the broad spectrum of university members who come together in cross-functional settings. It is for the person who can tolerate failure, and who can endure hierarchy, authority, and accountability.

In the final analysis, I spend my time based on what I like doing and based on an assessment of my strengths and weaknesses relative to all of the professional options available (and, by implication, not available) to me at this point in time. To be sure, my choices are not nearly as consciously rational as presented here, and there are certain elements of my present career situation that I would most certainly change. However, for the most part, I like the balance of internal and external activities that my role as project director has led to, and I enjoy preserving certain portions of my life as professor, as it has evolved over time.

I am still learning a lot about working within, across, and outside the university. I recognize that despite my inclination to dwell on all that is yet to be accomplished, we have managed a lot, and the positive dimensions of these experiences have been multifaceted (learning in several content areas) and multilayered (emotional, cognitive, and behavioral). IBM is content with our progress—we were among the few grantees that continued to receive full funding after 2 years. I am excited about what lies ahead. In fact, I am teaching in the IBM-TQ electronic classroom to stretch myself into practicing what I preach. This has required a whole new way of organizing myself for teaching, in addition to the learning of new tools. I was also promoted to full professor, primarily on the basis of my research record, but I do think that my service activities added at the margin. Should I choose to pursue a career direction other than pure professorship, my experiences outside the research/teaching tracks will probably provide me with a distinguishing feature among similarly situated faculty members.

As I said at the outset—part of the objective was to experiment with a new configuration of the frame that constitutes my career, and I believe the experiment was successfully implemented. On certain days, I say to myself that I'd like my work life to be exactly as it was before—I like the relatively focused life of the university professor, being more in command of my time and agenda. On other days, I experience deep satisfaction as the source of jolts (albeit small) to the status quo in some aspects of the university's values or operating procedures, by experimenting with changes—I hope for the better—in teaching, learning, or service processes. There is no question in my mind that even if I elect to retain the career frame as originally configured, my career picture has been enriched through these "reaching out" experiences. I have also enjoyed the opportunity to experience a realistic preview of a reshaped career structure, constructed from the planes of the original frame. Either way, I'm looking at the next 25 years (it's no longer 30—time has passed!) through a different set of lenses.

Postscript

Since I completed the first draft of this chapter, I have been appointed associate dean of the school here at Maryland. As I approach this new role, my attachments have become clearer to me. I have found myself incapable of cutting all ties to my previous life, especially in areas in which I am emotionally vested. I continue as the "codirector" of the IBM-TQ Project, and I still teach one course a semester, at least for the time being. This career move into some form of deanship is a continuation of a journey of discovery—I am obviously moving in an incremental, somewhat linear mode, though with a healthy degree of caution. For an associate dean, experimentation with the role content and boundaries is expected. Many of my predecessors have stepped back from the brink of full-fledged administration and returned to faculty status. I retain that option. This career story is continuing.

Working With Policy Makers

Finally, what do people hope to accomplish through careers in academia? Although some are just trying to make a living, many have larger aspirations. Put simply, we want to make a difference. We want to leave the world a better place than we found it as a result of the work we do.

Paul R. Sackett (p. 416)

Instead of "breaking out, inside the university," some academics find themselves breaking out outside, in fairly unique ways, helping to shape the course of public policy. Although working with policy makers is unlikely to be something an individual intentionally plans to undertake during the course of an academic career, it can, as Paul Sackett notes, result from a distinguished research record on a policy-related topic or from holding an officer position in a professional organization. In the following essay, Sackett discusses his own experiences in shaping policy as a member of a multidisciplinary committee formed to examine the staffing guidelines for a large federal agency and as the president of a professional association invited to testify before a congressional hearing. He reminds us of the huge impacts such activities may have for the academics involved and also for society at large, impacts that contrast sharply with our everyday tasks of teaching, conducting research, and publishing.

What attributes enable an academic to work effectively with policy makers? Perhaps it is not surprising that Sackett identifies one as the ability to be brief: "Brevity is seen by those with experience in this area as an absolute necessity in writing to policy makers.... [The advice of the American Psychological Association is] that letters should be kept to a single page and to a single issue" (p. 414). Yet this requirement is not an easy one for academics, whose work typically requires acknowledging all sides of a question. As Sackett notes: "Following this advice can be difficult and uncomfortable for academics. We want the opportunity to provide background on an issue, to offer the evidence that leads to the position we are endorsing, and to offer the appropriate cautions and limitations about the evidence we are citing" (pp. 414-415).

Like most of the other career paths shared in this volume, working with policy makers brings its own unique set of costs and benefits. The costs include significant time investment and sacrifices in other arenas, such as in research and personal time. Further there is no guarantee that policy makers will heed the advice of academics who make such investments; their efforts may be unsuccessful, even ignored. However, the benefits of such endeavors—such as the broadening of one's views of other dis-

ciplines and the increased likelihood that one's academic career will "make a difference" in the work and lives of others in the larger society—seem worth some risk.

For academics who may be called on to play a role in policy making, Sackett provides a fascinating look at the nature of this path. He also identifies outside source material and provides sufficient insights from his own experience to guarantee that those who choose this path will not be left on their own to muddle through the experience.

42 Working With Policy Makers

Paul R. Sackett

Over the past decade, I have found myself involved in working with policy makers and attempting to influence public policy in a number of different contexts. My background is in industrial and organizational psychology, and a considerable amount of my research has focused on personnel selection issues; my involvement with public policy is an outgrowth of my work in this domain. I spent several years serving on a National Academy of Sciences committee charged with evaluating the controversial practice of race-based adjustment of scores on employment tests. As a result of my work on integrity in the workplace, I was asked to provide input as the U.S. Congress considered the possibility of legislation to restrict the use of paper-and-pencil integrity tests. I was asked by the American Psychological Association to testify before a congressional committee about Goals 2000: The Educate America Act, which called for the creation of a system of workplace skills assessments. As an officer of the Society for Industrial and Organizational Psychology, I have met with representatives of federal agencies to discuss proposed interpretations of employment-related legislation, such as the Americans with Disabilities Act and the Civil Rights Act of 1991. In this same context, I have been involved in preparing letters and position papers about proposed legislation and interpretive guidelines.

The examples outlined above illustrate a variety of mechanisms for input into public policy. They vary on a number of dimensions, one of which is the basis for participation in the policy process. The above examples reflect two bases: content expertise and formal role within an organization with interests in an issue (i.e., president of a professional society). A second dimension is how participation is initiated, ranging from self-initiation based on a decision that a particular policy issue is important to you personally or to an organization for which you speak to reacting to a request for input from a third party (e.g., a federal agency inviting you personally or inviting an organization for which you speak to offer input). A third dimension is time duration, ranging from being allotted 5 minutes for testimony during a congressional hearing to being asked to devote large amounts of time over a multiyear period to serving on a national commission studying a policy issue.

My assigned tasks in this chapter are to describe my experiences in working to influence public policy and to reflect on the role of such experiences in an academic career. Work in this domain was not something that I had seen in my future as I began my academic career. As is the case for a great many of the roles those in academic life find themselves thrust into, I had no formal preparation for the kinds of activities outlined above. Perhaps there is some value in my describing my experiences in muddling through. In this essay I will focus on various ways in which academics can influence public policy in areas linked to their professional fields of study. I will not address issues of working to influence policy in areas external to one's professional field (e.g., lobbying your local city council regarding property taxes, or writing to your state legislators encouraging their financial support for your university).

Serving on a National Commission on a Public Policy Issue

In 1987 I was invited to serve on a National Academy of Sciences committee to study employment testing practices in the U.S. Employment Service (USES). USES operates as a government-supported job placement service. About 19 million job seekers register with USES annually; about 7 million receive referrals to employers, and about 3 million are placed annually. At issue were three things. The first was the technical soundness of the General Aptitude Test Battery (GATB) as a device for matching people to jobs. The second was the theory of validity generalization, which USES was proposing as the basis for using the GATB for all jobs in the U.S. economy. The third was USES's practice of converting raw scores to percentile scores within an applicant's racial/ethnic group as a means of eliminating the adverse impact on protected groups that is found when raw scores are used.

Controversy over this practice of score adjustment led to the commissioning of a study of the issue by the National Academy of Sciences. Established by congressional charter in 1863, the NAS has a mandate to advise the federal government on scientific and technical matters. When a policy issue with scientific underpinnings leads to the commissioning of a study, the NAS assembles a committee of highly regarded scholars to study and report on the issue.

The strategy of the NAS is to assemble committees with wide-ranging areas of expertise. In the case of this group, labeled the Committee on the GATB, individuals with backgrounds in economics, history, law, sociology, education, statistics, and psychology were included. Committee members serve as individuals—that is, they do not represent specific organizations—and they serve without compensation. There is a conflict-of-interest review at the beginning of a committee's work in which members must certify that they do not have any a priori commitments to particular points of view and that there are no impediments to their endorsing whatever conclusion the committee's work leads to.

Let me offer a number of observations about the process of working on the GATB committee. First, I was immediately struck by the potential consequences of the committee's work. Here I was, toiling away in my academic job. I hoped that my writing and teaching would touch and influence a number of lives, but I recognized that progress is slow and I had learned to take comfort in "little victories." I was pleased when a fellow academic reported being influenced by something I wrote. I took pride in evidence that a student had made significant progress in his or her personal or professional development as a result of interactions with me. But suddenly I was looking at a different type of impact. Some 3 million individuals were placed in jobs annually by USES; to use or not use the GATB in screening candidates for jobs and to apply or not apply race-based score adjustment were decisions that could affect the lives and employment opportunities of very large numbers of people.

Second, I felt a staggering sense of responsibility as the committee began meeting. There was no safety in numbers: I was the sole academically based industrial/organizational psychologist on the committee, and was regularly asked to characterize the knowledge base of I/O psychology on a particular topic, or to explain the perspectives and underlying assumptions of the field.

Third, working with the committee members was alternately extremely stimulating and extremely frustrating. Without exception, the committee members were top-flight scholars—

sharp, articulate, and ready to challenge anything they disagreed with. However, the disciplinary differences were such that we often found ourselves not communicating well. We had to spend a lot of time developing a common vocabulary and bringing everyone up to speed on the issues under discussion. We all viewed issues through our own disciplinary filters, often without clearly recognizing that we were doing so. For example, I recall one committee member arguing that the GATB was clearly lacking sufficient validity for us to endorse its use, because the correlations between the GATB and job performance were lower than the correlations between scholastic aptitude tests and academic performance. That committee member had developed rules of thumb for evaluating validity evidence in the education context, and applied them uncritically to the employment context. Learning to recognize the impact of my disciplinary filter was, for me, one of the most useful outcomes of serving on the committee.

Fourth, serving on this committee took a very large amount of time. We met four times a year, usually for 2-3 days, but with a full 5-day meeting in summer. Add to this the actual work of the committee, which in my case included a reanalysis of the database of about 700 validity studies of the GATB, and I estimate that I devoted 30 workdays per year to this project. The question is, What gives way to permit this amount of time to be devoted to such a project? The options are reduced involvement in teaching, research, university service, consulting, or extrawork activities (you know, those nonessential things, like family and sleep). In my case, I had already made as large a dent in extrawork time as I was willing to make by taking on the editorship of the journal *Personnel Psychology,* which I was trying to edit during evenings and weekends. I ended up curtailing my consulting activities and cutting back my research. I think I can say in all honesty that my motivations at the time were altruistic: The issue was clearly important and the potential consequences high.

At the time, I did not view agreeing to serve as an investment in my future. In retrospect, I see that there have been a variety of consequences from my working on this project. It got me deeper into issues of the trade-off between productivity and diversity in selection decisions, and influenced my subsequent research. The exposure to ways of thinking beyond that of the

discipline in which I was trained has had a profound influence on the ways in which I now approach problems. I discovered that the GATB database that I reanalyzed for this project contained data that could be used to address a number of research questions beyond the scope of the GATB committee's mission, and I have now published five journal articles that make use of different aspects of this database.

Other consequences have been less pleasant, though not unexpected. The committee's position supporting score adjustment was controversial, and the report was widely praised in some quarters and roundly condemned in others. Now, I don't mind controversy; in fact, I relish it. I've long taken the view that the worst thing that can happen is that no one cares about your work; that your work is objectionable to some is a sign that you're doing something interesting. By taking a public stance on a controversial topic, however, I did end up straining relationships with some colleagues who disagreed with the perspective taken by the committee.

Congressional Testimony

In sharp contrast to the multiyear commitment entailed in serving on a national commission on a public policy issue is the opportunity to present testimony before a congressional committee. To illustrate, I will describe my experiences in representing the American Psychological Association (APA) in testifying before the House Subcommittee on Elementary, Secondary and Vocational Education regarding Goals 2000: The Educate America Act, which was enacted in April 1994. This bill called for the creation of new systems to assess workplace skills, and thus groups such as APA, with interests in testing and assessment issues, were concerned about the content of the bill.

APA employs a number of staff members to monitor legislative developments, to lobby legislators on issues relevant to psychology, and to seek opportunities for formal testimony on bills relevant to psychology. It is common for congressional committees to hold public hearings on bills under consideration, and interested groups and individuals seek time slots in these hearings. Advance notice is often very limited; in this case APA received 4 days' notice that the association had been allotted 5 minutes to testify.

I had served as chair of APA's Committee on Psychological Tests and Assessments and was currently president of APA Division 14—the Society for Industrial and Organizational Psychology. In these roles I was familiar with the pending legislation and was seen by APA staff as a credible spokesperson on the issue. Thus I was approached and asked if I could clear my schedule on short notice to prepare and deliver testimony. I agreed to do so, and spent a weekend in the office writing and faxing draft after draft of testimony back and forth with APA staff members. The written version of congressional testimony is part of the formal record, and so must be carefully crafted.

We had a number of key messages we needed to deliver, including a call for requiring that assessment systems developed under the act comply with professional testing and assessment standards. The most controversial and sensitive issue revolved around language in early drafts of the bill mandating that assessment systems developed under the act be free of adverse impact. We argued that the bill should instead mandate valid measurement, and that if there are inequities in our society, they will be reflected in the outcomes of the assessment and can serve as the basis for identifying deficiencies in achievement.

The procedure for the public hearing is imposing. A fixed block of time is set aside for the hearing. The individuals testifying are seated at a table in the center of the chamber; the members of the House Subcommittee are seated behind an elevated partition, so that they are looking down from on high at those who speak. Each speaker is given 5 minutes, and time limits are relentlessly enforced using a small "traffic light": When the light turns red, your time is up.

The testimony itself isn't the hard part; by the time it is delivered it's been well rehearsed and carefully timed. The challenging part comes after each of four to six presenters has delivered his or her prepared testimony. The members of the committee are then each given 5 minutes to question any of the presenters. After I testified, many of the questions were addressed to me, and I found myself trying to respond clearly, concisely, and without jargon to a variety of "what if" questions: What would happen if the bill were passed without language requiring that assessments be valid? What would happen if assessments turned out to produce adverse impact? I had tried to anticipate possible questions, as had the APA staff, and I had rehearsed answers to each. Some of the questions I received were anticipated; others were not.

I believe that I acquitted myself well, and I attribute that to a combination of the degree of preparation in the days before the testimony, my years of working in the content domain of the bill, and my years of struggling to become an effective classroom presenter of complex material. I would have been much less effective had any of these three been lacking. I note that in this case I was able to fill two roles: spokesperson for APA and content expert. It is not uncommon for someone serving primarily a spokesperson role (e.g., an officer of an organization) to offer testimony and yet have content expertise going no deeper than a pretestimony briefing by staff. Handling questions under those circumstances clearly involves a markedly different skill set, as the individual giving testimony is not equipped to respond to technically oriented questions.

Writing to and Meeting With Policy Makers

Over the past several years there have been a number of occasions on which I have been asked to draft letters or position statements on behalf of APA or the Society for Industrial and Organizational Psychology. A common context is that of proposed legislation or proposed interpretive guidelines to accompany legislation, where there is a public call for comment from interested groups or individuals.

Writing to legislators about proposed legislation requires a style dramatically different from the scientific writing style to which we've become accustomed. Brevity is seen by those with experience in this area as an absolute necessity in writing to policy makers. The American Psychological Association has a useful publication available titled *Advancing the Science: A Psychologist's Guide to Advocacy,* which advises that letters should be kept to a single page and to a single issue.

Following this advice can be difficult and uncomfortable for academics. We want the opportunity to provide background on an issue, to offer the evidence that leads to the position we are endorsing, and to offer the appropriate cautions and limitations about the evidence we are citing. Yet all that you can do in a brief letter is to state the nature of your concern and offer the briefest of explanations. If you are writing in support of proposed legislation, your task is easier than if you are writing to oppose. In a supporting letter, your primary purpose is to encourage a legislator to support a particular course of action. In a letter opposing proposed legislation, you need to state what it is you object to, the reason for the objection, and suggested alternative language that would be acceptable.

Unsolicited letters to policy makers are constrained by these demands for brevity, but you have more flexibility in situations in which you are invited to offer written policy advice. For example, the Equal Employment Opportunity Commission was given the charge of preparing interpretive guidelines to accompany the Civil Rights Act of 1991, and EEOC staff contacted the American Psychological Association to request advice as to the interpretation of the act. In response, APA's Division 14, the Society for Industrial and Organizational Psychology, developed a four-page position paper on the topic. Although brevity remains a concern in such situations, there is more opportunity to develop ideas and lines of argument. Clarity of thoughts and expression and the use of clear, jargon-free language become central concerns.

A variant on the above theme of influencing policy through written communication is the opportunity to meet one-on-one or in small groups with policy makers. I view this as requiring the same skills as congressional testimony, as discussed above, but without the formality of the public setting. Being effective in this setting requires advance preparation so that you can make a clear statement of your position and have the depth of knowledge and clarity of thought you need to respond to questions and the ability to express key ideas without resorting to technical jargon.

Impact on Academic Careers

Some of the topics treated in this volume are part of the common experience that many, if not all, academics share as they progress through their careers. Other topics involve roles in which relatively few find themselves, such as dean or journal editor. Involvement in public policy falls into this latter category: It certainly is not part of the standard course of a career. The likelihood of an individual's becoming involved in public policy work is linked to a number of factors. The first is the development of a scholarly reputation in an area with public policy implications. This strikes me as hard to plan in advance in many cases; it is often hard to project at the beginning of a career when you are choosing where to carve out a research niche which topics are likely to be the focus of public policy attention a decade down the road. Another factor is involvement in professional organizations, which may lead to election or appointment to positions that place one in a spokesperson role for an organization. Service in such roles is typically limited to specific terms, and it may be a matter of chance as to whether policy issues of importance to an organization surface during a given individual's term of office. Thus I see it as likely that involvement in public policy will be an unplanned aspect of an academic career.

Should one seek out such opportunities if it proves possible to do so? Personally, I've found my public policy involvement to have been extraordinarily valuable. First, involvement with policy issues that can affect very large numbers of people has led me to pay much more attention to the potential consequences of various lines of research that I'm considering. Although I pursue research questions for a variety of reasons, including at times pure and simple curiosity, I find that I give more and more emphasis to the potential breadth of application of research findings.

Second, work in the policy area has led me to a greatly increased knowledge of and appreciation for scholarly disciplines other than my own, and to greater insight into my own discipline. Serving on an interdisciplinary commission to examine a public policy issue forces you out of the comforts of working with and talking to people quite similar to you in perspective, and forces you to figure out how and why other disciplines see the world in different ways. Few other events force you to work as hard to think thoroughly, clearly, and precisely about the knowledge base of your field, its implicit assumptions, and its limitations (preparing for cross-examination in the courtroom in an expert witness context is another).

Third, I've learned to place a great premium on economy of expression and the avoidance of unnecessarily technical language. At one level, these issues seem so obvious that one might assert that there's little value in discussing them here. Yet my experience is that many prominent scholars prove ineffective in settings such as those described in this chapter for precisely these reasons. We can all nod our heads at the notion that jargon should be avoided, but I believe that it is easy to become so caught up in our discipline that we fail to recognize the idiosyncratic ways words are used in that context. The way the field of personnel selection uses the term *criterion* is a classic example. This field uses the term *predictor* to refer to information available prior to hire that can be used as the basis for a prediction of some future workplace behavior, and *criterion* to refer to that future workplace behavior that we're interested in predicting. Yet in common usage, *criteria* is used to refer to what this field calls *predictors,* as in

"The criteria I use for screening applicants include their grade point averages and their work histories." I find myself thinking carefully about word choices and terminology, and try to put myself in the position of someone encountering the concepts I'm talking about for the first time.

Finally, what do people hope to accomplish through careers in academia? Although some are just trying to make a living, many have larger aspirations. Put simply, we want to make a difference. We want to leave the world a better place than we found it as a result of the work we do; for many, these same aspirations apply to family and community roles as well as to work roles. Part of the appeal of work related to influencing public policy is the potential scope of impact of these activities; this is work that can make a difference. Thus when I'm asked to donate time and effort to a particular piece of policy work, these concerns about being of use come into play, and I view it as a privilege to participate.

Pause Point 3:
Another Look at Integrating Work and Nonwork Lives

As scholars of organizations, we are sometimes more sophisticated about the management of organizations than we are about the management of our own lives. In striving for success we somehow find disaster. One contributor to this phenomenon is the blind pursuit of some single success principle.

Robert E. Quinn, Regina M. O'Neill,
and Gelaye Debebe (p. 421)

These aggravations illustrate the tension between home and work—a tension that can't be escaped even if one stays in the same place, elects not to marry, and has no children. I argue, however, that management scholars must seek this tension. We study human organizations. Most of us are too often removed from our subject of study as it is. Focusing on professional life alone makes it highly unlikely that we will understand the human content of management.

Anne Sigismund Huff (p. 429)

Diverging from a number of nontraditional paths in the preceding section, we have once again reached a pause point in our journey. Here we should pause, take the pulse of our trip, and decide what, if anything, must be done to bring us back on track. At this point, we reexamine the delicate balance between our work and nonwork lives through the lenses of those in midcareer. It is clear to those of us who have reached midcareer that being an academic for a lengthy period of time does not lessen the importance of periodically

monitoring and reassessing the balance between our professional and personal lives. As activities change over time, the balance between them also shifts. It becomes all too easy to realize with a start one day that one's work life or one's nonwork life is not particularly satisfying and has not been for some time.

In this section, two essays address the topic of balancing work and nonwork lives from a midcareer vantage point. In the first essay, Bob Quinn, Regina O'Neill, and Gelaye Debebe address the issue of balance using a different methodology from that appearing in most of essays in this volume. Concerned that academics tend to recommend their own preferred methods of work and life as the best or only ways when asked, Quinn and his colleagues chose to survey a group of academics working in the administrative sciences. They asked participants to identify the primary sources of satisfaction and dissatisfaction in academic life and to discuss the ways they allocate time to various work and nonwork activities. The results provide some interesting information on the primary source of satisfaction for many academics—namely, engaging in tasks felt to be consistent with one's personal values and those that require ongoing or continuous learning. Quinn, O'Neill, and Debebe's findings also showed much consensus among survey participants concerning the demotivating experience of having to spend more and more time engaging in tasks other than research. As one commented, "The one activity upon which you are most centrally evaluated is the one activity for which there is no scheduled time" (p. 423).

Differences among respondents concerning their approaches to work are also noteworthy. Returning to a theme mentioned by Dutton, Bartunek, and Gersick in Chapter 24, some academics prefer to choose their research topics based on critical detached analysis, whereas others are shaped more by their emotional engagement with particular topics. For example: "I feel my best work is done when I am least happy.... The unhappy frame of mind is good for intellectual work because it is critical, self-critical. It is not exuberant. It does not get carried away with things" (p. 423). In contrast: "When the right criteria come together, I get very excited and it gives me the energy to go on. I need to be energized and excited" (p. 424). Similarly, some participants said they prefer a theoretical ba-

sis for their research, whereas others prefer more inductive and experiential approaches. Finally, some participants reported they actively maintain sharp differentiation between their work and nonwork lives, whereas others clearly hold a rather seamless view of the interconnections between work and nonwork activities. For instance, one participant noted: "There is some value, it seems to me, in divorcing the personal and professional sides of yourself. Throw yourself into work, work very hard while you are at work, and have other interests outside, so that when you go home, there's pleasure waiting for you there too of another kind" (p. 426). Another, on the other hand, had this to say: "Think of every day as having 24 hours; don't think of dividing up your time for school or personal life. Don't cut it up like that, just think of you, and what you want to accomplish" (p. 426).

Quinn, O'Neill, and Debebe's essay provides an interesting look at how academics at midcareer view their work and nonwork activities. Although comfortable with the ability of contributors to be personally informative in their accounts rather than overly prescriptive, we welcome the triangulation this methodology adds to the volume.

In the second essay, Anne Huff recalls her surprise at realizing, some 10 years into her academic career, that she was not devoting the same level of attention to her current occupation as she did to her first, as a manager in the private sector. As a result, both her productivity and her satisfaction were diminished. She also reports being startled at the recognition that a similar approach was needed in managing her personal life, that a satisfying and fulfilling personal life would not simply emerge without some systematic planning and management activities on her part: "Having an agenda at work gave me a chance to focus and develop a line of inquiry through to publication. My personal life didn't have comparable 'shape' and was languishing as a result" (p. 432).

Huff then offers a series of guidelines for managing the professional life, her own approach to her professional tasks, inviting readers to consider whether the suggestions may be generalizable to their own situations. The companion set of suggestions she proposes for the management of a satisfying and fulfilling private life are equally powerful. As she notes in the quotation that opens this introduction, without the insights gained from our personal lives, our professional contributions to the understanding and explanation of human behavior in organizations are certain to be less valuable. Finally, she provides an important caveat to readers regarding the guidelines offered; specifically, she warns that the dangers of overmanaging our professional and personal arenas may exceed those of not managing them at all.

Both of these essays converge around the importance of actively managing the balance between work and nonwork activities, suggesting that the abdication of this responsibility is likely to yield dissatisfaction, if not disaster in the long term. Further, the authors seem to concur with the observations made by contributors Montagno (Chapter 34) and Rynes (Chapter 35) in describing their experiences as full professors—namely, that the academic life is a privileged one that eliminates all major obstacles to self-actualization except perhaps the most critical, our own indecision about which path to take.

43 Confronting the Tensions in an Academic Career

Robert E. Quinn

Regina M. O'Neill

Gelaye Debebe

Once there was a panel of significant people who were asked to address the topic of success in professional life. They had much wisdom to impart and the session went very well. Toward the end, a young member of the audience raised his hand and asked about the integration of professional and personal life. There was a hesitation, and then members of the panel shared some useful advice on the topic. Afterward, one of the members of the panel was talking to a close colleague. The panel member indicated that the last question had been very sobering, and when his colleague asked why, he replied, "I looked down the table and noted that everyone there had either just completed a divorce, was in the middle of a divorce, or was in a battle with alcoholism."

As scholars of organizations, we are sometimes more sophisticated about the management of organizations than we are about the management of our own lives. In striving for success we somehow find disaster. One contributor to this phenomenon is the blind pursuit of some single success principle. In our field we have long been suspicious of literature suggesting that there is one best way to do something in the managerial world. Yet imagine the following scenario:

A group of four academics are asked to come together and give advice to doctoral students about to enter the dissertation process. The discussion begins, and Professor A suggests that there are several key characteristics of a successful dissertation. Professor B agrees, but adds two additional characteristics. Professor C takes issue with a characteristic suggested by both A and B. Professor D then suggests an entirely different perspective. The discussion heats up. Two hours later, the meeting ends.

From this scenario we learn three lessons. Lesson 1 is that if you ask an academic for advice, the academic will give you advice. Lesson 2 is that no group of academics is likely to agree in terms of advice given. Lesson 3 is that each academic will feel strongly about his or her own prescription. Why? Because each has an implicit "one best way" theory of action. When asked to describe the successful dissertation process, for example, each academic describes his or her own life experience. Each one did a dissertation, and each one succeeded; each one knows how a dissertation should be done. Yet all do not describe the same path to success.

This process tends to extend to nearly all issues of career development. Our colleagues, who do not believe in one-best-way management prescriptions, do not hesitate to give one-best-way career prescriptions. Such well-meaning guidelines may actually be dangerous.

The objective of this chapter is to make readers aware of the need to search for alternative prescriptions and to choose those that best fit themselves. Our method is to surface a few of the key tensions that readers might face and help them to see the contrasting alternatives that are available. In order to do this, we interviewed 14 tenured faculty members from various branches of the administrative sciences at the University of Michigan. Our respondents were from several disciplines, including organizational behavior, psychology, sociology, political science, and nursing; 64% were male and 36% were female.

Our purpose in doing these interviews was not intended to be scientific. We sought neither to build nor to test theory. Our purpose was simply to surface a few illustrations of our thesis. We asked the respondents to share their insights on three issues: integration of work and self, integration of personal and professional life, and the management of professional relationships. We then analyzed the interview data, looking for common and contrasting perspectives on the three issues.

In analyzing the data, we looked for commonalities as well as tensions among the comments made by these tenured faculty members. In particular, we searched for tensions where at least two different people clearly disagreed on how to manage various aspects of an academic career. We do not seek to make a comprehensive statement of all tensions in the career process, but simply to illustrate the need to apply complex thinking to the issue of career choices. We bring these tensions forth because the fact that there are many discrepancies suggests that these opposite perspectives are worthy of consideration by individuals contemplating their academic careers. Our purpose is not to give prescriptions, but to surface some of the issues that every young professional should consider. Rather, we want readers to consider carefully these opposing poles to try to determine where they fall along each continuum. Our hope is that readers will find the contrasts we have identified to be informative and thought-provoking, and that these contrasts will serve as reference points throughout their academic careers. We also hope that consideration and discussion of these issues will lead some individuals to greater insights, more intelligent choices, and more satisfying life paths.

This chapter is organized around commonalities and contrasts. The commonalities we found among our respondents include the alignment of work and core values, the ability to overcome failure and blockage, and the demands of multiple roles. The topics on which our respondents had differing opinions included how best to conduct research, how the research process is viewed, how research and applied work should be connected, the motives that drive scholars, the level of interdependence among scholars, mentoring relationships, and the boundaries between their personal and professional lives. We hope that in reading about these differences, readers are provoked to think about their career strategies in complex ways. To assist readers in this process, we conclude the essay with a set of questions designed to stimulate such thinking.

Commonalities

People find meaning in their work when that work is aligned with their core values (Hackman & Oldham, 1980). Alignment brings meaning, and meaning brings energy. When there is no alignment, people tend to become alienated from their tasks and disengage from their work. In considering the integration of work and self, we begin with several points of near consensus.

Our interviews suggest that academics are most happy when they are learning new things. That happiness intensifies when the learning is relevant to key issues of intellectual interest.

Happiness turns to agony when investments fail to bear fruit. This is particularly manifest when major research efforts stall or collapse, or when papers or presentations of central personal importance fail to excite others and are rejected in some fashion. It is important to realize that these two sources of agony are experienced with some regularity by even the most well-known scholars. The capacity to live with and overcome failure is a crucial element of academic success.

A second source of difficulty is the frustration that is associated with the lack of progress in generating new knowledge. Some people reach periods when they feel blocked and frustrated. Sometimes the block has psychological roots, and sometimes it is embedded in the social system. In the latter case, because of social and political pressures, people often find themselves involved in projects they simply do not care about.

Social and political pressures are also manifest in terms of multiple role demands. Nearly all of our respondents referred to the difficulty of meeting a complex array of expectations while also finding the time to execute the research process successfully. As one person indicated, "The one activity upon which you are most centrally evaluated is the one activity for which there is no scheduled time." The pressure always is to engage in tasks other than research, and the pressure increases over the course of a career. As another person said, "The more senior I become, the more administration I do, and I doubt a dean does more administration than I sometimes have to do." Like managers who must get their most important tasks done on the margins of their schedules (Mintzberg, 1973), academics must also fight to find the time to do the task they consider most important. Choices around time allocation are critical determinants of satisfaction in both personal life and professional life. It is here that the most precious resource is allocated. The problem is that no one prescription can best serve to guide the allocation process. Differences must be taken into account.

Differences

Planning/Adaptation

Some people have a mechanistic view of the research process and emphasize a rational plan-

ning approach to a research career. They have values that lead them to be interested in given subjects. They identify sets of issues to be addressed and then lay out plans of execution that may extend for a decade. In contrast, others see the process in a much more organic way. A person has values and interests, then encounters opportunities and barriers, and then makes choices. These choices shape a process of exploration and learning. The process is not very predictable, but it is possible to look back and impose a linear story line on what has transpired. These people believe that reality is messy and that continuous adaptation is critical to success.

This differentiation between planning and adaptation suggests that people act according to their need for and beliefs about control and interaction. Some feel much better when they have a sense of complete control over their long-term direction, whereas others feel better when they are continually considering new relationships, projects, and ideas. Some seem to be rational convergers and others organic divergers.

Critical Analysis/ Emotional Engagement

Some people see the research process as an exercise in detached objectivity. The phenomenon under study should be an object distant from the self. The task is a highly rigorous cognitive analysis that is free of emotion. Consider the following illustration:

I feel my best work is done when I am least happy. Happiness is not necessarily a desirable thing. The unhappy frame of mind is good for intellectual work because it is critical, self-critical. It is not exuberant. It does not get carried away with things.

Other people seem to need to embrace psychologically the phenomenon they study. Emotion is a very important part of the research process. Excitement and happiness provide energy to endure the pain of rigorous analysis. Contrast the following statement to the one above:

And, when I start to futz with some idea, concept, or project, I'm looking for certain things to come together. It may be, for example, a question that is both significant and answerable. When the right criteria come together, I get very excited and it gives me the energy to go on. I need to be energized and excited.

Theory/Action

This differentiation is in some ways similar to the above-discussed split between detached analysis and emotional engagement, but it has more to do with the nature of the work that is done. Some people prefer to do work that is disconnected from the real world. It is a purely intellectual activity. It may be highly theoretical and abstract. Such people seem to have little difficulty in splitting their work from the world of action. They are often content to have their work read by only a handful of qualified people. Although some people do actually split their work from their values, they tend to experience some internal conflict in doing so. Consider the following comments of one respondent:

A lot of my work is highly intellectual and theoretical, and that work does not connect with my values except insofar as my values are intellectual. I feel a little guilty about that side of my work since it has so little direct relevance to the real world, and I do have values that say that the world is in bad shape, and I believe it is incumbent on people who have advantages to help out in some way.

Other people have a need to integrate theory and action. They seem to have a lower tolerance for pure abstraction and seek to be more inductive and experiential. They seek to make sense of the world immediately around them. They are usually anxious to have an impact on many people. Contrast the following statement with the one above:

I need to bridge the theoretical and the applied. I find stimulation in applying ideas, in action learning. I feel best in moving from the concrete to the conceptual. I also feel better when I am having an impact. I need to feel like I am making a difference in the world, making it a better place. I feel like my

work is most worthwhile when it bridges the gap.

Extrinsically Driven/ Intrinsically Driven

For some of our interviewees, the starting point for developing a logic of strategic action is the long-term strategic objective. If the goal of the young scholar is to get tenure, then he or she must identify the most likely process for getting there. Given that the determining factor is publication in good journals, then the scholar must ask what the gatekeepers want and then practice deferred gratification in a disciplined effort to please the gatekeepers. For 6 years, you do what you must to get tenure:

Well, the main advice I would give to young scholars is to do what they need to do to become old scholars. . . . I think that young scholars ought to forget their own values for the most part and just do the work that will get them tenure. Now I would not say that in order to get tenure they have to go rape and pillage and murder . . . they just have to get some articles published in journals and it might not be exactly what they love to do best, but nevertheless the thing to do is to get that done.

A contrasting perspective begins with the question, Who am I? The logic of strategic action starts with the clarification of personal values. If an individual searches deeply within, he or she will find a unique vision, an innovative contribution he or she can make to the world. This perspective assumes that the best work is innovative, that it diverges from the expectations that the field has etched into the heads of the gatekeepers. Because the work is surprising and of quality, it causes the gatekeepers to value it even more highly than the expected incremental contributions. It begins by finding vision within, exercising disciplined faith in the vision, and then sacrificing to deliver a product of high impact:

My advice is to interconnect the personal and professional as closely as you can. And then look for what feeds you and try to do work in that stream because good work takes a lot of effort, a lot of faith. If you do not do this, I think the quality is lower and I think that you will have a harder time persisting in the face of setbacks.

Independence/Mutuality

People have different perspectives on interdependence in the research process. Some tend toward independence. These people may prefer to work alone, and may be concerned about the need for a unique professional identity. People with such an orientation are likely to be very careful in approaching the formation of a research relationship:

Be very selective about what you get involved with because every project lasts a couple years. . . . Nothing is done easily in this world, everything takes a couple years, and you're just going to get sucked into this world of doing somebody else's work.

In contrast, others are proactive in looking for working relationships. They sometimes seek to create communities of research activity. They tend not to see the academic life as inherently lonely, and strive for a synergy in which the parts are greater than the whole:

My best work has never been individual work. I love relationships when there is complementarity of skills, trust, and commonly produced output. Credit doesn't matter so much when you are both doing better than either of you could do individually.

Positive/Negative Mentoring Experiences

The above-described difference between independence and mutuality is probably deeply rooted in personality and also influenced by career stage. It may, however, also be influenced by early professional experiences.

In the professional realm, relationships are very important, particularly hierarchical relationships, and career success is often tied to mentoring relationships. Our interviewees tended to agree on the desired characteristics of a mentor. As one person suggested, "You need some-

one to demand that you do more than you think you're capable of doing; on the other hand you need someone who supports you, loves you, tells you you can do it." Unfortunately, there is not a heavy supply of such talented mentors, and young professionals have a variety of experiences with the mentoring process. In fact, the same person described two completely different experiences in two mentoring relationships with different people. About one mentor:

He was the one who patted me on the back and said don't worry, you're going to make it, you're going to be okay. You need to publish in these journals, forget about these journals. You need to do this kind of stuff at the Academy. . . . He gave me good advice.

In contrast, about the other:

Never have I had an experience in my life where I felt more worthless, more undervalued, more ignorant, and so on. To this day, I feel subordinate, I feel incompetent, I feel undervalued, I feel defensive, I feel like I have to protect myself, I feel like I'm not, I can't really be a person—to this very day.

Divergent Life Domains/ Seamless Life Domains

People differ in how they think about structuring their professional lives. Some create definite boundaries between the professional and the personal. One person, for example, described the need to separate from the painful experience of professional life and find support in a highly differentiated domain:

Because the academic world is so cruel, you have to have someplace to retreat. The pressures are enormous and there's very little warm and cuddly positive feedback. If you do not have any other way to get a boost in self-esteem, it can be pretty rough.

People who take this perspective tend to believe that there is value in separation and often advise young people to structure the split consciously into their lives:

There is some value, it seems to me, in divorcing the personal and professional sides of yourself. Throw yourself into work, work very hard while you are at work, and have other interests outside, so that when you go home, there's pleasure waiting for you there too of another kind, relating to family and friends and hobbies that don't have anything to do with work.

For some people, particularly men with relatively traditional marital relationships, it is easier to blur the boundaries between the professional and personal domains. Some reported relatively seamless relationships:

I don't have many activities other than what I do professionally, so personal life/professional life defined differently in terms of activities would be indistinguishable. Weekends you would be just as likely to find me reading, puzzling over stuff, as you would during weekdays. Nights, as much as early mornings.

The people who hold this perspective have very different advice for young professionals on the idea of separating personal and professional activities.

Think of every day as having 24 hours; don't think of dividing up your time for school or personal life. Don't cut it up like that, just think of you, and what you want to accomplish. . . . I really believe that young people coming along would do well to think . . . there is no such thing as a separation of personal and professional work.

Conclusion

Young scholars embarking upon the beginnings of an academic career are certain to encounter many important and challenging issues. Clearly, some of these issues will reflect common pressures of the profession that all scholars face. Others will be unique. Moreover, these issues are likely to change continually and to be redefined throughout the course of a career. In coping, each person must take a critical look at him- or herself, seek to know who he or she is, and decide what is most important. Each person must find his or her own way to the meaningful academic life.

The idea of each person finding his or her own way to success is very similar to the idea of individual performance myths explored by Quinn, Spreitzer, and Fletcher (1993). They argue that people have myths about their individual need to perform and that these myths drive key decisions. In a constantly changing environment, people must construct new myths as appropriate. Construction of new myths requires action under uncertainty, and action under uncertainty requires courage. To find meaning, each person must take the "hero's journey" by engaging in the unknown, overcoming barriers, and experiencing personal growth. Each individual's success story is consequently his or hers alone.

All young scholars are likely to need very different things in order to find success. We think it is helpful for each person to identify the critical steps that he or she will want to take on his or her own path. To help young scholars identify salient issues, we have developed the following set of questions. We encourage our readers to attempt to extend the list.

- What conditions stimulate you to do your best work? When are you most happy and most frustrated in your work? What is it about that situation that makes you happy or frustrated?
- Given your unique personal situation, what challenges do you expect to face in finding life balance? Do you have a specific plan to manage these challenges or will you wait to see what happens and then decide what to do?
- Do you prefer to do work that is detached from you and is purely an intellectual exercise or are you happiest when your work is something you can embrace closely?
- What are your long-term goals? Is it more important for you to attain tenure regardless of the research stream or would you prefer that you do research that you find personally important?
- Do you do your best work independently, or as part of a collaborative effort? To what activities and/or relationships do you attribute your prior successes?
- What expectations do you have about professional relationships? What have your experi-

ences with professional relationships been thus far? Have those experiences influenced your willingness to be involved in future professional relationships?

- What activities and relationships in your professional and personal lives are the most important to you? How much time would you like to spend on each? Would you prefer that your professional and personal lives remain separate, or will you be happiest if they are highly integrated?

These questions cover a wide range of topics, but each person would do well to assess them all. This set of questions is not meant to be exhaustive. We encourage readers to meet with others and attempt to extend the list. Our hope is that young scholars will find such questions to be informative, thought-provoking, and painfully helpful.

The many issues and challenges of managing the academic life may seem daunting to those embarking on the beginnings of an academic career. However, we believe that these challenges are balanced by many rewards and benefits. Consider the following comments made by one of our respondents:

I think academic life is a privileged life, and I am either amused or outraged, depending on my mood, at my colleagues who have somehow persuaded themselves, and intend to persuade others, that this is a burdened, difficult kind of career. Few people can earn a living doing things that are so close to their major life interests. Instead, they end up pouring their time and their energy into tasks defined by others. As academics, we have a high degree of choice. We ought to be profoundly grateful.

References

Hackman, J. R., & Oldham, G. R. (1980). *Work redesign.* Reading, MA: Addison-Wesley.

Mintzberg, H. (1973). *The nature of managerial work.* New York: Harper & Row.

Quinn, R. E., Spreitzer, G. M., & Fletcher, J. (1993). *Excavating the paths to meaning, renewal, and empowerment: A typology of individual high performance myths* (Working paper). Ann Arbor: University of Michigan.

44 Professional and Personal Life

Anne Sigismund Huff

I am drafting this essay (later than promised) on my new computer, which is on my lap in an empty home office pending the installation of new carpet. Our son, David, and two new friends may be wrestling into trouble downstairs in another empty room—so I'm keeping one ear open to the need for intervention. We bought the laptop to keep our work progressing even though we were moving this summer. It hasn't really helped. With new WordPerfect 6.0 installed, I had to call a friend just to create a new document. And a few of the keys are not where I expect, so I'm making more typos than usual. More important, of course, this is only the third time I've turned on this "do your work anywhere" device in the past month.

These aggravations illustrate the tension between home and work—a tension that can't be escaped even if one stays in the same place, elects not to marry, and has no children. I argue, however, that management scholars must seek this tension. We study human organizations. Most of us are too often removed from our subject of study as it is. Focusing on professional life alone makes it highly unlikely that we will understand the human content of manage-

ment. We must—even if we choose quantitative, noninterpretive methods—assume that we need rich personal lives to understand the complications of our subject.

Beyond that, we need rich personal lives to be human ourselves. Academic life can be intensely involving, but it does not ask us to use all of our capabilities. I particularly value my nonacademic activities because of their immediacy and because they make me feel an intensity of emotion that academics rarely delivers. On the other hand, I have not been seriously tempted to leave academia; I would miss the abstract thinking, the teaching opportunities, and many other aspects of this life. No one life seems likely to satisfy any of us; we need to think in portfolio terms. Dichotomizing our choices into the "personal" and the "professional" captures the importance of balancing emotion with abstraction, public with private.

The underlying theme of this essay is that this important equilibrium is unlikely to be achieved without effort. A decade after becoming an academic, I realized with a shock that I wasn't giving my research life the same organizing attention that I'd given the managerial jobs I'd undertaken. I'd assumed without conscious deliberation that I shouldn't manage research—that it should be driven by purer ideals. That attitude clearly undercut my productivity, however, and over the past few years I've been much more careful to think about priorities and support systems. More of my work has found an audience as a result.

In a doctoral seminar last year, I formalized some of these ideas into a brief lecture on improving the chances of getting published. You'll see here the influence of my professional interest in strategy—a discipline that focuses on understanding action in a broader context. Then as I thought about my assignment for this essay, which is to consider the importance of nonacademic life, it occurred to me that my experience with trying to manage research better was also applicable to the question of managing personal life. Once again I'd tacitly assumed it wasn't necessary to manage; once again I was missing things I wanted as a result.

I don't really like the idea of "managing" personal life. The lure of the *non*professional is that it gives me respite from professional life. To introduce the subject of my work is thus an intrusion. But I found it interesting to think about how the advice I'd given to doctoral students wanting to publish fit what I've been trying to achieve in my personal life. Perhaps you'll find something here too, so let me first summarize the lecture.

Getting Published

My advice to doctoral students was phrased in 10 "rules." Because class members had different subject interests and were fairly far along in programs under different advisers, I didn't presume to say anything about the content of their research. These are generic guidelines to increase the probability that they recognize the work they want to do and have the energy to get it done.

1. Choose a setting that values publication. The percentage of ABDs who never get PhDs is amazingly high. I used to wonder why. Now I think that ABDs who leave the university also leave a setting that promotes research in many ways, not all of which they recognize or appreciate. The most important thing about a re-

search university is that it is a setting in which many people are actively trying to generate new knowledge and communicate the results of those efforts to others. Those who move to corporate or other settings find atmospheres that support very different agendas. Even those in intellectually active teaching settings appear to find it difficult to be among a small number trying to test their ideas and put the results in writing; it is very hard to be the only one around you working with an eye toward publication. To finish the dissertation and go on to publish, my best advice is to work in a place where many people publish.

2. Associate with people who publish; observe and learn from them. Form supportive relationships with a few people who will read and respond to your work. Unfortunately, the limited availability of university jobs now makes it impossible for everyone who wants to publish to choose a research-active setting. Wherever one works, however, it is possible to pay attention to people who publish. Reading, attending lectures, going to conferences can all provide exposure to the mind-set that leads to publication. These activities are necessary, but rarely sufficient, to generate publication, however. I think that it is essential to make some personal contacts. Researchers need people who can be counted on to respond to early drafts with criticism, but also with encouragement. New PhDs generally find these supporters among their cohort and with a few mentors, but we never outgrow the need for attention from our colleagues. Without the supportive few, I suspect that observing those who publish from afar will have little effect; a few fellow observers are needed for help and inspiration.

3. Set up daily routines that support writing for publication. People often equate writing with inspiration, and it is certainly true for me that when "the stars are right" the work goes much faster. When the work flows easily, my decision rule is to devote as much time as I possibly can to staying in a writing mode; I make deals for child care, cancel dinners, and so on because I know that I'm making three or four times the amount of progress I can on other days. However, I don't just wait for inspiration to strike. My second decision rule is to do something almost every day to keep close to the writing; if

I'm not "hot," I type tables, write background description, or do something else mechanical. I've kept a backlog of these more easily accomplished tasks that might also lead me back to inspiration ever since I read that Ernest Hemingway always left something easy on his desk at the end of every day, so that he had something to warm up with in the morning. Though my ambitions are a bit less lofty than his were, I too have found that something like checking tense agreement can lead me back into substantive issues.

In addition to arranging the task, I pay attention to time and place. I know, for example, that I do my best work in the morning, and so I try not to teach or make appointments before noon. I've also found that it's usually better to leave the house, *and* my office, in favor of a place that is associated solely with thinking. In fact, the ambience of time and place is even more conducive to my getting work done than the easy task.

4. Plan, establish a calendar, reflect, and update your plan. The larger issue, of course, is to know where one is going. Many papers might be written—which ones should gain one's commitment? I am trying to be more purposeful about such things, and less responsive to immediate opportunities and demands. Lou Pondy used to emphasize that the *ci* root in *decide* means "to cut." Thus *decide* is cousin to *incisor* and *scissor,* and the key part of deciding what to do is deciding what not to do. The more carefully one prunes one's agenda, the more likely it is that one's research will have an impact on the field. It is interesting that we already know how to do this—establish goals, specify alternatives, and so on—but most of us just don't do it often enough.

5. Invest in your career. My doctoral adviser, Sam Doctors, taught me this valuable lesson. He hired assistants with his own money for the projects the university wouldn't support, and he encouraged me to do the same. His advice helped me to buy my own high-speed printer and my own fax machine. My productivity is higher as a result, because I can do work at home, at odd hours, that I otherwise would have to return to the university to accomplish. Convinced that I should invest in my career, I've also had an easier time deciding to attend

interesting but unfunded conferences and to subscribe to new journals.

6. Think about inputs. "Garbage in/garbage out" is a phrase from my student computing training that has stayed with me. For the researcher, the best books, the clearest thinkers, the subtlest arguments are the quality inputs that will improve published output. It's important to be open to a great variety of effort, and it's a good rule of thumb to try to learn from everything, but in a busy world I try to screen toward the things that deserve the greatest attention. I have a small list of people whose work I make a conscious attempt to follow, for example, and a small set of journals that get my greater attention.

7. Rethink, rewrite, put in everything you have. The works that are published are not written, they are rewritten many times before they appear. In the process of drafting, thinking over commentary from colleagues, and submitting to formal review and editorial advice, authors almost always rethink their initial ideas in very basic ways. Those who aim to publish should be aware of this cycle, accept it, and initiate more of it before risking the possibility of rejection under review.

I also think that the objective of rewriting/rethinking should be to say everything one knows about an increasingly well specified subject. I usually have to edit drastically to eliminate many ideas that distract attention from the major trail of thought I'm trying to establish; but that leaves room to elaborate on my major theme. I try to say everything I currently know about that topic, not saving anything for a second paper. The pressure to publish is so great that we are all tempted to make deli slices out of our work, but the papers I want to read, and that I'm more likely to accept as an editor, are far more nourishing. I think the likelihood of publishing is increased when an author follows through on a line of reasoning. Furthermore, I find that my best new ideas grow out of articulating what I now know.

8. Enjoy the process. All this sounds too serious. It's rarely easy to get work published, which makes it even more important to enjoy the tasks involved. A number of people seem to be instrumental in their approach to research, searching for the topics that are currently popular, trying to write the kinds of article they think will most easily be published. One can't totally ignore these issues, but I strongly believe they should be dominated by personal interest, intellectual curiosity, and the insight that comes from experience. Build in pleasure, move toward strength—that's my advice. The energy that flows into the work will keep it moving and ultimately attract others.

9. Celebrate the victories. The time that elapses over the course of thinking of a topic that's worth pursuing, designing the study, gathering the data, analyzing the data, drafting, presentation, redrafting, submission, redrafting, journal acceptance, and final publication is so long that I often feel disconnected from the words that ultimately appear on the printed page, and publication doesn't seem like such a victory. But it is, and so are all the steps along the way. We can keep ourselves publishing, I believe, by staying connected to the work, noting and celebrating these way stations.

10. Choose to do the work. All along I've been talking about doing the work, but it's worth emphasizing that the plan, the investment in a fax machine, the table waiting to be formatted, the champagne waiting to be drunk, all come to naught if we cave in to the many other pressures of life. Early in my career I was often asked to be on affirmative action committees, to serve on student review committees, and so on. Gradually I learned I had to say no to some of these requests if I was to get my own work done. As I've advanced, the requests come more and more frequently and are joined by Cub Scout and other demands from my private life. Most of these calls on my time come from worthwhile tasks that I approve of and want to support, but it's easy to let oneself be "nibbled to death by ducks," in Emerson's words. It takes continuing, very conscious attention to *do the work* that I think I prize so highly. I often tally the hours I spent on publishing-related activities at the end of the day. It's usually a small, sobering number that I achieved only by letting something else remain undone.

Managing Personal Life

You may have wondered if I've gotten my assignment right for this volume. In fact, the previous pages are an elaborate setup for the point I now wish to reiterate—I don't think a rewarding personal life "just happens," any more than publications "just happen." Both benefit from serendipity and luck, but consistent publication comes to those who value it and work at it. Ditto personal life. We need luck, but we can go a long way toward making our own luck if we think about what we want and what we can do to get it.

A few years after I decided to apply more managerial attention to my research life, Jim and I realized that our personal lives would benefit from similar attention. The point of private life, for me, is that it does not feel like "work," so I haven't organized myself in the same way. The basic reality, however, is that the organization necessary to accomplish research, teaching, administration, and service tasks tends to drive out disorganization. Having an agenda at work gave me a chance to focus and develop a line of inquiry through to publication. My personal life didn't have comparable "shape" and was languishing as a result.

It's been fun to play with the idea of recycling for my personal use the advice I gave students for maximizing the chances of publication— and thus I'll reiterate the "rules." In my case they are rules for putting energy into life with my family. There are many other choices, but I believe they all require the same regard. Paint or sail, collect antiques or volunteer—whatever it is, these personal choices will be a sustaining balance to professional life only if they are pursued with energy and attention. People often say something like, "Oh, I'm a photographer in my spare time" or "My family is very important to me." These are not balancing choices, in my view, unless we can point to the equivalent of publication—satisfying outcomes from sustained attention. Here are some thoughts about what it takes to achieve this balance:

1. Choose a setting that values the personal life you have chosen. Jim and I made an important choice when we moved from Los Angeles to Champaign-Urbana when our daughter was 2 years old. Obviously, many people successfully raise children in big cities like L.A., but it made us nervous. Having grown up in a small town, we didn't feel as if our reflexes were working well as we began to raise a child in L.A. The move to a small town like the one we grew up in made more of a difference than we realized at the time. People were doing the kinds of things we recognized. That encouraged us to do more of the same. It's easier to make time to take your child to soccer practice if most of the people you know are doing the same thing. Similar logic applies to attending concerts or painting pictures, biking, or becoming a better photographer. The best advice for achieving a sustaining personal life is to find a context where that life is supported.

2. *Value diversity, but don't forget to associate with people who focus on similar life issues so that you can observe and learn from them.* Though varied stimuli are a key part of creativity in both professional and personal endeavors, it is very helpful to have role models. It is even more helpful to form supportive relationships with a few people who can contribute to your life work. People with children learn a lot from other people who are absorbed in the same task, for example, and this cohort of known and trusted friends is invaluable when critical insights and support are needed in hard times.

3. *Set up routines that support personal life.* On a more mundane level, personal lives are lived day by day. Jim and I had gradually built a way of life I really valued, one that includes things like eating breakfast as a family every day and spending an afternoon a week with each of our children. As we began to pay more conscious attention to our family life, we added more of these routines. For example, I began to put extra effort into making a formal Sunday dinner. Then we added "Thursday date night" (rules: shower and dress before going out, and no coparent/cohouseholder talk). Our children weren't too happy with this new idea, but we also added "Friday family date night" (rules: kids choose both pizza topping and the rental movie)—this worked until our daughter became a teenager; now we're back to Sunday dinner. Such routines are placeholders in the calendar that should demand equal time with page proof deadlines. They make it easier to say no to an impromptu Sunday-night invitation from friends or colleagues. They ensure that regular attention is spent on core relationships and activities.

4. *Plan, establish a calendar, reflect, and update your plan.* There is also a larger rhythm to personal life. If it is to be as rich and sustaining as professional life, it needs the equivalent of con-ferences and journal deadlines. We don't do very many things as a family that match a conference in Paris, but we do try to identify and make room for special events. For example, we like to take long drives together. We now have complicated enough schedules that we might more conveniently fly to a destination from more than one location, but we choose instead to make the drive (even if it's more than a thousand miles) part of the event.

5. *Invest in your personal life.* Most of us make personal life choices that have significant costs, but it's worth noting that deepening personal life may require going beyond the requisite. When I encourage my doctoral students to invest in their careers, I want them to consider how they could enhance their work by purchasing additional tools or services. For those who choose to build personal lives around their families, paying for extra household services may be the equivalent, or a trip to see grandparents. The "necessary" can be so expensive that we neglect to think about the extra rewards of these additional expenditures.

6. *Think about inputs.* Publishing is supported by the books we read, the conferences we go to, the classes we teach, the students we mentor. What are the equivalents for personal life? Time in the woods? Listening to a favorite uncle? The specifics depend upon the life, but here again "personal life" is so taken for granted we may neglect to think about nourishing sources.

7. *Rethink, "rewrite" your life.* Using publication as a metaphor also reminds me of the many times I rethink a model or rewrite an article. Private life offers the same opportunities, but perhaps we don't always recognize them. It's pretty clear that practice leads to improved sailing; it also leads to better loving, improved parenting, and so on.

8. *Enjoy the process.* When I was about 14, I realized with considerable panic that most of the people around me did not seem happy. I still think the same thing, though encountering more of the genuine hardships of life makes it more understandable. My brother-in-law (after reading Joseph Campbell) says, "Follow your bliss"— it's good advice.

9. *Celebrate the victories.* We build joy, in part, by pausing to make things worth remembering. Our children have taught me more about doing this. One Valentine's Day we set up a trail of clues ending in a small toy for our daughter—we've done it every year since. Since our son invented it one year, we've celebrated Saint Patrick's Day every year by turning white grape juice green with food coloring. As we've built up these and other celebrations, I think we've been a bit more attentive to having champagne when a paper finally comes out too.

10. *Choose to do the work.* Of all these bits of advice this is the most important: *Take the time.* Just as it's easy to fool oneself about how much productive academic time one has been logging every day, it's easy to fool oneself about how much time is going into sustaining relationships, really improving one's backhand, or diversifying one's portfolio.

It's worth noting as a separate point how easily professional life crowds out personal life. An opportunity to present a paper, a grading deadline that suddenly looms, an important committee assignment—all can lure us away from simpler pleasures that have no inherent deadlines. Many professional demands are so tangible, their cost/benefit trade-offs so clear, that they seem to overrule taking the time to read to a child or trying to capture the late afternoon light. Nevertheless, if we are to have rich private lives, we must choose sometimes to ignore professional demands. Many people seem to think that they must establish their careers first, then work on their personal lives. Certainly the pressures of publishing universities push us all, and especially those who do not have tenure, in this direction. Yet tenure and other rewards are uncertain, whereas we are clearly missing life if we totally give in to these pressures.

This is not a decision that is made once and for all. The professional/personal choice must be made over and over again. I worry that I may have misjudged the balance myself when I agreed to be nominated for the election that leads to becoming the president of the Academy of Management. It's very flattering to be asked to run for such a position. It's not too hard to think of things one might try to do for the Academy if elected and to write these down on the ballot.

It made me feel more connected to many friends and to the organization when I was elected. But now I have to be very careful to pay attention to my family and to my professional life. I don't want to neglect these things that are far more important than an organizational role.

Furthermore, I don't want to work all the time. Peter Frost made a comment to me several years ago that is highly relevant to the problem-solving tone of this essay. "I have to be careful," he said, "that I don't fill up every minute I save with another task." I need to remember that I'm not trying to manage the balance of my life better just so that I can pile one more thing on the scale. (I really should exercise more; I wish I could start a new research project using option theory; I'd like to have more art and music in my life; I'd like to make more contact with colleagues outside the United States; it would be great to have a few more fruit trees in the yard. . . .) Ultimately, I am trying to balance "doing the work" with being still—avoiding the siren voices that inevitably make the balance lopsided again.

Conclusion

In the past few decades an increasing number of people have become concerned about the quality, or absence of quality, in their personal lives. Judging from the titles on bookstore shelves, as well as from more direct sources, such as conversations I've had with friends and colleagues, many of us feel we need to find a more sustaining counterpart to professional life.

I work on achieving this needed balance in the belief that the personal doesn't have to challenge the professional. It can fold back on and replenish professional life, make my research and teaching more insightful. I don't know if this is possible for mathematicians, but I believe it is true for those who study organizational life. Mathematicians supposedly do their best work early. I think business professors are much more likely to do their best work late in their careers. To gain the requisite insight, however, we have to have personal lives.

Even if they don't ultimately support our professional lives, we can't afford to ignore our private lives. Life is short—publication cannot possibly be all that we should accomplish.

V

Rhythms of Renewal

Taking a Sabbatical

What are you willing to give up to lead a healthier life?

Robert Tannenbaum, quoted by André L. Delbecq (p. 438)

Every time I had said yes in my career when my stomach said no, I had regretted it.

André L. Delbecq (p. 440)

My need for renewal thankfully pushed aside my best-laid plans.

Meryl Reis Louis (p. 452)

In this section of stories, we turn our attention to matters of significant renewal of our knowledge, of our skills, of ourselves. Up to this point in the volume, most of the experiences reported by our authors that have focused on balance and change have tended to deal with fine-tun-ing the directions of their lives. Exceptions include the transitions and relocations reported by Vance Mitchell (Chapter 4), Stewart Clegg (Chapter 5), and Marcy Crary (Chapter 22). On perhaps a deeper level are those times when scholars change from one major activity to another and/or when

they attempt to redefine themselves as individuals. The way they approach their
craft and/or their presentation of themselves changes significantly. This section
deals with such changes.

We are extremely fortunate, in our profession, to have sabbatical periods during
which we have time to retool, to complete
and start initiatives, and to address issues
of change in our lives. These provide unparalleled opportunities for us to pause
and to reframe what we do and who we
are. As Meryl Louis points out, we can use
sabbaticals to work on academic projects,
to continue our teaching and research in
different surroundings (usually without administrative responsibilities), or to undertake some fundamental renewal, or we can
combine these and other intentions in some
fashion. (In Chapter 3 of this volume, Miriam
Erez speaks of using sabbaticals to meet
new scholars and to discover and explore
new researchable issues.)

How we choose to use sabbaticals is influenced in part by the current rhythms of
our careers. The directions we take, the
emotions we feel, the rhythms we encounter after we have achieved tenure are likely
to be different from those at midlife (Meryl
Louis's story); from those we encounter
when moving from one major role to another, such as when stepping down as a
dean (André Delbecq's tale); or from those
we experience when contemplating the latter years of a career (Vance Mitchell's experience; see Chapter 4). We may be very

excited by and involved in a stream of
work and want to spend time with others,
extending our knowledge and skills to finish a project in the area. Our choices of
sabbatical focus are also tempered and
shaped by what our institutions will allow
as legitimate pursuits. Typically, the pressure in and on academic institutions is to
encourage academics to take leaves that
facilitate upgrading knowledge, retooling
skills, and completing tangible products
(e.g., books, papers, other projects). Our
own "drivenness" to produce and to be
constantly active also makes the more reflective aspects of a sabbatical period difficult to envisage or to implement. Nevertheless, we think that we and our fields
benefit when some significant part of our
sabbatical periods is devoted to "nondo-
ing," to listening to ourselves at rest.

Investment in personal renewal can be of
significant benefit to individuals and to their
institutions. In the essays in this section,
both Louis and Delbecq report much happiness resulting from their journeys. Both
feel they were enhanced by their experiences. Both emerged from their sabbaticals
excited about their work, bringing to it new
insights and fresh energy. At the same time,
neither conveys a sense that the work begun
on the sabbatical was complete. Each feels
that the process of change will likely continue for some time. These two stories illustrate vividly the rhythms of renewal. They
suggest the importance and value of this
undertaking for academics and for the field.

45 What's Next After 10 Years as Dean?

REFLECTIONS OF A REEMERGING PROFESSOR

André L. Delbecq

The Context

I had been the dean of the Leavey School of Business at Santa Clara University for 10 years. After a decade as an academic administrator, I stood at a crossroads, with signs pointing to a number of possible different paths. I could seek a position as dean at a similar school or a position as dean at a larger school. I could consider a position in industry through the extensive executive network that I had developed as dean. I could return to the faculty.

There was no certainty in my thinking at the time I stepped down. I promised myself that I would keep an open mind during my sabbatical year, explore a variety of options, and avoid making a hasty decision just to relieve the sense of displacement that tends to pervade one's consciousness when one is "between jobs."

For me the first order of business was to rest and restore my health. There are certain positions that take a great toll on body and spirit— hospital president and combat general, to name

only two. I would add dean to this list. Burnout is associated with positions that have great responsibility but offer limited control. I spent much of each workday as dean advocating, buffering, and dealing with problems over which I had limited control. Further, these were often problems that were "unsolvable," or they would have been dealt with by very bright individuals at other levels of the university community. Although I enjoyed my adventure as dean, and was proud of what I had accomplished, I was also aware of fatigue that had penetrated deep into my very bones. The thought of such simple pleasures as eating meals with my family (instead of alumni, advisory board members, distinguished guests, faculty) and having time to establish a regular exercise schedule had great appeal. I knew I needed time for just physical and mental recuperation.

For 60 days I rested, read, exercised, and meditated. It was the first real rest I had had in a decade without the obligatory daily check with the office, dealing with unmitigated problems by telephone, and preoccupation with how to solve major problems upon return to campus. At the end of these 2 months that I had allocated just for myself before serious exploration of my "next career," I felt 10 years younger.

The Advice of
Other Deans Who Stood Down

During this period I did speak to wise and experienced deans I had known who had finished their terms of office, to see what their experiences had been relative to their next career steps, and to gain a sense of what each alternative path would be like.

My first informant, a former dean of a professional school, had served for a similar period of time as I at a similar institution. He was very clear regarding his pleasure in returning to the faculty. He indicated that his blood pressure had dropped 20 points and that he was happy rediscovering his field of scholarship. There was no ambiguity in his response—he was happy to be a professor once again.

My second informant was a dean of a smaller business school who had gone on to serve as dean in a larger institution. He was equally pleased with his choice. He felt all the lessons he had learned in his first position had prepared him for an even more successful deanship at his present, more challenging, institution.

My third informant had chosen to accept a position as provost. "It was clear to me that I had become a professional academic administrator and no longer thought of myself as a faculty member. I plan to become a university president before my career is completed," he reported. In fact, he achieved that goal just recently.

This pattern of happy individuals, each of whom had made a different choice and each of whom seemed to be fulfilled having made his decision, repeated itself across a dozen informants. There was no pattern of regret, with one exception. The only informant who seemed unhappy with his choice was a dean who had gone on to another institution. He was very successful as perceived by the outside world, but he was not happy inside himself. "The first deanship was an adventure," he said. "This position is simply a job. I know what needs to be done and

do it well. Everyone judges me to be very skilled as a dean. But deep inside I am bored and increasingly cynical. The same human nature I met in my prior position is present in this institution, but I have lost my sense of humor about the normal faculty eccentricities and the power games in top administration."

Whether due to postdecision rationalization or wise personal choices (with the one exception), most informants were content with the paths they had chosen to walk. This left the crossroads signs still in front of me, with no clarity as to the best choice for me personally. Nonetheless, the words of each informant would return to me later when I was closer to a personal decision.

Rediscovering My
Academic Discipline

Meanwhile, I had promised myself that I would also take time during my sabbatical year to redevelop my intellectual capital in areas of interest within my management discipline. My emphases were organizational design and managing innovation, the topics that would be included in my teaching if I returned to the classroom.

There is an old saying: "Department chairs don't have time to write, and deans don't have time to read." In the early phase of my deanship I remember speaking to Robert Tannenbaum and telling him how overextended I felt as dean, and how difficult it was to balance my intellectual interests with academic administration. He replied, "What are you willing to give up to lead a healthier life?" It was a profound question. I gave up teaching because I felt that continuing to write and be active in the Academy of Management were important for my academic self-respect. I did not want to become "simply an administrator" with no continuing intellectual life. But while dean I needed to cut back even further, to limit my intellectual efforts to a much narrower range of topics. However, I did continue to be active in the Academy, and did continue to write at a limited pace.

In truth, however, I soon discovered there was much reality behind the aphorism that deans don't have time to read. During my sabbatical, as I delved once more into the literature, I discovered just how far behind current research and theory I was in areas in which I had considered myself to be competent. Not only was I unfamiliar with much of the new literature, more important, I did not grasp subtleties and could not engage in the creative theoretical development that had once been my forte. I decided during this sabbatical that I must "go back to school." I phoned a number of colleagues at the cutting edge of theoretical work (e.g., Andrew Van de Ven in innovation research, Robert House in leadership studies, Joseph Weiss in management culture studies, Edward Lawler in organizational design, just to mention a few) and asked if I could visit them after reading their current theories and related research findings. Off I trooped to campuses in both North America and Europe. What a joy! I now had the chance to sit at the feet of my colleagues who had spent the decade while I was an administrator thinking carefully about the topics in which I was most interested. In the process of my visits to campuses, I discovered two things: I was very much behind in the theoretical and research nuances, but I was ahead in the relationship of theory to practice. My monthly meetings with executives in Silicon Valley and my research with Joseph Weiss on regional technology cultures provided me with a rich understanding of current organizational designs. I began the fascinating mental game of relating the best of contemporary theory to evolving practices within the high-performing firms with which I was familiar in technology settings. It was an exciting time of intellectual stimulation and discovery. However, the "discoveries" were preliminary insights, not well-developed theoretical positions. I was certainly unable to describe the insights aloud with clarity, let alone put my reflections to paper. Still, I began to recover a sense of intellectual self-respect as I began to feel that I could make mental maps of important issues in my field.

Interviews for Administrative Positions

Then the phone began to ring. I was asked by institutions and executive recruiters to consider deanships, a provost position, and later a college presidency. I began to schedule interviews, feeling I would discover the proper choice for me in weighing real options as opposed to engaging in abstract self-debate. I was about 5

months into my sabbatical year as the actual interviews for new administrative positions began. I interviewed on campus for two deanships, and for the position of provost. I also interviewed in a preliminary context off campus for several other posts. I found the experience challenging, and found my administrative skills well honed. It was obvious to me that I was intellectually quicker in administrative diagnosis and institutional strategy than I was in theoretical synthesis in my discipline. Clearly, I had developed my skills as an academic administrator to a sharp point. This was a rewarding discovery. It was also refreshing to explore a new set of academic settings, meet new faculty cohorts, and visit new geographic communities. The tensions between my reemerging interest in problems in my discipline and the career potential associated with new academic administrative positions were not mitigated by these interviews but exacerbated. What should I do? What was best for my career? What did I really want to do?

The issue came to a head when I received a splendid offer from a major doctoral-granting institution in one of North America's most exciting cities. I liked the president of the university and the provost and respected the faculty, and the conditions of the offer were appealing. In addition, my wife was enthusiastic regarding the offer and the potential new location; she felt the position was a natural fit for my skills. I was no longer at a point where I could play Hamlet. I needed to decide. Was I going to go on with a career in academic administration, or would I return to my discipline and be a professor once again?

There was much to be said for accepting the offer to be dean; a prestigious position, an attractive location, a substantial financial improvement—and, perhaps most important, very little risk. I knew what needed to be done in terms of the strategic agenda at this institution, and I felt I could perform well. By contrast, I didn't know how well I would do in the classroom after a decade's absence, or whether I could rebuild a program of scholarship. I would certainly suffer a substantial personal financial cutback if I returned to the faculty. Besides, how would the faculty feel about a former dean roaming the halls? All the rational arguments seemed to point toward the path of continuing my career as an academic administrator.

An Unlikely Choice

I remember the day I made the choice very well. It was a gray day and I took my 212-pound mastiff with me for a walk along the San Francisco Bay. I couldn't clearly articulate my rationale for saying no to the new deanship, but I decided to say no. I wasn't happy in my stomach saying yes. Every time I had said yes in my career when my stomach said no, I had regretted it. I sat down on a rock, looked at the bay and at my dog, Bonaparte, and said, "I am going to be a professor again." Bonaparte was the only friend who seemed to approve of my decision. My wife, many colleagues, and most friends thought I was making a mistake. It was a decision that certainly did not play to immediate applause. Yet it was the decision I felt was right for me at that time.

Why Be a Professor Again?

I had, of course, a number of reasons to support my decision. First and foremost, I wanted to have time for my family. I had just spent a decade in a position whose demands often took precedence over family. It is inherent in the extraordinary time demands of such positions as dean that family time is both scarce and often interrupted—interrupted in terms of demands that took me away from home, but also in the sense of mental focus and energy. There was, at this time, an important challenge facing one of my adult children. In the past decade I was not really "there" in terms of available time. I felt that on this occasion I had an opportunity to help see a young family through an important and difficult period. I felt it was time to focus more clearly on family.

Health is another sacrificial lamb on the altar of central administrative positions. In Woodward's book *The Commanders,* he speaks about General Colin Powell's two different high blood pressure medicines and Secretary of Defense Cheney's bypass surgery. I knew that it was time to take control of my weight, regain my aerobic capacity, and rebuild my health, or I would face a similar scenario. After 5 months of aching muscles, I was just feeling a glimmer of a physically fit body again. I was hesitant to give up the reconditioning program I had under way.

There was also a sense of increasing mortality. Whatever I did next might be "the last mission." I wanted to choose a career path that allowed slack for me to "do good," and not just "do well." I was not sure what this meant, but I was sure I wanted to have the slack to "do good" when opportunities occurred.

Another concern that haunted me, although at the time I am not sure just how conscious the reflection might have been, were the words of the dean who had said, "The first deanship was an adventure. This position is simply a job." All the tasks associated with the deanship position I was offered were challenging and exciting, but they did seem to be more of a "job" than the fun I was having once again pursuing the intellectual puzzles of my discipline. When I spent effort pursuing my scholarly topics, time flew and I felt refreshed at the end of a challenging day's effort. It had been a long time since workdays deaning had flown by with equal speed.

All of these reasons seem more full-blown now in retrospect than they did at the time I made the decision. Are some just postdecision rationalizations? The only real certitude I had at the time was that I had decided to say no.

Returning to the Faculty

If the reality of moving to a new city is symbolized by moving cartons, the reality of moving back to the faculty is symbolized by the move into a faculty office: smaller than the dean's suite, remote from central offices, without a private secretary, and with somewhat shabby furniture. Also, there is no celebration of your arrival "back" as there is for the arrival of a new faculty member. Meanwhile, your successor is having the honeymoon period of his leadership. How does it feel?

My transition felt perfectly okay, at least in part because I had made several parameter decisions. I would take a vow of silence for 2 years with respect to college politics. I would avoid serving on major committees within the school to give space to those with legitimate desires for change. I would major in teaching and scholarship, and that would be sufficient in the short run.

It was not only sufficient, it was totally absorbing. In many ways it reminded me of that short, halcyon period when one is a new assistant professor: qualified to pursue one's own scholarly direction and not important enough to serve on committees.

Teaching Once Again

It is hard to convey the delight I felt in teaching after a decade out of the classroom. Although I had taught in executive programs, I had not had my own classes. This is not to say that everything went smoothly. I had all the problems of a new assistant professor. My pacing was poor. I often had far too much scheduled for a particular class period. The course was not well organized. My jokes were too intellectual and out-of-date. Examples were missing or not quite appropriate. Not surprisingly, my courses were hardly seamless. I was still "thinking out loud" in a number of areas where my ideas had not jelled into a coherent pattern. But very bright working-professional MBA students were the perfect honing stone. Gradually, though painfully, the "course" did emerge. It was hard work.

During this period I invested heavily in myself. I will be forever grateful to the Organizational Behavior Teaching Society, which provides a legitimate forum in which individuals can present teaching problems (not just solutions) to obtain input from skilled colleagues. Members of this splendid group of master teachers helped me solve a number of course issues, such as organization design for project teams and criteria for grading group assignments.

I also continued to invest in my schooling. I paid my registration and attended executive programs where colleagues at other universities presented on topics included in my courses. I found a wealth of resources by listening to these skilled instructors. I gave myself an unlimited book budget and read ravenously, like a parched plant seeking water following a drought. Like an assistant professor, I wondered if I could ever feel competent again as a contributor to the literature relating to my course topics.

However, despite the difficulties, over the course of 2 years I was renewed. I was once again mastering a scholarly niche. I found my intellectual self-respect in place. During the 10 years I served as dean I felt I had been writing checks on my intellectual capital, but not renewing the account. Now I had time and opportunity to reinvest in my personal intellectual stock. It was wonderful to feel competent again in my field. It also was a reminder of how much art, effort, and skill are required to make a classroom worthy of bright MBA students.

Returning to Scholarship

The return to scholarship was an equally slow and challenging task. In the beginning, I had so much new material to learn that I felt very much like the graduate student who wonders if there is anything left to be said that has not been written recently, and if he will ever be able to make an original contribution. In time, of course, you begin to discover gaps, feel confident regarding your own insights, and "venture out" through papers and symposia until you can confidently approach a new scholarly endeavor. Working with colleagues helped. I established partnerships on two projects with senior scholars (Robert House and Frank Friedlander) where my access to technological executives and intimate knowledge of Silicon Valley practices complemented their theoretical insights. I was very much their junior partner while I regained my scholarly skills. Once again, I now believe that some forthcoming personal scholarship will make a meaningful contribution. However, it has been a slow process.

How It Looked 4 Years Later

Joseph Campbell, the legendary storyteller and professor of myths, speaks of the importance of "following your bliss." The route back to the professorship has not been all silver linings. It involved substantial financial hardship. Rebuilding consulting relationships is as slow as rebuilding a program of scholarship (I had given up most consulting during my period as dean because of time constraints and the demands of administrative availability). It is not easy when you were once a master teacher to see that you are once again a novice teacher. Scholarship, which is always a slow and painful path, is no easier a path to climb when you are older.

There was also a change in status. There are a certain number of community members who feel you have fallen from grace when you become "only a professor." The former editor of

Harper's magazine reported on Public Radio, "The day after I was no longer editor I found that individuals who used to return my phone calls screened me out." I certainly felt a shift in my status in the eyes of some.

Yet for me there is no ambivalence. I entered education because I delighted in the intellectual life and the life of theoretical discovery. I enjoyed the adventure of being dean because there were many lessons to learn from being a manager, not simply studying managers. But clearly, after 10 years, when many of those lessons were learned, the greater reward for me was to return to the life of scholarly discovery. I rejoice in the sheer excitement of having time to "sift and winnow" intellectual problems, as my friends at the University of Wisconsin used to say. I am appreciative of the time I have to read, write, and study. I find my classes a fountain of youth, having my ideas tested and improved upon by my MBAs. I am a much better teacher of management for having been a manager, but now I am also grateful for time to study, interview, and assimilate the lessons.

There are other benefits. I feel very wealthy with a rich satisfying family life as well as time to exercise. I have found several social welfare projects to which I can make a meaningful contribution given my now more flexible schedule. In short, although Monday morning may not be my favorite time of the week, it is not a day I dread. I feel privileged to participate once again in my society as a professor.

Summary

Are there transferable lessons from my story? Perhaps a few are notable. The most important is to "follow your bliss" (or stomach) no matter what social pressures or "typical career paths" might otherwise dictate. I cannot claim to be happier than other former deans who went on to serve as deans at other institutions, or who became provosts or presidents. I stay in touch with these colleagues, rejoice in their success, and appreciate their service to our profession. Certainly there are days when I feel a twinge of envy or wish I could share in some aspect of their adventures. But on a daily basis I am totally content with the choice that I made. It has been a choice that has been good for me. I followed my own need to renew my family and intellectual life, and I feel fulfilled having done so.

While I was a dean, I laid some groundwork for this choice. Robert Tannenbaum's question, "What are you willing to give up?" inspired me to remain active in the Academy of Management. Without my involvement in this network, my reentry as a professor would have been much more difficult. From this, I also realized how foolish it would be to lose the network of contacts with the executive community I had forged as a dean. I continue to be a member of several CEO groups, and this participation assists my ability to link my scholarship to the perspectives of top management.

I learned the importance of reinvesting in myself. Even during a time of reduced income, I invest in travel to visit other universities, in registration fees for attendance at conferences where master teachers present, and in time and travel to spend several days with individuals doing research on topics of mutual interest. Investing in self-development is never a source of regret, and it has accelerated my reentry as a professor.

I am a much better professor for having learned the many lessons of managerial practice that were part of the richness of my 10 years as dean. I count my years as dean as an important and formative part of my academic career, but, as with my doctoral studies, I am for the moment glad those lessons are part of the past. For the present, I am enjoying being a professor. Will I ever accept an administrative post again? Perhaps, when my stomach agrees the time is right and my mastiff nods his head on the shores of San Francisco Bay.

46 A Sabbatical Journey

TOWARD PERSONAL AND PROFESSIONAL RENEWAL

Meryl Reis Louis

> Sabbatical: of the nature of a Sabbath or period of rest; pertaining to or appropriate to the Sabbath; root = to rest. Sabbatical year: the 7th year, prescribed by the Mosaic law to be observed as a "Sabbath" in which the land was to remain untilled and all debtors and Israelitish slaves were to be released.
>
> New English Dictionary, *1914*

> Sabbath: a Scriptural period (as the sabbatical year) of solemn rest or cessation from usual activity.
>
> Webster's 3rd New International Dictionary, *1986*

Overview

Traditionally, the purpose of a sabbatical has been to provide for a time of renewal in the broadest sense of intellectual and personal refreshment through a leave of absence from one's regular duties. In common practice, faculty often use sabbaticals to begin, continue, or complete work on academic projects. Others continue with research and teaching, but do so in different surroundings, serving as temporary faculty at other universities. Some undertake more fundamental renewal at personal and/or professional levels. And no doubt there are some who combine renewal with other agendas. I planned a sabbatical of the first sort—completing a project—and ended up pursuing one of the third sort—undertaking renewal of a personal nature that has fueled my professional work as well.

This chapter is the story of that sabbatical—of what I thought it was going to be and what it turned out to be. Most especially, it is the story of how I came to recognize the journey I

AUTHOR'S NOTE: In addition to the helpful comments of the editors, this chapter has benefited from the careful readings of Tony Athos, Jean Bartunek, Michael Brown, and Kate Warden, each of whom has also played an important role in my journey.

needed to pursue. The part of my sabbatical experience on which I will focus actually took place during the year between submission of my sabbatical application and its official beginning in January 1992. During this period I came to recognize that my original sabbatical plans were inappropriate. In response, I undertook a "life audit," a review of my past experiences, to surface issues I would need to address in undertaking personal and professional renewal. Results of the life audit led me to begin exploring the meaning of these issues in my own life and in others' lives, looking closely at my reactions to contemporary experiences. In addition, I gleaned guidance for the design of my sabbatical from conversations with people who shared my journey or reflected its effects back to me. A final and fundamental source of guidance came from a surprisingly vocal (though previously quiet) inner voice. Guidance from these several sources together shaped what was to be my 15-month experience of personal and professional renewal—including the official semester of sabbatical and relevant periods before and after it. In this essay I will describe and illustrate each of these sources of guidance, in the hopes of revealing signposts that might be of use to those considering a sabbatical agenda of renewal.

Plans and Life Collide: Guidance From Within

In December 1990 I applied for a sabbatical to begin 13 months later. This would be my first sabbatical in 14 years of tenure-track teaching. In moving between universities, I had forgone the normal sabbatical opportunities that accrue every 7 years. In my sabbatical application I indicated that I would use the time to write a book based on a study I had done following MBA graduates through the first 10 years of their post-MBA careers. The book would represent the completion of the project. Somewhere, I had absorbed the message that a book is a necessary product of such a project. I had also absorbed the message that finishing a project is an appropriate use of a sabbatical. On all counts, I would come to question the messages I had taken in.

As John Lennon has pointed out, life is what happens while you're making other plans. In

this case, life bubbled up from within me in the form of unease about the wrongheadedness of the plans I was making. Within a few months of submitting my application, a minor sense of unease about my plans had ripened into clarity that I had made a mistake. In many ways the project had long been complete. Theoretical and empirical findings from the study had been distilled and disseminated. I had written at length about career transitions, sensemaking processes by which newcomers cope with unfamiliar organizational settings, and the (in)adequacy of MBA education in preparing graduates for the jobs they held 1, 5, and 10 years out of school. A book, I had reasoned, would bring what I had learned from this study together in one place. But by March 1991, I had come to question whether such a book would serve the needs of researchers, employers, or graduates any better than the publications already available. And I questioned whether it would be the best use of my time. Thus a strong sense of unease signaled a need to reconsider my best-laid plans.

Another experience contributed to my unease about the sabbatical described in my December proposal. In February 1991, I turned 44, and with that anniversary I became aware that I was reaching midlife. I was surprised to find that this marker had meaning for me. Up to this point, I had been relatively immune to societal age typing. But by March I had accepted that "midlife" was significant for me. At about this time, I heard myself saying to friends that I was doing my midlife as a "review" rather than a "crisis." I used the term *life audit* to describe my review process, appropriating somewhat facetiously the notion of an audit gleaned from my years after college on the consulting staff at Arthur Andersen & Co. By *life audit*, I meant to convey (mostly to myself) my intention to be systematic in my review of my personal life—what was satisfying and not, what was needed though missing—and to take seriously what it might reveal. As I wrote in my journal, I wanted to identify the themes on which I would be working, personally and professionally, for the next 20 years. (No doubt the time frame is a bit overlong, but that is how I phrased my purpose to myself and to others at the time.) With this experience I became aware of an internal dialogue taking place, with one part of me as a slightly amused though increasingly attentive listener and learner.

In spring 1991, I was granted a sabbatical for spring 1992 and the reduced load I had requested for fall 1991. Although I would be teaching a course and serving on committees in the fall, I envisioned treating the entire 15 months from June 1991 to September 1992 as the leave. It seemed important to do so. I recognized, in the best symbolic interactionist tradition, that what I defined as the sabbatical period would affect my attitudes and behavior. In this sense, I considered "sabbatical" to be a state of mind. In fact, I heard myself saying to myself and others that my sabbatical work, including the preparation for the formal spring term off, needed to begin when the spring 1991 term ended.

I must note that I and others consider me to be action oriented, intuitive, and analytic. In most situations, I am willing if not eager to take charge, solve problems, and get on with it. So the idea of being responsive to guidance from an interior source that I could not clearly describe was foreign to me. Yet throughout the period, I experienced an uncharacteristic and surprisingly prevalent interior dialogue. Coming to listen to what the voice within had to offer was part of the ongoing learning. In addition to sentences and images that arose as powerful messages from within me, I found the upwelling of strong feelings of unease or peacefulness served as a guide for me during my sabbatical journey. So my sabbatical experience is also the story of my learning to listen within, of my coming to recognize or discern guidance from within. In my struggle to make sense of this experience, I have found Gerald May's (1983) distinction between being willing and being willful helpful in characterizing the contrast between my openness or willingness to be guided by signs, an inner voice, echoes, and emotional movements and my more normal take-charge or willful self.

Conducting a Life Audit: Using History to Surface Themes

In spring 1992 I undertook my life audit. As part of this review, I found myself reflecting rather systematically and analytically on contrasting experiences in my past. I assembled an array of what could be considered case data from my own life and the lives of friends. Selection of case data was guided by the sensitizing question "When have I had a sense of complete-

ness or deep satisfaction?" which seemed to arise from deep within me. In response to this question, I found myself enumerating moments in the past in which I had felt quite complete, as well as those I had found unsatisfying. I also searched my friends' lives for relevant situations, noting what I was being drawn toward in others' lives and what I was glad I did not have to endure. I found myself sketching out descriptions of moments, teasing out conditions associated with a sense of completeness and satisfaction as well as missing elements. For instance, recollections of myself in the woods were quite pleasurable but were accompanied by a sense of poignancy on occasions when there was no like-minded person to share them with.

Setting one instance against another, I found myself engaged in a kind of comparative case analysis in which complete moment was compared with complete moment in a search for the common characteristics. What gives me joy thus emerged. Conditions of pain or emptiness were revealed similarly through examination of unsatisfactory moments, events, situations. What emerged were sets of circumstances that gave me a sense of completeness. Among them were music, especially singing with others; my own playfulness, particularly in consort with others; being in nature with others who shared my awe and delight at what was put in our paths; and "hanging out"—that is, spontaneous, emergent conversation or outings with kindred souls. Although it interested me to see that music, playfulness, being in nature, and hanging out emerged as activities and settings that have given me great joy, these substantive themes were not what conveyed the most powerful message. I was surprised to see that beyond the distinctive aesthetic form of expression of each activity or setting, there were two broader themes underlying what I found pleasurable about making music and appreciating it, about being playful and being in nature, and about hanging out. First, when each of these activities had been most satisfying, it had been shared with like-minded comrades, fellow travelers, soul mates. Thus there was a communal aspect to the experience. Second, I was aware that at their best, each entailed a moment of awareness of the expression of a gift or appreciation of one. Thus there was a spiritual aspect to the experience.

Insights from the life audit left me with more questions than answers, but with a fairly clear direction. So, as of late spring 1991, my sense was that I would need to find out how spiritual and communal experiences might look and feel in my life. I was left with a longing to be part of something larger—not a specific task-based endeavor, but something open-ended, ongoing. I imagined that in having a more populated and stable social context than I was then experiencing in my life I would have more ready access to the kind of spiritual and communal experiences I seemed to find satisfying.

Thus the life audit entailed several tasks. I developed a sensitizing question to guide me in reviewing my past experiences. The review yielded a set of specific case situations the analysis of which revealed substantive themes that were in turn grounded in the two underlying themes of community and spirituality. Different sensitizing questions in pursuit of renewal in another's life or in my life at another time would no doubt yield quite different case instances and underlying themes. It seems likely that the steps constituting the life audit process are relevant and adaptable to others' renewal quests.

Four Events in May: Harvesting Moments From Current Experiences

As school ended in early May, I felt myself moving into the next phase of the journey. This phase was marked by a shift from reviewing past experiences to a close inspection of my current life experiences. That is, I was looking at what was unfolding in my life, not yet designing a specific experience in which to immerse. My particular orienting themes were spirituality and community, though I could not yet define or ever describe very well what I meant by either term. I began addressing the personal issue, "What is my experience of a sense of community?" My process during these explorations was to note moments of completeness in which I felt nourished and moments in which I felt unsatisfied in my current life.

Several relevant events occurred in mid-May. It is instructive to consider how they aided my journey. Within a 4-day period, I had occasion to spend time with each of two foursomes with which I had been involved over several years (one a hiking group and the other a social support group), to attend my first Quaker meeting, and to take my third walk with a new neighbor.

During these days, I cataloged two very unsatisfactory experiences and two very nourishing ones. Their proximity in time and difference in emotional tone made them salient as a set. I undertook a close examination of them, not unlike the process of reviewing cases revealed during the life audit. The contrasts were striking and fueled my sense that I was now on a fruitful path.

Time with one foursome left me embarrassed at my lack of enthusiasm for yet another round of reporting on our lives, a conversation it seemed we had been having over our monthly dinners for several years. I felt little engagement as the serial monologues and advice giving continued, and regretted that my past efforts to alter the dynamics had produced no change. Time with the other foursome began with a confirming impatience welling up in me. One more time they had voiced a desire to be in nature, but walked through the woods engrossed in discussions of their remodeling efforts, oblivious to our surroundings. I felt insulted on behalf of the woods and embarrassed at my holier-than-thou judgment, wishing I had come to the woods alone. I found I could no longer ignore my dissatisfaction with either of these groups and began trying to describe analytically what led to my reactions and disappointment.

On the third day I went to my first Quaker meeting. In partial response to the quasi-oracular messages produced through my life audit, I had been exploring several spiritual traditions. In the worshipful silence of Quaker meeting, I felt "at home." It was an experience that spread over me like a soft blanket as I sat on a bench in the growing silence in a large, unadorned room filled with people of every age. But my sense was of a blanket over all of us there in the room. There was something familiar in this breathing reverence—a collective awe, a kinship.

On the fourth day I walked with a new neighbor, Kate. We walked energetically (by middle-aged standards) along the river, our laughter providing the aerobic workout that our pace did not. We shared frustrations and commiserated about our experiences working/living inside academic institutions. Kate listened well, shared candidly, and lived 40 yards from my front door. She was savvy and funny. Irony, humor, and camaraderie characterized this, our third early-morning jaunt, as we made plans to walk together several days a week. I felt as if we had known each other for years, as if we had been longtime confidantes.

The striking contrast among these experiences emerged in language I by then did not find surprising. Through my walk with Kate and in Quaker meeting, I felt nourished. With the foursomes I did not. Kate and Quaker meeting have remained part of my journey, fueling lessons about community and spirituality. It is instructive to look at an example of how such lessons were provoked. My relationship with Kate made me aware that community must be something other than friendship. For instance, even as I felt nourished through our early-morning walks together, the shadow of potential dependency crossed my mind and left me wondering whether I would have such feelings in a community setting. Alternatively, she was my confidante and someone whose opinion I valued too much to share what I considered unsavory, flaky, or at odds with her values or what I imagined she would consider "good for me." It took some time before I could and did put words to these feelings. Ultimately, my coming clean was a relief in itself, and her reaction confronted me with the magnitude of my projections. Thus the weaknesses inherent in strong ties, in friendship, and the potential strength of a network of weak ties, community, were revealed in the contrasts between my experiences with Kate, a friend, and at Quaker meeting, a community setting.

So in this phase I continued the process of comparing salient moments of experience but shifted from a focus on the past to the present—first comparing satisfying moments (Kate and Quaker meeting) with unsatisfying moments (the foursomes), then comparing satisfying moments in the context of friendship (Kate) with those in the context of community (Quaker meeting). In doing so, additional questions and insights were revealed that further sparked my journey.

Thus by June I was aware that I had moved beyond the reflective mode of the life audit and had begun testing the issues in my contemporary life. I had a sense that the path was unfolding and I was on it. But even as I was unclear about where the path would lead or how I would know which direction to take at a crossroads, I was fiercely loyal to what came to me as "the integrity of the journey." This was another phrase that arose from within and seemed to warrant my respect before I could articulate its meaning. Somehow I trusted that the path would unfold as necessary. I trusted that in making a commitment to the unfolding path and the journey, I would be okay. It was as if from the other side a contract had been entered into as well. I carried an inner peace, a faith, I would later come to call it, in the integrity of the journey, just as I respected the source of the phrase itself.

Roles People and Settings Played

As I came to understand that I needed to use my sabbatical for renewal, I came to recognize that other people would play important and varied roles in my journey. Among the roles I came to distinguish were informants, or people who shared about their lives; mirrors, people I saw annually or at other periodic intervals whose comments and reactions served to help me take stock of changes in my perspective and behavior; fellow travelers, people pursuing similar issues with whom I felt a kinship; and witnesses or sympathetic onlookers, people involved in my life on a regular basis who were supportive of my journey but who were pursuing other issues in their own lives. In addition, I came to recognize that some people who were normally involved in my life would remain outsiders to my journey and that I would need to be able to help such outsiders appreciate the boundaries of my journey. Incidents from the summer of 1991 illustrate these roles.

Informants

In addition to my own life as a source of information, I needed to hear from others about their relevant experiences. But I had recognized early on that it was not useful to use the term *community*. It meant nothing and everything, anything the listener wanted it to mean. Instead, I came to ask people to consider "the interactions, relationships, and settings that had been nurturing and sustaining" and to talk with me about what came to mind. This query arose as did the notion of the integrity of the journey, from within. I asked it of friends, colleagues, acquaintances, and strangers in a variety of settings. I saw opportunities to inquire about it everywhere. It was my cocktail-party topic and the subject of conversation when I got my hair cut. Responses to it generated information about the location and extent of the sense of community in people's lives, what it looked like and felt like to them, as well as conditions that supported it. Sometimes I could see a faraway look in people's eyes as they talked about these experiences, seeming to revisit them in their minds as we talked. Having this as a virtual preoccupation allowed me to search broadly for leads in others' lives, to hear what their responses provoked in me, and to track potentially relevant features of the situation and persons. I find it ironic though not surprising that I had harnessed my methodical nature to what had become for me a deeply spiritual quest.

Mirrors: People and Settings as Annual and Long Mirrors

In anticipation of using summer to work with what the life audit was revealing, I planned to bookend my summer with the Organizational Behavior Teaching Conference at the beginning and the Academy of Management meetings at the end. I also signed up for a 2-week NTL lab to begin the day after my return from OBTC. Each of these settings illustrates a different type of mirroring.

Most noteworthy at the OBTC were long evenings with others singing around a piano and intense conversations with a few friends about issues with which we were each working. These were longtime friends, colleagues with whom friendships had developed over our years in the field together. Our approximately annual check-ins at this and other conferences help me monitor how I'm doing personally and professionally. My current state was mirrored against the backdrop of their mental snapshots of me from our previous periodic talks, providing data points, if you will, from which I could plot trends in my life's performance. Thus at the OBTC particular *people served as mirrors*.

An experience at the NTL lab illustrates what I have come to call the *long mirror*. As I arrived at registration, I ran into a dear friend with whom I had lost touch. Our sense of kinship was as visceral then as it had been 17 years

before. We were at Bethel to attend different labs, but spent an afternoon on a float in a lake catching up on one another's lives. By virtue of the hiatus in our contact, I found my life's broader trajectory plotted, rather than my recent progress. In addition, the strength of our connection made my then current life seem pale in comparison and provoked questions about the relationship between a sense of family and a sense of community.

The Academy of Management meetings I attended in Miami that August illustrate how some *settings serve as mirrors* as well. I arrived at the meetings feeling relatively peaceful, if damp, and departed 3 days later with a deep sense of affirmation. The cumulative effect of my experiences during these days mirrored the changes I was experiencing and gave legitimacy to the issues I was working. Numerous people commented that I seemed radiant. I recall that I was startled by their comments, but on reflection found they fit. Conversations with friends, discovering a colleague with whom to meditate in the mornings before the sessions began, a deeply moving symposium on spirituality in the workplace, as well as the reactions of friends and even acquaintances to my appearance confirmed that what I was pursuing had substance and suited me. The final touch was ending up flying home with a Boston University colleague, discovering that we both wished to find ways to provide support for our spiritual practices, and agreeing to meet for half an hour of silence in my office each week, which we did through the fall semester. Perhaps I would not need to live in small compartments after all. The opportunity to put together the emerging spiritual and professional pieces of my life made me aware that I had assumed that a lack of integration among important parts of my life was inevitable.

As at the OBTC 2 months earlier, I saw at the Academy meetings the value of returning briefly to familiar settings so that those who knew me well and might be in attendance could mirror to me how I seemed. But I was also aware that it was important to keep the exposure brief, so as not to be pulled back into old modes and response patterns. Another thing I learned—unanticipated but, on reflection, not surprising—was that fellow travelers into novel territory may be found among familiar faces, in familiar settings.

Fellow Travelers

The 2-week NTL lab engaged the 45 of us in intensive psychological work and served as a testing ground for material coming up about community, friendship, and spirituality. Through it, I found a fellow traveler. In climbing a mountain together, working with our dreams, and enduring at middle age the rigors of group living and psychological probing—all in the context of a hot and humid July in western Maine—Dennis and I became allies. He was deeply spiritual, a philosopher-theologian, Irish Catholic in heritage and practice, but he seemed to me Hasidic in appearance and conversational style. We held in common an appreciation of the ironic and a conspiratorial irreverence that aided us in bearing our sentence and bound us together. He represented a potential fellow traveler on the journey; that is, he was someone for whom the same life issues were central. In conversations with Dennis and other fellow travelers, my experiences did not seem like a foreign language. I did not censor myself for fear they would find me flaky. Because most people I considered fellow travelers lived far away, our interactions were periodic but intense, tapping into a deep connection, not unlike the kinship I felt on reconnecting with my friend at Bethel.

Witnesses or Sympathetic Onlookers

In contrast to fellow travelers, it was important for me to have sympathetic onlookers or witnesses to my journey. These people were supporters of my explorations, though they did not share my enthusiasm for the issues. They were personal friends who knew me more broadly than just through this journey. They were there for me, not for the issues. In contrast with my mirrors, who provided data for taking stock by virtue of our periodic meetings, I was in more frequent contact with people serving as my witnesses. In addition to my neighbor Kate, about whom you read earlier, Mary Ellen was my other local witness. We had weekly end-of-the-day get-togethers throughout this time at her house about three blocks away. She invariably inquired in detail about my journey. She followed up on events unfolding from the previous week and listened with great interest. Our long-term friendship and common Jewish heritage were a backdrop against which the contrasts of our present experiences—hers of having a baby, mine of the sabbatical journey—stood out. I worried she would find my explorations into Quaker and Ignatian traditions heretical, but she held firm in her interest in my ventures even into these foreign territories. Mary Ellen was truly a supportive onlooker, trusting with me, it seemed, in the integrity of the journey. As witnesses or sympathetic onlookers, Mary Ellen and Kate served as tethers between my journeying self and the historical me. They were at once outsiders to my journey and insiders to my life. In their very presence, they provided an alternative but sympathetic perspective on my insider experience (Louis & Bartunek, 1992). Their steadfastness freed me to immerse, to explore deeply, to pursue as I felt led. I question whether without their constancy in my life— their presence, interest, and support—I would have felt as free to pursue the path that was unfolding.

Outsiders

With most of my colleagues and some family members, I felt a need to put boundaries around my availability and my journey. I knew or anticipated that some would be skeptical and others would simply expect me to behave as usual. As the sabbatical experience unfolded, I did not want my normal "role senders" (e.g., colleagues) conveying expectations that would circumscribe my exploration. I did not want to be called back into my "normal" mode of being, into the reasoned, assertive, problem-solving mode. This was a particular concern during the period of the official sabbatical beginning in January 1992. For instance, I needed to have colleagues understand that although I was not leaving town, I would not be available to come to meetings. On reflection, there is likely to have been some truth to this concern as well as some projection of my own insecurities. I might have better handled my concerns about outsiders by providing early on a "cover story," that is, a clear, more complete statement of what I was up to and why I therefore needed to maintain boundaries. If I made intelligible my purpose and process, colleagues could shift their expectations of me or at least make sense of my nonresponse to requests consistent with my nonsabbatical roles. However, it took me some time to realize what was needed. Before I did, it was not uncommon for me to feel misunderstood, put-upon, and occasionally quite alienated from my colleagues. But once I did, the cover story helped me secure boundaries around my endeavor, alleviating the concerns of others, helping others appreciate my need for boundaries and see how they might be helpful.

Designing and Immersing in the Sabbatical Experience

During fall 1991 I became quite enthusiastically engaged, feeling momentum and confidence about the journey from both personal and professional perspectives. I sensed that pursuing the unfolding path would lead me to a deeper understanding of community—its meaning and dynamics as well as its relevance in and for work settings. This seemed a logical extension of my long-standing commitment to research on organizational culture.

On the personal side, I was convinced that by the end of the sabbatical "I would have a greater sense of community in my life" than I had had at the outset. This was another piece of language that emerged whole from the voice within. At the time it emerged, I did not grasp the weight of the distinction between "a sense of community" and the empirical fact of a community of people. But by then I did respect the language as it arose from within and would carry forward with it until its full meaning was revealed. By then as well I had the wisdom to know that I had no idea what form this "greater sense of community" would take. The NTL lab had helped me to recognize faulty assumptions embedded in my earlier framing of the issue. I could see that there was no greater likelihood that one would have a sense of community in one's life merely because one lived with other people. I was as likely to enhance my sense of community through a dramatically altered living situation (e.g., living with others) or one that from the outside would look precisely as it did now. By "becoming convinced" that this would occur I do not mean to suggest that I set a goal for myself. Instead, I trusted that my circumstances or rather my experience of them would be altered.

Because I now had a clear belief that the experience of community I had in my life would be changed by the time I completed the sabbatical, I incorporated it into my planning. To effect such a change in my local life suggested that I needed to be here, to be present in order for the change to occur. So in pursuit of this agenda, physically leaving the area made no sense. It made no sense for other reasons as well. Given the experiential quality of the issues as I had framed them, the idea emerged of immersing in settings in which I could expect a sense of community to form. I would use myself as a meter, an indicator of the sense of community engendered in me as I participated in a setting. For example, I anticipated that by participating in a variety of settings and comparing my experiences across them, I would be able to begin noting features characteristic of settings that foster a sense of community and features of the experience of a sense of community. Thus, for a number of reasons, it made the most sense to stay put and vary my experience rather than my geography, so that changes I would detect would be those associated not with change in locale but with the presence of or difference in my sense of community.

The mix of settings in which I wished to immerse varied on a number of dimensions relevant to what was emerging as my longer-term analytic task of ferreting out characteristics and dynamics of a sense of community. Among the dimensions were the size of the group and the frequency with which it convened, the extent to which it was secular and/or spiritual, stability of membership, whether it was an ongoing or newly forming setting, whether it had a fixed life span or was open-ended, the degree to which the group was formally constituted and whether it was connected with a larger institution (e.g., a course at an academic institution, a community chorus, a book group), and whether the group had a designated leader.

As the sabbatical began in January 1992, I was admitted to Boston University's School of Theology as a nondegree student and cross-registered for classes at two schools in the eight-school consortium of the Boston Theological Institute. I also arranged to audit a class at the Kennedy School of Government. In each case, the instructor was reputed to have special skills at convening community and/or creating an environment hospitable to the spirit in the classroom. For two of the classes, small groups met weekly outside of class time.

Beyond participating in these fixed-term, institution-based settings to track my experience of community forming as a class unfolded, I participated in a number of less formal groups in both secular and spiritual contexts. I helped organize a book group, a group of women who met monthly for dinner and discussion of a book we had agreed to read. After 5 months we disbanded, recognizing the press of demands on several of us as well as the artificiality and lack of compellingness of what we had created. I also helped organize a study group of 8 of the 40 people who had attended a Quaker history class in the fall. In contrast with the book group, the study group continued for 2 years, reviewing progress and renewing commitment at regular intervals. We came together every 3 weeks for dinner and to discuss a previously chosen question about the link between a particular spiritual issue and our daily lives, to hear the history of one another's spiritual journeys, and to close with a brief period of silent worship. This was one of the settings that most engendered in me a sense of community. Contrasts between the Quaker study group and the book group—both new, small, informal groups—have provoked numerous insights, hunches, and questions for ongoing research into the dynamics of creating a sense of community.

During the official sabbatical, I also continued to participate in a monthly support group of five of us from the NTL lab, which had begun meeting a couple of months after the lab. I continued to participate in a biweekly Quaker village group that I had first visited in the fall and began attending a Wednesday-morning Quaker worship group. For an experience in a different medium, I joined a community chorus, the Mystic Chorale. We came together, 150 of us, to rehearse one evening a week for 3 months in preparation for two public performances of a gospel mass and other gospel music. It was organized and led by a well-known local song leader unaffiliated with any larger institution, but over the years the Chorale had become its own institution. Participating in this setting was enormously instructive about community, spirituality, and leadership, and provided a deeply moving experience. Contrasts among the chorus, the NTL group, and others of the settings have raised critical questions about the relevance of task characteristics and subgroup formation in the crafting of commitment and sense of community. Contrasts among the song leader and each of the three instructors of the formal courses I was taking have highlighted leadership characteristics potentially relevant to the development of a sense of community.

In addition to these periodically (e.g., weekly, monthly) convening settings, I sought out appropriate intensive experiences in order to compare the formation of community and my sense of community in regularly convening settings of less intensity with what I would experience in brief but total systems. Among the intensive settings in which I participated were two Tavistock labs, two community-building workshops sponsored by the Foundation for Community Encouragement, a Quaker silent retreat, and a Jesuit-directed retreat. Contrasts among these intensive experiences as well as between particular intensive settings and ongoing settings have provoked insights and questions about the roles of energy, intimacy, and emotionality in forming and sustaining a sense of community.

My schedule during spring 1992 was demanding. The opportunity for more spontaneous reflection was somewhat lost for part of each week as I kept up with my calendar. My time on some days felt narrowly sliced. I would be preparing for and attending classes, meetings, and rehearsals, feeling some urgency to get home or to a quiet place after each to record and debrief my experience. On other days I had long periods for reflection. My desire to be able to compare my experiences of community forming in groups that differed on several dimensions and the momentum generated by my enthusiasm led me to overindulge. But perhaps I was ready to engage furiously and intellectually as well as in the more contemplative mode that had characterized my involvements during the fall. The emotional tempo of my journey had changed. At the time I did not monitor that very closely, or consider its impact on my judgment. I might have benefited from doing so—but then that would have been a different journey. I see little in my journals signaling that others were observing an overload, or, if they were, that I was able to hear such observations.

Conclusion

As you have seen, the story of my sabbatical is really several stories in one. It is the story of a personal exploration in the context of a professional career. In this vein, it is the story of my struggle to accept the centrality of my personal renewal agenda and to trust that it would feed my professional agenda. Pursuit of this renewal agenda has grounded me emotionally and empirically in the long-term study of the meaning of a sense of community, the dynamics entailed in fostering and sustaining it, and its relevance for the workplace (see Louis, 1994).

From this experience I have learned that attending to my personal need for renewal contributed to my professional interests and development, and that my need for renewal thankfully pushed aside my best-laid plans. I was forced to see that the message I had taken in about use of a sabbatical to complete ongoing work was not appropriate for me. I have come to appreciate the traditional meaning of sabbatical as relevant for my personal and professional life, and will seek to build into my life periods of rest and discontinuity, of immersion in a different set of life activities, in order to revitalize myself and refresh my perspective.

This is also a story about discerning a path to follow rather than designing it, of following rather than pursuing a path, and of the faith and insecurity, trust, and self-consciousness that characterized my following that path. Accordingly, to tell this story has been to describe the interior movements, the internal voice that guided me on the path as well as the external events along the way. I am convinced that what I experienced would not have been within my grasp had I relied on my normal mode. In following this path, I have been renewed, and I sense that "my normal way" has been transformed. Along those lines, I have seen the value of opening the space for reflection and contemplation in my life.

I realize that I am more likely to see a shooting star when I stop concentrating on a particular spot in the sky, when I unfocus my eyes and let my gaze be drawn to moving objects anywhere in the sky. This metaphor seems apt in thinking about personal and professional renewal processes. In the rush of our normal professional lives, we are pushed to focus narrowly on the task at hand. We may rest our eyes and minds by unfocusing them for brief periods. Separating oneself from one's normal daily life—temporally, spatially, psychologically—is at the core of what sabbatical has meant historically in both secular and religious settings. Many faculty travel during their leaves. Others take up residency at other universities, acquiring new colleagues, students, and physical surroundings for the sabbatical period. By changing the contexts in which they do their work, these faculty hope to bring fresh eyes and ideas to it.

There are several things I have learned from my renewal journey that may be relevant for others who might wish to pursue sabbaticals (or other periods) of personal renewal. I have come to realize that attentiveness to an inner voice may provide better guidance on journeys of renewal than the best my intellectual resources alone can provide. I have seen the value of a life audit, of a systematic review of what I have found satisfying, what I would wish for more of in my life, as a guide in a personal renewal process. I have seen the value of reflection-in-action, of taking a close look at specific experiences, comparing and contrasting them for what they reveal about my pursuits. I have come to appreciate the need for people to fill different roles along such a path, for some to mirror periodically, for others to serve as more regular sympathetic onlookers or witnesses, and for still others to take the role of fellow travelers. Similarly, I have realized that some will remain outsiders to the journey and to my life during the period of the journey; they may be helped by an honest cover story explaining my need for separateness during the journey. I have seen that it may be possible for me to integrate into my professional life what is coming to matter to me as a person, that I may be able to be more fully present in professional settings and relationships than might be suggested by the stereotypical narrowly defined roles.

I have no idea whether a final lesson from my journey has relevance for others, but it has been of great significance to me. In returning to my regular responsibilities, I find that I have carried from my sabbatical experience a more attentive ear. I find myself making room in my once again hectic life to be still and to listen for the voice within. And I am amazed at the benefit of a moment of silence in my office, in meetings, or in the classroom, and the ease with which such moments may be created.

References

Louis, M. R. (1994). In the manner of friends: Learnings from Quaker practice for organizational renewal. *Journal of Organizational Change Management, 7*(1), 42-60.

Louis, M. R., & Bartunek, J. M. (1992). Insider/outsider research teams: Collaboration across diverse perspectives. *Journal of Management Inquiry, 1*(2), 101-110.

May, G. G. (1983). *Will and spirit: A contemplative psychology.* New York: Harper & Row.

VI

Rhythms of the Field

A LOOK AT THE FUTURE

As a former dean, I am not certain that faculty are fully aware of all the pressures being brought to bear on the modern business school by its many stakeholders. Clearly, we can be both relevant and rigorous. We can produce a theory-based business education with great practical value. However, to this point, the current period of transition has not, in my view, produced the levels of commitment and insight needed to achieve our goals.

Raymond E. Miles (p. 458)

Our challenge as faculty members is to understand more fully the external and institutional context in which we are working, to become better at "dancing with change." We must accommodate and effectively utilize emerging technologies; become more globally literate; contribute to the enhancement, measurement, and understanding of academic productivity; and help our administrators communicate effectively with multiple external constituencies.

William H. Mobley (p. 463)

This is a challenging time for business schools, and as faculty we must become more involved in the leadership of our universities if business schools are going to continue to thrive in the next decade.

Robert B. Duncan (p. 467)

It has frequently been my experience that, unfortunately, members of some stakeholder groups truly believe that their group is "the customer," or the only really important stakeholder group. This has been one of the biggest surprises to me in my role as senior associate dean. One of the more difficult challenges is to help different constituencies understand that there are others to which the business school must also listen and respond, and that everyone is not speaking with the same voice. It is very challenging to try to determine the best responses.

Marcia P. Miceli (p. 471)

Like all other organizations, universities have reached the point where they must give stakeholders their due deference. Whether we do so too frequently or too intensely will prove the issue of greatest controversy for most faculties for many years to come. All of this is easy to predict. What is more difficult to discern is what these changing tides will mean for academics at any of the institutions that employ them throughout their careers. Understanding the effects of this strategic issue on the internal cultures and structures of our organizations will make our lives as scholars more productive and more pleasant.

Janet P. Near (p. 479)

The reports and stories of the contributors to this volume have addressed issues that affect the various rhythms that we as academics experience as we go about our work. All these activities and rhythms take place in the broader technological, economic, and sociocultural contexts of our times. There are dramatic changes taking place in each of these contexts, and they are having major impacts on our institutions and on us. We would be remiss if we did not include some attention to this more macro perspective of academic life. We are very fortunate to be able to incorporate in this volume some reflections on this very salient issue from several academics who have had experience in or are currently serving as senior administrators in university institutions.

A symposium titled "The Changing Institutional Context" was presented at a doctoral consortium organized by Art Brief, Jim Walsh, and Dick Woodman during the August 1995 Academy of Management meetings in Vancouver, Canada. The panel for the symposium was chaired by Ray Miles, former dean of the Haas School of Business at the University of California, Berkeley, and presented by Bill Mobley, former president of Texas A&M University and former chancellor of the Texas University System; and included Bob Duncan, former provost of Northwestern University; Marcia Miceli, senior associate dean for academic affairs at the Fisher College of Business at Ohio University; and Janet Near, department chair in the School of Business at Indiana University. The charge to this panel from Jim Walsh stressed the following:

> Our fundamental premise for the session is that many of our stakeholders are more alert (if not agitated) than they have been in some time. Many of us clearly feel pressures on our teaching and research that we did not ten years ago. So the first thing we want to do is identify and then sort out whether or not these "market pressures" represent a paradigm shift of some sort. This is the *institutional* issue we want to address. Next we want to talk about development of our human capital in this context. The audience is advanced Ph.D. students, so it is appropriate to talk about individual development issues at this career stage. Nevertheless, this session will be filmed in the hope of showing it to faculty groups throughout the Academy. With this broader audience in mind, it would be good if you could also speak to faculty development at various career stages as well. This is the *individual* issue we want to appear in this session. (memo dated June 19, 1995)

We invited the panel members to translate their presentations into text, and we present their work here. The reflections, predictions, and prescriptions of these authors were originally intended primarily for an audience of junior scholars. However, they make interesting reading for any academic who has a stake in the long-term viability of the enterprise.

Ray Miles briefly traces the past hundred years in business education. He points out that in that time business schools "have enjoyed periods of enormous success interspersed with periods of major transition" (p. 457) and adds that we are in the midst of one of these latter downswings. He identifies the current era as one in which we are searching as an enterprise for increased relevance in ways that do not sacrifice the quality of our teaching and research. As noted above, in the quote from his chapter, he has doubts about the extent to which academics as members of faculties have a good grasp of the nature and magnitude of the response that is required of them to meet this challenge.

Bill Mobley evokes the metaphor of dancing when he asks readers to think about their careers in the context of many different changes facing higher education: "Periodically, [you might want to] reflect on who is composing the music, who is conducting the music, who is leading, and what all this means for your career" (p. 459). Mobley discusses changes in demographics, in the size and scope of education, in the nature of work as well as in time, space, and information flows. He draws attention to the effects on higher education of rising costs and "increasing calls for demonstrable performance measurement" in higher education (p. 461). As we strive to do well in our teaching and our research, it is worth noting that the opinions held by external players of our value and our contributions are increasingly coming to influence our reputations as educators. Mobley, citing surveys, observes that these stakeholders do not necessarily find laudable what we do. If we do not examine carefully, counter wisely, and, where appropriate, respond constructively to these assessments, we may find much that we hold important being placed at risk.

Bob Duncan points out that fiscal and other crises facing universities translate into significant pressures on business schools. University administrations, in such times, tend to centralize decision making and make increased financial demands on business schools. Duncan points out that central university administrations fail to recognize the scholarship dimension of business schools, nor do they appreciate the diversity and sophistication of their constituencies.

He argues that we need to become more active in our efforts to educate the leaders in universities about the nature of the modern business school. He urges us to become more involved in the governance of universities and to find ways to make available business school expertise to help universities improve the quality of leadership on campus.

Marcia Miceli continues the theme of the growing need for academics to respond to change. She focuses on the many stakeholders of business schools and the importance of understanding their varied needs and wishes. "Each may raise questions, articulate expectations, and exert influence, because each provides resources to the business school" (p. 472). She traces some important differences between business enterprises and the university, in terms of what constitutes a "customer" and how customers' needs are addressed. Although members of some of a university's stakeholder groups "truly believe that their group is 'the customer,' or the only really important stakeholder group" (p. 471), this is not the case. Faculty members and administrators need to exercise judgment in how they respond to these needs and demands. Miceli points out that the values and goals of institution members provide an important part of the context within which such needs and demands must be weighed: "One of the more difficult challenges is to help different constituencies understand that there are others to which the business school must also listen and respond, and that everyone is not speaking with the same voice" (p. 471). Miceli believes strongly in faculty involvement in discussions about responses to change, and she traces out some of the ethical and political dilemmas that faculty need to discuss as they engage and respond to "players" from outside the university.

Janet Near examines the changing roles and impacts of three groups: faculty, students, and publics. Drawing on a strategic contingencies perspective of power, she traces the relative shifts in power from faculty to students, from departments to programs. Such shifts bring changes in roles and goals: "Whereas departments may have demanded excellent research (and probably still do), programs are more likely to demand outstanding teaching. Perhaps service demands related to the program will also increase. . . . In addition, the technology for measuring teaching performance has received far more discussion, and sparked more controversy, than in the past" (p. 476). Near draws attention to two other trends affecting universities, bringing into sharp relief the likely changes to our institutions and to the profession of shifts in demographics and of downsizing. Among other structural effects of these changes, she predicts that business schools "are far more likely to select women or people of color than would have been the case 30 years ago, thereby changing the overall composition of faculties" (p. 478).

Jim Walsh comments on the ideas expressed in these reports and adds several insights of his own. In particular, he points out the need for us to think and act as a community of scholars as we face these challenges. Academics, as individuals, cannot simultaneously attend to and excel on all the dimensions that need to be addressed in these turbulent times. This is an observation that deserves our careful and considered attention in the years ahead.

47 Business Schools in Transition

A BRIEF HISTORY OF BUSINESS EDUCATION

Raymond E. Miles

Over the past 100 years, business schools have enjoyed periods of enormous success interspersed with periods of major transition. Unfortunately, we are in one of those latter periods at the moment, one that will probably continue for another 5 years or so. The business community, the faculty of business schools, other departments on campus, and the campus as a whole become matters of concern in periods of transition. I am going to look at all the stakeholders and the role of the business school and business education in that process. My task in this essay is to provide a brief history, some current perspectives, and later on some views from a former dean.

Let me begin with a very brief history of business education. I will run through the past hundred years in rapid-fire order and make just a few comments about that history. Business education was born in the United States in the latter part of the nineteenth century. The Wharton School claims that birthplace and probably rightfully so, although the precise date is a mat-

ter of question. Shortly after Wharton's beginnings, schools emerged at the Universities of California and Chicago and immediately after that at Dartmouth, New York University, and the University of Wisconsin.

By 1916, business education was relatively well established in the United States, sufficiently so that an institutional association was created: the American Association of Collegiate Schools of Business, today the American Assembly of Collegiate Schools of Business. It began in 1916 with 16 charter members. Those were the premier schools of the day, and they set about to form an association to maintain standards within their own ranks. These early attempts at setting standards for accreditation marked a major transition.

The early growth is impressive for a new institution: 5 business schools by 1900, 55 by 1920, 84 by 1940, even with the Great Depression as an impediment to that growth, and by 1958, 112 schools. The late 1950s brought a second, more dramatic transition. Business education in the immediate postwar period was booming with an influx of veterans. Business schools were being created with great speed, and there was broadscale recognition that business education was frequently not a high-quality process.

By and large, throughout its early history business education focused on the art of business and not on the science of business and business education. Two major reports modeled on the earlier Flexner report on medical education emerged in the 1950s. Sponsored by the Ford Foundation, Robert Gordon and James Howell produced the more impactful of the two reports, a critique that evoked a major period of introspection in business schools across the country. Their report was seized on by the American Association of Collegiate Schools of Business (AACSB), the accrediting body, and their criteria for quality business education immediately became part of the AACSB accreditation process.

The second report, the Pierson Report, sponsored by the Carnegie Foundation, arrived at many of the same findings as Gordon and Howell, but had some special insights of its own. That report, too, was incorporated into the criteria by which people began to evaluate business education.

The bottom line from both reports was that business education would respond positively to a massive infusion of science—bringing the social sciences into business education. I was teaching at a business school in 1958 when Gordon and Howell's report was published, and their prescriptions became very salient to me, not only because my business school was seeking accreditation but because they represented something I was quite convinced needed to occur: a major reform brought about from external sources.

With the impetus of Gordon and Howell's and Pierson's reports, business schools brought sociologists, psychologists, operations researchers,

and econometricians, among others, into their faculties. Curriculum programs expanded to include new analytic tools and subjects, and faculty research took on new topics with enhanced scholarly standards.

By the late 1980s, the push for a true science of business had brought major gains in such areas as operations and inventory management, financial theory and practice, information systems, and consumer behavior. Numerous new journals displayed faculty research across dozens of new areas of specialization.

Indeed, the press for rigorous research and publication quantity ultimately raised questions concerning the focus of faculty and business school curricula. In the late 1980s, numerous critiques by prominent executives raised questions about curriculum and research relevance and called for program reforms to produce "practical" skills and knowledge. A 1988 AACSB-sponsored report by Lyman Porter and Lawrence McKibbon added to concerns about research and curriculum quality and directions.

The current transition represents a search for increased relevance while simultaneously maintaining research and curriculum quality. Leveling enrollments have added pressure for faculty to improve teaching quality and meet higher levels of student expectations. Slowed enrollment growth has increased competition for faculty slots and placed a premium on both research and teaching accomplishments.

As a former dean, I am not certain that faculty are fully aware of all the pressures being brought to bear on the modern business school by its many stakeholders. Clearly, we can be both relevant and rigorous. We can produce a theory-based business education with great practical value. However, to this point, the current period of transition has not, in my view, produced the levels of commitment and insight needed to achieve our goals.

48 The External and Institutional Context of Business Higher Education

William H. Mobley

After 14 years of university administration, I find it a pleasure to be back on the faculty and among faculty and would-be faculty. I consider this a promotion. I am not among those who define a faculty as a group of anarchists bound together by a common concern for parking. Nor am I one who believes that faculty members are concerned only about unlimited travel budgets, unlimited Pentium upgrades, unlimited graduate students, and very limited undergraduate teaching, although this list has grown more appealing since my return to the faculty.

I have been invited to contribute to this discussion from the perspective of the external and institutional context in which faculty careers develop. My remarks are organized around the elements presented in Table 48.1, which, as you will note, summarizes five general contextual categories and suggests some examples of needed responses from higher education. I have left the last column of the table, where personal responses belong, blank, in the hope that you will want to fill it out after you have had an opportunity to reflect on all the preceding and subsequent presentations.

Dancing With Change

The title of this first contextual category comes from the Pew Higher Education Roundtable (1994) report focusing on change in higher education. As you think about your career and the external environment and your personal responses to the right-hand column in Table 48.1, you might want to adopt this metaphor of dancing. Periodically, reflect on who is composing the music, who is conducting the music, who is leading, and what all this means for your career.

The first general categories of contextual change have to do with changing demographics, changes in the size and scope of higher education, and the changing nature of work. Demographically, the U.S. population has grown from 151 million in 1950 to some 260 million today. This growth includes increased diversity

TABLE 48.1   The Changing Context and Possible Responses

Context	Example Responses	
	Higher Education	Personal
Dancing with change	Responsiveness to changing markets; accommodation of diversity; reduction of polarizing rhetoric; improved demonstration of value	
Time, space, and information flows	Improved cyberspace literacy; evaluation and embrace of new technologies; focus on new forms of instruction and learning	
The global village	Decrease in ethnocentric research; expansion of resources to promote global literacy of faculty and students	
Costs and criteria	Improved productivity measurement and communication of criteria; enhancement of productivity through technology, resource management, networking, and leveraging	
Public perceptions	Improved communication with public and opinion leaders; open discussion of tenure; strengthened management and governance systems; attempts to address the contexts and responses listed in this table	

in schools and at work in almost every dimension of diversity. This demographic change is continuing in the workplace and in educational institutions at every level. As institutions of higher learning we must continue to be more responsive to the market and personal learning requirements of an older and more diverse population with a variety of education and reeducation needs. One of my concerns is that the rhetoric of both the extreme left and the extreme right has made reasoned and civil debate on issues of diversity and multiculturalism very difficult, even though diversity is a defining characteristic of our time.

Higher education has changed in its size and scope. We have gone from 1,800 institutions of higher learning in the United States in 1950 to more than 3,500 today. Enrollment in our universities has grown from 2.3 million students to more than 14 million. In 1950, 2% of the U.S. population older than 25 years of age had at least a bachelor's degree; by 1990, this figure had reached more than 21%.

Changes in the nature of work are evident. Manufacturing jobs have declined from some 19 million in 1981 to fewer than 18 million a decade later. Service sector jobs have grown from 18 million to more than 25 million, a 38% increase in a decade. Increasingly, a college degree is a necessary but insufficient credential for access to a place in the professional workforce.

As public expectations regarding education in general changed in the 1970s and 1980s, it was K-12 that received the most attention and criticism. Higher education, with some exceptions, remained out of the fray. But in the mid-1980s and continuing into the 1990s, higher education, with its rising costs and budget-strapped state legislatures, and in the face of growing public cynicism about all forms of institutions, found itself at the front of the battle. We were no longer in favored status and increasingly had to justify the cost and quality of all that we do (Mobley, 1994). The public policy lesson of the 1990s, in the view of the Pew Higher Education Roundtable (1994, 1995), is that most Americans are prepared to trust markets more than governments and, at every level, the willingness of society to tax itself to promote the public good, including higher education, has receded.

An editorial that appeared in the *Vancouver Sun* during the August 1995 Academy of Management meetings focused on the fact that taxpayers will continue to underwrite some two-thirds of the cost of higher education in Canada. (U.S. residents will recognize that this is a considerably higher level of support than in the United States, where many public-assisted universities are below one-third, some well below, in taxpayer support of the budget.) The editorial stated: "This means lower income Canadians will continue to subsidize the education of middle and upper class people in the college classroom. Although some taxpayer subsidy is warranted since society as a whole benefits from higher education, there is inequity at the heart of the system. That inequity remains." A variant of this editorial is being written in many parts of the free world. The point is that taxpayer support for higher education increasingly is going to have to be earned and justified; it is no longer awarded as an act of faith.

Changes in Time, Space, and Information Flows

Deregulation of communications and advances in technology have created a whole new environment for movement of information and knowledge. How many of you have used the Internet today to communicate with a colleague abroad, to retrieve information from a distant library, to forward a manuscript to an editor, or to witness once again the musings of an undergraduate who has not yet learned the responsibility that accompanies the freedom provided by such technology? Speed, power, and connectiveness we did not contemplate a short time ago now define our age. With live interactive video technology about to penetrate the mass market, and with more power and speed at ever lower costs available worldwide, we are experiencing significant compression in time and space.

Sheila Creth (1995) recently published a very interesting article on the true collaboration, beyond cooperation and communication, afforded by modern technology. She articulates the growing clash between "moving matter" and culture. What is moving? Markets, people, currency, goods, and information all are moving, and with increased speed and fewer restraints. However, culture—including religion, values, preferences, and manners—is slower and more difficult to change. The collision of high-velocity technological change and less pliable

culture results in conflict. The infusion of technology into developing countries and into some quarters of the university provides good examples.

Information technology is facilitating increased focus on lifelong learning and self-directed learning. In a decade, universities and students will not be as place-bound as they are today. Much of what we transmit in a classroom can easily be transmitted on demand from digitally stored video, and the interactive component can be done with interactive delivery systems relatively unconstrained by place. Technology will support a level of learning effectiveness not now attained, but only in the face of a reticent culture in too many quarters of the academy.

The Global Village

Global competition for ideas, markets, and talent is very evident. Educators must become more internationally active and competent. In so doing, we must recognize our cultural filters and blinders. Hofstede (1994) reminds us that management science by definition cannot be universal. He asserts that assuming universality of management science means assuming that everyone thinks, feels, and acts like oneself, and that is supremely ethnocentric and myopic.

Boyacigiller and Adler (1991) draw a parallel between the evolution of global corporations and the evolution of scholarship and academic organizations such as the Academy of Management. The Academy is still far from a global organization, and most of us are far from globally literate in our research and teaching. We are at best exporters of our models and theories, and do not yet have adequate understanding of the indigenous cultures around the world and how theories and models developed in those cultures might generalize to our own.

Costs and Criteria

My fourth contextual point focuses on the rising costs of higher education and increasing calls for demonstrable performance measurement. Contrary to some projections, college enrollments in the United States have not gone down; they are continuing to rise. The U.S. Department of Education's 1995 forecast through 2005 is that we will have an approximately 8%

growth in higher education enrollment. Expenditures are projected to rise some 34% over the coming decade, compared with a 55% growth in expenditures over the past decade. It is interesting to note that the Department of Education is predicting a decrease in master's and doctoral degrees awarded over the next decade, −6% and −11%, respectively. This will have budget implications as well as implications for faculty staffing and teaching preference.

The former chancellor of the SUNY system, Bruce Johnstone (1993), has written a very insightful analysis on productivity in higher education. He argues that escalating costs, uneven demographics, faltering revenues, and erosion of public confidence beg for increased productivity in higher education. This needs to be accomplished not through the creation of larger section sizes, not by the use of more graduate assistants in the classroom, not by increasing the input by lowering entrance standards, not by lowering graduation requirements, not by allowing students to park in universities for extended stays, and not by turning research universities into predominantly undergraduate teaching universities. Rather, true productivity gain must be attained through such steps as better utilization of technology, year-round education, minimization of course sequencing problems, additional teaching loads (in some cases), and better evaluation of and communication concerning all dimensions of academic performance. Those in the academy must rise to the challenge of helping measure performance, increase productivity, and communicate our effectiveness to our various constituents. Greater accountability in higher education will come from within or externally, and the former is infinitely better.

Public Perceptions

Public opinion about higher education has been mentioned several times already, but it requires further comment. At the 1995 meeting of the Council for the Advancement and Support of Education (CASE), Jim Harvey (1995), who is with the National Institute of Education and is coauthor of *A Nation at Risk* (National Commission on Excellence in Education, 1983), reported on a major study of the general public and opinion leaders that used both survey and focus group methods. He found that the general public generally likes higher education, views a college degree as worth what a high school diploma was worth a few years ago, views access as more important than quality, and believes faculty are okay and not overpaid like doctors and lawyers. Respondents from the general public felt that if a student fails it is the student's fault rather than the institution's, and said that they would redirect funds from senior universities to vocational postsecondary and community colleges.

Opinion leaders, on the other hand, had some markedly different perceptions from those of the general public. According to Harvey (1995), opinion leaders believe the following:

- Tenure should be abolished.
- A faculty member would have to commit a felony to be fired.
- Most college graduates cannot compose a decent letter.
- While corporate America is downsizing, most colleges are not slimming down.
- Both access and quality are important.
- Professors are not up-to-date in state-of-the-art techniques, especially those in business.
- Faculty avoid the big issues in research, teach too little, and rely too much on TAs.
- Costs are rising, but productivity enhancement is not seen as forthcoming.

Opinion leaders express understanding and support for academic goals, but they perceive an inadequate level of change. You may be assured that our elected officials are hearing these things from both the general public and opinion leaders, but are we communicating these opinions to every faculty member?

Barry Munitz (1995) provides some valuable information about the transformations that surround us. He quotes both Tom Kean and Clark Kerr. Kean, former governor of New Jersey and cochair of a current panel on national investment in higher education, says, "Hear it plain and simple. Our ivory tower is under siege. People are questioning our mission and questioning who we are. They claim we cost too much, spend carelessly, teach poorly, plan myopically and when questioned, act defensively." Kerr, former University of California system president, suggests that "we need to learn to subtract as well as add, to reduce less useful areas in order to make way for the most useful." Munitz, in noting the public perception issue, relates a story about a Cézanne painting that was the subject of comment by critics. It was a painting of a sunset, and the critics said it did not look like a sunset. Cézanne responded that the critics must not see sunsets as he did. Indeed, our publics are not seeing our academic "artistry" in the same way we do, and that should concern us all.

Lest all this sound like a Dennis Miller rant, permit me to conclude on a more optimistic note. In a wonderful op-ed piece on why businesses should be run like universities, R. L. Woodbury (1993) makes seven points:

1. Higher education in the United States is one of the few U.S. industries to be viewed as the best in the world. Our colleges and universities are universally recognized as the best in the world and dominate the globe as do few other areas of the economy.

2. Universities generate a favorable balance of payments, some $5 billion and rising. Some 420,000 international students, most funded from abroad, study full-time on our campuses, and only 80,000 U.S. students are studying abroad.

3. Higher education is a growth industry, with enrollments continuing to rise as consumers continue to see higher education as a good investment.

4. Cases of college bankruptcies or defaults on institutional loans or high-level malfeasance are relatively rare. Certainly many institutions can be run better and management can be improved, but overall the record of stewardship is quite enviable.

5. No other industry has organized, retained, or energized so much human capital at such a low cost. At a given institution, thousands of people have studied an average of 6 years beyond their bachelor's degrees and earn an average of $45,000 per year.

6. Undergraduates get a bargain. A college provides housing, food, association with some of the best minds in the world, arts, athletics, entertainment of all sorts, and libraries, all for an average cost of $12,000 per year.

7. The return on investment is enviable. Aside from the intellectual and cultural development, a graduate of a 4-year institution will earn approximately 50% more than the non-college graduate. The economic and social contribution of university research and auxiliary enterprises is huge.

The brighter side of the story that Woodbury tells is encouraging, but it is not shared broadly with the public at large or our opinion leaders.

Conclusion

Our challenge as faculty members is to understand more fully the external and institutional context in which we are working, to become better at "dancing with change." We must accommodate and effectively utilize emerging technologies; become more globally literate; contribute to the enhancement, measurement, and understanding of academic productivity; and help our administrators communicate effectively with multiple external constituencies.

References

Boyacigiller, N. A., & Adler, N. J. (1991). The parochial dinosaur: Organizational science in a global context. *Academy of Management Review, 16,* 262-290.

Creth, S. (1995, April). Creating a virtual information organization. *Educom Review,* pp. 15-17.

Harvey, J. (1995). *Perceptions of higher education.* Paper presented at the annual meeting of the Council for the Advancement and Support of Education, Washington, DC.

Hofstede, G. (1994). Management scientists are human. *Management Science, 40,* 4-13.

Johnstone, B. D. (1993). *Learning productivity: A new imperative for American higher education.* Albany: State University of New York Press.

Mobley, W. H. (1994, April). *Tough times-tough choices in higher education.* Paper presented at a forum of the American Council on Education and the Council for the Advancement and Support of Education, Washington, DC.

Munitz, B. (1995, June). Managing transformation in an age of social triage. *Higher Education Management.*

National Commission on Excellence in Education. (1983). *A nation at risk: The imperative for educational reform.* Washington, DC: Government Printing Office.

Pew Higher Education Roundtable. (1994, April). To dance with change. *Policy Perspectives.*

Pew Higher Education Roundtable. (1995, April). Twice imagined. *Policy Perspectives.*

U.S. Department of Education, National Center for Education Statistics. (1995). *Projections of education statistics to 2005.* Washington, DC: Government Printing Office.

Woodbury, R. L. (1993, March 23). Why not run a business like a good university? *Christian Science Monitor.*

49 The Changing Role of the Business School's Environment

THE THREAT-RIGIDITY RESPONSE IS REAL

Robert B. Duncan

Bill Mobley has provided an excellent overview of the changing institutional context of universities from his perspective as a former university president. My remarks are from the perspective of a former provost/senior vice president for academic affairs. The provost is the chief operating officer primarily responsible for all academic activities in the university. If the university's environment is less benign and more crisis oriented, then the business school's environment will become more turbulent and hostile. Threat-rigidity theory would predict that there will be pressures in the university environment to centralize decision making, pull resources back to the central administration, and generally rein in business schools. Business schools will no longer be benignly neglected by university central administrations and left alone as islands unto themselves. All this has important implications for us as business school faculty, and I will provide some thoughts on how

we need to be proactive in responding to this environmental change.

Educating the University

The first thing we must do is realize that university administrators fundamentally do not understand what business schools are about. Most senior administrators come from arts and science backgrounds, so they are often inclined to view business schools as professional schools that are primarily practitioner oriented, and then in their simplistic mind-set they make the erroneous assumption that our faculty are not serious scholars. They do not understand the scholarly focus of what we do. Therefore, we must better educate presidents, provosts, and our university colleagues as a whole as to just what the mission of a business school is. We must help them understand that we have a

465

more diverse set of constituents that we must satisfy. We have students and alumni like every other school in the university. However, we also have to satisfy the increasingly demanding expectations of corporate recruiters, who are looking for students with leading-edge usable knowledge, and our executive education customers, who are also looking for leading-edge usable knowledge. As a result of the more sophisticated demands of these customer groups, our faculty members are under an increasingly expanded set of performance expectations. They must do their research and publish in their scholarly journals just like every other faculty member. However, they must also invest a significant amount of time in developing the usable knowledge component of their research so they can meet the demands of our professional students. In a real sense, professional school students are more demanding than other students. They want to understand theory, but they also want to understand the application value of the theory.

We also need to help presidents and provosts understand our practitioner community. They view practitioners as a pool of donors from which they can easily pluck to fill university coffers. However, presidents and provosts must learn that these practitioners are becoming much more sophisticated about what universities can and cannot provide in the way of leading-edge usable knowledge to both the students they might hire and the executives they might send to university training programs. These practitioners are our customers, and if they are not satisfied with what we provide in leading-edge usable knowledge, they will support another university. Therefore, we must help administrators understand that business school faculty must develop the applications component of their research. Here we can use the medical school analogy of basic science and clinical research. Business school faculty have to do their basic research for the academic journals and then also make clinical applications with the development of leading-edge usable knowledge connections.

Proactive Responses to Reduce Centralization

Once we have helped the university to understand our mission more fully, there are a number of things we can do to minimize the centralization efforts of the university, which can limit the autonomy and ability of business schools to deal with our demanding constituents. It is important to understand that business schools have no inalienable right to be autonomous and left alone by the university central administration. Business schools can retain control over their destiny by being viewed as more integral to the university's overall mission. Business schools can earn this in a number of ways:

1. We can create alliances with other parts of the university. Joint MBA programs in manufacturing management with engineering schools and joint programs in law and medicine have been typical alliance programs in the past. New opportunities now exist to link up with arts and sciences as we all try to become more global. For example, the School of Business at the University of Texas has a joint program in which MBA students take a semester of a foreign language as part of their global management curriculum. Other opportunities exist to link up with programs in international relations and area studies as we become more global. We can also create links with computer science departments as we increase our efforts to understand the effects of the information technology revolution on organizations.

2. Business schools can become a resource in leadership expertise for the university. Universities are complex organizations with multimillion-dollar budgets, with many of the same strategic and operating problems that business organizations face as a result of leadership crises. University presidents are often selected because they are great academics. However, they may be poorly prepared for their new role. They may understand academic issues but often have no comprehension of the leadership requirements for running universities with multimillion-dollar budgets, billion-dollar endowments, and thousands of employees and students. They have no sense of strategic issues, setting priories, being able to say no and make tough decisions, and do not have the emotional toughness to stand up to the constant pressures that various constituents will make on them in often contentious ways. As provost I was yelled at, was the subject of

demonstrations, and had to close a school. There was nothing in my background to prepare me for that. However, as business school faculty, we can provide our usable knowledge in strategic decision making, organizational change, leadership, and so on to presidents and provosts to help them become better prepared to deal with many of these issues. It is also critical for business school faculty to be on search committees, so that some consideration is given to these leadership requirements in selecting presidents and provosts. Today, most universities get into a crisis *not* because their leaders are not good academics, but rather because these good academics *cannot* be competent strategic change leaders.

3. Business school faculty need to get more involved in university governance. General faculty committees and university senates are having increasing influence in shaping the strategic priorities of universities as presidents seek their input as a way to get support for controversial decisions. It is imperative that business school interests be represented in these groups, so that the business school is not viewed just as a cash cow to be raided to fix the economic problems of a university that from a strategic perspective has been mismanaged.

This is a challenging time for business schools, and as faculty we must become more involved in the leadership of our universities if business schools are going to continue to thrive in the next decade.

50 Business Schools in Transition

AN ASSOCIATE DEAN'S PERSPECTIVE

Marcia P. Miceli

I am the senior associate dean for academic programs at the Max M. Fisher College of Business at Ohio State University. I also serve as the interim academic director of the MBA programs. My job involves hands-on management of the MBA programs as well as coordination of the comprehensive planning process to revise the full-time MBA this year. In addition, I oversee the activities of the academic directors of the other programs in the Fisher College—the undergraduate program in business administration, the master's and PhD programs in labor and human resources and public policy and management, the PhD in accounting, and the PhD in business. I also perform other duties of associate deans where the dean is heavily involved in external fund-raising, such as meeting prospective faculty candidates, resolving issues among Fisher College support units, and coordinating with other associate deans on faculty or budget matters, as well as interacting with central university administration or members of other colleges. I also attempt to maintain a faculty presence in research.

My objective in this essay is to discuss the changes in the environment that affect business schools and junior faculty members by (a) focusing primarily on stakeholders both inside and outside the business school and (b) describing some implications of the perspectives for emerging scholars entering the profession. [*Editors' note:* Although this presentation was geared to junior faculty members, we believe much of it is relevant to all academics. As a result, specific references to junior faculty in the text have been minimized.]

Stakeholders: Understanding Their Varied Needs and Wishes

The Importance of Stakeholders

My perspectives are derived primarily from observations about stakeholders and how they can affect the events occurring in business schools and colleges. Other authors in this volume have

469

also touched on some of these points, particularly those concerned with the influences of stakeholders at the university level.

There are three overarching points I would like to make. First, there are many different groups of stakeholders for business colleges, many more than for most organizations. It is important to identify these groups and to hear their needs and wishes. Listening and responding can greatly improve the quality of what we do. Second, although in some cases there is congruence in stakeholder needs and wishes, these often conflict within and between groups. Resources offered by stakeholders also may vary substantially. Third, faculty and other college members must exercise judgment in determining how to sort out and respond to stakeholder voices, given the values and goals of the institution's members. This is a difficult process, but it is rewarding. A critical question for each faculty member concerns the extent to which he or she wants to participate in this process. The first order of business, as others have emphasized, is to get tenure, which requires productivity primarily in research and teaching. Faculty time devoted to sorting out environmental pressures is generally viewed as "service," and time spent in service can detract from more highly valued productivity on other fronts. I return now to each of the above three points.

Multiple Stakeholders

Some stakeholders can be classified as members of the college and university, whereas others are more clearly viewed as operating in the external environment. Internal stakeholders include faculty, staff, and current students; the central administration of the university; and members of other units in the university (e.g., other departments). External stakeholders include prospective students and parents, members of the profession (e.g., journal editors and reviewers) and colleagues at other academic institutions, donors and potential donors, recruiters, the business community, alumni, taxpayers (in state- and federally assisted institutions), grantors, and the federal government. A comprehensive analysis is obviously beyond the scope of this essay, but I hope to touch on some examples of stakeholder interests and influence.

These stakeholders are important obviously because they provide resources to the organization—though many other reasons can also be identified. For example, students pay tuition, employers hire students and perhaps faculty as consultants, citizens provide tax dollars, grantors and government agencies support research, society, and perhaps the international community, and so forth. Central administration (e.g., the president or provost) is particularly important if it is the primary decision maker in allocating the resources that flow into the university from a variety of sources.

Conflicting Needs and Wants

Because many constituents provide resources, they understandably want their expressions of needs and wishes heard; perhaps to encourage this, they point out to the faculty that they are "the customer." But these needs and wishes often conflict with those of other stakeholders, a key point that is often obscured when one or more of these groups views itself as "the customer."

Speaking very broadly and generally (there are many complexities and exceptions), I believe there are important ways in which customers of businesses differ from stakeholders in universities. For example, customers pay the full costs of a product or service; businesses that are not responsive to them do not thrive. Other stakeholders, such as shareholders and boards of directors, may also play a role, but if managers take actions that displease most customers, these other stakeholders will also be disadvantaged, and thus stakeholder voices are in harmony. In contrast, none of the stakeholders pays "full freight" at the university. Many different groups share the costs, and they do not all reap and value the same rewards. One possible business parallel is that of a publisher that must sell magazines to consumers while also pleasing advertisers and perhaps desiring to meet high critical standards.

As another example of a difference, most businesses must do what customers want in order to survive, and they do not require any action on the part of customers other than ability to pay. The salesperson shouldn't care whether she or he sells a car to me or to the next customer if we both have the money. But to survive, the university must require the group that perhaps can best claim to be a "customer" to meet its or its competitors' standards. If students insisted that there be no grading standards of any type, or that faculty do no more research and instead teach more classes, should the university agree? There are many factors (and other stakeholder wishes and needs) to consider here. In this sense the university is more like the fitness coach or physician, who may have to alienate some clients by being demanding or saying no.

Exercising Judgment in Responding to Stakeholders

The voices of stakeholders should be heard by the faculty (including college administration), and responses should be considered in the context of the values and goals of the institution's members (and other factors). Further, certain stakeholders may have greater impact at different institutions and faculty may be differentially affected.

It has frequently been my experience that, unfortunately, members of some stakeholder groups truly believe that their group is "the customer," or the only really important stakeholder group. This has been one of the biggest surprises to me in my role as senior associate dean. One of the more difficult challenges is to help different constituencies understand that there are others to which the business school must also listen and respond, and that everyone is not speaking with the same voice. It is very challenging to try to determine the best responses.

Stakeholder Wishes and Needs

From the junior faculty member's perspective, the primary stakeholder is probably the student. Students want us to teach the classes that they want, taught as they prefer, at convenient times. They may want small classes or evening classes; they may want instructors to be conversant in the latest technology and may desire lots of individual advising. I believe these preferences are much more likely to be expressed now than even 5 years ago. Faculty may agree with some of these preferences (e.g., small classes). Yet, at the same time, because students are not paying the full costs of their education

(nor the costly forms they would like it to take) at most institutions, budget constraints likely prevent our doing all of these things, and hard choices must be made. Similarly, faculty time constraints must be recognized. It is not possible for a junior faculty member to teach many sections, all with the latest technology, and give much individual attention to students while also being a generator as well as a consumer of the best, more recent research.

The profession has been a dominant stakeholder in the past, and it continues to be very important, particularly for junior faculty. If their research does not meet the standards of the editors and reviewers for the journals their colleges value, then at most universities they cannot get tenure, no matter how well they may satisfy other stakeholders. All too frequently, other stakeholders do not understand how important the profession is as a stakeholder, or why this is so.

Unfortunately, sometimes even the university administration has an incomplete view of business schools' research. Administrators and other university colleagues may view the business college as primarily a teaching and consulting unit that only generates funds. Thus faculty may hear of more pressures to "generate credit hours," and they need to understand that the universities, like other organizations, are facing many demands for accountability and economic viability. At the same time, it is the job of college administration and senior faculty to continue to communicate with other stakeholders about the value of research and the research community's importance as a stakeholder.

State legislatures and related entities determine significant portions of some budgets, and increasingly they want to know how these budgets are spent. One example is occurring in the state of Ohio. Legislators noticed that subsidies to PhD programs had increased dramatically, and they asked the board of regents to explore the growth in enrollment in PhD programs at state-assisted institutions. Legislators were concerned about the proliferation of programs and their quality. They provided that, if programs did not meet standards of quality, with criteria to be determined by the regents, such programs would be eliminated.

This is a very reasonable and laudable inquiry. In a positive sense, it forces schools to focus greater attention on data collection. In practice, it was very time- and resource-consuming to respond, because many criteria were chosen for evaluation for which records were not kept, and some criteria changed over time. More important, some of the criteria were questioned as indicators of quality. For example, initially, one important issue to be addressed was the extent to which the program met the needs of the state's residents; for example, did the graduates later join Ohio school faculties or provide services to local residents? Although this is very understandable from this constituent's perspective, it is problematic from other perspectives, and these criteria may be very much at odds with the goals of most PhD programs of quality that have limited resources. The quality of most PhD programs is more likely to be reflected in national or international rather than local or regional placements, for example. Fortunately, this criterion was weighed less heavily as more was learned about PhD program evaluation. But I think the example still serves to illustrate how important this type of stakeholder can be in influencing the activities of a business college in perhaps unexpected ways.

Donors can exercise important influence on faculty and college activity. On the one hand, a donor can ask if we would be willing to engage in an activity he or she would find interesting, such as an accounting honors program. The donor may be unwilling to contribute unless we conduct the activity in the way the donor desires. On the other hand, donors may simply say, "We want you to do well what you choose to do; we don't want to dictate to you, but rather to support you in your endeavors." It is easy to see how differently influence could play out, depending on the stance taken by the donor and the extent to which the college solicits and accepts each type of donation. A dialogue is needed to determine whether goals and expectations are congruent, and faculty can play a key role here.

Recruiters of graduates have always been important to the business school. Increasingly, some recruiters view the business school as a "training ground" for their particular needs, or as a "supplier." Employers may view themselves as the primary customer and the graduate as "the product" of the business school. Although in some ways faculty may agree with these sentiments, in other ways they may disagree. This dialogue, like others, should continue.

As other contributors to this section have noted, the business community may want research that it sees as "cutting edge" in a practical sense. It may or may not understand the importance of fundamental, sound, basic research. This poses obvious difficulties, particularly when one remembers the needs and wishes of the profession, described earlier.

Alumni are often the most supportive of external stakeholders. They want us to do well because many are fond of their institutions and want their degrees to continue to be respected. They want to try to help if they can, but they're not always as involved as we would like them to be.

Alumni are very interested in the rankings of business schools, for example, those published by *Business Week* and *U.S. News & World Report*. These rankings are exerting a strong influence in business schools, and this may be because many of the stakeholder groups care a great deal about these ratings—alumni, donors, recruiters, prospective students, even central university administration. This may surprise you. But one reason is that administrators generally must determine budgets across competing and different units, and it is helpful to them to have some type of external measure of relative quality or productivity. Departments and colleges all may profess to be "the best" in their respective fields, and so these external measures provide a basis for judging the claims. The federal government may be overlooked as a stakeholder. Government officials will want to know whether the business college is meeting diversity goals.

In summary, there are many stakeholder groups for business colleges, and these groups may have different needs and wishes or may attempt to impose different demands on business schools. Each may raise questions, articulate expectations, and exert influence, because each provides resources to the business school.

Implications for Faculty

Faculty Involvement in Determining Priorities

Given the many different stakeholders and their varied and often conflicting interests, a major task for each business school is to determine priorities. It is not possible to meet all stakeholders' needs and wishes in the ways they desire. If we really aspire to excellence, we must be frank with ourselves and others about what we are able and not able to do and what we really want to do. We have to determine what truly are our priorities and then behave that way. And we need to commit to the college priorities over time—a "priority du jour" is not truly a priority. If, for example, producing a certain level of research that is highly respected in the profession is a top priority, this will mean that some other goals dear to other constituencies will not be accomplished. Trade-offs must be made, not only with money, but with equipment and facilities, and faculty time—particularly junior faculty time. We in administration often have difficulty accepting these trade-offs, because we want to see everything done well or because we have to face the stakeholder groups who are not pleased or do not understand.

Faculty discussions are particularly important. Faculty must be drawn into the process to consider the conflicting pressures or inputs, to understand what the trade-offs are, and to evaluate options in terms of shared values and objectives. Yet these discussions will take time away from activities that perhaps should be higher in priority for junior faculty as individuals. Ideally, perhaps there are institutions in which senior faculty are willing to carry on these discussions with an awareness of junior faculty's concerns and interests but without requiring a great deal of participation, but even where this occurs, junior faculty will likely be affected and thus need to have an understanding of the implications of stakeholder influences. I would like to discuss three examples of the many questions that could be raised during discussions of priorities, and the translation of these priorities into faculty actions.

Should decisions about course pedagogy and content be centralized? In the past, faculty members generally made such decisions as individuals. More and more, stakeholders directly or indirectly push colleges of business to appoint course coordinators or provide another means of centralization to determine what gets taught and how it gets taught. For example, in MBA program planning, there may be controversy about the extent to which the program, versus individual faculty, will determine which topics will be covered in the required MIS class, the finance class, and so on. There are advantages to centralization and to decentralization.

To what extent should interdisciplinary research be encouraged? Senior administrators often celebrate the emergence of cross-college programs of research or teaching, such as those between business and engineering. I believe that one of the barriers to such cooperation is that our journals generally don't reward interdisciplinary research, and I'm not sure that they should. Do the professions and universities tell chemists that they need to have very broad experiences, or do we tell them they need to delve deeply into their research so that they are very, very focused on important issues? Should the answer be so different for business scholars? Does interdisciplinary research foster greater growth and knowledge, or does it throw us back into an earlier era during which we were not very scientific? In my opinion, faculty in each college of business will probably need to debate these questions, and they should do so through dialogue and consideration of the views of others in the profession and what it will reward, as well as the views of other stakeholders.

Under what conditions should we join in partnerships with business? Business organizations are approaching business schools and saying, "Look, you're trying to figure out what we want, and we are investing too much in retraining graduates. You're doing research, and we have interesting problems that require research to solve and we don't have the time or expertise to investigate them. Why don't we put our heads together and form a partnership? Then we both can benefit." That offer sounds very exciting, but in my opinion faculty must be very careful to make sure the goals of the business are congruent with those of the college.

For example, would the business partners support the kind of research that the profession and the university will reward? Would they support the programmatic changes that the faculty judge to be desirable, that respond to the needs of a number of constituents, or would the partners insist that the curriculum be tailored to the needs of that particular business? It seems to me that the answers to these questions are necessary for a business school to determine whether or not a particular partnership should be pursued.

Faculty should discuss these issues or determine whether they want to trust the administration of the college to carry out these conversations with faculty input and consultation. Given the obvious potential benefits, faculty may also want to consider whether they wish to seek such partnerships actively. Faculty could obviously gain from research site access, but there would be costs involved in developing or responding to proposals.

Special Abilities of Management Faculty

As an associate dean who is also a member of a management faculty, I am increasingly struck by the extent to which the management faculty have special expertise that can be particularly helpful to the college in sorting out conflicting pressures from the environment. Faculty may be called upon to share this expertise, but again, my advice to incoming junior faculty is that they must be particularly careful in responding to the call, because their first orders of business are to get their research done, develop teaching competency, and so on. However, an emerging scholar may be comfortable doing all of those things and also participating, and it may also be helpful to be supportive of other faculty who are responding to the call.

What are some examples of the application of special expertise? First, environmental analysis and planning are needed. Those academics with a more strategic framework can help sort out how to respond to conflicting needs of stakeholders.

Second, some faculty may have knowledge of and a comfort level with participation, teamwork, change agency, and so on. Colleges of business—relative to many large private businesses—are more participative, I believe, for a variety of reasons; for example, many faculty like to participate in decisions—the formal rights

and responsibilities in the governance rules may require faculty voting on many issues. Working effectively in such cultures requires special skills. Colleagues in other fields, and corporate friends, may have difficulty accepting or understanding this, but participative change is something with which many academics in the organizational sciences are comfortable and skillful.

Third, many emerging scholars in the organizational sciences are knowledgeable about reward systems, justice, motivation, and related issues. There are many opportunities to use such knowledge. Promotion and tenure systems may require change to be more congruent with revised goals of the college.

Fourth, some colleges are restructuring or considering replacing department chairs with area coordinators or reassigning certain responsibilities to program chairs—are these good ideas? Questions may be posed, and emerging scholars may be particularly helpful in responding.

Fifth, those with training and development backgrounds and interests will likely see many applications within their own colleges. They may be asked to assist the business college (or university) to help faculty and staff adjust to changing pressures.

Conclusion

Increasingly, faculty find their professional lives affected by some important trends within business schools and in the environment that affects these schools. Stakeholders are important, and faculty can and should play an important role in determining how colleges will interact with stakeholders. They can determine the extent to which partnerships are beneficial not only for the college but for their own research and teaching. My hope is for current PhD students (and other academics) to be aware of the changes that are occurring so that they can more successfully navigate their careers as they work in business colleges in the future.

51 Stakeholders and You

Janet P. Near

In Marcia Miceli's preceding essay, we learned about the pressures exerted by stakeholders on schools of business. In considering stakeholders, we usually focus on how the organization can best respond to their concerns. The stakeholders are classified as being part of the external environment, and the organization is seen as responding to these pressures from the external environment, whether proactively or reactively. The goal, of course, is organization effectiveness, or—ultimately—survival. In this chapter I will focus specifically on three specific stakeholder groups and their effects over time on schools: faculty, students, and publics.

Faculty, Students, and Strategic Contingencies

What mechanisms do business schools—or any organizations, for that matter—use to respond to stakeholder pressures in the external environment? To approach this question we can turn to resource dependence theory (Pfeffer & Salancik, 1978) or its predecessor, strategic contingencies theory (Hickson, Hinings, Lee, Schneck, & Pennings, 1971). At a very basic level, the main premise of this theory is that the unit in any organization that has the strategic contingencies or provides those to the organization is the unit that has more power, relatively speaking. In other words, the unit of the organization that provides the most needed resource will have the most power internally. To link this to stakeholder theory, we could expect then that the unit that deals with the dominant stakeholder would gain power relative to other units. Because power is always relative (Pfeffer & Salancik, 1978), no one unit will have all the power; likewise, because several of the stakeholders will have some power—and conflicting goals—the units who best represent each stakeholder's interests will have corresponding power.

Now, to apply this admittedly simplistic description of strategic contingencies theory to business schools is straightforward, but it helps to explain recent events in many schools. In the 1980s, the critical resource in business schools

AUTHOR'S NOTE: I would like to thank Dan Dalton and Joe Near for comments on an earlier draft of this essay.

was faculty. It was impossible to find enough faculty. In fact, at one point our business school decided that we would no longer bring in 2,400 undergraduates a year; we would limit ourselves to 1,200 because we could not find enough talented faculty. So faculty were the critical resource. That meant that the units that had power relatively speaking were the departments, because the departments were the units that hired faculty.

What's changed now? At least for ours and most state schools, and some private schools as well, the critical resource is students. The result of that, for us, is that the units that have power are those that provide the raw material, so in our organization those are the programs. In our organization, these programs are the MBA program, the undergraduate program (which is the key cash cow), and the doctoral program. Among these, the MBA program is dominant in most schools, because the *Business Week* ratings, and other student-based ratings of MBA programs, have had the effect of giving this stakeholder stronger, more consensual, and therefore more legitimate voice relative to undergraduate students and doctoral students (that is, as groups of students, not individual students). But all three student programs bring in students and enrollment dollars, as do executive education programs for some schools. Faculty, as a group, do not represent a critical resource at this point for most schools, because the market is now sufficiently robust that replacement faculty can easily be obtained if any current faculty leave.

The effects of this shift in critical resources (or dominant stakeholder) have been clear in many business schools. Where previously the academic departments had relatively greater power than other units, now the program units have greater power than others. Now the department chairperson, who would have had much more power in the 1980s, has far less, relative to the MBA chairperson especially.

What are the implications for faculty of this power shift among units? First, roles will shift. Whereas departments may have demanded excellent research (and probably still do), programs are more likely to demand outstanding teaching. Perhaps service demands related to the program will also increase; for example, in our institution faculty are now called upon to attend ceremonial events, such as graduation,

with far greater urgency than in the past, because these events are thought to build student loyalty. In addition, the technology for measuring teaching performance has received far more discussion, and sparked more controversy, than in the past. Although most institutions always required some combination of great research and teaching, there has been a subtle shift in emphasis and a more explicit shift in emphasis in some.

What are the effects of this change on internal department politics? We can argue that the department chairperson is important in at least two ways, based on related research results. First, educational research suggests that the department chairperson is usually the best link between a junior faculty member and the rest of the university: a poor relationship can significantly reduce the junior faculty member's chances of success, not only because the individual feels alienated from the institution, but also because the chairperson can deny tangible resources and information needed to succeed, whether formally or informally. Second, even for established faculty, the chairperson is important symbolically and perhaps politically. As we know from classic leadership research, the most important attribute of good leaders is that they bring home resources to subordinates. This role is even more obvious in a relatively organic structure, which is typical of the academic side of most universities (Mintzberg, 1983). In this setting, departmental budgets, faculty lines, and other resources may be directly based on the chairperson's ability to argue the department's case before the deans.

Clearly, these are not functions that the program chairperson can serve. The MBA chairperson is in no position to argue for one of our departments, because that person, of necessity, has other vested interests. In fact, unless the departments and programs find shared interests and goals, neither is likely to make much progress. Increasingly, then, we should see "strategic alliances" internally—or coalition formation—as weaker department chairpersons collude with stronger program chairpersons in order to pursue shared goals. Often this will benefit the institution, as when the shared goals in fact benefit the entire business school. Where "horse trading" results, however, and chairpersons trade support for projects they might not otherwise favor, we may see schools reduced to the worst characteristics of the highly politi-cized decision-making processes described by the Carnegie school many years ago (Cyert & March, 1963; March & Simon, 1958).

Publics, Demographics, and Downsizing

Two related trends have increased uncertainty for institutions even further: downsizing and a shift of demographics. Downsizing may have occurred in response to environmental pres-sures from stakeholders, specifically concerned publics (e.g., legislatures in the case of state schools, society at large in the case of private), to increase efficiency (as opposed to effective-ness) of teaching. Or downsizing may have re-sulted from what institutional theorists describe as a process of isomorphism (DiMaggio & Pow-ell, 1983), so that academic institutions en-gaged in this process may have emulated both other universities and business firms. Quite prob-ably both pressures have resulted in the down-sizing we now see. Either way, the pertinent stakeholder is the public, however defined.

In terms of demographics, probably the av-erage age in most business school faculties is around 50, so we can expect some retirement over the next decade or so. Because business schools engaged in substantial hiring much later than the social sciences (late 1970s to early 1980s versus a decade earlier in most social science departments), the various predictions that half of all university faculty will retire by the year 2000 probably do not apply to business schools. Nonetheless, retirements are on the horizon for most departments. Schools are re-sponding with several strategic actions.

Strategic Responses

First of all, not everyone who retires will be replaced automatically by an assistant profes-sor. Most institutions are discussing distance learning, higher teaching loads, and larger classes to increase efficiency. All of these will have the effect of reducing the number of faculty relative to the number of students. In many institu-tions, the driving force is the legislature for public universities or the corresponding public for private universities. The purpose is to econo-mize so that tuition costs will not have to in-crease at the same rates as in the past.

Second, to improve teaching quickly, institu-tions are increasingly hiring at senior levels, rather than developing junior faculty; even though this may be more expensive than hiring at jun-ior levels, it is apparently perceived by deans to improve teaching reputation quickly. Thus even retiring faculty are being replaced by senior faculty rather than assistant professors. Again, the impetus comes from the public as stake-holder, and its concern for high-quality teach-ing. This has several unanticipated effects at all levels. At the department level, the effect is to bring in senior people from diverse experiences, who are often tenured and therefore enter di-rectly into the decision-making efforts of the department. Given that these individuals have not been socialized into the department's cul-ture as assistant professors, they likely have varying standards and norms; blending them together into a cohesive decision-making group is sometimes problematic. At the level of the school, the overall effect is to create a more mature group of scholars, with mature inter-ests: in consulting, in service, and perhaps less so in teaching and research. Further, this group is likely less energetic and open to change than junior faculty at the beginning of their careers. Finally, at a macro level, the effect is radically changed mobility patterns. If recent graduates from prestigious PhD programs are not hired by similarly prestigious institutions because they've been displaced by more senior indi-viduals moving to those institutions, then they will accept jobs at what have traditionally been regarded as teaching schools. Research expecta-tions at those institutions will change, in turn, as more research-oriented junior faculty are hired. The effect overall is to distribute well-trained scholars across a diverse group of insti-tutions, including both traditional teaching and research schools, thereby resulting in a different professional context. This is actually healthy for the field, because individuals from more di-verse schools will go on to leadership positions within the field, whether in professional asso-ciations or informally, but it may lead to con-siderable disappointment among the junior fac-ulty who expected the hiring market to be similar to that of past years.

Further, contextual constraints on faculty pro-ductivity are far less than in the past. Junior faculty selecting schools 20 years ago needed strong mainframe computers, well-stocked libraries, and supportive clerical staff; bright doctoral students were almost required, because research assistants were necessary to collect and analyze data owing to the slowness of the process; collaborative coauthors or senior faculty were needed on-site to give advice. In an era when data can be coded from computer files or generated on questionnaires that can be printed in a day rather than 6 weeks, when quality of libraries and mainframes doesn't matter because CD-ROM journals and statistics packages for personal computers are readily available, when few faculty use secretarial services, and when coauthors and knowledgeable experts both can be contacted via the Internet, a scholar can produce good research at virtually any school.

Finally, to increase flexibility, departments are hiring adjunct faculty, either with PhDs or without, who won't expect tenure. Again, administrators concerned about cutting costs to meet public concern have focused on this as a strategy for keeping short-term costs low and maintaining control over long-term costs associated with tenured faculty. The former category of adjuncts were termed *gypsies* or *nomads* when this phenomenon occurred in other areas of the university a decade or more ago. The sciences resolved the issue by creating postdoctoral requirements for hiring, but the social sciences continued to hire gypsies, which is not healthy for either the individuals involved or the institution. Clearly adjuncts of either sort will not contribute to the school or the department in the same way as more stable faculty, because it is not in their best interests to engage in service; typically the school will not invest in the development of their research skills, so these contributions are also lacking in many cases. The result, then, is the creation of a class of faculty who focus solely on teaching and individual pursuits (e.g., consulting). Clearly this composition change in departments will affect the way we operate.

Structural Effects

An unanticipated effect of downsizing on composition is increased departmental diversity. The people who will be retiring will be primarily white males, so the faculty members who remain will be by definition more diverse than they have been in the past. To the extent that departments do not replace those retiring with senior faculty, but rather select adjunct faculty or assistant professors, they are far more likely to select women or people of color than would have been the case 30 years ago, thereby changing the overall composition of faculties. This is happening already in the composition of the Academy of Management, and over the next decade we will find it occurring in schools to a greater extent. It obviously raises a number of problems and opportunities for both departments and schools.

Myths About Faculty

We have discussed the effects of these stakeholders' demands primarily in terms of effects on organizations and their subunits, but it is also useful to think about their direct effects on you. In particular, stakeholders often ascribe to some commonly held myths about academics. This folklore influences administrators' behavior toward faculty as a result, and they often find themselves in defensive positions because of the myths. As a result, it's important for you to be aware of the myths as well, so that you can anticipate and deflect them.

The first one, perhaps the primary one, is that all faculty quit doing research after tenure. In fact that is a myth; in my experience, people who do research before tenure seem to keep doing it after tenure. Perhaps this is because they've simply been reinforced for research efforts, so they continue. Perhaps it is that the same social pressures from colleagues that influenced them to do research in the first place continue to influence their behavior. Perhaps it is habit—but in any case, they seem to continue, for the most part.

The second myth is that the best researchers are not good teachers. The truth is that they are often the best teachers as well. My potential explanation for this is that clear thinkers also tend to be clear writers and clear lecturers. Although time constraints certainly make it feel as if there is role conflict between our roles as teachers and researchers, the fact seems to be that my colleagues who teach well also are the most productive scholars, with rare exceptions.

The third myth is one that we as faculty try to put over on our deans: that you can't measure academic performance, so they should just leave us alone and go away. As you've read in previous chapters in this volume, we have to realize that this is a myth and that we can't accept it.

One of my favorite theories for looking at performance is Ouchi and Maguire's (1975) theory of behavior control and output control. One of the difficulties for faculty is that we would like to say that neither behavior control nor output control should be used for looking at our performance, whereas deans would like to use both. In the first year in particular I think you'll find that your chairperson or dean and in fact your whole department will be using a lot of behavior control with you. They'll want to make sure that you show up, that you're in your office, that you attend meetings, that you appear to be a good citizen, even though that may have absolutely no impact on your abilities as a teacher or researcher. They'll also be looking at output measures; when you persuade them that you can in fact meet their output standards, they will tend to be less concerned about behavior. I remember that the image I carried with me as an untenured junior faculty member was that I had a number branded on my forehead indicating how many articles I'd authored to date. When that number reached a level deemed acceptable to my colleagues, I felt less pressure to show appropriate behaviors and greater freedom to try to improve my output in any way I thought would actually work. Of course, all of this may have been simple paranoia on my part!

In our institution we've recently gone to an incentive system in which we look at two very simple criteria: Over the past 5 years, how many articles did you publish, and over the past 5 years, what was your average teaching rating on a single item from our teaching evaluation scale? Many faculty have said something like the following: "Even though I did very well on those criteria, those aren't the right criteria, they are too simplistic." Certainly, they probably are very simplistic criteria, but the fact is you'll never get measures that all faculty will agree on. And that's the bad news. The good news is that this creates a system where you don't have to become a friend of the dean, or be part of his or her network or of the good old boys' network, or whatever the dominant coalition is at your school, in order to do well, because a more objective output measure has been used. In fact, academic performance has always been measured; what has varied is the degree of agreement among faculty on the measures.

Predictions

With this mind-set, some predictions can be made with almost absolute certainty. Like all other organizations, universities have reached the point where they must give stakeholders their due deference. Whether we do so too frequently or too intensely will prove the issue of greatest controversy for most faculties for many years to come. All of this is easy to predict. What is more difficult to discern is what these changing tides will mean for academics at any of the institutions that employ them throughout their careers. Understanding the effects of this strategic issue on the internal cultures and structures of our organizations will make our lives as scholars more productive and more pleasant.

References

Cyert, R. M., & March, J. G. (1963). *A behavioral theory of the firm.* Englewood Cliffs, NJ: Prentice Hall.

DiMaggio, P. J., & Powell, W. W. (1983). The iron cage revisited: Institutional isomorphism and collective rationality in organizational fields. *American Sociological Review, 48,* 147-160.

Hickson, D. J., Hinings, C. R., Lee, C. A., Schneck, R. E., & Pennings, J. M. (1971). A strategic contingencies theory of intraorganizational power. *Administrative Science Quarterly, 16,* 216-229.

March, J. G., & Simon, H. A. (1958). *Organizations.* New York: John Wiley.

Mintzberg, H. (1983). *Structure in fives: Designing effective organizations.* Englewood Cliffs, NJ: Prentice Hall.

Ouchi, W. G., & Maguire, M. A. (1975). Organizational control: Two functions. *Administrative Science Quarterly, 20,* 559-571.

Pfeffer, J., & Salancik, G. R. (1978). *The external control of organizations: A resource dependence perspective.* New York: Harper & Row.

◆ 52 Embracing Change

WE GET BY WITH A LOT OF
HELP FROM OUR FRIENDS

James P. Walsh

The life of a business school faculty member is at once more exacting and less defined than ever before. When Art Brief, Dick Woodman, and I were talking about how to organize our doctoral consortium, we decided that our new faculty colleagues might benefit from a discussion of possible changes in our institutional environment and what they might mean for career development. And so we invited a university president and provost, as well as a business school dean, associate dean, and department chair to address these issues for them. In truth, we were as interested in all of this as they were. Many of us have been struggling to come to terms with the seemingly unrelenting pressure for "world-class performance" in our many faculty roles. Now that everyone has had a chance to read our colleagues' comments, I will serve as a faculty representative in this discussion and offer a few observations about these insights and how they might inform the choices we make in our faculty lives.

Nearly everyone has argued that we need to understand the changes in our institutional environment before we can consider how to address them. Let me see if I can summarize the changes articulated by our colleagues in a nutshell. To begin, changes in demographics, the technology of work, and the sanctity of national boundaries are prompting society to ask for both more contribution and more accountability from higher education. These pressures affect the business school in two broad ways. First, the pressure for contribution and accountability asks us to reconcile our age-old trade-off between practical relevance and scientific rigor in favor of the simultaneous pursuit of both relevance and rigor in our work. And second, when senior university administrators perceive these challenges as a threat (note Bill Mobley's quote from Tom Kean, "Our ivory tower is under siege"), these administrators then centralize authority and, in so doing, severely limit

481

the degrees of freedom the business school has to address its own changing environment. Close to home, these changes are manifest in stakeholder activism. Students of all kinds, recruiters, funding agencies, and the like all see themselves as our "customers" and, worse, clamor for "first among equals" status as they stake claims on our time and talent. Moreover, the changing resource picture has both altered our faculty labor markets and shifted the balance of power within the business school to create an emotionally charged and often contested work environment. Hearing this, it is no wonder that many of us have sensed that our professional lives today are under stress, if not under siege.

What to do? Again, let me try to distill the essence of our administrators' advice. At first blush, nothing much has changed. They point to challenges in the familiar areas of research, teaching, and service. Only a close reading of their prescriptions, however, reveals how conceptions of valuable research, teaching, and service have changed. It seems to me that we are exhorted to conduct theoretically and methodologically rigorous research that bears practical relevance to undergird our teaching and consulting. We are asked to embrace the latest in pedagogical technology to serve a range of domestic and international students from undergraduates to MBA students to PhD students and to executives of all ages and responsibilities. In the end, we are to help society meet the challenge of postindustrial work in our new global village. Our job does not end there, however. We are also encouraged to take the time to educate our presidents and provosts about the place of the business school in the university (and in society), while also contributing our management expertise to the training and development of a variety of local administrators as they come to grips with the human resource management challenges posed by operating in this new world. And, of course, many of us are trying to earn tenure under these expectations, just when tenured positions are becoming more precious thanks to outsourcing and technology-enhanced faculty downsizing. If the shock of the diagnosis of our problem does not kill us, these prescriptions surely will! None of us can meet these challenges alone.

That said, I would like to consider two principles invoked by this discussion and then close by sharing the two conclusions that I draw from

these chapters. The principles center on the ideas of power and division of labor. Janet Near asks us to consider the strategic contingencies theory of power. Let's apply it to the broad set of issues Bill Mobley has raised. If Reich (1991), Drucker (1993), and Casey (1995) are correct in their views about the central role knowledge plays in postindustrial, postcapitalist, postoccupational society, then the ivory tower is under siege by society precisely because what goes on in the university is absolutely central to the well-being of society. If you will, "we" have the power here. There is no reason for us to assume a defensive and reactionary position with respect to all those who demand our services. Consistent with Bill Mobley's closing sentiment, these are the best of times for the university (imagine the reverse scenario!). That said, we need to offer our own clear and compelling voice to the debates about higher education. The lingering question, of course, is, Just who is the "we" I am talking about?

The second principle is the division of labor. I fear that many of us read the kinds of prescriptive aphorisms offered here and elsewhere as a mandate for individual accomplishment. Obviously, the freshly minted PhD is not in the best position to articulate the university's voice to society; similarly, the university president is not poised to make the kinds of scholarly contributions the new assistant professor is. This same principle applies to how we allocate our talent to address the more nuanced distinctions between research and teaching, theory and practice, domestic and international business, PhD and executive education, and the like. We need to address the fiction that any one person can deliver "world-class performance" in all of these domains.

The conclusions I draw from this discussion, for us as individual faculty members, are very modest. First, at a time when so many of our different stakeholders are asking so much of us, it is important to remember that we cannot do everything alone. My sense is that we all need to acknowledge our particular passions and talents, continually develop them, and deliver "world-class performance" in these domains. We do not need mediocre contributions from talented individuals who are stretched too thin. And second, as we self-consciously contribute to only a portion of the range of possible roles that a business school faculty member might fulfill, we need to be sure to appreciate the contributions of our colleagues who are gifted in ways that we are not. None of us deserves to work in an environment where our colleagues dismiss our contributions simply because they are different. As dedicated basic and clinical researchers, executive educators and undergraduate educators, administrators and faculty, we need to be able to work side by side to understand and promote the effective management of organizations in these changing times.

Beyond noting the seemingly inescapable conclusion that we must simultaneously focus our professional activities and broaden our appreciation for others' work, I have to agree with Bill Mobley when he says that is up to each of us to draw our own specific conclusions from the chapters presented here. My hope is that our colleagues' comments will stimulate us all to discuss and reflect upon what just may be a period of disjunctive change in our profession.

References

Casey, C. (1995). *Work, self and society after industrialism.* New York: Routledge.

Drucker, P. F. (1993). *Post-capitalist society.* New York: Harper Business.

Reich, R. B. (1991). *The work of nations.* New York: Vintage.

Commentary

Peter J. Frost
M. Susan Taylor

Becoming a productive scholar is a developmental journey. It involves understanding the research terrain, comparing alternative routes, choosing a personal path, recognizing critical crossroads, navigating roadblocks, sustaining personal commitment, and celebrating the joys of the expedition.

Joan V. Gallos (p. 16)

In my salad days, I could routinely spend 14-16 hours a day locked in my study revising a textbook. The burnout that ultimately resulted, and the death of a well-known contemporary, actually found dead at his desk, occasioned a simple question: Did I want to spend the rest of my life writing textbooks? My answer was no.

Looking back, I now see how I cheated not only my family but myself of irretrievable time together. Would I have achieved in my career as I have without such sacrifice? Who knows? Was it worth it? I honestly can't say.

Arthur G. Bedeian (p. 8)

We think that the sentiments expressed in both these quotes have relevance to the rhythms of academic life. It is a privileged life but also a challenging one, requiring at times high levels of focus, self-absorption, and isolation. The reports in this book have addressed a number of different roles and activities within the academic enterprise. Each set of roles and activities has its own rhythms, each provides paradoxes to the scholar who takes it on. Inherent within each role and set of activities are opportunities to learn, to make mistakes, to create new knowledge, to make a difference to others, to see the academic world from a different vantage point. There are decisions to be made about what to do within a role, how long to stay in or to attend to it, and when and how best to move on to another one.

The nature of early rhythms in an academic career, when one is relatively unknown and busy establishing oneself as a teacher and as a researcher, are different from those of an established scholar, when there are additional pressures to serve in administrative or professional association roles; when one is in demand as an adviser, a reviewer, perhaps even as an editor; when one is more likely to be doing consulting and in other ways interacting with various external communities. Of course, there are other possible pressures on scholars in their early years, including starting a family (especially demanding on women academics) and representing actively, through service and teaching, some category that has taken on a high political profile in the profession or in the community. Such demands on junior faculty do not replace the primary requirement to establish a presence in their fields and institutions through research and/or teaching.

We expect that readers will focus on different roles, on different rhythms represented in the book. They will likely draw different inferences about academic practice based on their own perspectives, needs, and expectations as well as on the circumstances and stages of their current professional lives.

The contributors to this volume have been shaped by the events and conditions of the past 30 or so years. In some sense, the lessons learned and the suggestions and prescriptions offered are based on a world that is changing rather quickly. This may bound the lessons of this book in a time that is passing. Doubtless we will need to reexamine the rhythms of academic life anew in the future. Having said this, we think there are some themes within this book that seem to be fairly persistent and important; we discuss these in the pages that follow.

Early Rhythms

Choosing a Job

Choosing the "right" school or university to join requires attention to the fit between one's own intended career path and that of the hiring institution. As Marilyn Gist points out, it is important to clarify what the real priorities of the organization are: Is it rewarding performances that build research portfolios and thus emphasize national visibility for the academic and the institution? Or are the important goals focused on local accomplishments that may be assessed according to teaching performance or service contributions? Typically, the goals and

the criteria are intermingled; academic institutions often want to meet both local and cosmopolitan objectives, and beginning academics must investigate carefully to sort out the mix and to assess what the true criteria are for success in the institution. The alternative is to find out the hard way that what is expected of a junior scholar on a day-to-day basis may not be either what that scholar is trained for or what he or she prefers to do to develop a career, as Toni King found out. Or the discovery may be that what is encouraged as professional behavior in the short run is not what really counts when tenure decisions are made.

Finally, as Arthur Bedeian points out, and other contributors implicitly corroborate, it is important that one seek out settings where one can encounter other colleagues who can support and extend the interests and skills one brings to the first job. It is invaluable to have colleagues who can provide advice and guidance on teaching and on getting research projects going. Junior faculty need the help of seasoned colleagues to interpret the meanings of editorial reviews of their work, to learn the ropes of publishing. They need mentoring on the politics of the institution.

Teaching and Research

In the early years of an academic career, emphases are on learning one's craft, learning the ropes in one's institution and profession, and adjusting one's professional and personal lives to the complex demands of being a scholar. The primary career stress in these years tends to be to get tenure, particularly in North America, and within most institutions the assessment of worth as a scholar lies in producing an exemplary research portfolio, teaching competently, and, to an extent, being seen as a "good colleague." This usually means, in these early years, that one does what one is asked to do in accepting teaching assignments and fulfilling service duties. In a growing number of schools, the expectation of pretenure academics, from students and from administrators, is that they perform very well in the classroom. It is becoming less acceptable that they be simply competent teachers. Christina Shalley's initial mantra going into her academic career—"Publish, plain and simple, and be competent at teaching so they don't have to get rid of you" (p. 64)—is becoming increasingly untenable in light of the expectations of students, parents, legislators, and the media. The performance bar is being raised for teaching performance. However, it has not simultaneously been lowered on the research dimension. Academics need to do well on both dimensions.

It seems likely that at some point in the not-too-distant future, business faculties and the profession will have to examine the implications of this shift for new faculty, for institutions, and for the field. Providing training in doctoral programs in teaching as is done for research is one strategic response to the change in the game. However, in one sense, this simply intensifies the pressure on junior scholars. Once they have been trained to teach and can, presumably, perform better in the classroom sooner, they will be expected to do more as teachers. Although this provides a benefit to the institution and to students, the need for academics to do first-rate research to get tenure remains. Doing research requires long blocks of uninterrupted time, as several authors in this book have pointed out. Adding to teaching responsibilities can conflict with this need. We think that, on balance, greater contributions will be made by academics who are both teachers and researchers. Jointly, these roles require scholars to contribute to a continuously developing knowledge base and to communicate their contributions to others, perhaps in less technical or sophisticated forms than originally stated. However, working in and across both activities will better preserve the spirit and the substance of the ideas and findings while conveying them in ways useful to practitioners and other potential users.

It is going to take a conscious and concerted effort by academics, administrators, and the profession to figure out how this new equation translates into assessment of academic performance and how it keeps vital the quality of scholarship, the creation and dissemination of knowledge. It may require a lengthening of the tenure clock. It may require educating a smaller cadre of doctoral students but providing them a richer experience that produces strong teachers and competent researchers. Unquestionably, it will require that we find creative ways to facilitate for junior faculty the development of their crafts, so that they can make effective use of them more quickly when they start their first jobs.

Tensions Between Creativity and Instrumentality

A common theme throughout this book is the trade-off between choices, about research emphases and teaching efforts that draw primarily on the creative and passionate aspects of one's abilities versus those that are more instrumental or political, that stress "playing the game" to get ahead. This issue is likely to be highly salient for individuals on the tenure trail. One hears all kinds of advice offered to junior scholars on this matter, ranging from encouragement to "keep your nose clean and do the work that is needed to get tenure" and "save your creativity for the time after you have tenure" to those that urge scholars to "follow their bliss" and to do the things that they consider important and intellectually satisfactory, no matter what the politics of the situation are. This latter strategy rests in part on an assumption that following one's creative instincts and one's passion will lead to high-quality work that will reflect well on the scholar. It is also based, implicitly at least, on the view that the success of one's career does not rest exclusively on whether one's work is judged favorably or as acceptable by one's initial colleagues or by the institution.

As will become evident in our discussion below on finding and developing one's voice, we do not side with those who advise suppression of an individual's creativity and passion until after tenure is secured. We believe that new scholars are ill-advised to avoid or abandon research endeavors that are interesting and creative until it is "safe" or "convenient" for them to undertake such pursuits. There is considerable evidence that in the physical sciences, at least, the greatest discoveries are more often made by researchers in their early career stages (see Gladwell, 1990). It is worth noting also that three of the seven exemplary research publications reported in *Doing Exemplary Research* (Frost & Stablein, 1992) were based on pioneering work done by doctoral students and junior faculty. Although we do not believe that only new scholars do pathbreaking work as researchers or teachers, we suspect that creativity is at least partly determined by a strong and broad familiarity with the current literature in the field, by a weak commitment to established paradigms and ways of viewing research questions, and by a healthy desire to prove oneself as a serious scholar. All these characteristics are likely to be found in greater abundance in new scholars than in their more established counterparts. It seems likely to us that those who postpone their creative interests for 7 years or more are placing a precious quality at serious risk. (We do agree with Anne Huff, having made this pitch for attention to creativity among junior scholars, that ours is a field that also facilitates the doing of breakthrough work by senior scholars, given the human nature of many of the phenomena we study and the value of personal experiences as stimuli for creative insights.)

In Chapter 12, Susan Ashford captures this issue rather poignantly:

> Doing research that "they" seem to want, doing the types of studies that seem to be all that the journals are publishing (as opposed to what will best answer the question), and choosing a topic based on what is hot or accepted rather than because you are passionate about it are all examples of letting the instrumental dominate. Making such choices amounts to choosing death. These are small deaths, to be sure, and may go many years without detection, but it seems to me that they are death all the same. (p. 127)

We suspect that the passion versus politics dilemma does not yield to a simple all-or-none response. Whereas we argue against a postponement of passion and creativity in the service of one's intellectual and professional career, we believe it is prudent for junior scholars to learn the political ropes of their institutions and profession and then to make informed choices about how to manage their careers. One needs to keep in mind that at least some of one's research must reach publication in acceptable outlets, that others may have ideas and understanding about research and about teaching from which one can learn, and that, as Kevin Murphy and Keith Murnighan note, we need to understand our various audiences and be able to communicate with them so that our work can be understood.

Other Demands

Other pressures on early academic life include time needed to nurture a personal life and the service demands placed on some new faculty by administrators and professional associations. Miriam Erez points out in Chapter 3 that having a child soon after completing her PhD slowed down her productivity as a researcher. The demands on Toni King in her first job to be active in student and other communities thwarted her efforts to produce a strong research record. These and other major events that occur in people's lives in this testing period may make their emergence as scholars slower than is the current norm for progress. Of course, we expect that individuals faced with, or choosing to have, experiences that draw them away from a single-minded pursuit of attaining tenure will want to take responsibility for the way they manage their research and teaching agendas. Further, we believe that it is important for junior scholars to be active, selectively, in service of their academic community. The alternative is isolation of these scholars from this life, which, for several years, robs them and their institution of valuable contributions and understanding about the way academic life proceeds.

Nevertheless, the conventional wisdom on publishing in the pretenure period, epitomized by Art Bedeian's dictum to "hit the ground running" as a researcher, may not always apply to starting scholars. The expectations of tenure committees and of deans about sustained productivity levels of junior scholars will need some recalibration to accommodate a more diverse pool of scholars and a greater variation in life experiences and responsibilities of current junior academics than was the case in this cohort a decade ago. These demands on junior faculty may also require senior faculty to take on more responsibility for teaching courses than is currently the norm. This charge is unlikely to be accepted unless thoughtfully implemented, as the demands and pressures of later rhythms of academic life may change somewhat in nature, but they do not lessen. If anything, the pace of scholarship quickens. We turn now to a discussion of these later rhythms.

Middle Rhythms . . . and Later

In the early days of a career, the scholar may have a somewhat limited range of research projects to manage and a relatively preordained set of courses to teach. (Personally, we recall having relatively empty bookshelves, the excitement and expectation of publishing our doctoral dissertations, and not much more. There was a touch of awe in our observations of the multitude of ongoing and planned research projects being undertaken by our more experienced colleagues!)

The tenor of life begins to change as one becomes established as a scholar. This can and does happen even before one gets tenure, so that although the rite of passage that is tenure is a distinctive marker, and should be treated as such, it is also, as Marilyn Gist observes, but one point on the continuum of an academic career. The academic experience, initially largely focused on teaching and research, begins to include opportunities to work with and to supervise doctoral students, to serve as occasional and eventually as a regular reviewer of manuscripts for scholarly journals, later perhaps to become a journal editor, to serve in an administrative role for one's school or profession. Participating as an instructor in executive education becomes more likely. Increased visibility and mobility enhance opportunities for the scholar to do collaborative work, as a researcher, as a teacher. It becomes more plausible at this stage to contemplate programmatic research, as Mats Alvesson points out, and to link with others on more ambitious and potentially risky projects. If anything, one faces an overabundance of choices. The heavy press to produce published products relatively quickly, as is often the case in the start-up time of a career, diminishes with the development of assurance and visibility. One may need, in fact, to attend to the trap of "publishing *and* perishing," as Keith Murnighan notes.

The late middle years also offer opportunities for more institutional nurturance and building activities. There is a chance to "give something back to the field." Art Bedeian, Jan Beyer, Larry Cummings, and Mary Ann Von Glinow all made this contribution through their terms leading up to and during periods as president of the Academy of Management, for example. Stewart Clegg describes establishing the Australian Pacific Researchers in Organization Studies. Most of the contributors to this book have given considerable amounts of time to community service within their institutions and the profession.

Overenrichment can also be a feature of an academic's career as it moves through the mid-

dle and later years. There are so many arenas in which to perform, and within each, as we grow in experience and visibility, there are many possibilities to explore. This is the period when scholars are being invited to do this, that, or the other by their institutions, the profession, and other communities. Learning to say no, learning to decide what to do and what to avoid or to let go, becomes a necessary skill, as Susan Jackson and Anne Huff, among others, underscore in their chapters.

Finally, there are more opportunities in the middle and later years for individuals to differentiate themselves, to develop along dimensions that reflect their strengths. They may begin to "specialize" as teachers rather than as researchers, as administrators rather than teachers. Given the increasing demands and diversity of the environments facing academic institutions, we will need to develop attitudes and reward systems that encourage the desires and the needs for different contributions to the common good of the enterprise. In the current system, we are likely to find those who emphasize teaching or administration consigned to second-class status, seeing few extrinsic rewards for their endeavors. This is not to deny the importance of a vital research spirit in our institutions; rather, it is a plea for a more evenhanded acknowledgment of portfolios of skills and interests as a basis for an effective academic enterprise.

Developing One's Voice

An important aspect of the distinctive contribution that each scholar strives to make seems to hinge on the ability to find and define his or her voice, as a researcher, a teacher, an administrator, an editor, and so forth, and to continue to refine and redefine that voice throughout a career. Joan Gallos makes the point eloquently:

Having a clear scholarly voice involves the willingness and ability to speak out, but it is more than just taking a stand. It entails a personal commitment to your own research agenda and a push to explore multiple facets of that agenda before moving on to something else. It requires identifying a passion for some set of issues and setting out to explore that deep interest, even in the face of opposition and critique. It means believing you have a worthwhile contribution to make. It involves finding a style of writing and expression that is uniquely and comfortably yours. (p. 15)

This sense of voice occurs in the contributions of many of our authors. Susan Ashford deals with the development of voice when she describes her interactions with adviser Larry Cummings, who believed in her, saw something in her that she had not yet discovered in herself, and challenged and stretched her to realize her potential as a scholar. She also addresses voice when she notes the importance of standing up to an adviser so that one does not become a clone of someone else. Walter Nord captures some of the self-initiated aspects of this process when he describes his experiences as a doctoral student and as a junior faculty member. It is also evident in his tendency to teach graduate students topics that he needs to learn. It becomes part of the practice of developing his own voice as a teacher and a scholar. Roderick Kramer and Joanne Martin identify the need to "let go" of their desire to emulate the styles of their own mentors as they became advisers of doctoral students. Stewart Clegg's story contains many similar themes of exploration and inquiry that helped him become an authority on organizational power.

Finding and shaping one's voice may be enhanced by one's locating in a context that is supportive as well as challenging, that can provide resources and opportunities to practice one's crafts and to discover and/or to express one's voice. This is in part Art Bedeian's message when he emphasizes "location, location, location" as a basis for choosing a job.

Doctoral training and the tempering and shaping influences of the pretenure years in academia help socialize junior faculty into the profession, and provide the means for developing the skills of the scholarly crafts of research and teaching. They are perhaps a necessary but not sufficient basis for developing the distinctiveness of each scholar's impact in the field. It seems necessary that an academic have opportunities to wrestle with challenging, even perverse, situations within the task and or in the context. Coming to terms with such conditions and with the consequences of acting on or in these conditions seems to facilitate the develop-

ment and expression of the scholar's voice. Individuals may have to make stands in the face of resistance to their innovations, as did both Dave Whetten and Bob Marx when developing their distinctive new teaching texts, or to their theories, as did Ed Locke in the early days of his goal-setting theory, when cognitive approaches to behavior were ignored or discounted in the field. Individuals may need to respond assertively to the insights they get from feedback concerning their own actions or those of others, as John Miller did when he recognized from the teaching critique of a student what direction he needed to take his teaching and what focus was needed in his university's management program. Kramer and Martin report how the influence of a persevering doctoral student changed the direction of the research of one of them in a significant way. Although one's voice seems to need to come from within, as Gallos notes, it is also influenced by situations and people in one's environment.

Sometimes feedback from others comes in the form of messages or actions designed to deter one from a particular course of action, or a career move can have the opposite voice-defining or -strengthening effect, as happened in Joan Gallos's case. She relates how apparently well-meaning advice to stay away from gender research seemed to be the spark that helped her decide who she wanted to be as a researcher and confirmed her desire to do gender-related research. Vance Mitchell seemed to have been strengthened in his resolve to complete a PhD in his middle years when he was told by an academic that he was too old to undertake the program.

We have focused thus far on voice development and expression in research and teaching, but it seems to apply to other areas of academic life as well. Allan Cohen suggests that it is difficult to sustain the pace and loneliness of the academic role, particularly at strategic levels, unless one has a strong personal vision of what one wants to accomplish in the role. Jan Beyer and Bob Sutton's stories reveal their commitment to visions and practices that shape their influences as editors. Alan Meyer has a very distinctive approach to reviewing, as do others who do this work well.

The development of one's voice as an academic entails the development of integrity and distinctiveness in one's work. Treated unreflectively, over time, a vibrant voice may lose its flexibility, may become stilted, uninteresting—even shrill. Openness to change and to growth seems to be an essential orientation if the academic is to continue to contribute to the creation and communication of new ideas and knowledge, to have a voice worth listening to. Suggestions from several authors seem applicable to this challenge. Bedeian suggests that we keep upgrading our skills by taking new courses that stretch us and add new dimensions to our repertoire. Nord teaches "without a net" when working with graduate students. Erez transports herself to new situations and new scholars to help her see new challenges. Ashford uses a particular strategy for getting feedback from reviewers so that she can "hear" the critiques and respond constructively. Locke advocates idea champions rather than idea defenders who are interested in keeping change out of their work. Clegg and others seek new and different coauthors to work with who stretch and challenge them. These and other strategies may help redefine the academic's voice when this is warranted.

Managing One's Academic Portfolio: Keeping the Plates Spinning

The story Susan Ashford attributes to Lyman Porter about carnival plate spinners is worth repeating here:

> At carnivals . . . there is a man who spins plates on top of various poles. . . . The plate spinner gives one plate a vigorous spin and moves on to the second. As he walks back and forth across the stage, he amazes the audience with the number of plates he is able to keep up and spinning. (p. 121)

This story evokes one of the central challenges faced by academics as they pursue their work. They typically have many projects, committees, assignments, classes, and so forth to keep "spinning." Keeping everything moving satisfactorily takes large investments of energy and uses up the nonrenewable resource called *time*. It takes time to prepare and to teach classes, to counsel students, to evaluate performance. It takes time to initiate, conduct, analyze, interpret, report, and publish research. Reviewing

the work of others takes time, large blocks if one is a member of an editorial board of a journal and even more if one is an editor. We write research proposals and conference proposals, prepare consulting proposals. We present our ideas at workshops, in conferences, to administrators, to the business community. We supervise graduate students, write letters of assessment on colleagues for tenure and promotion, serve on faculty and university committees, as administrators, as officers in our professional associations. All these activities contribute to the academic enterprise, all consume hours and hours of time. Not specified in this list are the things we might do or wish to do that constitute personal lives, away from the academy.

The simultaneity of many of our various tasks compounds the busyness of our lives. We are not arguing that this condition is necessarily wrong—it can be a very exciting way to live. Most of us do live very productive and happy lives under these conditions, and there are many benefits to our institutions and our clients that stem from these large commitments of time, talent, and energy. We are suggesting, however, that we can get stuck in the rhythms of our work and that this can have detrimental effects on our creativity and the quality of our own lives and those around us.

Most of the time, adjustments we might make when things are not working out are a matter of "retuning on the run." Many of the insights of our authors are geared to on-line adjustments. At other times we need to "stop the action" and take an extended period of time to refresh ourselves and perhaps to reorient what it is that we know and do. Sabbaticals provide a useful means to look at our lives with this intensity. When we do this, we are in effect reducing the number of plates we choose or have to keep spinning, or we hand them to someone else or we put them in storage, at least for a while. We will discuss the use of extended time-outs to manage our careers and ourselves later.

Retuning on the Run

We are struck by the many useful ideas and suggestions our contributors offer for managing time, for creating ways to keep a focus on priorities and to get things done. These include

Marilyn Gist's suggestion that one ought to have clear strategies for choosing a school when starting out in one's career as an academic and for getting done what needs to be done to get tenure. She acknowledges the difficulties faced in this era where one has to learn "to balance what's urgent with *all* of what's important" (p. 191). Christina Shalley suggests that junior faculty keep down the number and types of course preparations they do at the beginning of their careers. She further argues that one should spend enough time in preparation to be a very good teacher, but that it may be a poor use of one's energies and time to try to be an excellent teacher when one's research also requires serious attention. Susan Ashford's practice of making appointments with herself to ensure time to think and to tackle extended projects makes sense for all scholars. Learning to do this early on is likely to be a useful tactic.

Distinguishing one's roles as clearly as one can and discerning accurately what they entail can be a useful way to manage time. One needs to have some evocative ways to differentiate the requirements of one's various roles and to make the appropriate kind of time and space for each of them. In addition, recognizing what one has accomplished through successfully completing the tenure process can provide a useful context for making the next steps as an academic. Although this probably is most beneficial if one can take an extended period of time to evaluate the lessons of the pretenure years, even acknowledgment of the rite of passage may help prepare the scholar for the next round of plate spinning.

Managing one's time as a more visible and accomplished academic requires additional tools. Susan Jackson's suggestions are appropriate here. She identifies many of the techniques used by others to get us to say yes to projects and commitments in which we cannot afford to involve ourselves. These include flattery; offering flexible, even distant deadlines; offering control over the shape and content of the assignment; and more. Of course, once we all know the game, can any of us really successfully deflect the advances made on us by well-meaning others?

Learning to say no is likely to be an important way to keep one's priorities clear and effective. Clarifying the relationship between one's work and nonwork responsibilities may be another facet of the process. Marcy Crary pro-

vides an example of this when she responds to her sense of discomfort with the small amount of time she is devoting to her young daughter and renegotiates with a sympathetic dean the terms of her academic contract.

Strategic leadership roles are among the more demanding arenas in which academics can find themselves. These tend to be at the rank of assistant or associate dean or above, though many department chairs will attest to the complexity of their roles. As Allan Cohen points out, the turbulence stems from having to deal with so many different stakeholders—faculty, administrators, students, parents, the business community, the legislature, other faculties on campus. The combinations are demanding and often require contradictory responses. Not only are academics rarely trained for these jobs, but the work they do is usually not understood or particularly appreciated by those in the ranks from which the incumbents have come and to which they will likely return. Coping with such complex and multiple demands as an associate dean with two portfolios felt often, to Peter Frost, like operating simultaneously in five or six Harvard Business School cases without having any of the teaching notes to assist in the journey. One might be ahead in one situation, behind in several others, and unaware of yet others and their relationship to those that are visible. Having a personal vision of what might be accomplished and the support and buffering of competent executive assistance can make such roles more manageable.

One other important ingredient for keeping the plates spinning may be, as André Delbecq found while serving as a dean, consciously to let something go, to take one of the plates out of circulation, to ask oneself, What are you willing to give up to lead a healthier life? That is a question one might build into any academic life, given the multiple demands of the profession. (It may also form a macro question to the institution, as it tries to balance the many demands and priorities of its existence.)

While one is retuning on the run, it may also make sense to take note of the findings of Bob Quinn, Regina O'Neill, and Gelaye Debebe, who surveyed academics in the administrative sciences. Doing activities that are consistent with one's central values and that require continuous learning seems to energize us and keep us vital. Doing things we do not wish to do because of social and/or political pressures tends to demotivate us and burn us out. It may not be possible always to do the things we most want to do, and there are times when the institution requires us to make "sacrifices." However, knowing what we value and spending most of our time in those arenas is probably healthy for us and for our organizations.

Perhaps as valuable as any strategies and tactics for retuning, for staying vital, is our orientation to the meaning of our activities as academics. We can too easily and too quickly shift our attention from what we are doing to what needs to be done next, "looking beyond" the present to anticipate what is next on the horizon. It is built into the nature of our work, perhaps. However, this can blind us to the enjoyment and the lessons to be found in what we are doing. The following comment from Nathaniel Branden (1995) captures the sense of this point:

> Many years ago, in the '60s, I was writing a book called *The Psychology of Self-Esteem.* . . . I was a young man at the time, in my thirties, and one day I was sitting at my typewriter, impatient for the book to be finished, thinking that my life would really begin to unfold only when this book was finished. Yet I knew something was instinctively wrong with this line of thought. So I asked myself what I thought I would be doing when the book was finished, and I immediately answered: Planning the next book. And when that book was finished? Planning the book after that. I saw that my life, first and foremost, was about writing; that was and is my passion. So in the middle of writing *The Psychology of Self-Esteem,* I finally realized: This is it. This is my life. If I can't enjoy it now every day, there is no reason to believe I'll be better able to enjoy it in the future, after the seventh, eighth or ninth book. That realization was a turning point for me. (p. 81)

Stopping the Action: Refocusing One's Journey

At other times, we need to pause for more extended periods of time, to take stock more extensively of our efforts and our intentions. Anne Huff describes many of the issues academics face in trying to energize and sustain both their professional and personal lives. Her advice is cogent and insightful. Her personal aim to try to "balance 'doing the work' with being still" is one eloquent representation of the challenge. Getting in touch with our values and preferences as academics and as human beings may take more time than we have available when we are in the trenches of our work. We may feel a need to change and not have time to do anything about it. We may not even be consciously aware that it is time to change except for some feelings of discontent or burnout that are not being attended to. We may need to look at our priorities and our path because change is mandated by the end of a period in a particular role. We may need to take a more leisurely, though not passive, journey to clarify our preferences to discover what we need to do next. One important feature of a journey of renewal appears to be the availability of plenty of open space, to allow experiences and events simply to unfold. Meryl Reis Louis describes her experience as being about "discerning a path to follow rather than designing it, of following rather than pursuing a path, and of the faith and insecurity, trust, and self-consciousness that characterized my following that path" (p. 452). André Delbecq, describing his actions on stepping down as dean, notes: "For 60 days I rested, read, exercised, and meditated. It was the first real rest I had had in a decade without the obligatory daily check with the office. . . . At the end of these 2 months that I had allocated just for myself before serious exploration of my 'next career,' I felt 10 years younger" (p. 438).

Coupled with a willingness to stop, slow down, or alter daily routines and pursuits, there seems to be a need to listen to oneself, particularly when external events emerge and require decisions or responses that may affect what one does next along the journey:

> Coming to listen to what the voice within had to offer was part of the ongoing learning. In addition to sentences and images that arose as powerful messages from within me, I found the upwelling of strong feelings of unease or peacefulness served as a guide for me during my sabbatical journey. (Meryl Reis Louis, p. 445)

> I remember the day I made the choice very well. It was a gray day and I took my 212-

pound mastiff with me for a walk along the San Francisco Bay. I couldn't clearly articulate my rationale for saying no to the new deanship, but I decided to say no. I wasn't happy in my stomach saying yes. Every time I had said yes in my career when my stomach said no, I had regretted it. I sat down on a rock, looked at the bay and at my dog, Bonaparte, and said, "I am going to be a professor again." Bonaparte was the only friend who seemed to approve of my decision. (André Delbecq, p. 440)

The journeys of Louis and Delbecq also involved careful attention to analysis of themselves and others to identify some of the content of their exploration. Louis conducted a "life audit" on herself. Her sensitizing question was: "When have I had a sense of completeness or deep satisfaction?" Delbecq asked himself Tannenbaum's question, "What are you willing to give up to lead a healthier life?" (He asked this question at an earlier reflective period of his deanship.) Both authors examined the experiences of others. Louis "searched my friends' lives for relevant situations." Delbecq talked with other deans who had made transitions from initial deanships. They made different decisions from one another, but "the words of each informant would return to me later when I was closer to a personal decision" (p. 438).

Both Louis and Delbecq sought out structured experiences to enhance their renewal. They invested time and money in themselves. Louis spent time at an NTL lab and joined different interest groups that widened her experience base. Delbecq traveled to and attended executive programs taught by outstanding teachers presenting topics he would later be teaching. He also spent time visiting colleagues whom he judged to be working on the cutting edge of their subject matter. Both attended professional conferences and used them for renewal and to talk through thorny issues.

The journey Louis describes deals with an attempt to reorient herself spiritually, personally, and professionally. Her candor and her descriptions are instructive for those who are embarking on a similar process. Delbecq, on the other hand, is most concerned with his decision about whether to stay an administrator or return to the professorial ranks. Having decided on the latter role, he focuses in his

report on the strategies he used for getting his research and teaching performance back on track. His ideas are valuable for academics who are contemplating ways to upgrade their skills. He also attests to the magnitude of the challenge that faces individuals who have been out of this game for a long while: "During the 10 years I served as dean I felt I had been writing checks on my intellectual capital, but not renewing the account" (p. 441). Discussing his return as a teacher (formerly a master teacher), he says: "The course was not well organized. My jokes were too intellectual and out-of-date. . . . Gradually, though painfully, the "course" did emerge. It was hard work" (p. 441).

During a time of major personal exploration and change, it seems to be particularly important to "protect the integrity" of the journey, as Louis describes it. Those outside the process are unlikely to appreciate or to understand the actions and attitudes that accompany deep change. Others tend to look for cues to confirm the previous identity of the person they have known. Their well-meaning efforts to affirm their perceptions can put an often fragile experiment at risk. Louis indicates that, in retrospect, it would probably have been more helpful to everyone if she had constructed a cover story, "that is, a clear, more complete statement of what I was up to and why I therefore needed to maintain boundaries" (p. 449).

Returning on the Run

Ending a sabbatical and returning to one's institution are important transition points, whatever has been the purpose of the leave. This is particularly true if one has traveled a long distance psychologically from that community. Although neither Delbecq nor Louis deals with this matter in detail, it seems likely that there is a need to acknowledge and manage the transition. This includes providing time for returnees and others to digest the lessons of the experience. Research from the expatriate training literature has some relevance here. At repatriation, most managers experience unexpected difficulties for several reasons—a sense of being left out of the loop of information while they have been gone; a feeling of having undergone many changes during the assignment, changes that sometimes generate disapproval and suspicion in colleagues; and finally, a feeling of having acquired significant new knowledge and skills that are not being used by the organization after repatriation. Many readers may recall similar feelings on returning from sabbaticals spent separated from their home universities. We suspect that both academics and their institutions would benefit from better management of the "sabbatical repatriation," yielding scholars who are better prepared to "return on the run" after their time away.

Again, it is possible to use the expatriate literature as a guide for the design of a functional reorientation process, including regular communications from the department during the sabbatical to keep those away in touch with the department (some academics may choose to ignore them, but at least the information would be available); verbal reminders to the individual not to underestimate the transition difficulties of the return home; flexibility in teaching assignments that allow the returnee to introduce new knowledge or methodologies acquired while away; "front-stage" opportunities, such as colloquia or brown-bag invitations to share sabbatical experiences with colleagues; and service assignments that confirm the individual's value to the department or school. We believe that judicious use of activities such as these would maximize the benefits of a return from sabbatical for both the individual and the institution.

Future Rhythms of the Academic Enterprise

Our final theme reflects the discussions in the last section of the book, on rhythms of the future. We highlight the following points from those discussions, although there is much more that is significant in the section that is available as readers draw their own maps of the future. It is likely that the rate of change experienced by academics and their professions and institutions will accelerate as it has for every other industry. As Janet Near points out, the demographics of business schools are changing. There is a large cohort of scholars who will retire in the next decade, and most of them are white males. It is likely that some will not be replaced, and that replacements that occur will increase the representation of women and of ethnic mi-

norities in schools and the profession. There may be a larger proportion of part-time faculty in business schools than is currently the case. These changes will undoubtedly alter some of the emphases on what is valued in academia and how institutions are managed. There will be a greater variety of different distinctive voices in the community.

The power shift that Near suggests from faculty members and their departments to programs and to students is already happening in many schools. It may continue. It is unlikely that we will easily return to the power arrangements of the earlier era, and academics and administrators will need to devote more time and attention to these constituents if resources are to continue to flow to scholarly agendas. As a general challenge, we need to figure out how we respond to our various and many stakeholders. As Marcia Miceli points out cogently, we need to establish what it means to have "customers" for our products and to learn how to educate customers about how our responses to them may differ from those encountered in business settings.

We have already noted the increased visibility of teaching as an academic craft. What remains to be addressed is how this shift (and others like it) away from an exclusive focus on research is going to be managed and rewarded. It is not clear that we have a good handle on how to assess teaching and service contributions for purposes of tenuring and promoting individuals. We expect that more explicit and public processes for rewarding and training academics will be needed to meet the demands of legislators and other resource givers in the system.

The dramatic changes in technology that continue to take place will have strong impacts on research and teaching practices. It is now much less necessary to be attached to one location in order to conduct research. Bedeian's belief in the importance of location must be refined to include virtual locations that are linked by e-mail, fax, and teleconferencing. It is possible to build a network of colleagues that meets physically mainly at conferences. For better and worse, scholars can pursue research with the support of colleagues who are not at their home institutions. We expect, however, that proximity to mentors and colleagues who are "just down the hall" will remain an important contribution to the research environment.

Distance education will surely challenge, likely supplement, and perhaps supplant conventional teaching methods. Just as we begin to teach doctoral students how to teach in classrooms, that task is evolving. The classroom, like the research network, may not be in the same building as the teacher. The attractiveness of connecting someone like Karl Weick or Jim March or Rosabeth Moss Kanter to a national or international audience of students is appealing and potentially lucrative to hosting institutions. It would also change or at least complement in very vital ways what and how we teach the subject matter of our field to our students. We see the electronic component of teaching as an inevitable feature of the classroom of the future. We may also need fewer people to teach, given these changes. We do not see a diminishing of importance of the academic-as-teacher, however. It is likely that the roles of teachers as facilitators and interpreters of learning to those who watch on monitors or search for knowledge electronically and as developers of learning situations will become increasingly important. Teaching the skills of investigation and assessment of the meaning of new knowledge will assume even higher importance, in our opinion.

We think there will be competition from other institutions to educate students in business and other disciplines. We will need increasingly able administrators to manage increasingly flexible organizations. In a world of tenure, where faculty can with some impunity refuse to partici-

pate in changes that they may not perceive as important, it is and will be a challenge to move our institutions in appropriate new directions. Deans, department chairs, and other administrators will need to exhibit effective leadership skills to persuade faculty and influence commitment to new visions and practices. As academics, we are typically buffered from what deans and other boundary spanners see and experience, and we are understandably reluctant to give up hard-won freedoms and privileges. Nevertheless, the need to innovate, to think about new ways of accomplishing good research and all the other requirements of a business school of the next century, will not go away. If we do not adjust our rhythms to the needs and demands of the times, if we do not become more proactive in responding to change, others will do it for us. At the very least, we need to attract and keep active in our institutions and in the profession individuals who have the will and the skills to administer and to lead.

References

Branden, N. (1995, August). Nurturing the soul. *New Age Journal,* p. 81.

Frost, P. J., & Stablein, R. (Eds.). (1992). *Doing exemplary research.* Newbury Park, CA: Sage.

Gladwell, M. (1990, April 16). Why, in some fields, do early achievers seem to be the only kind? *Washington Post,* p. A3.

Conclusion

There is so much richness in the reports from our authors that it is difficult to do justice to all the insights they have generated. We have attended to many of these in the preceding commentary. In addition, however, we would like to note some of the "truths" that we have taken away from our reading of the essays in this book. In no particular order of importance, they are as follows:

1. As many of our contributors note, the discovery of their own voices has served as a source of great creativity, high productivity, and continuing renewal as they have moved through their careers.

2. Several contributors reference the opportunity to engage in new learning as perhaps the most critical source of their motivation. In this time of diminished resources, it seems important to remind university administrators and academics themselves of the power of this resource.

3. Academics, like most other people, have a tendency to overlook and undernourish their "nonwork" responsibilities. Many of our contributors point to the importance, although frequently retrospectively, of periodically setting aside time to put "first things first."

4. Perhaps, not surprisingly, given the continuing expansion of role demands throughout the academic career, several contributors offer tips for dealing with the demands of an overenriched work life. Somewhat contrary to the job design literature, some note the importance of breaking tasks down to fairly small components in order to get something done each day and allow one to keep up with the workload. Such strategies clearly place the rewards for a task in its completion rather than in its process—in finishing, rather than in doing. We can't help but wonder, however, if the effectiveness of such strategies does not also explain why many incredibly productive people report deriving so little enjoyment from their work. This suggests the need to maintain a proportionality in the academic workload between those tasks that are enjoyed most because they have been *completed* and those that are enjoyed

most simply through the *process* of doing them.

5. For some academics, synergies between teaching and research are frequent and direct. Not surprisingly, such individuals seem to have little trouble accepting the importance of teaching in the academic role. However, for others, perhaps because of their research areas or the level of students taught, such synergies are generally more indirect, often resulting more from the psychic energy that teaching generates, with its requirement for intense student-professor interactions, than from its intellectual requirements. Yet the current external environment makes it clear that teaching will continue to be an important, and even growing, part of the academic role. Thus it is important that synergies between teaching and research, particularly indirect ones, not be overlooked. We concur with author and professor Mary Catherine Bateson (1990), who notes, "Most of us run out of [psychic] 'energy' before we run out of energy. . . . An activity that affects vitality is not directly competitive or subtractive from other activities—on the contrary, it may enhance them" (pp. 169-170). The challenge for us as academics is to find novel ways of increasing the frequency and the directness of synergies between our teaching and research activities.

6. The very nature of an academic career requires considerable focus, self-absorption, and isolation. Thus it is not surprising to find mature and productive researchers reporting a different excitement and renewed commitment to their craft after the discovery of a collaborator or collaborators who bring new synergies at both the intellectual and affiliative levels.

7. Another unanticipated truth emerging from this volume is derived from the experiences of academics who have taken on the role of administrator for a period of time. Our authors found parts of that role onerous and demanding, and most were pleased to leave it behind after a period of time. More surprising, however, are their reports of profound changes in the ways they view the faculty role and its relationship to the institution. Even the most reluc-

tant administrators generally argued the importance of faculty assuming the roles of administrator for a period of time.

8. The publishing process is frequently criticized for its inconsistent and political nature. Yet, as many of us have noted, criticisms of the process spring more readily from our lips when we wear our author hats than when we wear our reviewer or editor ones. Several contributions to this volume serve as reminders of the critical but largely unrecognized contributions that editors and reviewers make to the development of the organizational sciences. Journal editors comment in this volume about the thought and effort devoted to developing and implementing their own agendas to improve the publication process. They strive to minimize instances of political behavior in the process. Their actions provide a reaffirmation of the constructive aspects of the publication process. Similarly, reviewers' portrayals of the careful, conscientious manner in which they approach their tasks encourages authors to look beyond the "black box" of the publication process. These accounts challenge us to push the boundaries of our work, sharpening our methodologies, logic, and conclusions.

9. Many authors in this volume comment on the importance of renewal times in the academic career, when obsessive and career-driven academics turn off their achievement striving for a period of time and listen to their inner voices concerning what future directions they should move in with respect to career and life. We suspect that renewal periods will become even more important for academics in the future, given the pace and continuous nature of change now affecting our institutions of learning.

10. Perhaps the greatest tribute to the quality of the academic life lies in the large numbers of scholars who return to it time and time again after enjoyable sabbaticals, after demanding periods as administrators, "heady" periods as consultants, and even after retirement.

We believe that much of the hard-won wisdom shared by our authors will prove to be a resource for those who join the community of scholars and who must deal with the challenges in the rhythms they encounter and initiate. We think there will always be a mix of creativity and instrumentality, of passion and the prosaic, in the work we do in the institutions we inhabit. The reports of our authors lead us to conclude that the field has imbued its members strong norms of initiative and integrity. We think that those among us (and we believe there will be many) who take up the challenge to reshape our forums and our practices will be encouraged, perhaps even inspired, by the energy, the capacities, and the humanity of the authors who grace these pages with their ideas, experiences, and reflections.

We close with a quote from one of the academics interviewed by Bob Quinn and his coauthors. It reflects our own sense of academic life, from living it but also from having experienced it vicariously through this book:

I think academic life is a privileged life, and I am either amused or outraged, depending on my mood, at my colleagues who have somehow persuaded themselves, and intend to persuade others, that this is a burdened, difficult kind of career. Few people can earn a living doing things that are so close to their major life interests. Instead, they end up pouring their time and their energy into tasks defined by others. As academics, we have a high degree of choice. We ought to be profoundly grateful. (p. 427)

Reference

Bateson, M. C. (1990). *Composing a life*. New York: Penguin.

About the Editors

Peter J. Frost is in the Faculty of Commerce and Business Administration at the University of British Columbia. He holds the Edgar F. Kaiser Chair in Organizational Behavior and is a former Associate Dean of the Faculty. He is currently a senior editor for *Organization Science* and served for several years as Executive Director of the Organizational Behavior Teaching Society. He has published books on organizational culture, most recently *Reframing Organizational Culture*, with Larry Moore, Meryl Louis, Craig Lundberg, and Joanne Martin (1992), and on management, including *Managerial Reality: Balancing Technique, Practice and Values*, with Vance Mitchell and Walter Nord (1995). He has coedited a special issue of the *Leadership Quarterly* titled "Leadership for Environment and Social Exchange" with Carolyn Egri (October 1994) and published with Carolyn several papers on the politics of innovation. He is working with Rae Andre on the final stages of a book that showcases the reports of noted researchers on their *teaching* experiences, titled *Hooked on Teaching*. He received a 3M Teaching Excellence Fellowship in 1988, the CASE Canada Professor of the Year Award in 1989, and the David L. Bradford Outstanding Educator Award in 1993. He is a Fellow of the Academy of Management. Dr. Frost has a keen interest in the politics and processes of leadership and will shortly begin work on a project about leading in times of crisis and ambiguity. He is an avid movie fan, enjoys birding, hiking, meditating, and Scottish country dancing.

M. Susan Taylor is Professor and Chair of the Department of Management and Organization at the College of Business and Management, University of Maryland, College Park. She received her doctorate in industrial/organizational psychology from Purdue University, was once a faculty member at the University of Wisconsin—Madison, and has been a visiting faculty member at the Amos Tuck School, Dartmouth College, SDA Boconni University in Milan, Italy, and the University of Washington, Seattle. She serves on the editorial boards of the *Journal of Applied Psychology* and the *Academy of Management Journal*, and is a past Chair (1994) of the Human Resources Division within the

National Academy of Management. Her current research focuses on the effects of procedurally just human resource systems on the reactions of employees and managers and on the determinants of managers' career mobility. With the editing of this volume completed, she looks forward to taking more frequent outdoor romps with her cocker spaniel, Cassandra; to relocating her tennis serve; and to searching for her Scottish-Irish ancestors in their homelands.

About the Contributors

Mats Alvesson works in the Department of Business Administration at the University of Lund, Sweden. He is engaged in the areas of organizational culture and symbolism, critical theory, communication, power, and gender. He has also written (with Kaj Sköldberg) on philosophy of science and qualitative method, and tries to relate these two themes through pragmatizing the former and intellectualizing (detechnifying) the latter. He is currently writing a book on organization and gender (with Yvonne Billing) and another on method in critical management research (with Stan Deetz). He lives in Copenhagen, Denmark, and commutes to his workplace. He and his wife, Yvonne Billing, have recently adopted Miha, a little girl from Vietnam.

Susan J. Ashford received her PhD degree in organizational behavior from Northwestern University and currently serves as Professor on the Business School faculty at the University of Michigan. She joined the Michigan faculty in 1991, after spending 8 years at Dartmouth College's Amos Tuck School of Business Administration. Her research focuses on the ways that individuals are proactive in their organizational lives, whether in assessing their own performance by seeking feedback, enhancing their managerial effectiveness by staying "tuned in" to various constituents, facilitating their own socialization during organizational entry, or attempting to sell particular issues to top management from the middle ranks of organizations. Her work has been published in a variety of outlets, including the *Academy of Management Review, Academy of Management Journal, Organizational Behavior and Human Decision Processes,* and *Research in Organizational Behavior*. A member of the *Academy of Management Journal* editorial board since 1984, she served as a consulting editor for *AMJ* from 1990 to 1993 and has reviewed for several other journals.

Jean M. Bartunek is Professor and Chairperson of the Organizational Studies Department at Boston College. Her substantive research interests concern the varieties of ways social cognition, conflict, and organizational change and transformation might intersect. Currently she is particularly interested in ways external researchers and insider members of a particular setting can collaborate in carrying out research there, and she has been involved in a number of joint insider-outsider research projects. She and Meryl Louis are currently completing a book on insider-outsider joint research teams to be published in Sage's Qualitative Research Methods series. She is a true midwesterner— she grew up in Cleveland and went to high school in Cincinnati, college in St. Louis, and graduate school in Chicago—but she has worked in the Northeast, at Boston College, since 1977. She is a member of the Society of the Sacred Heart, an international Catholic religious congregation. Prior to her graduate training in social and organizational psychology at the University of Illinois at Chicago, she was an elementary and high school teacher.

Arthur G. Bedeian (DBA, 1973, Mississippi State University) is the Ralph and Kacoo Olinde Distinguished Professor of Management, and Chairman, Department of Management, at Louisiana State University, where he specializes in the study of organization design and employee behavior. A Past President of the Academy of Management, he has also been President of the Allied Southern Business Association, the Southern Management Association, the Southeastern Institute for Decision Sciences, and the Foundation for Administrative Research. He was elected a Fellow of the Academy of Management in 1979 and of the International Academy of Management in 1992. In 1987 he received the Distinguished Scholar Award from the Southern Management Association. He is a former editor of the *Journal of Management,* and his work has appeared in the *Academy of Management Journal, Journal of Applied Psychology, Journal of Management, Journal of Vocational Behavior, Academy of Management Review, Applied Psychological Measurement, Personnel Psychology, Strategic Management Journal,* and *Organizational Behavior and Human Decision Processes.* In addition to being author of a text on the principles of management, he is coauthor of *Organization Design: Structure, Strategy, and Environment.* Both texts have appeared in numerous international and foreign-language editions. Dr. Bedeian has received numerous teaching awards as well as the 1991 LSU Alumni Association Distinguished Faculty Award. He has been involved in management development and consulting for the Veterans Administration, CBS College Publishing, the U.S. Air Force, and the LSU Executive Program. He currently serves as a member of the Fulbright Scholar Advisory Committee in Business Administration. Taking his own advice about "having fun," he is an avid golfer, a 1950s rock 'n' roll aficionado, and a long-time jogger. He still, however, feels guilty watching television.

Janice M. Beyer is Rebecca L. Gale Professor in Business, Professor of Sociology, and Director of the Center for Organizations Research at the University of Texas at Austin. She earned a Bachelor of Music degree at the University of Wisconsin—Madison, and MS and PhD degrees in organizational behavior from Cornell University. She is currently Past President of the International Federation of Scholarly Associations in Management. Previously, she has served as President of the Academy of Management and as editor of the *Academy of Management Journal.* She has also held a variety of editorial positions on other journals and administrative positions in other professional associations. She is especially interested in exploring the effects of people's individual and shared cognitions. In this vein, her early research investigated the effects of paradigm development in scientific fields, scientific journals, and universities. Her later work has looked at how managerial ideologies and values influence decision making. Her current research centers on organizational cultures, how individuals' self-concepts are shaped during organizational socialization, and the social values reflected in imagery about child care for working parents. She has two beautiful daughters—Claire, a veterinarian, and Andrea, a lawyer—and five delightful grandchildren.

Stewart R. Clegg studied behavioral science (sociology) at Aston University, graduating in 1971. He received his PhD from Bradford in 1974, after which he received a postdoctoral research fellowship from the European Group for Organization Studies. He moved to Australia for a job in 1976 and has been there ever since, apart from an interregnum in Scotland in the early 1990s. He has held chairs at the University of New England in sociology, 1985-1989; the University of St. Andrews in organization studies, 1990-1993; and the Foundation Chair in Management at the University of Western Sydney, Macarthur, 1993- , as well as having been Reader at Griffith University, where he worked from 1976 to 1984. He was a founder of Asian and Pacific Researchers in Organization Studies in the early 1980s, and has been the coeditor of the *Australian and New Zealand Journal of Sociology* as well as editor of a leading European journal, *Organization Studies.* He serves on the editorial boards of many other leading journals. Among the 15 books he has published are *Power, Rule and Domination* (1975), *Organization, Class and Control* (1980, with David Dunkerley), *Frameworks of Power* (1989), *Organization Theory and Class Analysis* (1989), *Modern Organizations: Organization Studies in the Postmodern World* (1990), and *Capitalism in Contrasting Cultures* (1990). He has published widely in the journals, including *Administrative Science Quarterly, Organization Studies, Organization, Organization Science, Sociological Review, Theory and Society*, and *British Journal of Management.* He researched "the leadership and management needs of embryonic industries" for the Taskforce on Leadership and Management in the Twenty-First Century, commissioned by the Australian federal government, which reported in 1995, and has been Head of the Department of Management and Marketing since his appointment at the University of Western Sydney, Macarthur, in 1993.

Allan R. Cohen is Academic Vice President and Dean of Faculty at Babson College, where he is responsible for academic activities including undergraduate and MBA programs, the School of Executive Education, and the development of 120 full-time faculty. Previously, he was gainfully employed as chaired Professor of Management, at Babson and the University of New Hampshire, teaching organizational behavior, negotiations, and other courses aimed at helping aspiring and current managers learn skills required by those in positions such as academic vice president. In the spirit of continuous learning, he persists in conceptualizing about management. His books include *Managing for Excellence* and *Influence Without Authority* (both coauthored with David Bradford); *The Portable MBA in Management* (editor); *Alternative Work Schedules* (coauthored with Herman Gadon), winner of the 1978 ASPA best book prize; and six editions of a textbook, *Effective Behavior in Organizations* (written with Fink, Gadon, and Willits), that introduced the classroom-as-organization to teaching organizational behavior. His consulting clients have included General Electric, Digital Equipment, Polaroid, and Lafarge Coppee, few of which seem to have suffered permanent damage. His education includes an AB in English literature from Amherst College, MBA and DBA from Harvard, and an

applied behavioral science internship from National Training Labs.

Marcy Crary is an Associate Professor of Management at Bentley College in Waltham, Massachusetts. She in involved in an institutional diversity change project at Bentley and team teaches a course called Managing Diversity in the Workplace with three other colleagues. Her personal and professional development is tied to the challenges of making the classroom and workplace more inclusive environments. She admires an elder who, when describing her life, said, "I never tried to have a 'career'—I just worked on what interested me." Dr. Crary is 43, married, and has an 8-year-old at home and two stepchildren in their 20s. She lives in Newton, Massachusetts, where she is currently involved in holding it all together. She is enjoying this challenge and all it is teaching her.

Larry L. Cummings is Professor of Management and Organization at the University of Minnesota. Formerly, he served as the J. L. Kellogg Professor of Organizational Behavior at Northwestern University and as the Slichter Research Professor, H. I. Romnes Faculty Fellow, and Director of the Center for the Study of Organizational Performance in the Graduate School of Business, University of Wisconsin—Madison. He also has served as an Associate Dean of the Graduate School there. He teaches and conducts research in the areas of organizational behavior, organizational theory, and management. He is author, coauthor, or coeditor of 24 books and has published more than 120 journal articles, which have appeared in the *Academy of Management Journal, Administrative Science Quarterly, Journal of Applied Psychology, Organizational Behavior and Human Decision Processes, Psychological Bulletin,* and other scholarly journals. He is a Fellow of the American Psychological Association, a Charter Fellow of the American Psychological Society, and a Fellow of the Decision Sciences Institute and has served as President (1980-1981) of the Academy of Management as well as Dean (1990-1993) of the Fellows of the Academy. He is a founding member and past Chair (1992) of the Society of Organizational Behavior. In 1995 he was awarded the Distinguished Educator Award by the Academy of Management.

Gelaye Debebe is a doctoral student in the Department of Organizational Behavior at the University of Michigan Business School. She received her BS in political science from the University of Maryland and her MS in human resources development from the American University. Her major research interest is in the organizational dimensions of economic development activities in both domestic and international contexts. Her experiences living in Ethiopia, Liberia, and the United States have led her to become increasingly interested in the ways in which cultural differences pose some interesting issues for how we think about the organizing problems inherent in the economic development process, where organizations embedded in different cultural and technological contexts attempt to cooperate.

André L. Delbecq is Professor of Management in the Leavey School of Business and Administration at Santa Clara University, where he served as Dean from 1979 to 1989. During his career his research interests have focused on three topics: executive decision-making processes, organization structure and design, and managing innovation in science-driven organizations. Recently he has conducted extensive research with CEOs in technology firms, which has included both professional challenges and a study of role impact on personal and family life. He has also done research on the business culture of Silicon Valley and the reasons for its innovative character. He has served on the Board of Governors and as chair of three divisions of the Academy of Management, and as President of the Midwest and Western Divisions. In 1975 he was elected Fellow of the Academy of Management and is currently the eighth Dean of Fellows. He is an avid sailor and lives at the water's edge in Alameda, where he and his wife, Mili, welcome their four children and six grandchildren to summer boating adventures on the San Francisco Bay.

Robert B. Duncan is currently the J. L. Kellogg Distinguished Professor of Strategy and Organizations and Chair of the Organization Behavior Department at Northwestern University. From 1987 to 1992, he served as the Provost of Northwestern, the chief operating officer of the university, responsible for the operating budget, educational policy, academic planning, and faculty personnel. All 10 of Northwestern's schools and their associated academic programs report through the Provost, who also serves as acting president in the absence of the president. Dr. Duncan teaches extensively in Kellogg's executive programs, where his courses include strategy implementation and the management of strategic change. He is also a Faculty Director of the Advanced Executive Program, which is Kellogg's 4-week program for senior managers. He is the author of numerous journal articles and two books: *Innovations* and *Organizations* (with G. Zaltman and J. Holbeck, 1977). His research deals with strategy formulation and implementing strategic change. His most recent research focuses on how top management shapes corporate strategy, with a specific emphasis on how CEOs develop and implement corporate strategic visions. He is a Fellow of the Academy of Management and served as its President in 1983. He has been on the editorial boards of the *Academy of Management Journal, Academy of Management Executive, Administrative Science Quarterly,* and the *Strategic Management Journal.* He is a frequent consultant to senior management and chief executive officers on strategy formulation, managing corporate culture, organizational design, and implementing strategic change.

Jane E. Dutton is Professor of Organization Behavior and Corporate Strategy at the University of Michigan Business School. Her major research interest is in the area of organizational change, an interest sparked 20 years ago when she worked as a research assistant on an NSF-funded study of innovation adoption in the footwear industry. Her experience as a research assistant hooked her and prompted her to travel to Evanston, Illinois, to attend Northwestern's PhD program. Today she looks at organizational change through a lens that sits at the intersection of micro organization behavior and strategic management. She is fascinated by the question of how organizational strategy affects the everyday behaviors of organizational members, and how members contribute to changes in organizational strategy. In her role as coeditor of *Advances in Strategic Management* (with Paul Shrivastava and Anne Huff), she is committed to opening up the conversation about theories relevant to strategic management. She is currently adjusting to her new role as Chair of the Organization Behavior and Human Resource Management Department. She is married to Lance Sandelands and they have two wonderful daughters, ages 8 and 11.

Miriam Erez is Professor of Industrial/Organizational Psychology at the Technion-Israel Institute of Technology, where she also serves as Dean of the Faculty of Industrial Engineering and Management. Her research focuses on two major areas: work motivation, with an emphasis on participation in goal setting; and cross-cultural organizational behavior, with an emphasis on the differential effects of motivational techniques across cultures. Her research in the first area examines the mediating processes between the motivational technique and performance quantity and quality, as well as the boundary conditions of the goal-setting method; this line of research has been expanded from the individual to the group level of analysis. She is the coauthor of two books and coeditor of two others on culture and organizational behavior, and has published more than 50 articles and book chapters. She is a Fellow of the American Psychological Association and of the Society for Industrial and Organizational Psychology. She serves on the editorial boards of *Organizational Behavior and Human Decision Processes* and *Human Performance* and is associate editor of *Applied Psychology: An International Review*. She is President-Elect of the Division of Organizational Psychology of the International Association of Applied Psychology.

Päivi Eriksson is Senior Research Fellow and Docent in Management and Marketing at the School of Business Administration, University of Tampere, Finland. She completed her doctoral degree at the Helsinki School of Economics and Business Administration in 1991. She has worked at the Scandinavian Consortium for Organizational Research at Stanford University, at the University of Tampere, and at the Centre for Corporate Strategy and Change at the Warwick Business School in the United Kingdom. She has published on management of change and organizational aspects of professional expertise and has presented papers at numerous European and international conferences and workshops, including the meetings of the British Academy of Management. Central themes in her research include the logics of action and the interaction of different management groups as well as the historical development of the confectionery industry. She is currently leading a 3-year research project on management and professional expertise funded by the Academy of Finland, and is also working on several comparative research projects in cooperation with researchers from the United Kingdom, Canada, and Sweden.

Cynthia V. Fukami is Associate Professor and Chair in the Department of Management in the College of Business Administration, University of Denver. She teaches organizational behavior and human resources management and has conducted research in the areas of employee commitment, turnover, absenteeism, employee discipline, and total quality management. She was awarded the 1992 Willemssen Distinguished Research Professorship by US WEST and the University of Denver, and was the recipient of the University of Denver's 1992 Distinguished Teaching Award. She is a member of the Academy of Management, the Organizational Behavior Teaching Society, the Industrial Relations Research Association, and the Society of Industrial Psychologists. She received her PhD from Northwestern University.

Joan V. Gallos is Associate Professor in the Division of Urban Leadership and Policy Studies in Education, School of Education, University of Missouri, Kansas City, where she teaches courses in organizations, power and influence, leadership, and gender. Raised in a tight-knit Slovak community in New Jersey, she was educated in parochial schools and at Princeton (BA in English, cum laude) and Harvard (EdM and EdD, with a concentration in organizational theory and behavior). She is currently editor of the *Journal of Management Education,* a dedicated wife and the mother of two sons, a member of the board of directors of the Organizational Behavior Teaching Society, an avid dog lover and dalmatian owner, and a member of the national steering committee for the joint AACSB-GMAC New Models of Management Education project. When she is not teaching, reading books with her children, or fantasizing about her comeback as a cabaret singer, she can be found at her computer, writing. She has published widely on management education, performance and learning, gender, and individual development; has just completed a book on teaching workplace diversity (with V. Jean Ramsey) and is currently hard at work on another book about the art and craft of good teaching.

Connie J. G. Gersick is Associate Professor at the Anderson Graduate School of Management at the University of California, Los Angeles. Her first profession, as a college administrator, reflected her interest in women's career development. She was on the staffs of Radcliffe's Offices of Admissions and Women's Education, and she directed Yale's Office on the Education of Women before earning her PhD there, in organizational behavior. Her research and writing have centered on theories of punctuated equilibrium at multiple levels of analysis and on growth, change, creative adaptation, and timing in human systems from project groups to start-up companies. She has used both field and laboratory methods. Most recently, she has edited an anthology of articles on groups in the workplace. Her collaboration with Jane Dutton and Jean Bartunek addresses her long-standing fascination with adult development and returns to her particular interest in women's issues. She and her husband, an organizational psychologist, have a son in college and a daughter in high school.

Marilyn E. Gist is Professor at the University of Washington, where she teaches at all levels, including executive degree and nondegree programs. She earned a bachelor's degree in education from Howard University and an MBA and PhD in business administration from the University of Maryland. Her research interests center on the study of self-regulatory factors in motivation and training. Her background includes several years' experience as a manager in both the public and private sectors. In addition, she has served as a consultant or trainer in the areas of performance motivation, career development, managing cultural diversity, and managerial assessment and development. She is a widely published scholar; in recent years her articles have appeared in *Personnel Psychology, Academy of Management Review, Journal of Applied Psychology,* and *Journal of Management.*

Royston Greenwood is the AGT Professor of Strategic Management in the Department of Organizational Analysis, Faculty of Business, University of Alberta. He is a cofounder of the Centre for Professional Service Firm Management. His research is concentrated on the management of professional service firms, and recently he has been particularly concerned with the development of new organizational forms at the global level. He is very involved with local business in Edmonton. He spends his time working with Bob Hinings and coaching girls' soccer. His teams have won gold medals at the provincial level and silver and bronze at the national level.

C. R. Hinings is the Thornton A. Graham Professor of Business in the Department of Organizational Analysis, Faculty of Business, University of Alberta, Director of the PhD Programme, and Director of the Centre for Professional Service Firm Management. He is on the editorial boards of *Administration Science Quarterly* and *Organization Studies.* His research is focused on understanding processes of strategic change in organizations, with special concentration on professional service firms. he spends his time working with Royston Greenwood, interacting with his seven grandchildren, and attending St. Paul's Anglican Church.

Anne Sigismund Huff is Professor of Strategic Management at the University of Colorado and Cranfield University. She has an MA in sociology and a PhD in management from Northwestern University. Her research interests focus on strategic change. She has used cognitive mapping to understand more about the thinking processes associated with change, has looked at group political processes as an important component of organizational change processes, and has considered industry-level causes and consequences of change. Her publications include articles and chapters on these topics as well as a book, *Mapping Strategic Thought* (1990). She is currently on the editorial boards of the *Strategic Management Journal* and the *British Journal of Management,* and is a senior editor for *Organization Science.* She also helps to edit two book series: Advances in Strategic Management and Foundations for Organizational Science.

James G. (Jerry) Hunt is Paul Whitfield Horn Professor of Management, Professor of Health Organization Management, Management Department Chair, and Director of the Program in Leadership Studies in the Institute for Management and Leadership Research at Texas Tech University, where he has been since 1981. He received his doctorate from the University of Illinois in 1966, back when the "new look" business administration programs that have so strongly affected the field were first being put in place. The systematic study of organizational behavior and organization theory in business schools was barely more than a glimmer in scholars' eyes, and work crossing cultural borders was not even that. By the late 1970s, however, developments were such that he first seriously considered working across national, if not cultural, borders, and in 1980 visited for a semester at the University of Aston in Birmingham, England. That led to his co-organizing leadership symposia in 1983 and 1985, emphasizing international work. Since the late 1980s, his international work has involved the Finnish connection described in his essay in this volume, where he has worked closely with coauthor Arja Ropo and more recently with Päivi Eriksson and has had professional and personal contacts with several other Finns. His career journey discussions have been strongly influenced by international collaborations such as they describe.

Susan E. Jackson is currently Professor of Management at New York University. She received her MA and PhD degrees from the University of California at Berkeley and her undergraduate degree from the University of Minnesota at Morris. Since beginning her academic career, she has moved back and forth between holding faculty positions in psychology (first at the University of Maryland and most recently at New York University) and in management/organizational behavior/human resources management (at New York University, then at the University of Michigan, and now again at New York University). Her research interests and publications mirror this dual orientation and span a variety of topics, including strategic human resources management and its relationship to firm performance, group processes within diverse work teams, job stress and burnout, as well as a few other topics. Recently, her energies have been split between service activities for the Academy of Management (these have included serving as editor of the *Academy of Management Review* and holding various offices in the

OB Division), writing and editing several books, and relearning the unique skill of teaching organizational behavior to MBAs. Unconfirmed rumors indicate that she has a variety of interests that keep her busy outside the office as well.

John M. Jermier is Professor of Organizational Behavior in the College of Business at the University of South Florida. His PhD is from the Ohio State University. Much of his work has focused on the development of a critical science of organizations, with a particular interest in research philosophy and methodology. Currently, he serves on the editorial review boards of *Administrative Science Quarterly, Leadership Quarterly,* and *Organization Science,* and he is coeditor of *Organization & Environment.* He looks forward to the day when the dolphins once again dominate the sea at Indian Shores, to the day when basketball replaces baseball as the American national pastime, and to the day when a complete anthology of Bob Marley's music is released on compact disc. He also looks forward to the day when the majority of the people of the state of Florida begin to value education, when a genuine third party emerges in the United States to represent the interests of the exploited, and when a global consciousness replaces provincialism in the minds of the many.

Toni C. King is an educator whose focus is human relationships and interaction. She has a PhD in organizational behavior from Case Western Reserve University, a master of arts degree in guidance and counseling from The Ohio State University, and a bachelor of arts degree in psychology from Oklahoma State University. Her research on African American female bonding relationships and on cross-race relationships among women has led to the development of numerous presentations, workshops, and curriculum design. She is currently an Assistant Professor within the Division of Human Development in the School of Education and Human Development at the State University of New York at Binghamton. She teaches courses at the graduate and undergraduate levels in group dynamics, multicultural diversity, and gender in organizations. In these courses she utilizes an interdisciplinary approach, drawing upon counseling competencies, group process skills, and systems analysis to explore race, class, and gender in society. Her work is based on the

philosophy that relational bonds have high potential to promote personal growth and to motivate behaviors that contradict forms of oppression based on differences (race, class, gender,
sexuality). Her work as an educator and researcher seeks to further understanding and
enhancement of human relationships.

Roderick M. Kramer is Associate Professor of
Organizational Behavior at the Stanford University Graduate School of Business. He received his PhD in social psychology from UCLA
in 1985. His research focuses on decision making in conflict situations, such as social dilemmas, negotiations, and international disputes.
Most recently, his research has explored the role
of cognitive illusions in conflicts and the dynamics of trust and distrust in organizations.
His work has appeared in journals such as the
*Annual Review of Psychology, Journal of Person-
ality and Social Psychology, Journal of Experimental Social Psychology, Journal of Conflict Resolution,* and *Organizational Behavior and Human
Decision Processes.* He is coeditor, with David
Messick, of *Negotiation as a Social Process* (1995)
and, with Tom Tyler, of *Trust in Organizations*
(1995). He teaches courses on organizational
conflict, negotiation, group decision making,
and power and politics, as well as an introductory course on organizational behavior.

Huseyin Leblebici is Professor of Business Administration at the University of Illinois Urbana-Champaign. He received his MBA and
PhD from the same institution. After receiving
his PhD, he went back to his native Turkey to
teach at the Middle East Technical University in
Ankara, with no idea that he would be back to
the University of Illinois. He has been an editorial board member of *Administrative Science
Quarterly, Academy of Management Review,* and
Organizational Science. For the past 7 years he
has been working on projects that attempt to
understand the essence of organizing. He has
focused on questions of how our collective rules
and resources come together and generate organized patterns of activities, and how this process can be described within a grammar of organizing. He is married and has two daughters.

Edwin A. Locke is Professor of Business and
Management and of Psychology at the University of Maryland. He received his undergradu-

ate degree from Harvard University in 1960 and
his MA and PhD degrees in industrial psychology
from Cornell University in 1962 and 1964, respectively. He is the author of *A Guide to Effective
Study* (1975), *Goal Setting: A Motivational Technique That Works* (with G. Latham, 1984), *Generalizing From Laboratory to Field Settings* (1986), *A
Theory of Goal Setting and Task Performance* (with
G. Latham, 1990), and *The Essence of Leadership*
(with others, 1991). He is an internationally
known behavioral scientist whose work is included in leading textbooks and acknowledged in
books on the history of management. He has been
elected a Fellow of the American Psychological
Association, of the American Psychological Society, and of the Academy of Management, and is a
member of the Society of Organizational Behavior. He is on the editorial boards of *Organizational
Behavior and Human Decision Processes* and the
Journal of Applied Psychology. In 1993 he received
the Distinguished Scientific Contribution Award
from the Society of Industrial and Organizational Psychology.

Meryl Reis Louis is an Associate Professor of
Organizational Behavior at Boston University's
School of Management. For 5 years, she was
also a Senior Research Associate at the Center
for Applied Social Science at Boston University.
Prior to returning to UCLA for a PhD in the
organizational sciences, she served on the management consulting staff of Arthur Andersen &
Co. and worked as a paraprofessional counselor
at a community mental health center in Los
Angeles. Her research has focused on workplace
cultures, career transitions, organizational entry
and socialization, and cognitive processes of
people in work settings. For 10 years, she studied "life after MBA school" with a panel of
graduates from four major MBA programs. She
has long advocated supplementing traditional
positivist approaches with interpretive approaches
to organizational research. Most recently, she
has been exploring issues of community and
spirituality as they may be relevant to the workplace and her life. She serves as a member of the
leader corps of the Foundation for Community
Encouragement, an organization that provides
community-building workshops and related assistance to the public and to intact groups.

Joanne Martin is the Fred H. Merrill Professor
of Organizational Behavior at the Graduate

School of Business and, by courtesy, in the Department of Sociology, Stanford University. She has been at Stanford since 1977. She recently served as Director of the Graduate School of Business's seven doctoral programs. Her PhD in social psychology is from the Department of Psychology and Social Relations, Harvard University. Her current research interests include organizational culture, with particular emphasis on subcultural identities and ambiguities; judgments about the justice of unequal pay levels; and gender and race in organizations as subtle barriers to acceptance and advancement. Her most recent books are *Reframing Organizational Culture,* coedited and cowritten with Peter Frost, Larry Moore, Meryl Louis, and Craig Lundberg (1991), and *Cultures in Organizations* (1992).

Robert D. Marx is Associate Professor of Management at the University of Massachusetts, Amherst. He is the coauthor of *Management Live! The Video Book* and the 1991 recipient of the Bradford Outstanding Educator Award from the Organizational Behavior Teaching Society. His research efforts have focused on the problem of skill retention following management development programs. He has published on the topic of relapse prevention in management training in numerous journals, including the *Academy of Management Review, Journal of Management Development,* and the *Training and Development Journal.* His recent writing has focused on the optimal use of video in management education and the development of classroom activities to teach awareness of race and gender inequities in the workplace. He has recently taught MBA classes in Russia and Greece, and has traveled also to South Africa and China. He consults with many organizations on issues of leadership, communication, teamwork, and improving skill retention in management training.

Alan D. Meyer is the Cone Professor of Management at the University of Oregon. He received his BA in economics from the University of Washington and his doctorate in organizational behavior and industrial relations from the University of California, Berkeley. He is senior editor of organization theory and design for *Organization Science.* Previously, he has served as consulting editor for the *Academy of Management Journal,* and as a member of the edito-

rial boards of *AMJ* and *Administrative Science Quarterly.* He likes using multiple research methods and collecting data by talking with informants on their own turf. He is interested in organizational behavior away from equilibrium, which leads him to ask questions that cross levels of analysis, address temporal changes, and focus on cognitive events in organizations. His early work focused on reactions to "environmental jolts" when a doctors' strike against San Francisco hospitals set up a natural experiment in organizational change. He is now studying the impacts of quantum changes in the structure and boundaries of the health care, electric utility, and savings and loan industries. Before entering academia, he worked as an industrial engineer, a market researcher, and a ski instructor. He currently is training a new golden retriever puppy to neutralize reviewers' unkind barbs.

Marcia P. Miceli is Senior Associate Dean for Academic Programs and Professor of Human Resources in the Max M. Fisher College of Business at Ohio State University. Her research interests are currently in the process of transition. She remains interested in learning why whistleblowing occurs and the consequences it has for individuals and organizations, and in the factors that determine pay satisfaction. Her spending the past 5 years in administrative positions has stimulated interests in many new areas. With Janet Near, she wrote *Blowing the Whistle: The Organizational and Legal Implications for Companies and Employees* (1992). She has taught courses in human resources management, compensation, and staffing, and has served on the editorial boards of *Academy of Management Review* and *Journal of Management.* Her doctorate of business administration degree was awarded by Indiana University in 1982.

Raymond E. Miles is Eugene E. and Catherine M. Trefethen Professor of Organizational Behavior and Dean Emeritus in the Walter A. Haas School of Business at the University of California at Berkeley. He joined the faculty in 1963, after receiving his PhD in organizational behavior and industrial relations at Stanford University. He served as Dean of the Walter A. Haas School of Business from 1983 to 1990. He has also served as Director of the Institute of Industrial Relations at the University of California at Berkeley and as editor of the journal *Industrial Relations*. He has been a Visiting Professor at the Amos Tuck School of Business at Dartmouth College and at the Graduate School of Business at the University of Texas, Austin, and a Visiting Scientist at the Tavistock Institute in London. He has been consultant to numerous private, public, labor, and academic organizations across the United States and throughout the world. For the past 10 years, his research and writing have focused on the interaction of organizational strategy, structure, and managerial processes. The conceptual framework and organizational typology emerging from this research (done in conjunction with Professor Charles C. Snow of Pennsylvania State University and others) are broadly used and have stimulated a continuing research stream. Dr. Miles is a Fellow of the Academy of Management and a regular participant in its programs, including its doctoral consortia. He was a founding member of the Organizational Behavior Teaching Society (Berkeley, 1974). He is the author of five books and more than 50 articles and chapters. He has lectured in Europe, Asia, Canada, and Latin America.

John A. Miller is Professor of Organization and Management at Bucknell University and serves as Executive Director of the Organizational Behavior Teaching Society. He received his BA with honors in economics and international relations from Stanford, did graduate work in languages and literature at the University of Munich (Germany), and received his MBA from the European Institute of Business Administration (INSEAD, France). His PhD in management is from the University of Rochester. He taught management at INSEAD, Rochester, and Yale prior to going to work at Bucknell. Although he has been active as a researcher and consultant on managerial career development, leadership, organizational politics, organization design, and team management for a number of business and service organizations in the United States, Europe, and Africa, his current scholarly, consulting, and teaching interests are focused on developing active, problem-based, and collaborative pedagogical methods designed to meet the special needs of undergraduate management students. He directed an interdisciplinary "Technologies of Management" curriculum and software development project funded by

the General Electric Educational Foundation, and currently directs a collaborative learning laboratory project funded by Johnson & Johnson and Andersen Consulting. He established Management 101, Bucknell's popular undergraduate management project course, in 1979. He has designed and taught versions of MG 101 at various universities in the United States and abroad, including Doshisha University in Kyoto, Japan, and the École Supérieure de Commerce in Tours, France. He has received teaching and community service prizes, but claims that his greatest rewards, and his own most productive experiential learning, have come from MG 101, from OBTS, and from music. He served as musical director and conductor for a number of Stanford's musical theater productions, and as Director of the Stanford Men's Glee Club and of a choral society in France. He has sung with community chorales in Germany, France, New Haven, and Pennsylvania's Susquehanna Valley.

Philip H. Mirvis is an organizational psychologist whose research and private practice concern large-scale organizational change and the character of the workforce and workplace. A regular contributor to academic and professional journals, he has authored six books, including *Failures in Organization Development and Change*, a study of national attitudes, *The Cynical Americans*, and, most recently, a survey of corporate human resource strategies, *Building the Competitive Workforce*. He has led seminars all over the United States, addressed many university faculties and professional groups, and lectured throughout Europe and in China, India, Japan, Latvia, and Russia. His consulting work concerns organizational development, the human side of mergers and acquisitions, innovation and technological change, corporate social responsibility, environmental practices, and cultural change. His corporate clients include Ben & Jerry's, Hewlett-Packard, Unisys, Chemical Bank, Caterpillar Tractor, and Graphic Controls. He has also studied organization and human resources issues in government and the nonprofit sector, where his clients include Blue Cross/Blue Shield, the National Association of Meal Providers, the National Council on Aging, and U.S. Aid for International Development. He also leads outdoor management education programs, contributes to seminars by the American Management Association and Federal Executive Institute, and is a member of the board of directors of the Foundation for Community Encouragement. He has a BA from Yale University and a PhD in organizational psychology from the University of Michigan. He lives in Sandy Spring, Maryland, with his wife, Katherine Farquhar; three daughters, Alexa, Lucy, and Suzanne; and assorted animals—domestic and wild.

Vance F. Mitchell entered this world on March 30, 1923, in Baltimore, Maryland, as the caboose fifth child of a Presbyterian minister. His father, like himself, earned his PhD while raising a young family. His nearest brother was 8 years his senior, and the others were already grown and out in the world, so for the latter part of his childhood he was the only nestling. He attended public school through grade 9 and West Nottingham Academy in Maryland for the remainder of his secondary education. The rest of his education and progressions through the U.S. Air Force and academe you already know if you have read his chapter in this volume. His hobbies, until recently, included fishing and boating. Now his recreation is mostly confined to reading, his two sons, his grandson, baking bread in a bread machine, and the many interesting places his position with Embry-Riddle Aeronautical University takes him. In June 1995 he and his wife celebrated their fiftieth wedding anniversary. He has no idea what his fourth career will be, but he hopes that whatever it is, it is as rewarding as the first three have been.

William H. Mobley is Visiting Professor of Management at the Hong Kong University of Science and Technology and Professor of Human Resources Management at Texas A&M University. He returned to faculty life in 1994 after serving for more than 14 years in various administrative roles, including department head, dean, vice chancellor, president, and chancellor. He is best known for his research on employee motivation, employee turnover, and human resources management. Most recently, he has been focusing on strategy and human resources management and on international human resources issues. A Fellow of the American Psychological Society and the Society for Industrial-Organizational Psychology, he also is a member of the Academy of Management and

the Academy of International Business. He grew up in Ohio and earned his doctorate at the University of Maryland in 1971. He served as head of HR Research and Planning at PPG Industries before starting his faculty career in 1973. He serves on a number of corporate and foundation boards and is President of PDI's International Institute for Research and Applications. He and his wife, Jayne, have two daughters and three grandchildren.

Ray V. Montagno received his PhD in industrial/organizational psychology in 1980 from Purdue University. He has a master's degree from Western Michigan University and his undergraduate degree is from the University of Dayton. He is currently Professor of Management at Ball State University, where his responsibilities include teaching courses at the graduate and undergraduate levels in the areas of human resources management, organizational behavior, international management, and research methodology. He also serves as Chair of the College of Business Committee on Internationalization, a position focused on improving the level of international activity for students and faculty, as well as outreach to the business community. He has completed more than 40 publications on numerous organizational topics, including manufacturing strategies, fostering innovation within organizations, job design, small business management, and productivity measurement. His publications have appeared in such outlets as *Strategic Management Journal, Journal of Small Business Management, International Journal of Production Research, Training and Development Journal,* and *Academy of Management Journal.* His current research interests include global competitiveness and organizational strategy to improve performance. He has also served as a reviewer for numerous journals, professional organizations, and publishers. He has served as an adviser to state, community, and university boards and committees and has provided consulting services to a broad spectrum of organizations, including hospitals, small businesses, governments, and Fortune 500 companies.

J. Keith Murnighan is the W. J. Van Dusen Professor at the University of British Columbia. In the fall of 1996, he will become the Harold H. Hines Jr. Distinguished Professor at the Kellogg School of Management at Northwestern University. He received his PhD in social psychology from Purdue University, and taught at the University of Illinois for 19 years before moving to UBC. His research focuses on negotiation and interpersonal interaction, and currently addresses altruism, fairness, cooperation, and repentance. His work has appeared in many journals, in organizational behavior, social psychology, and economics. His recent books include *Bargaining Games: A New Approach to Strategic Thinking in Negotiations* (1992) and an edited volume, *Social Psychology in Organizations: Advances in Theory and Research* (1993). He currently serves as associate editor of the *Administrative Science Quarterly*.

Kevin R. Murphy is Professor of Psychology at Colorado State University. He has held regular or visiting positions at Rice University, New York University, the University of Stockholm, and University of California, Berkeley. He received his BA (1974) from Siena College, his MS (1976) from Rensselaer Polytechnic University, and his PhD (1979) from the Pennsylvania State University, all in psychology. He is a Fulbright scholar, has served as a member of two National Academy of Sciences committees, and is a member of the Department of Defense Advisory Committee on Military Personnel Testing. He serves as associate editor of the *Journal of Applied Psychology* and as a member of the editorial boards of *Personnel Psychology, Human Performance,* and *International Journal of Selection and Assessment.* He is the author of more than 50 articles and book chapters and author or editor of four books: *Psychological Testing: Principles and Applications* (with C. Davidshofer), *Psychology in Organizations: Integrating Science and Practice* (with F. Saal), *Performance Appraisal: An Organizational Perspective* (with J. Cleveland), and *Honesty in the Workplace.* His research interests include performance appraisal, judgment and decision making, honesty in the workplace, and research methodology. He has collaborated with Jan Cleveland on several books and chapters on performance appraisal, but their most successful collaboration has been their long and happy marriage.

Nancy K. Napier (PhD, Ohio State University) is currently Professor of Management and In-

ternational Business at Boise State University, where she also oversees the College of Business and Economics International Business Programs, including the university's Vietnam MBA program. She previously has held the positions of Chairman of the Management Department and Associate Dean for Academic and Student Affairs at Boise State. Her research interests include international human resources management and women working overseas. Her publications have appeared in such journals as *Strategic Management Journal, Sloan Management Review, Journal of International Management,* and *Journal of Management Inquiry.* With Sully Taylor, she recently published *Western Women Working in Japan: Breaking Corporate Barriers* (1995).

Janet P. Near is Dow Professor of Management, School of Business, Adjunct Professor, Sociology Department, and Adjunct Professor, Philanthropic Studies Department, Indiana University. Her research focuses on the effects of organization structure on people, most recently in two areas: the effects of whistle-blowing on both the organization and the whistle-blower and the effects of work life on life away from work. She teaches organization theory, design, and development. She has been Chairperson of the Department of Management for the past 5 years, where she has had a chance to participate in organization theory issues on a daily basis. She escaped from teenage experience with family business to academia via undergraduate school at the University of California, Santa Cruz, in an independent major (psychology of power) and graduate school at the State University of New York, Buffalo, in sociology. Her husband is a faculty member in pharmacology who teaches medical students about drugs. They have two sons, ages 7 and 11.

Stella M. Nkomo in Professor in the Department of Management in the Belk College of Business Administration at the University of North Carolina at Charlotte. Her research focuses on race and gender in organizations. With Ella Bell, she is completing a book, *Our Separate Ways: Life Journeys of Black and White Women in Corporate America.* In her fifth year of teaching at the University of North Carolina, she received the University's Teaching Excellence Award. She offers this reflection on that experience: "When I was told that I would be receiving the award, I experienced a range of feelings from extreme joy to extreme anxiety. My feelings of anxiety seemed strange until I realized that my anxiety stemmed from two things. First, those who are fortunate to get teaching awards are usually expected to have profound and illuminating insights into the art of teaching. I had nightmares about what I would say when the time came to answer that dreaded question. Second, I realized that receiving the award placed a tremendous burden upon me for repeat performances. I had to sustain the level of performance that led to the award or otherwise risk the utterances of disbelieving new students—Is she really the one who received the teaching award?"

Walter R. Nord is Professor of Management at the University of South Florida. Previously, he was affiliated with Washington University-St. Louis (1967-1989). His current interests center on developing a critical political economic perspective of organizations, organizational innovation, and organizational conflict. He has published widely in scholarly journals and has edited/authored a number of books. His recent books include *The Meanings of Occupational Work* (with A. Brief), *Implementing Routine and Radical Innovations* (with S. Tucker), *Organizational Reality: Reports From the Firing Line* (with P. Frost and V. Mitchell), and *Resistance and Power in Organizations* (with J. Jermier and D. Knights). He is currently coeditor of *Employee Responsibilities and Rights Journal* and a recent past book review editor for the *Academy of Management Review.* He has served as consultant on organizational development and change for a variety of groups and organizations. He is currently coediting the *Handbook of Organization Studies* (with S. Clegg and C. Hardy).

Judy D. Olian is Professor of Management and Organization and Associate Dean at the Maryland Business School, University of Maryland. In this role she is responsible for all faculty issues, academic programs, technology support, and administrative oversight of the college. Her research interests include strategic human resources management and especially the alignment of organizational systems with business strategies. She has published widely in these areas. She is a member of the board of editors of the *Academy of Management Review* and *Jour-*

nal of Quality Management. Between 1990 and 1992, she was Assistant to the President of the University of Maryland at College Park to support the design and implementation of the university's continuous improvement strategy, the delivery of training, and the establishment of corporate partnerships to support TQ. She works with executives to implement total quality management in private sector organizations and in higher education. She has written on total quality concepts and implementation, and has conducted numerous executive and professional workshops on management and total quality principles and tools. She has been the recipient of an American Council on Education Fellowship and was the team leader for the University of Maryland's submission to the IBM-TQ Competition for Higher Education, which culminated in a multimillion-dollar award to the university. In addition to her faculty appointment, she was the first director of the IBM-TQ program.

Regina M. O'Neill is earning her doctorate in organizational behavior and human resources management at the University of Michigan Business School. She is currently completing her dissertation, which is a conceptual and empirical integration of mentoring and social support in the workplace. Her research interests also include organizational context, empowerment, integration of work and family, and issue selling in organizations. Before coming to Michigan, she earned her MBA at the Amos Tuck School of Business Administration in Dartmouth College, and her undergraduate degree from the University of Massachusetts. She also worked as a CPA in a large international accounting firm.

Robert E. Quinn is Professor of Organizational Behavior and Human Resource Management at the University of Michigan Business School. His central interest is in organizational change, and he particularly focuses on culture, leadership, and management. He has recently completed work on three book manuscripts: *Deep Change: Discovering the Leader Within; Diagnosing and Changing Organizational Culture;* and *Becoming a Master Manager* (second edition). All three are scheduled to be published in the fall of 1996. He has extensive experience in the field of organizational development and has been involved in the design of many large-scale organizational interventions.

Elaine Romanelli is Associate Professor of Management and Director of the Global Entrepreneurship Studies Program at the Georgetown University School of Business, where she teaches courses in the areas of strategic management, organization design, and entrepreneurship. Her research focuses on processes and patterns in organizational transformation as well as the role of organizational foundings in influencing the transformation of industries. Her current research projects focus on the strategic and entrepreneurial development of two industries, international biotechnology and U.S. motion picture production. She has published articles in *Administrative Science Quarterly, Academy of Management Journal, Organization Science,* and *Research in Organizational Behavior,* among other outlets. She has served on numerous editorial review boards for academic journals and has been an officer of the Organization and Management Theory Division of the Academy of Management. She received her AB degree in English literature from the University of California, Berkeley, and her MBA and PhD degrees in marketing and management from Columbia University.

Arja Ropo is Associate Professor in the School of Business Administration at the University of Tampere in Finland. She received both her master's and doctoral degrees in Tampere; her dissertation, *Leadership and Organization Change,* was published in 1989. Her interests involve leadership in and of organizations and organizational competence development. She prefers studying organizational processes across time: how things evolve; what forces support, hinder, delay, or accelerate organizational life; how individual and organizational competencies are configured. Her research most often involves different types of service organizations, such as banks, cultural organizations, and university departments. She has published recently in such international outlets as *Leadership Quarterly, Entrepreneurship Theory and Practice,* and *Personnel Review.* She served as the Director of the Business School in Tampere from 1992 to 1994, as well as serving on several university- and national-level task forces covering different assignments over the past 10 years. She has also taken responsible roles in the Tampere Business School's Management Development Program as well as in other continuing education programs and in-house training for companies across Finland.

Sara L. Rynes is the John F. Murray Professor of Management & Organizations at the College of Business, University of Iowa. Her research and teaching interests are in the areas of human resource strategy, compensation, total quality management, recruitment and selection, and career management. She has served as consultant to a wide range of private and public sector organizations, and is on the editorial boards of the *Academy of Management Journal, Personnel Psychology,* and *Journal of Applied Psychology.* She is a Fellow of the American Psychological Association and the Society for Industrial and Organizational Psychology. Prior to joining the University of Iowa faculty, she was on the faculties of the University of Minnesota and Cornell University.

Paul R. Sackett holds the Carlson Professorship in Industrial Relations at the University of Minnesota. He received his PhD in industrial and organizational psychology at the Ohio State University, and has served on the faculties of the University of Kansas and the University of Illinois at Chicago. His research interests include the assessment of managerial potential, honesty in the workplace, psychological testing in workplace settings, and methodological issues in employee selection. He served as the editor of *Personnel Psychology* from 1984 to 1990, and coauthored the text *Perspectives on Employee Staffing and Selection.* He served in 1993-1994 as President of the Society for Industrial and Organizational Psychology, Division 14 of the American Psychological Association. When not working, he and his wife, Pat, run marathons (40 to date), build harpsichords, read widely on topics having nothing to do with business or psychology, strive to get their passports stamped in as many countries as possible, build character by enduring Minnesota winters, and enjoy the company of three charming and lovely cats.

Christina E. Shalley is Associate Professor of Organizational Behavior and Human Resource Management in the School of Management at

Georgia Institute of Technology. Her MA in labor and industrial relations and PhD in business administration are from the University of Illinois, Urbana-Champaign. Prior to joining Georgia Tech, she was an Assistant Professor of Management and Policy at the University of Arizona. Her research interests include examining the effects of social and contextual factors on creative performance. She is also involved in exploring the boundaries of traditional goal-setting programs, such as the effects of multiple goals and competing goals on resource allocation and performance outcomes. Her research has appeared in such places as the *Academy of Management Journal, Journal of Applied Psychology, Organizational Behavior and Human Decision Processes,* and *Research in Personnel and Human Resource Management.* She has been the recipient of a number of teaching awards, including Outstanding Undergraduate Teacher and Business Teacher of the Year.

Robert I. Sutton is Professor of Organizational Behavior in Stanford University's Department of Industrial Engineering and Engineering Management. He received his PhD degree in organizational psychology from the University of Michigan in 1984 and has been at Stanford since he left graduate school, except for 2 years (1986-1987, 1994-1995) spent at the Center for Advanced Study in the Behavioral Sciences at Stanford. Most of his research uses psychological theory, alone or in combination with sociological perspectives, to help understand how people influence and are influenced by their organizational contexts. His research style emphasizes the development of theory on the basis of direct observation of organizational life and interviews with engineers, managers, and other organization members. He also does survey research studies now and then, and is thinking about trying an experiment in the next couple of years. He has done a lot of work on job stress and organizational decline and death in the past, but he is not interested in these areas any longer. He also continues to work on organizational impression management, although he seems to be losing interest in this topic as well. These days, he is interested in felt and expressed emotion in organization, intense public scrutiny, brainstorming, managerial rhetoric, how organizations try to innovate routinely, and performance as a strange and sometimes dysfunctional obsession for organizational researchers. He has served on the editorial boards of the *Academy of Management Journal, Academy of Management Executive, Administrative Science Quarterly,* and *Organization Science,* and recently resigned as associate editor of the *Administrative Science Quarterly.* He would rather do research than any other part of his job; he finds writing the most fun. He doesn't like being an administrator very much, and he doesn't like tasks where he has to judge other people or their work, but the pressures to do these kinds of tasks keep increasing as he gets older.

Linn Van Dyne is Assistant Professor at Michigan State University, where she teaches organization behavior. She received her PhD from the University of Minnesota with a concentration in strategic management and organization. She also holds an MBA from the University of Minnesota and has 15 years of work experience, including executive-level responsibility for worldwide human resources in a multinational manufacturing firm. She has published in the *Journal of Applied Psychology* and the *Academy of Management Journal,* and has contributed several book chapters. Her major research interests focus on proactive employee behaviors involving initiative, such as affiliative and challenging extrarole behavior, minority influence, and feedback-seeking behavior. She is also interested in group composition, employee attachment, cross-cultural research, and research on human resources policy issues.

Mary Ann Von Glinow is Professor of Management and International Business at Florida International University. She was previously on the Business School Faculty at the University of Southern California. She has an MBA, MPA, and PhD in management science from the Ohio State University. She was 1994-1995 President of the Academy of Management, the world's largest association of academicians in management, and is a member of 10 editorial review boards. In the past 8 years she has authored numerous journal articles and six books: *The New Professionals: Managing Today's High Technology Employees* (1988), *Managing Complexity in High Technology Organizations* (1990), *United States-China Technology Transfer* (1990), *Technology Transfer in International Business* (1991), *A Resource Guide for Internationalizing the*

Business School Curriculum (1993), and *International Technology Transfer and Management* (1993). She is currently writing a book titled *International Management* and is heading an international consortium of researchers delving into "best international HRM practices." She consults to a number of domestic and multinational enterprises and serves as a mayoral appointee to the Shanghai Institute of Human Resources in China. Since 1989, she has been a consultant in General Electric Company's Workout program, and she serves as a lead Workout consultant to Southern California Edison, Kaiser Permanente, First Bank of Chicago, New York Life, and the State of Florida.

James P. Walsh is Professor of Organizational Behavior and Corporate Strategy in the University of Michigan Business School. His research on corporate governance attempts to blend perspectives from organization theory, corporate strategy, international business, and corporate finance. He currently serves the profession as a consulting editor at the *Academy of Management Review,* senior editor at *Organization Science,* board member of the *Strategic Manage-*

ment Journal, Chair of the OMT Division of the Academy of Management, and Chair of the College on Organization within INFORMS. On the home front, he is busy raising three daughters and scheming to find more ways to ski beyond the borders of Michigan.

David A. Whetten is the Jack Wheatley Professor of Organizational Behavior and Director of the Center for the Study of Values in Organizations at Brigham Young University. Before he joined the Marriott School of Management at BYU, he spent 20 years as a faculty member at the University of Illinois, where he supervised the teaching of management skills in a large undergraduate course. He has coauthored several articles on management skills education based on that experience. He has served as an editor of the *Academy of Management Review,* as a member of the Academy's Board of Governors, and as Chair of the OMT Division. He is the recipient of the Academy of Management's Distinguished Service Award and the Organizational Behavior Teaching Society's Distinguished Educator Award.